Classical and Object-Oriented Software Engineering

with UML and Java™

FOURTH EDITION

CLASSICAL AND OBJECT-ORIENTED SOFTWARE ENGINEERING

with UML and Java™

FOURTH EDITION

Stephen R. Schach
Vanderbilt University

Boston • Burr Ridge, IL • Dubuque, IA • Madison, WI • New York
San Francisco • St. Louis • Bangkok • Bogotá • Caracas • Lisbon
London • Madrid • Mexico City • Milan • New Delhi • Seoul
Singapore • Sydney • Taipei • Toronto

WCB/McGraw-Hill

*A Division of The **McGraw-Hill** Companies*

CLASSICAL AND OBJECT-ORIENTED SOFTWARE ENGINEERING WITH UML AND JAVA
International Editions 1999

1 2 3 4 5 6 7 8 9 10 CMO UPE 2 0 9

Library of Congress Cataloging-in-Publication Data

Schach, Stephen R.
Classical and object-oriented software engineering with UML and Java / Stephen R. Schach. – 4th ed.
p. cm.
ISBN 0-07-230226-7
Rev. ed. of: Classical and object-oriented software engineering. – 3rd ed. c1996.
Includes bibliographical references and index.
1. Software engineering. 2. Object-oriented programming (Computer science) 3. UML (Computer science) 4. Java (Computer program language) I. Schach, Stephen R. Classical and object-oriented software engineering. II. Title.
QA76.758.S33 1999
005.1–dc21 98-39274

www.mhhe.com

When ordering this title, use ISBN 0-07-116760-9

Printed in Singapore

To Sharon, David, and Lauren

The following are registered trademarks:

Access
ActiveX
ADF
ADW
Aide-de-Camp
Analyst/Designer
Apple
AT&T
Bachman Product Set
Battlemap
Borland
Bull
CA-Tellaplan
CCC
Coca-Cola
COM
DB2
Demo II
Emeraude
Excel
Excelerator
Ford
Foundation
FoxBASE
Guide
Hewlett-Packard
Honeywell
Hypercard
Hypertalk
IBM
IEW
IMS/360
Informix
Iona
Java
Lotus 1-2-3
Lucent Technologies
Macintosh
MacProject
Method/1
Microsoft
Motif
MS-DOS
MVS/360
Natural
Netscape
The New York Times
Newton
Nomad
Object C
ObjectBroker
Objective-C
OLE
OMTool
1-800-FLOWERS
OpenWindows
OpenDoc
Oracle
ORB Plus
ORBIX
OS/360
OS/370
OS/VS2
Post-it
PowerBuilder
Project
PVCS
QAPartner
RAMIS-II
Rational
Rose
SoftBench
Software through Pictures
Source Safe
SPARCstation
SQL
Statemate
Sun
Sun Microsystems
SunView
System Architect
Teamwork
UNIX
VAX
Visigenic
VM/370
VMS
The Wall Street Journal
Windows 95
Word
X11
XRunner

To the Instructor

The software engineering process is essentially language-independent. However, it is necessary to choose a specific programming language for implementing a software product.

Java™ and C++ are currently the two most popular implementation languages for software engineering courses. For ease of use, this book is therefore published in two versions, the C++ version and the Java version. Other than the few code examples and the Case Study, the two versions are identical.

PREFACE

The title of this book, *Classical and Object-Oriented Software Engineering with UML and Java,* is somewhat surprising. After all, there is virtually unanimous agreement that the object-oriented paradigm is superior to the classical (structured) paradigm. It would seem obvious that an up-to-date software engineering textbook should describe only the object-oriented paradigm, and treat the classical paradigm at best as a historical footnote.

That is not the case. Despite the widespread enthusiasm for the object-oriented paradigm and the rapidly accumulating evidence of its superiority over the classical paradigm, it is nevertheless essential to include material on the classical paradigm. There are three reasons for this. First, it is impossible to appreciate why object-oriented technology is superior to classical technology without fully understanding the classical approach and how it differs from the object-oriented approach.

The second reason why both the classical and object-oriented paradigms are included is that technology transfer is a slow process. The vast majority of software organizations have not yet adopted the object-oriented paradigm. It is therefore likely that many of the students who use this book will be employed by organizations that still use classical software engineering techniques. Furthermore, even if an organization is now using the object-oriented approach for developing new software, existing software still has to be maintained, and this legacy software is not object-oriented. Thus, excluding classical material would not be fair to the students who use this text.

A third reason for including both paradigms is that a student who is employed at an organization that is considering the transition to object-oriented technology will be able to advise that organization regarding both the strengths and the weaknesses of the new paradigm. Thus, as in the previous edition, the classical and object-oriented approaches are compared, contrasted, and analyzed.

The Fourth Edition differs from the Third Edition in two ways. First, many new topics are introduced in this edition. Second, the material has been rearranged to support both one- and two-semester software engineering curricula; this is described in the next section.

With regard to new topics, Unified Modeling Language (UML) permeates this edition; this is reflected in the title of the book. In addition to utilizing UML for object-oriented analysis and object-oriented design, UML has also been used wherever there are diagrams depicting objects and their interrelationships. UML has become a de facto software engineering standard and this is reflected in the Fourth Edition.

Another new topic is design patterns. This material is part of a new chapter on reuse, portability, and interoperability. Other reuse topics in this chapter include software architecture and frameworks. Underlying all the reuse material is the importance of object reuse. The portability sections include material on Java. With regard to interoperability, there are sections on topics like OLE, COM, ActiveX, and CORBA.

There is also a new chapter on planning and estimating, especially for the object-oriented paradigm. The chapter therefore includes new material on feature points and COCOMO II.

The synchronize-and-stabilize life-cycle model used by Microsoft has been included in this edition. The associated team organization method is also described.

As in the previous edition, particular attention is also paid to object-oriented life-cycle models, object-oriented analysis, object-oriented design, management implications of the object-oriented paradigm, and to the testing and maintenance of object-oriented software. Metrics for objects are also included. In addition, there are many briefer references to objects, a paragraph or even just a sentence in length. The reason is that the object-oriented paradigm is not just concerned with how the various phases are performed, but rather permeates the way we think about software engineering. Object technology pervades this book.

The software process is still the concept that underlies the book as a whole. In order to control the process, we have to be able to measure what is happening to the project. Accordingly, the emphasis on metrics is retained. With regard to process improvement, material on SPICE has been added to the sections on the Capability Maturity Model (CMM) and ISO 9000.

Another topic that still is stressed is CASE. I also continue to emphasize the importance of maintenance and the need for complete and correct documentation at all times.

The software process is essentially language-independent and this is again reflected in the Fourth Edition. The few code examples are in Java. However, care has been taken to make this material accessible to readers with little or no knowledge of Java by providing explanations of constructs that are specific to Java.

With regard to prerequisites, it is assumed that the reader is familiar with one high-level programming language such as Pascal, C, C++, Ada, BASIC, COBOL, FORTRAN, or Java. In addition, the reader is expected to have taken a course in data structures.

How the Fourth Edition Is Organized

The Third Edition of this book was written for a one-semester, project-based software engineering course. The book accordingly consisted of two parts. Part 2 covered the life cycle, phase by phase; the aim was to provide the students with the knowledge and skills needed for the Term Project. Part 1 contained the theoretical material needed to understand Part 2. For example, Part 1 introduced the reader to CASE, metrics, and testing because each chapter of Part 2 contained a section on CASE tools for that phase, a section on metrics for that phase, and a section on testing during that phase. Part 1 was kept short to enable the instructor to start Part 2 relatively early in the semester. In this way, the class could begin developing the Term Project as soon as possible. The need to keep Part 1 brief meant that I had to include topics like reuse, portability, and team organization in Part 2. Thus, while the students were working on their term projects, they learned additional theoretical material.

However, there is a new trend in software engineering curricula. More and more computer science departments are realizing that the overwhelming preponderance of their graduates find employment as software engineers. As a result, many colleges and universities have introduced a two-semester (or two-quarter) software engineering sequence. The first course is largely theoretical (but there is almost always a small project of some sort). The second course is a major team-based term project, usually a capstone project. When the Term Project is carried out in the second semester, there is no need for the instructor to rush to start Part 2.

In order to cater to both the one- and two-semester course sequences, I have rearranged the material of the previous edition and added to it. Part 1 now includes two more chapters, but the material of those two chapters is not a prerequisite for Part 2. First, Chapter 7 is entitled "Reusability, Portability, and Interoperability." The theme of this chapter is the need to develop reusable portable software that can run on a distributed heterogeneous architecture such as client-server.

Second, some instructors who adopted the Third Edition have told me that they were uncomfortable with a separate planning and estimating phase between the specification phase and the design phase. They agreed that accurate estimates of cost and duration are not possible until the specifications are complete (although sometimes we are required to produce estimates earlier in the life cycle). However, they felt that these planning and estimating activities did not merit a complete phase, particularly because they comprise only about 1 percent of the total software life cycle. Accordingly, I have dropped the separate planning phase and incorporated these activities at the end of the specifications phase. The various planning activities that are performed are described in Chapter 8, entitled "Planning and Estimating." This material, too, may be delayed in order to start Part 2. In addition to these two chapters, certain sections of other chapters (such as Section 2.12) may also be deferred and taught in parallel with Part 2. All material that can be postponed in this way is marked with ❖.

Thus, an instructor who is teaching a one-semester (or one-quarter) sequence using the Fourth Edition covers most of Chapters 1 through 6, and then starts Part 2 (Chapters 9 through 15). Chapters 7 and 8 can then be taught in parallel with Part 2. When teaching the two-semester sequence, the chapters of the book are taught in order; the class is now fully prepared for the semester-long team-based Term Project.

In order to ensure that the key software engineering techniques of Part 2 are truly understood, each is presented twice. First, whenever a technique is introduced, it is illustrated by means of the elevator problem. The elevator problem is the correct size for the reader to be able to see the technique applied to a complete problem, and it has enough subtleties to highlight both the strengths and weaknesses of the technique being taught. Then, at the end of each chapter there is a new continuing major Case Study. A detailed solution to the Case Study is presented. The solution to each phase of the Case Study is generally too large to appear in the chapter itself. Instead, only key points of the solution are presented in the chapter, and the complete material appears at the end of the book (Appendices C through I). The rapid prototype and detailed Java implementation are available via the World-Wide Web at www.mhhe.com/engcs/compsci/schach.

THE PROBLEM SETS

As in the previous edition, there are four types of problems. First, at the end of each chapter there are a number of exercises intended to highlight key points. These exercises are self-contained; the technical information for all of the exercises can be found in this book.

Second, there is a major Term Project. It is designed to be solved by students working in teams of three, the smallest number of team members that cannot confer over a standard telephone. The Term Project comprises 15 separate components, each tied to the relevant chapter. For example, design is the topic of Chapter 12, so in that chapter the component of the Term Project is concerned with designing the software for the project. By breaking a large project into smaller, well-defined pieces, the instructor can monitor the progress of the class more closely. The structure of the Term Project is such that instructors may freely apply the 15 components to any other project they choose.

Because this book is written for use by graduate students as well as upper-class undergraduates, the third type of problem is based on research papers in the software engineering literature. In each chapter an important paper has been chosen; wherever possible, a paper related to object-oriented software engineering has been selected. The student is asked to read the paper and to answer a question relating to its contents. Of course, the instructor is free to assign any other research paper; the "For Further Reading" section at the end of each chapter includes a wide variety of relevant papers.

The fourth type of problem relates to the Case Study. This type of problem was introduced in the Third Edition in response to instructors who told me that they believe their students learn more by modifying an existing product than by developing a product from scratch. Many senior software engineers in the industry agreed with that viewpoint. Accordingly, each chapter in which the Case Study is presented has at least three problems that require the student to modify the Case Study in some way. For example, in one chapter the student is asked to redesign the Case Study using a different design technique than the one used for the Case Study. In another chapter, the student is asked what the effect would have been of performing the steps of the object-oriented analysis in a different order. To make it easy to modify the source code of the Case Study, it is readily available as described at the end of the previous section.

The *Instructor's Solution Manual,* available from McGraw-Hill, contains detailed solutions to all the exercises, as well as to the Term Project. In addition, the *Instructor's Solution Manual* contains transparency masters for all the figures in this book. The transparency masters can also be downloaded from www.mhhe.com/engcs/compsci/schach.

ACKNOWLEDGMENTS

I am indebted to those who reviewed this edition, including:

Thaddeus R. Crews, Jr., Western Kentucky University
Eduardo B. Fernandez, Florida Atlantic University
Michael Godfrey, Cornell University
Thomas B. Horton, Florida Atlantic University
Gail Kaiser, Columbia University
Laxmikant V. Kale, University of Illinois
Chung Lee, California State Polytechnic University at Pomona
Susan Mengel, Texas Tech University
David S. Rosenblum, University of California at Irvine
Shmuel Rotenstreich, George Washington University
Wendel Scarbrough, Azusa Pacific University
Gerald B. Sheble, Iowa State

I am particularly grateful to two of the reviewers. Thad Crews made many creative pedagogic suggestions. As a consequence, it is easier to teach from this book and to learn from it. Laxmikant Kale pointed out a number of weaknesses. I am grateful to him for his meticulous reading of the entire manuscript.

I should like to thank three individuals who have also made contributions to earlier books. First, Jeff Gray has once again made numerous insightful suggestions. In particular, I am grateful for his many ideas regarding Chapter 7. Also, he is once again a coauthor of the *Instructor's Solution Manual.* Second, my son David has made a number of helpful contributions to the book and is also a coauthor of the *Instructor's Solution Manual.* Third, I thank Saveen Reddy for drawing my attention to the quotation from Marcus Aurelius that appears in the last Just in Case You Wanted to Know box.

With regard to my publishers, McGraw-Hill, I am especially grateful to executive editor Betsy Jones, sponsoring editor Brad Kosirog, senior project manager Jean Lou Hess, and project manager Paula Buschman.

Finally, as always, I thank my family for their continual support. When I started writing books, my limited free time had to be shared between my family and my current book project. Now that my children are assisting with my books, writing has become a family activity. For the seventh time, it is my privilege to dedicate this book to my wife, Sharon, and my children, David and Lauren, with love.

Stephen R. Schach

Brief Contents

CONTENTS

CHAPTER 4
Teams and the Tools of Their Trade 90

CHAPTER 5
Testing 134

CHAPTER 6
Introduction to Objects 171

PART 2
The Phases of the Software Life Cycle 299

CHAPTER 9
Requirements Phase 301

CHAPTER 10
Specification Phase 329

CHAPTER 11
Object-Oriented Analysis Phase 376

CHAPTER 14
Implementation and Integration Phase 479

CHAPTER 15
Maintenance Phase 502

APPENDIX A
Air Gourmet 523

APPENDIX B
Software Engineering Resources 526

APPENDIX C
Osbert Oglesby Case Study: Rapid Prototype 529

PART

1

INTRODUCTION TO THE SOFTWARE LIFE CYCLE

The first eight chapters of this book serve a dual role. They introduce the reader to the software process, and they also provide an overview of the book. The software process is the way we produce software. It starts with concept exploration and ends when the product is finally decommissioned. During this period the product goes through a series of phases such as requirements, specification, design, implementation, integration, maintenance, and, ultimately, retirement. The software process also includes the tools and techniques we use to develop and maintain software, as well as the software professionals involved.

In Chapter 1, Scope of Software Engineering, it is pointed out that techniques for software production must be cost effective and must also promote constructive interaction between the members of the software production team. The importance of objects is stressed throughout the book, starting with this chapter.

The Software Process is the title of Chapter 2. Each phase of the process is discussed in detail. Many problems of software engineering are described, but no solutions are put forward in this chapter. Instead, the reader is informed about where in the book each problem is addressed. In this way, the chapter serves as a guide to the rest of the book. The chapter concludes with material on software process improvement.

A variety of different software life-cycle models are discussed in detail in Chapter 3, Software Life-Cycle Models. These include the waterfall model, the rapid prototyping model, the incremental model, the synchronize-and-stabilize model, and the spiral model. To enable the reader to decide on an appropriate life-cycle model for a specific project, the various life-cycle models are compared and contrasted.

Chapter 4 is entitled Teams and the Tools of Their Trade. Today's projects are too large to be completed by a single individual within the given time constraints. Instead, a team of software professionals collaborate on the project. The first topic of this chapter is how teams should be organized so that team members work together productively. Also, a software engineer needs to be able to use a number of different tools, both theoretical and practical. In the remainder of this chapter, the reader is introduced to a variety of software engineering tools. One such tool is stepwise refinement, a technique for decomposing a large problem into smaller, more tractable problems. Another tool is cost–benefit analysis, a technique for determining whether a software project is financially feasible. Then, computer-aided software engineering (CASE) tools are described. A CASE tool is a software product that assists software engineers to develop and maintain software. Finally, in order to manage the software process, it is necessary to measure various quantities to determine whether the project is on track. These measures (metrics) are critical to the success of a project.

The last two topics of Chapter 4, namely CASE tools and metrics, are treated in detail in Chapters 9 through 15, which describe the specific phases of the software life cycle. There is a discussion of the CASE tools that support each phase, as well as a description of the metrics needed to manage that phase adequately.

An important theme of this book is that testing is not a separate phase to be carried out just before delivering the product to the client or even at the end of each phase of the software life cycle. Instead, testing is performed in parallel with all software production activities. In Chapter 5, Testing, the concepts underlying testing are discussed. Testing techniques specific to individual phases of the software life cycle are deferred until Chapters 9 through 15.

Chapter 6 is entitled Introduction to Objects. A detailed explanation is given of classes and objects, and why the object-oriented paradigm is proving to be more successful than the structured paradigm. The concepts of this chapter are then utilized in the rest of the book, particularly Chapter 11, Object-Oriented Analysis Phase, and in Chapter 12, Design Phase, in which object-oriented design is presented.

The ideas of Chapter 6 are extended in Chapter 7, Reusability, Portability, and Interoperability. It is important to be able to write reusable software that can be ported to a variety of different hardware and can run on distributed architectures such as client-server. The first part of the chapter is devoted to reuse; topics include a variety of reuse case studies as well as reuse strategies such as object-oriented patterns and frameworks. Portability is the second major topic; portability strategies are presented in some depth. The chapter concludes with interoperability topics such as CORBA and COM. A recurring theme of this chapter is the role of objects in achieving reusability, portability, and interoperability.

The last chapter in Part One is Chapter 8, Planning and Estimating. Before starting a software project, it is essential to plan the entire operation in detail. Once the project begins, management must closely monitor progress, noting deviations from the plan and taking corrective action where necessary. Also, it is vital that the client be provided with accurate estimates of how long the project will take and how much it will cost. Different estimation techniques are presented, including function points and COCOMO II. A detailed description of a software project management plan is given. The material of this chapter is utilized in Chapters 10 and 11. When the classical paradigm is used, major planning and estimating activities take place at the end of the specification phase, as explained in Chapter 10. When software is developed using the object-oriented paradigm, this planning takes place at the end of the object-oriented analysis phase (Chapter 11).

chapter

1

SCOPE OF SOFTWARE ENGINEERING

There is a well-known story about an executive who received a computer-generated bill for $0.00. After having a good laugh with friends about "idiot computers," the executive tossed the bill away. A month later a similar bill arrived, this time marked 30 days. Then came the third bill. The fourth bill arrived a month later, accompanied by a message hinting at possible legal action if the bill for $0.00 was not paid at once.

The fifth bill, marked 120 days, did not hint at anything—the message was rude and forthright, threatening all manner of legal actions if the bill was not immediately paid. Fearful of his organization's credit rating in the hands of this maniacal machine, the executive called an acquaintance who was a software engineer and related the whole sorry story. Trying not to laugh, the software engineer told the executive to mail a check for $0.00. This had the desired effect, and a receipt for $0.00 was received a few days later. The executive carefully filed it away in case the computer at some future date might allege that $0.00 was still owing.

This well-known story has a less well-known sequel. A few days later the executive was summoned by his bank manager. The banker held up a check and asked, "Is this your check?"

The executive agreed that it was.

"Would you mind telling me why you wrote a check for $0.00?" asked the banker.

So the whole story was retold. When the executive had finished, the banker turned to him and she quietly asked, "Have you any idea what your check for $0.00 did to *our* computer system?"

A computer professional can laugh at this story, albeit somewhat nervously. After all, every one of us has designed or implemented a product that, in its original form, would have resulted in the equivalent of sending dunning letters for $0.00. Up to now, we have always caught this sort of fault during testing. But our laughter has a hollow ring to it, because at the back of our minds there is the fear that someday we will not detect the fault before the product is delivered to the customer.

A decidedly less humorous software fault was detected on November 9, 1979. The Strategic Air Command had an alert scramble when the worldwide military monitoring command and control system (WWMCCS) computer network reported that the Soviet Union had launched missiles aimed toward the United States [Neumann, 1980]. What actually happened was that a simulated attack was interpreted

JUST IN CASE YOU WANTED TO KNOW

In the case of the WWMCCS network, disaster was averted at the last minute. However, the consequences of other software faults have sometimes been tragic. For example, between 1985 and 1987 at least two patients died as a consequence of severe overdoses of radiation delivered by the Therac-25 medical linear accelerator [Leveson and Turner, 1993]. The cause was a fault in the control software.

During the 1991 Gulf War, a Scud missile penetrated the Patriot anti-missile shield and struck a barracks near Dhahran, Saudi Arabia. In all, 28 Americans were killed and 98 wounded. The software for the Patriot missile contained a cumulative timing fault. The Patriot was designed to operate for only a few hours at a time, after which the clock was reset. As a result, the fault never had a significant effect and was therefore not detected. In the Gulf War, however, the Patriot missile battery at Dhahran ran continuously for over 100 hours. This caused the accumulated time discrepancy to become large enough to render the system inaccurate.

During the Gulf War, the U.S. shipped Patriot missiles to Israel for protection against the Scuds. Israeli forces detected the timing problem after only 8 hours and immediately reported it to the manufacturer in the United States. They corrected the fault as quickly as they could but, tragically, the new software arrived the day after the direct hit by the Scud [Mellor, 1994].

as the real thing, just as in the movie *WarGames* some 5 years later. Although the U.S. Department of Defense has understandably not given details about the precise mechanism by which test data were taken for actual data, it seems reasonable to ascribe the problem to a software fault. Either the system as a whole was not designed to differentiate between simulations and reality, or the user interface did not include the necessary checks for ensuring that end users of the system would be able to distinguish fact from fiction. In other words, a software fault, if indeed the problem was caused by software, could have brought civilization as we know it to an unpleasant and abrupt end. (See the Just In Case You Wanted to Know box above for information on disasters caused by other software faults.)

Whether we are dealing with billing or air defense, much of our software is delivered late, over budget, and with residual faults. Software engineering is an attempt to solve these problems. In other words, software engineering is a discipline whose aim is the production of fault-free software, delivered on time and within budget, that satisfies the user's needs. Furthermore, the software must be easy to modify when the user's needs change. In order to achieve these goals, a software engineer has to acquire a broad range of skills, both technical and managerial. These skills have to be applied not just to programming but to every phase of software production, from requirements to maintenance.

The scope of software engineering is extremely broad. Some aspects of software engineering can be categorized as mathematics or computer science; other aspects fall into the areas of economics, management, or psychology. In order to display the wide-reaching realm of software engineering, five different aspects will now be examined.

1.1 HISTORICAL ASPECTS

It is a fact that electric power generators fail, but far less frequently than payroll products do. It is true that bridges sometimes collapse, but considerably less often than operating systems do. In the belief that software design, implementation, and maintenance could be put on the same footing as traditional engineering disciplines, a NATO study group in 1967 coined the term *software engineering*. The claim that building software is similar to other engineering tasks was endorsed by the 1968 NATO Software Engineering Conference held in Garmisch, Germany [Naur, Randell, and Buxton, 1976]. This endorsement is not too surprising; the very name of the conference reflected the belief that software production should be an engineeringlike activity. A conclusion of the conferees was that software engineering should use the philosophies and paradigms of established engineering disciplines to solve what they termed the *software crisis,* namely, that the quality of software was generally unacceptably low and that deadlines and cost limits were not being met.

Although there have been many software success stories, a considerable amount of software is still being delivered late, over budget, and with residual faults. That the software crisis is still with us, 30 years later, tells us two things. First, the software production process, while resembling traditional engineering in many respects, has its own unique properties and problems. Second, the software crisis should perhaps be renamed the *software depression,* in view of its long duration and poor prognosis.

It is certainly true that bridges collapse less frequently than operating systems. Why then cannot bridge-building techniques be used to build operating systems? What the NATO conferees overlooked is that bridges are as different from operating systems as ravens are from writing desks.

A major difference between bridges and operating systems lies in the attitudes of the civil engineering community and the software engineering community to the act of collapsing. When a bridge collapses, as the Tacoma Narrows bridge did in 1940, the bridge almost always has to be redesigned and rebuilt from scratch. The original design was faulty and posed a threat to human safety; certainly the design requires drastic changes. In addition, the effects of the collapse will in almost every instance have caused so much damage to the bridge fabric that the only reasonable thing to do is to demolish what is left of the faulty bridge, then completely redesign and rebuild it. Furthermore, other bridges built to the same design have to be carefully inspected and, in the worst case, redesigned and rebuilt.

In contrast, an operating system crash is not considered unusual and rarely triggers an immediate investigation into its design. When a crash occurs, it may be possible simply to reboot the system in the hope that the set of circumstances that caused the crash will not recur. This may be the only remedy if, as is often the case, there is no evidence as to the cause of the crash. The damage caused by the crash will usually be minor: a database partially corrupted, a few files lost. Even when damage to the file system is considerable, back-up data can often restore the file system to a state not too far removed from its precrash condition. Perhaps if software engineers treated an operating system crash as seriously as civil engineers treat a bridge collapse, the overall level of professionalism within software engineering would rise.

Now consider a real-time system, that is, a system able to respond to inputs from the real world as fast as they occur. An example is a computer-controlled intensive care unit. Irrespective of how many medical emergencies occur virtually simultaneously, the system must continue to alert the medical staff to every new emergency without ceasing to monitor those patients whose condition is critical but stable. In general, the failure of a real-time system, whether it controls an intensive care unit, a nuclear reactor, or the climatic conditions aboard a space station, has significant effects. Most real-time systems, therefore, include some element of fault tolerance to minimize the effects of a failure. That is, the system is designed to attempt an automatic recovery from any failure.

The very concept of fault tolerance highlights a major difference between bridges and operating systems. Bridges are engineered to withstand every reasonably anticipated condition such as high winds, flash floods, and so on. An implicit assumption of all too many software builders is that we cannot hope to anticipate all possible conditions that the software must withstand, so we must design our software to try to minimize the damage that an unanticipated condition might cause. In other words, bridges are assumed to be perfectly engineered. In contrast, most operating systems are assumed to be imperfectly engineered; many are designed in such a way that rebooting is a simple operation that the user may perform whenever needed. This difference is a fundamental reason why so much software today cannot be considered as *engineered.*

It might be suggested that this difference is only temporary. After all, we have been building bridges for thousands of years, and we therefore have considerable experience and expertise in the types of conditions a bridge must withstand. We have only 50 years of experience with operating systems. Surely with more experience, the argument goes, we will understand operating systems as well as we understand bridges and so eventually will be able to construct operating systems that will not fail.

The flaw in this argument is that hardware, and hence the associated operating system, is growing more complex faster than we can master it. In the 1960s, we had multiprogramming operating systems, in the 1970s we had to deal with virtual memory, and now we are attempting to come to terms with multiprocessor and distributed (network) operating systems. Until we can handle the complexity caused by the interconnections of the various components of a software product such as an operating system, we cannot hope to understand it fully, and if we do not understand it, we cannot hope to engineer it.

Part of the reason for the complexity of software is that, as it executes, software goes through discrete states. Changing even one bit causes the software to change state. The total number of such states can be vast, and many of them have not been considered by the development team. If the software enters such an unanticipated state, the result will often be software failure. In contrast, bridges are continuous (analog) systems. They are described using continuous mathematics, essentially calculus. However, discrete systems such as operating systems have to be described using discrete mathematics [Parnas, 1990]. Software engineers therefore have to be skilled in discrete mathematics, a primary tool in trying to cope with complexity.

A second major difference between bridges and operating systems is maintenance. Maintaining a bridge is generally restricted to painting it, repairing minor cracks, resurfacing the road, and so on. A civil engineer, if asked to rotate a bridge through 90° or to move it hundreds of miles, would consider the request to be outrageous. However, we think nothing of asking a software engineer to convert a batch operating system into a time-sharing one or to port it from one machine to another machine with totally different architectural characteristics. It is not unusual for 50 percent of the source code of an operating system to be rewritten over a 5-year period, especially if it is ported to new hardware. But no engineer would consent to replacing half a bridge; safety requirements would dictate that a new bridge be built. The area of maintenance is thus a second fundamental aspect in which software engineering differs from traditional engineering. Further maintenance aspects of software engineering are described in Section 1.3. But first, economic-oriented aspects are presented.

1.2 ECONOMIC ASPECTS

An insight into the relationship between software engineering and computer science can be obtained by comparing and contrasting the relationship between chemical engineering and chemistry. After all, computer science and chemistry are both sciences, and both have a theoretical component and a practical component. In the case of chemistry, the practical component is laboratory work; in the case of computer science, the practical component is programming.

Consider the process of extracting gasoline from coal. During World War II, the Germans used this process to make fuel for their war machine because they were largely cut off from oil supplies. While the anti-apartheid oil embargo was in effect, the government of the Republic of South Africa poured billions of dollars into SASOL (an Afrikaans acronym standing for "South African coal into oil"). About half of South Africa's liquid fuel needs were met in this way.

From the viewpoint of a chemist, there are many possible ways to convert coal into gasoline, and all are equally important. After all, no one chemical reaction is more important than any other. But from the chemical engineer's viewpoint there is, at any one time, exactly one important mechanism for synthesizing gasoline from coal—namely, the reaction that is economically the most attractive. In other words, the chemical engineer evaluates all possible reactions, and then rejects all but that one reaction for which the cost per liter is the lowest.

A similar relationship holds between computer science and software engineering. The computer scientist investigates a variety of ways to produce software, some good and some bad. But the software engineer is interested in only those techniques that make sound economic sense.

For instance, a software organization that is currently using coding technique CT_{old} discovers that new coding technique CT_{new} would result in code being produced in only nine-tenths of the time needed by CT_{old} and, hence, at nine-tenths of the cost. Common sense seems to dictate that CT_{new} is the appropriate technique to use. In fact, although common sense certainly dictates that the faster technique is the technique of choice, the economics of software engineering may imply the opposite.

One reason is the cost of introducing new technology into an organization. The fact that coding is 10 percent faster when technique CT_{new} is used may be less important than the costs incurred in introducing CT_{new} into the organization. It may be necessary to complete two or three projects before recouping the costs of training. Also, while software personnel are attending courses on CT_{new}, they are unable to do productive work. Even when they return, there may be a steep learning curve involved; it may take months of practice with CT_{new} before software professionals become as proficient with CT_{new} as they currently are with CT_{old}. Thus, initial projects using CT_{new} may take far longer to complete than if the organization had continued to use CT_{old}. All these costs need to be taken into account when deciding whether to change to CT_{new}.

A second reason why the economics of software engineering may dictate that CT_{old} be retained is the maintenance consequence. Coding technique CT_{new} may indeed be 10 percent faster than CT_{old} and the resulting code may be of comparable quality from the viewpoint of satisfying the client's current needs. But the use of technique CT_{new} may result in code that is difficult to maintain, thereby making the cost of CT_{new} higher over the life of the product. Of course, if the software developer is not responsible for any maintenance, then, from the viewpoint of just that developer, CT_{new} is a most attractive proposition. After all, use of CT_{new} would cost 10 percent less. The client should insist that technique CT_{old} be used, and pay the higher initial costs with the expectation that the total lifetime cost of the software will be lower. Unfortunately, it is often the case that the sole aim of both the client and the software provider is to produce code as quickly as possible. The long-term effects of using a particular technique are generally ignored in the interests of short-term gain. Applying economic principles to software engineering requires the client to choose techniques that reduce long-term costs.

We now consider the importance of maintenance.

1.3 MAINTENANCE ASPECTS

The series of steps that software undergoes, from concept exploration through final retirement, is termed the *life cycle*. During this time the product goes through a series of phases: requirements, specification, design, implementation, integration, maintenance, and retirement. Life-cycle models are discussed in greater detail in Chapter 3; the topic is introduced at this point so that the concept of maintenance can be defined.

Until the end of the 1970s most organizations were producing software using as their life-cycle model what is now termed the *waterfall model.* There are many variations of this model, but by and large, the product goes through seven broad phases. These phases probably do not correspond exactly to the phases of any one particular organization, but they are sufficiently close to most practices for the purposes of this book. Similarly, the precise name of each phase varies from organization to organization. The names used here for the various phases have been chosen to be as general as possible in the hope that the reader will feel comfortable with them. For easy reference, the phases are summarized in Figure 1.1, which also indicates the chapters in this book in which they are presented.

1. *Requirements phase:* The concept is explored and refined, and the client's requirements are elicited.
2. *Specification (analysis) phase:* The client's requirements are analyzed and presented in the form of the *specification document,* "what the product is supposed to do." This phase is sometimes called the analysis phase. At the end of this phase a plan is drawn up, the *software project management plan,* describing the proposed software development in detail.
3. *Design phase:* The specifications undergo two consecutive design processes. First comes *architectural design* in which the product as a whole is broken down into components, called *modules.* Then each module in turn is designed; this process is termed *detailed design.* The two resulting *design documents* describe "how the product does it."
4. *Implementation phase:* The various components are coded and tested.
5. *Integration phase:* The components of the product are combined and tested as a whole. When the developers are satisfied with the product, it is tested by the client (*acceptance testing*). This phase ends when the product is accepted by the client and goes into operations mode. (We will see in Chapter 14 that the

1. Requirements phase (Chapter 9)
2. Specification (analysis) phase (Chapters 10 and 11)
3. Design phase (Chapter 12)
4. Implementation phase (Chapters 13 and 14)
5. Integration phase (Chapter 14)
6. Maintenance phase (Chapter 15)
7. Retirement

Figure 1.1 The phases of the software life cycle, and the chapters in this book in which they are presented.

integration phase should be performed in parallel with the implementation phase.)

6. *Maintenance phase:* Maintenance includes all changes to the product once the client has agreed that it satisfies the specification document. Maintenance includes *corrective maintenance* (or *software repair*), which consists of the removal of residual faults while leaving the specifications unchanged, as well as *enhancement* (or *software update*), which consists of changes to the specifications and the implementation of those changes. There are, in turn, two types of enhancement. The first is *perfective maintenance,* changes that the client thinks will improve the effectiveness of the product, such as additional functionality or decreased response time. The second is *adaptive maintenance,* changes made in response to changes in the environment in which the product operates, such as new government regulations. Studies have indicated that, on average, maintainers spend approximately 17.5 percent of their time on corrective maintenance, 60.5 percent on perfective maintenance, and 18 percent on adaptive maintenance [Lientz, Swanson, and Tompkins, 1978].
7. *Retirement:* The product is removed from service.

Returning to the topic of maintenance, it is sometimes said that only bad software products undergo maintenance. In fact, the opposite is true; bad products are thrown away, whereas good products are repaired and enhanced, for 10, 15, or even 20 years. Furthermore, a software product is a model of the real world, and the real world is perpetually changing. As a consequence, software has to be maintained constantly in order for it to remain an accurate reflection of the real world.

For instance, if the sales tax rate changes from 6 percent to 7 percent, almost every software product that deals with buying or selling has to be changed. Suppose the product contains the Java statement

```
public static final float salesTax = (float) 6.0;
```

declaring that salesTax is a floating-point constant and is initialized to the value 6.0. In this case maintenance is relatively simple. With the aid of a text editor the value 6.0 is replaced by 7.0, and the code is recompiled and relinked. However, if instead of using the name salesTax, the actual value 6.0 has been used in the product wherever the value of the sales tax is invoked, then such a product will be extremely difficult to maintain. For example, there may be occurrences of the value 6.0 in the source code that should be changed to 7.0 but are overlooked, or instances of 6.0 that do not refer to sales tax, but will incorrectly be changed to 7.0. Finding these faults is almost always difficult and time-consuming. In fact, with some software it might be less expensive in the long run to throw the product away and recode it, rather than try to determine which of the many constants need to be changed and how to make the modifications.

The real-time real world is also constantly changing. The missiles with which a jet fighter is armed may be replaced by a new model, requiring a change to the weapons control component of the associated avionics system. A six-cylinder engine is to be offered as an option in a popular four-cylinder automobile; this

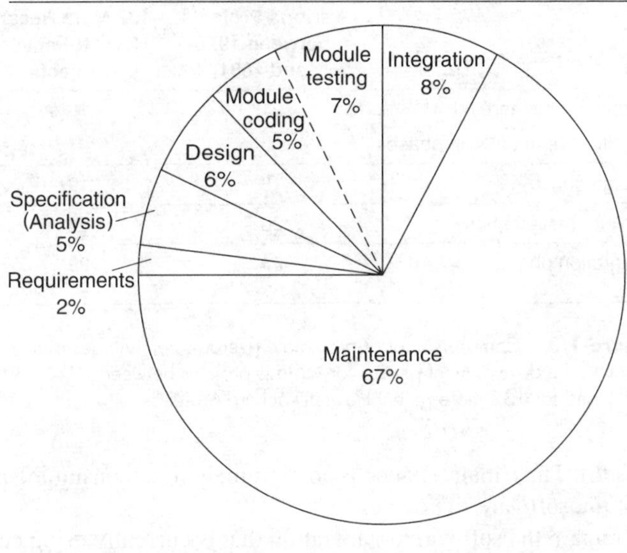

Figure 1.2 Approximate relative costs of the phases of the software life cycle.

implies changing the onboard computer that controls the fuel injection system, timing, and so on.

Healthy organizations change; only dying organizations are static. This means that maintenance in the form of enhancement is a positive part of an organization's activities, reflecting that the organization is on the move.

But just how much time is devoted to maintenance? The pie chart in Figure 1.2 was obtained by averaging data from various sources, including [Elshoff, 1976], [Daly, 1977], [Zelkowitz, Shaw, and Gannon, 1979], and [Boehm, 1981]. Figure 1.2 shows the approximate percentage of time (= money) spent on each phase of the software life cycle. About 15 years later, the proportion of time spent on the various development phases had hardly changed. This is shown in Figure 1.3, which compares the data in Figure 1.2 with more recent data on 132 Hewlett-Packard projects [Grady, 1994]. The data from Figure 1.2 has been grouped to make it comparable to the newer data.[1]

As can be seen in Figure 1.2, about two-thirds of total software costs are devoted to maintenance. Newer data confirm the continuing emphasis on maintenance. For example, in 1992 between 60 and 80 percent of research and development personnel at Hewlett-Packard were involved in maintenance, and maintenance constituted between 40 and 60 percent of the total cost of software [Coleman, Ash, Lowther, and Oman, 1994]. However, there are many organizations that devote as much as 80 percent of their time and effort to maintenance

[1] Figure 1.3 reflects only the development phases. Thus the proportion of development time devoted to the requirements and specification phases in Figure 1.2 is (2 + 5)/33, or 21%, as shown in Figure 1.3.

	Various Projects between 1976 and 1981	132 More Recent Hewlett-Packard Projects
Requirements and specification (analysis) phases	21%	18%
Design phase	18	19
Implementation phase	36	34
Integration phase	24	29

Figure 1.3 Comparison of approximate average percentages of time spent on the development phases for various projects between 1976 and 1981 and for 132 more recent Hewlett-Packard projects.

[Yourdon, 1996]. Thus, maintenance is an extremely time-consuming and expensive phase of the software life cycle.

Consider again the software organization that is currently using coding technique CT_{old} but learns that CT_{new} will reduce coding time by 10 percent. Even if CT_{new} has no adverse effect on maintenance, an astute software manager will think twice before changing coding practices. The entire staff will have to be retrained, new software development tools purchased, and perhaps additional staff hired who are experienced in the new technique. All this expense and disruption will have to be endured for a possible 0.5 percent decrease in software costs because, as shown in Figure 1.2, module coding consumes on average only 5 percent of total software costs.

Now suppose a new technique that reduces maintenance by 10 percent is developed. This should probably be introduced at once because, on average, it will reduce overall costs by 6.7 percent. The overhead involved in changing to this technique is a small price to pay for such large overall savings.

Because maintenance is so important, a major aspect of software engineering consists of those techniques, tools, and practices that lead to a reduction in maintenance costs.

1.4 SPECIFICATION AND DESIGN ASPECTS

Software professionals are human, and therefore sometimes we make an error while developing a product. As a result, there will be a fault in the software. If the error is made during the requirements phase, then the resulting fault will probably also appear in the specifications, the design, and the code. It is clear that the earlier we correct a fault, the better.

The relative costs of fixing a fault at various phases in the software life cycle are shown in Figure 1.4 [Boehm, 1981]. The figure reflects data from IBM [Fagan, 1974], GTE [Daly, 1977], the Safeguard project [Stephenson, 1976], and some

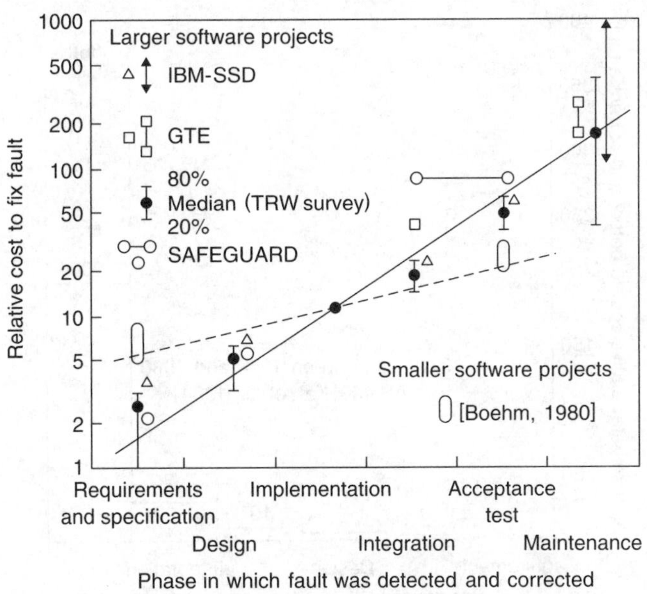

Figure 1.4 Relative cost of fixing a fault at each phase of the software life cycle. The solid line is the best fit for the data relating to the larger software projects, and the dashed line is the best fit for the smaller software projects. (Barry Boehm, *Software Engineering Economics,* © 1981, p. 40. Adapted by permission of Prentice Hall, Inc., Englewood Cliffs, NJ.)

smaller TRW projects [Boehm, 1980]. The solid line in Figure 1.4 is the best fit for the data relating to the larger projects, and the dashed line is the best fit for the smaller projects. For each of the phases of the software life cycle, the corresponding relative cost to detect and correct a fault is depicted in Figure 1.5. Each step on the solid line in Figure 1.5 is constructed by taking the corresponding point on the solid straight line of Figure 1.4 and plotting the data on a linear scale.

Suppose that it costs $40 to detect and correct a specific fault during the design phase. From the solid line in Figure 1.5 (projects between 1974 and 1980), that same fault would cost only about $30 to fix during the specification phase. But during the maintenance phase, that fault would cost around $2,000 to detect and correct. Newer data show that it is now even more important to detect faults early. The dashed line in Figure 1.5 shows the cost of detecting and correcting a fault during the development of system software for the IBM AS/400 [Kan et al., 1994]. On average, the same fault would have cost $3,680 to fix during the maintenance phase of the AS/400 software.

The reason that the cost of correcting a fault increases so steeply is related to what has to be done to correct a fault. Early in the development life cycle the product essentially exists only on paper, and correcting a fault may simply mean

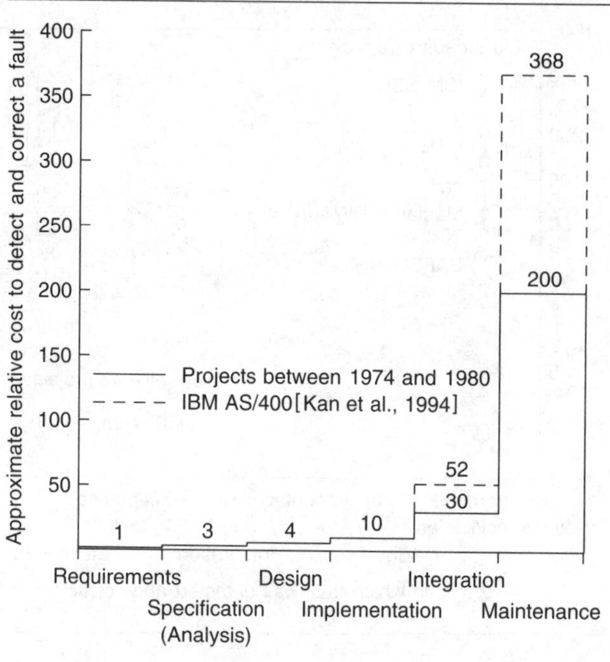

Figure 1.5 Solid line depicts points on solid line of Figure 1.4 plotted on a linear scale. Dashed line depicts newer data.

using an eraser and pencil. The other extreme is a product that has already been delivered to a client. At the very least, correcting a fault will mean editing the code, recompiling and relinking it, and then carefully testing that the problem has been solved. Next, it is critical to check that making the change has not created a new problem elsewhere in the product. All the relevant documentation, including manuals, then needs to be updated. Finally, the corrected product must be delivered and installed. The moral of the story is: We must find faults early, or else it will cost us money. We should therefore employ techniques for detecting faults during the requirements and specification (analysis) phases.

There is a further need for such techniques. Studies have shown [Boehm, 1979] that between 60 percent and 70 percent of all faults detected in large-scale projects are specification or design faults. Newer results bear out this preponderance of specification and design faults. An inspection is a careful examination of a document by a team (Section 5.2.3). During 203 inspections of Jet Propulsion Laboratory software for the NASA unmanned interplanetary space program, on average about 1.9 faults were detected per page of a specification document, 0.9 faults per page of a design, but only 0.3 faults per page of code [Kelly, Sherif, and Hops, 1992].

Thus it is important that we improve our specification and design techniques not only so that faults can be found as early as possible, but also because specification and design faults constitute such a large proportion of all faults. Just as the example in the previous section showed that reducing maintenance costs by 10 percent will reduce overall costs by nearly 7 percent, reducing specification and design faults by 10 percent will reduce the overall number of faults by 6 percent to 7 percent.

Newer data on a number of projects are reported in [Bhandari et al., 1994]. For example, a compiler was undergoing extensive changes. At the end of the design phase, the faults detected during the project were categorized. Only 13 percent of the faults were carry-overs from previous versions of the compiler. Of the remaining faults, 16 percent were introduced during the specification phase, and 71 percent were introduced during the design phase. The fact that so many faults are introduced early in the software life cycle highlights another important aspect of software engineering, namely, techniques that yield better specifications and designs.

Most software is produced by a team of software engineers rather than by a single individual who is responsible for every phase of the development and maintenance life cycle. We now consider the implications of this.

1.5 TEAM PROGRAMMING ASPECTS

The performance–price factor of a computer may be defined as follows:

$$\text{performance–price factor} = \text{time to perform one million additions} \times \text{cost of CPU and main memory}$$

This quantity has decreased by an order of magnitude with each succeeding generation of computers. That is, the performance–price factor has decreased by an order of magnitude eight times over the past 40 years. This decrease has been a consequence of discoveries in electronics, particularly the transistor, and very large scale integration (VLSI).

The result of these discoveries has been that organizations can easily afford hardware that can run large products, that is, products too large to be written by one person within the allowed time constraints. For example, if a product has to be delivered within 18 months but would take a single programmer 15 years to complete, then the product must be developed by a team. However, team programming leads to interface problems among code components and communications problems among team members.

For example, Joe and Freda code modules p and q respectively, where module p calls module q. When Joe codes p he writes a call to q with five arguments in the argument list. Freda codes q with five arguments, but in a different order from those of Joe. Unless function prototypes are used, this will not be detected by an ANSI C compiler. A few software tools such as the Java interpreter and loader, *lint* for C (Section 7.7.4), or an Ada linker will detect such a type violation, but only if the interchanged arguments are of different types; if they are of the same type, then the problem may not be detected for a long period of time. It may be debated that this is a design problem and that if the modules had been more carefully designed, this problem would not have happened. That may be true, but what happens in practice is that the design is often changed after coding commences, but notification of a change is sometimes not distributed to all members of the development team. Thus, when a design that affects two or more programmers has been changed, poor communications can lead to the interface problems Joe and Freda experienced. This sort of problem does not occur when only one individual is responsible for every aspect of the product, as was the case before powerful computers that can run huge products became affordable.

But interfacing problems are merely the tip of the iceberg when it comes to problems that can arise when software is developed by teams. Unless the team is properly organized, an inordinate amount of time can be wasted in conferences between team members. Suppose that a product takes a single programmer 1 year to complete. If the same task is assigned to a team of three programmers, the time for completing the task is frequently closer to 1 year than the expected 4 months, and the quality of the resulting code may well be lower than if the task had been assigned to one individual. Because a considerable proportion of today's software is being developed and maintained by teams, the scope of software engineering must also include techniques for ensuring that teams are properly organized and managed.

As has been shown in the preceding sections, the scope of software engineering is extremely broad. It includes every phase of the software life cycle, from requirements to retirement. It also includes human aspects, such as team organization; economic aspects; and legal aspects, such as copyright law. All these aspects are implicitly incorporated in the definition of software engineering given at the beginning of this chapter, namely that software engineering is a discipline whose aim is the production of fault-free software that is delivered on time, within budget, and satisfies the user's needs.

1.6 THE OBJECT-ORIENTED PARADIGM

Before 1975, most software organizations did not use any specific techniques; each individual worked his or her own way. Major breakthroughs were made between approximately 1975 and 1985 with the development of the so-called structured paradigm. The techniques constituting the structured paradigm include structured systems analysis (Section 10.3), composite/structured design (Section 6.1), structured programming, and structured testing (Section 13.8.2). These techniques seemed extremely promising when first used. However, as time passed, they proved to be somewhat less successful in two respects. First, the techniques were sometimes unable to cope with the increasing size of software products. That is, the structured techniques were adequate when dealing with products of (say) 5000 or even 50,000 lines of code. Today, however, products containing 500,000 lines of code are not considered large; even products of 5,000,000 or more lines of code are not that unusual. However, it turned out that the structured techniques frequently could not scale up sufficiently to be able to handle today's larger products.

The maintenance phase is the second area in which the structured paradigm did not live up to earlier expectations. A major driving force behind the development of the structured paradigm 20 years ago was the fact that, on average, two-thirds of the software budget was being devoted to maintenance (see Figure 1.2). Unfortunately, the structured paradigm has not solved this problem; as pointed out in Section 1.3, there are still many organizations that spend up to 80 percent of their time and effort on maintenance [Yourdon, 1996].

The reason for the limited success of the structured paradigm is that the structured techniques are either action oriented or data oriented, but not both. The basic components of a software product are the actions[2] of the product and the data on which those actions operate. For example, determine average height is an action that operates on a collection of heights (data) and returns the average of those heights (data). Some structured techniques, such as data flow analysis (DFA) (Section 12.3), are action oriented. That is, such techniques concentrate on the actions of the product; the data are of secondary importance. Conversely, techniques such as Jackson system development (Section 12.5) are data oriented. The emphasis here is on the data; the actions that operate on the data are of less significance.

In contrast, the object-oriented paradigm considers both data and actions to be of equal importance. A simplistic way of looking at an object is as a unified software component that incorporates both the data and the actions that operate on that data. This definition is incomplete and will be fleshed out later in the book, once *inheritance* has been defined (Section 6.7). Nevertheless, the definition captures much of the essence of an object.

A bank account is one example of an object (see Figure 1.6). The data component of the object is the account balance. The actions that can be performed on that account balance include deposit money, withdraw money, and determine balance. From the viewpoint of the structured paradigm, a product that deals with banking would have to incorporate a data element, namely, the account balance, and three actions, namely, deposit, withdraw, and determine balance. From the object-oriented viewpoint, a bank account is an object. This object combines a data element together with the three actions performed on that data element in a single unit.

Up to now, there seems to be little difference between the two approaches. However, a key point is the way in which an object is implemented. Specifically, details as to how the data element of an object is stored are not known from outside the object. This is an instance of "information hiding" and is discussed in more detail in Section 6.6. Thus, in the case of the bank account object shown in Figure 1.6(b), the rest of the software product is aware of the fact that there is such a

[2] The word *action* is used here rather than *process* in order to avoid confusion with the term *software process*.

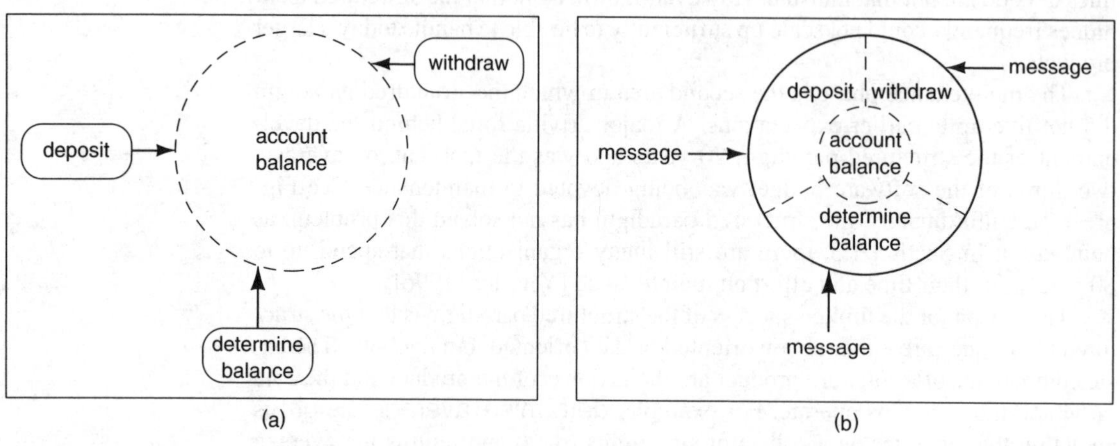

Figure 1.6 Comparison of implementations of bank account using (a) structured paradigm and (b) object-oriented paradigm. Solid black line surrounding object denotes that details as to how account balance is implemented are not known outside object.

thing as a balance within a bank account object, but it has no idea as to the format of account balance. That is, there is no knowledge outside the object as to whether the account balance is implemented as an integer or a floating-point number, or whether it is a field (component) of some larger structure. This information barrier surrounding the object is denoted by the solid black line in Figure 1.6(b), which depicts an implementation using the object-oriented paradigm. In contrast, there is a dashed line surrounding account balance in Figure 1.6(a), because all details of account balance are known to the modules in the implementation using the structured paradigm, and the value of account balance can therefore be changed by any of them.

Returning to Figure 1.6(b), the object-oriented implementation: If a customer deposits $10 in an account, then a *message* is sent to the deposit action (*method*) of the relevant object telling it to increment the account balance data element (*attribute*) by $10. The deposit method is within the bank account object and knows how the account balance is implemented; this is denoted by the dashed line inside the object. But there is no need for any entity external to the object to have this knowledge. The fact that the three methods in Figure 1.6(b) shield account balance from the rest of the product symbolizes this localization of knowledge.

At first sight, the fact that implementation details are local to an object may not seem to be terribly useful. The payoff comes during maintenance. First, suppose that the banking product has been constructed using the structured paradigm. If the way that an account balance is represented is changed from (say) an integer to a field of a structure, then every part of that product that has anything to do with an account balance has to be changed, and these changes have to be made consistently. In contrast, if the object-oriented paradigm is used, then the only changes that need be made are within the bank account object itself. No other part of the product has knowledge of how an account balance is implemented, so no other part can have access to an account balance. Consequently, no other part of the banking product needs to be changed. Thus, the object-oriented paradigm makes maintenance quicker and easier, and the chance of introducing a regression fault (that is, a fault inadvertently introduced into one part of a product as a consequence of making an apparently unrelated change to another part of the product) is greatly reduced.

In addition to maintenance benefits, the object-oriented paradigm makes development easier. In many instances, an object has a physical counterpart. For example, the object bank account in the bank product corresponds to an actual bank account in the bank for which this product is being written. As will be shown in Chapter 11, modeling plays a major role in the object-oriented paradigm. The close correspondence between the objects in a product and their counterparts in the real world promotes better software development.

There is yet another way of looking at the benefits of the object-oriented paradigm. Well-designed objects are independent units. As has been explained, an object consists of both data and the actions that are performed on the data. If all the actions that are performed on the data of an object are included in that object, then the object can be considered a conceptually independent entity. Everything in the product that relates to the portion of the real world modeled by that object can be found in the object itself. This conceptual independence is sometimes termed *encapsulation* (Section 6.4). But there is an additional form of independence, namely physical independence. In a well-designed object, information hiding ensures that implementation details are hidden from everything outside that object. The only allowable form of communication is the sending of a message to the object to carry out a specific action. The way that the action is carried out is entirely the responsibility of the object itself. For this reason, object-oriented design is sometimes referred to as *responsibility-driven design* [Wirfs-Brock, Wilkerson, and Wiener, 1990] or *design by contract* [Meyer, 1992a]. (For another view of responsibility-driven design, see the Just in Case You Wanted to Know box on page 20.)

A product that has been built using the structured paradigm is essentially a single unit. This is one reason why the structured paradigm has been less successful when applied to larger products. In contrast, when the object-oriented paradigm is correctly used, the resulting product consists of a number of smaller, largely independent units. The object-oriented paradigm reduces the level of complexity of a software product and hence simplifies both development and maintenance.

Another positive feature of the object-oriented paradigm is that it promotes reuse; because objects are independent entities, they can be utilized in future products. This reuse of objects reduces the time and cost of both development and maintenance, as explained in Chapter 7.

JUST IN CASE YOU WANTED TO KNOW

Suppose that you live in New Orleans, and you want to have a floral arrangement delivered to your aunt in Iowa City on her birthday [Budd, 1991]. One way would be to try to obtain a list of all the florists in Iowa City, and then determine which one is located closest to your aunt's home. An easier way is to call 1-800-FLOWERS and leave the entire responsibility for delivering the floral arrangement to that organization. You do not need to know the identity of the Iowa City florist who will deliver the flowers.

In exactly the same way, when a message is sent to an object, not only is it entirely irrelevant how the request is carried out, but the unit that sends the message is not even allowed to know the internal structure of the object. The object itself is entirely responsible for every detail of carrying out the message.

When the object-oriented paradigm is utilized, the software life cycle (Figure 1.1) has to be modified somewhat. Figure 1.7 shows the software life cycles of both the structured and object-oriented paradigms. To appreciate the difference, first consider the design phase of the structured paradigm. As stated in Section 1.3, this phase is divided into two subphases, namely, architectural design followed by detailed design. In the architectural design subphase, the product is decomposed into components, called modules. Then, during the detailed design subphase, the data structures and algorithms of each module are designed in turn. Finally, during the implementation phase, these modules are implemented.

If the object-oriented paradigm is used instead, one of the steps during the object-oriented analysis phase is to determine the objects. Because an object is a kind of module, architectural design is therefore performed during the object-oriented analysis phase. Thus, object-oriented analysis goes further than the corresponding specification (analysis) phase of the structured paradigm. This is shown in Figure 1.8.

Structured Paradigm		Object-Oriented Paradigm	
1.	Requirements phase	1.	Requirements phase
2.	Specification (analysis) phase	2′.	Object-oriented analysis phase
3.	Design phase	3′.	Object-oriented design phase
4.	Implementation phase	4′.	Object-oriented programming phase
5.	Integration phase	5.	Integration phase
6.	Maintenance phase	6.	Maintenance phase
7.	Retirement	7.	Retirement

Figure 1.7 Comparison of life cycles of structured paradigm and object-oriented paradigm.

Structured Paradigm	Object-Oriented Paradigm
2. Specification (analysis) phase • Determine what the product is to do	2′. Object-oriented analysis phase • Determine what the product is to do • Extract the objects
3. Design phase • Architectural design (extract the modules) • Detailed design	3′. Object-oriented design phase • Detailed design
4. Implementation phase • Implement in appropriate programming language	4′. Object-oriented programming phase • Implement in appropriate object-oriented programming language

Figure 1.8 Differences between structured paradigm and object-oriented paradigm.

This difference between the two paradigms has major consequences. When the structured paradigm is used, there is almost always a sharp transition between the analysis (specification) phase and the design phase. After all, the aim of the specification phase is to determine *what* the product is to do, whereas the purpose of the design phase is to decide *how* to do it. In contrast, when object-oriented analysis is used, objects enter the life cycle from the very beginning. The objects are extracted in the analysis phase, designed in the design phase, and coded in the implementation phase. Thus, the object-oriented paradigm is an integrated approach; the transition from phase to phase is far smoother than with the structured paradigm, thereby reducing the number of faults during development.

As already mentioned, it is inadequate to define an object merely as a software component that encapsulates both data and actions and implements the principle of information hiding. A more complete definition is given in Chapter 6 when objects are examined in depth. But first, the terminology used in this book must be considered in greater detail.

1.7 TERMINOLOGY

A word that is used on almost every page of this book is *software.* Software consists of not just code in machine-readable form, but also all the documentation that is an intrinsic component of every project. Thus software includes the specification document, the design document, legal and accounting documents of all kinds, the software project management plan and other management documents, as well as all types of manuals.

Since the 1970s the difference between a *program* and a *system* has become blurred. In the "good old days" the distinction was clear. A program was an autonomous piece of code, generally in the form of a deck of punched cards, that could be executed. A system was a related collection of programs. Thus a system might consist of programs P, Q, R, and S. Magnetic tape T_1 was mounted, then program P was run. It caused a deck of data cards to be read in and produced as output tapes T_2 and T_3. Tape T_2 was then rewound, and program Q was run, producing tape T_4 as output. Program R now merged tapes T_3 and T_4 into tape T_5; T_5 served as input for program S, which printed a series of reports.

Compare that situation with a product, running on a machine with a front-end communications processor and a back-end database manager, that performs real-time control of a steel mill. The single piece of software controlling the steel mill does far more than the old-fashioned system, but in terms of the classic definitions of program and system this software is undoubtedly a program. To add to the confusion, the term *system* is now also used to denote the hardware–software combination. For example, the flight control system in an aircraft consists of both the in-flight computers and the software running on them. Depending on who is using the term, the flight control system may also include the controls, such as the joystick, that send commands to the computer, and the parts of the aircraft, such as the wing flaps, that are controlled by the computer.

In order to minimize confusion, this book uses the term *product* to denote a nontrivial piece of software. There are two reasons for this convention. The first is simply to obviate the program versus system confusion by using a third term. The second reason is more important. This book deals with the *process* of software production, and the end result of a process is termed a *product. Software production* consists of two phases: *software development* followed by *maintenance.* Finally, the term *system* is used in its modern sense, that is, the combined hardware and software; or as part of universally accepted phrases, such as operating system and management information system.

Two words that are widely used within the context of software engineering are *methodology* and *paradigm.* Both are used in the same sense, namely, a collection of techniques for carrying out the complete life cycle. This usage offends language purists; after all, "methodology" means the science of methods, and a "paradigm" is a model or a pattern. Notwithstanding the best efforts of the author and others to encourage software engineers to use the words correctly, the practice is now so widespread that, in the interests of clarity, both words are used in this book in the sense of a *collection of techniques.* Erudite readers who are offended by this corruption of the English language are warmly invited to take up the cudgels of linguistic accuracy on the author's behalf; he is tired of tilting at windmills!

One term that is avoided as far as possible is *bug* (the history of this word is in the Just in Case You Wanted to Know box on page 23). The term *bug* nowadays is simply a euphemism for *error.* Although there is generally no real harm in using euphemisms, the word bug has overtones that are not conducive to good software production. Specifically, instead of saying, "I made an error," a programmer will say, "A bug crept into the code" (not *my* code, but *the* code), thereby transferring responsibility for the error from the programmer to the bug. No one blames a programmer for coming down with a case of influenza, because flu is caused by

JUST IN CASE YOU WANTED TO KNOW

The first use of the word "bug" to denote a fault is attributed to the late Rear Admiral Grace Murray Hopper, one of the designers of COBOL. On September 9, 1945, a moth flew into the Mark II computer that Hopper and her colleagues used at Harvard, and lodged between the contact plates of a relay. Thus there was literally a bug in the system. Hopper taped the bug to the log book and wrote, "First actual case of bug being found." The log book, with moth still attached, is in the Naval Museum at the Naval Surface Weapons Center, in Dahlgren, Virginia.

Although this may have been the first use of "bug" within a computer context, the word was used in engineering slang in the nineteenth century [Shapiro, 1994]. For example, Thomas Alva Edison wrote on November 18, 1878, "This thing gives out and then that—'Bugs'—as such little faults and difficulties are called . . ." [Josephson, 1992]. One of the definitions of a bug in the 1934 Edition of *Webster's New English Dictionary* is "A defect in apparatus or its operation." It is clear from Hopper's remark that she, too, was familiar with the use of the word in that context, otherwise she would have explained what she meant.

the flu bug. Referring to an error as a bug is a way of casting off responsibility. In contrast, the programmer who says, "I made an error," is a computer professional who takes responsibility for his or her actions.

There is considerable confusion regarding object-oriented terminology. For example, in addition to the term *attribute* for a data component of an object, the term *state variable* is sometimes used in the object-oriented literature. In Java, the term is *instance variable;* in C++ the term *field* is used. With regard to the actions of an object, the term *method* is usually used; in C++, however, the term is *member function.* In C++, a *member* of an object refers to either an attribute ("field") or a method. In Java, the term *field* is used to denote either an attribute ("instance variable") or a method. In order to avoid confusion, wherever possible the generic terms *attribute* and *method* are used in this book.

Thankfully, some terminology is widely accepted. For example, when a method within an object is invoked, this is almost universally termed *sending a message* to the object.

In this section we have defined the various terms used in this book. One of those terms, "process," is the subject of the next chapter.

CHAPTER REVIEW

Software engineering is defined (Section 1.1) as a discipline whose aim is the production of fault-free software that satisfies the user's needs and that is delivered on time and within budget. In order to achieve this goal, appropriate techniques have to be used in all phases of software production, including specification (analysis) and design (Section 1.4) and maintenance (Section 1.3). Software engineering addresses all phases of the software life cycle and incorporates aspects of many different areas of human knowledge, including economics (Section 1.2) and the social sciences (Section 1.5). In Section 1.6, objects are introduced, and a brief comparison between the structured and object-oriented paradigms is made. In the final section (Section 1.7), the terminology used in this book is explained.

FOR FURTHER READING

Boehm is a valuable source of further information on the scope of software engineering [Boehm, 1976; Boehm and Papaccio, 1988]. Other excellent papers on that topic include [Goldberg, 1986], [Mathis, 1986], and [Card, McGarry, and Page, 1987]. [DeMarco and Lister, 1989] is a report on the extent to which software engineering techniques are actually used in practice. For an analysis of the extent to which software engineering can be considered to be a true engineering discipline, see [Shaw, 1990] and [Wasserman, 1996]. The future of software engineering is discussed in [Lewis et al., 1995a], [Ramamoorthy and Tsai, 1996], [Lewis 1996a; 1996b], and [Leveson, 1997].

The current practice of software engineering is described in [Yourdon, 1996]. For a view on the importance of maintenance in software engineering and how to plan for it, see [Parnas, 1994]. The unreliability of software and the resulting risks (especially in safety-critical systems) are discussed in [Littlewood and Strigini, 1992], [Mellor, 1994], and [Neumann, 1995]. A modern view of the software crisis appears in [Gibbs, 1994].

The fact that mathematics underpins software engineering is stressed in [Parnas, 1990]. For an introduction to the importance of economics in software engineering, consult [Boehm, 1981].

Two classic books on the social sciences and software engineering are [Weinberg, 1971] and [Shneiderman, 1980]. Neither book requires prior knowledge of psychology or the behavioral sciences in general. A newer book on the topic is [DeMarco and Lister, 1987].

Brooks's timeless work, *The Mythical Man-Month* [Brooks, 1975], is a highly recommended introduction to the realities of software engineering. The book includes sections on all the topics mentioned in this chapter.

Excellent introductions to the object-oriented paradigm are [Budd, 1991] and [Meyer, 1997]. A balanced perspective of the paradigm is given in [Radin, 1996]. [Khan, Al-A'ali, and Girgis, 1995] explains the differences between the classical and object-oriented paradigms. Three successful projects carried using the object-oriented paradigm are described in [Capper, Colgate, Hunter, and James, 1994]. Lessons learned from developing large-scale object-oriented products are presented in [Maring, 1996] and [Fichman and Kemerer, 1997]. [Scholtz et al., 1993] is a report on a workshop held in April 1993 on the state of the art and the practice of object-oriented programming. A variety of short articles on recent trends in the object-oriented paradigm can be found in [El-Rewini et al., 1995]. Important articles on the object-oriented paradigm are found in the October 1992 issue of *IEEE Computer,* the January 1993 issue of *IEEE Software,* and the January 1993 and November 1993 issues of the *Journal of Systems and Software*. Potential pitfalls of the object-oriented paradigm are described in [Webster, 1995].

PROBLEMS

1.1 You are in charge of developing a software product for an Internet service provider that will handle all aspects of billing and of ensuring that the product will be delivered on time and within budget. Your development budget is $290,000. Approximately how much money should you devote to each phase of the software life cycle?

1.2 You are a software-engineering consultant. The vice-president for sales of a regional casual clothing retailing chain wants you to develop a product that will carry out all the accounting functions of the company and will also provide online information to the head office staff regarding orders and inventory in the various company warehouses. Terminals are required for 15 accounting clerks, 32 order clerks, and 42 warehouse clerks. In addition, 18 managers must be able to access the data. The president is willing to pay $30,000 for the hardware and the software together and wants the complete product in 4 weeks. What do you tell him? Bear in mind that, as a consultant, you want his business, no matter how unreasonable his request.

1.3 You are an air vice-marshal of the Air Force of the Republic of Hermanus. It has been decided to call in a software development organization to develop the control software for a new generation of ship-to-ship missiles. You are in charge of supervising the project. In order to protect the government of Hermanus, what clauses do you include in the contract with the software developers?

1.4 You are a software engineer and your job is to supervise the development of the software in Problem 1.3. List ways that your company can fail to satisfy the contract with the Air Force. What are the probable causes of such failures?

1.5 Fifteen months after delivery, a fault is detected in a mechanical engineering product that determines the optimal viscosity of oil in internal combustion engines. The cost of fixing the fault is $18,250. The cause of the fault is an ambiguous sentence in the specification document. Approximately how much would it have cost to have corrected the fault during the specification phase?

1.6 Suppose that the fault in Problem 1.5 had been detected during the implementation phase. Approximately how much would it have cost to have fixed it then?

1.7 You are the president of an organization that builds large-scale software. You show Figure 1.5 to your employees, urging them to find faults early in the software life cycle. Someone responds that it is unreasonable to expect anyone to remove faults before they have entered the product. For example, how can anyone remove a fault during the design phase if the fault in question is a coding fault? What do you reply?

1.8 Look up the word *system* in a dictionary. How many different definitions are there? Write down those definitions that are applicable within the context of software engineering.

1.9 It is your first day at your first job. Your manager hands you a listing and says, "See if you can find the bug." What do you reply?

1.10 You are in charge of developing the product in Problem 1.1. Will you use the object-oriented paradigm or the structured paradigm? Give reasons for your answer.

1.11 (Term Project) Suppose that the Air Gourmet product of Appendix A has been implemented exactly as described. Now, instead of using postcards, perceived meal quality is to be determined by means of a telephone interview. In what ways will the existing product have to be changed? Would it be better to discard everything and start again from scratch?

1.12 (Readings in Software Engineering) Your instructor will distribute copies of [Capper, Colgate, Hunter, and James, 1994]. To what extent are you convinced that the object-oriented paradigm is superior to the classical paradigm?

REFERENCES

[Bhandari et al., 1994] I. BHANDARI, M. J. HALLIDAY, J. CHAAR, R. CHILLAREGE, K. JONES, J. S. ATKINSON, C. LEPORI-COSTELLO, P. Y. JASPER, E. D. TARVER, C. C. LEWIS, AND M. YONEZAWA, "In-Process Improvement through Defect Data Interpretation," *IBM Systems Journal* **33** (No. 1, 1994), pp. 182–214.

[Boehm, 1976] B. W. BOEHM, "Software Engineering," *IEEE Transactions on Computers* **C-25** (December 1976), pp. 1226–41.

[Boehm, 1979] B. W. BOEHM, "Software Engineering, R & D Trends and Defense Needs," in: *Research Directions in Software Technology,* P. Wegner (Editor), The MIT Press, Cambridge, MA, 1979.

[Boehm, 1980] B. W. BOEHM, "Developing Small-Scale Application Software Products: Some Experimental Results," *Proceedings of the Eighth IFIP World Computer Congress,* October 1980, pp. 321–26.

[Boehm, 1981] B. W. BOEHM, *Software Engineering Economics,* Prentice Hall, Englewood Cliffs, NJ, 1981.

[Boehm and Papaccio, 1988] B. W. BOEHM AND P. N. PAPACCIO, "Understanding and Controlling Software Costs," *IEEE Transactions on Software Engineering* **14** (October 1988), pp. 1462–77.

[Brooks, 1975] F. P. BROOKS, JR., *The Mythical Man-Month: Essays on Software Engineering,* Addison-Wesley, Reading, MA, 1975. Twentieth Anniversary Edition, Addison-Wesley, Reading, MA, 1995.

[Budd, 1991] T. A. BUDD, *An Introduction to Object-Oriented Programming,* Addison-Wesley, Reading, MA, 1991.

[Capper, Colgate, Hunter, and James, 1994] N. P. CAPPER, R. J. COLGATE, J. C. HUNTER, AND M. F. JAMES, "The Impact of Object-Oriented Technology on Software Quality: Three Case Histories," *IBM Systems Journal* **33** (No. 1, 1994), pp. 131–57.

[Card, McGarry, and Page, 1987] D. N. CARD, F. E. MCGARRY, AND G. T. PAGE, "Evaluating Software Engineering Technologies," *IEEE Transactions on Software Engineering* **SE-13** (July 1987), pp. 845–51.

[Coleman, Ash, Lowther, and Oman, 1994] D. COLEMAN, D. ASH, B. LOWTHER, AND P. OMAN, "Using Metrics to Evaluate Software System Maintainability," *IEEE Computer* **27** (August 1994), pp. 44–49.

[Daly, 1977] E. B. DALY, "Management of Software Development," *IEEE Transactions on Software Engineering* **SE-3** (May 1977), pp. 229–42.

[DeMarco and Lister, 1987] T. DEMARCO AND T. LISTER, *Peopleware: Productive Projects and Teams,* Dorset House, New York, 1987.

[DeMarco and Lister, 1989] T. DEMARCO AND T. LISTER, "Software Development: The State of the Art vs. State of the Practice," *Proceedings of the 11th International Conference on Software Engineering,* Pittsburgh, May 1989, pp. 271–75.

[El-Rewini et al., 1995] H. EL-REWINI, S. HAMILTON, Y.-P. SHAN, R. EARLE, S. MCGAUGHEY, A. HELAL, R. BADRACHALAM, A. CHIEN, A. GRIMSHAW, B. LEE, A. WADE, D. MORSE, A. ELMAGRAMID, E. PITOURA, R. BINDER, AND P. WEGNER, "Object Technology," *IEEE Computer* **28** (October 1995), pp. 58–72.

[Elshoff, 1976] J. L. ELSHOFF, "An Analysis of Some Commercial PL/I Programs," *IEEE Transactions on Software Engineering* **SE-2** (June 1976), 113–20.

[Fagan, 1974] M. E. FAGAN, "Design and Code Inspections and Process Control in the Development of Programs," Technical Report IBM-SSD TR 21.572, IBM Corporation, December 1974.

[Fichman and Kemerer, 1997] R. G. FICHMAN AND C. F. KEMERER, "Object Technology and Reuse: Lessons from Early Adopters," *IEEE Computer* **30** (October 1997), pp. 47–59.

[Gibbs, 1994] W. W. GIBBS, "Software's Chronic Crisis," *Scientific American* **271** (September 1994), pp. 86–95.

[Goldberg, 1986] R. GOLDBERG, "Software Engineering: An Emerging Discipline," *IBM Systems Journal* **25** (No. 3/4, 1986), pp. 334–53.

[Grady, 1994] R. B. GRADY, "Successfully Applying Software Metrics," *IEEE Computer* **27** (September 1994), pp. 18–25.

[Josephson, 1992] M. JOSEPHSON, *Edison, A Biography,* John Wiley and Sons, New York, 1992.

[Kan et al., 1994] S. H. KAN, S. D. DULL, D. N. AMUNDSON, R. J. LINDNER, AND R. J. HEDGER, "AS/400 Software Quality Management," *IBM Systems Journal* **33** (No. 1, 1994), pp. 62–88.

[Khan, Al-A'ali, and Girgis, 1995] E. H. KHAN, M. AL-A'ALI, AND M. R. GIRGIS, "Object-Oriented Programming for Structured Procedural Programming," *IEEE Computer* **28** (October 1995), pp. 48–57.

[Kelly, Sherif, and Hops, 1992] J. C. KELLY, J. S. SHERIF, AND J. HOPS, "An Analysis of Defect Densities Found during Software Inspections," *Journal of Systems and Software* **17** (January 1992), pp. 111–17.

[Leveson, 1997] N. G. LEVESON, "Software Engineering: Stretching the Limits of Complexity," *Communications of the ACM* **40** (February 1997), pp. 129–31.

[Leveson and Turner, 1993] N. G. LEVESON AND C. S. TURNER, "An Investigation of the Therac-25 Accidents," *IEEE Computer* **26** (July 1993), pp. 18–41.

[Lewis, 1996a] T. LEWIS, "The Next $10{,}000_2$ Years: Part I," *IEEE Computer* **29** (April 1996), pp. 64–70.

[Lewis, 1996b] T. LEWIS, "The Next $10{,}000_2$ Years: Part II," *IEEE Computer* **29** (May 1996), pp. 78–86.

[Lewis et al., 1995a] T. LEWIS, H. EL-REWINI, J. GRIMES, M. HILL, P. LAPLANTE, J. LARUS, B. MEYER, G. POMBERGER, M. POTEL, D. POWER, W. PREE, R. VETTER, B. W. WEIDE, D. WOOD, "Where Is Software Headed?" *IEEE Computer* **28** (August 1995), pp. 20–32.

[Lientz, Swanson, and Tompkins, 1978] B. P. LIENTZ, E. B. SWANSON, AND G. E. TOMPKINS, "Characteristics of Application Software Maintenance," *Communications of the ACM* **21** (June 1978), pp. 466–71.

[Littlewood and Strigini, 1992] B. LITTLEWOOD AND L. STRIGINI, "The Risks of Software," *Scientific American* **267** (November 1992), pp. 62–75.

[Maring, 1996] B. MARING, "Object-Oriented Development of Large Applications," *IEEE Software* **13** (May 1996), pp. 33–40.

[Mathis, 1986] R. F. MATHIS, "The Last 10 Percent," *IEEE Transactions on Software Engineering* **SE-12** (June 1986), pp. 705–12.

[Mellor, 1994] P. MELLOR, "CAD: Computer-Aided Disaster," Technical Report, Centre for Software Reliability, City University, London, UK, July 1994.

[Meyer, 1992a] B. MEYER, "Applying 'Design by Contract,' " *IEEE Computer* **25** (October 1992), pp. 40–51.

[Meyer, 1997] B. MEYER, *Object-Oriented Software Construction,* Second Edition, Prentice Hall, Upper Saddle River, NJ, 1997.

[Naur, Randell, and Buxton, 1976] P. NAUR, B. RANDELL, AND J. N. BUXTON (Editors), *Software Engineering: Concepts and Techniques: Proceedings of the NATO Conferences,* Petrocelli-Charter, New York, 1976.

[Neumann, 1980] P. G. NEUMANN, Letter from the Editor, *ACM SIGSOFT Software Engineering Notes* **5** (July 1980), p. 2.

[Neumann, 1995] P. G. NEUMANN, *Computer-Related Risks,* Addison-Wesley, Reading, MA, 1995.

[Parnas, 1990] D. L. PARNAS, "Education for Computing Professionals," *IEEE Computer* **23** (January 1990), pp. 17–22.

[Parnas, 1994] D. L. PARNAS, "Software Aging," *Proceedings of the 16th International Conference on Software Engineering,* Sorrento, Italy, May 1994, pp. 279–87.

[Radin, 1996] G. RADIN, "Object Technology in Perspective," *IBM Systems Journal* **35** (No. 2, 1996), pp. 124–26.

[Ramamoorthy and Tsai, 1996] C. V. RAMAMOORTHY AND W.-T. TSAI, "Advances in Software Engineering," *IEEE Computer* **29** (October 1996), pp. 47–58.

[Scholtz et al., 1993] J. SCHOLTZ, S. CHIDAMBER, R. GLASS, A. GOERNER, M. B. ROSSON, M. STARK, AND I. VESSEY, "Object-Oriented Programming: The Promise and the Reality," *Journal of Systems and Software* **23** (November 1993), pp. 199–204.

[Shapiro, 1994] F. R. SHAPIRO, "The First Bug," *Byte* **19** (April 1994), p. 308.

[Shaw, 1990] M. SHAW, "Prospects for an Engineering Discipline of Software," *IEEE Software* **7** (November 1990), pp. 15–24.

[Shneiderman, 1980] B. SHNEIDERMAN, *Software Psychology: Human Factors in Computer and Information Systems,* Winthrop Publishers, Cambridge, MA, 1980.

[Snyder, 1993] A. SNYDER, "The Essence of Objects: Concepts and Terms," *IEEE Software* **10** (January 1993), pp. 31–42.

[Stephenson, 1976] W. E. STEPHENSON, "An Analysis of the Resources Used in Safeguard System Software Development," Bell Láboratories, Draft Paper, August 1976.

[Wasserman, 1996] A. I. WASSERMAN, "Toward a Discipline of Software Engineering," *IEEE Software* **13** (November/December 1996), pp. 23–31.

[Webster, 1995] B. F. WEBSTER, *Pitfalls of Object-Oriented Development,* M&T Books, New York, 1995.

[Weinberg, 1971] G. M. WEINBERG, *The Psychology of Computer Programming,* Van Nostrand Reinhold, New York, 1971.

[Wirfs-Brock, Wilkerson, and Wiener, 1990] R. WIRFS-BROCK, B. WILKERSON, AND L. WIENER, *Designing Object-Oriented Software,* Prentice Hall, Englewood Cliffs, NJ, 1990.

[Yourdon, 1996] E. YOURDON, *Rise and Resurrection of the American Programmer,* Yourdon Press, Upper Saddle River, NJ, 1996.

[Zelkowitz, Shaw, and Gannon, 1979] M. V. ZELKOWITZ, A. C. SHAW, AND J. D. GANNON, *Principles of Software Engineering and Design,* Prentice Hall, Englewood Cliffs, NJ, 1979.

chapter

2

THE SOFTWARE PROCESS

The software process is the way we produce software. It incorporates the software life-cycle model (Section 1.3), the tools we use (Sections 4.6 through 4.15) and, most important of all, the individuals building the software.

Different organizations have different software processes. For example, consider the issue of documentation. Some organizations consider the software they produce to be self-documenting, that is, the product can be understood simply by reading the source code. Other organizations, however, are documentation intensive. They punctiliously draw up specifications and check them methodically. Then they perform careful design activities, check and recheck their designs before coding commences, and give detailed descriptions of each module to the programmers. Test cases are preplanned, the result of each test run is logged, and the test data are carefully filed. Once the product enters the maintenance phase, any suggested change must be proposed in writing, with detailed reasons for making the change. The proposed change can be made only with written authorization, and the modification is not integrated into the product until the documentation has been updated and the changes to the documentation approved.

Intensity of testing is another measure by which organizations can be compared. Some organizations devote up to half their software budgets to the testing of software, whereas others feel that only the user can thoroughly test a product. Consequently, some companies devote minimal time and effort to testing the product but spend a considerable amount of time fixing faults detected by users.

Maintenance is a major preoccupation of many software organizations. Software that is 5, 10, or even 20 years old is continually enhanced to meet changing needs; in addition, residual faults continue to appear, even after the software has been in successful operations mode for many years. In contrast, other organizations are essentially concerned with research, leaving development—let alone maintenance—to others. This applies particularly to university computer science departments, where graduate students build software to prove that a particular design or technique is feasible. The commercial exploitation of the validated concept is then left to other organizations. (See the Just in Case You Wanted to Know box on page 31 regarding the wide variation in the ways different organizations develop software.)

However, regardless of the exact procedure, the software process broadly follows the seven phases outlined in Section 1.3, namely, requirements, specification, design, implementation, integration, maintenance, and retirement. Some of these phases are known by other names. One example is that the requirements and specification phases together are sometimes called *systems analysis*. Another example is

JUST IN CASE YOU WANTED TO KNOW

Why does the software process vary so drastically from organization to organization? A major reason is lack of software engineering skills. All too many software professionals simply do not keep up to date. They continue to develop software the Olde Fashioned Way, because they do not know any other way.

Another reason for differences in the software process is that many software managers are excellent managers but know precious little about software development or maintenance. Their lack of technical knowledge can result in the project slipping so badly behind schedule that there is no point in continuing. This is frequently the reason that many software projects are never completed.

Another reason for differences among processes is management outlook. For example, one organization may decide that it is better to deliver a product on time, even if it is not adequately tested. Given the identical circumstances, a different organization might conclude that the risk of delivering that product without comprehensive testing would be far greater than taking the time to test the product thoroughly and consequently delivering it late.

The bottom line is that software is developed by human beings, and the process within a given organization depends first and foremost on the individuals working in that organization. If those individuals are ethical, hard-working, intelligent, sensible, and up-to-date, then the chances are good that the software process within that organization will be satisfactory. Unfortunately, the converse is equally true.

the maintenance phase. Once the client agrees that the product has passed its acceptance test, the product can be used to perform useful work. For this reason, the maintenance phase is sometimes referred to as *operations mode*. Furthermore, certain phases may be subdivided; for instance, the design phase is almost always broken down into *architectural design* and *detailed design*.

In the preceding list of phases there is no separate testing phase. This omission is deliberate. Testing is not a separate phase but rather an activity that takes place all the way through software production. The requirements have to be tested, the specification document has to be tested, the design has to be tested, and so on. There are times in the process when testing is carried out to the almost total exclusion of other activities. This occurs toward the end of each phase (*verification*) and is especially true before the product is handed over to the client (*validation*). Although there are times when testing predominates, there should never be times when no testing is being performed. If testing is treated as a separate phase, then there is a very real danger that testing will not be carried out constantly throughout every phase of the product development and maintenance process.

There is also no separate documentation phase. It is important that each phase be fully documented before the next phase begins. First, the pressures to deliver a product on time are such that postponed documentation may never be completed. Second, the individual responsible for an early phase in the software process may have been transferred to a different area of responsibility or be working for another organization by the time the documentation has to be produced. Third, a product is constantly changing during development. For example, the design will usually have to be modified during the implementation phase to take into account new information about the product. Unless the design has been fully documented by the design team, modifications to the design will be extremely difficult to achieve. Furthermore, it will not be easy for the original designers to document their design after it has been modified. For all these reasons, the documentation for each phase of the software development process must be completed by the team responsible for that phase—before the next phase starts. Furthermore, the documentation must be updated continually to reflect the current version of the product.

In this chapter the phases through which a product passes are described, together with potential difficulties that may arise during each phase. In addition, testing procedures appropriate to each phase are described. Solutions to the difficulties associated with the production of software are usually nontrivial, and the rest of this book is devoted to describing suitable techniques. In the first part of this chapter only the difficulties are highlighted, but the reader is guided to the relevant sections or chapters for solutions. Thus this part of the chapter is not only an overview of the software process, it is also a guide to much of the rest of this book.

After this description of problems appertaining to each phase, inherent difficulties of software production as a whole are presented. The chapter concludes with national and international initiatives to improve the software process.

2.1 CLIENT, DEVELOPER, AND USER

Some preliminary definitions are needed here. The *client* is the individual or organization who wants a product to be developed. The *developers* are the members of the organization responsible for building that product. The developers may be responsible for every aspect of the development process, from the beginning of the requirements phase until the product passes its acceptance test, or they may be responsible for only the implementation of an already designed product. The term *software development* covers all aspects of software production before the product enters the maintenance phase. Any task that is a step toward building a piece of software, including specifying, planning, designing, testing, or documenting, constitutes software development. And after it has been developed, the software is maintained.

The client and developers may both be part of the same organization. For example, the client may be the head actuary of an insurance company and the developers a team headed by the vice-president for management information systems of that insurance company. This is termed *internal software* development. On the other hand, with *contract software* the client and developers are two totally independent organizations. For instance, the client may be the Department of Defense and the developers a major defense contractor specializing in software for weapons systems. On a much smaller scale, the client may be an accountant in a one-person practice and the developer a student who earns income by writing software on a part-time basis.

The third party involved in software production is the *user*. The user is the person or persons on whose behalf the client has commissioned the product and who will utilize the software. In the insurance company example, the users may be insurance agents who will use the software to select the most appropriate policy. In some instances the client and the user will be the same person (for example, the accountant discussed previously).

In the next part of this chapter we present the seven phases of the software life cycle and carefully analyze the role played by testing in each phase. The first phase is the requirements phase.

2.2 REQUIREMENTS PHASE

Software development is an expensive process. The development process usually begins when the client approaches a development organization with regard to a piece of software that, in the opinion of the client, is either essential to the profitability of his or her enterprise or can somehow be economically justified. At any stage of the process, if the client stops believing that the software will be cost effective, development will immediately terminate. Throughout this chapter the assumption is made that the client feels that the cost is justified.

At an initial meeting between client and developers, the client will outline the product as he or she conceptualizes it. From the viewpoint of the developers, the client's description of the desired product may be vague, unreasonable, contradictory, or simply impossible to achieve. The task of the developers at this stage is to determine exactly what it is that the client needs and to find out from the client what constraints exist. Typical constraints are cost and deadline (for example, the finished product must cost less than $370,000 and must be completed within 14 months), but a variety of other constraints are often present such as reliability (the product must be operational 99 percent of the time) or the size of the object code (it has to run on the client's personal computer). This preliminary investigation is sometimes called *concept exploration*. In subsequent meetings between members of the development team and the client team, the functionality of the proposed product is successively refined and analyzed for technical feasibility and financial justification.

Up to now, everything seems to be straightforward. Unfortunately, the requirements phase is frequently inadequately performed. When the product is finally delivered to the user, perhaps a year or two after the specifications have been signed off by the client, the client may call the developers and say, "I know that this is what I asked for, but it isn't really what I wanted." What the client asked for, and therefore, what the developers thought the client wanted, was not what the client actually *needed*. There can be a number of reasons for this predicament. First, the client may not truly understand what is going on in his or her own organization. For example, it is no use asking the software developers for a faster operating system if the cause of the current slow turnaround is a badly designed database. Or, if the client operates an unprofitable chain of retail stores, the client may ask for a financial management information system that reflects such items as sales, salaries, accounts payable, and accounts receivable. Such a product will be of little use if the real reason for the losses is shrinkage (shoplifting, and theft by employees). If that is the case, then a stock control product rather than a financial control product is required.

But the major reason that the client frequently asks for the wrong product is that software is complex. If it is difficult for a software professional to visualize a piece of software and its functionality, the problem is far worse for a client who is barely computer literate. There are a number of ways of coping with this; one of them is rapid prototyping.

A *rapid prototype* is a piece of software hurriedly put together that incorporates much of the functionality of the target product but omits those aspects generally invisible to the client, such as file updating or error handling. The client and users then experiment with the prototype to determine whether it indeed meets their needs. The rapid prototype can be changed until the client and users are satisfied that it encapsulates the functionality they desire. Rapid prototyping and other requirements analysis techniques are discussed in detail in Chapter 9.

2.2.1 REQUIREMENTS PHASE TESTING

Within every software development organization there should be a group whose primary responsibility is to ensure that the delivered product is what the client ordered, that the product has been correctly built in every way. This group is called the software quality assurance (SQA) group. The quality of software is the extent to which it meets its specifications. Quality and software quality assurance are described in more detail in Chapter 5, as is the role of SQA in setting up and enforcing standards.

The SQA group must play a role right from the start of the development process. In particular, it is vital that the product satisfy the client's needs. The SQA group must, therefore, verify with the client that the final version of the rapid prototype is totally satisfactory.

It is essential that the rapid prototype be carefully checked by both client and users to be certain that it reflects their current needs. Nevertheless, no matter how meticulously this is done, there is always the possibility that forces beyond the control of the development team will necessitate changes in the requirements while the product is being developed. Further development will then have to be put on hold until the necessary modifications have been made to the partially completed product.

A major issue in software development is the so-called moving target problem. That is, the client changes the requirements during development. One reason this occurs is an unforeseeable change in circumstances. For example, if a company expands its operations, or is taken over by another company, then many products will have to be modified, including those still under development. However, the major cause of the moving target problem is a client who keeps changing his or her mind. As explained in Section 15.4.4, there is nothing that can be done about it if the client has sufficient clout.

2.3 SPECIFICATION PHASE

Once the client agrees that the developers understand the requirements, the *specification document* is drawn up by the specification team. As opposed to the informal requirements phase, the specification document (or *specifications*) explicitly describes the functionality of the product—that is, precisely what the product is supposed to do—and lists any constraints that the product must satisfy. The specification document will include the inputs to the product and the required outputs. For example, if the client needs a payroll product, then the inputs will include the pay scales of each employee, data from a time clock, as well as information from personnel files so that taxes can be computed correctly. The outputs will be paychecks and reports such as Social Security deductions. In addition, the specification document will include stipulations that the product must be able to handle correctly a wide range of deductions such as medical insurance payments, union dues, and pension fund contributions.

The specification document of the product constitutes a contract. The software developers will be deemed to have completed the contract when they deliver a product that satisfies the acceptance criteria of the specification document. For this reason, the specification document should not include imprecise terms like suitable, convenient, ample, or enough, or similar terms that sound exact but which in practice are equally imprecise, such as optimal or 98 percent complete. Whereas contract software development can lead to a lawsuit, there is no chance of the specification document forming the basis for legal action when the client and developers are from the same organization. Nevertheless, even in the case of internal software development, the specification document should always be written as if it will be used as evidence in a trial.

A variety of difficulties can arise during the specification phase. One possible mistake that can be made by the specification team is that the specifications may be *ambiguous*—certain sentences or sections may have more than one possible valid interpretation. Consider the specification, "A part record and a plant record are read from the database. If it contains the letter A directly followed by the letter Q, then compute the cost of transporting that part to that plant." To what does the *it* in the preceding sentence refer: the part record or the plant record? In fact, the *it* could conceivably even refer to the database!

The specifications may also be *incomplete*, that is, some relevant fact or requirement may have been omitted. For instance, the specifications may not state what actions are to be taken if the input data contain errors. Moreover, the specifications may be *contradictory*. For example, in one place in the specification document for a product that controls a fermentation process, it is stated that if the pressure exceeds 35 psi, then valve M17 must immediately be shut. However, in another place it is stated that if the pressure exceeds 35 psi, then the operator must immediately be alerted; only if the operator takes no remedial action within 30 seconds should valve M17 be shut automatically. Software development cannot proceed until such problems in the specification document have been corrected.

Once the specifications are complete, detailed planning and estimating commences. No client will authorize a software project without knowing in advance how long the project will take and how much it will cost. From the viewpoint of the developers, these two items are just as important. If the developers underestimate the cost of a project, then the client will pay the agreed fee, which may be significantly less than the actual cost to the developers. Conversely, if the developers overestimate what the project will cost, then the client may turn the project down or have the job done by other developers whose estimate is more reasonable. Similar issues arise with regard to duration estimation. If the developers underestimate how long it will take to complete a project, then the resulting late delivery of the product will, at best, result in a loss of confidence on the part of the client. At worst, lateness penalty clauses in the contract will be invoked, causing the developers to suffer financially. Again, if the developers overestimate how long it will take for the product to be delivered, the client may well award the job to developers who promise faster delivery.

For the developers, merely estimating the duration and total cost is not enough. The developers need to assign the appropriate personnel to the various stages of the development process. For example, the coding team cannot start until the design documents have been approved by the SQA group, and the design team is not needed until the specification team has completed its task. In other words, the developers have to plan ahead. A software project management plan (SPMP) must be drawn up that reflects the separate phases of the development process and that shows which members of the development organization are involved in each task, as well as the deadlines for completing each task.

The earliest that such a detailed plan can be drawn up is when the specifications have been finalized. Before that time, the project is too amorphous to undertake complete planning. Some aspects of the project can certainly be planned right from the start, but until the developers know exactly what is to be built, they cannot specify all aspects of the plan for building it.

Thus, once the specification document has been finished and checked, preparation of the software project management plan commences. Major components of the plan are the deliverables (what the client is going to get), the milestones (when the client gets them), and the budget (how much it is going to cost).

The plan describes the software process in fullest detail. It includes aspects such as the life-cycle model to be used, the organizational structure of the development organization, project responsibilities, managerial objectives and priorities, the techniques and CASE tools to be used, and detailed schedules, budgets, and resource allocations. Underlying the entire plan are the duration and cost estimates; techniques for obtaining such estimates are described in Section 8.2.

The specification phase is described in Chapters 10 and 11; structured techniques are described in Chapter 10, whereas object-oriented analysis is the subject of Chapter 11. (The term *analysis* is sometimes used to describe activities of the specification phase, hence the phase *object-oriented analysis*.)

2.3.1 SPECIFICATION PHASE TESTING

As pointed out in Chapter 1, a major source of faults in delivered software is faults in the specification document that are not detected until the software has gone into operations mode; that is, it is being used by the client's organization for the intended purpose for which it was developed. The SQA group must therefore carefully check the specifications, looking for contradictions, ambiguities, and any signs of incompleteness. In addition, the SQA group must ensure that the specifications are feasible, for example, that any specified hardware component is fast enough or that the client's current online disk storage capacity is adequate for handling the new product. If a specification document is to be testable, then one of the properties it must have is *traceability*. It must be possible to trace every statement in the specification document back to a statement made by the client team during the requirements phase. If the requirements have been methodically presented, properly numbered, cross-referenced, and indexed, then the SQA group should not have too much difficulty tracing through the specification document and ensuring that it is indeed a true reflection of the client's requirements. If rapid prototyping has been used in the requirements phase, then the relevant statements of the specification document should be traceable to the rapid prototype.

An excellent way of checking the specification document is by means of a review. Representatives of the specification team and of the client are present. The meeting is usually chaired by a member of the SQA group. The aim of the review is to determine whether the specifications are correct. The reviewers go through the specification document, ensuring that there are no misunderstandings about the document. Walkthroughs and inspections are two types of reviews, and they are described in Section 5.2.

Consider now the testing of the detailed planning and estimating that takes place once the client has signed off the specifications. Whereas it is essential that every aspect of the SPMP be meticulously checked by the SQA group, particular attention must be paid to the plan's duration and cost estimates. One way to do this is for management to obtain two (or more) independent estimates of both duration and cost at the start of the planning phase, and then to reconcile any significant differences. With regard to the SPMP document, an excellent way to verify it is by a review similar to the review of the specification document.

If the duration and cost estimate are satisfactory, then the client will give permission for the project to proceed. The next stage is to design the product.

2.4 DESIGN PHASE

The specifications of a product spell out *what* the product is to do. The aim of the design phase is to determine *how* the product is to do it. Starting with the specification document, the design team determines the internal structure of the product.

During the design phase, algorithms are selected and data structures chosen. The inputs to and outputs from the product are laid down in the specifications, as are all other external aspects of the product. During the design phase, the internal data flows are determined. The design team decomposes the product into *modules*, independent pieces of code with well-defined interfaces to the rest of the product. (An object is a specific type of module.) For each module, the designer specifies what that module has to do and how it has to do it. The interface of each module, that is, the arguments passed to the module and the arguments returned by the module, must be specified in detail. For example, a module might measure the water level in a nuclear reactor and cause an alarm to sound if the level is too low. A module in an avionics product might take as input two or more sets of coordinates of an incoming enemy missile, compute its trajectory, and advise the pilot as to possible evasive action.

While this decomposition is being performed, the design team must keep a careful record of the design decisions that are made. This information is essential for two reasons. First, while the product is being designed there will be times when a dead end is reached and the design team feels the need to backtrack and redesign certain pieces. Having a written record of why specific decisions were made will assist the team when this occurs and help them get back on track.

The second reason for keeping the design decisions concerns maintenance. Ideally, the design of the product should be open-ended, meaning future enhancements can be done by adding new modules or replacing existing modules without affecting the design as a whole. Of course, in practice this ideal product is difficult to achieve. Deadline constraints in the real world are such that designers struggle against the clock to complete a design that will satisfy the original specification document, without worrying about any later enhancements. If future enhancements (to be added after the product has gone into operations mode) are included in the specification document, then these must be allowed for in the design, but this situation is extremely rare. In general, the specification document, and hence the design, will deal with only present requirements. In addition, there is no way of determining, while the product is still in the design phase, what all possible future enhancements might be. And finally, if the design has to take *all* future possibilities into account, at best it will be unwieldy; at worst it will be so complicated that implementation will be impossible. So the designers have to compromise, putting together a design that can be extended in many reasonable ways without the need for total redesign. But in a product that undergoes major enhancement, the time will come when the design simply cannot handle further changes. When this stage is reached, it is time to redesign the product as a whole. If the redesign team has a record of the reasons for all the original design decisions, its job will be easier.

The major output from the design phase is the *design* itself that has two parts: the *architectural design*, a description of the product in terms of its modules, and the *detailed design*, a description of each module. The latter descriptions are given to the programmers for implementation. Chapter 6 is devoted to the theory of design in general and the design of objects in particular. Design techniques, including object-oriented design, are described in Chapter 12, together with ways of describing the design, such as graphics and pseudocode.

2.4.1 DESIGN PHASE TESTING

As mentioned in Section 2.3.1, a critical aspect of testability is *traceability.* In the case of design, this means that every part of the design can be linked to a statement in the specification document. A suitably cross-referenced design gives the SQA group a powerful tool for checking whether the design agrees with the specification document and whether every statement of the specification document is reflected in some part of the design.

Design reviews are similar to the reviews that the specifications undergo. However, in view of the technical nature of most design documents, the client is not usually present. Members of the design team and the SQA group work through the design as a whole as well as through each separate module, ensuring that the design is correct. The types of faults to look for include logic faults, interface faults, lack of exception handling (processing of error conditions), and, most important, nonconformance to the specifications. In addition, the review team should always be aware of the possibility that some specification faults were not detected during the previous phase. A detailed description of the review process is given in Section 5.2.

2.5 IMPLEMENTATION PHASE

During the implementation phase, the various component modules of the design are coded. Implementation is discussed in detail in Chapters 13 and 14. The major documentation associated with implementation is the source code itself, suitably commented. But the programmer should provide additional documentation to assist in maintenance, including all test cases against which the code was tested, the expected results, and the actual output. These documents will be used in regression testing, as explained in Section 2.7.1.

2.5.1 IMPLEMENTATION PHASE TESTING

The modules should be tested while they are being implemented (*desk checking*) and, after they have been implemented, they are run against test cases. This informal testing is done by the programmer. Thereafter, the quality assurance group tests the modules methodically. A variety of module testing techniques are described in Chapter 13.

In addition to running test cases, a code review is a powerful and successful technique for detecting programming faults. Here the programmer guides the members of the review team through the listing of the modules. The review team must include an SQA representative. The procedure is similar to reviews of specifications and designs described previously.

2.6 INTEGRATION PHASE

The next stage is to combine the modules and determine whether the product as a whole functions correctly. The way in which the modules are integrated (all at once or one at a time) and the specific order (from top to bottom in the module interconnection diagram or bottom to top) can have a critical influence on the quality of the resulting product. For example, suppose the product is integrated bottom-up. If there is a major design fault, then it will show up late, necessitating an expensive rewrite. Conversely, if the modules are integrated top-down, then the lower-level modules usually will not receive as thorough a testing as would be the case if the product were integrated bottom-up. These and other problems are discussed in detail in Chapter 14. A careful explanation is given in that chapter as to why implementation and integration must be performed in parallel.

2.6.1 INTEGRATION PHASE TESTING

The purpose of *integration testing* is to check that the modules combine together correctly to achieve a product that satisfies its specifications. During integration testing, particular care must be paid to testing the module interfaces. It is important that the number, order, and types of formal arguments match the number, order, and types of actual arguments. This strong type checking [van Wijngaarden et al., 1975] is best performed by the compiler and linker. However, many languages are not strongly typed. When such a language is used, checking of interfaces must be done by members of the SQA group.

When the integration testing has been completed, the SQA group performs *product testing*. The functionality of the product as a whole is checked against the specifications. In particular, the constraints listed in the specification document must be tested. A typical example is whether the response time is short enough. Because the aim of product testing is to determine whether the specifications have been correctly implemented, many of the test cases can be drawn up once the specification document is complete.

Not only must the correctness of the product be tested, but also its robustness. That is, intentionally erroneous input data are submitted to determine whether the product will crash or whether its error-handling capabilities are adequate for dealing with bad data. If the product is to be run together with the client's currently installed software, then tests must also be performed to check that the new product will not have an adverse effect on the client's existing computer operations. Finally, a check must also be made as to whether the source code and all other types of documentation are complete and internally consistent. Product testing is discussed in Section 14.4.

The final aspect of integration testing is *acceptance testing*. The software is delivered to the client, who tests the software on the actual hardware, using actual data as opposed to test data. No matter how careful the development team or the SQA group might be, there is a significant difference between test cases, which by their very nature are artificial, and actual data. A software product cannot be considered to satisfy its specifications until the product has passed its acceptance tests. Mor details about acceptance testing are given in Section 14.5.

As opposed to expensive custom software written for one client, multiple copies of shrink-wrapped software, such as word processors or spreadsheets, are sold at much lower prices to a large number of buyers. That is, the manufacturers of shrink-wrapped software (such as Microsoft or Borland) recover the cost of developing a product by volume selling. (The term *shrink-wrapped software* comes from the fact that the box containing the CD or diskettes, the manuals, and the license agreement is almost always shrink-wrapped. An alternative term is *commercial off-the-shelf* software, usually referred to by the acronym *COTS*.) As soon as product testing is complete, versions of the complete shrink-wrapped product are shipped to the client for testing on site. The first such version is termed the alpha version. The corrected alpha version is called the beta version; in general, the beta version is intended to be close to the final version.

Faults in shrink-wrapped software usually result in poor sales of the product and huge losses for the development company. In order for as many faults as possible to come to light as early as possible, developers of shrink-wrapped software frequently give alpha or beta versions to selected companies, in the expectation that on-site tests will uncover any latent faults. In return, the alpha and beta sites are frequently promised free copies of the delivered version of the software. There are risks involved for a company participating in alpha or beta testing. In particular, alpha test versions can be fault-laden, resulting in frustration, time wasting, and possible damage to databases. However, the company gets a head start in using the new shrink-wrapped software, which can give it an advantage over its competitors. A problem occurs sometimes when software organizations use alpha testing by potential clients in place of thorough product testing by the SQA group. Although alpha testing at a number of different sites will usually bring to light a large variety of faults, there is no substitute for the methodical testing that the SQA group can provide.

2.7 MAINTENANCE PHASE

Once the product has been accepted by the client, any changes constitute maintenance. Maintenance is not an activity that is grudgingly carried out after the product has gone into operations mode. On the contrary, it is an integral part of the software process that must be planned for from the beginning. As explained in Section 2.4, the design should, as far as is feasible, take future enhancements into account. Coding must be performed with future maintenance kept in mind. After all, as pointed out in Section 1.3, more money is spent on maintenance than on all other software activities combined. It is therefore almost always a vital aspect of software production. Maintenance must never be treated as an afterthought. Instead, the entire software development effort must be carried out in such a way as to minimize the impact of the inevitable future maintenance.

A common problem with maintenance is documentation, or rather a lack of it. In the course of developing software against a time deadline, the original specification and design documents are frequently not updated and are, consequently, almost useless to the maintenance team. Other documentation such as the database manual or the operating manual may never be written, because management decided that delivering the product to the client on time was more important than developing the documentation in parallel with the software. In many instances, the source code is the only documentation available to the maintainer. The high rate of personnel turnover in the software industry exacerbates the maintenance situation in that none of the original developers may be working for the organization at the time when maintenance is performed.

Maintenance is frequently the most challenging phase of software production for the reasons stated previously and for the additional reasons to be given in Chapter 15.

2.7.1 MAINTENANCE PHASE TESTING

There are two aspects to the testing of changes to a product in operations mode. The first is checking that the required changes have been correctly implemented. The second aspect is ensuring that, in the course of making the required changes to the product, no other inadvertent changes were made. Thus, once the programmer has determined that the desired changes have been implemented, the product must be tested against previous test cases to make certain that the functionality of the rest of the product has not been compromised. This procedure is called *regression testing*. To assist in performing regression testing, it is necessary that all previous test cases be retained, together with the results of running those test cases. Testing during the maintenance phase is discussed in greater detail in Chapter 15.

2.8 RETIREMENT

The final phase in the software life cycle is retirement. After many years of service, a stage is reached when further maintenance is no longer cost effective. Sometimes the proposed changes are so drastic that the design as a whole would have to be changed. In such a case it is less expensive to redesign and recode the entire product. Or perhaps so many changes may have been made to the original design that interdependencies have inadvertently been built into the product, and there is a real danger that even a small change to one minor module might have a drastic effect on the functionality of the product as a whole. Third, the documentation may not have been adequately maintained, thus increasing the risk of a regression fault to the extent that it would be safer to recode than to maintain. A fourth possibility is that the hardware (and operating system) on which the product runs is to be replaced; it may be more economical to rewrite from scratch than to modify. In each of these instances the current version is replaced by a new version, and the software process continues.

True retirement, on the other hand, is a somewhat rare event that occurs when a product has outgrown its usefulness. The client organization no longer requires the functionality provided by the product, and it is finally removed from the computer.

After this review of the complete software process, together with some of the difficulties attendant on each phase, it is time to consider difficulties associated with software production as a whole.

2.9 Problems with Software Production: Essence and Accidents

Over the past 40 years hardware has become cheaper and faster. It was mentioned in Section 1.5 that the performance–price factor has decreased by an order of magnitude eight times during this period. Furthermore, hardware has shrunk in size. In the 1950s, companies paid hundreds of thousands of preinflation dollars for a machine as large as a room that was no more powerful than today's desktop personal computer selling for under $1,000. It would seem that this trend is inexorable, and that computers will continue to become smaller, faster, and cheaper.

Unfortunately, this is not the case. There are a number of physical constraints that must eventually impose limits on the possible future size and speed of hardware. The first of these constraints is the speed of light. Electrons, or more precisely, electromagnetic waves, simply cannot travel faster than 186,300 miles per second. One way to speed up a computer is therefore to miniaturize its components. In that way, the electrons will have shorter distances to travel. Second, there are also lower limits on the size of a component. An electron travels along a path that can be as narrow as three atoms in width. But if the path along which the electron is to travel is any narrower than that, then the electron can stray onto an adjacent path. For the same reason, parallel paths must not be located too close to one another. Thus the speed of light and the nonzero width of an atom impose physical limits on hardware size and speed. We are nowhere near these limits yet—computers can easily become at least two orders of magnitude faster and smaller without reaching these physical limits. But there are intrinsic laws of nature that will eventually prevent computers from becoming arbitrarily fast or arbitrarily small.

Now what about software? Software is essentially conceptual, and therefore nonphysical, although it is of course always stored on some physical medium such as paper or magnetic disk. Superficially, it might appear that with software

JUST IN CASE YOU WANTED TO KNOW

The "silver bullet" in the title of Brooks's article refers to the recommended way of slaying werewolves, otherwise perfectly normal human beings who suddenly turn into wolves. Brooks's line of inquiry is to determine whether a similar silver bullet can be used to solve the problems of software. After all, software usually appears to be innocent and straightforward but, like a werewolf, software can be transformed into something horrifying, in the shape of late deadlines, exceeded budgets, and residual specification and design faults not detected during testing.

anything is possible. But Fred Brooks, in a landmark article entitled "No Silver Bullet" [Brooks, 1986], exploded this belief. He argued that, analogous to hardware speed and size limits that cannot physically be exceeded, there are inherent problems with current techniques of software production that can never be solved. To quote Brooks, "... building software will always be hard. There is inherently no silver bullet." (An explanation of the term "silver bullet" is in the Just in Case You Wanted to Know box above.)

Recall that the title of Brooks's article is "*No* Silver Bullet" (author's italics). Brooks's theme is that the very nature of software makes it highly unlikely that a silver bullet will be discovered that will magically solve all the problems of software production, let alone help achieve software breakthroughs comparable to those that have occurred with unfailing regularity in the hardware field. He divides the difficulties of software into two Aristotelian categories: *essence,* the difficulties inherent in the intrinsic nature of software, and *accidents,* the difficulties encountered today that are not inherent in software production. That is, essence constitutes those aspects of software production that probably cannot be changed, whereas accidents are amenable to research breakthroughs, or silver bullets.

What then are the aspects of software production that are inherently difficult? Brooks lists four, which he terms complexity, conformity, changeability, and invisibility. Brooks's use of the word *complexity* is somewhat unfortunate in that the term has many different meanings in computer science in general and in software engineering in particular. In the context of his article, Brooks uses the word *complex* in the sense of *complicated* or *intricate.* In fact, the names of all four aspects are used in their nontechnical sense.

Each of the four aspects is now examined.

2.9.1 COMPLEXITY

Software is more complex than any other construct made by human beings. Even hardware is almost trivial compared to software. To see this, consider a 16-bit word W in the main memory of a computer. Because each of the 16 bits comprising the word can take on exactly two values, namely, 0 and 1, word W as a whole can be in any of 2^{16} different states. If we have two words, w_1 and w_2, each 16 bits in length, then the number of possible states of words w_1 and w_2 together is 2^{16} times 2^{16}, or 2^{32}. In general, if a system consists of a number of independent pieces, then the number of possible states of that system is the product of the numbers of possible states of each component.

Now suppose the computer is to be used to run a software product p, and the 16-bit word w is to be used to store the value of an integer x. If the value of x is read in by a statement such as read(x), then, because the integer x can take on 2^{16} different values, at first sight it might seem that the number of states in which the product could be is the same as the number of states in which the word could be. If the product p consisted only of the single statement read (x), then the number of states of p would indeed be 2^{16}. But in a realistic, nontrivial software product the value of a variable that is input is later used elsewhere in the product. There is thus an interdependence between the read (x) statement and any statement that uses the value of x. The situation is more complex if the flow of control within the product depends on the value of x. For example, x may be the control variable in a **switch** statement, or there may be a **for** loop or **while** loop whose termination depends on the value of x. Thus the number of states in any nontrivial product is greater, because of this interaction, than the product of the number of states of each variable. As a consequence of this combinatorial explosion in the number of states, complexity does not grow linearly with the size of the product, but much faster.

Complexity is an inherent property of software. No matter how a nontrivial piece of software is designed, the pieces of the product will interact. For example, the states of a module will depend on the states of its arguments, and the states of global variables (variables that can be accessed by more than one module) will also affect the state of the product as a whole. Certainly, complexity can be reduced, for example by using the object-oriented paradigm. Nevertheless, it can never be totally eliminated. In other words, complexity is an essential property of software, not an accidental one.

Brooks points out that complex phenomena can be described and explained in disciplines such as mathematics and physics. Mathematicians and physicists have learned how to abstract the essential features of a complex system, to build a simple model that reflects only those essential features, to validate the simple model, and to make predictions from it. In contrast, if software is simplified the whole exercise is useless; the simplifying techniques of mathematics and physics work only because the complexities of those systems are accidents, not essence, as is the case with software products.

The consequence of this essential complexity of software is that a product becomes difficult to understand. In fact, it is often true that no one really understands a large product in its entirety. This leads to imperfect communication between team members that, in turn, results in the time and cost overruns that characterize the development of large-scale software products. In addition, errors in specifications are made simply because of a lack of understanding of all aspects of the product.

This essential complexity affects not only the software process itself, but also the management of the process. Unless a manager can obtain accurate information regarding the process that he or she is managing, it is difficult to determine personnel needs for the succeeding stages of the project and to budget accurately. Reports to senior management regarding both progress-to-date and future deadlines are likely to be inaccurate. Drawing up a testing schedule is difficult when neither the manager nor anyone reporting to the manager knows what loose ends still have to be tied. And if a project staffer leaves, trying to train a replacement can be a nightmare.

A further consequence of the complexity of software is that it complicates the maintenance process. As shown in Figure 1.2, about two-thirds of the total software effort is devoted to maintenance. Unless the maintainer really understands the product, there is always the danger that corrective maintenance or enhancement can damage the product in such a way that further maintenance is required to repair the damage caused by the original maintenance. The possibility of this sort of damage being caused by carelessness is always present, even when the original author makes the change, but it is exacerbated when the maintenance programmer is effectively working in the dark. Poor documentation; or worse, no documentation; or still worse, incorrect documentation is often a major cause of incorrectly performed maintenance. But no matter how good the documentation may be, the inherent complexity of software transcends all attempts to cope with it, and this complexity will unfavorably impact maintenance. Again, the object-oriented paradigm can help reduce complexity (and hence improve maintenance), but it cannot eliminate it completely.

2.9.2 CONFORMITY

A manually controlled gold refinery is to be computerized. Instead of the plant being operated via a series of buttons and levers, a computer will send the necessary control signals to the components of the plant. Although the plant is working perfectly, management feels that a computerized control system will increase the gold yield. The task of the software development team is to construct a product that will interface with the existing plant. That is, the software must conform to the plant, not the plant to the software. This is the first type of conformity identified by Brooks, where software acquires an unnecessary degree of complexity because it has to interface with an existing system.

What if a brand-new computerized gold refinery were to be constructed? It would appear that the mechanical engineers, metallurgical engineers, and software engineers could sit down together and come up with a plant design in which the machinery and the software fit together in a natural and straightforward manner. In practice, however, there is generally a perception that it is easier to make the software interface conform to the other components, rather than to change the way the other components have been configured in the past. As a result, even in a new gold refinery the other engineers will insist on designing the machinery as before, and the software will be forced to conform to the hardware interfaces. This

JUST IN CASE YOU WANTED TO KNOW

According to Section 1.4, pages 15–17 of the Technical Manual for the U.S.S. Enterprise, NCC-1701-D, much of the software development was started before the hardware development [Sternbach and Okuda, 1991]. I hope that, in this respect at least, *Star Trek* turns out to be science fact rather than science fiction!

is the second type of conformity identified by Brooks, where software acquires an unnecessary degree of complexity because of the misconception that software is the component that is the most conformable.

The problems caused by this forced conformity cannot be removed by redesigning the software, because the complexity is not due to the structure of the software itself. Instead, it is due to the structure of software caused by the interfaces, to humans or to hardware, imposed on the software designer (but see the Just in Case You Wanted to Know box above for details of how this may change in the future).

2.9.3 CHANGEABILITY

As pointed out in Section 1.1, it is considered unreasonable to ask a civil engineer to move a bridge 300 miles or rotate it through 90°, but it is perfectly acceptable to tell a software engineer to rewrite half an operating system over a 5-year period. Civil engineers know that redesigning half a bridge is expensive and dangerous; it is both cheaper and safer to rebuild it from scratch. Software engineers are equally well aware that, in the long run, extensive maintenance is unwise and that rewriting the product from scratch will sometimes prove to be less expensive. Nevertheless, clients frequently demand major changes to software.

Brooks points out that there will always be pressures to change software. After all, it *is* easier to change software than, say, the hardware on which it runs; that is the reason behind the terms *soft*ware and *hard*ware. In addition, the functionality of a system is embodied in its software, and changes in functionality are achieved through changing the software. It has been suggested that the problems caused by frequent and drastic maintenance are merely problems caused by ignorance, and if the public at large were better educated with regard to the nature of software, then demands for major changes would not occur. But Brooks points out that changeability is a property of the essence of software, an inherent problem that cannot be surmounted. That is, the very nature of software is such that, no matter how the public is educated, there will always be pressures for changes in software, and often these changes will be drastic.

There are four reasons why useful software has to undergo change. First, as pointed out in Section 1.3, software is a model of reality, and as the reality changes, so the software must adapt or die. Second, if software is found to be useful, then there are pressures, chiefly from satisfied users, to extend the functionality of the product beyond what is feasible in terms of the original design. Third, one of the greatest strengths of software is that it is so much easier to change than hardware. Fourth, successful software survives well beyond the lifetime of the hardware for which it was written. In part this is due to the fact that, after 4 or 5 years, hardware often does not function as well as it did. But more significant is the fact that technological change is so rapid that more appropriate hardware components, such as larger disks, faster CPUs, or more powerful monitors, become available while the software is still viable. In general, the software will have to be modified to some extent in order to run on the new hardware.

For all these reasons, part of the essence of software is that it has to be changed, and this inexorable and continual change has a deleterious effect on the quality of software.

2.9.4 INVISIBILITY

A major problem with the essence of software is that it is "invisible and unvisualizable" [Brooks, 1986]. Anyone who has been handed a 200-page listing and told to modify the software in some way will know exactly what Brooks is saying. Unfortunately, there is no acceptable way to represent either a complete product or some sort of overview of the product. In contrast, architects, for example, can provide 3-dimensional models that give an idea of the overall design, as well as 2-dimensional blueprints and other detailed diagrams that, to the trained eye, will reflect every detail of the structure to be built. Chemists can build models of molecules, engineers can construct scale models, and plastic surgeons can use the computer to show potential clients exactly how their faces will look after surgery. Diagrams can be drawn to reflect the structure of silicon chips and other electronic components; the components of a computer can be represented by means of various sorts of schematics, at various levels of abstraction.

Certainly there are ways in which software engineers can represent specific views of their product. For example, a software engineer can draw one directed graph depicting flow of control, another showing flow of data, a third with patterns of dependency, and a fourth depicting time sequences. The problem is that few of these types of graphs are planar, let alone hierarchical. The many crossovers in these graphs are a distinct obstacle to understanding. Parnas [Parnas, 1979] suggests cutting the arcs of the graphs until one or more becomes hierarchical. The problem is that the resulting graph, though comprehensible, makes only a subset of the software visualizable, and the arcs that have been cut may be critical from the viewpoint of comprehending the interrelationships between the components of the software.

The result of this inability to represent software visually not only makes software difficult to comprehend, it also severely hinders communication among software professionals—there does not seem to be an alternative to handing a colleague a 200-page listing together with a list of modifications to be made.

It must be pointed out that visualizations of all kinds, such as flowcharts, data flow diagrams (Section 10.3.1), or module interconnection diagrams, are extremely useful and powerful ways of visualizing certain aspects of the product. Visual representations are an excellent means of communicating with a client as well as with other software engineers. The problem is that such diagrams cannot embody *every* aspect of the product, nor is there a way of determining what is missing from any one visual representation of the product.

2.9.5 NO SILVER BULLET?

Brooks's article [Brooks, 1986] is by no means totally gloom-filled. He describes what he considers to be the three major breakthroughs in software technology, namely, high-level languages, time sharing, and software development environments (such as the UNIX Programmer's Workbench), but stresses that they solved only accidental, and not essential, difficulties. He evaluates various technical developments that are currently advanced as potential silver bullets, including proofs of correctness (Section 5.5), object-oriented design (Section 12.6), Ada, and artificial intelligence and expert systems. Although some of these approaches may solve remaining accidental difficulties, Brooks feels that they are irrelevant to the essential difficulties.

In order to achieve comparable future breakthroughs, Brooks suggests that we change the way that software is produced. For example, whenever possible, software products should be bought off the shelf (that is, shrink-wrapped software) rather than custom-built. For Brooks, the hard part of building software lies in the requirements, specification, and design phases—not in the implementation phase. The use of rapid prototyping (Section 9.2) is for him a major potential source of an order-of-magnitude improvement. Another suggestion that, in Brooks's opinion, may lead to a major improvement in productivity is greater use of the principle of incremental development, where instead of trying to build the product as a whole, it is constructed stepwise. This concept is described in Section 4.6.

For Brooks, the greatest hope of a major breakthrough in improving software production lies in training and encouraging great designers. As stated previously, in Brooks's opinion one of the hardest aspects of software production is the design phase, and to get great designs, we need great designers. Brooks cites UNIX, APL, Pascal, Modula-2, Smalltalk, and FORTRAN as exciting products of the past. He points out that they have all been the products of one, or a very few, great minds. On the other hand, more prosaic but useful products like COBOL, PL/I, ALGOL, MVS/360, and MS-DOS have all been products of committees. Nurturing great designers is for Brooks the most important objective if we wish to improve software production.

Parts of Brooks's paper make depressing reading. After all, from the title onwards he states that the inherent nature (or essence) of current software production makes the finding of a silver bullet a dubious possibility. Nevertheless, he concludes on a note of hope, suggesting that if we change our software production strategies by buying ready-made software wherever possible, using rapid prototyping and incremental building techniques, and attempting to nurture great designers, we may increase software productivity. However, an order-of-magnitude breakthrough, the "silver bullet," is most unlikely.

Brooks's pessimism must be put into perspective. Over the past 20 years there has been a steady productivity increase in the software industry of roughly 6 percent per year. This productivity increase is comparable to what has been observed in many manufacturing industries. What Brooks is looking for, though, is a "silver bullet," a way of rapidly obtaining an order-of-magnitude increase in productivity. It is difficult to disagree with his view that we cannot hope to double productivity overnight. At the same time, the compound growth rate of 6 percent means that productivity is doubling every 12 years. This improvement may not be as rapid and spectacular as we would like, but the software engineering process is steadily improving from year to year.

The remainder of this chapter is devoted to national and international initiatives aimed at process improvement.

2.10 IMPROVING THE SOFTWARE PROCESS

Our global economy is critically dependent on computers, and hence on software. For this reason, the governments of many countries are concerned about the software process. For example, in 1987 a task force of the U.S. Department of Defense (DoD) reported:

"After two decades of largely unfulfilled promises about productivity and quality gains from applying new software methodologies and technologies, industry and government organizations are realizing that their fundamental problem is the inability to manage the software process" [DoD, 1987].

In response to this and related concerns, DoD founded the Software Engineering Institute (SEI) and set it up at Carnegie Mellon University in Pittsburgh on the basis of a competitive procurement process. One of the major successes of the SEI has been the capability maturity model (CMM) initiative. Related software process improvement efforts include the ISO 9000-series standards of the International Standards Organization, and the software process improvement capability determination (SPICE), an international initiative involving more than 20 countries. We begin by describing CMM.

2.11 CAPABILITY MATURITY MODELS

The *capability maturity models* (CMMs) of the SEI are a related group of strategies for improving the software process, irrespective of the actual life-cycle model used. (The term *maturity* is a measure of the goodness of the process itself.)

There are CMMs for software (SW–CMM), for management of human resources (P–CMM; the *P* stands for "people"), for systems engineering (SE–CMM), for integrated product development (IPD–CMM), and for software acquisition (SA–CMM). In addition, there is now an initiative to unify these five partially overlapping capability maturity models [Konrad et al., 1996].

For reasons of space, only one capability maturity model, SW–CMM, is examined here. The SW–CMM was first put forward in 1986 by Watts Humphrey [Humphrey, 1989]. Recall that a software process encompasses the activities, techniques, and tools used to produce software. It thus incorporates both technical and managerial aspects of software production. Underlying the SW–CMM is the belief that the use of new software techniques will not in itself result in increased productivity and profitability, because the cause of our problems is how we manage the software process. The strategy of the SW–CMM is to improve the management of the software process in the belief that improvements in techniques will be a natural consequence. The resulting improvement in the process as a whole should result in better quality software and fewer software projects that suffer from time and cost overruns.

Bearing in mind that improvements in the software process cannot occur overnight, the SW–CMM induces change incrementally. More specifically, five different levels of *maturity* are defined, and an organization then advances slowly in a series of small evolutionary steps toward the higher levels of process maturity [Paulk, Weber, Curtis, and Chrissis, 1995]. In order to understand this approach, the five levels are now described.

Maturity Level 1: Initial Level At this the lowest level, there are essentially no sound software engineering management practices in place in the organization. Instead, everything is done on an ad hoc basis. If one specific project happens to be staffed by a competent manager and a good software development team, then that project may be successful. However, the usual pattern is time and cost overruns caused by a lack of sound management in general and planning in particular. As a result, most activities are responses to crises, rather than preplanned tasks. In level 1 organizations the software process is unpredictable, because it depends totally on the current staff; as the staff changes, so does the process. As a consequence, it is impossible to predict with any accuracy such important items as the time it will take to develop a product or the cost of that product.

It is an unfortunate fact that the vast majority of software organizations all over the world are level 1 organizations.

Maturity Level 2: Repeatable Level At this level, basic software project management practices are in place. Planning and management techniques are based on experience with similar products; hence the name *repeatable*. At level 2, measurements are taken, an essential first step in achieving an adequate process. Typical measurements include the careful tracking of costs and schedules. Instead of functioning in crisis mode as in level 1, managers identify problems as they arise and take immediate corrective action to prevent them from becoming crises. The key point is that without measurements it is impossible to detect problems before they get out of hand. Also, measurements taken during one project can be used to draw up realistic duration and cost schedules for future projects.

Maturity Level 3: Defined Level At level 3 the process for software production is fully documented. Both the managerial and technical aspects of the process are clearly defined, and continual efforts are made to improve the process wherever possible. Reviews (Section 5.2) are used to achieve software quality. At this level, it makes sense to introduce new technology such as CASE environments (Section 4.10) in order to increase quality and productivity further. In contrast, "high tech" only makes the crisis-driven level 1 process even more chaotic.

Although a number of organizations have attained maturity levels 2 and 3, few have reached levels 4 or 5. The two highest levels are thus targets for the future.

Maturity Level 4: Managed Level A level 4 organization sets quality and productivity goals for each project. These two quantities are continually measured and corrective action is taken when there are unacceptable deviations from the goal. Statistical quality controls [Deming, 1986; Juran, 1988] are in place to enable management to distinguish a random deviation from a meaningful violation of quality or productivity standards. (A simple example of a statistical quality control measure is the number of faults detected per 1000 lines of code. A corresponding objective is to reduce this quantity over time.)

Maturity Level 5: Optimizing Level The goal of a level 5 organization is continuous process improvement. Statistical quality and process control techniques are used to guide the organization. The knowledge gained from each project is utilized in future projects. The process thus incorporates a positive feedback loop, resulting in a steady improvement in productivity and quality.

These five maturity levels are summarized in Figure 2.1. In order to improve its software process, an organization first attempts to gain an understanding of its current process and then formulates the intended process. Next, actions that will result in achieving this process improvement are determined and ranked in priority order. Finally, a plan to accomplish this improvement is drawn up and executed. This series of steps is then repeated, with the organization successively improving its software process; this progression from level to level is reflected in Figure 2.1. Experience with the capability maturity model has shown that advancing a complete maturity level usually takes from 18 months to 3 years, but moving from level 1 to level 2 sometimes takes 3 or even 5 years. This is a reflection of how difficult it is to instill a methodical approach in an organization that up to now has functioned on a purely ad hoc and reactive basis.

For each maturity level, the SEI has highlighted a series of key process areas (KPAs) that an organization should target in its endeavor to reach the next maturity level. For example, the KPAs for Level 2 (Repeatable Level) include

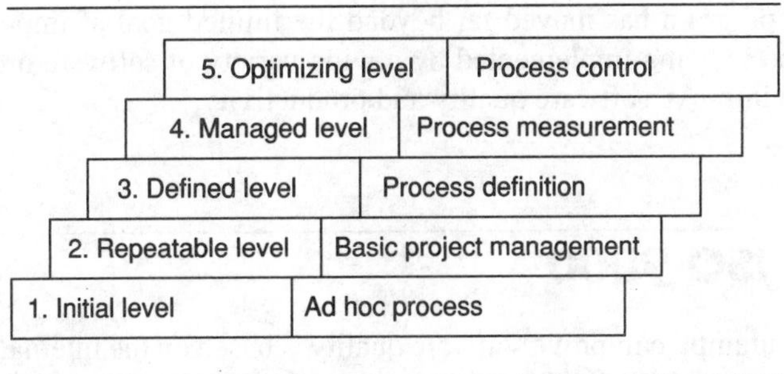

Figure 2.1 The five levels of the capability maturity model.

configuration control (Section 4.13); software quality assurance (Section 5.1.1); project planning (Chapter 8); project tracking (Section 8.2.5); and requirements management (Chapter 9). These areas cover the basic elements of software management: Determine the client's needs (requirements management); draw up a plan (project planning); monitor deviations from that plan (project tracking); control the various pieces that make up the software product (configuration management); and ensure that the product is fault-free (quality assurance). Within each KPA is a group of between two and four related goals which, if achieved, will result in the next maturity level being attained. For example, one of the project planning goals is the development of a plan that appropriately and realistically covers the activities of software development.

At the highest level, maturity level 5, the KPAs include defect prevention, technology innovation, and process change management. Comparing the KPAs of the two levels, it is clear that a level 5 organization is far in advance of one that is at level 2. For example, a level 2 organization is concerned with software quality assurance, that is, with detecting and correcting faults (software quality is discussed in more detail in Chapter 5). In contrast, the process of a level 5 organization incorporates defect prevention, that is, trying to ensure that there are no faults in the software in the first place.

To aid an organization to reach the higher maturity levels, the SEI has developed a series of questionnaires that form the basis for an assessment by an SEI team. The purpose of the assessment is to highlight current shortcomings in the organization's software process and to indicate ways in which the organization can improve its process.

The CMM program of the Software Engineering Institute was sponsored by the U.S. Department of Defense (DoD). One of the original goals of the CMM program was to raise the quality of defense software by evaluating the processes of contractors who produce software for DoD and awarding contracts to those contractors who demonstrate a mature process. The U.S. Air Force has stipulated that any software development organization that wishes to be an Air Force contractor must conform to SW–CMM level 3 by 1998, and the Department of Defense as a whole subsequently issued a similar directive. Thus, there is pressure for organizations to improve the maturity of their software processes. However, the

SW–CMM program has moved far beyond the limited goal of improving DoD software and is being implemented by a wide variety of software organizations that wish to improve software quality and productivity.

❖ 2.12 ISO 9000

A different attempt to improve software quality is based on the International Standards Organization (ISO) 9000-series standards. As described in the previous section, the SEI Capability Maturity Model (CMM) initiative is an attempt to improve software quality by improving the process by which software is developed.

ISO 9000 is a series of five related standards that are applicable to a wide variety of industrial activities, including design, development, production, installation, and servicing; ISO 9000 is certainly not just a software standard. Within the ISO 9000 series, standard ISO 9001 for quality systems [ISO 9001, 1987] is the standard that is most applicable to software development. Because of the broadness of ISO 9001, ISO has published specific guidelines to assist in applying ISO 9001 to software, namely, ISO 9000-3 [ISO 9000-3, 1991].

ISO 9000 has a number of features that distinguish it from the CMM [Dawood, 1994]. In ISO 9000 there is stress on documenting the process in both words and pictures in order to ensure consistency and comprehensibility. Also, the ISO 9000 philosophy is that adherence to the standard does not guarantee a 100 percent quality product, but rather reduces the risk of a poor quality product. ISO 9000 is only part of a quality system. Also required are management commitment to quality, intensive training of workers, and setting and achieving goals for continual quality improvement.

Like the CMM, ISO 9000 emphasizes measurement. Both models stress the corrective actions that need to be taken to ensure process improvement. Finally, both strongly underline the need for continuous training of software professionals, not just when introducing quality-improvement measures.

ISO 9000-series standards have been adopted by over 60 countries, including the U.S., Japan, Canada, and the countries of the European Union (E.U.). This means, for example, that if a U.S. software organization wishes to do business with a European client, the U.S. organization must first be certified as ISO 9000-compliant. A certified registrar (auditor) has to examine the company's process and certify that its process complies with the ISO standard.

Although the CMM and ISO 9000 both have the same objective, namely, improved software quality, each considers different attributes when determining maturity level or compliance with ISO 9000. Thus, even though there are major areas of overlap, it has been reported that at least two level 1 organizations have been certified as compliant with ISO 9000 [Bishop, 1994]. Conversely, it

❖As explained in the Preface, the material of this section may be taught in parallel with Part 2.

is possible in principle for an organization to demonstrate a high level of maturity without complying with ISO 9000 [Bamford and Deibler, 1993a]. In general, however, there is a high probability that a mature organization will have a software process that is ISO 9000-compliant.

Following their European counterparts, more and more U.S. organizations are requiring ISO 9000 certification. For example, General Electric Plastic Division insisted that 340 vendors achieve the standard by June 1993 [Dawood, 1994]. It is unlikely that the U.S. government will follow the E.U. lead and require ISO 9000 compliance for non-U.S. companies that wish to do business with organizations in the United States. Nevertheless, there are pressures both within the U.S. and from its major trading partners that may ultimately result in significant worldwide ISO 9000 compliance.

❖ 2.13 SPICE

SPICE, like ISO 9000, is an international process improvement initiative (the name *SPICE* is an acronym formed from Software Process Improvement Capability dEtermination). Over 40 countries are actively contributing to the SPICE endeavor. SPICE was initiated by the British Ministry of Defence (MOD) with the long-term aim of establishing SPICE as an international standard (MOD is the U.K. counterpart of the U.S. DoD, which initiated the CMM). The first version of SPICE was completed in 1995.

The original study that led to the SPICE initiative, the "ImproveIT" report [Dorling and Simms, 1991], examined a wide variety of existing process assessment methods, including CMM and ISO 9000. In addition, some organizations stated that they were interested in replacing their own internal assessment methods with a standardized public domain method. Although SPICE is nominally a process assessment initiative, it goes far beyond that to include process improvement and software procurement. Thus, SPICE is intended to extend and improve on existing software process improvement models like SW–CMM and ISO 9000.

SW–CMM, ISO 9000, and SPICE all have the common aim of process improvement. SPICE goes further than the other two in that it sets out a framework for assessment methods that conform to SPICE but does not lay down a specific method (both SW–CMM and ISO 9000 are conformant methods).

Another difference between SPICE and SW–CMM is that SPICE generates a separate assessment of each component of the overall process, such as requirements analysis and configuration management. In contrast, the KPAs of each level of the SW–CMM and their associated goals appertain to the overall process used by the organization being assessed [Kitson, 1996].

Since July 1997, much of the SPICE initiative has been taken over by a joint committee of the International Standards Organization and the International Electrotechnical Commission. For this reason, SPICE is now sometimes referred to as ISO/IEC 15504, or 15504 for short.

2.14 COSTS AND BENEFITS OF SOFTWARE PROCESS IMPROVEMENT

Does implementing software process improvement lead to increased profitability? Preliminary results indicate that this is indeed the case. For example, the Software Engineering Division of Hughes Aircraft in Fullerton, California, spent nearly $500,000 between 1987 and 1990 for assessments and improvement programs [Humphrey, Snider, and Willis, 1991]. During this 3-year period, Hughes Aircraft moved up from maturity level 2 to level 3, with every expectation of future improvement to level 4 and even level 5. As a consequence of improving its process, Hughes Aircraft estimates its annual savings to be of the order of $2 million. These savings have accrued in a number of ways, including decreased overtime hours, fewer crises, improved employee morale, and lower turnover of software professionals.

Comparable results have been reported at other organizations. For example, the Equipment Division at Raytheon moved from level 1 in 1988 to level 3 in 1993. A twofold increase in productivity has resulted, as well as a return of $7.70 for every dollar invested in the process improvement effort [Dion, 1993]. Schlumberger has had similar successes [Wohlwend and Rosenbaum, 1993]. As a consequence of results like these, the capability maturity models are being applied relatively widely within the U.S. software industry and also abroad.

Figure 2.2 is taken from an SEI report on 13 large organizations that participated in the initial CMM study [Herbsleb et al., 1994]. The sample consisted of a broad range of software developers, including DoD contractors, military organizations, and commercial software organizations. Because each organization measured quantities such as costs and productivity in a different way, the study focused on how these quantities changed with time. As shown in the figure, productivity and early defect detection increased, and time to market and post-release

Category	Range	Median	Number of Data Points
Years engaged in software process improvement (SPI)	1–9	3.5	24
Yearly cost of SPI per software engineer	$490–$2004	$1375	5
Productivity gain per year	9%–67%	35%	4
Early defect detection gain per year	6%–25%	22%	3
Yearly reduction in time to market	15%–23%	19%	2
Yearly reduction in post-release defect reports	10%–94%	39%	5
Business value (saving/cost of SPI)	4.0–8.8:1	5.0:1	5

Figure 2.2 SW–CMM software improvement data [Herbsleb et al., 1994].

CMM Level	Number of Projects	Relative Decrease in Duration	Faults per MEASL Detected during Development	Relative Productivity
Level 1	3	1.0	—	—
Level 2	9	3.2	890	1.0
Level 3	5	2.7	411	0.8
Level 4	8	5.0	205	2.3
Level 5	9	7.8	126	2.8

MEASL stands for million equivalent assembler source lines.
[Diaz and Sligo, 1997]. ©1997, IEEE.

Figure 2.3 Results of 34 Motorola GED projects.

defect reports decreased. Figure 2.2 also shows that for every dollar spent on software process improvement, the savings were in the range of $4 to $8.80, with a median of $5. It must be pointed out that the 13 organizations in the study were actively engaged in a variety of process improvement activities, not just the SEI SW-CMM.

Motorola Government Electronics Division (GED) has been actively involved in SEI's software process improvement program since 1992 [Diaz and Sligo, 1997]. Figure 2.3 depicts 34 GED projects, categorized according to the maturity level of the group that developed each project. As can be seen from the figure, the relative duration (that is, the duration of a project relative to a baseline project completed before 1992) decreased with increasing maturity level. Quality was measured in terms of faults per million equivalent assembler source lines (MEASL); in order to be able to compare projects implemented in different languages, the number of lines of source code was converted into the number of equivalent lines of assembler code [Jones, 1996]. As shown in Figure 2.3, quality increased with increasing maturity level. Finally, productivity was measured as MEASL per person-hour. For reasons of confidentiality, Motorola does not publish actual productivity figures, so Figure 2.3 reflects productivity relative to the productivity of a level 2 project. (There are no quality or productivity figures for the level 1 projects because these quantities cannot be measured when the team is at level 1.)

As a consequence of published studies such as those described in this section and those listed in the For Further Reading section of this chapter, more and more organizations worldwide are realizing that process improvement is cost effective.

CHAPTER REVIEW

After some preliminary definitions (Section 2.1), the various phases of the software process, from requirements (Section 2.2) to retirement (Section 2.8), are described. Special attention is paid to the problems associated with each phase.

Testing is not considered to be a separate phase, because testing must be carried out in parallel with all software production activities. A description of testing activities during each of the life-cycle phases is given in Sections 2.2.1 through 2.7.1.

In addition to the problems associated with each separate software life-cycle phase, Brooks's views regarding the inherent difficulties of software production are presented (Section 2.9). Brooks's four aspects of essential software difficulty, namely, complexity, conformity, changeability, and invisibility, are described and discussed in Sections 2.9.1 through 2.9.4. Brooks's viewpoint is analyzed in Section 2.9.5.

The last part of the chapter is devoted to software process improvement (Section 2.10). Details are given of various national and international software improvement initiatives, including SW–CMM (Section 2.11), ISO 9000 (Section 2.12), and SPICE (Section 2.13). The cost-effectiveness of software process improvement is discussed in Section 2.14.

FOR FURTHER READING

The review articles in the For Further Reading section of Chapter 1, namely, [Brooks, 1975], [Boehm, 1976], [Goldberg, 1986], [Mathis, 1986], [Card, McGarry, and Page, 1987], [Boehm and Papaccio, 1988], [DeMarco and Lister, 1989], [Yourdon, 1992], and [Wasserman, 1996] also highlight the problems associated with software production.

With regard to testing during each of the phases of the life cycle, a good general source is [Beizer, 1990]. More specific references are given in Chapter 5 of this book and in the For Further Reading section at the end of that chapter.

No summary such as that presented here can do justice to Brooks's "No Silver Bullet"—the article must be read in the original [Brooks, 1986]. Among the many thoughtful responses to Brooks's article, Cox suggests [Cox, 1990] that there is indeed a silver bullet, namely, reuse of objects (described in Chapter 7). The view expressed in [Harel, 1992], although largely agreeing with Brooks, is that as a consequence of the newer technologies, the future will be less bleak than in Brooks's opinion. [Mays, 1994] provides another interesting view on the silver bullet issue. The issue of software complexity is addressed by a number of articles in the July 1997 issue of *IEEE Computer.*

A detailed description of the original SEI capability maturity model (CMM) is given in [Humphrey, 1989]. A newer version is described in [Paulk, Curtis, Chrissis, and Weber, 1993] and [Paulk, Weber, Curtis, and Chrissis, 1995]. [Humphrey, 1996] describes a personal software process (PSP); results of applying the PSP appear in [Ferguson et al., 1997]. Successes of the CMM are described in [Hicks and Card, 1994], and criticism of the assessment process appears in [Bollinger and McGowan, 1991]. The July 1993 issue of *IEEE Software* contains a number of papers on the CMM.

An overview of SEI software process assessments between 1987 and 1991 is given in [Kitson and Masters, 1993]; newer results are incorporated in [Herbsleb et al., 1997]. A number of articles have been written on industry experiences from the viewpoint of a specific company that has introduced the SEI process improvement program; typical examples include Shlumberger [Wohlwend and Rosenbaum, 1993] and Raytheon [Haley, 1996]. The impact of SEI on the software industry is discussed in [Saiedian and Kuzara, 1995] and in [Brodman and Johnson, 1996]. An interesting view of the CMM is given in [Bamberger, 1997]. [Bamford and Deibler, 1993b] is a detailed comparison of ISO 9000 and the CMM; an overview appears in [Bamford and Deibler, 1993a]. [Paulk, 1995] is another comparison. A wealth of information on the CMM is available at the SEI CMM web site[1], www.sei.cmu.edu. The ISO/IEC 15504 ("SPICE") home page is at www.sei.cmu.edu/technology/process/spice/.

The June 1997 issue of *Proceedings of the ACM* contains a number of papers on software quality and the CMM; [Herbsleb et al., 1997] is of particular interest. Yet another process improvement program, namely, that of the Software Engineering Laboratory, is described in [Basili et al., 1995]. [Fuggetta and Picco, 1994] is an annotated bibliography on process improvement.

PROBLEMS

2.1 Describe a situation in which the client, developer, and user are one and the same person.

2.2 What problems can arise if the client, developer, and user are one and the same person? How can these problems be solved?

2.3 What are the potential advantages if the client, developer, and user are one and the same person?

2.4 Consider the requirements phase and the specification phase. Would it make more sense to combine these two activities into one phase rather than treating them separately?

2.5 List the documentation that should be produced during each phase of the software life cycle.

2.6 More testing is performed during the integration phase than in any other development phase. Would it be better to divide this phase into two separate phases, one incorporating the nontesting aspects, the other all the testing?

2.7 Maintenance is one of the most important phases of software production and also the most difficult to perform. Nevertheless, it is looked down on by many software

[1] This and the other URLs cited in this book were correct at the time of going to press. Web addresses tend to change frequently, however, and without prior or subsequent notification. If this happens, the reader should consult the Web site for this book, www.mhhe.com/engcs/compsci/schach, where the new address will be given.

professionals, and maintenance programmers are often paid less than developers. Do you think that this is reasonable? If not, how would you try to change it?

2.8 Why do you think that, as stated in Section 2.8, true retirement is a rare event?

2.9 Due to a fire at Constantia Software, all documentation for a product is destroyed just before it is delivered. What is the impact of the resulting lack of documentation?

2.10 Brooks says that software production is inherently difficult because of complexity, conformity, changeability, and invisibility. Other areas of human endeavor, including law, medicine, theology, and engineering, are also difficult. To what extent is each of these areas affected by complexity, conformity, changeability, and invisibility?

2.11 Brooks considers the most important breakthroughs in software technology to be high-level languages, time-sharing, and software development environments. What do *you* consider to be the major software breakthroughs? Give reasons for your answer.

2.12 Draw a detailed flowchart of the software distributed by your instructor. Is it easy to understand? Now make the flowchart planar by deleting all edges that cross over another edge. Is the resulting flowchart easier to understand? How much of the original functionality has been lost? Translate the resulting planar flowchart back into the original programming language and run it. Do you agree with Brooks's statement that software is "invisible and unvisualizable"?

2.13 You have just purchased Medieval Software Developers, an organization that is on the verge of bankruptcy because the company is at maturity level 1. What is the first step that you will take to restore the organization to profitability?

2.14 (Term Project) Discuss how the four essential problems of software production (complexity, conformity, changeability, and invisibility) affect the Air Gourmet product of Appendix A.

2.15 (Readings in Software Engineering) Your instructor will distribute copies of [Herbsleb et al., 1997]. If you were in charge of a software organization, would you embark on CMM-based software process improvement?

REFERENCES

[Bamford and Deibler, 1993a] R. C. BAMFORD AND W. J. DEIBLER, II, "Comparing, Contrasting ISO 9001 and the SEI Capability Maturity Model," *IEEE Computer* **26** (October 1993), pp. 68–70.

[Bamford and Deibler, 1993b] R. C. BAMFORD AND W. J. DEIBLER, II, "A Detailed Comparison of the SEI Software Maturity Levels and Technology Stages to the Requirements for ISO 9001 Registration," Software Systems Quality Consulting, San Jose, CA, 1993.

[Bamberger, 1997] J. BAMBERGER, "Essence of the Capability Maturity Model," *IEEE Computer* **30** (June 1997), pp. 112–14.

[Basili et al., 1995] V. Basili, M. Zelkowitz, F. McGarry, J. Page, S. Waligora, and R. Pajerski, "SEL's Software Process-Improvement Program," *IEEE Software* **12** (November 1995), pp. 83–87.

[Beizer, 1990] B. Beizer, *Software Testing Techniques,* Second Edition, Van Nostrand Reinhold, New York, NY, 1990.

[Bishop, 1994] M. Bishop, Usenet posting <2p8pab$rv0@source.asset.com> on comp.software-eng, April 22, 1994.

[Boehm, 1976] B. W. Boehm, "Software Engineering," *IEEE Transactions on Computers* **C-25** (December 1976), pp. 1226–41.

[Boehm and Papaccio, 1988] B. W. Boehm and P. N. Papaccio, "Understanding and Controlling Software Costs," *IEEE Transactions on Software Engineering* **14** (October 1988), pp. 1462–77.

[Bollinger and McGowan, 1991] T. Bollinger and C. McGowan, "A Critical Look at Software Capability Evaluations," *IEEE Software* **8** (July 1991), pp. 25–41.

[Brodman and Johnson, 1996] J. G. Brodman and D. Johnson, "Return on Investment from Software Process Improvement as Measured by U.S. Industry," *CrossTalk* **9** (April 1996), pp. 23–28.

[Brooks, 1975] F. P. Brooks, Jr., *The Mythical Man-Month: Essays on Software Engineering,* Addison-Wesley, Reading, MA, 1975. Twentieth Anniversary Edition, Addison-Wesley, Reading, MA, 1995.

[Brooks, 1986] F. P. Brooks, Jr., "No Silver Bullet," in: *Information Processing '86,* H.-J. Kugler (Editor), Elsevier North-Holland, New York, NY, 1986. Reprinted in: *IEEE Computer* **20** (April 1987), pp. 10–19.

[Card, McGarry, and Page, 1987] D. N. Card, F. E. McGarry, and G. T. Page, "Evaluating Software Engineering Technologies," *IEEE Transactions on Software Engineering* **SE-13** (July 1987), pp. 845–51.

[Cox, 1990] B. J. Cox, "There *Is* a Silver Bullet," *Byte* **15** (October 1990), pp. 209–18.

[Dawood, 1994] M. Dawood, "It's Time for ISO 9000," *CrossTalk* (March 1994) pp. 26–28.

[DeMarco and Lister, 1989] T. DeMarco and T. Lister, "Software Development: The State of the Art vs. State of the Practice," *Proceedings of the 11th International Conference on Software Engineering,* Pittsburgh, May 1989, pp. 271–75.

[Deming, 1986] W. E. Deming, *Out of the Crisis,* MIT Center for Advanced Engineering Study, Cambridge, MA, 1986.

[Diaz and Sligo, 1997] M. Diaz and J. Sligo, "How Software Process Improvement Helped Motorola," *IEEE Software* **14** (September/October 1997), pp. 75–81.

[Dion, 1993] R. Dion, "Process Improvement and the Corporate Balance Sheet," *IEEE Software* **10** (July 1993), pp. 28–35.

[DoD, 1987] "Report of the Defense Science Board Task Force on Military Software," Office of the Undersecretary of Defense for Acquisition, Washington, DC, September 1987.

[Dorling and Simms, 1991] A. Dorling and P. Simms, "ImproveIT," Ministry of Defence, London, UK, June 1991.

[Fuggetta and Picco, 1994] A. Fuggetta and G. P. Picco, "An Annotated Bibliography on Software Process Improvement," *ACM SIGSOFT Software Engineering Notes* **19** (July 1995), pp. 66–68.

[Ferguson et al., 1997] P. Ferguson, W. S. Humphrey, S. Khajenoori, S. Macke, and A. Matvya, "Results of Applying the Personal Software Process," *IEEE Computer* **30** (May 1997), pp. 24–31.

[Goldberg, 1986] R. GOLDBERG, "Software Engineering: An Emerging Discipline," *IBM Systems Journal* **25** (No. 3/4, 1986), pp. 334–53.

[Haley, 1996] T. J. HALEY, "Raytheon's Experience in Software Process Improvement," *IEEE Software* **13** (November 1996), pp. 33–41.

[Harel, 1992] D. HAREL, "Biting the Silver Bullet," *IEEE Computer* **25** (January 1992), pp. 8–24.

[Herbsleb et al., 1994] J. HERBSLEB, A. CARLETON, J. ROZUM, J. SIEGEL, AND D. ZUBROW, "Benefits of CMM-Based Software Process Improvement: Initial Results," Technical Report CMU/SEI-94-TR-13, Software Engineering Institute, Carnegie Mellon University, August 1994.

[Herbsleb et al., 1997] J. HERBSLEB, D. ZUBROW, D. GOLDENSON, W. HAYES, AND M. PAULK, "Software Quality and the Capability Maturity Model," *Communications of the ACM* **40** (June 1997), pp. 30–40.

[Hicks and Card, 1994] M. HICKS AND D. CARD, "Tales of Process Improvement," *IEEE Software* **11** (January 1994), pp. 114–15.

[Humphrey, 1989] W. S. HUMPHREY, *Managing the Software Process,* Addison-Wesley, Reading, MA, 1989.

[Humphrey, 1995] W. S. HUMPHREY, *A Discipline for Software Engineering,* Addison-Wesley, Reading, MA, 1995.

[Humphrey, 1996] W. S. HUMPHREY, "Using a Defined and Measured Personal Software Process," *IEEE Software* **13** (May 1996), pp. 77–88.

[Humphrey, Snider and Willis, 1991] W. S. HUMPHREY, T. R. SNIDER, AND R. R. WILLIS, "Software Process Improvement at Hughes Aircraft," *IEEE Software* **8** (July 1991), pp. 11–23.

[ISO 9000-3, 1991] "ISO 9000-3, Guidelines for the Application of ISO 9001 to the Development, Supply, and Maintenance of Software," International Organization for Standardization, Geneva, 1991.

[ISO 9001, 1987] "ISO 9001, Quality Systems—Model for Quality Assurance in Design/Development, Production, Installation, and Servicing," International Organization for Standardization, Geneva, 1987.

[Jones, 1996] C. JONES, *Applied Software Measurement,* McGraw-Hill, New York, 1996.

[Juran, 1988] J. M. JURAN, *Juran on Planning for Quality,* Macmillan, New York, 1988.

[Kitson, 1996] D. H. KITSON, "Relating the SPICE Framework and the SEI Approach to Software Process Assessment," Proceedings of the Fifth European Conference on Software Quality, Dublin, Ireland, September 1996.

[Kitson and Masters, 1993] D. H. KITSON AND S. M. MASTERS, "An Analysis of SEI Software Process Assessment Results: 1987–1991," *Proceedings of the Fifteenth International Conference on Software Engineering,* Baltimore, MD, May 1993, pp. 68–77.

[Konrad et al., 1996] M. KONRAD, M. B. CHRISSIS, J. FERGUSON, S. GARCIA, B. HELFLEY, D. KITSON, AND M. PAULK, "Capability Maturity Modeling SM at the SEI," *Software Process—Improvement and Practice* **2** (March 1996), pp. 21–34.

[Mathis, 1986] R. F. MATHIS, "The Last 10 Percent," *IEEE Transactions on Software Engineering* **SE-12** (June 1986), pp. 705–12.

[Mays, 1994] R. G. MAYS, "Forging a Silver Bullet from the Essence of Software," *IBM Systems Journal* **33** (No. 1, 1994) pp. 20–45.

[Parnas, 1979] D. L. PARNAS, "Designing Software for Ease of Extension and Contraction," *IEEE Transactions on Software Engineering* **SE-5** (March 1979), pp. 128–138.

[Paulk, 1995] M. C. PAULK, "How ISO 9001 Compares with the CMM," *IEEE Software* **12** (January 1995), pp. 74–83.

[Paulk et al., 1993] M. C. PAULK, C. V. WEBER, S. GARCIA, M. B. CHRISSIS, AND M. BUSH, "Key Practices of the Capability Maturity Model, Version 1.1," Report CMU/SEI-93-TR-25, ADA263432, Software Engineering Institute, Carnegie Mellon University, Pittsburgh, February 1993.

[Paulk, Weber, Curtis, and Chrissis, 1995] M. C. PAULK, C. V. WEBER, B. CURTIS, AND M. B. CHRISSIS, *The Capability Maturity Model: Guidelines for Improving the Software Process,* Addison-Wesley, Reading, MA, 1995.

[Saiedian and Kuzara, 1995] H. SAIEDIAN AND R. KUZARA, "SEI Capability Maturity Model's Impact on Contractors," *IEEE Computer* **28** (January 1995), pp. 16–26.

[Sternbach and Okuda, 1991] R. STERNBACH AND M. OKUDA, *Star Trek: The Next Generation, Technical Manual,* Pocket Books, New York, 1991.

[van Wijngaarden et al., 1975] A. VAN WIJNGAARDEN, B. J. MAILLOUX, J. E. L. PECK, C. H. A. KOSTER, M. SINTZOFF, C. H. LINDSEY, L. G. L. T. MEERTENS, AND R. G. FISKER, "Revised Report on the Algorithmic Language ALGOL 68," *Acta Informatica* **5** (1975), pp. 1–236.

[Wasserman, 1996] A. I. WASSERMAN, "Toward a Discipline of Software Engineering," *IEEE Software* **13** (November/December 1996), pp. 23–31.

[Wohlwend and Rosenbaum, 1993] H. WOHLWEND AND S. ROSENBAUM, "Software Improvements in an International Company," *Proceedings of the 15th International Conference on Software Engineering,* Baltimore, MD, May 1993, pp. 212–20.

[Yourdon, 1992] E. YOURDON, *Decline and Fall of the American Programmer,* Yourdon Press, Englewood Cliffs, NJ, 1992.

chapter

3

SOFTWARE LIFE-CYCLE MODELS

A software product usually begins as a vague concept, such as "Wouldn't it be nice if the computer could plot our graphs of radioactivity levels," or "If this corporation doesn't have an exact picture of our cash flow on a daily basis, we will be insolvent in six months," or even "If we develop and market this new type of spreadsheet, we'll make a million dollars!" Once the need for a product has been established, the product goes through a series of development phases. Typically, the product is specified, designed, and then implemented. If the client is satisfied, the product is installed, and while it is operational it is maintained. When the product finally comes to the end of its useful life, it is decommissioned. The series of steps through which the product progresses is called the *life-cycle model*.

The life-cycle history of each product is different. Some products will spend years in the conceptual stage, perhaps because current hardware is just not fast enough for the product to be viable, or because fundamental research has to be done before an efficient algorithm can be developed. Other products will be quickly designed and implemented and then spend years in the maintenance phase being modified to meet the users' changing needs. Yet other products will be designed, implemented, and maintained; then after many years of radical maintenance, it will be cheaper to develop a completely new product rather than attempt to patch the current version yet again.

In this chapter a number of different life-cycle models are described. The two most widely used models are the waterfall model and the rapid prototyping model. In addition, the spiral model is now receiving considerable attention. To help shed light on the strengths and weaknesses of these three models, other life-cycle models will also be examined, including incremental models, the synchronize-and-stabilize model, and the highly unsatisfactory build-and-fix model.

3.1 BUILD-AND-FIX MODEL

It is unfortunate that many products are developed using what might be termed the *build-and-fix* model. The product is constructed without specifications or any attempt at design. Instead, the developers simply build a product that is reworked as many times as necessary to satisfy the client. This approach is shown in Figure 3.1. Although this approach may work well on short programming exercises 100 or 200 lines long, the build-and-fix model is totally unsatisfactory for products of

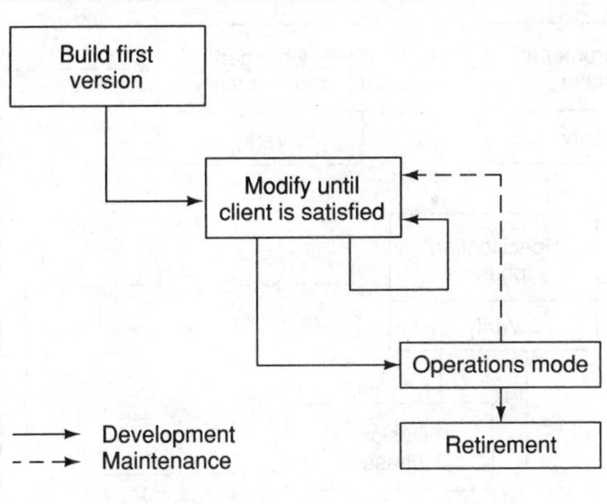

Figure 3.1 Build-and-fix model.

any reasonable size. Figure 1.5 shows that the cost of changing a software product is relatively small if the change is made at the requirements, specification, or design phases, but grows unacceptably large if changes are made after the product has been coded, or worse, if it is already in operations mode. Thus, the cost of the build-and-fix approach is actually far greater than the cost of a properly specified and carefully designed product. In addition, maintenance of a product can be extremely difficult without specification or design documents, and the chances of a regression fault occurring are considerably greater.

Instead of the build-and-fix approach, it is essential that before development of a product begins, an overall game plan or *life-cycle model* be chosen. The life-cycle model (sometimes abbreviated to just "model") specifies the various phases of the software process, such as the requirements, specification, design, implementation, integration, and maintenance phases, and the order in which they are to be carried out. Once the life-cycle model has been agreed to by all parties, development of the product can begin.

Until the early 1980s, the waterfall model was the only widely accepted life-cycle model. This model is now examined in some detail.

3.2 WATERFALL MODEL

The waterfall model was first put forward by Royce [Royce, 1970]. A version of the model appears as Figure 3.2. First, requirements are determined, and checked by the client and members of the SQA group. Then the specifications for the product are drawn up, that is, a document is produced stating what the product is to do. The specifications are now checked by the SQA group and then shown

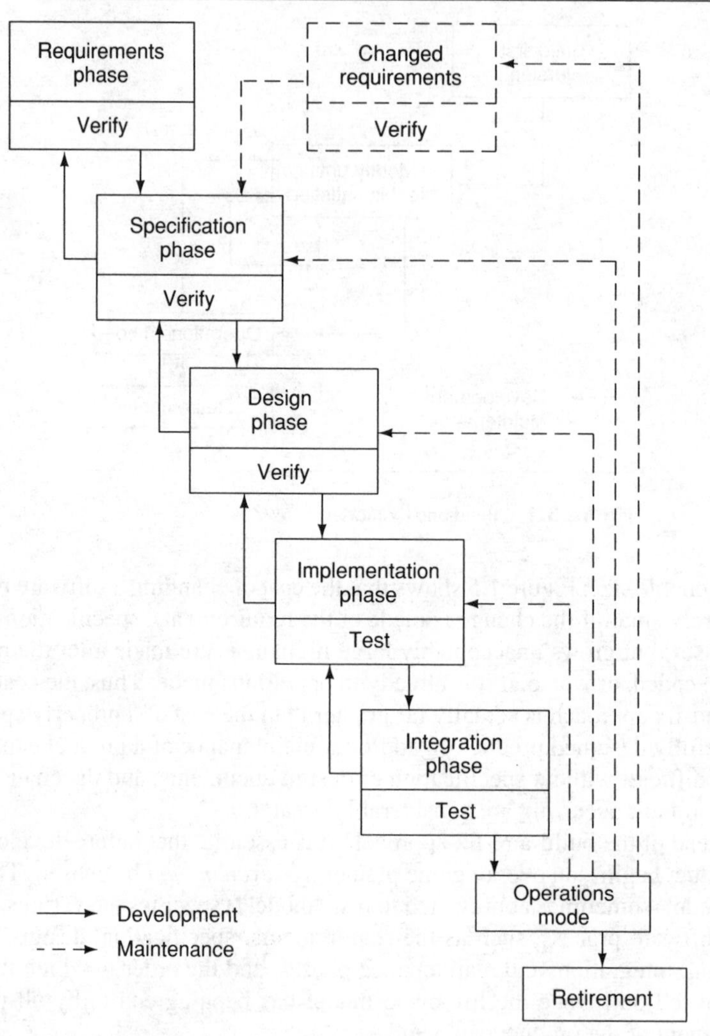

Figure 3.2 Waterfall model.

to the client. Once the client has signed off on the specification document, the next step is to draw up the software project management plan, a detailed timetable for developing the software. This plan is also checked by the SQA group. When the client has approved the developers' duration and cost estimates for the product, the design phase begins. In contrast to the specification document that describes *what* the product is to do, the design documents describe *how* the product is to do it.

During the design phase, it sometimes becomes apparent that there is a fault in the specification document. The specifications may be incomplete (some features of the product have been omitted), contradictory (two or more statements in the specification document define the product in an incompatible way), or ambiguous (the specification document has more than one possible interpretation). The presence of incompleteness, contradictions, or ambiguities necessitates a revision of the specification document before the software development process can continue. Referring again to Figure 3.2, the arrow from the left side of the design phase box back to the specification phase box constitutes a feedback loop. The software production process follows this loop if the developers have to revise the specification document during the design phase. With the client's permission, the necessary changes are then made to the specification document, and the planning and design documents are adjusted to incorporate these changes. When the developers are finally satisfied, the design documents are handed to the programmers for implementation.

Flaws in the design may appear during implementation. For example, the design of a real-time system may prove to be too slow when implemented. An example in FORTRAN of such a design flaw results from the fact that the elements of an array b are stored in column-major order, that is, in the order b(1, 1), b(2, 1), b(3, 1),..., b(n, 1), b(1, 2), b(2, 2), b(3, 2),..., b(n, 2), and so on. Suppose a 200 × 200 FORTRAN array b is stored on disk with one column to a block, that is, a 200-word column is read into a buffer in main memory each time a FORTRAN read statement is executed. The complete array is to be read from disk into main memory. If the array is read column by column, then exactly 200 blocks will have to be transferred from the disk to main memory to read all 40,000 elements. The first read statement will cause the first column to be put in the buffer, and the first 200 reads will use the contents of the buffer. Only when the 201st element is required will a second block need to be transferred from disk to main memory. But if the product reads the array row by row, then a fresh block will have to be transferred for every read, because consecutive reads access different columns and, hence, different blocks. Thus 40,000 block transfers would be required, instead of 200 when the array is read in column-major order, and the input/output time for that part of the product would be 200 times longer. Design faults of this type have to be corrected before the team can continue with software development.

During the implementation phase, the waterfall model with its feedback loops permits modifications to be made to the design documents, the specification document, and even the requirements, if necessary. Modules are implemented, documented, and then integrated to form a complete product. (In practice, the implementation and integration phases are usually carried out in parallel. As will be described in Chapter 14, each module is integrated as soon as it has been implemented and tested.) During integration it may be necessary to backtrack and make modifications to the code, preceded perhaps by modifications to the specification and design documents.

A critical point regarding the waterfall model is that no phase is complete until the documentation for that phase has been completed and the products of that phase have been approved by the SQA group. This carries over into modifications; if the products of an earlier phase have to be changed as a consequence of following a feedback loop, that earlier phase is deemed to be complete only when the documentation for the phase has been modified and the modifications have been checked by the SQA group.

When the developers feel that the product has been successfully completed, it is given to the client for acceptance testing. Deliverables at this stage include the user manual and other documentation listed in the contract. When the client agrees that the product indeed satisfies its specification document, the product is handed over to the client, installed, and put into operations mode.

Once the client has accepted the product, any changes, whether to remove residual faults or to extend the product in any way, constitute maintenance. As can be seen in Figure 3.2, maintenance may require not just implementation changes but also design and specification changes. In addition, enhancement is triggered by a change in requirements. This, in turn, is implemented via changes in the specification document, design documents, and code. The waterfall model is a dynamic model, and the feedback loops play an important role in this dynamism. Again, it is vital that the documentation be maintained as meticulously as the code itself and that the products of each phase be carefully checked before the next phase commences.

The waterfall model has been used with great success on a wide variety of products. However, there have also been failures. In order to decide whether or not to use the waterfall model for a project, it is necessary to understand both its strengths and weaknesses.

3.2.1 ANALYSIS OF THE WATERFALL MODEL

The waterfall model has many advantages, including the enforced disciplined approach—the stipulation that documentation be provided at each phase and the requirement that all the products of each phase (including the documentation) be carefully checked by SQA. An essential aspect of the milestone terminating each phase is approval by the SQA group of all the products of that phase, including all the documentation stipulated for that phase.

Inherent in every phase of the waterfall model is testing. Testing is not a separate phase to be performed only after the product has been constructed; it is not to be performed only at the end of each phase. Instead, as stated in Chapter 2, testing should proceed continuously throughout the software process. Specifically, while the requirements are being drawn up they must be verified, as must the specification document and the software project management plan as well as the design documents. The code must be tested in a variety of ways. During maintenance it is necessary to ensure not only that the modified version of the product still does what the previous version did—and still does it correctly (regression testing)—but that it totally satisfies any new requirements imposed by the client.

The specification document, design documents, code documentation, and other documentation such as the database manual, user manual, and operations manual are essential tools for maintaining the product. As stated in Chapter 1, on average, 67 percent of a software budget is devoted to maintenance, and adherence to the waterfall model with its documentation stipulations will make this maintenance easier. As mentioned in the previous section, the same methodical approach to software production continues during maintenance. Every change must be reflected in the relevant documentation. Many of the successes of the waterfall model have been due to the fact that it is essentially a documentation-driven model.

However, the fact that the waterfall model is documentation-driven can also be a disadvantage. To see this, consider the following two somewhat bizarre scenarios. First, Joe and Jane Johnson decide to build a house. They consult with an architect. Instead of showing them sketches, plans, and perhaps a model, the architect gives them a 20-page single-spaced typed document describing the house in highly technical terms. Despite the fact that neither Joe nor Jane have any previous architectural experience and hardly understand the document, they enthusiastically sign it and say, "Go right ahead, build the house!"

Another scenario is as follows. Mark Marberry buys his suits by mail order. Instead of mailing him pictures of their suits and samples of available cloths, the company sends Mark a written description of the cut and the cloth of their products. Mark then orders a suit solely on the basis of a written description.

The preceding two scenarios are highly unlikely. Nevertheless, they typify precisely the way software is often constructed using the waterfall model. The process begins with the specifications. In general, specification documents are long, detailed, and, quite frankly, boring to read. The client is usually inexperienced in the reading of software specifications, and this difficulty is compounded by the fact that specification documents are usually written in a style with which the client is unfamiliar. The difficulty is even worse when the specifications are written in a formal specification language like Z [Spivey, 1992] (Section 10.8). Nevertheless, the client proceeds to sign off the specification document, whether properly understood or not. In many ways there is little difference between Joe and Jane Johnson contracting to have a house built from a written description that they only partially comprehend and clients approving a software product described in terms of a specification document that they only partially understand.

Mark Marberry and his mail-order suits may seem bizarre in the extreme, but that is precisely what happens when the waterfall model is used in software development. The first time that the client sees a working product is only after the entire product has been coded. Small wonder that software developers live in fear of the sentence "I know this is what I asked for, but it isn't really what I wanted."

What has gone wrong? There is a considerable difference between the way a client understands a product as described by the specification document and the actual product. The specifications exist only on paper; the client therefore cannot really understand what the product itself will be like. The waterfall model, depending as it does so crucially on written specifications, can lead to the construction of products that simply do not meet clients' real needs.

In fairness it should be pointed out that, just as an architect can help a client to understand what is to be built by providing models, sketches, and plans, so the software engineer can use graphical techniques, such as data flow diagrams (Section 10.3.1), to communicate with the client. The problem is that these graphical aids do not describe how the finished product will work. For example, there is a considerable difference between a flowchart (a diagrammatic description of a product) and the working product itself.

The strength of the next life-cycle model to be examined, the rapid prototyping model, is that it can help to ensure that the client's real needs are met.

3.3 RAPID PROTOTYPING MODEL

A *rapid prototype* is a working model that is functionally equivalent to a subset of the product. For example, if the target product is to handle accounts payable, accounts receivable, and warehousing, then the rapid prototype might consist of a product that performs the screen handling for data capture and prints the reports, but does no file updating or error handling. A rapid prototype for a target product that is to determine the concentration of an enzyme in a solution might perform the calculation and display the answer, but without doing any validation or reasonableness checking of the input data.

The first step in the rapid prototyping life-cycle model depicted in Figure 3.3 is to build a rapid prototype and let the client and future users interact with the rapid prototype and experiment with it. Once the client is satisfied that the rapid prototype indeed does most of what is required, the developers can draw up the specification document with some assurance that the product meets the client's real needs.

Having constructed the rapid prototype, the software process continues as shown in Figure 3.3. A major strength of the rapid prototyping model is that the development of the product is essentially linear, proceeding from the rapid prototype to the delivered product; the feedback loops of the waterfall model (Figure 3.2) are less likely to be needed in the rapid prototyping model. There are a number of reasons for this. First, the members of the development team use the rapid prototype to construct the specification document. Because the working rapid prototype has been validated through interaction with the client, it is reasonable to expect that the resulting specification document will be correct. Second, consider the design phase. Even though the rapid prototype has (quite rightly) been hurriedly assembled, the design team can gain insights from it—at worst they will be of the "how not to do it" variety. Again, the feedback loops of the waterfall model are less likely to be needed here.

Implementation comes next. In the waterfall model, implementation of the design sometimes leads to design faults coming to light. In the rapid prototyping model, the fact that a preliminary working model has already been built tends to lessen the need to repair the design during or after implementation. The prototype will give some insights to the design team, even though it may reflect only partial functionality of the complete target product.

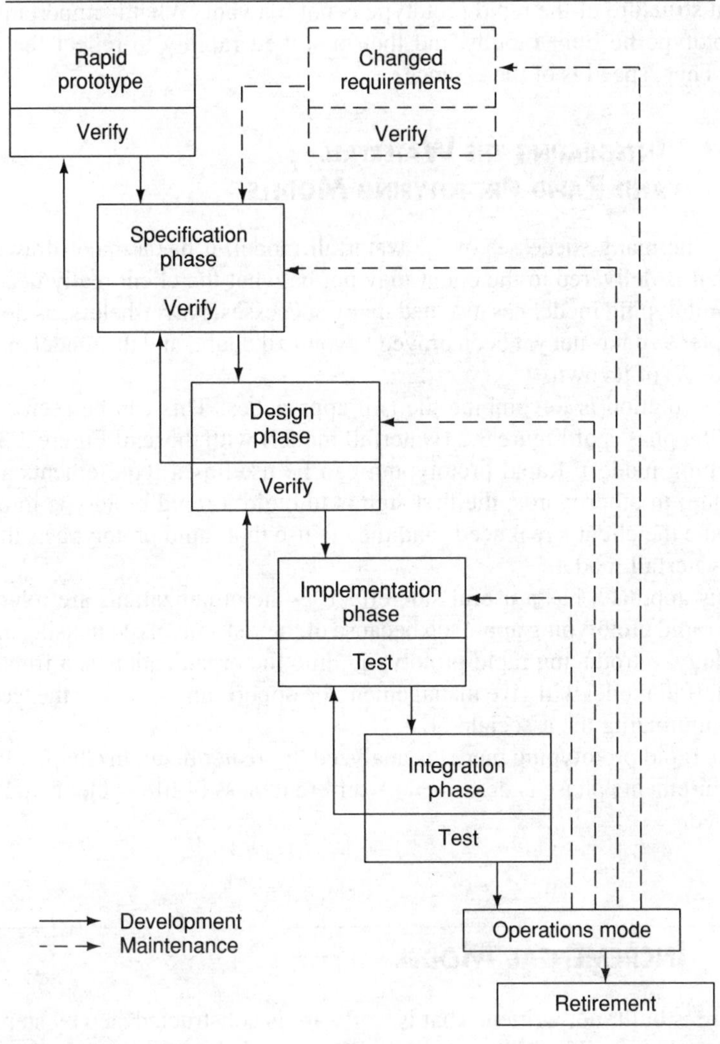

Figure 3.3 Rapid prototyping model.

Once the product has been accepted by the client and then installed, maintenance begins. Depending on the maintenance that has to be performed, the cycle is reentered either at the requirements, specification, design, or implementation phase.

An essential aspect of a rapid prototype is embodied in the word *rapid*. The developers should endeavor to construct the rapid prototype as rapidly as possible to speed up the software development process. After all, the sole use of the rapid prototype is to determine what the client's real needs are; once this has been determined, the rapid prototype is effectively discarded. For this reason, the internal structure of the rapid prototype is not relevant. What is important is that the prototype be built rapidly and then modified rapidly to reflect the client's needs. Thus, speed is of the essence.

3.3.1 INTEGRATING THE WATERFALL AND RAPID PROTOTYPING MODELS

Despite the many successes of the waterfall model, it has a major drawback in that what is delivered to the client may not be what the client really needs. The rapid prototyping model has also had many successes. Nevertheless, as described in Chapter 9, it has not yet been proved beyond all doubt, and the model may have weaknesses of its own.

One solution is to combine the two approaches: This can be seen by comparing the phases of Figure 3.2 (waterfall model) with those of Figure 3.3 (rapid prototyping model). Rapid prototyping can be used as a requirements analysis technique; in other words, the first step is to build a rapid prototype in order to determine the client's real needs and then to use that rapid prototype as the input to the waterfall model.

This approach has a useful side effect. Some organizations are reluctant to use the rapid prototyping approach because of the risks involved in using any new technology. Introducing rapid prototyping into the organization as a front end to the waterfall model will give management the opportunity to assess the technique while minimizing the associated risk.

The rapid prototyping model is analyzed in greater detail in Chapter 9 where the requirements phase is described. A different class of life-cycle model is now examined.

3.4 INCREMENTAL MODEL

Software is built, not written. That is, software is constructed step by step, in the same way that a building is constructed. While a software product is in the process of being developed, each step adds to what has gone before. One day the design is extended; the next day another module is coded. The construction of the complete product proceeds incrementally in this way until completion.

Of course, it is not quite true that progress is made every day. Just as a contractor occasionally has to tear down an incorrectly positioned wall or replace a pane of glass that a careless painter has cracked, it sometimes is necessary to respecify, redesign, recode, or at worst, throw away what has already been completed and start again. But the fact that the product sometimes advances in fits and starts does not negate the basic reality that a software product is built piece by piece.

The realization that software is engineered incrementally has led to the development of a model that exploits this aspect of software development, the so-called

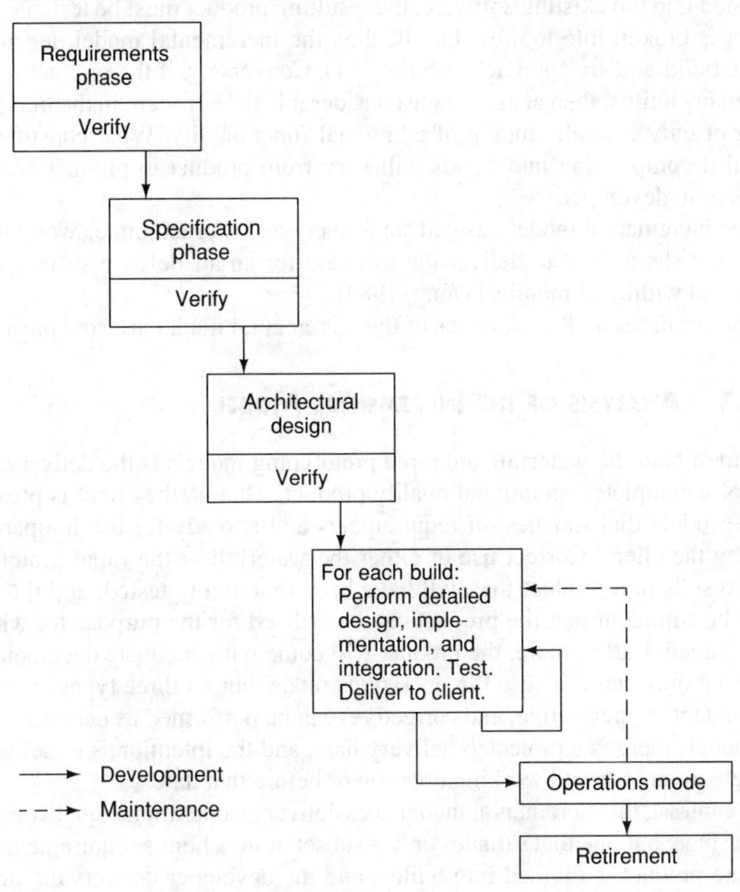

Figure 3.4 Incremental model.

incremental model shown in Figure 3.4. The product is designed, implemented, integrated, and tested as a series of incremental *builds,* where a build consists of code pieces from various modules interacting together to provide a specific functional capability.

For example, if the product is to control a nuclear submarine, then the navigation system could constitute a build, as could the weapons control system. In an operating system, the scheduler could be a build, and so could the file management system. At each stage of the incremental model, a new build is coded and then integrated into the structure that is tested as a whole. The process stops when the product achieves the target functionality, that is, when the product satisfies its specifications. The developer is free to break up the target product into builds as he or she sees fit, subject only to the constraint that as each build is integrated into the existing software, the resulting product must be testable. If the product is broken into too few builds, then the incremental model degenerates into the build-and-fix approach (Section 3.1). Conversely, if the product consists of too many builds, then at each stage considerable time is spent in the integration testing of only a small amount of additional functionality. What constitutes an optimal decomposition into builds will vary from product to product and from developer to developer.

The incremental model has had some successes. For example, Wong has reported that she used it to deliver the software for an air defense system within budget and within 25 months [Wong, 1984].

The strengths and weaknesses of the incremental model are now presented.

3.4.1 ANALYSIS OF THE INCREMENTAL MODEL

The aim of both the waterfall and rapid prototyping models is the delivery to the client of a complete, operational quality product. That is, the client is presented with a product that satisfies *all* requirements and is ready for use in operations mode by the client. Correct use of either the waterfall or the rapid prototyping model results in a product that will have been thoroughly tested, and the client should be confident that the product can be utilized for the purpose for which it was designed. Furthermore, the product will come with adequate documentation so that not only can it be used in operations mode, but all three types of maintenance (adaptive, perfective, and corrective) can be performed as necessary. With both models there is a projected delivery date, and the intention is to deliver the complete product in full working order on or before that date.

In contrast, the incremental model does deliver an operational quality product at each stage, but one that satisfies only a subset of the client's requirements. The complete product is divided into builds, and the developer delivers the product build by build. A typical product will usually consist of 10 to 50 builds. At each stage the client has an operational quality product that does a portion of what is required; from delivery of the first build, the client is able to do useful work. With the incremental model, portions of the total product might be available within weeks, whereas the client generally waits months or years to receive a product built using the waterfall or rapid prototyping models.

Another advantage of the incremental model is that it reduces the traumatic effect of imposing a completely new product on the client organization. The gradual introduction of the product via the incremental model provides time for the client to adjust to the new product. Change is an integral part of every growing organization; because a software product is a model of reality, the need for change is also an integral part of delivered software. Change and adaptation are natural to the incremental model, whereas change can be a threat when products are developed and introduced in one large step.

From the client's financial viewpoint, phased delivery does not require a large capital outlay. Instead, there is an excellent cash flow, particularly if the earliest builds are chosen on the basis of delivering a high return on investment. A related advantage of the incremental model is that it is not necessary to complete the product to get a return on investment. Instead, the client can stop development of the product at any time.

A difficulty with the incremental model is that each additional build somehow has to be incorporated into the existing structure without destroying what has been built to date. Furthermore, the existing structure must lend itself to extension in this way, and the addition of each succeeding build must be simple and straightforward. Although this need for an open architecture is certainly a short-term difficulty, in the long term it can be a real strength. Every product undergoes development, followed by maintenance. During development it is indeed important to have clear specifications and a coherent and cohesive design. But once a product enters the maintenance phase, the requirements for that product change, and radical enhancement can easily destroy a coherent and cohesive design to the extent that further maintenance becomes impossible. In such a case, the product must be rebuilt virtually from scratch. The fact that the design must be open-ended is not merely a prerequisite for development using the incremental model but is essential for maintenance, irrespective of the model selected for the development phase. Thus, although the incremental model may require more careful design than the holistic waterfall and rapid prototyping models, the payoff comes in the maintenance phase. If a design is flexible enough to support the incremental model, then it will certainly allow virtually any sort of maintenance without falling apart. In fact, the incremental model does not distinguish between developing a product and enhancing (maintaining) it; each enhancement is merely an additional build.

It happens all too frequently that the requirements change while development is in progress; this problem is discussed in greater detail in Section 15.4.4. The flexibility of the incremental model gives it a major advantage over the waterfall and rapid prototyping models in this regard. On the negative side, the incremental model can too easily degenerate into the build-and-fix approach. Control of the process as a whole can be lost, and the resulting product, instead of being open-ended, becomes a maintainer's nightmare. In a sense, the incremental model is a contradiction in terms, requiring the developer to view the product as a whole in order to begin with a design that will support the entire product, including future enhancements, but simultaneously to view that product as a sequence of builds, each essentially independent of the next. Unless the developer is skilled enough to be able to handle this apparent contradiction, the incremental model may lead to an unsatisfactory product.

In the incremental model of Figure 3.4, the requirements, specifications, and architectural design must all be completed before implementation of the various builds commences. A more risky version of the incremental model is depicted in Figure 3.5. Once the client's requirements have been elicited, the specifications of the first build are drawn up. When this has been completed, the specification team turns to the specifications of the second build while the design team designs the first build. Thus, the various builds are constructed in parallel, with each team making use of information gained in all the previous builds.

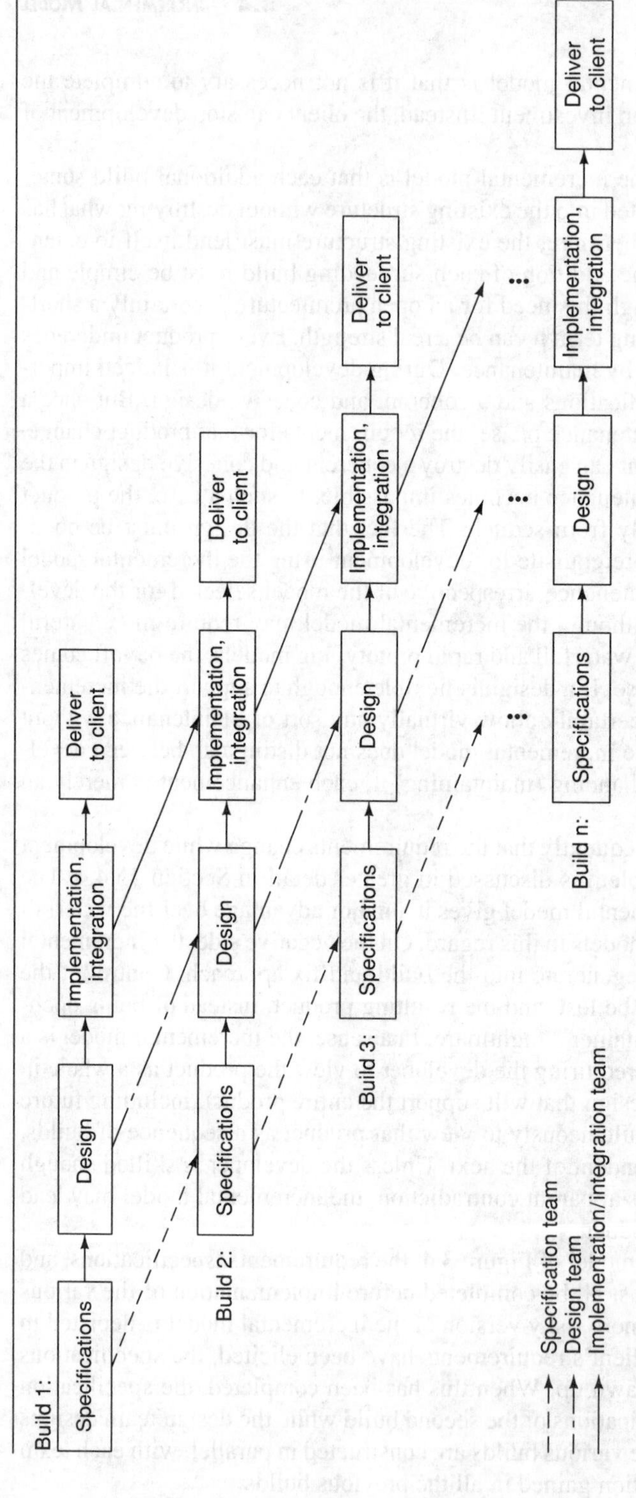

Figure 3.5 More risky incremental model.

This approach incurs the real risk that the resulting builds will not fit together. With the incremental model of Figure 3.4, the fact that the specification and architectural design must be completed before starting the first build means that there is an overall design at the start. With the incremental model of Figure 3.5, unless the process is carefully monitored, the entire project risks falling apart.

3.5 SYNCHRONIZE-AND-STABILIZE MODEL

Microsoft, Inc. is the world's largest manufacturer of shrink-wrapped software. The majority of their packages are built using a version of the incremental model that has been termed the synchronize-and-stabilize model [Cusamano and Selby, 1997].

The requirements analysis phase is conducted by interviewing numerous potential customers for the package and extracting a list of features prioritized by the customers. A specification document is now drawn up. Next, the work is divided into three or four builds. The first build consists of the most critical features, the second build consists of the next most critical features, and so on. Each build is carried out by a number of small teams working in parallel. At the end of each day all the teams *synchronize*, that is, they put the partially completed components together and test and debug the resulting product. *Stabilization* is performed at the end of each of the builds. Any remaining faults that have been detected so far are fixed and the build is now *frozen*, that is, no further changes will be made to the specifications.

The repeated synchronization step ensures that the various components always work together. Another advantage of this regular execution of the partially constructed product is that the developers obtain an early insight into the operation of the product and can modify the requirements if necessary during the course of a build. The model can even be used if the initial specification is incomplete. The synchronize-and-stabilize model is considered further in Section 4.5 where team organizational details are discussed.

The spiral model has been left to last because it incorporates aspects of all the other models.

3.6 SPIRAL MODEL

There is almost always an element of risk involved in the development of software. For example, key personnel can resign before the product has been adequately documented. The manufacturer of hardware on which the product is critically dependent can go bankrupt. Too much, or too little, can be invested in testing and quality assurance. After spending hundreds of thousands of dollars on developing a major software product, technological breakthroughs can render the entire product worthless. An organization may research and develop a database management system, but before the product can be marketed, a lower-priced, functionally equivalent package is announced. The components of a product built using the incremental model of Figure 3.5 may not fit together. For obvious reasons, software developers try to minimize such risks wherever possible.

One way of minimizing certain types of risk is to construct a prototype. As described in Section 3.3, an excellent way of reducing the risk that the delivered product will not satisfy the client's real needs is to construct a rapid prototype during the requirements phase. During subsequent phases, other sorts of prototypes may be appropriate. For example, a telephone company may devise a new, apparently highly effective algorithm for routing calls through a long-distance network. If the product is implemented but does not work as expected, the telephone company will have wasted the cost of developing the product. In addition, angry or inconvenienced customers may take their business elsewhere. This scenario can be avoided by constructing a prototype to handle only the routing of calls and testing it on a simulator. In this way the actual system is not disturbed, and for the cost of implementing just the routing algorithm, the telephone company can determine whether it is worthwhile to develop an entire network controller incorporating the new algorithm.

The idea of minimizing risk via the use of prototypes and other means is the concept underlying the *spiral model* [Boehm, 1988]. A simplistic way of looking at this life-cycle model is as a waterfall model with each phase preceded by risk analysis, as shown in Figure 3.6. (A portion of that figure is redrawn as Figure 3.7, to reflect the term *spiral model.*) Before commencing each phase, an attempt is made to control (or resolve) the risks. If it is impossible to resolve all the significant risks at that stage, then the project is immediately terminated.

Prototypes can be used effectively to provide information about certain classes of risk. For example, timing constraints can generally be tested by constructing a prototype and measuring whether the prototype can achieve the necessary performance. If the prototype is an accurate functional representation of the relevant features of the product, then measurements made on the prototype should give the developers a good idea as to whether the timing constraints can be achieved.

Other areas of risk are less amenable to prototyping. For example, there is often a risk that the software personnel necessary to build the product cannot be hired or that key personnel may resign before the project is complete. Another potential risk is that a particular team may not be competent enough to develop a specific large-scale product. A successful contractor who builds single-family homes would probably not be able to build a high-rise office complex. In the same way, there are essential differences between small-scale and large-scale software, and prototyping is thus of little use. This risk cannot be resolved by testing team performance on a much smaller prototype in which team organizational issues specific to large-scale software cannot arise. Another area of risk for which prototyping cannot be employed is evaluating the delivery promises of a hardware supplier. A strategy the developer can adopt is to determine how well previous

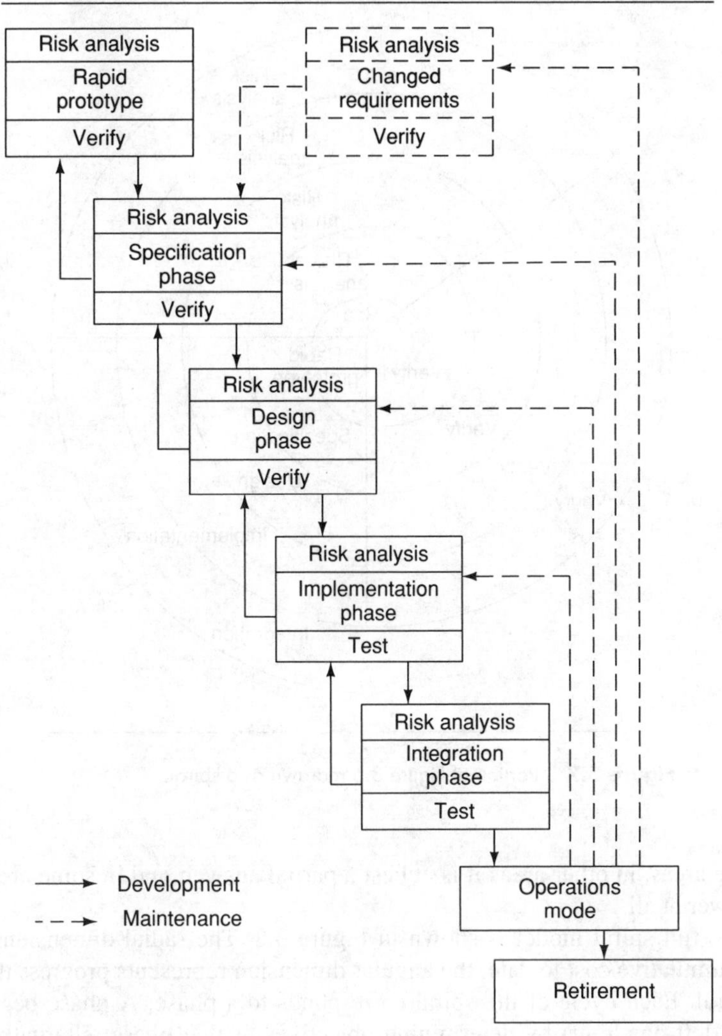

Figure 3.6 Simplistic version of spiral model.

clients of the supplier have been treated, but past performance is by no means a certain predictor of future performance. A penalty clause in the delivery contract is one way of trying to ensure that essential hardware will be delivered on time, but what if the supplier refuses to sign an agreement that includes such a clause? Even with a penalty clause, late delivery may occur and eventually lead to legal action that can drag on for years. In the meantime, the software developer may have gone bankrupt because nondelivery of the promised hardware caused nondelivery of the promised software. In short, whereas prototyping helps reduce risk

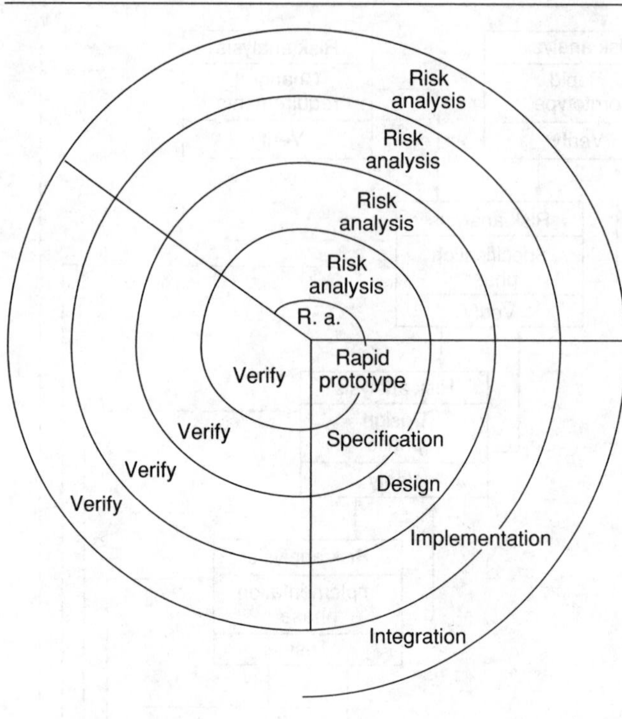

Figure 3.7 Portion of Figure 3.6 redrawn as a spiral.

in some areas, in other areas it is at best a partial answer, and in some areas it is no answer at all.

The full spiral model is shown in Figure 3.8. The radial dimension represents cumulative cost to date, the angular dimension represents progress through the spiral. Each cycle of the spiral corresponds to a phase. A phase begins (in the top left quadrant) by determining objectives of that phase, alternatives for achieving those objectives, and constraints imposed on those alternatives. This process results in a strategy for achieving those objectives. Next, that strategy is analyzed from the viewpoint of risk. Attempts are made to resolve every potential risk, in some cases by building a prototype. If certain risks cannot be resolved, the project may be terminated immediately; under some circumstances, however, a decision could be made to continue the project but on a significantly smaller scale. If all risks are successfully resolved, the next development step is started (bottom right quadrant). This quadrant of the spiral model corresponds to the pure waterfall model. Finally, the results of that phase are evaluated and the next phase is planned.

The spiral model has been used successfully to develop a wide variety of products. In one set of 25 projects in which the spiral model was used in

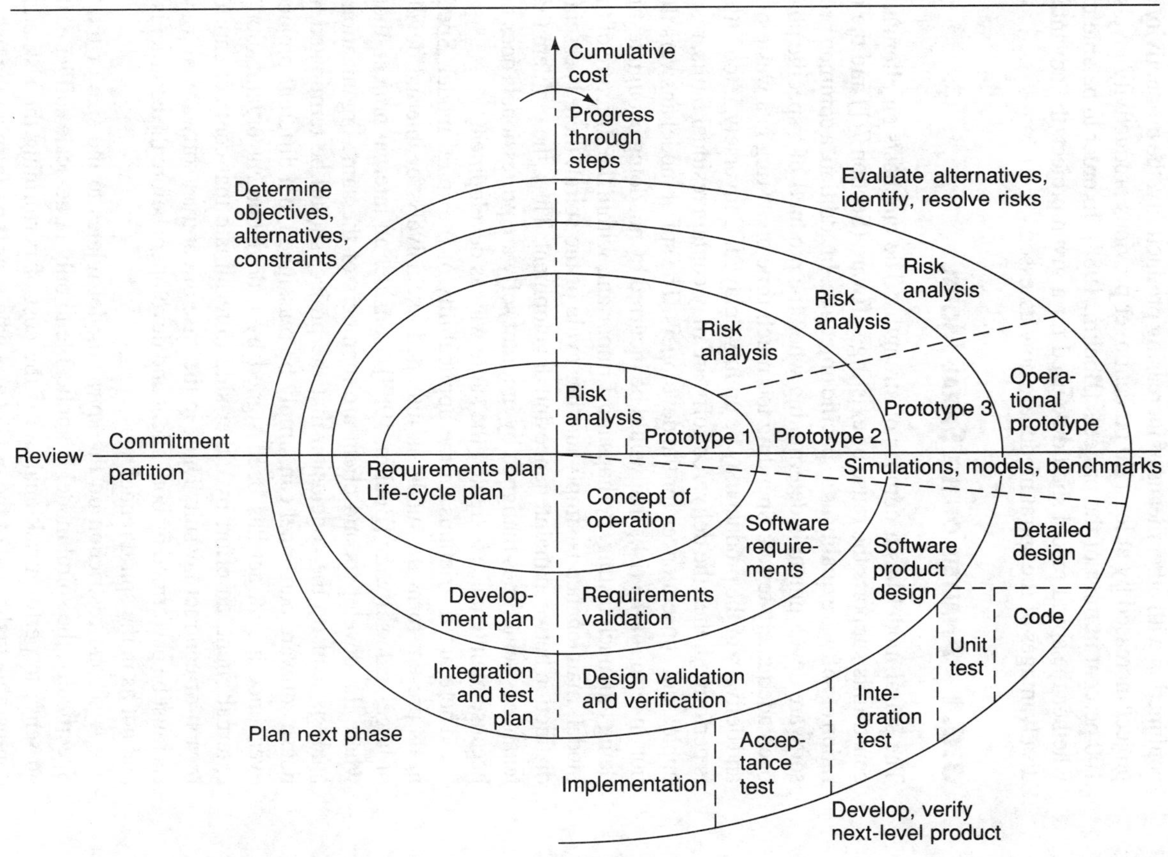

Figure 3.8 Full spiral model [Boehm, 1988]. (©1988 IEEE.)

conjunction with other means of increasing productivity, the productivity of every project increased by at least 50 percent over previous productivity levels and by 100 percent in most of the projects [Boehm, 1988]. In order to be able to decide whether the spiral model should be used for a given project, the advantages and disadvantages of the spiral model are now assessed.

3.6.1 ANALYSIS OF THE SPIRAL MODEL

The spiral model has a number of strengths. The emphasis on alternatives and constraints supports the reuse of existing software (Section 7.1) and the incorporation of software quality as a specific objective. In addition, a common problem in software development is determining when the products of a specific phase have been adequately tested. Spending too much time on testing is a waste of money, and delivery of the product may be unduly delayed. Conversely, if too little testing is performed, then the delivered software may contain residual faults, resulting in unpleasant consequences for the developers. The spiral model answers this question in terms of the risks that would be incurred by not doing enough testing or by doing too much testing. Perhaps most important, within the structure of the spiral model, maintenance is simply another cycle of the spiral; there is essentially no distinction between maintenance and development. Thus, the problem that maintenance is sometimes maligned by ignorant software professionals does not arise, because maintenance is treated the same way as development.

There are restrictions on the applicability of the spiral model. Specifically, in its present form the model is intended exclusively for internal development of large-scale software [Boehm, 1988]. Consider an internal project, that is, one where the developers and client are members of the same organization. If risk analysis leads to the conclusion that the project should be terminated, then in-house software personnel can simply be reassigned to a different project. However, once a contract has been signed by a development organization and an external client, an effort by either side to terminate that contract can lead to a breach-of-contract lawsuit. Thus, in the case of contract software, all risk analysis must be performed by both client and developers before the contract is signed, and not as in the spiral model.

A second restriction on the spiral model relates to the size of the project. Specifically, the spiral model is applicable to only large-scale software. It makes no sense to perform risk analysis if the cost of performing the risk analysis is comparable to the cost of the project as a whole, or if performing the risk analysis would significantly affect the profit potential. Instead, the developers should first decide how much is at risk and then decide how much risk analysis, if any, to perform.

A major strength of the spiral model is that it is risk-driven, but this can also be a weakness. Unless the software developers are skilled at pinpointing the possible risks and analyzing the risks accurately, there is a real danger that the team may believe that all is well at a time when the project, in fact, is headed for disaster. Only if the members of the development team are competent risk analysts should management decide to use the spiral model.

3.7 Object-Oriented Life-Cycle Models

Experience with the object-oriented paradigm has shown that the need for iteration between phases or portions of phases of the process appears to be more common with the object-oriented paradigm than with the structured paradigm. Object-oriented life-cycle models have been proposed that explicitly reflect the need for iteration. One such model is the fountain model [Henderson-Sellers and Edwards, 1990] shown in Figure 3.9. The circles representing the various phases overlap, explicitly reflecting an overlap between activities. The arrows within a phase represent iteration within that phase. The maintenance circle is smaller, to symbolize reduced maintenance effort when the object-oriented paradigm is used.

In addition to the fountain model, other object-oriented life-cycle models have been put forward, including Objectory [Jacobson, Christerson, Jonsson, and Overgaard, 1992], recursive/parallel life cycle [Berard 1993], and round-trip gestalt design [Booch, 1994]. All these models are iterative, incorporate some form of parallelism (overlap of activities), and support incremental development (Section 3.4). The danger of such life-cycle models is that they may be misinterpreted

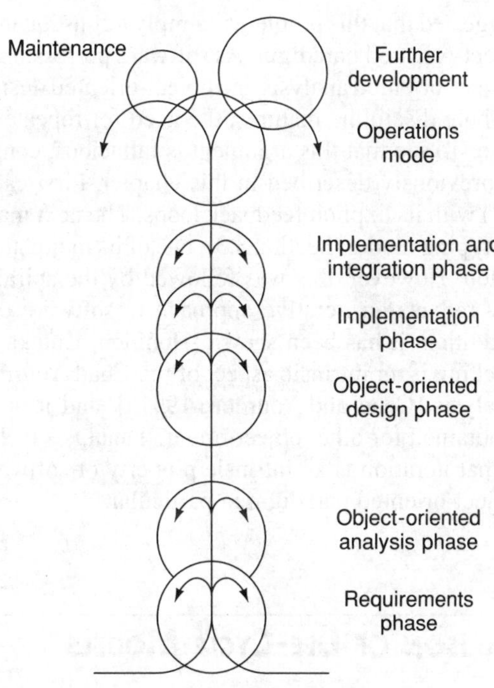

Figure 3.9 Fountain model.

JUST IN CASE YOU WANTED TO KNOW

When the members of the development team move in essentially haphazard fashion from one task to another, this is sometimes referred to as CABTAB (code a bit, test a bit). The acronym was initially used in a positive sense to refer to successful iterative models, such as those that have been used in conjunction with the object-oriented paradigm. However, just as the word *hacker* now has a pejorative context in addition to its original meaning, so CABTAB is now also used in a derogatory sense to refer to this undisciplined approach to software development.

as simply attempts to make a virtue out of necessity, and thereby lead to a totally undisciplined form of software development in which team members move almost randomly between phases, first designing one piece of the product, next analyzing another piece, and then implementing a third piece that has been neither analyzed nor designed; the Just in Case You Wanted to Know box above gives more on this undesirable approach. A better way to proceed is to have as an overall objective a linear process (such as the rapid prototyping model of Section 3.3 or the central vertical line in Figure 3.9), but to appreciate that the realities of the object-oriented paradigm are such that frequent iterations and refinements will certainly be needed.

It might be suggested that this problem is simply a consequence of the relative newness of the object-oriented paradigm. As software professionals acquire more experience with object-oriented analysis and object-oriented design, the argument goes, and as the whole discipline matures, the need for repeated review and revision will decrease. To see that this argument is fallacious, consider the various life-cycle models previously described in this chapter. First came the waterfall model (Section 3.2) with its explicit feedback loops. The next major development was the rapid prototyping model (Section 3.3); one of its major aims was to reduce the need for iteration. However, this was followed by the spiral model (Section 3.6) that explicitly reflects an iterative approach to software development and maintenance. In addition, it has been shown [Honiden, Kotaka, and Kishimoto, 1993] that backtracking is an intrinsic aspect of the Coad-Yourdon technique for object-oriented analysis [Coad and Yourdon, 1991a], and it is likely that similar results can be obtained for other object-oriented analysis techniques. In other words, it appears that iteration is an intrinsic property of software production in general and the object-oriented paradigm in particular.

3.8 COMPARISON OF LIFE-CYCLE MODELS

Six different classes of software life-cycle models have been examined with special attention paid to some of their strengths and weaknesses. The build-and-fix model (Section 3.1) should be avoided. The waterfall model (Section 3.2) is a known quantity. Its strengths are understood, and so are its weaknesses. The rapid prototyping model (Section 3.3) was developed as a reaction to a specific perceived weakness in the waterfall model; namely, that the delivered product may not be what the client really needs. Less is known about the newer rapid prototyping model than the familiar waterfall model, and the rapid prototyping model may have some problems of its own, as described in Chapter 9. One alternative is to combine the strengths of both models, as suggested in Section 3.3.1. Another is to use a different model, the incremental model (Section 3.4). This model, notwithstanding its successes, also has some drawbacks. The synchronize-and-stabilize model (Section 3.5) has been used with great success by Microsoft, but as yet there is no evidence of comparable successes in other corporate cultures. Yet another alternative is to use the spiral model (Section 3.6), but only if the developers are adequately trained in risk analysis and risk resolution. A further factor that needs to be considered is that when the object-oriented paradigm is used, the life-cycle model needs to be iterative, that is, it must support feedback (Section 3.7). The strengths and weaknesses of the various life-cycle models of this chapter are summarized in Figure 3.10.

Each software development organization should decide on a life-cycle model that is appropriate for that organization, its management, its employees, and its

Life-Cycle Model	Strengths	Weaknesses
Build-and-fix model (Section 3.1)	Fine for short programs that will not require any maintenance	Totally unsatisfactory for nontrivial programs
Waterfall model (Section 3.2)	Disciplined approach Document-driven	Delivered product may not meet client's needs
Rapid prototyping model (Section 3.3)	Ensures that delivered product meets client's needs	See Chapter 9
Incremental model (Section 3.4)	Maximizes early return on investment Promotes maintainability	Requires open architecture May degenerate into build-and-fix
Synchronize-and-stabilize model (Section 3.5)	Future users' needs are met Ensures components can be successfully integrated	Has not been widely used other than at Microsoft
Spiral model (Section 3.6)	Incorporates features of all the above models	Can be used only for large-scale, in-house products Developers have to be competent in risk analysis and risk resolution
Object-oriented models (Section 3.7)	Supports iteration within phases, parallelism between phases	May degenerate into CABTAB

Figure 3.10 Comparison of life-cycle models described in this chapter, including the section in which each is defined.

software process, and vary the model depending on the features of the specific product currently under development. Such a model will incorporate appropriate features from the various life-cycle models, utilizing their strengths and minimizing their weaknesses.

CHAPTER REVIEW

A number of different life-cycle models are described, including the build-and-fix model (Section 3.1), waterfall model (Section 3.2), rapid prototyping model (Section 3.3), incremental model (Section 3.4), synchronize-and-stabilize model (Section 3.5), spiral model (Section 3.6), and object-oriented life-cycle models (Section 3.7). In Section 3.8 these life-cycle models are compared and contrasted, and suggestions are made regarding choice of a life-cycle model for a specific project.

FOR FURTHER READING

A description of the waterfall model appears in Chapter 4 of [Boehm, 1981]. The same chapter also includes an example of an incremental model different from the one presented here in Section 3.4.

For an introduction to rapid prototyping, three suggested books are [Lantz, 1985], [Connell and Shafer, 1989], and [Gane, 1989]. The role of computer-aided prototyping is assessed in [Luqi and Royce, 1992]. The February 1995 issue of *IEEE Computer* contains several articles on rapid prototyping.

A description of the evolutionary delivery model, one version of the incremental model, can be found in [Gilb, 1988]. Another type of incremental model is described in [Currit, Dyer, and Mills, 1986] and [Selby, Basili, and Baker, 1987]. The synchronize-and-stabilize model is outlined in [Cusamano and Selby, 1997] and described in detail in [Cusamano and Selby, 1995]. Insights into the synchronize-and-stabilize model can be obtained from [McConnell, 1996]. The spiral model is explained in [Boehm, 1988], and its application to the TRW Software Productivity System appears in [Boehm et al., 1984]. Risk analysis is described in [Boehm, 1991], [Jones, 1994c], and [Karolak, 1996]. The May/June 1997 issue of *IEEE Software* contains 10 articles on risk management.

Object-oriented life-cycle models are described in [Jacobson, Christerson, Jonsson, and Overgaard, 1992], [Henderson-Sellers and Edwards, 1990], [Booch, 1994], and [Rajlich, 1994], as well as in the books on object-oriented analysis listed in the first paragraph of the For Further Reading section of Chapter 11.

Many other life-cycle models have been put forward. A life-cycle model that emphasizes human factors is presented in [Mantei and Teorey, 1988]. A life-cycle model recommended by the Software Engineering Laboratory is described in [Landis et al., 1992]. A method for comparing alternative life-cycle models is presented in [Davis, Bersoff, and Comer, 1988]. The proceedings of the International Software Process Workshops are a useful source of information on life-cycle models. [ISO/IEC 12207, 1995] is a standard for software life-cycle processes.

PROBLEMS

3.1 Suppose that you have to build a product to determine the cube root of 40,293.8473 to four decimal places. Once the product has been implemented and tested, it will be thrown away. Which life-cycle model would you use? Give reasons for your answer.

3.2 You are a software engineering consultant and have been called in by the vice-president for finance of Chocolate × 3, a corporation that manufactures and sells triple-chocolate cake to restaurants. She wants your organization to build a product that will monitor the company's product, starting with the purchasing of the various ingredients and keeping track of the cakes as they are manufactured and distributed to the various restaurants. What criteria would you use in selecting a life-cycle model for the project? (For the uninitiated, triple-chocolate cake consists of layers of chocolate cake and chocolate frosting, decorated with pieces of chocolate.)

3.3 List the risks involved in developing the software of Problem 3.2. How would you attempt to resolve each risk?

3.4 Your development of the stock control product for Chocolate × 3 is highly successful. As a result, Chocolate × 3 wants the product to be rewritten as a COTS package to be sold to a variety of different organizations that manufacture and sell food to restaurants as well as to retail organizations. The new product must therefore be portable and easily adapted to new hardware and/or operating systems. How do the criteria you would use in selecting a life-cycle model for this project differ from those in your answer to Problem 3.2?

3.5 Describe the sort of product that would be an ideal application for the incremental model.

3.6 Now describe the type of situation where the incremental model might lead to difficulties.

3.7 Describe the sort of product that would be an ideal application for the spiral model.

3.8 Now describe the type of situation where the spiral model is inappropriate.

3.9 What do waterfalls and fountains have in common? What do the waterfall model and fountain model have in common? How do they differ?

3.10 (Term Project) Which software life-cycle model would you use for the Air Gourmet project described in Appendix A? Give reasons for your answer.

3.11 (Readings in Software Engineering) Your instructor will distribute copies of [Cusamano and Selby, 1997]. Would you like to work in an organization that uses the synchronize-and-stabilize model?

REFERENCES

[Berard, 1993] E. V. BERARD, *Essays on Object-Oriented Software Engineering, Volume I,* Prentice Hall, Englewood Cliffs, NJ, 1993.

[Boehm, 1981] B. W. BOEHM, *Software Engineering Economics,* Prentice Hall, Englewood Cliffs, NJ, 1981.

[Boehm, 1988] B. W. BOEHM, "A Spiral Model of Software Development and Enhancement," *IEEE Computer* **21** (May 1988), pp. 61–72.

[Boehm, 1991] B. W. BOEHM, "Software Risk Management: Principles and Practices," *IEEE Software* **8** (January 1991), pp. 32–41.

[Boehm et al., 1984] B. W. BOEHM, M. H. PENEDO, E. D. STUCKLE, R. D. WILLIAMS, AND A. B. PYSTER, "A Software Development Environment for Improving Productivity," *IEEE Computer* **17** (June 1984), pp. 30–44.

[Booch, 1994] G. BOOCH, *Object-Oriented Analysis and Design with Applications,* Second Edition, Benjamin/Cummings, Redwood City, CA, 1994.

[Coad and Yourdon, 1991a] P. COAD AND E. YOURDON, *Object-Oriented Analysis,* Second Edition, Yourdon Press, Englewood Cliffs, NJ, 1991.

[Connell and Shafer, 1989] J. L. CONNELL AND L. SHAFER, *Structured Rapid Prototyping: An Evolutionary Approach to Software Development*, Yourdon Press, Englewood Cliffs, NJ, 1989.

[Currit, Dyer, and Mills, 1986] P. A. CURRIT, M. DYER, AND H. D. MILLS, "Certifying the Reliability of Software," *IEEE Transactions on Software Engineering* **SE-12** (January 1986), pp. 3–11.

[Cusamano and Selby, 1995] M. A. CUSAMANO AND R. W. SELBY, *Microsoft Secrets: How the World's Most Powerful Software Company Creates Technology, Shapes Markets, and Manages People*, The Free Press/Simon and Schuster, New York, 1995.

[Cusamano and Selby, 1997] M. A. CUSAMANO AND R. W. SELBY, "How Microsoft Builds Software," *Communications of the ACM* **40** (June 1997), pp. 53–61.

[Davis, Bersoff, and Comer, 1988] A. M. DAVIS, E. H. BERSOFF, AND E. R. COMER, "A Strategy for Comparing Alternative Software Development Life Cycle Models," *IEEE Transactions on Software Engineering* **14** (October 1988), pp. 1453–61.

[Gane, 1989] C. GANE, *Rapid System Development: Using Structured Techniques and Relational Technology*, Prentice Hall, Englewood Cliffs, NJ, 1989.

[Gilb, 1988] T. GILB, *Principles of Software Engineering Management*, Addison-Wesley, Wokingham, UK, 1988.

[Henderson-Sellers and Edwards, 1990] B. HENDERSON-SELLERS AND J. M. EDWARDS, "The Object-Oriented Systems Life Cycle," *Communications of the ACM* **33** (September 1990), pp. 142–59.

[Honiden, Kotaka, and Kishimoto, 1993] S. HONIDEN, N. KOTAKA, AND Y. KISHIMOTO, "Formalizing Specification Modeling in OOA," *IEEE Software* **10** (January 1993), pp. 54–66.

[ISO/IEC 12207, 1995] "Software Life Cycle Processes," ISO/IEC 12207, International Organization for Standardization, International Electrotechnical Commission, Geneva, 1995.

[Jacobson, Christerson, Jonsson, and Overgaard, 1992] I. JACOBSON, M. CHRISTERSON, P. JONSSON, AND G. OVERGAARD, *Object-Oriented Software Engineering: A Use Case Driven Approach*, ACM Press, New York, 1992.

[Jones, 1994c] C. JONES, *Assessment and Control of Computer Risks*, Prentice Hall, Englewood Cliffs, NJ, 1994.

[Karolak, 1996] D. W. KAROLAK, *Software Engineering Risk Management*, IEEE Computer Society, Los Alamitos, CA, 1996.

[Landis et al., 1992] L. LANDIS, S. WALIGARA, F. MCGARRY, ET AL., "Recommended Approach to Software Development: Revision 3," Technical Report SEL-81-305, Software Engineering Laboratory, Greenbelt, MD, June 1992.

[Lantz, 1985] K. E. LANTZ, *The Prototyping Methodology*, Prentice Hall, Englewood Cliffs, NJ, 1985.

[Luqi and Royce, 1992] LUQI AND W. ROYCE, "Status Report: Computer-Aided Prototyping," *IEEE Software* **9** (November 1992), pp. 77–81.

[Mantei and Teorey, 1988] M. M. MANTEI AND T. J. TEOREY, "Cost/Benefit Analysis for Incorporating Human Factors in the Software Development Lifecycle," *Communications of the ACM* **31** (April 1988), pp. 428–39.

[McConnell, 1996] S. MCCONNELL, "Daily Build and Smoke Test," *IEEE Computer* **13** (July 1996), pp. 144, 143.

[Rajlich, 1994] V. RAJLICH, "Decomposition/Generalization Methodology for Object-Oriented Programming," *Journal of Systems and Software* **24** (February, 1994), pp. 181–86.

[Royce, 1970] W. W. ROYCE, "Managing the Development of Large Software Systems: Concepts and Techniques," *1970 WESCON Technical Papers, Western Electronic Show and Convention*, Los Angeles, August 1970, pp. A/1-1–A/1-9. Reprinted in: *Proceedings of the 11th International Conference on Software Engineering*, Pittsburgh, May 1989, pp. 328–38.

[Selby, Basili, and Baker, 1987] R. W. SELBY, V. R. BASILI, AND F. T. BAKER, "Cleanroom Software Development: An Empirical Evaluation," *IEEE Transactions on Software Engineering* **SE-13** (September 1987), pp. 1027–37.

[Spivey, 1992] J. M. SPIVEY, *The Z Notation: A Reference Manual*, Prentice Hall, New York, 1992.

[Wong, 1984] C. WONG, "A Successful Software Development," *IEEE Transactions on Software Engineering* **SE-10** (November 1984), pp. 714–27.

chapter

4

TEAMS AND THE TOOLS OF THEIR TRADE

Without competent and well-trained software engineers, a software project is doomed to failure. However, having the right people is not enough; teams must be organized in such a way that the team members can work productively in cooperation with one another. Team organization is described in the first half of this chapter.

Software engineers need two types of tools. First, there are analytical tools used in software development, such as stepwise refinement and cost–benefit analysis. And then there are software tools, that is, products that assist the teams of software engineers in developing and maintaining software. These are usually termed *CASE tools* (CASE is an acronym that stands for computer-aided software engineering). The second half of the chapter is devoted to these two types of tools of the trade.

4.1 TEAM ORGANIZATION

Most products are too large to be completed by a single software professional within the given time constraints. As a result, the product must be assigned to a group of professionals organized as a *team.* For example, consider the specification phase. In order to specify the target product within 2 months, it may be necessary to assign the task to three specification specialists organized as a team under the direction of the specification manager. Similarly, the design task may be shared between members of the design team.

Suppose now that a product has to be coded within 3 months, even though there is 1 person-year of coding involved (a person-year is the amount of work that can be done by one person in 1 year). The solution is apparently simple: If one programmer can code the product in 1 year, four programmers can do it in 3 months.

This, of course, is nonsense. In practice, the four programmers may take nearly a year, and the quality of the resulting product may well be lower than if one programmer had coded the entire product. The reason is that some tasks can be shared; others must be done individually. For instance, if one farm hand can pick a strawberry field in 10 days, the same strawberry field can be picked by 10 farm hands in 1 day. On the other hand, one woman can produce a baby in 9 months, but this feat cannot possibly be accomplished in 1 month by nine women!

In other words, tasks like strawberry picking can be fully shared; others, like baby production, cannot be shared. Unlike baby production, it is possible to share implementation tasks between members of a team by distributing the coding among the team members. However, team programming is also unlike strawberry picking in that team members have to interact with one another in a meaningful and effective way. For example, suppose Jane and Ned have to code two modules, m1 and m2. A number of things can go wrong. For instance, both Jane and Ned may code m1 and ignore m2. Or Jane may code m1, and Ned may code m2. But when m1 calls m2 it passes four arguments; Ned has coded m2 in such a way that it requires five arguments. Or the order of the arguments in m1 and m2 may be different. Or the order may be the same, but the data types may be slightly different. Such problems are usually caused by a decision made during the design phase that is not propagated throughout the development organization. The issue has nothing whatsoever to do with the technical competency of the programmers. Team organization is a managerial issue; management must organize the programming teams so that each team is highly productive.

A different type of difficulty that arises from team development of software is shown in Figure 4.1. There are three channels of communication between the three computer professionals working on the project. Now suppose that the work is slipping, a deadline is rapidly approaching, but the task is not nearly complete. The obvious thing to do is to add a fourth professional to the team. But the first

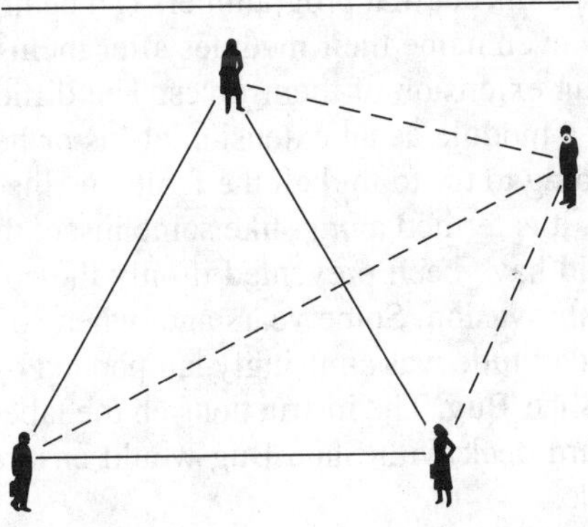

Figure 4.1 Communication paths between three computer professionals (solid lines), and when a fourth professional joins them (dashed lines).

thing that must happen when the fourth professional joins the team is for the other three to explain in detail what has been accomplished to date and what is still incomplete. In other words, adding personnel to a late software project makes it even later. This principle is now known as "Brooks's Law " after Fred Brooks who observed it while managing the development of OS/360 [Brooks, 1975].

In a large organization, teams are used in every phase of software production, but especially in the implementation phase during which programmers work independently on separate modules. Accordingly, the implementation phase is a prime candidate for sharing the task among several computer professionals. In some smaller organizations, one individual may be responsible for the requirements, specifications, and design, after which the implementation is done by a team of two or three programmers. Because teams are most heavily used during the implementation phase, the problems of team organization are most acutely felt during implementation. In the remainder of this chapter, team organization is therefore presented within the context of implementation, even though the problems and their solution are also applicable to all the other phases.

There are two extreme approaches to programming-team organization, namely, democratic teams and chief programmer teams. The approach taken here is to describe each of the two approaches, highlight their strengths and weaknesses, and then suggest other ways of organizing a programming team that incorporate the best features of the two extremes.

4.2 DEMOCRATIC TEAM APPROACH

The democratic team organization was first described by Weinberg in 1971 [Weinberg, 1971]. The basic concept underlying the democratic team is *egoless programming.* Weinberg points out that programmers can be highly attached to their code. Sometimes they even name their modules after themselves; they therefore see their modules as an extension of themselves. The difficulty with this is that if a programmer sees a module as an extension of his or her ego, that programmer is certainly not going to try to find all the faults in "his" code or "her" code. And if there is a fault, it is termed a *bug,* like some insect that has crept unasked into the code and could have been prevented if only the code had been guarded more zealously against invasion. Some years ago, when software was still input on punched cards, that attitude was amusingly lampooned by the marketing of an aerosol spray named Shoo-Bug. The instructions on the label solemnly explained that spraying one's card deck with Shoo-Bug would ensure that no bugs could possibly infest the code.

Weinberg's solution to the problem of programmers being too closely attached to their own code is egoless programming. The social environment must be restructured and so must programmer values. Every programmer must encourage the other members of the team to find faults in his or her code. The presence of a fault must not be considered something bad, but rather a normal and accepted event; the attitude of the reviewer should be appreciation at being asked for advice, rather than ridicule of the programmer for making coding errors. The team as a whole will develop an ethos, a group identity, and modules will belong to the team as a whole rather than to any one individual.

A group of up to 10 egoless programmers constitutes a *democratic team.* Weinberg warns that management may have difficulty working with such a team. After all, consider the managerial career path. When a programmer is promoted to a management position, his or her fellow programmers are not promoted and must strive to attain the higher level at the next round of promotions. In contrast, a democratic team is a group working for a common cause with no single leader, and with no programmers trying to get promoted to the next level. What is important is team identity and mutual respect.

Weinberg tells of a democratic team that developed an outstanding product. Management decided to give a cash award to the team's nominal manager (by definition, a democratic team has no leader). He refused to accept it personally, saying that it had to be shared equally among all members of the team. Management thought that he was angling for more money and that the team (and especially its nominal manager) had some rather unorthodox ideas. Management forced the nominal manager to accept the money, which he then divided equally among the team. Next, the entire team resigned and joined another company as a team.

The advantages and disadvantages of democratic teams are now presented.

4.2.1 ANALYSIS OF THE DEMOCRATIC TEAM APPROACH

A major advantage of the democratic team approach is the positive attitude toward the finding of faults. The more that are found, the happier are the members of a democratic team. This positive attitude leads to more rapid detection of faults, and hence to high-quality code. But there are some major problems. As pointed out previously, managers may have difficulty accepting egoless programming. In addition, a programmer with, say, 15 years of experience is likely to resent having his or her code appraised by fellow programmers, especially beginners.

Weinberg feels that egoless teams spring up spontaneously and cannot be imposed from outside. Little experimental research has been done on democratic programming teams, but the experience of Weinberg is that democratic teams are enormously productive. Mantei has analyzed the democratic team organization using arguments based on theories of and experiments on group organization in general, rather than specifically on programming teams [Mantei, 1981]. She points out that decentralized groups work best when the problem is difficult, and suggests that democratic teams should function well in a research environment. It has been the author's experience that a democratic team also works well in an industrial setting when there is a hard problem to solve. On a number of occasions he has been a member of democratic teams that have sprung up spontaneously among computer professionals with research experience. But once the task has been reduced to the implementation of a hard-won solution, the team must then be reorganized in a more hierarchical fashion, such as the chief programmer team approach described in the next section.

4.3 CLASSICAL CHIEF PROGRAMMER TEAM APPROACH

Consider the six-person team shown in Figure 4.2. There are 15 two-person communication channels. In fact, the total number of two-, three-, four-, five-, and six-person groups is 57. This multiplicity of communication channels is the major reason why a six-person team structured as in Figure 4.2 is unlikely to be able to perform 36 person-months of work in 6 months; many hours are wasted in meetings involving two or more team members at a time.

Now consider the six-person team shown in Figure 4.3. Again there are six programmers, but now there are only five lines of communication. This is the basic concept behind what is now termed the *chief programmer* team. A related idea was put forward by Brooks, who drew the analogy of a chief surgeon directing an operation [Brooks, 1975]. The surgeon is assisted by other surgeons, the anesthesiologist, and a variety of nurses. In addition, when necessary the team makes

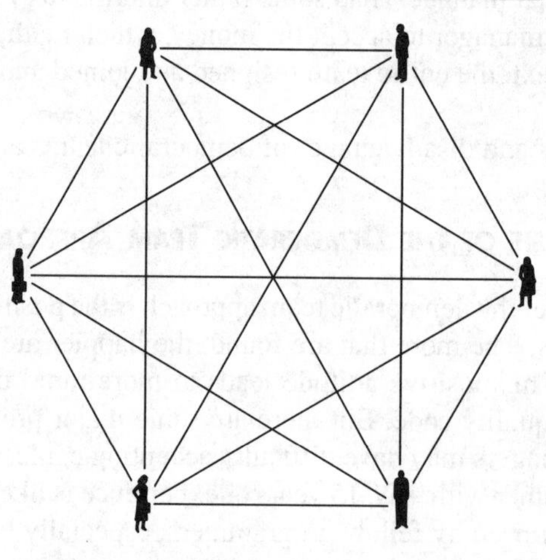

Figure 4.2 Communication paths between six computer professionals.

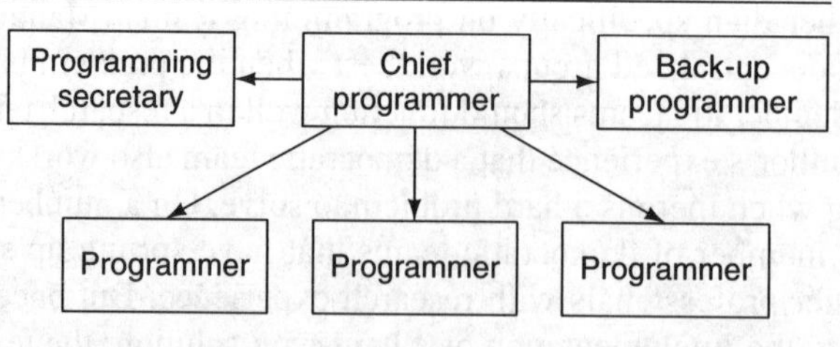

Figure 4.3 Structure of classical chief programmer team.

use of experts in other areas such as cardiologists or nephrologists. This analogy highlights two key aspects of a chief programmer team. The first is *specialization;* each member of the team carries out only those tasks for which he or she has been trained. The second aspect is *hierarchy.* The chief surgeon directs the actions of all the other members of the team and is responsible for every aspect of the operation.

The chief programmer team concept was formalized by Mills [Baker, 1972]. A classical chief programmer team, as described by Baker, is shown in Figure 4.3. It consists of the chief programmer, who is assisted by the back-up programmer, the programming secretary, and from one to three programmers. When necessary, the team is assisted by specialists in other areas, such as job control language (JCL) or legal or financial matters. The *chief programmer* is both a successful manager and a highly skilled programmer who does the architectural design and any critical or complex sections of the code. The other team members work on the detailed design and the coding, under the direction of the chief programmer. As shown in Figure 4.3 there are no lines of communication between the programmers; all interfacing issues are handled by the chief programmer. Finally, the chief programmer reviews the work of the other team members, because the chief programmer is personally responsible for every line of code.

The position of *back-up programmer* is necessary only because the chief programmer is human and may therefore become ill, fall under a bus, or change jobs. Thus the back-up programmer must be as competent as the chief programmer in every respect and must know as much about the project as the chief programmer. In addition, in order to free the chief programmer to concentrate on the architectural design, the back-up programmer does black-box test case planning (Section 13.7) and other tasks that are independent of the design process.

The word *secretary* has a number of meanings. On the one hand, a secretary assists a busy executive by answering the telephone, typing correspondence, and so on. But when we talk about the American Secretary of State or the British Foreign Secretary, we are referring to one of the most senior members of the Cabinet. The *programming secretary* is not a part-time clerical assistant but a highly skilled, well-paid, central member of a chief programmer team. The programming secretary is responsible for maintaining the project production library, the documentation of the project. This includes source code listings, JCL, and test data. The programmers hand their source code to the secretary who is responsible for its conversion to machine-readable form, compilation, linking, loading, execution, and running test cases. *Programmers* therefore do nothing but program. All other aspects of their work are handled by the programming secretary. (Because the programming secretary maintained the project production library, some organizations have used the title "librarian.")

Recall that what is described here are Mills's and Baker's original ideas, dating back to 1971, when keypunches were still widely used. Coding is no longer done that way. Programmers now have their own terminals or workstations in which they enter their code, edit it, test it, and so on. A modern version of the classical chief programmer team is described in Section 4.4.

4.3.1 The *New York Times* Project

The chief programmer team concept was first used in 1971 by IBM to automate the clipping file ("morgue") of the *New York Times.* The clipping file contains abstracts and full articles from the *New York Times* and other publications. Reporters and other members of the editorial staff use this information bank as a reference source.

The facts of the project are astounding. For example, 83,000 lines of code (LOC) were written in 22 calendar months, an effort of 11 person-years. After the first year, only the file maintenance system consisting of 12,000 LOC had been written. Most of the code was written in the last 6 months. Only 21 faults were detected in the first 5 weeks of acceptance testing; only 25 further faults were detected in the first year of operation. Principal programmers averaged one detected fault and 10,000 LOC per person-year. The file maintenance system, delivered 1 week after coding was completed, operated 20 months before a single fault was detected. Almost half the subprograms, usually 200 to 400 lines of PL/I, were correct on the first compilation [Baker 1972].

Nevertheless, after this fantastic success, no comparable claims for the chief programmer team concept have been made. Yes, many successful projects have been carried out using chief programmer teams, but the figures reported, although satisfactory, are not as impressive as those obtained for the *New York Times* project. Why was the *New York Times* project such a success, and why have similar results not been obtained on other projects?

One possible explanation is that this was a prestige project for IBM. It was the first real trial for PL/I, a language developed by IBM. An organization known for its superb software experts, IBM set up a team comprising what can only be described as their crème de la crème from one division. Second, technical backup was extremely strong. PL/I compiler writers were on hand to assist the programmers in every way they could and JCL experts assisted with the job control language. A third possible explanation was the expertise of the chief programmer, F. Terry Baker. He is what is now called a *superprogrammer,* a programmer whose output is four or five times that of an average good programmer. In addition, Baker is a superb manager and leader, and it could be that his skills, enthusiasm, and personality were the reasons underlying the success of the project.

If the chief programmer is competent, then the chief programmer team organization works well. Although the remarkable success of the *New York Times* project has not been repeated, many successful projects have employed variants of the chief programmer approach. The reason for the phrase *variants of the approach* is that the classical chief programmer team as described in [Baker, 1972] is impractical in many ways.

4.3.2 Impracticality of the Classical Chief Programmer Team Approach

Consider the chief programmer, a combination of a highly skilled programmer and successful manager. Such individuals are difficult to find; there is a shortage of highly skilled programmers, as well as a shortage of successful managers, and the job description of a chief programmer requires both abilities. It has also been suggested that the qualities needed to be a highly skilled programmer are different from those needed to be a successful manager; therefore, the chances of finding a chief programmer are small.

But if chief programmers are hard to find, back-up programmers are as rare as hen's teeth. After all, the back-up programmer is expected to be as good as the chief programmer, but has to take a back seat and a lower salary while waiting for something to happen to the chief programmer. Few top programmers or top managers would accept this role.

A programming secretary is also difficult to find. Software professionals are notorious for their aversion to paperwork, but the programming secretary is expected to do nothing but paperwork all day.

Thus chief programmer teams, at least as proposed by Baker, are impractical to implement. Democratic teams were also shown to be impractical, but for different reasons. Furthermore, neither technique seems to be able to handle products that require 20 or even 120 programmers for the implementation phase. What is needed is a way of organizing programming teams that makes use of the strengths of democratic teams and chief programmer teams and that can be extended to the implementation of larger products.

4.4 BEYOND CHIEF PROGRAMMER AND DEMOCRATIC TEAMS

Democratic teams have a major strength, namely, a positive attitude toward the finding of faults. A number of organizations use chief programmer teams in conjunction with code reviews (Section 5.2), creating a potential pitfall. The chief programmer is personally responsible for every line of code and must, therefore, be present during all code reviews. However, a chief programmer is also a manager, and as explained in Chapter 5, reviews should not be used for any sort of performance appraisal. Thus, because the chief programmer is also the manager responsible for the primary evaluation of the team members, it is strongly inadvisable for that individual to be present at a code review.

The way out of this contradiction is to remove much of the managerial role from the chief programmer. After all, the difficulty of finding one individual who is both a highly skilled programmer and successful manager has been pointed out previously. Instead, the chief programmer should be replaced by two individuals: a team *leader* who is in charge of the technical aspects of the team's activities and a team *manager* who is responsible for all nontechnical managerial decisions. The structure of the resulting team is shown in Figure 4.4. It is important to realize that this organizational structure does not violate the fundamental managerial principle that no employee should report to more than one manager. The areas of responsibility are clearly delineated. The team leader is responsible

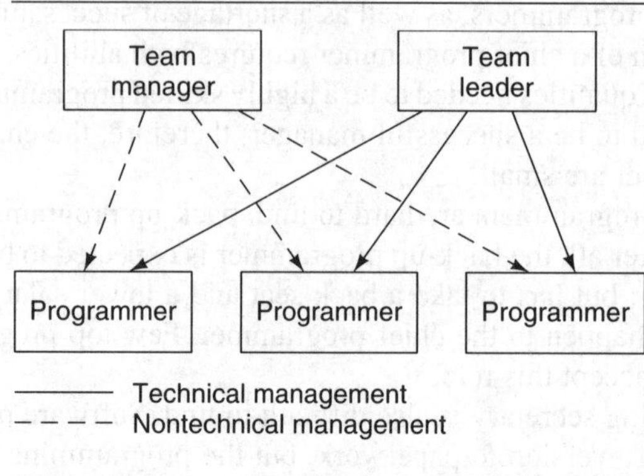

Figure 4.4 Structure of modern programming team.

for only technical management. Thus budgetary and legal issues are not handled by the team leader, nor are performance appraisals. On the other hand, the team leader has sole responsibility on technical issues. The team manager therefore has no right to promise, say, that the product will be delivered within four weeks; promises of that sort have to be made by the team leader. The team leader naturally participates in all code reviews; after all, he or she is personally responsible for every aspect of the code. At the same time, the team manager is not permitted at a review, because programmer performance appraisal is a function of the team manager. Instead, the team manager acquires knowledge of the technical skills of each programmer in the team during regularly scheduled team meetings.

Before implementation begins, it is important to demarcate clearly those areas that appear to be the responsibility of both the team manager and the team leader. For example, consider the issue of annual leave. The situation can arise that the team manager approves a leave application because leave is a nontechnical issue, only to find the application vetoed by the team leader because a deadline is approaching. The solution to this and related issues is for higher management to draw up a policy regarding areas that both the team manager and the team leader consider to be their joint responsibility.

What about larger projects? This approach can be scaled up as shown in Figure 4.5, which shows the technical managerial organizational structure; the nontechnical side is similarly organized. Implementation of the product as a whole is under the direction of the project leader. The programmers report to their team leaders, and the team leaders report to the project leader. For even larger products, additional levels can be added to the hierarchy.

Another way of drawing on the best features of both democratic and chief programmer teams is to decentralize the decision-making process where appropriate. The resulting channels of communication are shown in Figure 4.6. This scheme is useful for the sorts of problems for which the democratic approach is good, that is, in a research environment or whenever there is a hard problem that

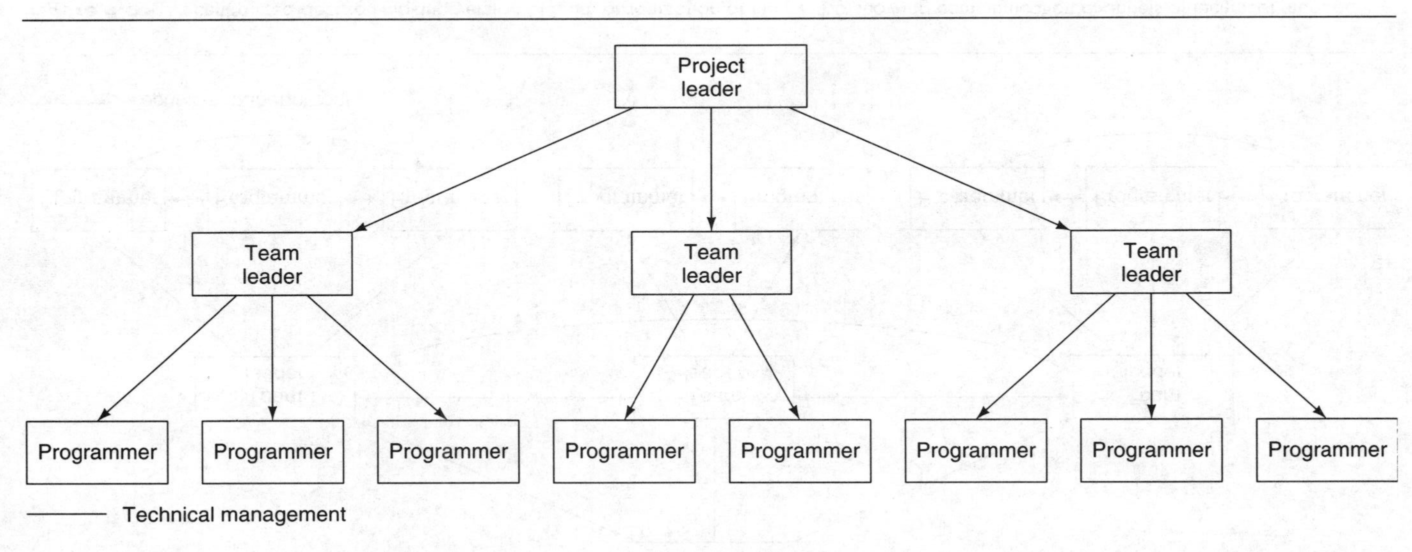

Figure 4.5 Technical managerial organizational structure for larger projects.

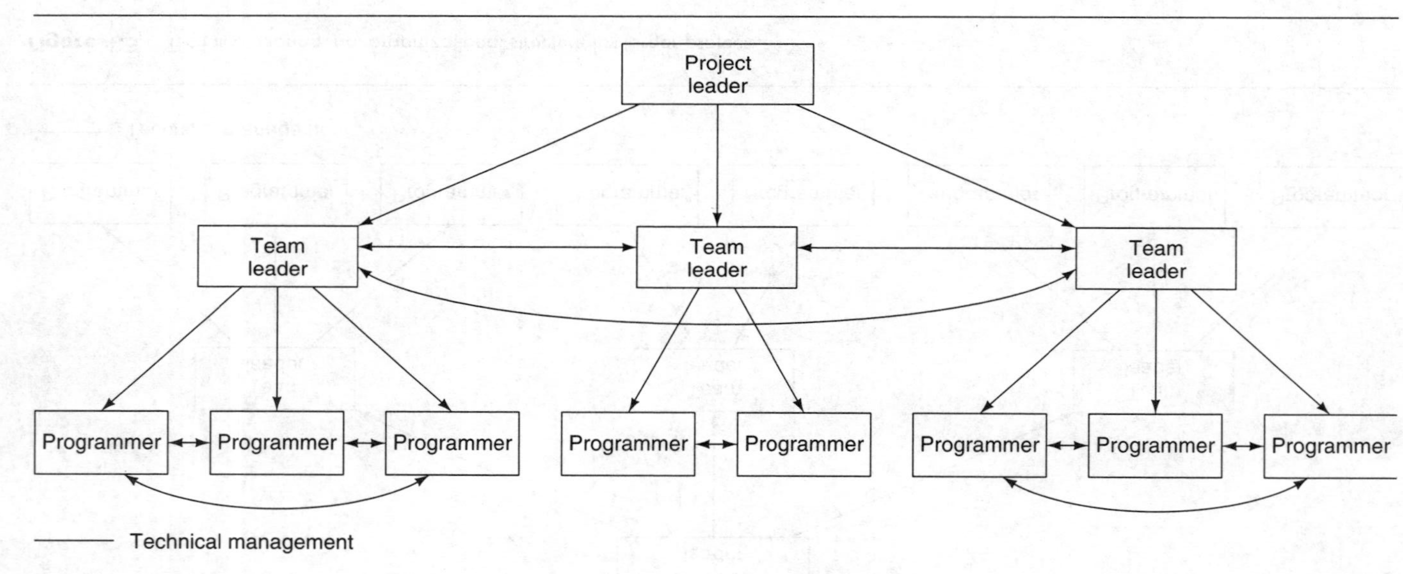

Figure 4.6 Decentralized decision-making version of team organization of Figure 4.5 showing communication channels of technical management.

requires the synergistic effect of group interaction for its solution. Notwithstanding the decentralization, the arrows from level to level still point downward; allowing programmers to dictate to the project leader can lead only to chaos.

Unfortunately, there is no one solution to the problem of programming team organization and, by extension, to the problem of organizing teams for all the other phases. The optimal way of organizing a team depends on the product to be built, on previous experience with various team structures, and on the outlook of the heads of the organization. For example, if senior management is uncomfortable with decentralized decision making, then it will not be implemented. Unfortunately, not much research has been done on software development team organization, and many of the generally accepted principles are based on research on group dynamics in general and not on software development teams. Until experimental results on team organization have been obtained within the software industry, it will not be easy to determine the optimal team organization for a specific product.

4.5 SYNCHRONIZE-AND-STABILIZE TEAMS

An alternative approach to team organization is the synchronize-and-stabilize team utilized by Microsoft [Cusamano and Selby, 1997]. Microsoft builds large products; for example, Windows 95 consists of more than 11 million lines of code, built by over 200 programmers and testers. Team organization is a vital aspect of the successful construction of a product of this size.

The synchronize-and-stabilize life-cycle model was described in Section 3.5. The success of this model is largely a consequence of the way the teams are organized. Each of the three or four sequential builds of the synchronize-and-stabilize model is constructed by a number of small parallel teams led by a program manager and consisting of between three and eight developers together with three to eight testers who work one-to-one with the developers. The team is provided with the specifications of their overall task; the individual team members are then given the freedom to design and implement their portion of that task as they wish. The reason that this does not rapidly devolve into hacker-induced chaos is the synchronization step that is performed each day; the partially completed components are tested and debugged on a daily basis. Thus, even though individual creativity and autonomy are nurtured, the individual components always work together.

The strength of this approach is that, on the one hand, individual programmers are encouraged to be creative and innovative, a characteristic of a democratic team. On the other hand, the daily synchronization step ensures that the hundreds of developers are working together toward a common goal without requiring the communication and coordination characteristic of a chief programmer team (Figure 4.3).

There are very few rules that Microsoft developers must follow, but one of them is that they must adhere strictly to the time laid down to enter their code into the product database for that day's synchronization. Cusamano and Selby liken this to telling children that they can do what they like all day, but have to be in bed by 9 PM [Cusamano and Selby, 1997]. Another rule is that if a developer's code prevents the product from being compiled for that day's synchronization, the problem must be fixed immediately so that the rest of the team can test and debug that day's work.

Will use of the synchronize-and-stabilize model and associated team organization guarantee that every other software organization will be as successful as Microsoft? This is extremely unlikely. Microsoft, Inc. is more than just the synchronize-and-stabilize model. It is an organization consisting of a highly talented set of managers and software developers with an evolved group ethos. Merely using the synchronize-and-stabilize model will not magically turn an organization into another Microsoft. At the same time, the use of many of the features of the model in other organizations could lead to process improvement. On the other hand, it has been suggested that the synchronize-and-stabilize model is simply a way of allowing a group of hackers to build large products. As stated at the end of the previous section, experimental data are needed before conclusions can be drawn regarding optimal programmer team organization.

This concludes our discussion on team organization. A comparison of the various types of team organization appears in Figure 4.7. The remainder of this chapter is devoted to the tools of the trade, first theoretical tools and then software (CASE) tools. We begin with stepwise refinement.

4.6 STEPWISE REFINEMENT

Stepwise refinement is a problem-solving technique that underlies many software engineering techniques. It can be defined as a means to "postpone decisions on

Team Organization	Strengths	Weaknesses
Democratic teams	High quality code as consequence of positive attitude to finding faults Particularly good with hard problems	Cannot be externally imposed
Classical chief programmer teams	Major success of *New York Times* project	Impractical
Modified chief programmer teams	Many successes	No successes comparable to *New York Times* project
Modern programming teams	Team manager/team leader structure obviates need for chief programmer Scales up Supports decentralization when needed	Problems can arise unless areas of responsibilities of team manager and team leader are clearly delineated

Figure 4.7 Comparison of approaches to team organization.

details until as late as possible in order to be able to concentrate on the important issues."

As will be seen during the course of this book, stepwise refinement underlies many specification techniques, design and implementation techniques, even testing and integration techniques. The reason stepwise refinement is so important is because of Miller's law [Miller, 1956], which states that at any one time a human being can concentrate on at most 7 ± 2 *chunks* (quanta of information).

The problem when developing software is that we need to concentrate on many more than seven chunks at a time. For example, a class usually has considerably more than seven attributes and methods, and a client has more than seven requirements. Stepwise refinement enables the software engineer to concentrate on those seven chunks that are the most relevant at the current phase of development.

The following example illustrates how stepwise refinement can be used in the design of a product.

4.6.1 STEPWISE REFINEMENT EXAMPLE

The example presented in this section seems almost trivial in that it involves updating a sequential master file, a common operation in many application areas. This choice of a familiar example is deliberate in order to enable the reader to concentrate on stepwise refinement rather than the problem in hand:

> Design a product to update the sequential master file containing name and address data for the monthly magazine, *True Life Software Disasters.* There are three types of transactions, namely insertions, modifications, and deletions, with transaction codes 1, 2, and 3 respectively. Thus the transaction types are:
>
> Type 1: INSERT (a new subscriber into the master file)
> Type 2: MODIFY (an existing subscriber record)
> Type 3: DELETE (an existing subscriber record)
>
> Transactions are sorted into alphabetical order by name of subscriber. If there is more than one transaction for a given subscriber, the transactions for that subscriber have been sorted so that insertions occur before modifications and modifications before deletions.

The first step in designing a solution is to set up a typical file of input transactions, such as that shown in Figure 4.8. The file contains five records, namely, DELETE Brown, INSERT Harris, MODIFY Jones, DELETE Jones, and INSERT Smith. (It is not unusual to perform both a modification and a deletion of the same subscriber in one run.)

The problem may be represented as shown in Figure 4.9. There are two input files:

1. Old master file name and address records
2. Transaction records

Transaction Type	Name	Address
3	Brown	
1	Harris	2 Oak Lane, Townsville
2	Jones	Box 345, Tarrytown
3	Jones	
1	Smith	1304 Elm Avenue, Oak City

Figure 4.8 Input transaction records for sequential master file update.

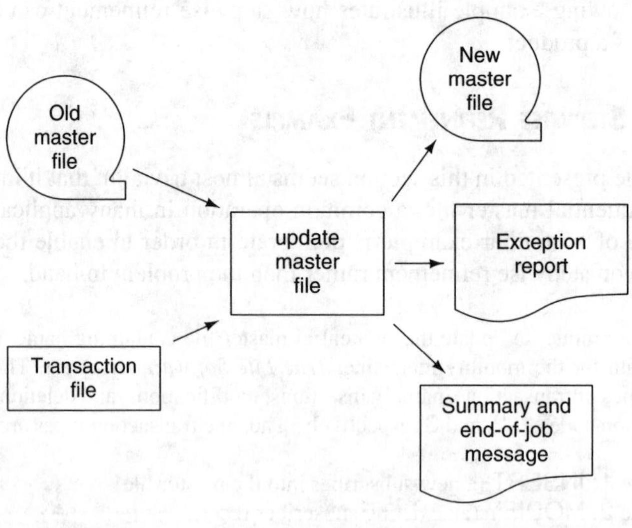

Figure 4.9 Sequential master file update.

and there are three output files:

3. New master file name and address records
4. Exception report
5. Summary and end-of-job message

To begin the design process, the starting point is the single box update master file shown in Figure 4.10. This box can be decomposed into three boxes, labeled input, process, and output. The assumption is that when process requires a record, our level of competence is such that the correct record can be produced at the right time. Similarly, we are capable of writing the correct record to the correct file at the right time. Therefore, the technique is to separate out the input and output aspects and concentrate on process. What is this process?

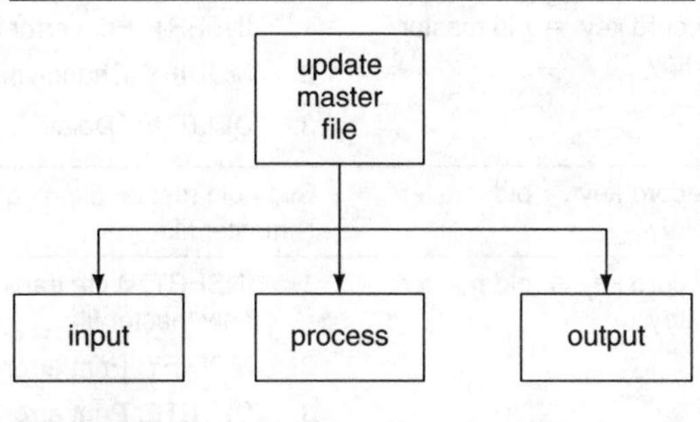

Figure 4.10 First refinement of design.

Transaction file
3 Brown
1 Harris
2 Jones
3 Jones
1 Smith

Old master file
Abel
Brown
James
Jones
Smith
Townsend

New master file
Abel
Harris
James
Smith
Townsend

Exception report
Smith

Figure 4.11 Transaction file, old master file, new master file, and exception report.

To determine what it does, consider the example shown in Figure 4.11. The key of the first transaction record (Brown) is compared with the key of the first old master file record (Abel). Because Brown comes after Abel, the Abel record is written to the new master file, and the next old master file record (Brown) is read. In this case the key of the transaction record matches the key of the old master file record, and because the transaction type is 3 (DELETE), the Brown record must be deleted. This is implemented by not copying the Brown record onto the new master file. The next transaction record (Harris) and old master file record (James) are read, overwriting the Brown records in their respective buffers. Harris comes before James and is, therefore, inserted into the new master file; the next transaction record (Jones) is read. Because Jones comes after James, the James record is written to the new master file, and the next old master file record is read; this is Jones. As can be seen from the transaction file, the Jones record is to be modified and then deleted, so the next transaction record (Smith) and the next old master file record (also Smith) are read. Unfortunately, the transaction type is 1 (INSERT), but Smith is already in the master file. So there is an error of some sort in the data, and the Smith record is written to the exception

Transaction record key = old master file record key	1. INSERT: Print error message 2. MODIFY: Change master file record 3. DELETE: *Delete master file record
Transaction record key > old master file record key	Copy old master file record onto new master file
Transaction record key < old master file record key	1. INSERT: Write transaction record to new master file 2. MODIFY: Print error message 3. DELETE: Print error message

*Deletion of a master file record is implemented by not copying the record onto the new master file.

Figure 4.12 Diagrammatic representation of process.

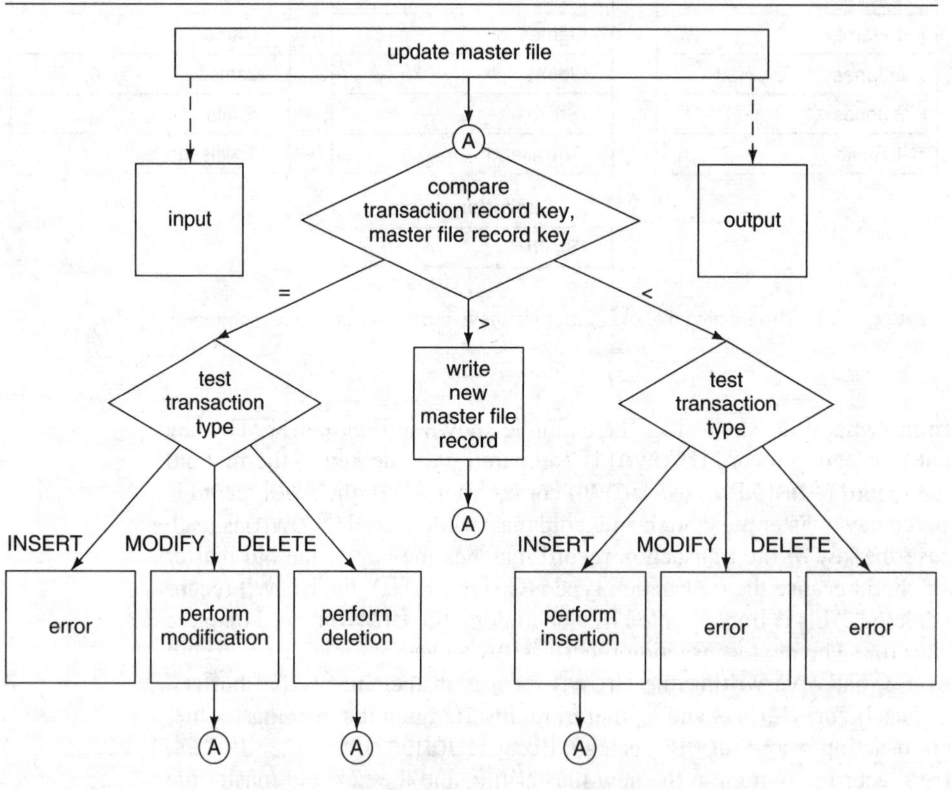

Figure 4.13 Second refinement of design.

report. To be more precise, the Smith transaction record is written to the exception report, the Smith old master file record is written to the new master file.

Now that process is understood, it may be represented as in Figure 4.12. Next, the process box of Figure 4.10 may be refined, resulting in the second refinement shown in Figure 4.13. The dashed lines to the input and output boxes denote that decisions as to how to handle input and output have been deferred until a later refinement. The remainder of the figure is the flowchart of the process, or rather, an early refinement of the flowchart. As already pointed out, input and output have been deferred. Also, there is no provision for an end-of-file condition, nor has it yet been specified what to do when an error condition is encountered. The strength of stepwise refinement is that these and similar problems can be solved in later refinements.

The next step is to refine the input and output boxes of Figure 4.13, resulting in Figure 4.14. End-of-file conditions have still not been handled, nor has the writing of the end-of-job message. Again, these can be done at a later iteration. What is critical, however, is that the design of Figure 4.14 has a major fault. To see this, consider the situation with regard to the data of Figure 4.11 when the current transaction is 2 Jones, that is, modify Jones, and the current old master file record is Jones. In the design of Figure 4.14, because the key of the transaction record is the same as the key of the old master file record, the leftmost path is followed to the test transaction type decision box. Because the current transaction type is MODIFY, the old master file record is modified and written to the new master file, and the next transaction record is read. This record is 3 Jones, that is, delete Jones. But the modified Jones record has already been written to the new master file.

The reader may be wondering why an incorrect refinement has deliberately been presented. The point is that, when using stepwise refinement, it is necessary to desk-check each successive refinement before proceeding to the next. If a particular refinement turns out to be faulty, it is not necessary to restart the process from the beginning, but merely to go back to the previous refinement and proceed from there. In this instance, the second refinement (Figure 4.13) is correct, so it may be used as the basis for another attempt at a third refinement. This time, the design uses *level-1 lookahead,* that is, a transaction record is processed only after the next transaction record has been analyzed. Details are left as an exercise; see Problem 4.3.

In the fourth refinement, details that have been ignored up to now, such as opening and closing files, have to be introduced. With stepwise refinement such details are handled last, after the logic of the design has been fully developed. Obviously, it is impossible to execute the product without opening and closing files. However, what is important here is the stage in the design process at which such details as file openings and closings are handled. While the design is being developed, the seven or so chunks on which the designer can concentrate at once should *not* include details like opening and closing files; file openings and closings have nothing to do with the design itself, they are merely implementation details that are part of any design. However, in later refinements, opening and closing files becomes vital. In other words, stepwise refinement can be

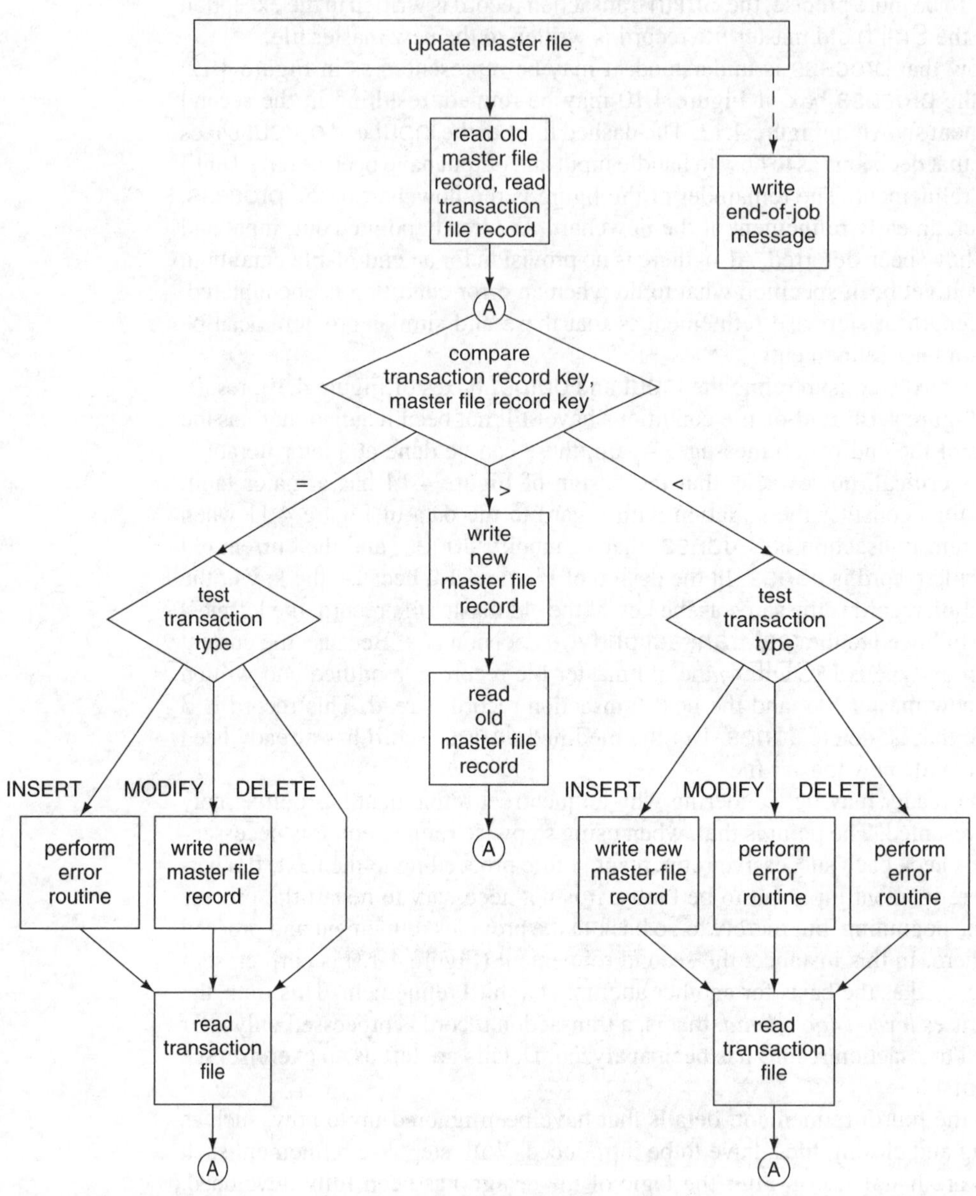

Figure 4.14 Third refinement of design (design has major fault).

considered to be a technique for prioritizing the various problems that have to be solved within a phase. Stepwise refinement ensures that every problem is solved and that each is solved at the appropriate time, but at no time need more than 7 ± 2 chunks be handled.

The term *stepwise refinement* was first introduced by Wirth [Wirth, 1971]. In the preceding example, stepwise refinement was applied to a flowchart, whereas Wirth applied the technique to pseudocode. The specific representation to which stepwise refinement is applied is not important; stepwise refinement is a general technique that can be used in every phase of software development and with almost every representation.

Miller's law is a fundamental restriction on the mental powers of human beings. Because we cannot fight our nature, we must live with it, accepting our limitations and doing the best we can under the circumstances.

The power of stepwise refinement is that it helps the software engineer to concentrate on the relevant aspects of the current development phase (design phase in the preceding example) and to ignore details that, though essential in the overall scheme, need not be considered, and in fact should be ignored, until later. Unlike a divide-and-conquer technique in which the problem is decomposed into pieces that are essentially of equal importance, in stepwise refinement the importance of a particular aspect of the problem changes from refinement to refinement. Initially, a particular issue may be irrelevant, but later that same issue will be of critical importance. The difficulty with stepwise refinement is appreciating which issues must be handled in the current refinement and which must be postponed until a later refinement.

Like stepwise refinement, cost–benefit analysis is another fundamental theoretical software engineering technique that is used throughout the software life cycle. This technique is described in the next section.

4.7 COST–BENEFIT ANALYSIS

One way of determining whether a possible course of action would be profitable is to compare estimated future benefits against projected future costs. This is termed *cost–benefit analysis.* As an example of cost–benefit analysis within the computer context, consider how Krag Central Electric Company (KCEC) decided in 1965 whether or not to computerize its billing system. Billing was then being done manually by 80 clerks who mailed bills every 2 months to KCEC customers. Computerization would require KCEC to buy or lease the necessary software and hardware, including data-capture equipment for recording the input data on punch cards or magnetic tape.

One advantage of computerization would be that bills could be mailed monthly instead of every 2 months, thereby improving the company's cash flow considerably. Furthermore, the 80 billing clerks would be replaced by 11 data-capture clerks. Salary savings were estimated to be \$1,575,000, and improved cash flow was projected to be worth \$875,000. The total benefits were therefore estimated at $2,450,000. On the other hand, a complete data processing department would have to be set up, staffed by well-paid computer professionals. Over a 7-year period, costs were estimated as follows. The cost of hardware and software, including maintenance, was estimated to be $1,250,000. In the first year there would be a conversion cost of $350,000, and the cost of explaining the new system to customers was estimated at an additional $125,000. Total costs were estimated at $1,725,000, about $750,000 less than the estimated benefits. KCEC immediately decided to computerize.

Cost–benefit analysis is not always straightforward. On the one hand, salary savings can be estimated by a management consultant; cash flow improvements can be projected by an accountant; the change in the cost of money with time can be handled in terms of net present value [Yourdon, 1989]; and the costs of hardware, software, and conversion can be estimated by a software engineering consultant. But how is the cost of dealing with customers trying to adjust to computerization to be determined? Or how can the benefits of inoculating an entire population against measles be measured?

The point is that tangible benefits are easy to measure, but intangible benefits can be hard to quantify directly. A practical way of assigning a dollar value to intangible benefits is to make *assumptions*. These assumptions must always be stated in conjunction with the resulting estimates of the benefits. After all, managers have to make decisions. If no data are available, then making assumptions from which such data can be determined is usually the best that can be done under the circumstances. This approach has the further advantage that if someone else reviewing the data and the underlying assumptions can come up with better assumptions, then better data can be produced and the associated intangible benefits can be computed more accurately. The same technique can be used for intangible costs.

Cost–benefit analysis is a fundamental technique in deciding whether a client should computerize his or her business, and if so, in what way. The costs and benefits of various alternative strategies are compared. For example, a product for storing the results of drug trials can be implemented in a number of different ways, including flat files and various database management systems. For each possible strategy the costs and benefits are computed, and the one for which the difference between benefits and costs is the largest will then be selected as the optimal strategy.

The final theoretical tool described in this chapter is software metrics.

4.8 SOFTWARE METRICS

As explained in Section 2.11, without measurements (or *metrics*) it is impossible to detect problems early in the software process, before they get out of hand. Metrics can thus serve as an early warning system for potential problems. A wide variety of metrics can be used. For example, lines of code (LOC) is one way of measuring the size of a product (see Section 8.2.1). If LOC measurements are taken at regular intervals, they will provide a measure of how fast the project is progressing. In addition, the number of defects (faults) per 1000 lines of code is a measure of software quality. After all, it is of little use if a programmer consistently turns out 2000 lines of code a month but half of it has to be thrown away because it is of unacceptable quality. Thus, LOC in isolation is not a very meaningful metric.

When a product is in operations mode, a metric such as mean time between failures provides management with an indication of the reliability of an installed product. If a certain product fails every other day, its quality is clearly lower than that of a similar product that on average runs for 9 months without a failure.

Certain metrics can be applied throughout the software process. For example, effort in person-months (one person-month is the amount of work that is done by one person in one month) can be measured for each phase. Staff turnover is another important metric. High turnover will adversely affect current projects because it takes time for a new employee to learn the relevant facts about the project (see Section 4.1). In addition, new employees may have to be trained in aspects of the software process; if new employees are less educated in software engineering than the individuals they replace, then the process as a whole may suffer. Of course, cost is an essential metric that must also be monitored continually throughout the entire process.

A number of different metrics are described in this book. Some are *product metrics,* that is, they measure some aspect of the product itself, such as its size or its reliability. In contrast, others are *process metrics;* these metrics are used by the developers to deduce information about their software process. A typical metric of this kind is the efficiency of fault detection during development, that is, the ratio of the number of faults detected during development to the total number of faults detected in the product over its lifetime.

Many metrics are specific to a given phase. For example, lines of code cannot be used before implementation begins, and the number of defects detected per hour in reviewing specifications is relevant to only the specification phase. In subsequent chapters describing the various phases of the software process, metrics that are relevant to that phase are discussed.

There is a cost involved in gathering the data needed to compute the values of metrics. Even if the data gathering is fully automated, the CASE tool (Section 4.9) that accumulates the required information is not free, and interpreting the output from the tool consumes human resources. Bearing in mind that literally hundreds (if not thousands) of different metrics have been put forward, an obvious question is: What should a software organization measure? There are five essential, fundamental metrics:

1. Size (in lines of code or, better, in a more meaningful metric such as those of Section 8.2.1)
2. Cost (in dollars)
3. Duration (in months)
4. Effort (in person-months)
5. Quality (number of faults detected)

Each of these metrics must be measured by phase. On the basis of the data from these fundamental metrics, management can identify problems within the software organization, such as high fault rates during the design phase or code output that is well below industry averages. Once problem areas have been highlighted, a strategy to correct these problems can be introduced. In order to monitor the success of this strategy, more detailed metrics can be introduced. For example, it may be deemed appropriate to collect data on fault rates of each individual programmer or to conduct a survey of user satisfaction. Thus, other than the five fundamental metrics, more detailed data gathering and analysis should be performed only toward a specific objective.

Finally, one aspect of metrics is still fairly controversial. Questions have been raised as to the validity of many of the popular metrics; some of these issues are discussed in Section 13.8.2. Although it is agreed that we cannot control the software process unless we can measure it, there is some disagreement as to precisely what should be measured [Fenton and Pfleeger, 1997].

We now turn from theoretical tools to software (CASE) tools.

4.9 CASE

During the development of a software product, a number of very different operations have to be carried out. Typical activities include estimating resource requirements, drawing up the specification document, performing integration testing, and writing the user manual. Unfortunately, neither these activities, nor the others in the software process, can yet be fully automated and performed by a computer without human intervention.

However, computers can *assist* every step of the way. The title of this section, CASE, stands for computer-aided (or computer-assisted) software engineering. Computers can help by carrying out much of the drudge work associated with software development, including the organization of documentation of all kinds such as plans, contracts, specifications, designs, source code, and management information. Documentation is essential for software development and maintenance, but the majority of individuals involved in software development are not fond of either creating or updating documentation. Maintaining diagrams on the computer is especially useful as it allows changes to be made with ease.

But CASE is not restricted to assisting with documentation. In particular, computers can assist software engineers to cope with the complexity of software development, especially in managing all the details. CASE involves all aspects of computer support for software engineering. At the same time, it is important to remember that CASE stands for computer-*aided* software engineering, and not computer-*automated* software engineering—no computer can yet replace a human being with respect to development or maintenance of software. For the foreseeable future at least, the computer must remain a tool of the software professional.

4.10 TAXONOMY OF CASE

The simplest form of CASE is the software *tool,* a product that assists in just one aspect of the production of software. CASE tools are currently being used in every phase of the life cycle. For example, there are a variety of tools on the market, many of them for use with personal computers, that assist in the construction of graphical representations of software products, such as flowcharts. CASE tools that help the developer during the earlier phases of the process, namely, the requirements, specification, and design phases, are sometimes termed *upperCASE* or *front-end* tools, whereas those that assist with implementation, integration, and maintenance are termed *lowerCASE* or *back-end* tools. Figure 4.15(a) represents a CASE tool that assists with part of the requirements phase.

One important class of CASE tools is the *data dictionary,* a computerized list of all data defined within the product. In a large product there will be tens (if not hundreds) of thousands of data items, and the computer is ideal for storing information such as variable names and types and the location where each is defined, and procedure names and parameters and their types. The power of a data dictionary can be enhanced by combining it with a *consistency checker,* a tool that can check that every data item in the specification document is reflected in the design and, conversely, that every item in the design has been defined in the specification document.

Another use of a data dictionary is to provide the data for report generators and screen generators. A *report generator* is used to generate the code needed for producing a report. A *screen generator* is used to assist the software developer

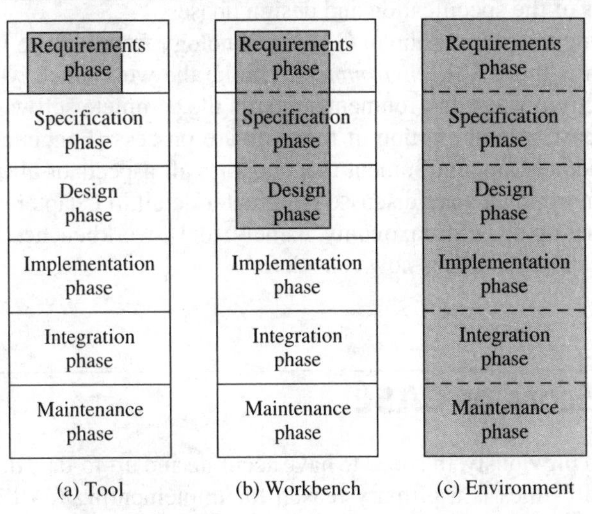

Figure 4.15 Representation of tool, workbench, and environment.

in producing the code for a data-capture screen. Suppose that a screen is being designed for entering the weekly sales at each branch of a chain of book stores. The branch number is a four-digit integer in the range 1000 to 4500 or 8000 to 8999, entered on the screen three lines from the top. This information is given to the screen generator. The screen generator then automatically generates code to display the string BRANCH NUMBER _ _ _ _ three lines from the top and to position the cursor at the first underline character. As the user enters each digit, it is displayed; and the cursor moves on to the next underline. The screen generator also generates code for checking that the user enters only digits and that the resulting four-digit integer is in the specified range. If the data entered are invalid, or if the user presses the ? key, help information is displayed.

Use of such generators can result in rapid prototypes being quickly constructed. Furthermore, a graphical representation tool combined with a data dictionary, consistency checker, report generator, and screen generator together constitute a specification and design *workbench* that supports rapid prototyping. Examples[1] of commercial workbenches that incorporate all these features include PowerBuilder, Software through Pictures, and System Architect.

A CASE workbench is thus a collection of tools that together support one or two *activities,* where an activity is a related collection of tasks. For example, the coding activity includes editing, compiling, linking, testing, and debugging. An activity is not the same thing as a phase of a life-cycle model. In fact, the tasks of an activity can even cross phase boundaries. For example, a project management workbench is used for every phase of the project, and a coding workbench can be used for rapid prototyping as well as for the implementation, integration, and maintenance phases. Figure 4.15(b) represents a workbench of upperCASE tools. The workbench includes the requirements phase tool of Figure 4.15(a), as well as tools for parts of the specification and design phases.

Continuing the progression of CASE technology from tools to workbenches, the next item is the CASE *environment.* Unlike the workbench which supports one or two activities, an environment supports the complete software process or, at the very least, a large portion of the software process [Fuggetta, 1993]. Figure 4.15(c) depicts an environment that supports all aspects of all phases of the life cycle. Environments are discussed in greater detail in Chapter 14.

Having set up a CASE taxonomy, namely, tools, workbenches, and environments, the scope of CASE is now considered.

4.11 SCOPE OF CASE

As mentioned previously, the need to have accurate and up-to-date documentation available at all times is a primary reason for implementing CASE technology.

[1]The fact that a specific CASE tool is cited in this book in no way implies any form of endorsement of that CASE tool by the author or publisher. Each CASE tool mentioned in this book has been included because it is a typical example of the class of CASE tools of which it is an instance.

For example, suppose that specifications are produced manually. A member of the development team has no way of telling whether a particular specification document is the current version or an older version. There is no way of knowing if the handwritten changes on that document are part of the current specification or were merely a suggestion that was later rejected. On the other hand, if the specifications of the product are produced using a CASE tool, then at any time there is only one copy of the specifications, namely, the online version accessed via the CASE tool. Then, if the specifications are changed, members of the development team can easily access the document and be sure that they are seeing the current version. In addition, the consistency checker will flag any design changes without corresponding changes to the specification document.

Programmers also need online documentation. For example, online help information must be provided for the operating system, editor, programming language, and so on. In addition, programmers have to consult manuals of many kinds, such as editor manuals and programming manuals. It is highly desirable that, wherever possible, these manuals be available online. Apart from the convenience of having everything at one's fingertips, it is generally quicker to query by computer than to try to find the appropriate manual and then plow through it to find the needed item. In addition, it is usually much easier to update an online manual than to try to find all hard-copy versions of a manual within an organization and make the necessary page changes. As a result, online documentation is likely to be more accurate than hard-copy versions of the same material—another reason for providing online documentation to programmers. An example of such online documentation is the UNIX *manual* pages [Sobell, 1995].

CASE can also assist with communications among team members. E-mail is rapidly becoming as much a part of an average office as a computer or a fax machine. There are many advantages to e-mail. From the viewpoint of software production, if copies of all e-mail relevant to a specific project are stored in a particular mailbox, then there will be a written record of the decisions that were made during the project. This can be used to resolve conflicts that may arise later. Many CASE environments and some CASE workbenches now incorporate e-mail systems. In other organizations the e-mail system is implemented via a World Wide Web browser such as Netscape. Other tools that are equally essential are spreadsheets and word processors.

The term *coding tools* refers to CASE tools such as text editors, debuggers, and pretty printers designed to simplify the programmer's task, to reduce the frustration that many programmers experience in their work, and to increase programmer productivity. Before discussing such tools, three definitions are required. *Programming-in-the-small* refers to software development at the level of the code of a single module, whereas *programming-in-the-large* is software development at the module level [DeRemer and Kron, 1976]. The latter includes aspects such as architectural design and integration. *Programming-in-the-many* refers to software production by a team. At times the team will be working at the module level, at times at the code level. Thus programming-in-the-many incorporates aspects of both programming-in-the-large and programming-in-the-small.

A *structure editor* is a text editor that "understands" the implementation language. That is, a structure editor is able to detect a syntax fault as soon as it has been keyed in by the programmer, thus speeding up the implementation phase because time is not wasted on futile compilations. Structure editors exist for a wide variety of languages, operating systems, and hardware. Because a structure editor has knowledge of the programming language, it is easy to incorporate a pretty printer (or formatter) into the editor to ensure that the code always has a good visual appearance. For example, a pretty printer for Java will ensure that each } is indented the same amount as its corresponding {. An example of a structured editor that incorporates a formatter is the Macintosh Pascal editor [Apple, 1984]. Reserved words are automatically put in boldface so that they stand out, and indentation has been carefully designed to aid readability. In fact, many Macintosh editors are totally or partially structured.

Now consider the problem of invoking a method within the code, only to discover at linkage time either that the method does not exist or that it has been wrongly specified in some way. What is needed is for the structure editor to support *online interface checking*. That is, just as the structure editor has information regarding the name of every variable declared by the programmer, so it must also know the name of every method defined within the product. For example, if the programmer enters a call such as

```
average = computeAverage (dataArray, numberOfValues);
```

but method computeAverage has not yet been defined, then the editor immediately responds with a message such as

```
Method computeAverage not known
```

At this point, the programmer is given two choices, either to correct the name of the method or to declare a new method named computeAverage. If the second option is chosen, the programmer must also specify the arguments of the new method. Argument types must be supplied when declaring a new method because the major reason for having online interface checking is precisely in order to be able to check full interface information, not just the names of methods. A common fault is for method p to call method q passing, say, four arguments, whereas method q has been specified with five arguments. It is more difficult to detect the fault when the call correctly uses four arguments, but two of the arguments are transposed. For example, the declaration of method q might be

```
void q (float floatVar, int intVar, String s1, String s2)
```

whereas the call is

```
q (intVar, floatVar, s1, s2);
```

The first two arguments have been transposed in the call statement. Java compilers and linkers will detect this fault, but only when they are later invoked. In contrast, an online interface checker immediately detects this and similar faults. In addition, if the editor has a help facility, the programmer can request online information as to the precise arguments of method q before attempting to code the call to q. Better yet, the editor should generate a template for the call, showing the type of each of the arguments. The programmer merely has to replace each formal argument by an actual argument of the correct type.

A major advantage of online interface checking is that hard-to-detect faults caused by the calling of methods with the wrong number of arguments, or with arguments of the wrong type, are immediately flagged. Online interface information is important for the efficient production of high-quality software, particularly when the software is produced by a team (programming-in-the-many). It is essential that online interface information regarding all modules be available to all programming team members at all times. Furthermore, if one programmer changes the interface of method vaporCheck, perhaps by changing the type of one argument from **int** to **float** or by adding an additional argument, then every component that calls vaporCheck must automatically be disabled until the relevant call statements have been altered to reflect the new state of affairs.

Even with a syntax-directed editor incorporating an online interface checker, the programmer still has to exit from the editor and invoke the compiler and linker. Clearly, there can be no compilation faults, but the compiler still has to be invoked to perform code generation. Then the linker has to be called. Again, the programmer can be sure that all external references will be satisfied as a consequence of the presence of the online interface checker, but the linker is still needed to link the product. The solution to this is to incorporate an *operating system front end* within the editor. That is, a programmer should be able to give operating system commands from within the editor. In order to cause the editor to invoke the compiler, linker, loader, and any other system software needed to cause the module to be executed, the programmer should be able to type a single command named GO or RUN, or use the mouse to choose the appropriate icon or menu selection. In UNIX, this can be achieved by using the *make* command (Section 4.13) or by invoking a shell script [Sobell, 1995]. Such front ends can also be implemented in other operating systems.

One of the most frustrating computing experiences is for a product to execute for a second or so, then terminate abruptly, printing a message such as

Overflow at 4B06

The programmer is working in a high-level language such as FORTRAN or Java, not a low-level language like assembler or machine code. But when debugging support is of the Overflow at 4B06 variety, then the programmer is forced to examine machine code core dumps, assembler listings, linker listings, and a variety of similar low-level documentation, thereby destroying the whole advantage of programming in a high-level language. A similar situation arises when the only information provided is the infamous UNIX message

Core dumped

or the equally uninformative

Segmentation fault

Here again, the user is forced to examine low-level information.

```
OVERFLOW ERROR
Class:      CyclotronEnergy
Method:     performComputation
Line 6:     newValue = (oldValue + tempValue)/tempValue;
                      oldValue = 3.9583        tempValue = 0.0000
```

Figure 4.16 Output from source level debugger.

In the event of a failure, the message shown in Figure 4.16 is a great improvement over the earlier terse error messages. The programmer can immediately see that the method failed because of an attempt to divide by zero. Even more useful is for the operating system to enter edit mode and automatically display the line at which the failure was detected, namely, line 6, together with the preceding and following four or five lines. The programmer can probably then see what caused the failure and make the necessary changes.

Another type of source level debugging is tracing. Before the advent of CASE tools, programmers had to insert appropriate print statements into their code by hand that, at execution time, would indicate the line number and the values of relevant variables. This can now be done by giving commands to a *source level debugger* that automatically causes trace output to be produced. Even better is an *interactive source level debugger.* Suppose that the value of variable escapeVelocity seems to be incorrect and that method computeTrajectory seems to be faulty. Using the interactive source level debugger, the programmer can set breakpoints in the code. When a breakpoint is reached, execution stops and debugging mode is entered. The programmer now asks the debugger to trace variable escapeVelocity and method computeTrajectory. That is, every time the value of escapeVelocity is subsequently either used or changed, execution again halts. The programmer then has the option of entering further debugging commands, for example, to request that the value of a specific variable be displayed. Alternatively, the programmer may choose to continue execution in debugging mode or to return to normal execution mode. The programmer can similarly interact with the debugger whenever method computeTrajectory is entered or exited. Such an interactive source level debugger offers almost every conceivable type of assistance to the programmer when the product fails. The UNIX debugger *dbx* is a good example of such a CASE tool.

As pointed out many times, it is essential that documentation of all kinds be available online. In the case of programmers, all documentation they might need should be accessible from within the editor.

What has now been described, namely, a structure editor with online interface checking capabilities, operating system front end, source level debugger, and online documentation, constitutes an adequate and effective programming workbench.

This sort of workbench is by no means new. All the preceding features were supported by the FLOW software development workbench as far back as 1980

[Dooley and Schach, 1985]. Thus, what has been put forward as a minimal, but essential, programming workbench does not require many years of research before a prototype can be tentatively produced. Quite the contrary, the necessary technology has been in place for about 20 years, and it is therefore somewhat surprising that there are programmers who still implement code "the old-fashioned way," instead of using a workbench like Sun WorkShop.

An essential tool, especially when software is developed by a team, is a version control tool.

4.12 SOFTWARE VERSIONS

Whenever a product is maintained, there will be at least two versions of the product, the old version and the new version. Because a product is comprised of modules, there will also be two or more versions of each of the component modules that have been changed.

Version control is first described within the context of maintenance and is then broadened to include earlier phases of the process.

4.12.1 REVISIONS

Suppose that a product is in operations mode at a number of different sites. If a fault is found in a module, then that module has to be fixed. After appropriate changes have been made, there will be two versions of the module, the old version and the new version intended to replace it. The new version is termed a *revision*. The presence of multiple versions is apparently easy to solve—any old versions should be thrown away, leaving just the correct one. But that would be most unwise. Suppose that the previous version of the module was revision n and that the new version is revision n + 1. First, there is no guarantee that revision n + 1 will be any more correct than revision n. Even though revision n + 1 may have been thoroughly tested by the SQA group, both in isolation and also linked to the rest of the product, there may be disastrous consequences when the new version of the product is run by the user on actual data. Revision n must be kept for a second reason. The product may have been distributed to a variety of sites, and not all of them may have installed revision n + 1. If a fault report is now received from a site that is still using revision n, then in order to analyze this new fault it is necessary to configure the product in exactly the same way it is configured at the user's site, that is, incorporating revision n of the module. It is therefore necessary to retain a copy of every revision of each module.

As described in Section 1.3, perfective maintenance is performed to extend the functionality of a product. In some instances new modules are written; in other cases existing modules are changed to incorporate this additional functionality. These new versions are also revisions of existing modules. So are modules that are changed when performing adaptive maintenance, that is, changes made to the product in response to changes in the portion of the real world modeled by the product. As with corrective maintenance, all previous versions must be retained.

These issues arise not just during the maintenance phase but from the implementation phase onwards. After all, once a module has been coded it continually undergoes changes as a consequence of faults being detected and corrected. As a result, there will be numerous versions of every module, and it is vital that there be some sort of control to ensure that every member of the development team always knows which version is the current version of a given module. Before we can present a solution to this problem, there is a further complication that must be taken into account.

4.12.2 VARIATIONS

Consider the following example. Most computers support more than one type of printer. For example, a personal computer may support an ink-jet printer and a laser printer. The operating system must therefore contain two *variations* of the printer driver, one for each type of printer. Unlike revisions, each of which is specifically written to replace its predecessor, variations are designed to coexist. Another situation where variations are needed is when a product is to be ported to a variety of operating systems and/or hardware. A different variation of many of the modules may have to be produced for each operating system/hardware combination.

Versions are schematically depicted in Figure 4.17, which shows both revisions and variations. To complicate matters further, in general there will be multiple revisions of each variation. In order for a software organization to avoid drowning in a morass of multiple versions, a CASE tool is needed.

4.13 CONFIGURATION CONTROL

The code for every module exists in three forms. First, there is the source code, nowadays generally written in a high-level language like Pascal, C++, COBOL, Java, or Ada. Then there is the object code, produced by compiling the source code. Finally, the object code for each module is combined with run-time routines to produce an executable load image. This is shown in Figure 4.18. The programmer can use various different versions of each module. The specific version of each module from which a given version of the complete product is built is called the *configuration* of that version of the product.

Suppose that a programmer is given a test report from SQA stating that a module failed on a specific set of test data. One of the first things that must be done is to attempt to recreate the failure. But how can the programmer determine which revisions of which variations went into the version of the product that crashed? Unless a configuration control tool (described in the following discussion) is used,

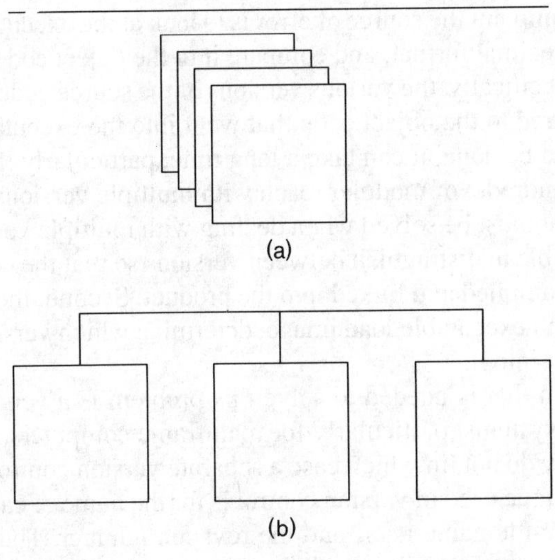

Figure 4.17 Schematic representation of multiple versions of modules, showing (a) revisions and (b) variations.

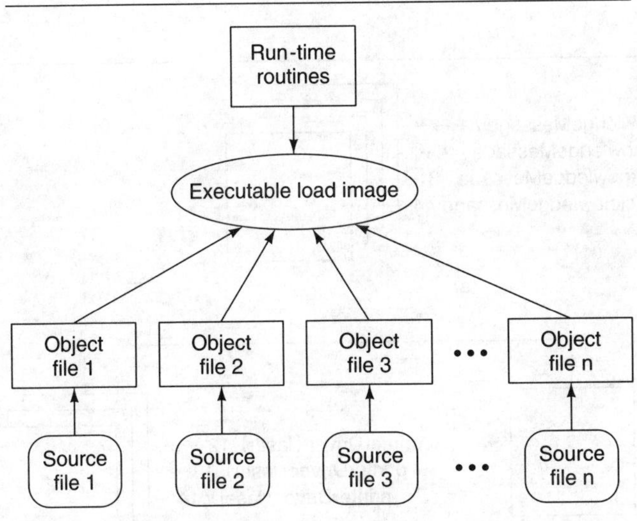

Figure 4.18 Components of executable load image.

the only way to pinpoint the source of error is to look at the executable load image, in octal or hexadecimal format, and compare it to the object code, also in octal or hexadecimal. Specifically, the various versions of the source code have to be compiled and compared to the object code that went into the executable load image. Although this can be done, it can take a long time, particularly if the product has dozens (if not hundreds) of modules, each with multiple versions. There are thus two problems that must be solved when dealing with multiple versions. First, it is necessary to be able to distinguish between versions so that the correct version of each module is compiled and linked into the product. Second, there is the inverse problem: Given an executable load image, determine which version of each of its components went into it.

The first item that is needed to solve this problem is a version control tool. Many operating systems, particularly for mainframe computers, support version control. But many do not, in which case a separate version control tool is needed. A common technique used in version control is for the name of each file to consist of two pieces, the file name itself and the revision number. Thus a module that acknowledges receipt of a message will have revisions acknowledgeMessage / 1, acknowledgeMessage / 2, and so on, as depicted in Figure 4.19(a). A programmer can then specify exactly which revision is needed for a given task.

With regard to multiple variations (slightly changed versions that fulfill the same role in different situations), one useful notation is to have a basic file name, followed by a variation name in parentheses [Babich, 1986]. Thus two printer drivers are given the names printerDriver (inkJet) and printerDriver (laser).

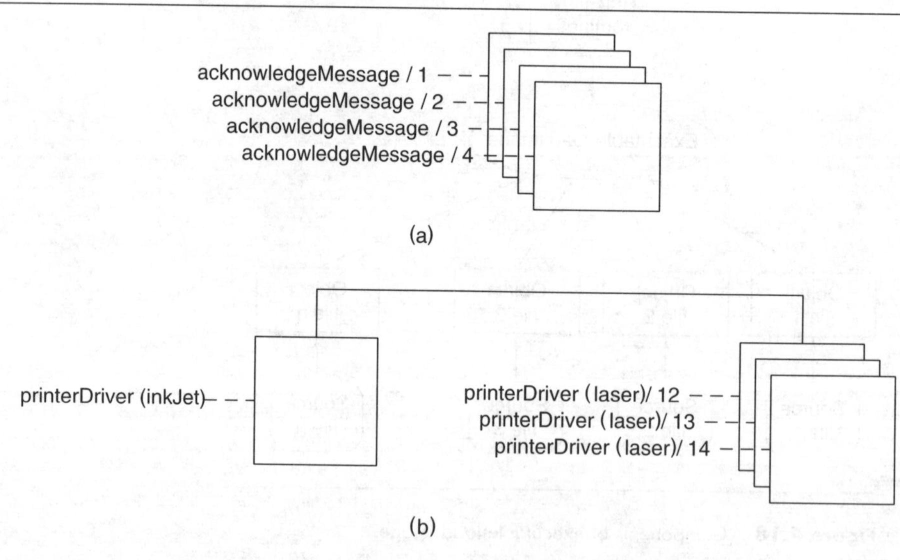

Figure 4.19 Multiple revisions and variations. (a) Four revisions of module acknowledgeMessage. (b) Two variations of module printerDriver, with three revisions of variation printerDriver (laser).

Of course, there will be multiple revisions of each variation, such as printerDriver (laser) / 12, printerDriver (laser) / 13, and printerDriver (laser) / 14. This is depicted in Figure 4.19(b).

A version control tool is the first step toward being able to manage multiple versions. Once it is in place, a detailed record (or *derivation*) of every version of the product must be kept. The derivation contains the name of each source code element, including the variation and revision, the versions of the various compilers and linker used, the name of the person who constructed the product, and, of course, the date and the time at which it was constructed.

Version control is a great help in managing multiple versions of modules and the product as a whole. But more than just version control is needed, because of additional problems associated with maintaining multiple variations.

Consider the two variations printerDriver (inkJet) and printerDriver (laser). Suppose that a fault is found in printerDriver (inkJet) and suppose that the fault occurs in a part of the module that is common to both variations. Then it is necessary to fix not only printerDriver (inkJet), but also printer Driver (laser). In general, if there are v variations of a module, all v of them have to be fixed. Not only that, but they have to be fixed in exactly the same way.

One solution to this problem is to store just one variation, say printerDriver (inkJet). Then any other variation is stored in terms of the list of changes that have to be made to go from the original to that variation. The list of differences is termed a *delta*. Thus what is stored is one variation and $v - 1$ deltas. Variation printerDriver (laser) is retrieved by accessing printerDriver (inkJet) and applying the delta. A change made just to printerDriver (laser) is implemented by changing the appropriate delta. However, any change made to printer Driver (inkJet), the original variation, will automatically apply to all the other variations.

A configuration control tool can automatically manage multiple variations. But configuration control goes beyond multiple variations. A configuration control tool can also handle problems caused by development and maintenance by teams, as described in the next sections.

4.13.1 CONFIGURATION CONTROL DURING PRODUCT MAINTENANCE

All sorts of difficulties can arise when more than one programmer is simultaneously maintaining a product. For example, suppose two programmers are each assigned a different fault report on a Monday morning. By coincidence, they both localize the fault they are to fix to different parts of the same module mDual. Each programmer makes a copy of the current version of the module, namely, mDual / 16, and they start to work on the faults. The first programmer fixes the first fault, has the changes approved, and replaces the module, now called mDual / 17. A day later the second programmer fixes the second fault, has the changes approved, and installs module mDual / 18. Unfortunately, revision 17 contains the changes of only the first programmer, whereas revision 18 contains those of only the second programmer. Thus all the changes of the first programmer have been lost.

Although the idea of each programmer making individual copies of a module is far better than both working together on the same piece of software, it is clear that it is inadequate for maintenance by a team. What is needed is some mechanism that allows only one user at a time to change a module.

4.13.2 BASELINES

The maintenance manager must set up a *baseline,* a configuration (set of versions) of all the modules in the product. When trying to find a fault, a maintenance programmer puts copies of any needed modules into his or her own *private workspace.* In this private workspace the programmer can change anything at all without having an impact on any other programmer in any way, because all changes are made to the programmer's private copy; the baseline version is left untouched.

Once it has been decided which module has to be changed to fix the fault, the programmer *freezes* the current version of the module that he or she is going to alter. No other programmer may ever make changes to any frozen version. After the maintenance programmer has made changes and they have been tested, the new version of the module is installed, thereby modifying the baseline. The previous version, now frozen, is retained because it may be needed in the future, as explained previously, but it cannot be altered. Once a new version has been installed, any other maintenance programmer can freeze the new version and make changes to it. The resulting module will, in turn, become the next baseline version. A similar procedure is followed if two or more modules have to be changed simultaneously.

This scheme solves the problem with module mDual. Both programmers make private copies of mDual / 16 and use those copies to analyze the respective faults that they have been assigned to fix. The first programmer decides what changes to make, freezes mDual / 16, and makes the changes to it to repair the first fault. After the changes have been tested, the resulting revision mDual / 17 becomes the baseline version. In the meantime, the second programmer has found the second fault by experimenting with a private copy of mDual / 16. However, changes cannot now be made to mDual / 16 because it was frozen by the first programmer. Once mDual / 17 becomes the baseline, it is frozen by the second programmer whose changes are made to mDual / 17. The resulting module is now installed as mDual / 18, a version that will incorporate the changes of both programmers. Revisions mDual / 16 and mDual / 17 are retained for possible future reference, but they can never be altered.

4.13.3 CONFIGURATION CONTROL DURING PRODUCT DEVELOPMENT

While a module is in the process of being coded, versions are changing too rapidly for configuration control to be helpful. However, once coding of the module has been completed, it should immediately be tested informally by its programmer, as described in Section 5.6. During this informal testing, the module will again pass through numerous versions. When the programmer is satisfied, it is handed over to the SQA group for methodical testing. As soon as the module has been passed by the SQA group, it is ready to be integrated into the product. From then on it should be subject to the same configuration control procedures as those of the maintenance phase. Any change to an integrated module can impact the product as a whole in the same way as a change made during the maintenance phase. Thus configuration control is needed not only during maintenance, but also during the implementation and integration phases. Furthermore, management cannot monitor the development process adequately unless every module is subject to configuration control as soon as is reasonable, namely, after it has been passed by SQA. When configuration control is properly applied, management is aware of the status of every module and can take early corrective action if it seems that project deadlines are slipping.

The three major UNIX version control tools are *sccs* (source code control system) [Rochkind, 1975], *rcs* (revision control system) [Tichy, 1985], and *cvs* (concurrent versions system) [Loukides and Oram, 1997]. Popular commercially available configuration control tools include CCC, PVCS, and Aide-de-Camp. Microsoft Source Safe is a configuration control tool for personal computers.

4.14 BUILD TOOLS

If a software organization does not wish to purchase a complete configuration control tool, then at the very least a *build* tool must be used in conjunction with a version control tool, that is, a tool that assists in selecting the correct version of each object-code module to be linked to form a specific version of the product. At any time there will be multiple variations and revisions of each module in the product library. Any version control tool will assist users in distinguishing between different versions of the modules of source code. But keeping track of object code is more difficult, because some version control tools do not attach revision numbers to object versions.

To cope with this, some organizations automatically compile the latest version of each module every night, thereby ensuring that all the object code is always up to date. Although this technique works, it can be extremely wasteful of computer time because a large number of unnecessary compilations will frequently be performed. The UNIX tool *make* can solve this problem [Feldman, 1979]. For each executable load image, the programmer sets up a Makefile specifying the hierarchy of source and object files that go into that particular configuration; such a hierarchy is shown in Figure 4.18. More complex dependencies, such as included files in C or C++, can also be handled by *make*. When invoked by a programmer, the tool works as follows: UNIX, like virtually every other operating system, attaches a date and time stamp to each file. Suppose that the stamp on a source file is Friday, June 6, at 11:24 AM, whereas the stamp on the corresponding object file is Friday, June 6, at 11:40 AM. Then it is clear that the source file has not been changed since the object file was created by the compiler. On the other hand, if the date and time stamp on the source file is later than that on the object file, then *make* calls the appropriate compiler or assembler to create a version of the object file that will correspond to the current version of the source file.

Next, the date and time stamp on the executable load image is compared to those on every object file in that configuration. If the executable load image was created later than all the object files, then there is no need to relink. But if an object file has a later stamp than that of the load image, then the load image does not incorporate the latest version of that object file. In this case *make* will call the linker and construct an updated load image.

In other words, *make* checks whether the load image incorporates the current version of every module. If so, then nothing further is done, and no CPU time is wasted on needless compilations and/or linkage. But if not, then *make* calls the relevant system software to create an up-to-date version of the product.

In addition, *make* simplifies the task of building an object file. There is no need for the user to specify each time what modules are to be used and how they are to be connected, because this information is already in the Makefile. Thus, a single *make* command is all that is needed to build a product with hundreds of modules and ensure that the complete product is put together correctly.

4.15 PRODUCTIVITY GAINS WITH CASE TECHNOLOGY

Reifer (as reported in [Myers, 1992]) conducted an investigation into productivity gains as a consequence of introducing CASE technology. He collected data from 45 companies in 10 industries. Half the companies were in the field of information systems, 25 percent in scientific areas, and 25 percent in real-time aerospace. Average annual productivity gains varied from 9 percent (real-time aerospace) to 12 percent (information systems). If only productivity gains are considered, then these figures do not justify the cost of $125,000 per user of introducing CASE technology. However, the companies surveyed felt that the justification for CASE is not merely increased productivity but also shorter development time and improvement in software quality. In other words, the introduction of CASE environments has boosted productivity, though less than some proponents of CASE technology have claimed. Nevertheless, there were other, equally important, reasons for introducing CASE technology into a software organization, such as faster development, fewer faults, better usability, easier maintenance, and improved morale.

Newer results on the effectiveness of CASE technology from over 100 development projects at 15 Fortune 500 companies reflect the importance of training and the software process [Guinan, Cooprider, and Sawyer, 1997]. When teams using CASE were given training in application development in general as well as tool-specific training, user satisfaction increased and development schedules

Theoretical tools
Cost–benefit analysis (Section 4.7)
Metrics (Section 4.8)
Stepwise refinement (Section 4.6)
CASE Taxonomy
Environment (Section 4.10)
LowerCASE tool (Section 4.10)
UpperCASE tool (Section 4.10)
Workbench (Section 4.10)
CASE Tools
Build tool (Section 4.14)
Coding tool (Section 4.11)
Configuration control tool (Section 4.13)
Consistency checker (Section 4.10)
Data dictionary (Section 4.10)
E-mail (Section 4.11)
Interface checker (Section 4.11)
Online documentation (Section 4.11)
Operating system front-end (Section 4.11)
Pretty printer (Section 4.11)
Report generator (Section 4.10)
Screen generator (Section 4.10)
Source level debugger (Section 4.11)
Spreadsheet (Section 4.11)
Structure editor (Section 4.11)
Version control tool (Section 4.12)
Word processor (Section 4.11)
World Wide Web browser (Section 4.11)

Figure 4.20 Summary of the theoretical tools and software (CASE) tools presented in this chapter and the sections in which each is described.

were met. However, when training was not provided, software was delivered late and users were less satisfied. Also, performance increased by 50 percent when teams used CASE tools in conjunction with a structured methodology. These results support the assertion in Section 2.11 that CASE environments should not be used by groups at maturity levels 1 or 2. To put it bluntly, a fool with a tool is still a fool [Guinan, Cooprider, and Sawyer, 1997].

The final figure in this chapter, Figure 4.20, is an alphabetical list of the theoretical tools and CASE tools described in this chapter, together with the section in which each is described.

CHAPTER REVIEW

The issue of team organization (Section 4.1) is approached by first considering the democratic team (Section 4.2) and the classical chief programmer team (Section 4.3) and then suggesting a team organization that makes use of the strengths of both approaches (Section 4.4). Synchronize-and-stabilize teams (used by Microsoft) are described in Section 4.5.

A number of theoretical tools are presented. Miller's law (Section 4.6) states that at any one time human beings can concentrate on at most only 7 ± 2 chunks of information. Stepwise refinement is a technique that allows the software engineer to concentrate on the currently relevant seven chunks. The application of stepwise refinement to design is illustrated. Another analytical tool, namely, cost–benefit analysis, is presented in Section 4.7. Software metrics are introduced in Section 4.8.

A variety of computer-aided software engineering (CASE) tools are described in Sections 4.9 through 4.11. When large products are constructed, version control, configuration control, and build tools are essential; these are presented in Sections 4.12 through 4.14. Productivity gains as a consequence of the use of CASE technology are described in Section 4.15.

FOR FURTHER READING

The classic works on team organization are [Weinberg, 1971], [Baker, 1972], and [Brooks, 1975]. Newer books on the subject include [Aron, 1983], [Licker, 1985], [DeMarco and Lister, 1987], and [Cusamano and Selby, 1995]. Articles on team organization and management can be found in the October 1993 issue of the *Communications of the ACM*. Synchronize-and-stabilize teams are outlined in [Cusamano and Selby, 1997] and described in detail in [Cusamano and Selby, 1995]. Insights into synchronize-and-stabilize teams can be obtained from [McConnell, 1996].

For further information regarding Miller's law, and for his theory of how the brain operates on chunks, the reader should consult [Tracz, 1979] and [Moran, 1981], as well as Miller's original paper [Miller, 1956]. An analysis of Miller's law from the viewpoint of cognitive psychology and software science is to be found in [Coulter, 1983].

Wirth's paper on stepwise refinement is a classic of its kind and deserves careful study [Wirth, 1971]. Equally significant from the viewpoint of stepwise refinement are the books by Dijkstra [Dijkstra, 1976] and Wirth [Wirth, 1975]. Mills applies stepwise refinement to box-structured design, a technique for producing a design from a specification [Mills, Linger, and Hevner, 1987; Mills, 1988]. Rajlich extends stepwise refinement to large-scale products [Rajlich, 1985]. Stepwise design of real-time systems is described in [Kurki-Suonio, 1993].

There are articles on CASE in the January 1995 issue of *Communications of the ACM,* as well as in the March 1995 and September 1996 issues of *IEEE Software.* [Chmura and Crockett, 1995] examines the role of CASE tools in software development. Case studies of tool evaluation are presented in [Kitchenham, Pickard, and Pfleeger, 1995]. CASE tools for the separate phases of the software process are described in the chapters on each phase. For information on workbenches or CASE environments, consult the For Further Reading section of Chapter 14.

[Whitgift, 1991] is a good introduction to configuration management. The impact of the choice of software life-cycle model is described in [Bersoff and Davis, 1991]. The proceedings of the International Workshops on Software Configuration Management are a useful source of information.

There are many excellent books on cost–benefit analysis, including [Dasgupta and Pearce, 1972] and [Mishan, 1982]. For information on cost–benefit analysis as applied to information systems, the reader should consult [King and Schrems, 1978].

Important books on metrics include [Conte, Dunsmore, and Shen, 1986], [Musa, Iannino, and Okumoto, 1987], [Sheppard, 1996], and [Fenton and Pfleeger, 1997]. A particularly clearly written text is [Grady, 1992]. [Jones, 1994a] highlights unworkable and invalid metrics that nevertheless continue to be mentioned in the literature. Object-oriented metrics are described in [Henderson-Sellers, 1996].

Over 120 papers on software metrics published between 1980 and 1988 are listed in [Côté, Bourque, Oligny, and Rivard, 1988]. Later articles on metrics appear in the September 1994 issue of *IEEE Computer* and the March/April 1997 issue of *IEEE Software.*

PROBLEMS

4.1 How would you organize a team to develop a payroll project? How would you organize a team for developing state-of-the-art military avionics software? Explain your answers.

4.2 You have just started a new software company. All your employees are recent college graduates; this is their first programming job. Is it possible to implement democratic teams in your organization, and if so, how?

4.3 Consider the effect of introducing *lookahead* to the design of the corrected third refinement of the sequential master file update problem. That is, before processing a transaction the next transaction must be read. If both transactions apply to the same master file record, then the decision regarding the processing of the current transaction will depend on the type of the next transaction. Draw up a 3×3 table with the rows labeled by the type of the current transaction and the columns labeled by the type of the next transaction and fill in the action to be taken in each instance. For example, two successive insertions of the same record are clearly an error. But two modifications may be perfectly valid—for example, a subscriber can change address more than once in a given month. Now develop a flowchart for the third refinement that incorporates lookahead.

4.4 Check whether your answer to Problem 4.3 can correctly handle a modification transaction followed by a deletion transaction, both transactions being applied to the same master file record. If not, modify your answer.

4.5 Check whether your answer to Problem 4.3 can also correctly handle an insertion followed by a modification followed by a deletion, all applied to the same master file record. If not, modify your answer.

4.6 Check whether your answer can also correctly handle n insertions, modifications, or deletions, $n > 2$, all applied to the same master file record. If not, modify your answer.

4.7 The last transaction record does not have a successor. Check whether your flowchart for Problem 4.3 takes this into account and processes the last transaction record correctly. If not, modify your answer.

4.8 In some applications an alternative to lookahead can be achieved by careful ordering of the transactions. For example, the original problem caused by a modification followed by a deletion of the same master file record could have been solved by processing a deletion before a modification. This would have resulted in the master file being correctly written and an error message appearing in the exception report. Investigate whether there is an ordering of the transactions that can solve all of the difficulties listed in Problems 4.4, 4.5, and 4.6.

4.9 A new form of gastrointestinal disease is sweeping the country of Veloria. Like histoplasmosis, it is transmitted as an airborne fungus. Although the disease is almost never fatal, an attack is very painful, and the sufferer is unable to work for about 2 weeks. The government of Veloria wishes to determine how much money, if any, to spend on attempting to eradicate the disease. The committee charged with advising the Department of Public Health is considering four aspects of the problem, namely, health care costs (Veloria provides free health care to all its citizens), loss of earnings (and hence loss of taxes), pain and discomfort, and gratitude toward the government. Explain how cost–benefit analysis can assist the committee. For each benefit or cost, suggest how a dollar estimate for that benefit or cost could be obtained.

4.10 Does a one-person software production organization need a version control tool, and if so, why?

4.11 Does a one-person software production organization need a configuration control tool, and if so, why?

4.12 You are the manager in charge of the software that controls the production line of a bottling plant for fruit juice. Three different user-reported faults have to be fixed, and you assign one each to Archie, Bella, and Claude. A day later you learn that in order to implement each of the three fixes, the same four modules must be changed. However, your configuration control tool is inoperative, so you will have to manage the changes yourself. How will you do it?

4.13 In Section 2.11 it was stated that it makes little sense to introduce CASE environments within organizations at maturity levels 1 or 2. Explain why this is so.

4.14 What is the effect of introducing CASE tools (as opposed to environments) within organizations with low maturity levels?

4.15 (Term Project) What types of CASE tools would be appropriate for developing the Air Gourmet product described in Appendix A?

4.16 (Readings in Software Engineering) Your instructor will distribute copies of [Wirth, 1971]. List the differences between Wirth's approach and the approach to stepwise refinement presented in this chapter.

REFERENCES

[Apple, 1984] *Macintosh Pascal User's Guide,* Apple Computer, Inc., Cupertino, CA, 1984.

[Aron, 1983] J. D. ARON, *The Program Development Process. Part II. The Programming Team,* Addison-Wesley, Reading, MA, 1983.

[Babich, 1986] W. A. BABICH, *Software Configuration Management: Coordination for Team Productivity,* Addison-Wesley, Reading, MA, 1986.

[Baker, 1972] F. T. BAKER, "Chief Programmer Team Management of Production Programming," *IBM Systems Journal* **11** (No. 1, 1972), pp. 56–73.

[Bersoff and Davis, 1991] E. H. BERSOFF AND A. M. DAVIS, "Impacts of Life Cycle Models on Software Configuration Management," *Communications of the ACM* **34** (August 1991), pp. 104–18.

[Brooks, 1975] F. P. BROOKS, JR., *The Mythical Man-Month: Essays in Software Engineering,* Addison-Wesley, Reading, MA, 1975. Twentieth Anniversary Edition, Addison-Wesley, Reading, MA, 1995.

[Chmura and Crockett, 1995] A. CHMURA AND H. D. CROCKETT, "What's the Proper Role for CASE Tools?" *IEEE Software* **12** (March 1995), pp. 18–20.

[Conte, Dunsmore, and Shen, 1986] S. D. CONTE, H. E. DUNSMORE, AND V. Y. SHEN, *Software Engineering Metrics and Models,* Benjamin/Cummings, Menlo Park, CA, 1986.

[Côté, Bourque, Oligny, and Rivard, 1988] V. CÔTÉ, P. BOURQUE, S. OLIGNY, AND N. RIVARD, "Software Metrics: An Overview of Recent Results," *Journal of Systems and Software* **8** (March 1988), pp. 121–31.

[Coulter, 1983] N. S. COULTER, "Software Science and Cognitive Psychology," *IEEE Transactions on Software Engineering* **SE-9** (March 1983), pp. 166–71.

[Cusamano and Selby, 1995] M. A. CUSAMANO AND R. W. SELBY, *Microsoft Secrets: How the World's Most Powerful Software Company Creates Technology, Shapes Markets, and Manages People,* The Free Press/Simon and Schuster, New York, 1995.

[Cusamano and Selby, 1997] M. A. CUSAMANO AND R. W. SELBY, "How Microsoft Builds Software," *Communications of the ACM* **40** (June 1997), pp. 53–61.

[Dasgupta and Pearce, 1972] A. K. DASGUPTA AND D. W. PEARCE, *Cost–Benefit Analysis,* Macmillan, London, 1972.

[DeMarco and Lister, 1987] T. DEMARCO AND T. LISTER, *Peopleware: Productive Projects and Teams,* Dorset House, New York, 1987.

[DeRemer and Kron, 1976] F. DEREMER AND H. H. KRON, "Programming-in-the-Large versus Programming-in-the-Small," *IEEE Transactions on Software Engineering* **SE-2** (June 1976), pp. 80–86.

[Dijkstra, 1976] E. W. DIJKSTRA, *A Discipline of Programming,* Prentice Hall, Englewood Cliffs, NJ, 1976.

[Dooley and Schach, 1985] J. W. M. DOOLEY AND S. R. SCHACH, "FLOW: A Software Development Environment Using Diagrams," *Journal of Systems and Software* **5** (August 1985), pp. 203–19.

[Feldman, 1979] S. I. FELDMAN, "Make—A Program for Maintaining Computer Programs," *Software—Practice and Experience* **9** (April 1979), pp. 225–65.

[Fenton and Pfleeger, 1997] N. E. FENTON AND S. L. PFLEEGER, *Software Metrics: A Rigorous and Practical Approach,* Second Edition, IEEE Computer Society, Los Alamitos, CA, 1997.

[Fuggetta, 1993] A. FUGGETTA, "A Classification of CASE Technology," *IEEE Computer* **26** (December 1993), pp. 25–38.

[Grady, 1992] R. B. GRADY, *Practical Software Metrics for Project Management and Process Improvement,* Prentice Hall, Englewood Cliffs, NJ, 1992.

[Guinan, Cooprider, and Sawyer, 1997] P. J. GUINAN, J. G. COOPRIDER, AND S. SAWYER, "The Effective Use of Automated Application Development Tools," *IBM Systems Journal* **36** (No. 1, 1997). pp. 124–39.

[Henderson-Sellers, 1996] B. HENDERSON-SELLERS, *Object-Oriented Metrics: Measures of Complexity,* Prentice Hall, Upper Saddle River, NJ, 1996.

[Jones, 1994a] C. JONES, "Software Metrics: Good, Bad, and Missing," *IEEE Computer* **27** (September 1994), pp. 98–100.

[King and Schrems, 1978] J. L. KING AND E. L. SCHREMS, "Cost–Benefit Analysis in Information Systems Development and Operation," *ACM Computer Surveys* **10** (March 1978), pp. 19–34.

[Kitchenham, Pickard, and Pfleeger, 1995] B. KITCHENHAM, L. PICKARD, AND S. L. PFLEEGER. "Case Studies for Method and Tool Evaluation," *IEEE Software* **12** (July 1995), pp. 52–62.

[Kurki-Suonio, 1993] R. KURKI-SUONIO, "Stepwise Design of Real-Time Systems," *IEEE Transactions on Software Engineering* **19** (January 1993), pp. 56–69.

[Licker, 1985] P. S. LICKER, *The Art of Managing Software Development People,* John Wiley and Sons, New York, 1985.

[Loukides and Oram, 1997] M. K. LOUKIDES AND A. ORAM, *Programming with GNU Software,* O'Reilly and Associates, Sebastopol, CA, 1997.

[Mantei, 1981] M. MANTEI, "The Effect of Programming Team Structures on Programming Tasks," *Communications of the ACM* **24** (March 1981), pp. 106–113.

[McConnell, 1996] S. MCCONNELL, "Daily Build and Smoke Test," *IEEE Computer* **13** (July 1996), pp. 144, 143.

[Miller, 1956] G. A. MILLER, "The Magical Number Seven, Plus or Minus Two: Some Limits on Our Capacity for Processing Information," *The Psychological Review* **63** (March 1956), pp. 81–97.

[Mills, 1988] H. D. MILLS, "Stepwise Refinement and Verification in Box-Structured Systems," *IEEE Computer* **21** (June 1988), pp. 23–36.

[Mills, Linger, and Hevner, 1987] H. D. MILLS, R. C. LINGER, AND A. R. HEVNER, "Box Structured Information Systems," *IBM Systems Journal* **26** (No. 4, 1987), pp. 395–413.

[Mishan, 1982] E. J. MISHAN, *Cost–Benefit Analysis: An Informal Introduction,* Third Edition, George Allen & Unwin, London, 1982.

[Moran, 1981] T. P. MORAN (EDITOR), Special Issue: The Psychology of Human-Computer Interaction, *ACM Computing Surveys* **13** (March 1981).

[Musa, Iannino, and Okumoto, 1987] J. D. MUSA, A. IANNINO, AND K. OKUMOTO, *Software Reliability: Measurement, Prediction, Application,* McGraw-Hill, New York, 1987.

[Myers, 1992] W. MYERS, "Good Software Practices Pay Off—or Do They?", *IEEE Software* **9** (March 1992), pp. 96–97.

[Rajlich, 1985] V. RAJLICH, "Stepwise Refinement Revisited," *Journal of Systems and Software* **5** (February 1985), pp. 81–88.

[Rochkind, 1975] M. J. ROCHKIND, "The Source Code Control System," *IEEE Transactions on Software Engineering* **SE-1** (October 1975), pp. 255–65.

[Shepperd, 1996] M. SHEPPERD, *Foundations of Software Measurement,* Prentice Hall, Upper Saddle River, NJ, 1996.

[Sobell, 1995] M. G. SOBELL, *A Practical Guide to the UNIX System,* Third Edition, Benjamin/Cummings, Menlo Park, CA, 1995.

[Tichy, 1985] W. F. TICHY, "RCS—A System for Version Control," *Software—Practice and Experience* **15** (July 1985), pp. 637–54.

[Tracz, 1979] W. J. TRACZ, "Computer Programming and the Human Thought Process," *Software—Practice and Experience* **9** (February 1979), pp. 127–37.

[Weinberg, 1971] G. M. WEINBERG, *The Psychology of Computer Programming,* Van Nostrand Reinhold, New York, 1971.

[Whitgift, 1991] D. WHITGIFT, *Methods and Tools for Software Configuration Management,* John Wiley and Sons, New York, 1991.

[Wirth, 1971] N. WIRTH, "Program Development by Stepwise Refinement," *Communications of the ACM* **14** (April 1971), pp. 221–27.

[Wirth, 1975] N. WIRTH, *Algorithms + Data Structures = Programs,* Prentice Hall, Englewood Cliffs, NJ, 1975.

[Yourdon, 1989] E. YOURDON, *Modern Structured Analysis,* Yourdon Press, Englewood Cliffs, NJ, 1989.

chapter

5

TESTING

Software life-cycle models all too frequently include a separate testing phase, after integration and before maintenance. Nothing could be more dangerous from the viewpoint of trying to achieve high-quality software. Testing is an integral component of the software process and an activity that must be carried out throughout the life cycle. During the requirements phase, the requirements must be checked; during the specification phase, the specifications must be checked; and the software production management plan must undergo similar scrutiny. The design phase requires careful checking at every stage. During the coding phase, each module must certainly be tested, and the product as a whole needs testing at the integration phase. After passing the acceptance test, the product is installed and goes into operations mode, and maintenance begins. And hand in hand with maintenance goes repeated checking of modified versions of the product.

In other words, it is not sufficient to test the end-product of a phase merely at the end of that phase. For example, consider the specification phase. The members of the specification team must consciously and conscientiously check the specifications while they develop them. It is not much use for the team to develop the complete specification document only to find, weeks or months later, that they made an error early in the process that necessitates rewriting almost all the specifications. Thus, what is needed is continual testing carried out by the development team while they perform each phase, in addition to more methodical testing at the end of each phase.

The terms *verification* and *validation* were introduced in Chapter 2. *Verification* refers to the process of determining whether a phase has been correctly carried out; this takes place at the end of each phase. On the other hand, *validation* is the intensive evaluation process that takes place just before the product is delivered to the client. Its purpose is to determine whether the product as a whole satisfies its specifications (but see the Just in Case You Wanted to Know box on page 135 for a somewhat different definition). Despite the fact that both these terms are defined in the IEEE Software Engineering Glossary [IEEE 610.12, 1990] in this way, and notwithstanding the common usage of the term *V & V* to denote testing, the words *verification* and *validation* are avoided as far as possible in this book. One reason is that, as explained in Section 5.5, the word *verification* has another meaning within the context of testing. A second reason is that the phrase *verification and validation* (or V & V) implies that the process of checking a phase can wait until the end of that phase. On the contrary, it is essential that this checking be carried out in parallel with all software development and maintenance activities. Thus, in order to avoid the undesirable implications of the phrase *V & V*, the term *testing* is used.

There are essentially two types of testing: execution-based testing and nonexecution-based testing. For example, it is impossible to execute a written specification document; the only alternatives are to

> **Just in Case You Wanted to Know**
>
> Barry Boehm is the author of the following definitions for verification and validation [Boehm, 1984a]:
>
> Verification: Are we building the product right?
> Validation: Are we building the right product?

review it as carefully as possible or to subject it to some form of analysis. However, once there is executable code, it becomes possible to run test cases, that is, to perform execution-based testing. Nevertheless, the existence of code does not preclude nonexecution-based testing because, as will be explained, carefully reviewing code will uncover at least as many faults as running test cases. In this chapter principles of both execution-based and nonexecution-based testing are described. These principles are applied in Chapters 9 through 15, where a description is given of each phase of the process model and the specific testing practices applicable to it.

The failures described in the first Just in Case You Wanted to Know box (page 4) had fatal consequences. Fortunately, in most cases the result of delivering software with residual faults are considerably less catastrophic. Nevertheless, the importance of testing cannot be stressed too strongly.

5.1 Quality Issues

The term *quality* is frequently misunderstood when used within the software context. After all, quality implies excellence of some sort, but this unfortunately is not the meaning intended by software engineers. To put it bluntly, the state of the art in software development is such that merely getting the software to function correctly is enough—excellence is an order of magnitude more than what is generally possible with our current software technology. The *quality* of software is the extent to which the product satisfies its specifications (see the Just in Case You Wanted to Know box on page 136).

The task of every software professional is to ensure, at all times, high quality software. Notwithstanding this, the software quality assurance (SQA) group has additional responsibilities with regard to software quality.

5.1.1 Software Quality Assurance

One aspect of the job of the SQA group is to ensure that the product is correct. More precisely, once the developers have completed a phase, members of the SQA group have to check that that phase has been carried out correctly. Also, when the product is complete, the SQA group has to check that the product as a whole is correct. However, software quality assurance goes further than just testing (or V & V) at the end of a phase or at the end of the development process; SQA applies

Just in Case You Wanted to Know

The use of the term "quality" to denote "adheres to specifications" (as opposed to "excellent" or "luxurious") is the practice in fields such as engineering and manufacturing. Consider, for example, the Quality Control Manager at a Coca-Cola bottling plant. The job of that Quality Control Manager is to ensure that every single bottle or can that leaves the production line satisfies the specifications for Coca-Cola in every way. There is no attempt to produce "excellent" Coca-Cola or "luxurious" Coca-Cola; the sole aim is to be certain that each bottle or can of Coca-Cola stringently adheres to the company's formula (specifications) for that carbonated beverage.

The word *quality* is used identically in the automobile industry. "Quality is Job One" is a former slogan of the Ford Motor Company. In other words, the aim of Ford is to ensure that every car that comes off a Ford production line adheres rigorously to the specifications for that car; in common software engineering parlance, the car must be "bug free" in every way.

to the software process itself. For example, the responsibilities of SQA include the development of the various standards to which the software must conform, as well as the establishment of the monitoring procedures for assuring compliance with those standards. In brief, the role of the SQA group is to ensure the quality of the software process and thereby ensure the quality of the product.

5.1.2 Managerial Independence

It is important to have *managerial independence* between the development team and the SQA group. That is, development should be under one manager, SQA under a different manager, and neither manager should be able to overrule the other. The reason is that all too frequently serious faults are found in a product as the delivery deadline approaches. The software organization must now choose between two unsatisfactory options. Either the product can be released on time but full of faults, leaving the client to struggle with faulty software; or, the developers can fix the software but deliver it late. No matter what, the client will probably lose confidence in the software organization. The decision to deliver faulty software on time should not be made by the manager responsible for development, nor should the SQA manager be able to make the decision to perform further testing and deliver the product late. Instead, both managers should report to a more senior manager who can decide which of the two choices would be in the best interest of both the software development organization and the client.

At first sight, having a separate SQA group would appear to add considerably to the cost of software development. But this is not so. The additional cost is relatively small compared to the resulting benefit, namely, higher quality software. Without an SQA group, every member of the software development organization would have to be involved to some extent with quality assurance activities. Suppose that there are 100 software professionals in an organization and that they each devote about 30 percent of their time to quality assurance activities. Instead, the 100 individuals should be divided into two groups, with 70 individuals performing software development and the other 30 people responsible for SQA. The same amount of time is still devoted to SQA, the only additional expense being a manager to lead the SQA group. Quality assurance can now be performed by an independent group of specialists, leading to products of higher quality than when SQA activities are performed throughout the organization.

In the case of a very small software company (four employees or fewer), it may simply not be economically viable to have a separate SQA group. The best that can be done under such circumstances is to ensure that the specification document be checked by someone other than the person responsible for producing those specifications, and similarly for the design, code, and so on. The reason for this is explained in the next section.

5.2 NONEXECUTION-BASED TESTING

It is not a good idea for the person responsible for drawing up a document to be the only one responsible for reviewing it. Almost everyone has blind spots that allow faults to creep into a document, and those same blind spots will prevent the faults from being detected on review. Thus, the review task must be assigned to someone other than the original author of the document. In addition, having only one reviewer may not be adequate; we have all had the experience of reading through a document many times while failing to detect a blatant spelling error that a second reader picks up almost immediately. This is one of the principles underlying review techniques like walkthroughs or inspections. In both types of review, a document (such as a specification document or design document) is carefully checked by a team of software professionals with a broad range of skills. The advantage of a review by a team of experts is that the different skills of the participants increase the chances of finding a fault. In addition, a team of skilled individuals working together often generates a synergistic effect.

Walkthroughs and inspections are two types of reviews. The fundamental difference between them is that walkthroughs have fewer steps and are less formal than inspections.

5.2.1 WALKTHROUGHS

A walkthrough team should consist of four to six individuals. A specification walkthrough team should include at least one representative from the team responsible for drawing up the specifications; the manager responsible for the specifications; a client representative; a representative of the team who will perform the next phase of the development (in this instance the design team, because they are the immediate users of the specification document [Dunn, 1984]); and a representative of the software quality assurance group. For reasons that will be explained in the next section, the SQA group member should chair the walkthrough.

The members of the walkthrough team should, as far as possible, be experienced senior technical staff because they tend to find the important faults. That is, they detect the faults that would have a major negative impact on the project [New, 1992].

The material for the walkthrough must be distributed to the participants well in advance to allow for careful preparation. Each reviewer should study the material and develop two lists: a list of items that the reviewer does not understand and a list of items the reviewer believes are incorrect.

5.2.2 Managing Walkthroughs

The walkthrough should be chaired by the SQA representative because the SQA representative has the most to lose if the walkthrough is poorly performed and faults slip through. In contrast, the representative responsible for the specification phase may be eager to have the specification document approved as quickly as possible in order to start some other task. The client representative may decide that any defects not detected at the review will probably show up during acceptance testing and will therefore be fixed at no cost to the client organization. But the SQA representative has the most at stake: The quality of the product is a direct reflection of the professional competence of the SQA group.

The person leading the walkthrough guides the other members of the walkthrough team through the document in order to uncover any faults. It is not the task of the team to correct faults, merely to record them for later correction. One reason is that a correction produced by a committee (that is, the walkthrough team) within the time constraints of the walkthrough is likely to be inferior in quality to a correction produced by an individual trained in the necessary techniques. Second, a correction produced by a walkthrough team of five individuals will take at least as much time as a correction produced by one person and, therefore, cost five times as much when the salaries of the five participants are considered. A third reason is that not all items that are flagged as faults are actually incorrect. In accordance with the dictum, "If it ain't broke, don't fix it," it is better for faults to be analyzed carefully and then corrected only if there really is a problem, rather than have a team attempt to "fix" something that is completely correct. The fourth reason is that there simply is not enough time in a walkthrough both to detect and to correct faults. No walkthrough should last longer than 2 hours. The time should be spent detecting and recording faults, not correcting them.

There are two ways of conducting a walkthrough. The first is participant-driven. Participants present their lists of unclear items and items that they think are incorrect. The representative of the specifications team must respond to each query, clarifying what is unclear to the reviewer, and will either agree that there is indeed a fault or will explain why the reviewer is mistaken.

The second way of conducting a review is document-driven. A person responsible for the document, either individually or as part of a team, walks the participants through that document, with the reviewers interrupting either with their prepared comments or with comments triggered by the presentation. This second approach is likely to be more thorough. In addition, it generally leads to the detection of more faults because the majority of faults at a document-driven walkthrough are spontaneously detected by the presenter. Time after time the presenter will pause in the middle of a sentence, his or her face will light up, and a fault, one that has lain dormant through many readings of the document, will suddenly become obvious. A fruitful field for research by a psychologist would be to determine why verbalization so often leads to fault detection during walkthroughs of all kinds, including specification walkthroughs, design walkthroughs, plan walkthroughs, and code walkthroughs. Not surprisingly, the more thorough document-driven review is the technique prescribed in the "IEEE Standard for Software Reviews and Audits" [IEEE 1028, 1988].

The primary role of the walkthrough leader is to elicit questions and facilitate discussion. A walkthrough is an interactive process; it is not supposed to be one-sided instruction by the presenter. It is also essential that the walkthrough not be used as a means of evaluating the participants. If that happens, the walkthrough will degenerate into a point-scoring session and will not detect faults, no matter how well the session leader tries to run the walkthrough. It has been suggested that the manager who is responsible for the document being reviewed should be a member of the walkthrough team. If this manager is also responsible for the annual evaluations of the members of the walkthrough team (and particularly of the presenter) the fault detection capabilities of the team will be compromised because the primary motive of the presenter will be to minimize the number of faults that show up. To prevent this conflict of interests, the person responsible for a given phase should not also be directly responsible for evaluating any member of the walkthrough team for that phase.

5.2.3 INSPECTIONS

Inspections were first proposed by Fagan for the testing of designs and code [Fagan, 1976]. An inspection goes far beyond a walkthrough and has five formal steps. First, an *overview* of the document to be inspected (specification, design, code, or plan) is given by one of the individuals responsible for producing that document. At the end of the overview session, the document is distributed to the participants. In the second step, *preparation,* the participants try to understand the document in detail. Lists of fault types found in recent inspections, with the fault types ranked by frequency, are excellent aids. These lists will help team members concentrate on the areas where the most faults have occurred. The third step is the *inspection.* To begin, one participant walks through the document with the inspection team, ensuring that every item is covered and that every branch is taken at least once. Then fault finding commences. As with walkthroughs, the purpose is to find and document the faults, not to correct them. Within one day the leader of the inspection team (the *moderator*) must produce a written report of the inspection to ensure meticulous follow-through. The fourth stage is the *rework* in which the individual responsible for that document resolves all faults and problems noted in the written report. The final stage is the *follow-up.* The moderator must ensure that every single issue raised has been satisfactorily resolved, either by fixing the document or by clarifying items that were incorrectly flagged as faults. All fixes must be checked to ensure that no new faults have been introduced [Fagan, 1986]. If more than 5 percent of the material inspected has been reworked, then the team reconvenes for a 100 percent reinspection.

The inspection should be conducted by a team of four. For example, in the case of a design inspection, the team will consist of a moderator, designer, implementer, and tester. The moderator is both manager and leader of the inspection team. There must be a representative of the team responsible for the current phase, as well as a representative of the team responsible for the next phase. The designer is a member of the team that produced the design, whereas the implementer will be responsible, either individually or as part of a team, for translating the design into code. Fagan suggested that the tester be any programmer responsible for setting up test cases; it is, of course, preferable that the tester be a member of the SQA group. The IEEE standard recommends a team of between three and six participants [IEEE 1028, 1988]. Special roles are played by the *moderator,* the *reader* who leads the team through the design, and the *recorder* who is responsible for producing a written report of the detected faults.

An essential component of an inspection is the checklist of potential faults. For example, the checklist for a design inspection should include items such as: Is each item of the specification document adequately and correctly addressed? For each interface, do the actual and formal arguments correspond? Have error-handling mechanisms been adequately identified? Is the design compatible with the hardware resources, or does it require more hardware than is actually available? Is the design compatible with the software resources—for example, does the operating system stipulated in the specification document have the functionality required by the design?

An important component of the inspection procedure is the record of fault statistics. Faults must be recorded by severity (major or minor—an example of a major fault is one that causes premature termination or damages a database) and by fault type. In the case of a design inspection, typical fault types include interface faults and logic faults. This information can be used in a number of useful ways. First, the number of faults in a given product can be compared with averages of faults detected at the same stage of development in comparable products, giving management an early warning that something is amiss and allowing timely corrective action to be taken. Second, if inspecting the design of two or three modules results in the discovery of a disproportionate number of faults of a particular type, management can begin checking other modules and take corrective action. Third, if the inspection of the design of a particular module reveals far more faults than were found in any other module in the product, then there is usually a strong case for redesigning that module from scratch. Finally, information regarding the number and types of faults detected at a design inspection will aid the team performing the code inspection of the same module at a later stage.

Fagan's first experiment was performed on a systems product [Fagan, 1976]. One hundred person-hours were devoted to inspections, at a rate of two 2-hour inspections per day by a four-person team. Of all the faults that were found during the development of the product, 67 percent were located by inspections before module testing was started. Furthermore, during the first 7 months of operations mode, 38 percent fewer faults were detected in the inspected product than in a comparable product reviewed using informal walkthroughs.

Fagan conducted another experiment on an applications product and found that 82 percent of all detected faults were discovered during design and code inspections [Fagan, 1976]. A useful side effect of the inspections was that programmer productivity rose because less time had to be spent on module testing. Using an automated estimating model, Fagan determined that, as a result of the inspection process, the savings on programmer resources were 25 percent—despite the fact that time had to be devoted to the inspections. In a different experiment Jones found that over 70 percent of detected faults could be detected by conducting design and code inspections [Jones, 1978].

More recent studies have produced equally impressive results. In a 6000-line business data processing application, 93 percent of all detected faults were found during inspections [Fagan, 1986]. As reported in [Ackerman, Buchwald, and Lewski, 1989], the use of inspections rather than testing during the development of an operating system decreased the cost of detecting a fault by 85 percent; in a switching system product, the decrease was 90 percent [Fowler, 1986]. At the Jet Propulsion Laboratory (JPL), on average each 2-hour inspection has exposed 4 major faults and 14 minor faults [Bush, 1990]. Translated into dollar terms, this meant a saving of approximately $25,000 *per inspection.* Another JPL study [Kelly, Sherif, and Hops, 1992] has shown that the number of faults detected decreases exponentially by phase. In other words, with the aid of inspections, faults can be detected early in the software process. The importance of this early detection is reflected in Figure 1.5.

A risk of the inspection process is that, like the walkthrough, it might be used for performance appraisal. The danger is particularly acute in the case of inspections because of the detailed fault information that is available. Fagan dismisses this fear by stating that over a period of 3 years he knew of no IBM manager who used such information against a programmer, or as he put it, no manager tried to "kill the goose that lays the golden eggs" [Fagan, 1976]. However, if inspections are not conducted properly, they may not be as wildly successful as they have been at IBM. Unless top management is aware of the potential problem, misuse of inspection information is a distinct possibility.

5.2.4 COMPARISON OF INSPECTIONS AND WALKTHROUGHS

Superficially, the difference between an inspection and a walkthrough is that the inspection team uses a checklist of queries to aid it in finding the faults. But the difference goes deeper than that. A walkthrough is a two-step process: preparation, followed by team analysis of the document. An inspection is a five-step process, namely overview, preparation, inspection, rework, and follow-up, and the procedure to be followed in each of those steps is formalized. Examples of such formalization are the careful categorization of faults and the use of that information in inspections of the documents of the succeeding phases, as well as in inspections of future products.

The inspection process takes much longer than a walkthrough. Is inspection worth the additional time and effort? The data of the previous section clearly indicate that inspections are a powerful and cost-effective tool for fault detection.

5.2.5 STRENGTHS AND WEAKNESSES OF REVIEWS

There are two major strengths of a review (walkthrough or inspection). First, a review is an effective way of detecting a fault and second, faults are detected early in the software process, that is, before they become expensive to fix. For example, design faults are detected before implementation commences and coding faults are found before the module is integrated into the product.

However, the effectiveness of a review can be reduced if the software process is inadequate. First, large-scale software is extremely hard to review unless it consists of smaller, largely independent components. One of the strengths of the object-oriented paradigm is that, if correctly carried out, the resulting product will indeed consist of largely independent pieces. Second, a design review team sometimes has to refer to the specification documents; a code review team often needs access to the design documents. Unless the documentation of the previous phases is complete, updated to reflect the current version of the project, and available online, the effectiveness of review teams will be severely hampered.

5.2.6 METRICS FOR INSPECTIONS

In order to determine the effectiveness of inspections, a number of different metrics can be used. The first is the *fault density.* When specifications and designs are inspected, faults per page inspected can be measured; for code inspections, an appropriate metric is faults per 1000 lines of code (KLOC) inspected. These metrics can be broken up into major faults per unit of material and minor faults per unit of material. Another useful metric is the *fault detection rate,* that is, the number of major/minor faults detected per hour. A third metric is the *fault detection efficiency,* that is, the number of major/minor faults detected per person-hour.

Although the purpose of these metrics is to measure the effectiveness of the inspection process, the results may instead reflect deficiencies of the development team. For example, if the fault detection rate suddenly rises from 20 defects per thousand lines of code to 30, this does not necessarily mean that the inspection team has suddenly become 50 percent more efficient. Another explanation could be that the quality of code has decreased and that there are simply more faults to be detected.

Having discussed nonexecution-based testing, the next topic is execution-based testing.

5.3 EXECUTION-BASED TESTING

It has been claimed that testing is a demonstration that faults are not present. (A *fault* is the IEEE standard terminology for what is popularly called a "bug," whereas a *failure* is the observed incorrect behavior of the product as a consequence of the fault [IEEE 610.12, 1990]. Finally, an *error* is the mistake made by the programmer.) Despite the fact that some organizations spend up to 50 percent of their software budget on testing, delivered "tested" software is notoriously unreliable.

The reason for this contradiction is simple. As Dijkstra put it, "Program testing can be a very effective way to show the presence of bugs, but it is hopelessly inadequate for showing their absence" [Dijkstra, 1972]. What Dijkstra is saying is that if a product is executed with test data and the output is wrong, then the product definitely contains a fault. But if the output is correct, then there still may be a fault in the product; all that particular test has shown is that the product runs correctly on that particular set of test data.

5.4 WHAT SHOULD BE TESTED?

In order to be able to describe what properties should be tested, it is first necessary to give a precise description of execution-based testing. According to Goodenough, execution-based testing is a process of inferring certain behavioral properties of a product based, in part, on the results of executing the product in a known environment with selected inputs [Goodenough, 1979].

This definition has three troubling implications. First, the definition states that testing is an inferential process. The tester takes the product, runs it with known input data, and examines the output. The tester has to infer what, if anything, is wrong with the product. From this viewpoint, testing is comparable to trying to find the proverbial black cat in a dark room, but without knowing whether or not there is a cat in the room in the first place. The tester has few clues to help find any faults: perhaps 10 or 20 sets of inputs and corresponding outputs, possibly a user fault report, and thousands of lines of code. From this the tester has to deduce if there is a fault, and if so, what it is.

A second problem with the definition arises from the phrase in a *known environment.* We can never really know our environment, either the hardware or the software. We can never be certain that the operating system is functioning correctly or that the run-time routines are correct. There may be an intermittent hardware fault in the main memory of the computer. So what is observed as the behavior of the product may in fact be a correct product interacting with a faulty compiler or faulty hardware or some other faulty component of the environment.

The third worrisome part of the definition of execution-based testing is the phrase *with selected inputs.* In the case of a real-time system, there is frequently no control over the inputs to the system. Consider avionics software. The flight control system has two types of inputs. The first type of input is what the pilot wants the aircraft to do. Thus, if the pilot pulls back on the joystick in order to climb or opens the throttle in order to increase the speed of the aircraft, these mechanical motions are transformed into digital signals that are sent to the flight control computer. The second type of input is the current physical state of the aircraft, such as its altitude, speed, and the elevations of the wing flaps. The flight control software uses the values of such quantities to compute what signals should be sent to the components of the aircraft such as the wing flaps and the engines in order to implement the pilot's directives. Whereas the pilot's inputs can easily be set to any desired values simply by setting the aircraft's controls appropriately, the inputs corresponding to the current physical state of the aircraft cannot be so easily manipulated. In fact, there is no way that one can force the aircraft to provide "selected inputs." How then can such a real-time system be tested? The answer is to use a simulator.

A *simulator* is a working model of the environment in which the product, in this case the flight control software, executes. The flight control software can be tested by causing the simulator to send selected inputs to the flight control software. The simulator has controls that allow the operator to set an input variable to any selected value. Thus, if the purpose of the test is to determine how the flight control software performs if one engine catches fire, then the controls of the simulator are set so that the inputs sent to the flight control software are indistinguishable from what the inputs would be if an engine of the actual aircraft were on fire. The output is analyzed by examining the output signals sent from the flight control software to the simulator. But a simulator can at best be a good approximation of a faithful model of some aspect of the system; it can never be the system itself. Using a simulator means that whereas there is indeed a "known environment," there is little likelihood that this known environment is in every way identical to the actual environment in which the product will be installed.

The preceding definition of testing speaks of "behavioral properties." What behavioral properties must be tested? An obvious answer is: Test whether the product functions correctly. But as will be shown, correctness is neither necessary nor sufficient. Before discussing correctness, four other behavioral properties will be considered, namely *utility, reliability, robustness,* and *performance* [Goodenough, 1979].

5.4.1 UTILITY

Utility is the extent to which a user's needs are met when a correct product is used under conditions permitted by its specifications. In other words, a product that is functioning correctly is now subjected to inputs that are valid in terms of the specifications. The user may test, for example, how easy the product is to use, whether the product performs useful functions, and whether the product is cost-effective compared to competing products. Irrespective of whether the product is correct or not, these are vital issues that have to be tested. If the product is not cost-effective, then there is no point in buying it. And unless the product is easy to use, it will not be used at all or it will be used incorrectly. Thus, when considering buying an existing product (including shrink-wrapped software), the utility of the product should be tested first, and if the product fails on that score, testing should stop.

5.4.2 RELIABILITY

Another aspect of a product that must be tested is its reliability. *Reliability* is a measure of the frequency and criticality of product failure; recall that a failure is an unacceptable effect or behavior, under permissible operating conditions, that occurs as a consequence of a fault. In other words, it is necessary to know how often the product fails (*mean time between failures*) and how bad the effects of that failure can be. When a product fails, an important issue is how long it takes, on average, to repair it (*mean time to repair*). But often more important is how long it takes to repair the *results* of the failure. This last point is frequently overlooked. Suppose that the software running on a communications front end fails, on average, only once every 6 months, but when it fails it completely wipes out a database. At best the database can be reinitialized to its status when the last checkpoint dump was taken, and the audit trail can then be used to put the database into a state that is virtually up to date. But if this recovery process takes the better part of 2 days, during which time the database and communications front end are inoperative, then the reliability of the product is low, notwithstanding the fact that the mean time between failures is 6 months.

5.4.3 ROBUSTNESS

Another aspect of every product that requires testing is its *robustness*. Although it is difficult to come up with a precise definition, robustness is essentially a function of a number of factors such as the range of operating conditions, the possibility of unacceptable results with valid input, and the acceptability of effects when the product is given invalid input. A product with a wide range of permissible operating conditions is more robust than a product that is more restrictive. A robust product should not yield unacceptable results when the input satisfies its specifications, for example, giving a valid command should not have disastrous consequences. A robust product should not crash when the product is *not* used under permissible operating conditions. To test for this aspect of robustness, test data that do not satisfy the input specifications are deliberately input, and the tester determines how badly the product reacts. For example, when the product solicits a name, the tester may reply with a stream of unacceptable characters such as `control-A escape-% ?$#@`. If the computer responds with a message such as `Incorrect data—Try again`, or better, informs the user as to why the data do not conform to what was expected, it is more robust than a product that crashes whenever the data deviate even slightly from what is required.

5.4.4 PERFORMANCE

Performance is another aspect of the product that must be tested. For example, it is essential to know the extent to which the product meets its constraints with regard to response time or space requirements. For an embedded computer system such as an onboard computer in a handheld antiaircraft missile, the space constraints of the system may be such that only 128 kilobytes (Kb) of main memory are available for the software. No matter how excellent the software may be, if it needs 256 Kb of main memory, then it cannot be used at all. (For more information on embedded software, see the Just in Case You Wanted to Know box below.)

Real-time software is characterized by hard time constraints, that is, time constraints of such a nature that if a constraint is not met, information is lost. For example, a nuclear reactor control system may have to sample the temperature of the core and process the data every 10th of a second. If the system is not fast enough to be able to handle interrupts from the temperature sensor every 10th of a second, then data will be lost, and there is no way of ever recovering the data; the next time that the system receives temperature data it will be the current temperature, not the reading that was missed. If the reactor is on the point of a meltdown, then it is critical that all relevant information be both received and processed as laid down in the specifications. With all real-time systems, the performance must meet every time constraint listed in the specifications.

5.4.5 CORRECTNESS

Finally, a definition of correctness can be given. A product is *correct* if it satisfies its output specifications, independent of its use of computing resources, when operated under permitted conditions [Goodenough, 1979]. In other words, if input that satisfies the input specifications is provided and the product is given all the resources it needs, then the product is correct if the output satisfies the output specifications.

This definition of correctness, like the definition of testing itself, has worrisome implications. Suppose that a product has been successfully tested against

JUST IN CASE YOU WANTED TO KNOW

An embedded computer is an integral part of a larger system whose primary purpose is not computation. The function of embedded software is to control the device in which the computer is embedded. Military examples include a network of avionics computers on board a warplane, or a computer built into an intercontinental ballistic missile. The embedded computer in the nose cone of a missile controls only that missile; it cannot be used, say, for printing the payroll checks for the soldiers on the missile base.

More familiar examples are the computer chip in a digital watch or a washing machine. Again, the chip in a washing machine is exclusively used for controlling the washing machine. There is no way that the owner of that washing machine could use the chip for balancing his or her checkbook.

Input specification:	p : array of n integers, n > 0.
Output specification:	q : array of n integers such that q[0] ≤ q[1] ≤ . . . ≤ q[n − 1]

Figure 5.1 Incorrect specification for a sort.

a broad variety of test data. Does this mean that the product is acceptable? Unfortunately, it does not. If a product is correct, all that it means is that it satisfies its specifications. But what if the specifications themselves are incorrect? To illustrate this difficulty, consider the specification shown in Figure 5.1. The specification states that the input to the sort is an array p of n integers, whereas the output is another array q that is sorted in nondecreasing order. Superficially, the specification seems to be perfectly correct. But consider method trickSort shown in Figure 5.2. In that method, all n elements of array q are set to 0. The method satisfies the specification of Figure 5.1 and is therefore correct!

What has happened? Unfortunately, the specification of Figure 5.1 is wrong. What has been omitted is a statement that the elements of q, the output array, are a permutation (rearrangement) of the elements of the input array p. An intrinsic aspect of sorting is that it is a rearrangement process. And the method of Figure 5.2 capitalizes on this specification fault. In other words, method trickSort is correct, but the specification of Figure 5.1 is wrong. A corrected specification appears in Figure 5.3.

```
void trickSort (int p[], int q[])
{
  int i;
  for (i = 0; i < n; i++)
    q[i] = 0;
}
```

Figure 5.2 Method trickSort which satisfies specification of Figure 5.1.

Input specification:	p : array of n integers, n > 0.
Output specification:	q : array of n integers such that q[0] ≤ q[1] ≤ . . . ≤ q[n − 1] The elements of array q are a permutation of the elements of array p, which are unchanged.

Figure 5.3 Corrected specification for the sort.

From the preceding example, it is clear that the consequences of specification faults are nontrivial. After all, the correctness of a product is meaningless if its specifications are incorrect.

The fact that a product is correct is not *sufficient,* because the specifications in terms of which it was shown to be correct may themselves be wrong. But is it *necessary?* Consider the following example. A software organization has acquired a superb new C++ compiler. The new compiler can translate twice as many lines of source code per minute as the old compiler, the object code runs nearly 45 percent faster, and the size of the object code is about 20 percent smaller. In addition, the error messages are much clearer and the cost of annual maintenance and updates is less than half of that of the old compiler. There is one problem, however: The first time that a `for` statement appears in any class, the compiler prints a spurious error message. The compiler is therefore not correct, because the specifications for a compiler implicitly or explicitly require that error messages be printed if, and only if, there is a fault in the source code. It is certainly possible to use the compiler—in fact, in every way but one the compiler is absolutely ideal. Furthermore, it is reasonable to expect that this minor fault will be corrected in the next release. In the meantime, the programmers will learn to ignore the spurious error message. Not only can the organization live with the incorrect compiler, but if anyone were to suggest replacing it by the old correct compiler there would be an outcry. Thus the correctness of a product is neither necessary nor sufficient.

Both the preceding examples are admittedly somewhat artificial. But they do make the point that correctness simply means that the product is a correct implementation of its specifications. In other words, there is more to testing than just showing that the product is correct.

With all the difficulties associated with execution-based testing, computer scientists have tried to come up with other ways of ensuring that a product does what it is supposed to do. One such nonexecution-based alternative that has received considerable attention for more than 40 years is correctness proving.

5.5 TESTING VERSUS CORRECTNESS PROOFS

A correctness proof is a mathematical technique for showing that a product is correct, in other words, that it satisfies its specifications. The technique is sometimes termed *verification.* However, as previously pointed out, the term *verification* is often used to denote all nonexecution-based techniques, not only correctness proving. For clarity, this mathematical procedure will be termed *correctness proving,* to remind the reader that it is a mathematical proof process.

5.5.1 EXAMPLE OF A CORRECTNESS PROOF

To see how correctness is proved, consider the code fragment shown in Figure 5.4. The flowchart equivalent to the code is given in Figure 5.5. It will now be

```
int     k, s;
int     y[] = new int[n];

k = 0;
s = 0;

while (k < n)
{
  s = s + y[k];
  k = k + 1;
}
```

Figure 5.4 Code fragment to be proved correct.

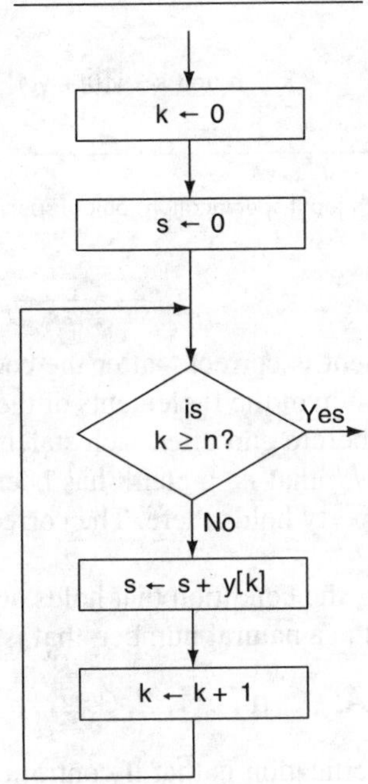

Figure 5.5 Flowchart of Figure 5.4.

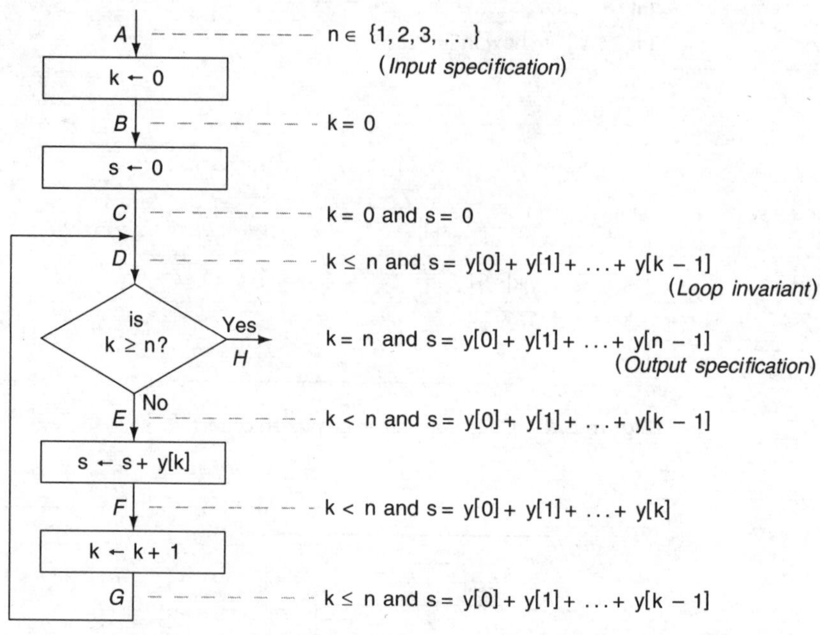

Figure 5.6 Figure 5.5 with input specification, output specification, loop invariant, and assertions.

shown that the code fragment is correct—after the code has been executed, the variable s will contain the sum of the n elements of the array y. In Figure 5.6, an *assertion* has been placed before and after each statement, at the places labeled with the letters *A* through *H*; that is, a claim has been made at each place that a certain mathematical property holds there. The correctness of each assertion is now proved.

The input specification, the condition that holds at *A* before the code is executed, is that the variable n is a natural number, that is,

$$A: \quad n \in \{1, 2, 3, \ldots\} \tag{5.1}$$

An obvious output specification is that if control reaches point *H*, the value of s contains the sum of the n values stored in array y, that is,

$$H: \quad s = y[0] + y[1] + \ldots + y[n-1] \tag{5.2}$$

In fact, the code fragment can be proved to be correct with respect to a stronger output specification, namely

$$H: \quad k = n \text{ and } s = y[0] + y[1] + \ldots + y[n-1] \tag{5.3}$$

A natural reaction to the last sentence is to ask: From where did output specification (5.3) come? By the end of the proof, the reader will hopefully have the answer to that question; also see Problems 5.10 and 5.11.

In addition to the input and output specifications, a third aspect of the proof process is to provide an invariant for the loop. That is, a mathematical expression must be provided that holds at point *D* irrespective of whether the loop has been executed 0, 1, or many times. The loop invariant that will be proved to hold is

$$D: \quad k \leq n \text{ and } s = y[0] + y[1] + \ldots + y[k-1] \qquad \textbf{(5.4)}$$

Now it will be shown that if specification (5.1) holds at point *A*, then specification (5.3) will hold at point *H*, that is, the code fragment will be proved to be correct.

First, the assignment statement $k \longleftarrow 0$ is executed. Control is now at point *B*, where the following assertion holds:

$$B: \quad k = 0 \qquad \textbf{(5.5)}$$

To be more precise, at point *B* the assertion should read $k = 0$ and $n \in \{1, 2, 3, \ldots\}$. However, the input specification (5.1) holds at all points in the flowchart. For brevity, the "and $n \in \{1, 2, 3, \ldots\}$" will therefore be omitted from now on.

At point *C*, as a consequence of the second assignment statement, namely $s \longleftarrow 0$, the following assertion is true:

$$C: \quad k = 0 \text{ and } s = 0 \qquad \textbf{(5.6)}$$

Now the loop is entered. It will be proved by induction that the loop invariant (5.4) is indeed correct. Just before the loop is executed for the first time, assertion (5.6) holds, that is, $k = 0$, and $s = 0$. Now consider loop invariant (5.4). Because $k = 0$ by assertion (5.6), and $n \geq 1$ from input specification (5.1), it follows that $k \leq n$ as required. Furthermore, because $k = 0$ it follows that $k - 1 = -1$, so the sum in (5.4) is empty and $s = 0$ as required. Loop invariant (5.4) is therefore true just before the first time the loop is entered for the first time.

Now the inductive hypothesis step is performed. Assume that at some stage during the execution of the code fragment the loop invariant holds. That is, for k equal to some value k_0, $0 \leq k_0 \leq n$, execution is at point *D*, and the assertion that holds is

$$D: \quad k_0 \leq n \text{ and } s = y[0] + y[1] + \ldots + y[k_0 - 1] \qquad \textbf{(5.7)}$$

Control now passes to the test box. If $k_0 \geq n$, then because $k_0 \leq n$ by hypothesis, it follows that $k_0 = n$. By inductive hypothesis (5.7), this implies that

$$H: \quad k_0 = n \text{ and } s = y[0] + y[1] + \ldots + y[n - 1] \qquad \textbf{(5.8)}$$

that is precisely the output specification (5.3).

On the other hand, if the test is $k_0 \geq n$? fails, then control passes from point *D* to point *E*. Because k_0 is not greater than or equal to n, $k_0 < n$, and (5.7) becomes

$$E: \quad k_0 < n \text{ and } s = y[0] + y[1] + \ldots + y[k_0 - 1] \qquad \textbf{(5.9)}$$

The statement $s \longleftarrow s + y[k_0]$ is now executed, so from assertion (5.9), at point *F* the following assertion must hold:

$$F: \quad k_0 < n \text{ and } s = y[0] + y[1] + \ldots + y[k_0 - 1] + y[k_0] \qquad \textbf{(5.10)}$$
$$= y[0] + y[1] + \ldots + y[k_0]$$

The next statement to be executed is $k_0 \longleftarrow k_0 + 1$. To see the effect of this statement, suppose that the value of k_0 before executing this statement is 17. Then the last term in the sum in (5.10) is y[17]. Now the value of k_0 is increased by 1 to 18. The sum s is unchanged, so the last term in the sum is still y[17], which is now $y[k_0 - 1]$. Also, at point *F*, $k_0 < n$. Increasing the value of k_0 by 1 means that if the inequality is to hold at point *G* then $k_0 \leq n$. Thus the effect of increasing k_0 by 1 is that the following assertion holds at point *G*:

$$G: \quad k_0 \leq n \text{ and } s = y[0] + y[1] + \ldots + y[k_0 - 1] \qquad \textbf{(5.11)}$$

Assertion (5.11) that holds at point *G* is identical to assertion (5.7) that, by assumption, holds at point *D*. But point *D* is topologically identical to point *G*. In other words, if (5.7) holds at *D* for $k = k_0$, then it will again hold at *D* with $k = k_0 + 1$. It has been shown that the loop invariant holds for $k = 0$. By induction it follows that loop invariant (5.4) holds for all values of k, $0 \leq k \leq n$.

All that remains is to prove that the loop terminates. Initially, by assertion (5.6), the value of k is equal to 0. Each iteration of the loop increases the value of k by 1 when the statement $k \longleftarrow k + 1$ is executed. Eventually, k must reach the value n, at which time the loop is exited, and the value of s is given by assertion (5.8), thus satisfying output specification (5.3).

To review, given the input specification (5.1), it was proved that loop invariant (5.4) holds whether the loop has been executed 0, 1, or more times. Furthermore, it was proved that after n iterations the loop terminates, and when it does so the values of k and s satisfy the output specification (5.3). In other words, the code fragment of Figure 5.4 has been mathematically proved to be correct.

5.5.2 Correctness Proof Case Study

An important aspect of correctness proofs is that they should be done in conjunction with design and coding. As Dijkstra put it, "The programmer should let the program proof and program grow hand in hand" [Dijkstra, 1972]. For example, when a loop is incorporated into the design, a loop invariant is put forward; and as the design is refined stepwise, so is the invariant. Developing a product in this way gives the programmer confidence that the product is correct and tends to reduce the number of faults. Quoting Dijkstra again, "The only effective way to raise the confidence level of a program significantly is to give a convincing proof of its correctness" [Dijkstra, 1972]. But even if a product is proved to be correct, it must be thoroughly tested as well. To illustrate the necessity for testing in conjunction with correctness proving, consider the following.

In 1969, Naur published a paper on a technique for constructing and proving a product correct [Naur, 1969]. The technique was illustrated by what Naur termed a *line-editing problem,* but today would be considered a text-processing problem. It may be stated as follows:

> Given a text consisting of words separated by blank characters or by newline (new line) characters, convert it to line-by-line form in accordance with the following rules:
>
> 1. line breaks must be made only where the given text contains a blank or newline;
> 2. each line is filled as far as possible, as long as
> 3. no line will contain more than maxpos characters

Naur constructed a procedure using his technique and informally proved its correctness. The procedure consisted of approximately 25 lines of ALGOL 60. The paper was then reviewed by Leavenworth in *Computing Reviews* [Leavenworth, 1970]. The reviewer pointed out that in the output of Naur's procedure, the first word of the first line is preceded by a blank unless the first word is exactly maxpos characters long. Although this may seem a trivial fault, it is a fault that would surely have been detected had the procedure been tested, that is, executed with test data rather than only proved correct. But worse was to come. London detected three additional faults in Naur's procedure [London, 1971]. One is that the procedure does not terminate unless a word longer than maxpos characters is encountered. Again, this fault is likely to have been detected if the procedure had been tested. London then presented a corrected version of the procedure and proved formally that the resulting procedure was correct; recall that Naur had used only informal proof techniques.

The next episode in this saga is that Goodenough and Gerhart found three faults that London had not detected, despite his formal proof [Goodenough and Gerhart, 1975]. These included the fact that the last word will not be output unless it is followed by a blank or newline. Yet again, reasonable choice of test data would have detected this fault without much difficulty. In fact, of the total of seven faults collectively detected by Leavenworth, London, and Goodenough and Gerhart, four could have been detected simply by running the procedure on test data, such as the illustrations given in Naur's original paper. The lesson from this saga is clear. Even if a product has been proved to be correct, it must still be tested thoroughly.

The example in Section 5.5.1 showed that proving the correctness of even a small code fragment can be a lengthy process. Furthermore, the case study of this section showed that it is a difficult and error-prone process, even for a 25-line procedure. The following issue must therefore be put forward: Is correctness proving just an interesting research idea, or is it a powerful software engineering technique whose time has come? This is answered in the next section.

5.5.3 CORRECTNESS PROOFS AND SOFTWARE ENGINEERING

A number of software engineering practitioners have put forward reasons why correctness proving should not be viewed as a standard software engineering technique. First, it is claimed that software engineers do not have adequate mathematical training. Second, it is suggested that proving is too expensive to be practical, and third, that proving is too hard. Each of these reasons will be shown to be an oversimplification.

Although the proof given in Section 5.5.1 can be understood with hardly more than high school algebra, nontrivial proofs require that input specifications, output specifications, and loop invariants be expressed in first- or second-order predicate calculus, or the equivalent. Not only does this make the proof process simpler for a mathematician, but it allows correctness proving to be done by a computer. To complicate matters further, predicate calculus is now somewhat outdated. To prove the correctness of concurrent products, techniques using temporal or other modal logics are required [Lamport, 1980; Manna and Pnueli, 1992]. There is no doubt that correctness proving requires training in mathematical logic. Fortunately, most computer science majors today either take courses in the requisite material or have the background to learn correctness-proving techniques on the job. Thus colleges are now turning out computer science graduates with sufficient mathematical skills for correctness proving. The claim that practicing software engineers do not have the necessary mathematical training may have been true in the past, but no longer applies in the light of the thousands of computer science majors joining the industry each year.

The claim that proving is too expensive for use in software development is also false. On the contrary, the economic viability of correctness proving can be determined on a project-by-project basis using cost–benefit analysis (Section 4.7). For example, consider the software for the NASA space station. Human lives are at stake, and if something goes wrong, a space shuttle rescue mission may not arrive in time. The cost of proving life-critical space station software correct is large. But the potential cost of a software fault that might be overlooked if correctness proving is not performed is even larger.

The third claim is that correctness proving is too hard. Despite this claim, many nontrivial products have been successfully proved to be correct, including operating system kernels, compilers, and communications systems [Landwehr, 1983; Berry and Wing, 1985]. Furthermore, many tools such as theorem provers exist to assist in correctness proving. A theorem prover takes as input a product, its input and output specifications, and loop invariants. The theorem prover then attempts to prove mathematically that the product, when given input data satisfying the input specifications, will produce output data satisfying the output specifications.

At the same time, there are some difficulties with correctness proving. For example, how can we be sure that a theorem prover is correct? If the theorem prover prints out `This product is correct`, can we believe it? To take an extreme case, consider the so-called theorem prover shown in Figure 5.7. No matter

```
void theoremProver ()
{
  System.out.println ("This product is correct");
}
```

Figure 5.7 Theorem prover.

what code is submitted to this theorem prover, it will print out This product is correct. In other words, what reliability can be placed on the output of a theorem prover? One suggestion is to submit a theorem prover to itself and see whether it is correct. Apart from the philosophical implications, a simple way of seeing that this will not work is to consider what would happen if the theorem prover of Figure 5.7 were submitted to itself for proving. It will, as always, print out This product is correct, thereby "proving" its own correctness.

A further difficulty is finding the input and output specifications, and especially the loop invariants or their equivalents in other logics such as modal logic. Suppose that a product is correct. Unless a suitable invariant for each loop can be found, there is no way of proving the product correct. Yes, tools do exist to assist in this task [Tamir, 1980]. But even with state-of-the-art tools, a software engineer may simply not be able to come up with a correctness proof. One solution to this problem is to develop the product and proof in parallel, as advocated in Section 5.5.2. When a loop is designed, an invariant for that loop is specified at the same time. With this approach, it is somewhat easier to prove the code modules correct.

Worse than not being able to find loop invariants, what if the specifications themselves are incorrect? An example of this is method trickSort (Figure 5.2). A good theorem prover, when given the incorrect specifications of Figure 5.1, will undoubtedly declare that the method shown in Figure 5.2 is correct.

Manna and Waldinger have stated that "We can never be sure that the specifications are correct" and "We can never be certain that a verification system is correct" [Manna and Waldinger, 1978]. These statements from two of the leading experts in the field encapsulate the various points made previously.

Does all this mean that there is no place for correctness proofs in software engineering? Quite the contrary. Proving products correct is an important, and sometimes vital, software engineering tool. Proofs are appropriate where human lives are at stake or where otherwise indicated by cost–benefit analysis. If the cost of proving software correct is less than the probable cost if the product fails, then the product should be proved. However, as the text-processing case study shows, proving alone is not enough. Instead, correctness proving should be viewed as an important component of the set of techniques that must be utilized together to check that a product is correct. Because the aim of software engineering is the production of quality software, correctness proving is indeed an important software engineering technique.

Even when a full formal proof is not justified, the quality of software can be markedly improved through the use of informal proofs. For example, a proof similar to that of Section 5.5.1 will assist in checking that a loop will be executed the correct number of times. A second way of improving software quality is to insert assertions such as those of Figure 5.6 into the code. Then, if at execution time an assertion does not hold, the product will be halted, and the software team can investigate whether the assertion that terminated execution is incorrect or whether there is indeed a fault in the code that was detected by triggering the assertion. Languages such as Eiffel [Meyer, 1992b] support assertions directly by means of an assert statement. Suppose that an informal proof requires that the value of variable xxx be positive at a particular point in the code. Even though the design team may be convinced that there is no way for xxx to be negative, for additional reliability they may specify that the statement

```
assert (xxx > 0)
```

appear at that point in the code. If xxx is less than or equal to zero, execution will terminate, and the situation can then be investigated by the software team. Unfortunately, *Assert* in C++ is a debugging statement, similar to *assert* in C; it is not part of the language itself. Ada 95 supports assertions via a pragma.

Once the users are confident that the product is working correctly, they have the option of switching off assertion checking. This will speed up execution, but if there is a fault that would have been detected by an assertion, it may not be found if assertion checking is switched off. Thus there is a trade-off between run-time efficiency and continuing assertion checking even after the product is in operations mode. (The Just in Case You Wanted to Know box below gives an interesting insight on this issue.)

JUST IN CASE YOU WANTED TO KNOW

One feature of languages such as Java and Ada (but not C or C++) is bounds checking. One example of bounds checking is examining every array index during execution to ensure that it is within its declared range. Another example is subrange checking, that is, checking during execution that when a value is assigned to a variable, that value is within the specific declared range for that variable.

Tony Hoare has suggested that using bounds checking while developing a product, but turning it off once the product is working correctly, can be likened to learning to sail on dry land wearing a life jacket and then taking the life jacket off when actually at sea. In his Turing Award lecture, Hoare described a compiler for ALGOL 60 that he developed in 1961 [Hoare, 1981]. When users were later offered the opportunity to turn off bounds checking in operations mode they unanimously refused, because they had experienced so many incidents of values out of range during earlier production runs.

Bounds checking can be viewed as a special case of a more general concept, namely assertion checking. Hoare's life jacket analogy is equally applicable to turning off assertion checking in operations mode.

A fundamental issue in execution-based testing is which members of the software development team should be responsible for carrying it out.

5.6 WHO SHOULD PERFORM EXECUTION-BASED TESTING?

Suppose a programmer is asked to test a module that he or she has written. Testing has been described by Myers as the process of executing a product with the intention of finding faults [Myers, 1979]. Testing is thus a destructive process. On the other hand, the programmer who is doing the testing will ordinarily not wish to destroy his or her work. If the fundamental attitude of the programmer toward the code is the usual protective one, then the chances of that programmer using test data that will highlight faults is considerably lower than if the major motivation were truly destructive.

A successful test is one that finds faults. This, too, poses a difficulty. It means that if the module passes the test, then the test has failed. Conversely, if the module does not perform according to specifications, then the test succeeds. When a programmer is asked to test a module he or she has written, the programmer is being asked to execute the module in such a way that a failure (incorrect behavior) ensues. This goes against the creative instincts of programmers.

An inescapable conclusion of this is that programmers should not test their own modules. After a programmer has been *con*structive and has built a module, testing that module requires the programmer to perform a *de*structive act, and to attempt to destroy the very thing that he or she has created. A second reason why execution-based testing should be done by someone else is that the programmer may have misunderstood some aspect of the design or specifications. If testing is done by someone else, such faults may be discovered. Nevertheless, debugging (finding the cause of the failure and correcting the fault) is best done by the original programmer, the person who is most familiar with the code.

The statement that a programmer should not test his or her own code must not be taken too far. Consider the programming process. The programmer begins by reading the detailed design of the module that may be in the form of a flowchart or, more likely, pseudocode. But whatever technique is used, the programmer must certainly desk-check the module before entering it into the computer. That is, the programmer must try out the flowchart or pseudocode with various test cases, tracing through the detailed design to check that each test case is correctly executed. Only when the programmer is satisfied that the detailed design is correct should the text editor be invoked and the module coded.

Once the module is in machine-readable form, it undergoes a series of tests. First, the programmer attempts to compile the module. When this has been successfully achieved, the following step is to link and load it. Then the programmer attempts to execute the module. If the module executes, then test data are used to determine that the module works successfully, probably the same test data that were used to desk-check the detailed design. Next, if the module executes correctly when correct test data are used, then the programmer tries out incorrect data to test the robustness of the module. When the programmer is satisfied that the module is operating correctly, systematic testing commences. It is this *systematic testing* that should not be performed by the programmer.

If the programmer is not to perform this systematic testing, who is to do it? As stated in Section 5.1.2, independent testing must be performed by the SQA group. The key word here is *independent.* Only if the SQA group is truly independent of the development team can its members fulfill their mission of ensuring that the product indeed satisfies its specifications, without software development managers applying pressures such as product deadlines that might hamper their work. SQA personnel must report to their own managers and thus protect their independence.

How is systematic testing performed? An essential part of a test case is a statement of the expected output before the test is executed. It is a complete waste of time for the tester to sit at a terminal, execute the module, enter haphazard test data, and then peer at the screen and say, "I guess that looks right." Equally futile is for the tester to plan test cases with great care and then execute each test case in turn, look at the output, and say, "Yes, that certainly looks right." It is far too easy to be fooled by plausible results. If programmers are allowed to test their own code, then there is always the danger that the programmer will see what he or she wants to see. The same danger can occur even when the testing is done by someone else. The solution is for management to insist that before a test is performed, both the test data and the expected results of that test be recorded. After the test has been performed, the actual results should be recorded and compared with the expected results.

Even in small organizations and with small products, it is important that this recording be done in machine-readable form, because test cases should never be thrown away. The reason for this is maintenance. While the product is being maintained, regression testing must be performed. Stored test cases that the product has previously executed correctly must be rerun to ensure that the modifications made to add new functionality to the product have not destroyed the product's existing functionality. This is discussed further in Chapter 15.

In the next two sections we discuss the testing of two somewhat specialized types of software, namely, distributed software and real-time software.

5.7 Testing Distributed Software

The difficulties of testing are considerably exacerbated when the product under test is implemented as a distributed product running on two or more different pieces of hardware. Examples of distributed computer systems are a hypercube [Seitz, 1985] and a network of computers connected by Ethernet [Silberschatz and Galvin, 1998]. In these systems the various component computers are loosely coupled, with the individual CPUs each having their own memory and communicating with one another by message passing.

The process of testing a product running on a uniprocessor is well understood. A vast literature exists on the subject, and tools have been constructed to aid the tester. Implicit in this uniprocessor testing process are a number of assumptions. It is assumed, for instance, that there is a global environment and that the execution of the product within that environment is deterministic. Furthermore, it is assumed that the instructions of the product are executed sequentially and that inserting debugging statements between source code statements will not modify the execution of the product in any way.

When attempting to test a product running on a distributed system, the familiar techniques of testing on a uniprocessor frequently are not very effective because the previous assumptions simply do not hold. In a distributed system there is no global environment. Instead, the instructions are executed in parallel on different processors. Furthermore, as a consequence of timing considerations, product execution behavior may not be reproducible from one execution to the next. Finally, adding debugging statements to one process could affect the behavior of other processes executing in parallel, resulting in timing-dependent faults, or so-called Heisenbugs. For example, suppose that process s is running on processor P_s, and process t is running on processor P_t. At some point process s sends a message to process t, that is, somewhere in process s there is a transmit command and a corresponding receive command in process t. Now suppose that the programmer has coded t incorrectly, so that if t reaches the receive instruction and the message from s is not waiting in the buffer, then process t fails. On the other hand, if the message from s is waiting, then process t works correctly. The programmer tests the product and it fails because process t is faster than process s, and the message is not waiting for t at the appropriate time. So the programmer attempts to debug process t by inserting a few output statements that will indicate to the programmer how much of process t has been executed before the failure. However, the additional output statements slow down process t, and process s has a chance to transmit the message before process t needs it. As a result, the product works perfectly. However, the moment the programmer removes the debugging statements from process t, it runs at its normal speed and reaches the receive before s can transmit; t therefore fails as it did before. Thus debugging causes the fault to disappear and to reappear when the process has apparently been successfully debugged.

Testing distributed software requires special tools for locating faults, especially distributed debuggers [Wahl and Schach, 1988]. Timing problems that arise when a distributed product is run on distributed hardware cannot be sorted out if the software is run on a uniprocessor. The distributed debugger must maintain history files, that is, a chronological record of events such as data inputs or messages transmitted from one process to another. The need for history files is a consequence of timing considerations. Suppose a distributed product is tested and fails. The programmer analyzes the output from the test run and concludes that a particular statement is in error. Once the statement has been changed, the test case must be rerun to determine whether the fault has in fact been correctly fixed. Because the modified product is now different from the original, if only slightly so, the processes will run at different relative rates, and the messages between processors may be sent in a different order. As a result, the execution sequence of the test case after the product has been modified may not be the same as the one in which the fault was detected, and the programmer may therefore not be able to determine if the fault has in fact been fixed. History files solve this problem in that the execution record they contain can be used by a distributed debugger to reproduce the exact sequence of events that caused the failure.

5.8 TESTING REAL-TIME SOFTWARE

There are a number of difficulties specific to the testing of real-time software. It is a characteristic of real-time systems that they are critically dependent on the timing of inputs and the order of inputs, two factors over which the developer has no control. The reason for this is that inputs to a real-time system, such as the temperature of a computer-controlled nuclear reactor, the arrival of an aircraft within the ambit of an air-traffic control system, or the heart rate of a patient in a computer-controlled intensive-care unit, come from the real world. From the testing viewpoint, a relatively large number of test cases are therefore needed to be reasonably sure that the real-time software is functioning correctly. Another difficulty is that inputs to the system may well occur in parallel, and many real-time systems are therefore implemented as parallel systems running on a number of processors, with the attendant problems of testing distributed software described in the previous section.

Real-time software, and especially embedded real-time software (Section 5.4.4), frequently must run without the supervision of computer operators. For example, the computers in a deep space probe or an orbiting satellite must run untended for the entire duration of the mission. The software must be able to cope with a wide variety of emergencies and exceptional conditions. If the worst happens and the software fails, it must be able to reinitialize itself and restart its actions. Embedded real-time systems on earth must be equally robust. Consider, for example, the software for a computer controlling the engine of an automobile; if it cannot recover by itself from an unexpected event, then the engine is immobilized until a mechanic trained in computers can restart the computer system.

This robustness requirement implies that real-time embedded software must incorporate a great number of exception-handling routines to enable the software to recover without human intervention from a wide variety of ordinarily unexpected circumstances. This means that real-time software has to be far more complicated than would be the case if a human operator were available to restart the product and perform the necessary recovery routines in the event of a failure. Testing real-time software is also far more complicated.

Yet another difficulty with testing real-time software arises in setting up test cases. The inputs to most real-time systems come from the real world. The timing and sequence of inputs constitute a major aspect of real-time software that must be tested, but it is often impossible to organize a specific set of inputs occurring in a specific order at a specific time. For example, it is impossible to arrange for all the patients in a 10-bed intensive care unit to develop cardiac failure at the same time or for a set of medical emergencies to occur in a given order during a certain time interval. In other instances, the test cases may theoretically be possible to arrange, but are too hazardous to risk. For example, it is difficult to determine whether the software controlling a nuclear power plant can successfully prevent accidents of the types that occurred at Three Mile Island and at Chernobyl, or whether a missile detection system would function correctly if an unfriendly power were to launch thousands of intercontinental ballistic missiles and submarine-launched ballistic missiles all at the same time.

Real-time software is frequently more complex than most people, even its developers, realize. As a result, there are sometimes subtle interactions among components that even the most skilled testers would not usually detect, and an apparently minor change can therefore have major consequences. A famous example of this is the fault that delayed the first space shuttle orbital flight in April 1981 [Garman, 1981]. The space shuttle avionics are controlled by four identical synchronized computers. There is also an independent fifth computer for back-up in case the set of four computers fails. A change had been made 2 years earlier to the module that performs bus initialization before the avionics computers are synchronized. An unfortunate side effect of this change was that a record containing a time just slightly later than the current time was erroneously sent to the data area used for synchronization of the avionics computers. The time that was sent was sufficiently close to the actual time for this fault not to be detected. About 1 year later the time difference was slightly increased, just enough to cause a 1 in 67 chance of a failure. Then on the day of the first space shuttle launch the synchronization failure occurred, and three of the four identical avionics computers were synchronized one cycle late relative to the first computer. A fail-safe device that prevents the independent fifth computer from receiving information from the other four computers unless they are in agreement had the unanticipated consequence of preventing initialization of the fifth computer, and the launch had to be postponed. An all too familiar aspect of this incident was that the fault was in the bus initialization module, a module that apparently had no connection whatsoever with the synchronization routines.

There are five main approaches to testing real-time software, namely, structure analysis, correctness proofs, systematic testing, statistical testing, and simulation [Quirk, 1985]. The first two approaches are nonexecution-based, the other three execution-based. *Structure analysis techniques* can be used to investigate control flow and data flow without executing the product. These techniques can then be used to prove that all parts of the product can be reached, that there is a path leading to termination from every node in the data flow graph, that all variables are assigned a value before they are used, and that all variables are referenced. These techniques are not perfect, however; for example, it is impossible to check that all elements of an array are assigned a value before they are used because the indices of array elements may be determined only at run time. Structure analysis can also assist in deadlock detection and can also be used for certain classes of timing checks [Quirk, 1983].

Correctness proofs were discussed in Section 5.5. Real-time systems were mentioned as one of the areas where correctness proving may be an economically viable technique. A number of theorem provers have been constructed to prove real-time systems correct. *Systematic testing* is carried out by running sets of test cases consisting of the same input data arranged in all possible orderings, thereby detecting faults caused by overlooking certain orderings of the inputs. Thus, if five different inputs are being tested, these inputs can be arranged in 5! different ways, yielding 120 different test cases. Clearly, the combinatorial explosion makes this technique infeasible when the number of different inputs is even moderately large. As a result, *statistical techniques* are employed to select a manageable sample from the huge number of possible test cases so that probabilistic statements can be made about the reliability of the product, for example, that the probability of software failure is below 0.0001 percent.

The most important testing technique for real-time software is *simulation.* A simulator is "a device which calculates, emulates or predicts the behavior of another device, or some aspect of the behavior of the world" [Bologna, Quirk, and Taylor, 1985]. A simulator can be considered as a test-bed on which the product can be run. The SQA group arranges for the simulator to provide selected inputs to the product, and then the simulator assists the SQA group in analyzing the outputs from the product to determine whether the product is functioning correctly.

Simulation is particularly important when it is impossible or too dangerous to test a product against suitable sets of test cases. Simulation can be used to check that a product can adequately handle situations like an aircraft stalling and about to crash, or a nuclear reactor about to go critical and explode. Another major use for a simulator is in the training environment. Perhaps the most common instance of this is a flight simulator used to train pilots. But a flight simulator can also be used to test avionics software without putting a human pilot at risk, as would be the case if an actual aircraft were flown with new and untested flight-control software.

5.9 WHEN TESTING STOPS

After a product has been successfully maintained for many years it may eventually lose its usefulness and be superseded by a totally different product, in much the same way that electronic valves were replaced by transistors. Alternatively, a product may still be useful, but the cost of porting it to new hardware or of running it under a new operating system may be larger than the cost of constructing a new product, using the old one as a prototype. Thus, finally, the software product is decommissioned and removed from service. Only at that point, when the software has been irrevocably discarded, is it time to stop testing.

Now that all the necessary background material has been covered, objects can be examined in greater detail. This is the subject of the next chapter.

CHAPTER REVIEW

A key theme of this chapter is that testing must be carried out in parallel with all activities of the software process. The chapter begins with a description of quality issues (Section 5.1). Next, nonexecution-based testing is described (Section 5.2), with a careful discussion of walkthroughs and inspections. This is followed by a definition of execution-based testing (Sections 5.3 and 5.4) and a discussion of behavioral properties of a product that must be tested, including utility, reliability, robustness, performance, and correctness (Sections 5.4.1 through 5.4.5). In Section 5.5 correctness proving is introduced and an example of such a proof is given in Section 5.5.1. The role of correctness proofs in software engineering is then analyzed (Sections 5.5.2 and 5.5.3). Another important issue is that systematic execution-based testing must be performed by the independent SQA group and not by the programmer (Section 5.6). Difficulties that arise in testing distributed software and real-time software are described in Sections 5.7 and 5.8, respectively. Finally, the issue of when testing can finally stop is discussed in Section 5.9.

FOR FURTHER READING

The attitude of software producers to the testing process has changed over the years, from viewing testing as a means of showing that a product runs correctly to the modern attitude that testing should be used to prevent requirement, specification, design, and implementation faults. This progression is described in [Gelperin and Hetzel, 1988].

Books on software quality assurance include [Dunn and Ullman, 1982] and [Schulmeyer and McManus, 1987]. There is also an IEEE Computer Society tutorial containing a number of useful papers on SQA [Chow, 1985]. Practical experiences with SQA are described in [Poston and Bruen, 1987]. The January 1996 issue of *IEEE Software* contains a number of articles on software quality, including [Tevonen, 1996]. The November 1996 issue of *IEEE Computer* also has articles on software quality. Yet another series of articles on software quality is in the June 1997 issue of the *Communications of the ACM*. Of particular interest are [Herbsleb, et al., 1997], which describes the effect on software quality of improving the software process; and [Arthur, 1997], a description of how total quality management (TQM) was used to improve software quality within McDonnell-Douglas. A different approach to achieving quality is described in [Onoma and Yamaura, 1995]. A way of assessing the overall quality of a software product is described in [Boloix and Robillard, 1995]. Metrics for software quality are discussed in [Schneidewind, 1994]. Reliability is discussed in a set of articles in the May 1995 issue of *IEEE Software.*

Good introductions to proving programs correct include Chapter 3 of [Manna, 1974], and [Baber, 1987]. One of the standard techniques of correctness proving is using so-called Hoare logic, as described in [Hoare, 1969]. An alternative approach to ensuring that products satisfy their specifications is to construct the product stepwise, checking that each step preserves correctness. This is described in [Dijkstra, 1968a], [Wirth, 1971], [Dahl, Dijkstra, and Hoare, 1972], and [Dijkstra, 1976]. Functional correctness is another approach. It has been developed by Mills and co-workers [Linger, Mills, and Witt, 1979; Mills, Basili, Gannon, and Hamlet, 1987] and is used in the IBM Cleanroom software development method [Dyer, 1992; Trammel, Binder, and Snyder, 1992] described in Section 13.11. A collection of research papers on correctness proving can be found in the August 1985 Special Issue of *ACM SIGSOFT Software Engineering Notes* devoted to the proceedings of the Third Formal Verification Workshop. An important article regarding acceptance of correctness proofs by the software engineering community is [DeMillo, Lipton, and Perlis, 1979].

The IEEE "Standard for Software Reviews and Audits" [IEEE 1028, 1988] is an excellent source of information on nonexecution-based testing. A paper on how to conduct inspections as well as their effectiveness is [Ackerman, Buchwald, and Lewski, 1989]. Inspection of a very large software product (2.5 million lines of code) is described in [Russell, 1991]. Other sources of information on experience with inspections are [Doolan, 1992] and [Weller, 1993]. Cost issues, such as reducing the size of a team and minimizing the time lost while waiting for reviewers to meet, are described in [Volta, 1993]. An experiment evaluating the costs and benefits of inspecting a large-scale software product is described in [Porter, Siy, Toman, and Votta, 1997]. A variety of useful papers on inspections appears in [Wheeler, Brykczynski, and Meeson, 1996].

The classic work on execution-based testing is [Myers, 1979], a work that has had a significant impact on the field of testing. [DeMillo, Lipton, and Sayward, 1978] is still an excellent source of information on selection of test data. [Beizer, 1990] is a compendium on testing, a true handbook on the subject. A similar work is [Hetzel, 1988].

Approaches to testing distributed software are presented in [Garcia-Molina, Germano, and Kohler, 1984] and [Wahl and Schach, 1988]. A wide-ranging source of material on testing real-time systems is [Quirk, 1985]. Glass has written a number of works on real-time systems, including [Glass, 1982] and [Glass, 1983]. Checking that real-time constraints have been satisfied is described in [Dasarathy, 1985].

The May 1989 issue of *IEEE Software* has a wide variety of papers on testing issues. Both execution-based and nonexecution-based testing are covered. The proceedings of the International Symposium on Software Testing and Analysis cover a similar broad spectrum of testing issues. Turning specifically to the object-oriented paradigm, the September 1994 issue of *Communications of the ACM* contains a number of articles on testing object-oriented software. The April 1997 issue of *Communications of the ACM* is devoted to debugging.

PROBLEMS

5.1 How are the terms *correctness proving, verification,* and *validation* used in this book?

5.2 A software development organization currently employs 78 software professionals, including 14 managers, all of whom do development as well as verification and validation of software. Latest figures show that 28 percent of their time is spent on verification and validation. The average annual cost to the company of a manager is $130,000, whereas nonmanagerial professionals cost $94,000 a year on average; both figures include overheads. Use cost–benefit analysis to determine whether a separate SQA group should be set up within the organization.

5.3 Repeat the cost–benefit analysis of Problem 5.2 for a firm with only seven software professionals, including two managers. Assume that the other figures remain unchanged.

5.4 You have been testing a module for 9 days and have found two faults. What does this tell you about the existence of other faults?

5.5 What are the similarities between a walkthrough and an inspection? What are the differences?

5.6 You are a member of the SQA group at Olde Fashioned Software. You suggest to your manager that inspections be introduced. He responds that he sees no reason why four people should waste their time looking for faults when one person can run test cases on the same piece of code. How do you respond?

5.7 You are the SQA manager at Hardy Hardware, a regional chain of 754 hardware stores. Your organization is considering buying a stock-control package for use throughout the organization. Before authorizing the purchase of the package, you decide to test it thoroughly. What properties of the package do you investigate?

5.8 All 754 stores in the Hardy Hardware organization are now to be connected by a communications network. A salesman is offering you a 4-week free trial to experiment with the communications package he is trying to sell you. What sort of software tests would you perform and why?

5.9 You are the admiral in charge of developing the software for controlling a new ship-to-ship missile. The software has been delivered to you for acceptance testing. What properties of the software do you test?

5.10 What happens to the correctness proof of Section 5.5.1 if loop invariant

$$s = y[0] + y[1] + \ldots + y[k-1]$$

is used instead of (5.4)?

5.11 Assume that you have some experience with loop invariants and that you know that invariant (5.4) is the correct invariant for the loop of Figure 5.6. Show that output specification (5.3) is a natural consequence of the loop invariant.

5.12 Consider the following code fragment:

```
k = 0;
g = 1;
while (k < n)
{
    k = k + 1;
    g = g * k;
}
```

Prove that this code fragment correctly computes $g = n!$ if $n \in \{1, 2, 3, \ldots\}$.

5.13 Can correctness proving solve the problem that the product as delivered to the client may not be what the client really needs? Give reasons for your answer.

5.14 How should Dijkstra's statement (Section 5.3) be changed to apply to correctness proofs rather than testing? Bear in mind the case study of Section 5.5.2.

5.15 Design and implement a solution to the Naur text-processing problem (Section 5.5.2) using the language specified by your instructor. Execute it against test data and record the number of faults that you find and also the cause of the faults (e.g., logic fault, loop counter fault). Do not correct any of the faults you detect. Now exchange products with a fellow student and see how many faults each of you finds in the other's product and whether or not they are new faults. Again record the cause of each fault and compare the fault types found by each of you. Tabulate the results for the class as a whole.

5.16 (Term Project) Explain how you would test the utility, reliability, robustness, performance, and correctness of the Air Gourmet product in Appendix A.

5.17 (Readings in Software Engineering) Your instructor will distribute copies of [Arthur, 1997]. Do you believe that TQM can improve software quality?

REFERENCES

[Ackerman, Buchwald, and Lewski, 1989] A. F. ACKERMAN, L. S. BUCHWALD, AND F. H. LEWSKI, "Software Inspections: An Effective Verification Process," *IEEE Software* **6** (May 1989), pp. 31–36.

[Arthur, 1997] L. J. ARTHUR, "Quantum Improvements in Software System Quality," *Communications of the ACM* **40** (June 1997), pp. 46–52.

[Baber, 1987] R. L. BABER, *The Spine of Software: Designing Provably Correct Software: Theory and Practice,* John Wiley and Sons, New York, 1987.

[Beizer, 1990] B. BEIZER, *Software Testing Techniques,* Second Edition, Van Nostrand Reinhold, New York, NY, 1990.

[Berry and Wing, 1985] D. M. BERRY AND J. M. WING, "Specifying and Prototyping: Some Thoughts on Why They Are Successful," in: *Formal Methods and Software Development, Proceedings of the International Joint Conference on Theory and Practice of Software Development, Volume 2,* Springer-Verlag, Berlin, 1985, pp. 117–28.

[Boehm, 1984a] B. W. BOEHM, "Verifying and Validating Software Requirements and Design Specifications," *IEEE Software* **1** (January 1984), pp. 75–88.

[Bologna, Quirk, and Taylor, 1985] S. BOLOGNA, W. J. QUIRK, AND J. R. TAYLOR, "Simulation and System Validation," in: *Verification and Validation of Real-Time Software,* W. J. Quirk (Editor), Springer-Verlag, Berlin, 1985, pp. 179–201.

[Boloix and Robillard, 1995] G. BOLOIX AND P. N. ROBILLARD, "A Software System Evaluation Framework," *IEEE Computer* **28** (December 1995), pp. 17–26.

[Bush, 1990] M. BUSH, "Improving Software Quality: The Use of Formal Inspections at the Jet Propulsion Laboratory," *Proceedings of the 12th International Conference on Software Engineering,* Nice, France, March 1990, pp. 196–99.

[Chow, 1985] T. S. CHOW (Editor), *Tutorial: Software Quality Assurance: A Practical Approach,* IEEE Computer Society Press, Washington, DC, 1985.

[Dahl, Dijkstra, and Hoare, 1972] O.-J. DAHL, E. W. DIJKSTRA, AND C. A. R. HOARE, *Structured Programming,* Academic Press, New York, 1972.

[Dasarathy, 1985] B. DASARATHY, "Timing Constraints of Real-Time Systems: Constructs for Expressing Them, Methods of Validating Them," *IEEE Transactions on Software Engineering* **SE-11** (January 1985), pp. 80–86.

[DeMillo, Lipton, and Perlis, 1979] R. A. DEMILLO, R. J. LIPTON, AND A. J. PERLIS, "Social Processes and Proofs of Theorems and Programs," *Communications of the ACM* **22** (May 1979), pp. 271–80.

[DeMillo, Lipton, and Sayward, 1978] R. A. DEMILLO, R. J. LIPTON, AND F. G. SAYWARD, "Hints on Test Data Selection: Help for the Practicing Programmer," *IEEE Computer* **11** (April 1978), pp. 34–43.

[Dijkstra, 1968a] E. W. DIJKSTRA, "A Constructive Approach to the Problem of Program Correctness," *BIT* **8** (No. 3, 1968), pp. 174–86.

[Dijkstra, 1972] E. W. DIJKSTRA, "The Humble Programmer," *Communications of the ACM* **15** (October 1972), pp. 859–66.

[Dijkstra, 1976] E. W. DIJKSTRA, *A Discipline of Programming,* Prentice Hall, Englewood Cliffs, NJ, 1976.

[Doolan, 1992] E. P. DOOLAN, "Experience with Fagan's Inspection Method," *Software—Practice and Experience* **22** (February 1992), pp. 173–82.

[Dunn, 1984] R. H. DUNN, *Software Defect Removal,* McGraw-Hill, New York, 1984.

[Dunn and Ullman, 1982] R. DUNN AND R. ULLMAN, *Quality Assurance for Computer Software,* McGraw-Hill, New York, 1982.

[Dyer, 1992] M. DYER, *The Cleanroom Approach to Quality Software Development,* John Wiley and Sons, New York, 1992.

[Fagan, 1976] M. E. FAGAN, "Design and Code Inspections to Reduce Errors in Program Development," *IBM Systems Journal* **15** (No. 3, 1976), pp. 182–211.

[Fagan, 1986] M. E. FAGAN, "Advances in Software Inspections," *IEEE Transactions on Software Engineering* **SE-12** (July 1986), pp. 744–51.

[Fowler, 1986] P. J. FOWLER, "In-Process Inspections of Workproducts at AT&T," *AT&T Technical Journal* **65** (March/April 1986), pp. 102–112.

[Garcia-Molina, Germano, and Kohler, 1984] H. GARCIA-MOLINA, F. GERMANO, JR., AND W. H. KOHLER, "Debugging a Distributed Computer System," *IEEE Transactions on Software Engineering* **SE-10** (March 1984), pp. 210–19.

[Garman, 1981] J. R. GARMAN, "The 'Bug' Heard 'Round the World," *ACM SIGSOFT Software Engineering Notes* **6** (October 1981), pp. 3–10.

[Gelperin and Hetzel, 1988] D. GELPERIN AND B. HETZEL, "The Growth of Software Testing," *Communications of the ACM* **31** (June 1988), pp. 687–95.

[Glass, 1982] R. L. GLASS, "Real-Time Checkout: The 'Source Error First' Approach," *Software—Practice and Experience* **12** (January 1982), pp. 77–83.

[Glass, 1983] R. L. GLASS (EDITOR), *Real-Time Software,* Prentice Hall, Englewood Cliffs, NJ, 1983.

[Goodenough and Gerhart, 1975] J. B. GOODENOUGH AND S. L. GERHART, "Toward a Theory of Test Data Selection," *Proceedings of the Third International Conference on Reliable Software,* Los Angeles, 1975, pp. 493–510. Also published in: *IEEE Transactions on Software Engineering* **SE-1** (June 1975), pp. 156–73. Revised version: J. B. Goodenough, and S. L. Gerhart, "Toward a Theory of Test Data Selection: Data Selection Criteria," in: *Current Trends in Programming Methodology, Volume 2,* R. T. Yeh (Editor), Prentice Hall, Englewood Cliffs, NJ, 1977, pp. 44–79.

[Goodenough, 1979] J. B. GOODENOUGH, "A Survey of Program Testing Issues," in: *Research Directions in Software Technology,* P. Wegner (Editor), The MIT Press, Cambridge, MA, 1979, pp. 316–40.

[Herbsleb et al., 1997] J. HERBSLEB, D. ZUBROW, D. GOLDENSON, W. HAYES, AND M. PAULK, "Software Quality and the Capability Maturity Model," *Communications of the ACM* **40** (June 1997), pp. 30–40.

[Hetzel, 1988] W. HETZEL, *The Complete Guide to Software Testing,*Second Edition, QED Information Systems, Wellesley, MA, 1988.

[Hoare, 1969] C. A. R. HOARE, "An Axiomatic Basis for Computer Programming," *Communications of the ACM* **12** (October 1969), pp. 576–83.

[Hoare, 1981] C. A. R. HOARE, "The Emperor's Old Clothes," *Communications of the ACM* **24** (February 1981), pp. 75–83.

[IEEE 610.12, 1990] "A Glossary of Software Engineering Terminology," IEEE 610.12-1990, Institute of Electrical and Electronic Engineers, Inc., 1990.

[IEEE 1028, 1988] "Standard for Software Reviews and Audits," IEEE 1028, Institute of Electrical and Electronic Engineers, Inc., 1988.

[Jones, 1978] T. C. JONES, "Measuring Programming Quality and Productivity," *IBM Systems Journal* **17** (No. 1, 1978), pp. 39–63.

[Kelly, Sherif, and Hops, 1992] J. C. KELLY, J. S. SHERIF, AND J. HOPS, "An Analysis of Defect Densities Found during Software Inspections," *Journal of Systems and Software* **17** (January 1992), pp. 111–17.

[Lamport, 1980] L. LAMPORT, "'Sometime' Is Sometimes 'Not Never': On the Temporal Logic of Programs," *Proceedings of the Seventh Annual ACM Symposium on Principles of Programming Languages,* Las Vegas, NV, 1980, pp. 174–85.

[Landwehr, 1983] C. E. LANDWEHR, "The Best Available Technologies for Computer Security," *IEEE Computer* **16** (July 1983), pp. 86–100.

[Leavenworth, 1970] B. LEAVENWORTH, Review #19420, *Computing Reviews* **11** (July 1970), pp. 396–97.

[Linger, Mills, and Witt, 1979] R. C. LINGER, H. D. MILLS, AND B. I. WITT, *Structured Programming: Theory and Practice,* Addison-Wesley, Reading, MA, 1979.

[London, 1971] R. L. LONDON, "Software Reliability through Proving Programs Correct," *Proceedings of the IEEE International Symposium on Fault-Tolerant Computing,* March 1971.

[Manna and Pnueli, 1992] Z. MANNA AND A. PNUELI, *The Temporal Logic of Reactive and Concurrent Systems,* Springer-Verlag, New York, 1992.

[Manna and Waldinger, 1978] Z. MANNA AND R. WALDINGER, "The Logic of Computer Programming," *IEEE Transactions on Software Engineering* **SE-4** (1978), pp. 199–229.

[Manna, 1974] Z. MANNA, *Mathematical Theory of Computation,* McGraw-Hill, New York, 1974.

[Meyer, 1992b] B. MEYER, *Eiffel: The Language,* Prentice Hall, New York, 1992.

[Mills, Basili, Gannon, and Hamlet, 1987] H. D. MILLS, V. R. BASILI, J. D. GANNON, AND R. G. HAMLET, *Principles of Computer Programming: A Mathematical Approach,* Allyn and Bacon, Newton, MA, 1987.

[Myers, 1979] G. J. MYERS, *The Art of Software Testing,* John Wiley and Sons, New York, 1979.

[Naur, 1969] P. NAUR, "Programming by Action Clusters," *BIT* **9** (No. 3, 1969), pp. 250–58.

[New, 1992] R. NEW, Personal communication, 1992.

[Onoma and Yamaura, 1995] A. K. ONOMA AND T. YAMAURA, "Practical Steps toward Quality Development," *IEEE Software* **12** (September 1995), pp. 68–77.

[Porter, Siy, Toman, and Votta, 1997] A. A. PORTER, H. P. SIY, C. A. TOMAN, AND L. G. VOTTA, "Assessing Software Review Meetings: Results of a Comparative Analysis of Two Experimental Studies," *IEEE Transactions on Software Engineering* **23** (March 1997), pp. 129–45.

[Poston and Bruen, 1987] R. M. POSTON AND M. W. BRUEN, "Counting Down to Zero Software Failures," *IEEE Software* **4** (September 1987), pp. 54–61.

[Quirk, 1983] W. J. QUIRK, "Recent Developments in the SPECK Specification System," Report CSS.146, Harwell, UK, 1983.

[Quirk, 1985] W. J. QUIRK (Editor), *Verification and Validation of Real-Time Software,* Springer-Verlag, Berlin, 1985.

[Russell, 1991] G. W. RUSSELL, "Experience with Inspection in Ultralarge-Scale Developments," *IEEE Software* **8** (January 1991), pp. 25–31.

[Schulmeyer and McManus, 1987] G. G. SCHULMEYER AND J. I. MCMANUS (Editors), *Handbook of Software Quality Assurance,* Van Nostrand Reinhold, New York, 1987.

[Seitz, 1985] C. L. SEITZ, "The Cosmic Cube," *Communications of the ACM* **28** (January 1985), pp. 22–33.

[Schneidewind, 1994] N. F. SCHNEIDEWIND, "Validating Metrics for Ensuring Space Shuttle Flight Software Quality," *IEEE Computer* **27** (August 1994), pp. 50–57.

[Silberschatz and Galvin, 1998] A. SILBERSCHATZ AND P. B. GALVIN, *Operating System Concepts,* Fifth Edition, Addison-Wesley, Reading, MA, 1998.

[Tamir, 1980] M. TAMIR, "ADI: Automatic Derivation of Invariants," *IEEE Transactions on Software Engineering* **SE-6** (January 1980), pp. 40–48.

[Tevonen, 1996] I. TEVONEN, "Support for Quality-Based Design and Inspection," *IEEE Software* **13** (January 1996), pp. 44–54.

[Trammel, Binder, and Snyder, 1992] C. J. TRAMMEL, L. H. BINDER, AND C. E. SNYDER, "The Automated Production Control Documentation System: A Case Study in Cleanroom Software Engineering," *ACM Transactions on Software Engineering and Methodology* **1** (January 1992), pp. 81–94.

[Volta, 1993] L. G. VOLTA, JR., "Does Every Inspection Need a Meeting?" *Proceedings of the First ACM SIGSOFT Symposium on the Foundations of Software Engineering, ACM SIGSOFT Software Engineering Notes* **18** (December 1993), pp. 107–14.

[Wahl and Schach, 1988] N. J. WAHL AND S. R. SCHACH, "A Methodology and Distributed Tool for Debugging Dataflow Programs," *Proceedings of the Second Workshop on Software Testing, Verification, and Analysis,* Banff, Canada, July 1988, pp. 98–105.

[Weller, 1993] E. F. WELLER, "Lessons from Three Years of Inspection Data," *IEEE Software* **10** (September 1993), pp. 38–45.

[Wheeler, Brykczynski, and Meeson, 1996] D. A. WHEELER, B. BRYKCZYNSKI, AND R. N. MEESON, JR., *Software Inspection: An Industry Best Practice,* IEEE Computer Society, Los Alamitos, CA, 1996.

[Wirth, 1971] N. WIRTH, "Program Development by Stepwise Refinement," *Communications of the ACM* **14** (April 1971), pp. 221–27.

chapter

6

Introduction to Objects

Some of the more lurid computer magazines seem to suggest that the object-oriented paradigm was a sudden and dramatic new discovery of the mid-1980s, a revolutionary alternative to the then popular structured paradigm. That is not the case. Instead, the theory of modularity underwent steady progress during the 1970s and the 1980s, and objects were simply a logical development within the theory of modularity (but see the Just in Case You Wanted to Know box on page 172). This chapter describes objects in the context of modularity.

This approach is taken because it is extremely difficult to use objects correctly without understanding why the object-oriented paradigm is superior to the structured paradigm. And to do that, it is necessary to appreciate that an object is merely the next step in the body of knowledge that begins with the concept of a module.

6.1 What Is a Module?

When a large product consists of a single monolithic block of code, maintenance is a nightmare. Even for the author of such a monstrosity, attempting to debug the code is extremely difficult; for another programmer to understand it is virtually impossible. The solution is to break the product into smaller pieces, called modules. What is a module? Is the way a product is broken into modules important in itself, or is it important only to break a large product into smaller pieces of code?

An early attempt to describe modules is the work of Stevens, Myers, and Constantine. They defined a module as "A set of one or more contiguous program statements having a name by which other parts of the system can invoke it, and preferably having its own distinct set of variable names" [Stevens, Myers, and Constantine, 1974]. In other words, a module consists of a single block of code that can be invoked in the way that a procedure, function, or method is invoked. This definition seems to be extremely broad. It includes procedures and functions of all kinds, whether internal or separately compiled. It includes COBOL paragraphs and sections, even though they cannot have their own variables, because the definition states that the property of possessing a distinct set of variable names

JUST IN CASE YOU WANTED TO KNOW

Object-oriented concepts were introduced as early as 1966 in the simulation language Simula 67 [Dahl and Nygaard, 1966]. However, at that time the technology was too radical for practical use, so it lay dormant until the early 1980s when it was essentially reinvented within the context of the theory of modularity.

There are other examples in this chapter of the way that leading edge technology lies dormant until the world is ready for it. For example, information hiding (Section 6.6) was first proposed within the software context by David Parnas in 1971 [Parnas, 1971], but the technology was not widely adopted until about 10 years later when encapsulation and abstract data types had become part of software engineering.

It seems that we human beings adopt new ideas only when we are ready to use them, not necessarily when they are first presented.

is merely "preferable." It also includes modules that are nested inside other modules. But broad as it is, the definition does not go far enough. For example, an assembler macro is not invoked and therefore, by the preceding definition, is not a module. In C and C++, a header file of declarations that is #**include**d in a product is similarly not invoked; neither is an Ada package (implementation of an abstract data type), nor an Ada generic (macro). In short, this definition is too restrictive.

Yourdon and Constantine give a broader definition, namely, "A module is a lexically contiguous sequence of program statements, bounded by boundary elements, having an aggregate identifier" [Yourdon and Constantine, 1979]. Examples of boundary elements are begin . . . end pairs in a block-structured language like Pascal or Ada, or {. . .} pairs in C++ or Java. This definition not only includes all the cases excluded by the previous definition, but is broad enough to be used throughout this book. In particular, procedures and functions of the classical paradigm are modules. In the object-oriented paradigm, an object is a module and so is a method within an object.

To understand the importance of modularization, consider the following somewhat fanciful example. John Fence is a highly incompetent computer architect. He has still not discovered that both NAND gates and NOR gates are complete, that is, every circuit can be built with only NAND gates or with only NOR gates. John therefore decides to build an ALU, shifter, and 16 registers using AND, OR, and NOT gates. The resulting computer is shown in Figure 6.1. The three components are connected together in a simple fashion. Now our architect friend decides that the circuit should be fabricated on three silicon chips, so he designs the three chips shown in Figure 6.2. One chip has all the gates of the ALU, a second contains the shifter, and the third is for the registers. At this point, John vaguely recalls that someone in a bar told him that it is best to build chips so that they have only one kind of gate, so he redesigns his chips. On chip 1 he puts all the AND gates, on chip 2 all the OR gates, and all the NOT gates go onto chip 3. The resulting "work of art" is shown schematically in Figure 6.3.

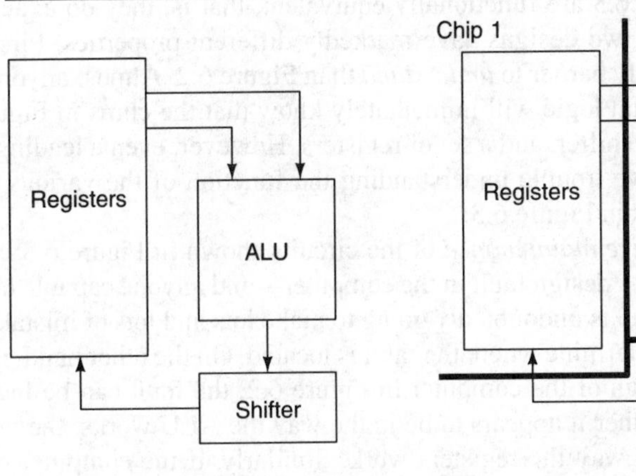

Figure 6.1 Design of computer.

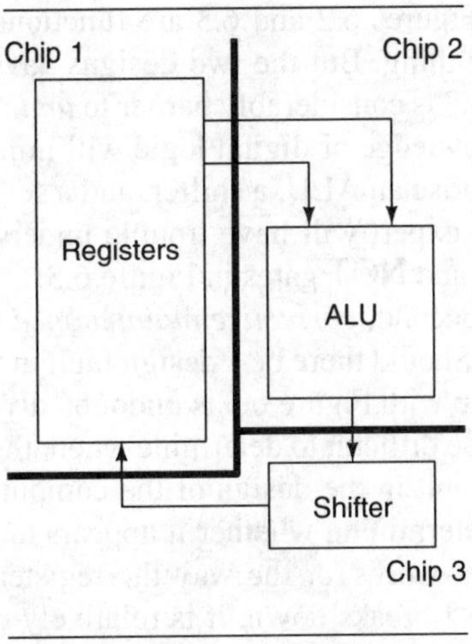

Figure 6.2 Computer of Figure 6.1 fabricated on three chips.

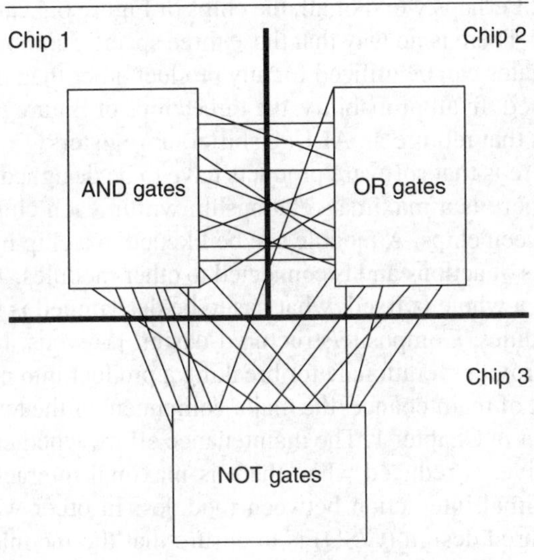

Figure 6.3 Computer of Figure 6.1 fabricated on three other chips.

Figures 6.2 and 6.3 are functionally equivalent, that is, they do exactly the same thing. But the two designs have markedly different properties. First, Figure 6.3 is considerably harder to *understand* than Figure 6.2. Almost anyone with a knowledge of digital logic will immediately know that the chips in Figure 6.2 comprise an ALU, a shifter, and a set of registers. However, even a leading hardware expert will have trouble understanding the function of the various AND, OR, and NOT gates in Figure 6.3.

Second, *corrective maintenance* of the circuits shown in Figure 6.3 is difficult. Should there be a design fault in the computer—and anyone capable of coming up with Figure 6.3 is undoubtedly going to make lots and lots of mistakes—it will be difficult to determine where the fault is located. On the other hand, if there is a fault in the design of the computer in Figure 6.2, the fault can be localized by determining whether it appears to be in the way the ALU works, the way the shifter works, or the way the registers work. Similarly, if the computer of Figure 6.2 breaks down, it is relatively easy to determine which chip to replace; if the computer in Figure 6.3 breaks down, it is probably best to replace all three chips.

Third, the computer of Figure 6.3 is difficult to *extend* or *enhance.* If a new type of ALU is needed or if faster registers are required, it is back to the drawing board. But the design of the computer of Figure 6.2 makes it easy to replace the appropriate chip. Perhaps worst of all, the chips of Figure 6.3 cannot be *reused* in any new product. There is no way that those three specific combinations of AND, OR, and NOT gates can be utilized for any product other than the one for which they were designed. In all probability, the three chips of Figure 6.2 can be reused in other products that require an ALU, a shifter, or registers.

The point here is that software products have to be designed to look like Figure 6.2, where there is a maximal relationship within each chip and a minimal relationship between chips. A module can be likened to a chip in that it performs an action or series of actions and is connected to other modules. The functionality of the product as a whole is fixed; what has to be determined is how to break the product into modules. Composite/structured design [Stevens, Myers, and Constantine, 1974] provides a rationale for breaking a product into modules as a way to reduce the cost of maintenance, the major component of the total software budget, as pointed out in Chapter 1. The maintenance effort, whether corrective, perfective, or adaptive, is reduced when there is maximal interaction within each module and minimal interaction between modules. In other words, the aim of composite/structured design (C/SD) is to ensure that the module decomposition of the product resembles Figure 6.2 rather than Figure 6.3.

Myers quantified the ideas of module *cohesion,* the degree of interaction within a module, and module *coupling,* the degree of interaction between two modules [Myers, 1978b]. To be more precise, Myers used the term *strength* rather than *cohesion.* However, cohesion is preferable because modules can have high strength or low strength, and there is something inherently contradictory in the expression *low strength*—if something is not strong, it is weak. In order to prevent terminological inexactitude, C/SD now uses the term *cohesion.* Some authors have used the term *binding* in place of *coupling*. Unfortunately, *binding* is also used in other contexts in computer science, such as the binding of values to variables. But *coupling* does not have these overtones and is therefore preferable.

It is necessary at this point to distinguish between the action of a module, the logic of a module, and the context of a module. The *action* of a module is what it does, that is, its behavior. For example, the action of module m is to compute the square root of its argument. The *logic* of a module is how the module performs its action; in the case of module m, the specific way of computing the square root is Newton's method [Young and Gregory, 1972]. The *context* of a module is the specific usage of that module. For example, module m is used to compute the square root of a double precision integer. A key point in C/SD is that the name assigned to a module is its action and not its logic or its context. Thus, in C/SD, module m should be named compute square root; its logic and its context are irrelevant from the viewpoint of its name.

6.2 COHESION

Myers defined seven categories or levels of cohesion [Myers, 1978b]. In the light of modern theoretical computer science, Myers's first two levels are considered to be equally good. More precisely, as will be shown, functional cohesion is optimal for the structured paradigm, whereas informational cohesion is optimal for the object-oriented paradigm. The resulting ranking is shown in Figure 6.4. This is not a linear scale of any sort. It is merely a relative ranking, a way of determining which types of cohesion are high (good) and which are low (bad).

In order to understand what constitutes a module with high cohesion, it is necessary to start at the other end and consider the lower cohesion levels.

6.2.1 COINCIDENTAL COHESION

A module has coincidental cohesion if it performs multiple completely unrelated actions. An example of a module with coincidental cohesion is a module named

7.	Functional cohesion Informational cohesion	(Good)
5.	Communicational cohesion	
4.	Procedural cohesion	
3.	Temporal cohesion	
2.	Logical cohesion	
1.	Coincidental cohesion	(Bad)

Figure 6.4 Levels of cohesion.

print next line, reverse the string of characters comprising the second argument, add 7 to the fifth argument, convert the fourth argument to floating point.

An obvious question is: How can such modules possibly arise in practice? The most common cause is as a consequence of rigidly enforcing rules such as "every module shall consist of between 35 and 50 executable statements." If a software organization insists that modules must neither be too big nor too small, then two undesirable things will happen. First, two or more otherwise ideal smaller modules will have to be lumped together to create a larger module with coincidental cohesion. Second, pieces hacked from well-designed modules that management considers too large will be combined, again resulting in modules with coincidental cohesion.

Why is coincidental cohesion so bad? Modules with coincidental cohesion suffer from two serious drawbacks. First, such modules degrade the maintainability of the product, both corrective maintenance and enhancement. From the viewpoint of trying to understand a product, modularization with coincidental cohesion is worse than no modularization at all [Shneiderman and Mayer, 1975]. Second, these modules are not reusable. It is extremely unlikely that the module with coincidental cohesion in the first paragraph of this section could be reused in any other product.

Lack of reusability is a serious drawback. The cost of building software is so great that it is essential to try to reuse modules wherever possible. Designing, coding, documenting, and above all, testing a module are time-consuming and hence costly processes. If an existing well-designed, thoroughly tested, and properly documented module can be used in another product, then management should insist that the existing module be reused. But there is no way that a module with coincidental cohesion can be reused, and the money spent to develop it can never be recouped. (Reuse is discussed in detail in Chapter 7.)

It is generally easy to rectify a module with coincidental cohesion—because it performs multiple actions, break the module into smaller modules that each perform one action.

6.2.2 LOGICAL COHESION

A module has logical cohesion when it performs a series of related actions, one of which is selected by the calling module. The following are all examples of modules with logical cohesion:

Example 1 Module new operation which is invoked as follows:

function code = 7;
new operation (function code, dummy 1, dummy 2, dummy 3);
// dummy 1, dummy 2, *and* dummy 3 *are dummy variables,*
// *not used if* function code *is equal to* 7

In this example, new operation is called with four arguments, but as stated in the pseudocode comment lines, three of them are not needed if function code is equal to 7. This degrades readability, with the usual implications for maintenance, both corrective and enhancement.

Example 2 An object that performs all input and output.

Example 3 A module performing editing of insertions and deletions and modifications of master file records.

Example 4 A module with logical cohesion in an early version of OS/VS2 performed 13 different actions; its interface contained 21 pieces of data [Myers, 1978b].

There are two problems when a module has logical cohesion. First, the interface is difficult to understand, Example 1 being a case in point, and comprehensibility of the module as a whole may suffer as a result. Second, the code for more than one action may be intertwined, leading to severe maintenance problems. For instance, a module that performs all input and output may be structured as shown in Figure 6.5. If a new tape unit is installed, it may be necessary to modify the sections numbered 1, 2, 3, 4, 6, 9, and 10. These changes may adversely affect other forms of input/output, such as laser printer output, because the laser printer will be affected by changes to sections 1 and 3. This intertwined property is characteristic of modules with logical cohesion. A further consequence of this intertwining is that it is difficult to reuse such a module in other products.

module performing all input and output
1. Code for all input and output
2. Code for input only
3. Code for output only
4. Code for disk and tape I/O
5. Code for disk I/O
6. Code for tape I/O
7. Code for disk input
8. Code for disk output
9. Code for tape input
10. Code for tape output
⋮
37. Code for keyboard input

Figure 6.5 Module that performs all input and output.

6.2.3 TEMPORAL COHESION

A module has temporal cohesion when it performs a series of actions related in time. An example of a module with temporal cohesion is one named open old master file, new master file, transaction file, and print file, initialize sales region table, read first transaction record, and first old master file record. In the bad old days before C/SD, such a module would be called perform initialization.

The actions of this module are weakly related to one another, but are more strongly related to actions in other modules. Consider, for example, the sales region table. It is initialized in this module, but actions such as update sales region table and print sales region table are located in other modules. Thus, if the structure of the sales region table is changed, perhaps because the organization is expanding into areas of the country where it has previously not done business, a number of modules will have to be changed. Not only is there more chance of a regression fault (a fault caused by a change being made to an apparently unrelated part of the product), but if the number of affected modules is large, there is a good chance that one or two modules will be overlooked. It is much better to have all the operations on the sales region table in one module, as described in Section 6.2.6. These operations can then be invoked, when needed, by other modules. In addition, a module with temporal cohesion is unlikely to be reusable in a different product.

6.2.4 PROCEDURAL COHESION

A module has procedural cohesion if it performs a series of actions related by the sequence of steps to be followed by the product. An example of a module with procedural cohesion is read part number from database and update repair record on maintenance file.

This is clearly better than temporal cohesion—at least the actions are procedurally related to one another. But even so, the actions are still weakly connected, and again the module is unlikely to be reusable in another product. The solution is to break up a module with procedural cohesion into separate modules each performing one action.

6.2.5 COMMUNICATIONAL COHESION

A module has communicational cohesion if it performs a series of actions related by the sequence of steps to be followed by the product and if all the actions are performed on the same data. Two examples of modules with communicational cohesion are update record in database and write *it* to the audit trail, and calculate new trajectory and send *it* to the printer. This is better than procedural cohesion because the actions of the module are more closely connected, but it still has the same drawback as coincidental, logical, temporal, and procedural cohesion, namely, that the module cannot be reused. Again the solution is to break such a module into separate modules performing one action.

In passing, it is interesting to note that Berry uses the term *flowchart cohesion* to refer to temporal, procedural, and communicational cohesion because the actions performed by such modules are adjacent in the product flowchart [Berry, 1978]. The actions are adjacent in the case of temporal cohesion because they are performed at the same time. They are adjacent in procedural cohesion because the algorithm requires the actions to be performed in series. They are adjacent in communicational cohesion because, in addition to being peformed in series, the actions are performed on the same data, and it is therefore natural that these actions should be adjacent in the flowchart.

6.2.6 INFORMATIONAL COHESION

A module has informational cohesion if it performs a number of actions, each with its own entry point, with independent code for each action, all performed on the same data structure. An example is given in Figure 6.6. This does not violate the tenets of structured programming; each piece of code has exactly one entry point and one exit point. A major difference between logical cohesion and informational cohesion is that the various actions of a module with logical cohesion are intertwined, whereas in a module with informational cohesion the code for each action is completely independent.

A module with informational cohesion is essentially an implementation of an abstract data type, as explained in Section 6.5, and all the advantages of using an abstract data type are gained when a module with informational cohesion is used. Because an object is essentially an instantiation (instance) of an abstract data type (Section 6.7), an object, too, is a module with informational cohesion.

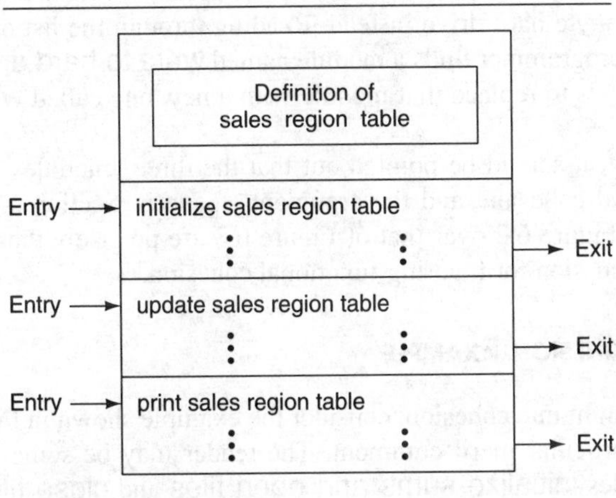

Figure 6.6 Module with informational cohesion.

This is why it was stated in Section 6.2 that informational cohesion is optimal for the object-oriented paradigm.[1]

6.2.7 Functional Cohesion

A module that performs exactly one action or achieves a single goal has functional cohesion. Examples of such modules are get temperature of furnace; compute orbital of electron; write to diskette; and calculate sales commission.

A module with functional cohesion can often be reused because the one action that it performs will often need to be performed in other products. A properly designed, thoroughly tested, and well-documented module with functional cohesion is a valuable (economic and technical) asset to any software organization and should be reused as often as possible (but see Section 7.5).

Maintenance is easier to perform on a module with functional cohesion. First, functional cohesion leads to fault isolation. If it is clear that the temperature of the furnace is not being read correctly, then the fault is almost certainly in module get temperature of furnace. Similarly, if the orbital of an electron is incorrectly computed, then the first place to look is compute orbital of electron.

Once the fault has been localized to a single module, the next step is to make the required changes. Because a module with functional cohesion performs one and only one action, such a module will generally be easier to understand than a module with lower cohesion. This ease in understanding also simplifies the maintenance task. Finally, when the change is made, the chance of that change impacting other modules is slight, especially if the coupling between modules is low (Section 6.3).

Functional cohesion is also valuable when a product has to be extended. For example, suppose that a personal computer has a 1 Megabyte hard drive but that the manufacturer now wishes to market a more powerful model of the computer with a 3 Megabyte hard drive instead. Reading through the list of modules, the maintenance programmer finds a module named write to hard drive. The obvious thing to do is to replace that module with a new one called write to larger hard drive.

In passing, it should be pointed out that the three "modules" of Figure 6.2 have functional cohesion, and the arguments made in Section 6.1 for favoring the design of Figure 6.2 over that of Figure 6.3 are precisely those made in the preceding discussion for favoring functional cohesion.

6.2.8 Cohesion Example

For further insight into cohesion, consider the example shown in Figure 6.7. Two modules in particular merit comment. The reader may be somewhat surprised that the modules initialize sums and open files and close files and print

[1] The discussion in this paragraph assumes that the abstract data type or object is well designed. If the methods of an object perform completely unrelated actions, then the object has coincidental cohesion.

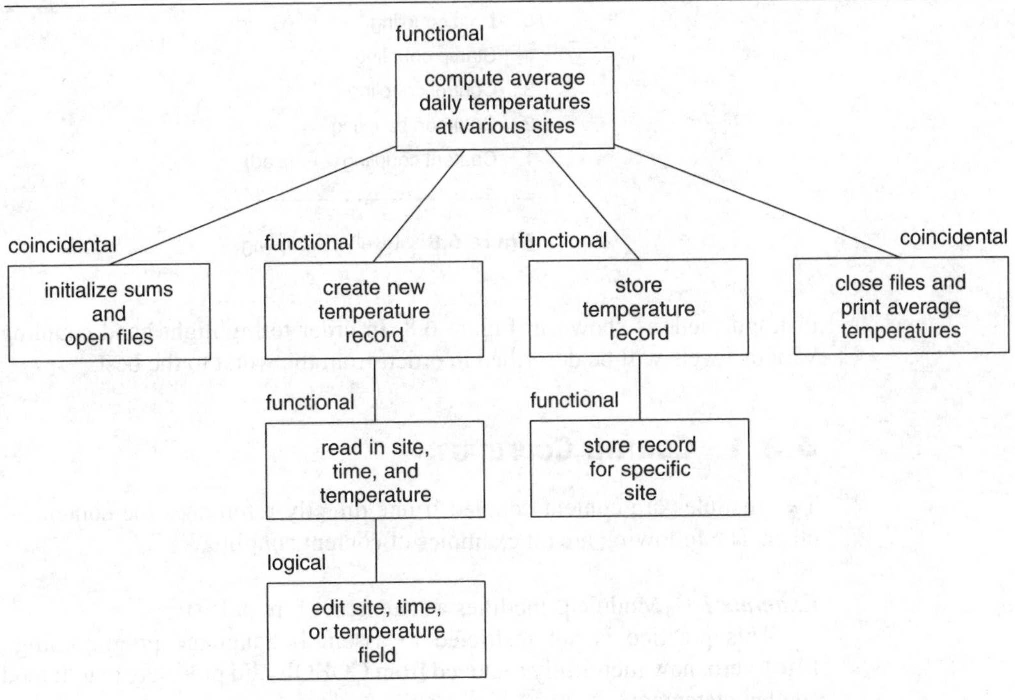

Figure 6.7 Module interconnection diagram showing cohesion of each module.

average temperatures have both been labeled as having coincidental cohesion, rather than temporal cohesion. First consider module initialize sums and open files. It performs two actions related in time in that both have to be done before any calculations can be performed, and therefore it seems that the module has temporal cohesion. Although the two actions of initialize sums and open files are indeed performed at the beginning of the calculation, there is another factor involved. Initializing the sums is related to the problem, but opening files has nothing to do with the problem itself. The rule when two or more different levels of cohesion can be assigned to a module is to assign the lowest possible level. Thus, because initialize sums and open files could have either temporal or coincidental cohesion, the lower of the two levels of cohesion, namely, coincidental, is assigned to that module. That is also the reason why close files and print average temperatures has coincidental cohesion.

6.3 COUPLING

Recall that cohesion is the degree of interaction within a module. *Coupling* is the degree of interaction between two modules. As before, a number of levels can be

5.	Data coupling	(Good)
4.	Stamp coupling	
3.	Control coupling	
2.	Common coupling	
1.	Content coupling	(Bad)

Figure 6.8 Levels of coupling.

distinguished, as shown in Figure 6.8. In order to highlight good coupling, the various levels will be described in order, from the worst to the best.

6.3.1 CONTENT COUPLING

Two modules are content-coupled if one directly references the contents of the other. The following are all examples of content coupling:

Example 1: Module p modifies a statement of module q.

This practice is not restricted to assembly language programming. The **alter** verb, now mercifully removed from COBOL, did precisely that; it modified another statement.

Example 2: Module p refers to local data of module q in terms of some numerical displacement within q.

Example 3: Module p branches to a local label of module q.

Suppose that module p and module q are content-coupled. One of the many dangers is that almost any change to q, even recompiling q with a new compiler or assembler, requires a change to p. Furthermore, it is impossible to reuse module p in some new product without reusing module q as well. When two modules are content-coupled, they are inextricably interlinked.

6.3.2 COMMON COUPLING

Two modules are common-coupled if they both have access to the same global data. The situation is depicted in Figure 6.9. Instead of communicating with one another by passing arguments, modules cca and ccb can access and change the value of global variable. The most common situation in which this arises is when both cca and ccb have access to the same database and can read and write the same record. For common coupling it is necessary that both modules can read *and* write to the database; if the database access mode is read-only, then this is not common coupling. But there are other ways of implementing common coupling, including use of the **common** statement in FORTRAN, the (nonstandard)

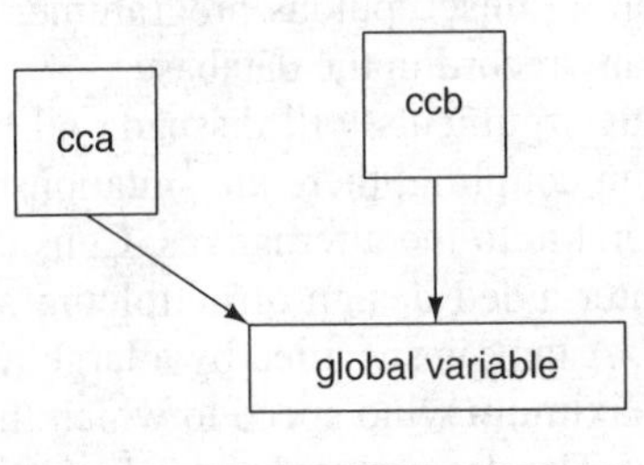

Figure 6.9 Common coupling.

```
while (global variable == 0)
{
  if (argument xyz > 25)
    module 3 ();
  else
    module 4 ();
}
```

Figure 6.10 Pseudocode fragment reflecting common coupling.

common statement in COBOL, the **global** statement in COBOL-80, and the C++ or Java modifier **public**.

This form of coupling is undesirable for a number of reasons. First, it contradicts the spirit of structured programming in that the resulting code is virtually unreadable. Consider the pseudocode fragment shown in Figure 6.10. If global variable is a global variable, then its value may be changed by module 3, module 4, or any module called by them. Determining under what conditions the loop terminates is then a nontrivial question; if a run-time failure occurs it may be difficult to reconstruct what happened, because any one of a number of modules could have changed the value of global variable.

A second difficulty is that modules can have side effects that affect their readability. To see this, consider the call edit this transaction (record 7). If there is common coupling, this call could change not just the value of record 7, but also any global variable that can be accessed by that module. In short, the entire module must be read to find out precisely what it does.

Third, if a maintenance change is made in one module to the declaration of a global variable, then every module that can access that global variable has to be changed. Furthermore, all changes must be consistent.

A fourth problem is that modules that are common-coupled are difficult to reuse because the identical list of global variables has to be supplied each time the module is reused.

The fifth problem is potentially the most dangerous. As a consequence of common coupling, a module may be exposed to more data than it needs. This defeats any attempts to control data access and may ultimately lead to computer crime. Many types of computer crime need some form of collusion. Properly designed software should not allow any one programmer to have access to all the data and/or modules needed to commit a crime. For example, a programmer writing the check printing part of a payroll product needs to have access to employee records, but in a well-designed product such access will be exclusively in read-only mode, thus precluding the programmer making unauthorized changes to his or her monthly salary. In order to make such changes, the programmer has to find another dishonest employee, one with access to the relevant records in update mode. But if the product has been badly designed and every module can access the payroll database in update mode, then an unscrupulous programmer acting alone can make unauthorized changes to any record in the database.

Although it is hoped that the previous arguments will dissuade all but the most daring of readers from using common coupling, there are situations where common coupling might seem to be preferable to the alternatives. Consider, for example, a product that performs computer-aided design of petroleum storage tanks [Schach and Stevens-Guille, 1979]. A tank is specified by a large number of descriptors such as height, diameter, maximum wind speed to which the tank will be subjected, and insulation thickness. The descriptors have to be initialized but do not change in value thereafter, and most of the modules in the product need to have access to the values of the descriptors. Suppose that there are 55 tank descriptors. If all these descriptors are passed as arguments to every module, then the interface to each module will consist of at least 55 arguments, and the potential for faults is huge. Even in a language like Ada, which requires strict type checking of arguments, it is still possible to interchange two arguments of the same type, a fault that would not be detected by a type checker.

One solution is to put all the tank descriptors in a database and to design the product in such a way that one module initializes the values of all the descriptors, whereas all the other modules access the database exclusively in read-only mode. However, if the database solution is impractical, perhaps because the specified implementation language cannot be interfaced with the available database management system, then an alternative is to use common coupling, but in a controlled way. That is, the product should be designed so that the 55 descriptors are initialized by one module, but none of the other modules changes the value of a descriptor. This programming style has to be enforced by management, unlike the database solution where enforcement is imposed by the software. Thus, in situations where there is no good alternative to the use of common coupling, close supervision by management can reduce some of the risks. A better solution, however, is to obviate common coupling by using information hiding, as described in Section 6.6.

6.3.3 CONTROL COUPLING

Two modules are control-coupled if one passes an element of control to the other module, that is, one module explicitly controls the logic of the other. For example, control is passed when a function code is passed to a module with logical cohesion (Section 6.2.2). Another example of control coupling is when a control switch is passed as an argument.

If module p calls module q, and q passes back a flag to p that says, "I am unable to complete my task," then q is passing *data.* But if the flag means, "I am unable to complete my task; accordingly, write error message ABC123," then p and q are control-coupled. In other words, if q passes information back to p and p then decides what action to take as a consequence of receiving that information, then q is passing data. But if q passes back not only information but also informs module p as to what action p must take, then control coupling is present.

The major difficulty that arises as a consequence of control coupling is that the two modules are not independent; module q, the called module, has to be aware of the internal structure and logic of module p. As a result, the possibility of reuse is reduced. In addition, control coupling is generally associated with modules that have logical cohesion, and the difficulties associated with logical cohesion will then be present.

6.3.4 STAMP COUPLING

In some programming languages only simple variables such as part number, satellite altitude, or degree of multiprogramming can be passed as arguments. But many languages also support the passing of data structures, such as records or arrays, as arguments. In such languages valid arguments would include part record, satellite coordinates, or segment table. Two modules are stamp-coupled if a data structure is passed as an argument, but the called module operates on only some of the individual components of that data structure.

Consider, for example, the call calculate withholding (employee record). It is not clear, without reading the entire calculate withholding module, which fields of the employee record the module accesses or changes. Passing the employee's salary is obviously essential for computing the withholding, but it is difficult to see how the employee's home telephone number is needed for this purpose. Instead, only those fields that it actually needs for computing the withholding should be passed to module calculate withholding. Not only is the resulting module, and particularly its interface, easier to understand, but it is likely to be reusable in a variety of other products that also need to compute withholding. (See the Just in Case You Wanted to Know box on page 186 for another perspective on this.)

Perhaps even more important, because the call calculate withholding (employee record) passes more data than strictly necessary, the problems of uncontrolled data access, and conceivably computer crime, once again can arise. This issue was discussed in Section 6.3.2.

There is nothing at all wrong with passing a data structure as an argument, provided that all the components of the data structure are used by the called module. For example, calls like invert matrix (original matrix, inverted matrix) or print inventory record (warehouse record) pass a data structure as an argument, but the called modules operate on all the components of that data structure. Stamp coupling is present when a data structure is passed as an argument, but only some of the components are used by the called module.

A subtle form of stamp coupling can occur in languages like C or C++ when a pointer to a record is passed as an argument. Consider the call check altitude (pointer to position record). At first sight, what is being passed is a simple variable. But the called module has access to all of the fields in the position record pointed to by pointer to position record. Because of the potential problems, it is a good idea to examine the coupling closely whenever a pointer is passed as an argument.

JUST IN CASE YOU WANTED TO KNOW

Passing four or five different fields to a module may be slower than passing a complete record. This situation leads to a larger issue: What should be done when optimization issues (such as response time or space constraints) clash with what is generally considered to be good software engineering practice?

In my experience, this question frequently turns out to be irrelevant. The recommended approach may slow down the response time, but by only a millisecond or so, far too small to be detected by users. Thus, in accordance with Don Knuth's First Law of Optimization: *Don't!*—there is rarely a need for optimization of any kind, including for performance reasons [Knuth, 1974].

But what if optimization really is required? In this case, Knuth's Second Law of Optimization applies. The Second Law (labeled "for experts only") is: *Not yet!* In other words, first complete the entire product using appropriate software engineering techniques. Then, if optimization really is required, make only the necessary changes, carefully documenting what is being changed and why. If at all possible, this optimization should be done by an experienced software engineer.

6.3.5 DATA COUPLING

Two modules are data-coupled if all arguments are homogeneous data items. That is, every argument is either a simple argument or a data structure in which all elements are used by the called module. Examples include display time of arrival (flight number), compute product (first number, second number, result), and determine job with highest priority (job queue).

Data coupling is a desirable goal. To put it in a negative way, if a product exhibits data coupling exclusively, then the difficulties of content, common, control, and stamp coupling will not be present. From a more positive viewpoint, if two modules are data-coupled, then maintenance is easier, because a change to one module is less likely to cause a regression fault in the other. The following example clarifies certain aspects of coupling.

6.3.6 COUPLING EXAMPLE

Consider the example shown in Figure 6.11. The numbers on the arcs represent interfaces that are defined in greater detail in Figure 6.12. Thus, for example, when module p calls module q (interface 1), it passes one argument, namely, the type of the aircraft. When q returns control to p, it passes a status flag back. Using the information in Figures 6.11 and 6.12, the coupling between every pair of modules can be deduced. The results are shown in Figure 6.13.

Some of the entries in Figure 6.13 are obvious. For instance, the data coupling between p and q (interface 1 in Figure 6.11), between r and t (interface 5), and between s and u (interface 6) is a direct consequence of the fact that a simple variable is passed in each direction. The coupling between p and s (interface 2) would be data coupling if all the elements of the list of parts passed from s to p are used and/or updated, but it is stamp coupling if p operates on only

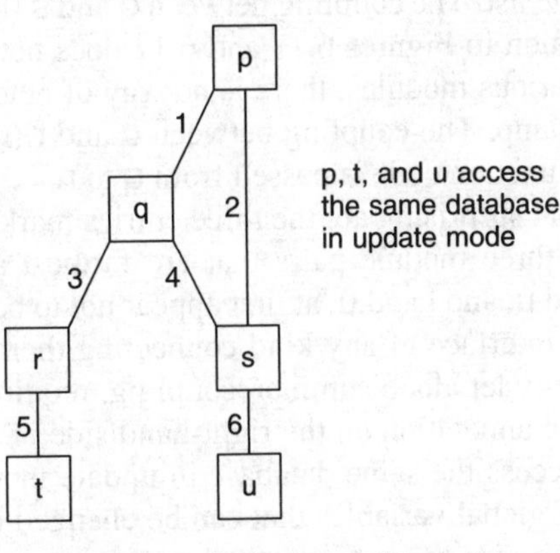

Figure 6.11 Module interconnection diagram for coupling example.

number	In	Out
1	aircraft type	status flag
2	—	list of aircraft parts
3	function code	—
4	—	list of aircraft parts
5	part number	part manufacturer
6	part number	part name

Figure 6.12 Interface description for Figure 6.11.

	q	r	s	t	u
p	Data	—	Data or Stamp	Common	Common
q		Control	Data or Stamp	—	—
r			—	Data	—
s				—	Data
t					Common

Figure 6.13 Coupling between pairs of modules of Figure 6.11.

certain elements of the list. The coupling between q and s (interface 4) is similar. Because the information in Figures 6.11 and 6.12 does not completely describe the function of the various modules, there is no way of determining whether the coupling is data or stamp. The coupling between q and r (interface 3) is control coupling, because a function code is passed from q to r.

Perhaps somewhat surprising are the three entries marked common coupling in Figure 6.13. The three module pairs that are farthest apart in Figure 6.11, namely, p and t, p and u, and t and u, at first appear not to be coupled in any way. After all, there is no interface of any kind connecting them, so the very idea of coupling between them, let alone common coupling, requires some explanation. The answer lies in the annotation on the right-hand side of Figure 6.11, namely, that p, t, and u all access the same database in update mode. The result is that there are a number of global variables that can be changed by all three modules, and hence they are pairwise common-coupled.

6.3.7 THE IMPORTANCE OF COUPLING

Coupling is an important metric. If module A is tightly coupled to module B, then a change to module B may require a corresponding change to module A. If this change is made, as required, during the integration or maintenance phase, then the resulting product will function correctly; however, progress during that phase will be slower than would have been the case had the coupling been looser. On the other hand, if the required change is not made to module A at that time, then the fault will manifest itself later. In the best case, the compiler or linker will inform the team right away that something is amiss, or a failure will occur while testing the change to module B. What usually happens, however, is that the product fails either during subsequent integration testing or while the product is in production mode. In both cases, the failure occurs after the change to module B has been completed. There is thus no longer any apparent link between the change to module B and the overlooked corresponding change to module A. The fault may therefore be hard to find.

The classical definition of coupling given in this chapter, namely, the degree of interaction between two modules, makes it hard to measure coupling. What is needed is a more complex type of metric targeted at a lower level of abstraction. One example of such a metric is the coupling dependency metric (CDM) [Binkley and Schach, 1997]. Given a module A, CDM(A) is a measure of the ways that a change to the product will require a corresponding change in A. For example, if A uses a global integer variable x, say, then A would have to be changed if the type of x were changed from **int** to **real**, or if the name of the variable x were changed to y.

Coupling metrics in general (and CDM in particular) are excellent metrics for predicting run-time faults. For example, CDM outperformed 17 other metrics in predicting which modules in an 80,000-line COBOL product were the most fault-prone [Binkley and Schach, 1998]. Coupling is equally effective at predicting maintenance measures, for example, the time required to make changes

Abstract data type a data type together with the actions performed on instantiations of that data type (Section 6.5)

Abstraction a means of achieving stepwise refinement by suppressing unnecessary details and accentuating relevant details (Section 6.4.1)

Class an abstract data type that supports inheritance (Section 6.7)

Cohesion the degree of interaction within a module (Section 6.1)

Coupling the degree of interaction between two modules (Section 6.1)

Data encapsulation a data structure together with the actions performed on that data structure (Section 6.4)

Encapsulation the gathering together into one unit of all aspects of the real-world entity modeled by that unit (Section 6.4.1)

Information hiding structuring the design so that the resulting implementation details will be hidden from other modules (Section 6.6)

Object an instantiation of a class (Section 6.7)

Figure 6.14 Key definitions of this chapter, and the sections in which they appear.

to a module or the number of faults per module. CDM outperformed a broad variety of other metrics in predicting maintenance of an 82,000-line comprehensive patient care management system written in C++ and a multilingual word-processing package written in C [Binkley and Schach, 1998]. Furthermore, CDM outperformed 15 other metrics in assessing the quality of a suite of object-oriented designs [Binkley and Schach, 1996]. It is thus apparent that coupling can be used to measure such disparate quantities as run-time failures, maintenance, and design quality. Also, coupling is equally effective as a metric for the classical paradigm or the object-oriented paradigm.

Given that a design in which modules have high cohesion and low coupling is a good design, the obvious question is: How can such a design be achieved? Because this chapter is devoted to theoretical concepts surrounding design, the answer to the question is presented in Chapter 12. In the meantime, those qualities that identify a good design are further examined and refined. For convenience, the key definitions in this chapter appear in Figure 6.14, together with the section in which each definition appears.

6.4 DATA ENCAPSULATION

Consider the problem of designing an operating system for a large mainframe computer. According to the specifications, any job submitted to the computer will be classified as high priority, medium priority, or low priority. In order to decide which job to load into memory next, which of the jobs in memory gets the next time slice, and how long that time slice should be, or which of the jobs that require

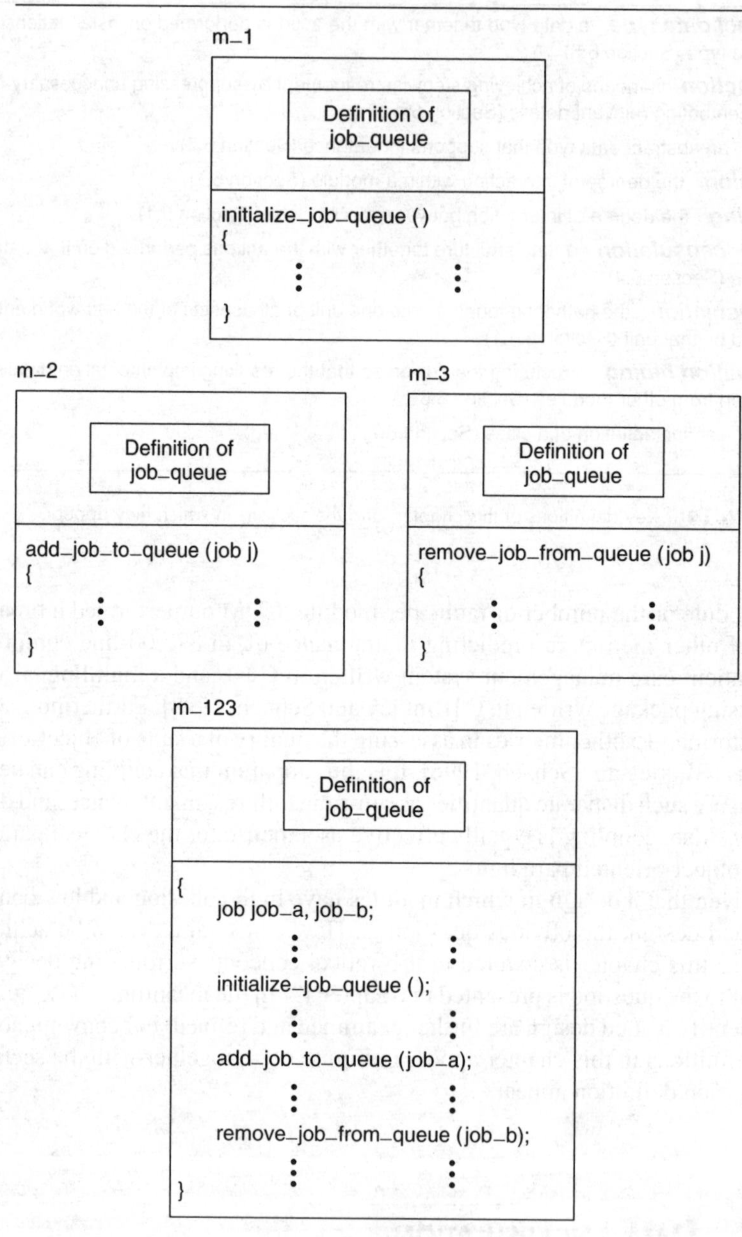

Figure 6.15 One possible design of job queue portion of operating system.

disk access has priority (that is, scheduling), the operating system must consider the priority of each job; the higher the priority, the sooner that job should be assigned the resources of the computer. One way of achieving this is to maintain separate job queues for each job-priority level. The job queues have to be initialized, and facilities must exist for adding a job to a job queue when the job requires memory, CPU time, or disk access, as well as for removing a job from a queue when the operating system decides to allocate the required resource to that job.

To simplify matters, consider the restricted problem of batch jobs queuing up for memory access. There are three queues for incoming batch jobs, one for each priority level. When a job is submitted by a user, the job is added to the appropriate queue, and when the operating system decides that a job is ready to be run, it is removed from its queue and memory is allocated to it.

There are a number of different ways to build this portion of the product. One possible design is shown in Figure 6.15 that depicts modules for manipulating one of the three job queues. A C-like pseudocode is used to highlight some of the problems that can arise in the classical paradigm. Later in this chapter, these problems will be solved using the object-oriented paradigm.

Consider Figure 6.15. Function initialize_job_queue[2] in module m_1 is responsible for the initialization of the job queue, and functions add_job_to_queue and remove_job_from_queue in modules m_2 and m_3, respectively, are responsible for the addition and deletion of jobs. Module m_123 contains invocations of all three functions in order to manipulate the job queue. In order to concentrate on data encapsulation, issues such as underflow (trying to remove a job from an empty queue) and overflow (trying to add a job to a full queue) have been suppressed here, as well as in the remainder of this chapter.

The modules of the design of Figure 6.15 have low cohesion, because actions on the job queue are spread all over the product. If a decision is made to change the way job_queue is implemented (for example, as a linked list of records instead of as a linear list), then modules m_1, m_2, and m_3 have to be drastically revised, and m_123 also has to be changed.

Now suppose that the design of Figure 6.16 is chosen instead. The module on the right-hand side of the figure has informational cohesion (Section 6.2.6) in that it performs a number of actions on the same data structure. Each action has its own entry point and exit point, and independent code. Module m_encapsulation in Figure 6.16 is an implementation of *data encapsulation,* that is, a data structure, in this case the job queue, together with the actions to be performed on that data structure.

An obvious question to ask at this point is: What is the advantage of designing a product using data encapsulation? This will be answered in two ways, from the viewpoint of development and from the viewpoint of maintenance.

[2]For added clarity, the underscore is used in function names like initialize_job_queue to highlight that the structured paradigm is used in this section. When the object-oriented paradigm is used in the next section, the corresponding method is named initializeJobQueue.

m_123

```
{
    job  job_a, job_b;
        :       :
    initialize_job_queue ( );
        :       :
    add_job_to_queue (job_a);
        :
    remove_job_from_queue (job_b);
        :       :
}
```

m_encapsulation

```
Definition of
job_queue

initialize_job_queue ( )
{
    :       :
}

add_job_to_queue (job j)
{
    :       :
}

remove_job_from_queue (job j)
{
    :       :
}
```

Figure 6.16 Design of job queue portion of operating system using data encapsulation.

6.4.1 DATA ENCAPSULATION AND PRODUCT DEVELOPMENT

Data encapsulation is an example of *abstraction.* Returning to the job queue example, a data structure, namely, the job queue, has been defined, together with three associated actions, namely, initialize the job queue, add a job to the queue, and delete a job from the queue. The developer is able to conceptualize the problem at a higher level, the level of jobs and job queues, rather than at the lower level of records or arrays.

The basic theoretical concept behind abstraction is, once again, stepwise refinement. First, a design for the product is produced in terms of high-level concepts such as jobs, job queues, and the actions that are performed on job queues. At this stage it is entirely irrelevant how the job queue is implemented. Once a complete high-level design has been obtained, the second step is to design the lower-level components in terms of which the data structure and actions on the data structure will be implemented. In C, for example, the data structure, that is, the job queue, will be implemented in terms of records (structures) or arrays; the three actions, namely, initialize the job queue, add a job to the queue, and remove a job from the queue, will be implemented as functions. The key point is that while this lower level is being designed, the designer totally ignores the intended use of the jobs, job queue, and actions. Thus, during the first step, the existence of the lower level is assumed, even though at that stage no thought has been given to that level; during the second step, that is, the design of the lower level, the existence of the higher level is ignored. At the higher level the concern is with the behavior of the data structure, namely, the job queue; at the lower level, the implementation of that behavior is the primary concern. Of course, in a larger product there will be many levels of abstraction. Examples of such multilevel products are now given.

The concept of levels of abstraction was described by Dijkstra in a different context in terms of architectural layers of an operating system [Dijkstra, 1968b]. The highest level, level 5, is the computer operator. Level 4 is the user program level. Each of the higher levels of abstraction is then implemented using some of the functions of the levels below it. For example, level 1, the memory-segment controller, utilizes some of the functions of level 0, where clock-interrupt handling and processor allocation are implemented. Suppose that the implementation of a lower-level function is changed. Provided that the interface between that function and the rest of the machine is not altered, that is, the number and types of the arguments are not changed, the higher levels should not even be aware that the change was made.

The same concept can be applied to computer organization. A computer can be thought of as consisting of levels of abstract machines [Tanenbaum, 1990]. The highest level, level 5, is the problem-oriented language level (Figure 6.17). Level 4 is the assembly language level. Level 3 is the operating system level, level 2 the machine code level. Suppose a product is written in C (level 5). It is compiled down to machine code (level 2). However, some compilers translate from C (level 5) to assembler (level 4), and then from assembler to machine code. Level 1 is the microprogramming level; machine code (level 2) is interpreted by the microprogram of level 1. The microcode is directly executed by the hardware of level 0, the digital logic level. This level is implemented in terms of silicon chips. Again there is independence of the various levels. Provided that the functionality and interfaces are not changed, it is possible to replace the digital logic level by faster hardware without altering any other aspect of the computer.

Level 5:	Problem-oriented language level
Level 4:	Assembly language level
Level 3:	Operating system level
Level 2:	Machine code level
Level 1:	Microprogramming level
Level 0:	Digital logic level

Figure 6.17 Levels of abstraction of a computer.

The microprogram can be rewritten to achieve further speed improvement, and provided again that the functionality and interfaces are not changed, this should not require any sort of change to products at level 5 or level 4, to the operating system level (level 3), or to the machine code level (level 2). By designing and implementing a computer in this way, each level of abstraction is independent. This allows a user working at level n to think conceptually at level n without having to descend to a lower level. Also, changes made at one level should not impact other levels in any way.

The description of abstraction in this section has glossed over the fact that different types of abstraction exist. Consider Figure 6.16. In that figure there are two types of abstraction. Data encapsulation, that is, a data structure together with the actions to be performed on that data structure, is an example of *data abstraction;* the C functions themselves are an example of *procedural abstraction.* Abstraction, as stated previously, is simply a means of achieving stepwise refinement by suppressing unnecessary details and accentuating relevant details. *Encapsulation* can now be defined as the gathering together into one unit of all aspects of the real-world entity modeled by that unit; this was termed conceptual independence in Section 1.6.

Data abstraction allows the designer to think at the level of the data structure and the actions performed on it, and only later be concerned with the details of how the data structure and actions are to be implemented. Turning now to procedural abstraction, consider the result of defining a C function, initialize_job_queue. The effect is to extend the language by supplying the developer with another function, one that is not part of the language as originally defined. The developer can now use initialize_job_queue in the same way as sqrt or printf.

The implications of procedural abstraction for design are as powerful as those of data abstraction. The designer can conceptualize the product in terms of high-level actions. These actions can be defined in terms of lower-level actions, until the lowest level is reached. At this level the actions are expressed in terms of the predefined constructs of the programming language. At each level the designer is concerned only with expressing the product in terms of actions appropriate to that level. The designer can ignore the level below, which will be handled at the next level of abstraction, that is, the next refinement step. The designer can also ignore the level above, a level that is irrelevant from the viewpoint of designing the current level.

6.4.2 DATA ENCAPSULATION AND PRODUCT MAINTENANCE

Approaching data encapsulation from the viewpoint of maintenance, a basic issue is to identify the aspects of a product that are likely to change and to design the product so as to minimize the effects of future changes. Data structures as such are unlikely to change; if a product includes job queues, for instance, then it is likely that future versions will incorporate them. At the same time, the specific way that job queues are implemented may well change, and data encapsulation provides a means of coping with that change.

```
//
// Warning:
// This code has been written in such a way so as to be accessible to readers
// who are not Java experts, as opposed to using good Java style. Also, vital
// features such as checks for overflow and underflow have been omitted, for simplicity.
// See the Just in Case You Wanted to Know box on page 196 for details.
//
class JobQueue
{
  // instance variables
  public int          queueLength;                 // length of job queue
  public int          queue[] = new int[25];       // queue can contain up to 25 jobs

  // methods
  public void initializeJobQueue ()
  /*
   * empty job queue has length 0
   */
  {
    queueLength = 0;
  }

  public void addJobToQueue (int jobNumber)
  /*
   * add job to end of job queue
   */
  {
    queue[queueLength] = jobNumber;
    queueLength = queueLength + 1;
  }

  public void removeJobFromQueue (int jobNumber)
  /*
   * set jobNumber equal to the number of the job stored at the head of the queue,
   * remove the job at the head of the job queue, and move up the remaining jobs
   */
  {
    jobNumber = queue[0];
    queueLength = queueLength – 1;
    for (int k = 0; k < queueLength; k++)
      queue[k] = queue[k + 1];
  }
} // class JobQueue
```

Figure 6.18 Java implementation of **class JobQueue**. (Problems caused by **public** attributes will be solved in Section 6.6.)

Figure 6.18 depicts an implementation in Java of the job queue data structure as **class JobQueue.** (The Just in Case You Wanted to Know box on page 196 has comments on the programming style in this and the following seven figures.) The queue is implemented as an array of up to 25 job numbers; the first

JUST IN CASE YOU WANTED TO KNOW

I deliberately wrote the code examples in this chapter in such a way as to highlight data abstraction issues at the cost of good programming practice. For example, the number 25 in the definition of **class JobQueue** in Figure 6.18 should certainly be coded as a parameter, that is, as a **public static final** variable.

In addition, because some readers may not be familiar with Java, language-specific features have been minimized. For instance, a Java programmer usually writes

```
queueLength++;
```

to increment the value of queueLength by 1, rather than

```
queueLength = queueLength + 1;
```

Also, for simplicity I have omitted checks for conditions such as underflow (trying to remove an item from an empty queue) or overflow (trying to add an item to a full queue). In any real product, it is absolutely essential to include such checks.

Another deliberate omission is constructors (for initializing a data structure when created) because the Java notion for constructors can be confusing to the uninitiated. Also, I have not included finalizers for explicit cleanup before deleting an object. Instead, as is usually the case, I have relied on the Java automatic garbage collector.

In summary, then, I wrote the code of Figures 6.18 through 6.25 for pedagogic purposes only. It should not be utilized for any other purpose!

element is queue[0] and the 25th is queue[24]. Each job number is represented as an integer. The reserved word **public** allows queueLength and queue to be visible everywhere in the operating system. The resulting common coupling is extremely poor practice and will be corrected in Section 6.6.

Because they are **public,** the methods in **class JobQueue** may be invoked from anywhere in the operating system. In particular, Figure 6.19 shows how **class JobQueue** may be used by method queueHandler. Method queueHandler invokes methods initializeJobQueue, addJobToQueue, and removeJobFromQueue of **JobQueue** without having any knowledge as to how the job queue is implemented; the only information needed to use **class JobQueue** is interface information regarding the three methods.

Now suppose that the job queue is currently implemented as a linear list of job numbers, but a decision has been made to reimplement it as a two-way linked list of job records. Each job record will have three components, namely, the job number as before, a reference (link) to the job record in front of it in the linked list, and a reference to the job record behind it. This is specified in Java as shown in Figure 6.20.

The question now is: What changes have to be made to the software product as a whole as a consequence of this modification to the way the job queue is implemented? In fact, only **JobQueue** itself has to be changed. Figure 6.21 shows the outline of a Java implementation of **JobQueue** using the two-way linked list of Figure 6.20. Implementation details have been suppressed to highlight the fact that the interface between **JobQueue** and the rest

```
class Scheduler
{
  ...
  public void queueHandler ()
  {
    int          jobA, jobB;
    JobQueue     jobQueueJ = new jobQueue ();

     // various statements
    jobQueueJ.initializeJobQueue ();
     // more statements
    jobQueueJ.addJobToQueue (jobA);
     // still more statements
    jobQueueJ.removeJobFromQueue (jobB);
     // further statements
  } // queueHandler
  ...
} // class Scheduler
```

Figure 6.19 Java implementation of queueHandler.

```
class JobRecord
{
  public int         jobNo;      // number of the job (integer)
  public JobRecord   inFront;    // reference to job record in front
  public JobRecord   inRear;     // reference to job record behind
} // class JobRecord
```

Figure 6.20 Java specification of two-way linked **class JobRecord.** (Problems caused by **public** data elements will be solved in Section 6.6.)

of the product (including queueHandler) has not changed in any way (but see Problem 6.10). That is, the three methods initializeJobQueue, addJobToQueue, and removeJobFromQueue are invoked in exactly the same way that they were before. Specifically, when method addJobToQueue is invoked it still passes an integer value to **JobQueue,** and removeJobFromQueue still returns an integer value from **JobQueue,** despite the fact that the job queue itself has been implemented in an entirely different way. Consequently, the source code of method queueHandler (Figure 6.19) need not be changed at all.

Thus data encapsulation supports the implementation of data abstraction in a way that simplifies product maintenance and reduces the chance of a regression fault.

```
class JobQueue
{
  public JobRecord frontOfQueue; // reference to front of queue
  public JobRecord rearOfQueue; // reference to rear of queue

  public void initializeJobQueue ()
  {
    /*
     * initialize the job queue by setting frontOfQueue and rearOfQueue to null
     */
  }

  public void addJobToQueue (int jobNumber)
  {
    /*
     * Create a new job record,
     * place jobNumber in its jobNo field,
     * set its inFront field to the current rearOfQueue
     * (thereby linking the new record to the rear of the queue),
     * and set its inRear field to null.
     * Set inRear field of current rearOfQueue
     * to the new record (thereby setting up a two-way link), and
     * finally, set rearOfQueue to this new record
     */
  }

  public void removeJobFromQueue (int jobNumber)
  {
    /*
     * set jobNumber equal to the jobNo field of the record at the front of the queue,
     * update frontOfQueue to the next item in the queue,
     * set the inFront field of the record that is now the head of the queue to null
     */
  }
} // class JobQueue
```

Figure 6.21 Outline of Java implementation of **class JobQueue** using a two-way linked list.

6.5 ABSTRACT DATA TYPES

Figures 6.18 and 6.21 are implementation of a job queue **class,** that is, a data type together with the actions to be performed on instantiations of that data type. Such a construct is called an *abstract data type.* A Java implementation of the job queue abstract data type is shown in Figure 6.22, which is identical to Figure 6.18.

```
class JobQueue
{
  // instance variables
  public int   queueLength;                  // length of job queue
  public int   queue[25] = new int[25];      // queue can contain up to 25 jobs

  // methods
  public void initializeJobQueue ()
  {
    // body of method unchanged from Figure 6.18
  }

  public void addJobToQueue (int jobNumber)
  {
    // body of method unchanged from Figure 6.18
  }

  public void removeJobFromQueue (int jobNumber)
  {
    // body of method unchanged from Figure 6.18
  }
} // class JobQueue
```

Figure 6.22 Job queue implemented in Java as abstract data type. (Problems caused by **public** data elements will be solved in Section 6.6.)

Figure 6.23 shows how this abstract data type may be utilized for the three job queues of the operating system. Three job queues are instantiated, namely, highPriorityQueue, mediumPriorityQueue and lowPriorityQueue. The statement highPriorityQueue.initializeJobQueue () means: apply method initializeJobQueue to data structure highPriorityQueue.

An abstract data type is a widely applicable design tool. For example, suppose that a product is to be written in which a large number of actions have to be performed on rational numbers, that is, numbers that can be represented in the form n / d, where n and d are integers, $d \neq 0$. Rational numbers can be represented in a variety of different ways, such as two elements of a one-dimensional array of integers or as two attributes of a class. To implement rational numbers in terms of an abstract data type, a suitable representation for the data structure is chosen. In Java it could be defined as shown in Figure 6.24, together with the various actions that are performed on rational numbers, such as constructing a rational number from two integers, adding two rational numbers, and multiplying two rational numbers. (The problems induced by **public** instance variables such as numerator and denominator in Figure 6.24 will be fixed in Section 6.6).

Abstract data types support both data abstraction and procedural abstraction (Section 6.4.1). In addition, when a product is modified, it is unlikely that the

```
class Scheduler
{
  ...
  public void queueHandler ()
  {
    int             job1, job2;
    JobQueue        highPriorityQueue = new JobQueue ();
    JobQueue        mediumPriorityQueue = new JobQueue ();
    JobQueue        lowPriorityQueue = new JobQueue ();

      // some statements
    highPriorityQueue.initializeJobQueue ();
      // some more statements
    mediumPriorityQueue.addJobToQueue (job1);
      // still more statements
    lowPriorityQueue.removeJobFromQueue (job2);
      // even more statements
  } // queueHandler
  ...
} // class Scheduler
```

Figure 6.23 Java method **queueHandler** implemented using abstract data type of Figure 6.22.

```
class Rational
{
  public int      numerator;
  public int      denominator;

  public void sameDenominator (Rational r, Rational s)
  {
    // code to reduce r and s to the same denominator
  }

  public boolean equal (Rational t, Rational u)
  {
    Rational      v, w;
    v = t;
    w = u;
    sameDenominator (v, w);
    return (v.numerator == w.numerator);
  }

// methods to add, subtract, multiply, and divide two rational numbers
} // class Rational
```

Figure 6.24 Abstract data type definition of a rational number. (Problems caused by **public** data elements will be solved in Section 6.6.)

abstract data types will be changed; at worst, additional actions may have to be added to an abstract data type. Thus, from both the product development and the product maintenance viewpoints, abstract data types are an attractive tool for software producers.

In addition to data abstraction and procedural abstraction, there is in fact a third type of abstraction, namely, *iteration abstraction* [Liskov and Guttag, 1986]. Iteration abstraction allows a programmer to specify at a higher level that a loop is to be used, and then to describe at a lower level the exact elements over which the iteration is to be performed and the order in which the elements are to be processed.

6.6 INFORMATION HIDING

The three types of abstraction discussed in the previous section, namely, data abstraction, procedural abstraction, and iteration abstraction, are in turn instances of a more general design concept put forward by Parnas, namely, *information hiding* [Parnas, 1971, 1972a, 1972b]. Parnas's ideas are directed toward future maintenance. Before a product is designed, a list should be made of implementation decisions likely to change in the future. Modules should then be designed so that the implementation details of the resulting design are hidden from other modules. Thus, each future change is localized to one specific module. Because the details of the original implementation decision are not visible to other modules, changing the design clearly cannot affect any other module. (See the Just in Case You Wanted to Know box on this page for a further insight into information hiding.)

To see how these ideas can be used in practice, consider the abstract data type implementation of Figures 6.22 and 6.23. A primary reason for using an abstract data type is to ensure that the contents of a job queue can be changed exclusively by invoking one of the three methods of Figure 6.22. Unfortunately, the nature of that implementation is such that job queues can be changed in other ways. Instance variables `queueLength` and `queue` are both declared to be **`public`** in Figure 6.22 and are therefore accessible everywhere within the product. As a result, it is perfectly legal Java to use an assignment statement such as

```
highPriorityQueue.queue[7] = −5678;
```

JUST IN CASE YOU WANTED TO KNOW

The term *information hiding* is somewhat of a misnomer. A more accurate description would be "details hiding," because what is hidden is not information, but rather implementation details.

```
class JobQueue
{
  // instance variables
  private int     queueLength;            // length of job queue
  private int     queue = new int [25];   // queue can contain up to 25 jobs

  // methods
  public void initializeJobQueue()
  {
    // body of method unchanged from Figure 6.18
  }

  public void addJobToQueue (int jobNumber)
  {
    // body of method unchanged from Figure 6.18
  }

  public void removeJobFromQueue (int jobNumber)
  {
    // body of method unchanged from Figure 6.18
  }
} // class JobQueue
```

Figure 6.25 Abstract data type implementation with information hiding, correcting the problem of Figures 6.18, 6.20, 6.22, and 6.24.

anywhere in **queueHandler** to change **highPriorityQueue**. In other words, it is possible to change the contents of a job queue without using any of the three actions of the abstract data type. In addition to the implications this might have with regard to lowering cohesion and increasing coupling, management must recognize that the product may be vulnerable to computer fraud as described in Section 6.3.2.

Fortunately, there is a way out. The designer of Java provided for information hiding within a class specification. This is shown in Figure 6.25. Other than the two changes of visibility modifier from **public** to **private**, Figure 6.25 is identical to Figure 6.22. Now the only information visible to other modules is that **JobQueue** is a **class** and that three actions with specified interfaces can operate on the resulting job queues. But the exact way that job queues are implemented is **private**, that is, invisible to the outside. The diagram in Figure 6.26 shows how a class with **private** instance variables enables a Java user to implement an abstract data type with full information hiding.

Information hiding techniques can also be used to obviate common coupling, as mentioned at the end of Section 6.3.2. Consider again the product described in that section, a computer-aided design tool for petroleum storage tanks specified by 55 descriptors. If the product is implemented with **private** actions for initializing a descriptor and **public** actions for obtaining the value of a descriptor, then there is no common coupling. This type of solution is characteristic of

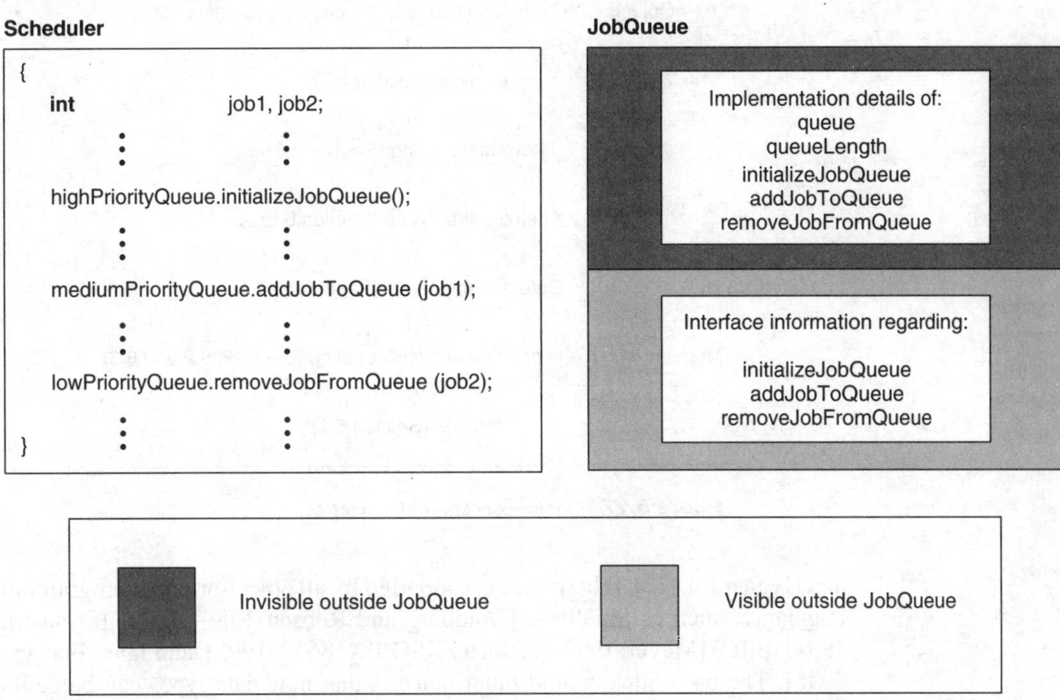

Figure 6.26 Representation of abstract data type with information hiding achieved via structure with private data (Figure 6.25 with Figure 6.23).

the object-oriented paradigm because, as described in the next section, objects support information hiding. This is another advantage of using object technology.

6.7 OBJECTS

As stated at the beginning of this chapter, objects are simply the next step in the progression shown in Figure 6.27. There is nothing special about objects; they are as ordinary as abstract data types or modules with informational cohesion. The importance of objects is that they have all the properties possessed by their predecessors in Figure 6.27, as well as additional properties of their own.

An incomplete definition of an object is that an object is an instantiation (instance) of an abstract data type. That is, a product is designed in terms of abstract data types, and the variables (objects) of the product are then instantiations of the abstract data types. But defining an object as an instantiation of an abstract data type is too simplistic. Something more is needed, namely, *inheritance*, a concept first introduced in Simula 67 [Dahl and Nygaard, 1966; Dahl, Myrhaug,

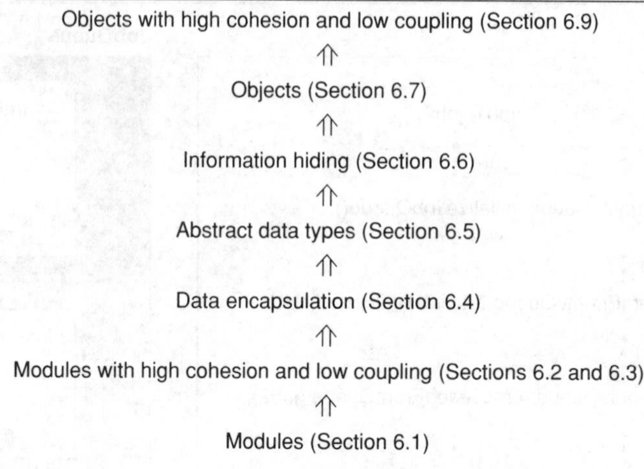

Figure 6.27 Major concepts of Chapter 6.

and Nygaard, 1973]. Inheritance is supported by all object-oriented programming languages, such as Smalltalk [Goldberg and Robson 1989], C++ [Stroustrup, 1991], Eiffel [Meyer, 1992b], Ada 95 [ISO/IEC 8652, 1995], and Java [Flanagan, 1996]. The basic idea behind inheritance is that new data types can be defined as extensions of previously defined types, rather than having to be defined from scratch [Meyer, 1986].

In an object-oriented language, a *class* can be defined. A class is an abstract data type that supports inheritance. An object is then an instantiation of a class. To see how classes are used, consider the following example. Define **HumanBeing** to be a class, and Joe to be an object, an instance of that class. Every **HumanBeing** has certain attributes such as age and height, and values can be assigned to those attributes when describing the object Joe. Now suppose that **Parent** is defined to be a *subclass* (or derived class) of **HumanBeing**. This means that a **Parent** has all the attributes of a **HumanBeing**, but in addition may have attributes of his or her own such as name of oldest child and number of children. This is depicted in Figure 6.28. In object-oriented terminology, a **Parent** *isA* **HumanBeing**. That is why the arrow in Figure 6.28 seems to be going in the wrong direction. In fact, the arrow is depicting the *isA* relation and therefore points from the derived class to the base class. (The use of the open arrowhead to denote inheritance is a UML convention; UML is described in Chapter 10.)

Class **Parent** *inherits* all the attributes of **HumanBeing**, because class **Parent** is a derived class (or subclass) of base class **HumanBeing**. If Fred is an object and an instance of class **Parent**, then Fred has all the attributes of a **Parent**, but also inherits all the attributes of a **HumanBeing**. A Java implementation is shown in Figure 6.29.

The property of inheritance is an essential feature of all object-oriented programming languages. However, neither inheritance nor the concept of a class is

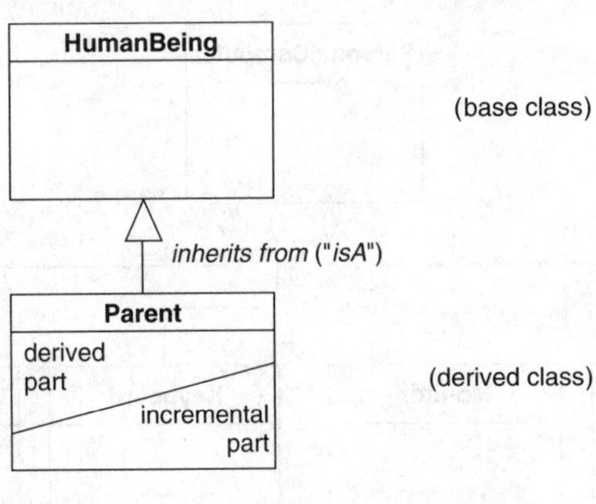

Figure 6.28 Derived types and inheritance.

```
class HumanBeing
{
  private int          age;
  private float        height;

  // public declarations of operations on HumanBeing
} // class HumanBeing


class Parent extends HumanBeing
{
  private String       nameOfOldestChild;
  private int          numberOfChildren ;


  // public declarations of operations on Parent
} // class Parent
```

Figure 6.29 Java implementation of Figure 6.28.

supported by classical languages such as C, COBOL, or FORTRAN. Thus the object-oriented paradigm cannot be directly implemented in these popular languages.

In the terminology of the object-oriented paradigm, there are two other ways of looking at the relationship between **Parent** and **HumanBeing** in Figure 6.28. We can say that **Parent** is a *specialization* of **HumanBeing**, or that **HumanBeing** is a *generalization* of **Parent**. In addition to specialization/generalization there are two other basic relationships between classes [Blaha,

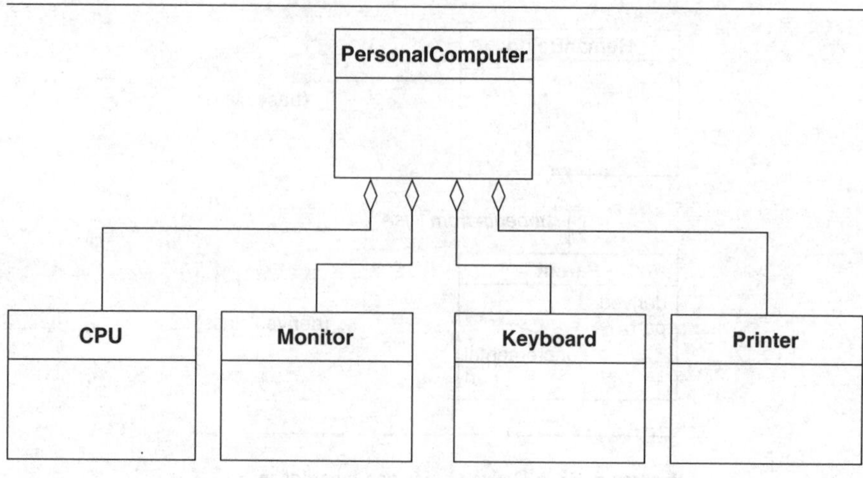

Figure 6.30 Aggregation example.

Premerlani, and Rumbaugh, 1988], namely, aggregation and association. *Aggregation* refers to the components of a class. For example, class **PersonalComputer** might consist of components **CPU**, **Monitor**, **Keyboard**, and **Printer**. This is depicted in Figure 6.30 (the use of a diamond to denote aggregation is another UML convention). There is nothing new about this; it occurs whenever a language supports records, such as a **struct** in C. Within the object-oriented context, however, it is used to group related items, resulting in a reusable class (Section 7.1).

Association refers to a relationship of some kind between two apparently unrelated classes. For example, there does not seem to be any connection between a radiologist and an artist, but a radiologist may consult an artist in regard to drawing the diagrams for a book describing how an MRI machine works. Association is depicted in Figure 6.31. The nature of the association in this instance is indicated by the word consults. In addition, there is a solid triangle to indicate the direction of the association; after all, an artist with a broken ankle might well consult a radiologist.

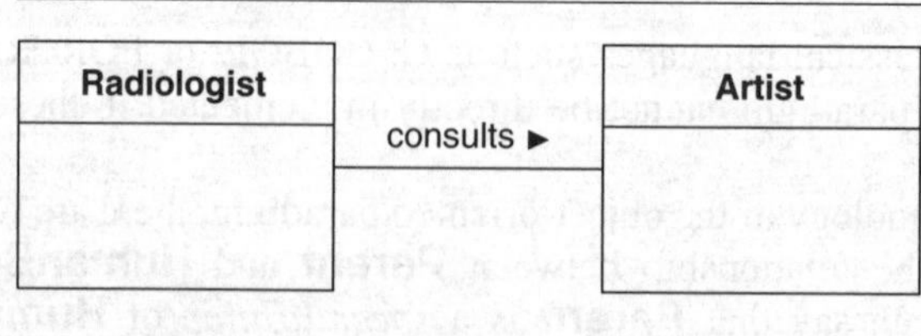

Figure 6.31 Association example.

In passing, one aspect of Java notation, like that of other object-oriented languages, explicitly reflects the equivalence of action and data. First, consider a classical language that supports records, C for example. Suppose that record_1 is a **struct** (record), and field_2 is a field within the class. Then, the field is referred to as record_1.field_2. That is, the period . denotes membership within the record. If function_3 is a function within a C module, then function_3 () denotes an invocation of that function.

In contrast, suppose that **ClassA** is a **class**, with attribute (instance variable) attributeB and method methodC. Suppose further that ourObject is an instance of **ClassA**. Then the field is referred to as ourObject.attributeB. Furthermore, ourObject.methodC () denotes an invocation of the method. Thus, the period is used to denote membership within an object, whether the member is an attribute or a method.

The advantages of using objects (or rather, classes) are precisely those of using abstract data types, including data abstraction and procedural abstraction. In addition, the inheritance aspects of classes provide a further layer of data abstraction, leading to easier and less fault-prone product development. Yet another strength follows from combining inheritance with polymorphism and dynamic binding, the subject of the next section.

6.8 INHERITANCE, POLYMORPHISM, AND DYNAMIC BINDING

Suppose that the operating system of a computer is called on to open a file. That file could be stored on a number of different media. For example, it could be a disk file, a tape file, or a diskette file. Using the structured paradigm, there would be three differently named functions, namely, open_disk_file, open_tape_file, and open_diskette_file; this is shown in Figure 6.32(a). If my_file is declared to be a file, then at run-time it is necessary to test whether it is a disk file, a tape file, or a diskette file in order to determine which of the three functions to invoke.

In contrast, when the object-oriented paradigm is used, a class named **FileClass** is defined, with three derived classes **DiskFileClass**, **TapeFileClass**, and **DisketteFileClass**. This is shown in Figure 6.32(b); recall that the open arrowhead denotes inheritance. Now, suppose that method open were defined in parent class **FileClass** and inherited by the three derived classes. Unfortunately, this would not work, because different actions need to be carried out to open the three different types of files.

The solution is as follows. In parent class **FileClass**, a dummy method open is declared. (In Java such a method is declared to be **abstract**.) A specific implementation of the method appears in each of the three derived classes and each method is given the identical name, that is, open, as shown in Figure 6.32(b). Again, suppose that myFile is declared to be a file. At run-time, the message myFile.open () is sent. The object-oriented system now determines

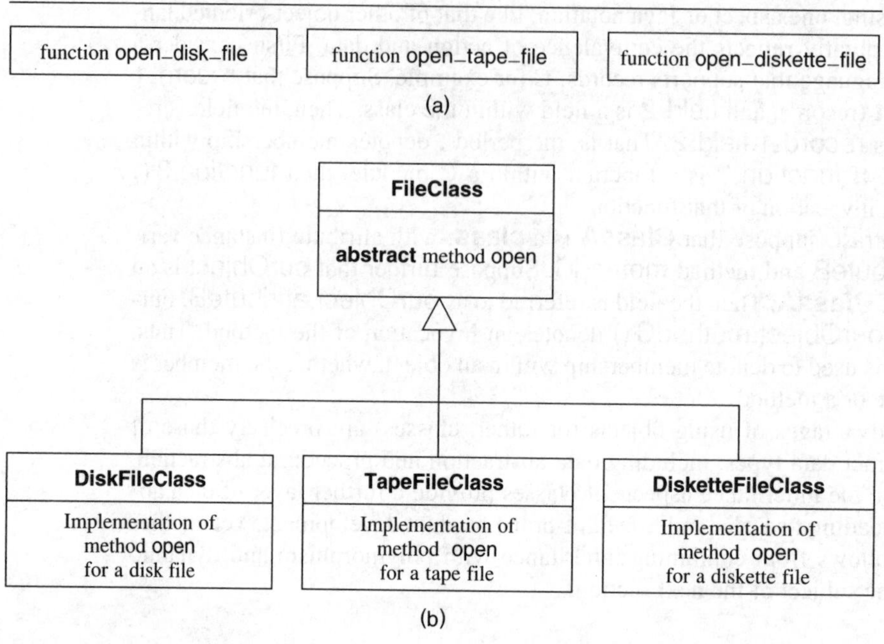

Figure 6.32 Operations needed to open file. (a) Structured implementation. (b) Object-oriented file class hierarchy.

whether myFile is a disk file, a tape file, or a diskette file and invokes the appropriate version of open. That is, the system determines at run-time whether object myFile is an instance of class **DiskFileClass**, class **TapeFileClass**, or class **DisketteFileClass** and automatically invokes the correct method. Because this has to be done at run-time (dynamically), and not at compile time (statically), the act of connecting an object to the appropriate method is termed *dynamic binding*. Furthermore, because the method open can be applied to objects of different classes, it is termed *polymorphic*. The term literally means "of different shapes." Just as carbon crystals come in different shapes, including hard diamonds and soft graphite, so method open comes in three different versions. In Java these versions are denoted DiskFileClass.open, TapeFileClass.open, and DisketteFileClass.open. However, because of dynamic binding, it is not necessary to determine which method to invoke to open a specific file. Instead it is only necessary to send the message myFile.open (), and the system will determine the type (class) of myFile and invoke the correct method.

These ideas are applicable to more than just **abstract** methods. Consider a hierarchy of classes, as shown in Figure 6.33. All classes are derived by inheritance from the **Base** class. Suppose method checkOrder (b : **Base**) takes as argument an instance of class **Base**. Then, as a consequence of inheritance, polymorphism, and dynamic binding, it is valid to invoke checkOrder with an argument not just of class **Base**, but also of any subclass of class **Base**, that is,

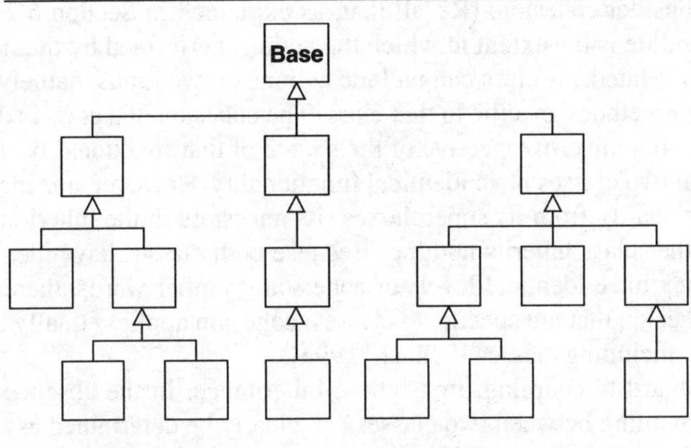

Figure 6.33 Hierarchy of classes

any class derived from **Base**. All that is needed is to invoke checkOrder, and everything will be taken care of at run-time. This technique is extremely powerful in that the software professional need not be concerned about the precise type of an argument at the time that a message is sent.

However, there are also major disadvantages of polymorphism and dynamic binding. First, it is generally not possible to determine at compilation time which version of a specific polymorphic method will be invoked at run-time. Accordingly, the cause of a failure can be extremely difficult to determine.

Second, polymorphism and dynamic binding can have a negative impact on maintenance. The first task of a maintenance programmer is usually to try to understand the product (as explained in Chapter 15, the maintainer is rarely the person who developed that code). However, this can be laborious if there are multiple possibilities for a specific method. The programmer has to consider all the possible methods that could be dynamically invoked at a specific place in the code; this can be a time-consuming task. Thus, polymorphism and dynamic binding add both strengths and weaknesses to the object-oriented paradigm.

The reasons for the superiority of the object-oriented paradigm given in Section 1.6 included conceptual and physical independence. To measure this independence, the concepts of cohesion and coupling must now be re-examined within the context of objects.

6.9 COHESION AND COUPLING OF OBJECTS

An object is a kind of module. Consequently, the material of Sections 6.2 and 6.3 concerning modules with high cohesion and low coupling applies equally to objects. The question arises as to whether special types of cohesion and coupling occur within the object-oriented paradigm.

First consider cohesion. (Recall that, as explained in Section 6.2, the cohesion of a module is the extent to which the actions performed by that module are functionally related.) A class can include actions of two kinds, namely, inherited methods and methods specific to that class. The cohesion of a class is determined from its functionality, irrespective of the source of that functionality. To see this, suppose that two classes have identical functionality. However, one class inherits all its functionality from its superclasses (its ancestors in the inheritance hierarchy); the other class inherits nothing. Because both classes have identical functionality, they have identical levels of cohesion. In other words, there can be no types of cohesion that are specific to classes; cohesion applies equally to all types of modules, including classes [Schach, 1996].

With regard to coupling, first ignore inheritance. In the absence of inheritance, the coupling between two classes can clearly be determined as in the classical paradigm. For example, if an attribute of a class is defined to be **public** (accessible to all other units within the product), then this can induce common coupling. What is somewhat surprising, however, is that inheritance does not induce new forms of coupling. That is, the forms of coupling that arise as a consequence of coupling can be shown to occur in the classical paradigm as well [Binkley and Schach, 1997]. Thus, despite the major differences between the classical and object-oriented paradigms, the object-oriented paradigm does not induce new forms of either cohesion or coupling.

However, a number of metrics specific to the object-oriented paradigm have been put forward, for example, the height of the inheritance tree [Chidamber and Kemerer, 1994]. Some of these metrics have been questioned on both theoretical and experimental grounds [Binkley and Schach, 1996, 1997]. In these cases, it remains to be shown that there is a need for specifically object-oriented metrics, as opposed to classical metrics (like cohesion and coupling) that can equally be applied to object-oriented software.

A number of different reasons for the superiority of the object-oriented paradigm were given in Section 1.6. A further reason is that the use of objects and classes promotes reuse. This is discussed in detail in the next chapter.

CHAPTER REVIEW

The chapter begins with a description of a module (Section 6.1). In the next two sections an analysis is given of what constitutes a well-designed module in terms of module cohesion and module coupling (Sections 6.2 and 6.3). Specifically, a module should have high cohesion and low coupling. Various types of abstraction are presented in Sections 6.4 through 6.7, including data abstraction and procedural abstraction. In data encapsulation (Section 6.4), a module comprises a data *structure*, together with the actions performed on that data structure. An abstract data type (Section 6.5) is a data *type*, together with the actions performed on instances of that type. Information hiding (Section 6.6) consists of designing a module in such a way that implementation details are hidden from other modules. The progression of increasing abstraction culminates in the description of a class, namely, an abstract data type that supports inheritance (Section 6.7). An object is then an instance of a class. Polymorphism and dynamic binding are the subjects of Section 6.8, and cohesion and coupling of objects are described in Section 6.9.

FOR FURTHER READING

Many of the ideas in this chapter were originally put forward by Parnas [Parnas, 1971, 1972a, 1972b]. Objects were first described in [Dahl and Nygaard, 1966].

The primary source on cohesion and coupling is [Stevens, Myers, and Constantine, 1974]; also important are [Myers, 1975, 1978b; Yourdon and Constantine, 1979]. The ideas of composite/structured design have subsequently been extended to objects [Binkley and Schach, 1997].

The use of abstract data types in software development was put forward in [Liskov and Zilles, 1974]. Another important early paper is [Guttag, 1977]. Later papers on abstraction include [Feldman, 1981], in which a practical approach to data abstraction is presented, and [Shaw, 1984], a discussion of how abstraction is achieved in modern programming languages. A useful book on abstraction is [Liskov and Guttag, 1986]. [Berry, 1985] discusses information hiding in Ada. The application of information hiding to the U.S. Navy A-7 project appears in [Parnas, Clements, and Weiss, 1985]. In [Neumann, 1986], a description is given of the use of abstraction for designing safer software for controlling life-critical systems in areas such as air-traffic control or medical care. An account of experiences with abstraction-based software development techniques in a university environment is found in [Berzins, Gray, and Naumann, 1986].

Introductory material on objects can be found in [Cox, 1986], [Stefik and Bobrow, 1986], [Korson and McGregor, 1990], [Snyder, 1993], and [Meyer, 1997]. Ways in which object-oriented programming promotes reuse are put forward in [Meyer, 1987, 1990]. Different types of inheritance are described in [Meyer, 1996b]. A number of short articles on recent trends in the object-oriented paradigm can be found in [El-Rewini et al., 1995]. The proceedings of the annual Conference on Object-Oriented Programming Systems, Languages, and Applications (OOPSLA) have a wide selection of research papers; the addendum to the proceedings (published annually in *ACM SIGPLAN Notices*) contains informal reports describing successful object-oriented projects. [Shriver and Wegner, 1987] contains many worthwhile earlier papers on various aspects of object-oriented software development. The successful use of the object-oriented paradigm in three IBM projects is described in [Capper, Colgate, Hunter, and James, 1994]. Other experiences with the paradigm are reported in the October 1995 issue of the *Communications of the ACM*. [Fayad, Tsai, and Fulghum, 1996] describes how to make the transition to object-oriented technology;

a number of recommendations for managers are included. A detailed account of object-oriented metrics is given in [Henderson-Sellers, 1996].

The October 1992 issue of *IEEE Computer* contains a number of important articles on objects, including [Meyer, 1992a] which describes "design by contract." A variety of articles on objects can be found in the January 1993 issue of *IEEE Software;* the paper by Snyder carefully defining key terms in the field [Snyder, 1993] is particularly useful. Possible drawbacks of polymorphism are described in [Ponder and Bush, 1994]. The October 1995 issue of the *Communications of the ACM* contains articles on object technology, as does Issue No. 2, 1996, of the *IBM Systems Journal.*

PROBLEMS

6.1 Choose any programming language with which you are familiar. Consider the two definitions of modularity given in Section 6.1. Determine which of the two definitions includes what you intuitively understand to constitute a module in the language you have chosen.

6.2 Determine the cohesion of the following modules:

edit composer and royalties record
edit composer record and royalties record
read sales record and check commission payments
compute the commission using Aksen's algorithm
measure alloy temperature and sound alarm if necessary

6.3 You are a software engineer involved in product development. Your manager asks you to investigate ways of ensuring that modules designed by your group will be as reusable as possible. What do you tell her?

6.4 Your manager now asks you to determine how existing modules can be reused. Your first suggestion is to break each module with coincidental cohesion into separate modules with functional cohesion. Your manager correctly points out that the separate modules have not been tested, nor have they been documented. What do you say now?

6.5 What is the influence of cohesion on maintenance?

6.6 What is the influence of coupling on maintenance?

6.7 Carefully distinguish between data encapsulation and abstract data types.

6.8 Carefully distinguish between abstraction and information hiding.

6.9 Carefully distinguish between polymorphism and dynamic binding.

6.10 Convert the comments in Figure 6.21 to Java. Make sure that the resulting module executes correctly.

6.11 It has been suggested that Java supports implementation of abstract data types, but only at the cost of giving up information hiding. Discuss this claim.

6.12 As pointed out in the "Just in Case You Wanted to Know" box at the beginning of this chapter, objects were first put forward in 1966. Only after essentially being reinvented nearly 20 years later did objects begin to receive widespread acceptance. Can you explain this phenomenon?

6.13 Your instructor will distribute a structured software product. Analyze the modules from the viewpoints of information hiding, levels of abstraction, coupling, and cohesion.

6.14 Your instructor will distribute an object-oriented software product. Analyze the modules from the viewpoints of information hiding, levels of abstraction, coupling, and cohesion. Compare your answer with that of Problem 6.13.

6.15 (Term Project) Suppose that the Air Gourmet product of Appendix A was developed using the structured paradigm. Give examples of modules of functional cohesion that you would expect to find. Now suppose that the product was developed using the object-oriented paradigm. Give examples of classes that you would expect to find.

6.16 (Readings in Software Engineering) Your instructor will distribute copies of [Meyer, 1996b]. Do you agree that it is necessary to consider so many different types of inheritance?

REFERENCES

[Berry, 1978] D. M. BERRY, Personal communication, 1978.

[Berry, 1985] D. M. BERRY, "On the Application of Ada and Its Tools to the Information Hiding Decomposition Methodology for the Design of Software Systems," in: *Methodologies for Computer System Design,* W. K. Giloi and B. D. Shriver (Editors), Elsevier North-Holland, Amsterdam, 1985, pp. 308–21.

[Berzins, Gray, and Naumann, 1986] V. BERZINS, M. GRAY, AND D. NAUMANN, "Abstraction-Based Software Developments," *Communications of the ACM* **29** (May 1986), pp. 402–15.

[Binkley and Schach, 1996] A. B. BINKLEY AND S. R. SCHACH, "A Comparison of Sixteen Quality Metrics for Object-Oriented Design," *Information Processing Letters,* Vol. 57, No. 6 (June 1996), pp. 271–75.

[Binkley and Schach, 1997] A. B. BINKLEY AND S. R. SCHACH, "Toward a Unified Approach to Object-Oriented Coupling," *Proceedings of the 35th Annual ACM Southeast Conference,* Murfreesboro, TN, April 2–4, 1997, pp. 91–97.

[Binkley and Schach, 1998] A. B. BINKLEY AND S. R. SCHACH, "Validation of the Coupling Dependency Metric as a Predictor of Run-Time Failures and Maintenance Measures," *Proceedings of the 1998 International Conference on Software Engineering,* Kyoto, Japan, April 1998, pp. 452–55.

[Blaha, Premerlani, and Rumbaugh, 1988] M. R. BLAHA, W. J. PREMERLANI, AND J. E. RUMBAUGH, "Relational Database Design Using an Object-Oriented Methodology," *Communications of the ACM* **31** (April 1988), pp. 414–27.

[Bruegge, Blythe, Jackson, and Shufelt, 1992] B. BRUEGGE, J. BLYTHE, J. JACKSON, AND J. SHUFELT, "Object-Oriented Modeling with OMT," *Proceedings of the Conference on Object-Oriented Programming, Languages, and Systems, OOPSLA '92, ACM SIGPLAN Notices* **27** (October 1992), pp. 359–76.

[Capper, Colgate, Hunter, and James, 1994] N. P. CAPPER, R. J. COLGATE, J. C. HUNTER, AND M. F. JAMES, "The Impact of Object-Oriented Technology on Software Quality: Three Case Histories," *IBM Systems Journal* **33** (No. 1, 1994), pp. 131–57.

[Chidamber and Kemerer, 1994] S. R. CHIDAMBER AND C. F. KEMERER, "A Metrics Suite for Object Oriented Design," *IEEE Transactions on Software Engineering* **20** (June 1994), pp. 476–93.

[Cox, 1986] B. J. COX, *Object-Oriented Programming: An Evolutionary Approach,* Addison-Wesley, Reading, MA, 1986.

[Dahl and Nygaard, 1966] O.-J. DAHL AND K. NYGAARD, "SIMULA—An ALGOL-Based Simulation Language," *Communications of the ACM* **9** (September, 1966), pp. 671–78.

[Dahl, Myrhaug, and Nygaard, 1973] O.-J. DAHL, B. MYRHAUG, AND K. NYGAARD, *SIMULA begin,* Auerbach, Philadelphia, 1973.

[Dijkstra, 1968b] E. W. DIJKSTRA, "The Structure of the 'THE' Multiprogramming System," *Communications of the ACM* **11** (May 1968), pp. 341–46.

[El-Rewini et al., 1995] H. EL-REWINI, S. HAMILTON, Y.-P. SHAN, R. EARLE, S. MCGAUGHEY, A. HELAL, R. BADRACHALAM, A. CHIEN, A. GRIMSHAW, B. LEE, A. WADE, D. MORSE, A. ELMAGRAMID, E. PITOURA, R. BINDER, AND P. WEGNER, "Object Technology," *IEEE Computer* **28** (October 1995), pp. 58–72.

[Fayad, Tsai, and Fulghum, 1996] M. E. FAYAD, W.-T. TSAI, AND M. L. FULGHUM, "Transition to Object-Oriented Software Development," *Communications of the ACM* **39** (February, 1996), pp. 108–21.

[Feldman, 1981] M. B. FELDMAN, "Data Abstraction, Structured Programming, and the Practicing Programmer," *Software—Practice and Experience* **11** (July 1981), pp. 697–710.

[Flanagan, 1996] D. FLANAGAN, *Java in a Nutshell,* O'Reilly and Associates, Sebastopol, CA, 1996.

[Goldberg and Robson, 1989] A. GOLDBERG AND D. ROBSON, *Smalltalk-80: The Language,* Addison-Wesley, Reading, MA, 1989.

[Guttag, 1977] J. GUTTAG, "Abstract Data Types and the Development of Data Structures," *Communications of the ACM* **20** (June 1977), pp. 396–404.

[Henderson-Sellers, 1996] B. HENDERSON-SELLERS, *Object-Oriented Metrics: Measures of Complexity,* Prentice Hall, Upper Saddle River, NJ, 1996.

[ISO/IEC 8652, 1995] "Programming Language Ada: Language and Standard Libraries," ISO/IEC 8652, International Organization for Standardization, International Electrotechnical Commission, 1995.

[Knuth, 1974] D. E. KNUTH, "Structured Programming with **go to** Statements," *ACM Computing Surveys* **6** (December 1974), pp. 261–301.

[Korson and McGregor, 1990] T. KORSON AND J. D. MCGREGOR, "Understanding Object-Oriented: A Unifying Paradigm," *Communications of the ACM* **33** (September 1990), pp. 40–60.

[Liskov and Guttag, 1986] B. LISKOV AND J. GUTTAG, *Abstraction and Specification in Program Development,* The MIT Press, Cambridge, MA, 1986.

[Liskov and Zilles, 1974] B. LISKOV AND S. ZILLES, "Programming with Abstract Data Types," *ACM SIGPLAN Notices* **9** (April 1974), pp. 50–59.

[Meyer, 1986] B. MEYER, "Genericity versus Inheritance," *Proceedings of the Conference on Object-Oriented Programming Systems, Languages and Applications, ACM SIGPLAN Notices* **21** (November 1986), pp. 391–405.

[Meyer, 1987] B. MEYER, "Reusability: The Case for Object-Oriented Design," *IEEE Software* **4** (March 1987), pp. 50–64.

[Meyer, 1990] B. MEYER, "Lessons from the Design of the Eiffel Libraries," *Communications of the ACM* **33** (September 1990), pp. 68–88.

[Meyer, 1992a] B. MEYER, "Applying 'Design by Contract'," *IEEE Computer* **25** (October 1992), pp. 40–51.

[Meyer, 1992b] B. MEYER, *Eiffel: The Language,* Prentice Hall, New York, 1992.

[Meyer, 1996b] B. MEYER, "The Many Faces of Inheritance: A Taxonomy of Taxonomy," *IEEE Computer* **29** (May 1996), pp. 105–8.

[Meyer, 1997] B. MEYER, *Object-Oriented Software Construction,* Second Edition, Prentice Hall, Upper Saddle River, NJ, 1997.

[Myers, 1975] G. J. MYERS, *Reliable Software through Composite Design,* Petrocelli/Charter, New York, 1975.

[Myers, 1978b] G. J. MYERS, *Composite/Structured Design,* Van Nostrand Reinhold, New York, 1978.

[Neumann, 1986] P. G. NEUMANN, "On Hierarchical Design of Computer Systems for Critical Applications," *IEEE Transactions on Software Engineering* **SE-12** (September 1986), pp. 905–20.

[Parnas, 1971] D. L. PARNAS, "Information Distribution Aspects of Design Methodology," *Proceedings of the IFIP Congress,* Ljubljana, Yugoslavia, 1971, pp. 339–44.

[Parnas, 1972a] D. L. PARNAS, "A Technique for Software Module Specification with Examples," *Communications of the ACM* **15** (May 1972), pp. 330–36.

[Parnas, 1972b] D. L. PARNAS, "On the Criteria to Be Used in Decomposing Systems into Modules," *Communications of the ACM* **15** (December 1972), pp. 1053–58.

[Parnas, Clements, and Weiss, 1985] D. L. PARNAS, P. C. CLEMENTS, AND D. M. WEISS, "The Modular Structure of Complex Systems," *IEEE Transactions on Software Engineering* **SE-11** (March 1985), pp. 259–66.

[Phillips, 1986] J. PHILLIPS, *The NAG Library: A Beginner's Guide,* Clarendon Press, Oxford, UK, 1986.

[Ponder and Bush, 1994] C. PONDER AND B. BUSH, "Polymorphism Considered Harmful," *ACM SIGSOFT Software Engineering Notes* **19** (April, 1994), pp. 35–38.

[Schach, 1996] S. R. SCHACH, "The Cohesion and Coupling of Objects," *Journal of Object-Oriented Programming* **8** (January 1966), pp. 48–50.

[Schach and Stevens-Guille, 1979] S. R. SCHACH AND P. D. STEVENS-GUILLE, "Two Aspects of Computer-Aided Design," *Transactions of the Royal Society of South Africa* **44** (Part 1, 1979), 123–26.

[Shaw, 1984] M. SHAW, "Abstraction Techniques in Modern Programming Languages," *IEEE Software* **1** (October 1984), pp. 10–26.

[Shneiderman and Mayer, 1975] B. SHNEIDERMAN AND R. MAYER, "Towards a Cognitive Model of Programmer Behavior," *Technical Report TR-37,* Indiana University, Bloomington, IN, 1975.

[Shriver and Wegner, 1987] B. SHRIVER AND P. WEGNER (Editors), *Research Directions in Object-Oriented Programming,* The MIT Press, Cambridge, MA, 1987.

[Snyder, 1993] A. SNYDER, "The Essence of Objects: Concepts and Terms," *IEEE Software* **10** (January 1993), pp. 31–42.

[Stefik and Bobrow, 1986] M. STEFIK AND D. G. BOBROW, "Object-Oriented Programming: Themes and Variations," *The AI Magazine* **6** (No. 4, 1986), pp. 40–62.

[Stevens, Myers, and Constantine, 1974] W. P. STEVENS, G. J. MYERS, AND L. L. CONSTANTINE, "Structured Design," *IBM Systems Journal* **13** (No. 2, 1974), pp. 115–39.

[Stroustrup, 1991] B. STROUSTRUP, *The C++ Programming Language,* Second Edition, Addison-Wesley, Reading, MA, 1991.

[Tanenbaum, 1990] A. S. TANENBAUM, *Structured Computer Organization,* Third Edition, Prentice Hall, Englewood Cliffs, NJ, 1990.

[Young and Gregory, 1972] D. M. YOUNG AND R. T. GREGORY, *A Survey of Numerical Mathematics, Volume I,* Addison-Wesley, Reading, MA, 1972.

[Yourdon and Constantine, 1979] E. YOURDON AND L. L. CONSTANTINE, *Structured Design: Fundamentals of a Discipline of Computer Program and Systems Design,* Prentice Hall, Englewood Cliffs, NJ, 1979.

chapter

7

REUSABILITY, PORTABILITY, AND INTEROPERABILITY

If reinventing the wheel were a criminal offense, many software professionals would today be languishing in jail. For example, there are tens of thousands (if not hundreds of thousands) of different COBOL payroll programs, all doing essentially the same thing. Surely all the world needs is one payroll program that can run on a variety of different hardware and that can be tailored, if necessary, to cater to the specific needs of an individual organization. However, instead of utilizing previously developed payroll programs, myriad organizations all over the world have built their own payroll program from scratch.

In this chapter we investigate why software engineers delight in reinventing the wheel over and over again, and what can be done to achieve portable software built using reusable components. We begin by distinguishing between portability and reusability.

7.1 REUSE CONCEPTS

A product is *portable* if it is significantly easier to modify the product as a whole in order to run it on another compiler/hardware/operating system configuration than to recode it from scratch. In contrast, *reuse* refers to taking components of one product in order to facilitate the development of a different product with different functionality. A reusable component need not necessarily be a module or a code fragment—it could be a design, a part of a manual, a set of test data, or a duration and cost estimate.

There are two types of reuse, accidental reuse and deliberate reuse. If the developers of a new product realize that a component of a previously developed product can be reused in the new product, then this is *accidental reuse.* On the other hand, utilization of software components constructed specifically for the purpose of possible future reuse is *deliberate reuse.* One potential advantage of deliberate reuse over accidental reuse is that components specially constructed for use in future products are more likely to be easy and safe to reuse; such components are generally well documented and thoroughly tested. In addition, they will usually display a uniformity of style that makes maintenance easier. The other side of the coin is that implementing deliberate reuse within a company can be expensive. It takes time to specify, design, implement, test, and document a software component. However, there can be no guarantee that such a component will ever be reused and thereby recoup the money invested in developing the potentially reusable component.

When computers were first constructed, nothing was reused. Every time a product was developed, items such as multiplication routines, input/output routines, or routines for computing sines and cosines were constructed from scratch. Quite soon, however, it was realized that this was a considerable waste of effort, and subroutine libraries were constructed. Programmers could then simply invoke square root or sine functions whenever they wished. These subroutine libraries have become more and more sophisticated and have developed into run-time support routines. Thus, when a programmer calls a C++ method, there is no need to write code to manage the stack or to pass the arguments explicitly; it is automatically handled by calling the appropriate run-time support routines. The concept of subroutine libraries has also been extended to large-scale statistical libraries such as SPSS [Norusis 1982] and to numerical analysis libraries like NAG [Phillips, 1986]. Class libraries are also playing a major role in assisting users of object-oriented languages. The environment for the language Eiffel incorporates seven libraries of classes [Meyer, 1990]. The success of Smalltalk is at least partly due to the wide variety of items in the Smalltalk library. In both instances, the presence of a browser, a CASE tool that assists the user to scan a class library, is of enormous assistance. With regard to C++ there are a large number of different libraries available, many in the public domain. One example is the C++ Standard Template Library (STL) [Musser and Saini, 1996].

An application programming interface (API) is generally a set of operating system calls that facilitate programming. For example, Win32 is an API for Microsoft operating systems such as Windows 95 and Windows NT, and the Macintosh Toolbox is an API for the Macintosh OS. Although an API is usually implemented as a set of operating system calls, to the programmer the routines comprising the API can be viewed as a subroutine library. For example, the Java Application Programming Interface (API) consists of a number of packages (libraries).

No matter how high the quality of a software product may be, it will not sell if it takes 4 years to get it onto the market when a competitive product can be delivered in only 2 years. The length of the development process is critical in a market economy. All other criteria as to what constitutes a "good" product are irrelevant if the product cannot compete timewise. For a corporation that has repeatedly failed to get a product to market first, software reuse offers a tempting technique. After all, if an existing component is reused, then there is no need to design, implement, test, and document that component. The key point is that, on average, only about 15 percent of any software product serves a truly original purpose [Jones, 1984]. The other 85 percent of the product could in theory be standardized and then reused in future products.

The figure of 85 percent is essentially a theoretical upper limit for the reuse rate; nevertheless, reuse rates of the order of 40 percent can be achieved in practice, as described in Section 7.3. This leads to an obvious question: If such reuse rates are attainable in practice and if reuse is by no means a new idea, why are so few organizations employing reuse to shorten the development process?

7.2 IMPEDIMENTS TO REUSE

There are a number of impediments to reuse. The first impediment is ego. All too many software professionals would rather rewrite a routine from scratch than reuse a routine written by someone else, the implication being that a routine cannot be any good unless they wrote it themselves, otherwise known as the "not invented here" (NIH) syndrome [Griss, 1993]. NIH is a management issue and can be solved if management is aware of the problem, usually by offering financial incentives to promote reuse. A second impediment is a quality issue. Many developers would be willing to reuse a routine provided he or she could be sure that the routine in question would not introduce faults into the product. This attitude is perfectly easy to understand. After all, every software professional has seen faulty software written by others. The solution here is to subject potentially reusable routines to exhaustive testing before making them available for reuse. A third impediment is the retrieval problem. That is, a large organization may have hundreds of thousands of potentially useful components. How should these components be stored for effective later retrieval? For example, a reusable components database might consist of 20,000 items, 125 of which are sort routines. The database must be organized so that the designer of a new product can quickly determine which (if any) of those 125 sort routines are appropriate for the new product. Solving the storage/retrieval problem is a technical issue for which a wide variety of solutions have been proposed, such as [Meyer, 1987; Prieto-Díaz, 1991]. Fourth, reuse is expensive. Tracz has stated that there are three costs involved, namely, the cost of making something reusable, the cost of reusing it, and the cost of defining and implementing a reuse process [Tracz, 1994]. He estimates that just making a component reusable increases its cost by at least 60 percent. Some organizations have reported cost increases of 200 percent and even up to 480 percent, whereas the cost of making a component reusable was only 11 percent in one Hewlett-Packard reuse project, as reported in Section 7.3.5 [Lim, 1994].

The preceding four impediments can be overcome, at least in principle. The fifth impediment is more problematic, namely, legal issues that arise with contract software. In terms of the type of contract that is usually drawn up between a client and a software development organization, the software product belongs to the client. Thus, if the software developer reuses a component of one client's product in a new product for a different client, this essentially constitutes a violation of the first client's copyright. For internal software, that is, when the developers and client are members of the same organization, this problem does not arise. Thus, other than certain legal issues, there are essentially no major impediments to implementing reuse within a software organization.

7.3 REUSE CASE STUDIES

Six case studies showing how reuse has been achieved in practice are now presented. They span the period from 1976 to 1996.

7.3.1 RAYTHEON MISSILE SYSTEMS DIVISION

In 1976 a study was undertaken at Raytheon's Missile Systems Division to determine whether deliberate reuse of designs and code was feasible [Lanergan and Grasso, 1984]. Over 5000 COBOL products in use were analyzed and classified. The researchers determined that only six basic actions are performed in a business application product. As a result, between 40 percent and 60 percent of business application designs and modules could be standardized and reused. The basic actions were found to be: sort data, edit or manipulate data, combine data, explode data, update data, and report on data. For the next 6 years, a concerted attempt was made to reuse both design and code wherever possible.

The Raytheon approach employed reuse in two ways, namely, what the researchers termed functional modules and COBOL program logic structures. In Raytheon's terminology a *functional module* is a COBOL code fragment designed and coded for a specific purpose, such as an edit routine, database procedure division call, tax computation routine, or date aging routine for accounts receivable. Use of the 3200 reusable modules resulted in applications that on average consisted of 60 percent reused code. Functional modules were carefully designed, tested, and documented. Products that used these functional modules were found to be more reliable, and less testing of the product as a whole was needed.

The modules were stored in a standard copy library and were obtained with the **copy** verb. That is, the code was not physically present within the application product, but was included by the COBOL compiler at compilation time; the mechanism is similar to **#include** in C or C++. The resulting source code was therefore shorter than if the copied code were physically present. As a consequence, maintenance was easier.

The Raytheon researchers also used what they termed a *COBOL program logic structure*. This is a framework that has to be fleshed out into a complete product. One example of a logic structure is the update logic structure. This is used for performing a sequential update, such as the case study in Section 4.6.1. Error handling is built in, as is sequence checking. The logic structure is 22 paragraphs (units of a COBOL program) in length. Many of the paragraphs can be filled in by using functional modules such as get_transaction, print_page_headings,

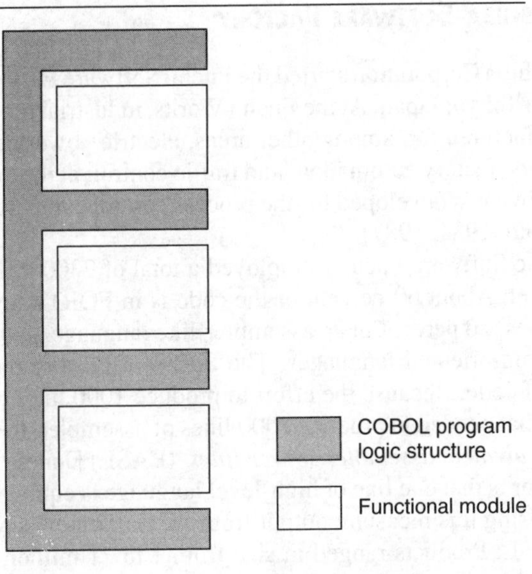

Figure 7.1 Symbolic representation of Raytheon Missile Systems Division reuse mechanism.

and print_control_totals. Figure 7.1 is a symbolic depiction of the framework of a COBOL program logic structure with the paragraphs filled in by functional modules.

There are many advantages to the use of such templates. It makes the design and coding of a product quicker and easier because the framework of the product is already present; all that is needed is to fill in the details. Fault-prone areas such as end-of-file conditions have already been tested. In fact, testing as a whole is easier. But Raytheon believed that the major advantage occurs when the user requests modifications or enhancements. Once a maintenance programmer is familiar with the relevant logic structure, it is almost as if that maintenance programmer had been a member of the original development team.

By 1983 logic structures had been used over 5500 times in developing new products. About 60 percent of the code consisted of functional modules, that is, reusable code. This meant that design, coding, module testing, and documentation time could also be reduced by 60 percent, leading to an estimated 50 percent increase in productivity in software product development. But for Raytheon, the real benefit of the technique lay in the hope that the readability and understandability resulting from the consistent style would reduce the cost of maintenance by between 60 percent and 80 percent. (Unfortunately, Raytheon closed the division before the necessary maintenance data could be obtained.)

It might seem that reuse is applicable only to business data processing applications. But that is not so, as is demonstrated by the second case study, the Toshiba Software Factory.

7.3.2 TOSHIBA SOFTWARE FACTORY

In 1977 the Toshiba Corporation started the Fuchu Software Factory at the Toshiba Fuchu Works in Tokyo, Japan. At the Fuchu Works, industrial process control systems are manufactured for, among other areas, electric power networks, nuclear power generators, factory automation, and traffic control; at the Software Factory, application software is developed for the process control computers for those systems [Matsumoto, 1984, 1987].

By 1985 the Software Factory employed a total of 2300 technical and managerial personnel. About 60 percent of the code is in FORTRAN augmented by real-time routines, 20 percent in an assembler-like language, and the rest in user-specified problem-oriented languages. The Software Factory measures productivity in lines of code. Because the effort to produce 1000 lines of FORTRAN is different from that needed to produce 1000 lines of assembler, the unit of productivity used is *equivalent assembler source lines,* (EASL) [Jones, 1996]; the usual conversion factor is that one line of high-level language is equivalent to four lines of assembler. Using this measure, output from the Software Factory in 1985 was 7.2 million EASL. Products ranged in size from 1 to 21 million EASL, with an average size of 4 million EASL.

Software was developed using the waterfall model, with detailed reviews and inspections at the end of each phase. Productivity, measured in EASL, is the driving force behind the Software Factory. It is monitored on both a projectwide basis as well as on an individual basis. Annual productivity increases for the Factory as a whole have been of the order of 8 percent to 9 percent. One of the items measured when appraising the performance of individuals is their fault rate. In the case of a programmer, for example, the number of faults per 1000 EASL is expected to decrease over time as a consequence of training and experience. Quality is an important aspect of the Factory and is achieved through a number of different mechanisms, including reviews, inspections, and quality circles (groups of workers who meet on a regular basis to find ways to improve quality).

Matsumoto attributes improvements in both productivity and quality to reuse of existing software (that is, accidental reuse) [Matsumoto, 1987]. This reusable software includes not only modules but also documentation of all kinds, such as designs, specifications, contracts, and manuals. A committee is responsible for deciding what components should be placed in the *reusable software components database* where they are indexed by keyword for later retrieval. Careful statistics are kept on the reuse rate of every component in the database. In 1985 the documentation reuse rate, that is, the number of reused pages divided by the total number of pages of documentation, was 32 percent. In the design phase, the reuse rate was 33 percent, whereas 48 percent of code was reused during the implementation phase. In addition, statistics were kept on the sizes of reused software components; about 55 percent were 1 to 10K EASL in size, and 36 percent were in the 10K to 100K EASL range.

Corresponding statistics for 25 software products developed by NASA follow in the next section.

7.3.3 NASA SOFTWARE

Selby has characterized the accidental reuse of software in a NASA software production group that produces ground support software for unmanned spacecraft control [Selby, 1989]. Altogether 25 software products were investigated. They ranged in size from 3000 to 112,000 lines of source code. The 7188 component modules were classified into four categories. Group 1 consisted of modules that were used without any changes. Group 2 were those modules reused with slight revisions, that is, less than 25 percent of the code was changed. Modules falling into group 3 were reused with major revisions; 25 percent or more of the code was changed. Group 4 modules were developed from scratch.

A total of 2954 FORTRAN modules in the sample were studied in detail. On average, 45 percent of the modules were reused in modified or unmodified form. More specifically, 28 percent fell into group 1, 10 percent into group 2, and 7 percent into group 3. In general, the reused modules were small, well documented, with simple interfaces and little input/output processing, and tended to be terminal nodes in a module interconnection diagram (such as Figure 6.7).

These results are not really surprising. Small, well-documented modules are easier to comprehend than large modules with poor documentation and are therefore more likely to be reused. In addition, a large module is likely to perform a number of different actions, or perhaps one rather specialized action, and is therefore less likely to be reused than its smaller counterpart. A complex interface implies a large number of arguments, which tends to reduce the reuse of a module. Input/output processing can be somewhat application-specific and therefore less reusable. Finally, comparing terminal modules in a module interconnection diagram with modules higher up in the diagram, a terminal module is more likely to carry out a specific task, whereas a module higher up is usually decision-oriented (this is discussed in more depth in Section 14.1.1). As a result, a terminal module is more likely to be reusable than a nonterminal one.

A more constructive way of looking at Selby's results is to utilize them to ensure that modules can be reused in future products. Management should ensure that a specific design objective should be small modules with simple interfaces. Input/output processing should be localized to a few modules. All modules must be properly documented.

There are considerable differences between the NASA group and the Fuchu software factory. In particular, the decision to reuse software was the personal choice of the NASA software developers; there were no managerial directives of any kind. The NASA staffers reused software simply because they believed that reuse is a worthwhile software engineering technique. In addition, there were no software tools to assist with the reuse process. This situation is in stark contrast to the reuse-oriented management of the Fuchu Works and the sophisticated software component retrieval mechanisms employed there. Despite this, surprisingly high reuse rates have been obtained at NASA.

The fourth case study highlights the effect of management commitment to reuse.

7.3.4 GTE DATA SERVICES

A successful accidental reuse scheme has been implemented at GTE Data Services [Prieto-Díaz, 1991]. Unlike the NASA case study, a key aspect of the GTE scheme was full management commitment to the reuse of source code modules. In order to promote reuse, cash incentives of between $50 and $100 were paid for a module that was accepted for possible reuse, and royalties were paid when that module was actually reused. In addition, managers' budgets were increased when projects they were managing achieved a high level of reuse. There was even a "Reuser of the Month" award.

The results of this scheme were as follows. In 1988 a reuse level of 14 percent was achieved; this saved the company an estimated $1,500,000. The following year it was estimated that the reuse level rose to 20 percent, and a 50 percent level was predicted for 1993. One of the reasons that GTE pushed their reuse scheme so strongly was that they had anticipated overall savings of well over $10 million by that date.

There are a number of interesting aspects of the GTE reuse program. First, the total number of modules available for reuse dropped from 190 in 1988 to 128 in 1990, despite the fact that new modules were added. It appears that, at least in organizations such as GTE Data Services, it is not necessary to build a huge inventory of reusable components. Second, the emphasis was on larger modules (10,000 lines of code or more), because of the greater payoff. In contrast to the NASA experience where smaller modules tended to be reused, GTE succeeded in reusing larger modules. This disparity emphasizes the importance of having management commitment to any reuse program.

7.3.5 HEWLETT-PACKARD

Hewlett-Packard has implemented reuse programs in many different divisions of the company [Lim, 1994]. In general, these programs have been successful from the viewpoint of improved software quality as a consequence of reuse. Two specific programs are discussed here.

The manufacturing productivity section of the software technology division has had an accidental reuse program in place since 1983. The section develops software for manufacturing resource planning. The components chosen for reuse are written in Pascal and SPL (the language for systems software on the HP 3000 computer system). The fault rate for new code is 4.1 faults per 1000 noncomment lines of code (KLOC), but only 0.9 faults per KLOC for the reused code. As a consequence of reuse, the overall fault rate has dropped to only 2.0 faults per KLOC, a 51 percent reduction. Productivity has increased 57 percent, to 1.1 KLOC per person-month in 1992. The program has cost $1 million, but has saved $4.1 million between 1983 and 1992. Amazingly, the project broke even in its second year.

Since 1987, there has been a planned reuse program in the San Diego Technical Graphics (STG) division of Hewlett-Packard. This division develops and maintains firmware for plotters and printers. A single product consisting of 20,000 noncomment lines of C was developed over a period of 3 years and then reused. The gross cost of the reuse program between 1987 and 1994 (1994 data estimated) was $2.6 million, and savings were $5.6 million. There was a 24 percent reduction in the fault rate to 1.3 faults per KLOC. Also, productivity increased by 40 percent to 0.7 KLOC per person-month. Finally, the delivery time for a product decreased by 24 percent.

The costs of the STG reuse program are also interesting. The cost of developing the reusable firmware component was only 11 percent more than the cost of a similar nonreusable component. Integration costs were 19 percent of the cost of developing a nonreusable component. That is, each time the component was reused, the cost was only about one-fifth of the cost of developing that component from scratch.

The overall lesson of these five case studies is that reuse is possible in practice and can result in significant cost savings. However, the major push for reuse must come from management.

The final case study is a cautionary tale, rather than a success story.

7.3.6 EUROPEAN SPACE AGENCY

On June 4, 1996, the European Space agency launched the Ariane 5 rocket for the first time. As a consequence of a software fault, the rocket crashed about 37 seconds after lift-off. The cost of the rocket and payload was about $500 million, making this the most costly software fault to date [Jézéquel and Meyer, 1997]. (Clearly, no financial value can possibly be attached to faults that have caused a loss of human life such as those listed in the Just in Case You Wanted to Know box on page 4.)

The primary cause of the failure was an attempt to convert a 64-bit integer into a 16-bit unsigned integer. The number being converted was larger than 2^{16}, so an Ada **exception** (run-time failure) occurred. Unfortunately, there was no explicit exception handler in the code to deal with this exception, so the software crashed. This caused the on-board computers to crash which, in turn, caused the Ariane 5 rocket to crash.

Ironically, the conversion that caused the failure was unnecessary. Certain computations are performed before lift-off to align the Inertial Reference System. These computations should normally stop 9 seconds before lift-off. However, if there is a subsequent hold in the countdown, resetting the Inertial Reference System after the countdown has recommenced can take several hours. To prevent that happening, the computations continue for 50 seconds after the start of flight mode, that is, well into the flight (notwithstanding the fact that, once lift-off has occurred, there is no way to align the Inertial Reference System). It was this futile continuation of the alignment process that caused the failure.

The European Space Agency uses a careful software development process that incorporates an effective SQA component. The obvious question is then: Why was there no exception handler in the Ada code to handle the possibility of such an overflow? In order not to overload the computer, conversions that could not possibly result in overflow were left unprotected. The code in question was 10 years old. It had been reused, unchanged and without any further testing, from the software controlling the Ariane 4 rocket (the precursor of the Ariane 5). Mathematical analysis had proved that the computation in question was totally safe for the Ariane 4. However, the analysis was performed on the basis of certain assumptions that were true for the Ariane 4 but did not hold for the Ariane 5. Thus, the analysis was no longer valid, and the code needed the protection of an exception handler to cater to the possibility of an overflow. Were it not for the performance constraint, there would surely have been exception handlers throughout the Ariane 5 Ada code. Alternatively, the use of the **assert** pragma both during testing and in production mode (Section 5.5.3) could have prevented the Ariane 5 crash if the relevant module had included an assertion that the number to be converted was smaller than 2^{16} [Jézéquel and Meyer, 1997].

The major lesson of this reuse experience is that software developed in one context must be retested when reused in another context. That is, a reused software module does not require to be retested by itself, but it must be retested after it has been integrated into the product in which it is reused. Another lesson is that it is unwise to rely exclusively on the results of mathematical proofs, as discussed in Section 5.5.2.

We now consider whether there is any evidence that designing a product in terms of objects encourages reuse, and hence improves software productivity.

7.4 Objects and Productivity

When the theory of composite/structured design (C/SD) was first put forward, the claim was made that an ideal module was one with functional cohesion (Section 6.2.7). That is, if a module performed one and only one action, it was thought to be an ideal candidate for reuse, and maintenance of such a module was expected to be easy. The flaw in this reasoning is that a module with functional cohesion is not self-contained and independent. Instead, it has to operate on data. If such a module is reused, then the data on which it is to operate must be reused, too. If the data in the new product are not identical to those in the original, then either the data have to be changed or the module with functional cohesion has to be changed. Similar issues arise with regard to maintenance.

According to C/SD the next best type of module is a module with informational cohesion (Section 6.2.6). Such a module is essentially an object, that is, an instance of a class. An object is the fundamental building block of software because it models all aspects of a particular real-world entity (conceptual independence, or encapsulation), but conceals the implementation of both its data and the actions that operate on the data (physical independence, or information hiding). This self-contained nature of an object is why use of the object-oriented paradigm can make both development and maintenance easier.

It is therefore not surprising that many organizations have reported that when they use object-oriented techniques for software development, their software costs appear to decrease and overall quality improves. Team organization (Section 4.1) is frequently a major cause of problems in the development of large-scale products. The object-oriented paradigm allows a large product to be treated, in many ways, as a collection of essentially independent smaller products, and managing the development is far easier. This is one of the reasons why the object-oriented paradigm is superior to the structured paradigm for large products.

Notwithstanding the many advantages of the object-oriented paradigm, some difficulties and problems have been reported. A frequently reported problem concerns development effort and size. The first time anything new is done, it takes longer than on subsequent occasions; this initial period is sometimes referred to as the *learning curve.* But when the object-oriented paradigm is used for the first time by an organization, it often takes longer than anticipated, even allowing for the learning curve. This is because the size of the product is larger than when structured techniques are used. This is particularly noticeable when the product has a graphical user interface (GUI) (see Section 9.3). Thereafter, however, things improve greatly. First, maintenance costs are lower, thus reducing the overall lifetime cost of the product. Second, the next time that a new product is developed, some of the classes from the previous project can be reused, further reducing software costs. This has been especially significant when a GUI has been used for the first time; much of the effort that went into the GUI can be recouped in subsequent products.

Problems of inheritance are harder to solve. A major reason for using inheritance is that a new subclass that differs slightly from its parent class can be created without affecting the parent class or any other ancestor class in the inheritance hierarchy. Conversely, however, once a product has been implemented, any change to an existing class directly affects all its descendants in the inheritance hierarchy; this is often referred to as the *fragile base class problem.* At the very least, the affected units will have to be recompiled. In some cases, the methods of the relevant objects (instantiations of the affected subclasses) will have to be recoded; this can be a nontrivial task. To minimize this problem it is important that all classes be carefully designed during the development process. This will reduce the ripple effect induced by a change to an existing class.

A second problem can result from a cavalier use of inheritance. Unless explicitly prevented, a subclass inherits all the attributes of its parent class(es). Usually, subclasses have additional attributes of their own. As a consequence, objects lower in the inheritance hierarchy can quickly get large, with resulting storage problems [Bruegge, Blythe, Jackson, and Shufelt, 1992]. One way to prevent this is to change the dictum "use inheritance wherever possible" to "use inheritance wherever appropriate." In addition, if a descendent class does not need an attribute of an ancestor, then that attribute should be explicitly excluded.

A third group of problems stem from polymorphism and dynamic binding. These were described in Section 6.8.

Despite these problems, there is no shortage of informal reports on the benefits of using object-oriented techniques. In addition, published papers such as

[Capper, Colgate, Hunter, and James, 1994] describe successful projects that have been carried out using the object-oriented paradigm. A large body of evidence is accumulating that indicates that the object-oriented paradigm is now the appropriate software process. This is discussed further in Chapter 11.

7.5 REUSE DURING THE DESIGN AND IMPLEMENTATION PHASES

Dramatically different types of reuse are possible during the design phase. The reused material can vary from just one or two modules to the architecture of the complete software product. We now examine various types of design reuse, some of which carry over into the implementation phase.

7.5.1 MODULE REUSE

When designing a product, a member of the design team may realize that a module or class from an earlier design can be reused in the current project, with or without minor modifications. This type of reuse is particularly common in an organization that develops software in one specific application domain, such as banking or air traffic control systems. The organization can promote this type of reuse by setting up a repository of design components that are likely to be reused in the future and encouraging designers to reuse them, perhaps by means of a cash bonus for each such reuse. There are two advantages of this type of reuse, limited though it may be. First, tested module designs are incorporated into the product. The overall design can therefore be produced more quickly and is likely to have a higher quality than when the entire design is produced from scratch. Second, if the design of a module can be reused, it is likely that the implementation of that module can also be reused, if not the actual code then at least conceptually.

This approach can be extended to library reuse, depicted in Figure 7.2(a). A library is a set of related reusable routines. For example, developers of scientific software rarely write the routines to perform such common tasks as matrix inversion or finding eigenvalues. Instead, a scientific library such as LAPACK 2.0 [Anderson et al., 1995] is purchased. Then, whenever possible, the routines in the scientific library are utilized in future software. With the rise in popularity of the object-oriented paradigm, class libraries for scientific software have also been developed, such as LAPACK++ [Dongarra et al., 1993], DiffPack [Langtangen, 1994], and C-XSC [Klatte et al., 1993].

Another example is a library for a graphical user interface (GUI). Instead of writing the GUI methods from scratch, it is far more convenient to use a GUI class library or *toolkit,* that is, a set of classes that can handle every aspect of the GUI. There are many GUI toolkits of this kind, including the Java Abstract Windowing Toolkit [Flanagan, 1996].

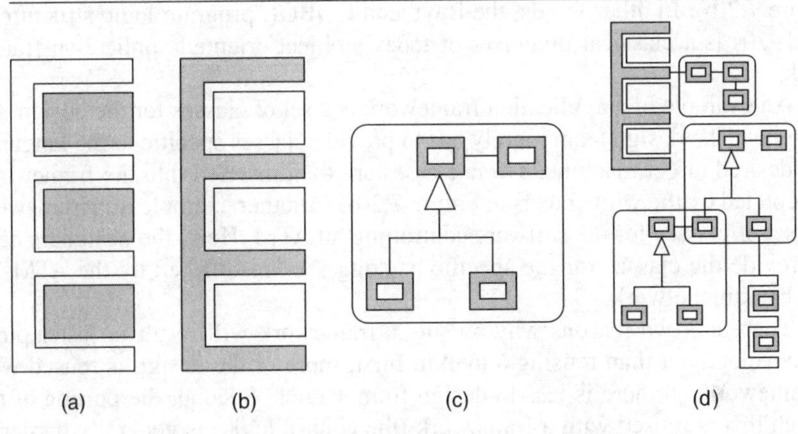

Figure 7.2 Symbolic representation of four types of design reuse. Shading denotes design reuse within (a) a library or a toolkit, (b) a framework, (c) a design pattern, and (d) a software architecture comprising a framework, a toolkit, and three design patterns.

A problem with library reuse is that libraries are frequently presented in the format of a set of reusable subroutines, rather than reusable designs. Toolkits, too, generally promote code reuse rather than design reuse. When the object-oriented paradigm is used, however, this problem can be alleviated with the help of a browser, that is, a CASE tool for displaying the inheritance tree. The designer can then traverse the inheritance tree of the library, examine the fields of the various classes, and determine which class is applicable to the current design.

A key aspect of library and toolkit reuse is that, as depicted in Figure 7.2(a), the designer is responsible for the control logic of the product as a whole. The library or toolkit contributes to the software development process by supplying parts of the design that incorporate the specific operations of the product.

On the other hand, an application framework is the converse of a library or toolkit in that it supplies the control logic; the developers are responsible for the design of the specific operations. This is described in the next section.

7.5.2 APPLICATION FRAMEWORKS

As shown in Figure 7.2(b), a *application framework* incorporates the control logic of a design. When a framework is reused, the developers have to design the application-specific operations of the product being built.

The term "framework" nowadays usually refers to an object-oriented application framework. For example, in [Gamma, Helm, Johnson, and Vlissides, 1995] a framework is defined as a "set of cooperating classes that make up a reusable design for a specific class of software." However, consider the Raytheon Missiles Systems Division case study of Section 7.3.1. Figure 7.1 is identical to

Figure 7.2(b). In other words, the Raytheon COBOL program logic structure of the 1970s is a classical precursor of today's object-oriented application framework.

An example of a application framework is a set of classes for the design of a compiler. The design team merely has to provide classes specific to the language and desired target machine. These classes are then inserted into the framework, as depicted by the white boxes in Figure 7.2(b). Another example of a framework is a set of classes for the software controlling an ATM. Here, the designers need to provide the classes for the specific banking services offered by the ATMs of that banking network.

There are two reasons why reusing a framework will result in faster product development than reusing a toolkit. First, more of the design is reused with a framework, so there is less to design from scratch. Second, the portion of the design that is reused with a framework (the control logic) is generally harder to design than the operations, so the quality of the resulting design is also likely to be higher than when a toolkit is reused. As with library/toolkit reuse, it is often possible that the implementation of the framework can be reused as well. The developers will probably have to use the names and calling conventions of the framework, but that is a small price to pay. Also, the resulting product is likely to be easily maintained because the control logic will have been tested in other products that have reused that application framework, and also because the maintainer may have previously maintained another product that reused that same framework.

In addition to application frameworks, there are many code frameworks. One of the first commercially successful code frameworks was MacApp, a framework for writing application software on the Macintosh [Wilson, Rosenstein, and Shafer, 1990]. The Microsoft Foundation Class Library (MFC) is a large collection of frameworks for building GUIs in Windows-based applications. MFC applications can perform standard windowing operations, such as moving and resizing windows, processing input via dialog boxes, and handling events like mouse clicks or menu selections [Holzner, 1993]. Borland's Visual Component Library (VCL), an update of the ObjectWindows Library (OWL), has functionality similar to that of MFC. However, VCL is fully object-oriented. This is one of the many reasons why some feel that VCL is superior to MFC [Wells, 1996].

We now consider design patterns.

7.5.3 DESIGN PATTERNS

Christopher Alexander (see the Just in Case You Wanted to Know Box on page 231) has said, "Each pattern describes a problem which occurs over and over again in our environment, and then describes the core of the solution to that problem, in such a way that you can use this solution a million times over, without ever doing it the same way twice" [Alexander et al., 1977]. Although he was writing within the context of patterns in buildings and other architectural objects, his remarks are equally applicable to design patterns.

A design pattern is a solution to a general design problem in the form of a set of interacting classes that have to be customized to create a specific design.

JUST IN CASE YOU WANTED TO KNOW

One of the most influential individuals in the field of object-oriented software engineering is Christopher Alexander, a world-famous architect who freely admits to knowing little or nothing about objects or software engineering. In his books, and especially in [Alexander et al., 1977], he describes a pattern language for architecture, that is, for describing towns, buildings, rooms, gardens, and so on. His ideas were adopted and adapted by object-oriented software engineers, especially the so-called "Gang of Four" (Erich Gamma, Richard Helm, Ralph Johnson, and John Vlissides). Their best-selling book on design patterns [Gamma, Helm, Johnson, and Vlissides, 1995] has resulted in Alexander's ideas being widely accepted by the object-oriented community.

Patterns occur in other contexts as well. For example, when approaching an airport, pilots have to know the appropriate landing pattern, that is, the sequence of directions, altitudes, and turns needed to land the plane on the correct runway. Also, a dressmaking pattern is a series of shapes that can be used repeatedly to create a particular dress. Thus, the concept of a pattern itself is by no means novel. What is new is the application of patterns to software development, especially design.

This is depicted in Figure 7.2(c). The shaded boxes connected by lines denote the interacting classes. The white boxes inside the shaded boxes denote that these classes must be customized for a specific design.

In order to understand how patterns can assist with software development, consider the following example. Suppose that a software organization wishes to build a GUI generator, a tool that assists developers in constructing a graphical user interface. Instead of having to develop the various *widgets* (such as windows, buttons, menus, sliders, and scroll bars) from scratch, a developer can make use of the set of classes of the GUI generator that defines the widgets to be utilized within the application program.

The problem is that there are many different GUIs, each with their own "look-and-feel," including Motif [Mione, 1998], SunView, and OpenWindows [OpenWindows, 1993]. The GUI generator is to support all three GUIs. However, if the GUI generator hard-codes one specific GUI into an application program, it will be difficult to modify that application program in the future by replacing the generated GUI with a different GUI. For example, suppose that the application program is to have a Motif GUI. Then, every time a menu is to be generated, message create Motif menu is sent. However, if that application program now needs to have a SunView GUI, every instance of create Motif menu must be replaced by create SunView menu. For a large application program, such a conversion from Motif to SunView is laborious and fault-prone.

The solution is to design the GUI generator in such a way that the application program is uncoupled from the specific GUI. This can be achieved using the design pattern named *Abstract Factory* [Gamma, Helm, Johnson, and Vlissides, 1995]. Figure 7.3 shows the resulting design. In this figure, the names of abstract classes and their abstract methods are in italics. (An abstract class is a class that cannot be instantiated, although it can be used as a base class. It usually contains at least one abstract method.) At the top of Figure 7.3 is abstract

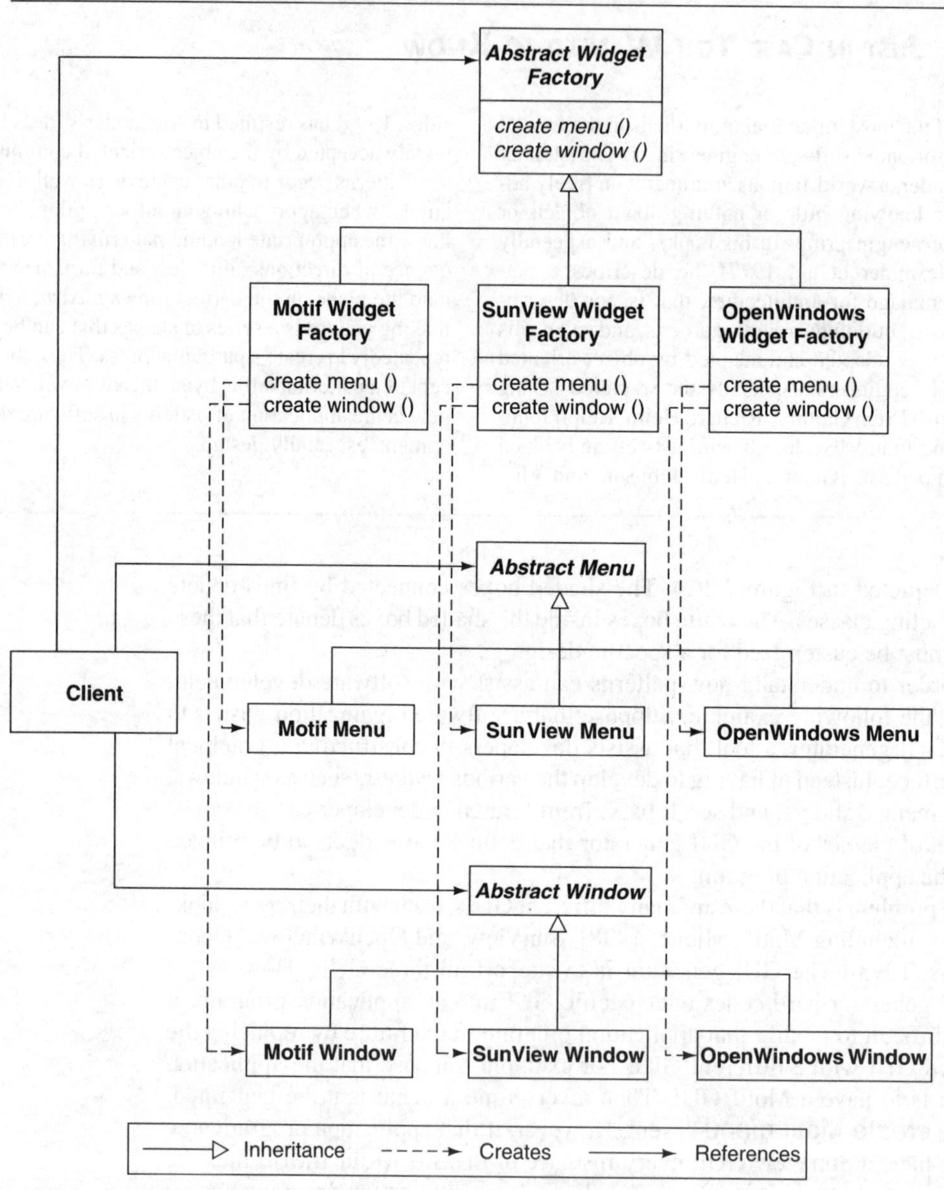

Figure 7.3 Design of graphical user interface toolkit. Names of abstract classes and their abstract methods are italicized.

class ***Abstract Widget Factory*** (the UML convention is that classes appear in boldface with the first letter of each word capitalized). This abstract class contains numerous abstract methods; for simplicity, only two are shown here: *create menu* and *create window*. Moving down in the figure, **Motif Widget Factory**, **SunView Widget Factory**, and **OpenWindows Widget Factory** are concrete subclasses of ***Abstract Widget Factory***. Each of these classes contains the specific methods for creating widgets for a given graphical user interface. For example, create menu within **Motif Widget Factory** will cause a menu object that conforms to the look-and-feel of Motif to be created.

There are also abstract classes for each widget. Two are shown here, ***Abstract Menu*** and ***Abstract Window***. Each has concrete subclasses, one for each of the three GUIs. For example, **Motif Menu** is one concrete subclass of ***Abstract Menu***. Method create menu within concrete subclass **Motif Widget Factory** will cause an object of type **Motif Menu** to be created.

To create a window, a **Client** object within the application program need only send a message to method *create window* of ***Abstract Widget Factory*** and polymorphism will ensure that the correct widget is created. Suppose that the application program is to have a Motif GUI. First, an object GUI Factory of type (class) **Motif Widget Factory** is created. Then a message to abstract method *create window* of ***Abstract Widget Factory*** passing GUI Factory as parameter is interpreted as a message to method create window within concrete subclass **Motif Widget Factory**. Method create window will in turn send a message to create a **Motif Window**; this is indicated by the leftmost vertical dashed line in Figure 7.3.

The critical aspect of this figure is that the three interfaces between the **Client** within the application program and the widget factory, namely, classes ***Abstract Widget Factory***, ***Abstract Menu***, and ***Abstract Window***, are all abstract classes. None of these interfaces are specific to any one GUI because the methods of the abstract classes are **abstract**. Thus, the design of Figure 7.3 has indeed uncoupled the application program from the GUI.

The design of Figure 7.3 is an instance of pattern ***Abstract Factory*** shown in Figure 7.4. To use this pattern, specific classes replace the generic names like **Concrete Factory 2** and **Product B3**. That is why Figure 7.2(c), the symbolic representation of a design pattern, contains white rectangles within the shaded rectangles; the white rectangles represent the details that have to be supplied to reuse this pattern in a design.

Patterns can interact with other patterns. This is symbolically represented in Figure 7.2(d) where the bottom-left block of the middle pattern is again a pattern. A case study of a document editor in [Gamma, Helm, Johnson, and Vlissides, 1995] contains eight different interacting patterns. That is what happens in practice; it is unusual for the design of a product to contain just one pattern.

As with toolkits and frameworks, if a design pattern is reused, then an implementation of that pattern can probably also be reused. In addition, there are also analysis patterns that can assist with object-oriented analysis [Coad, 1992; Fowler, 1997a].

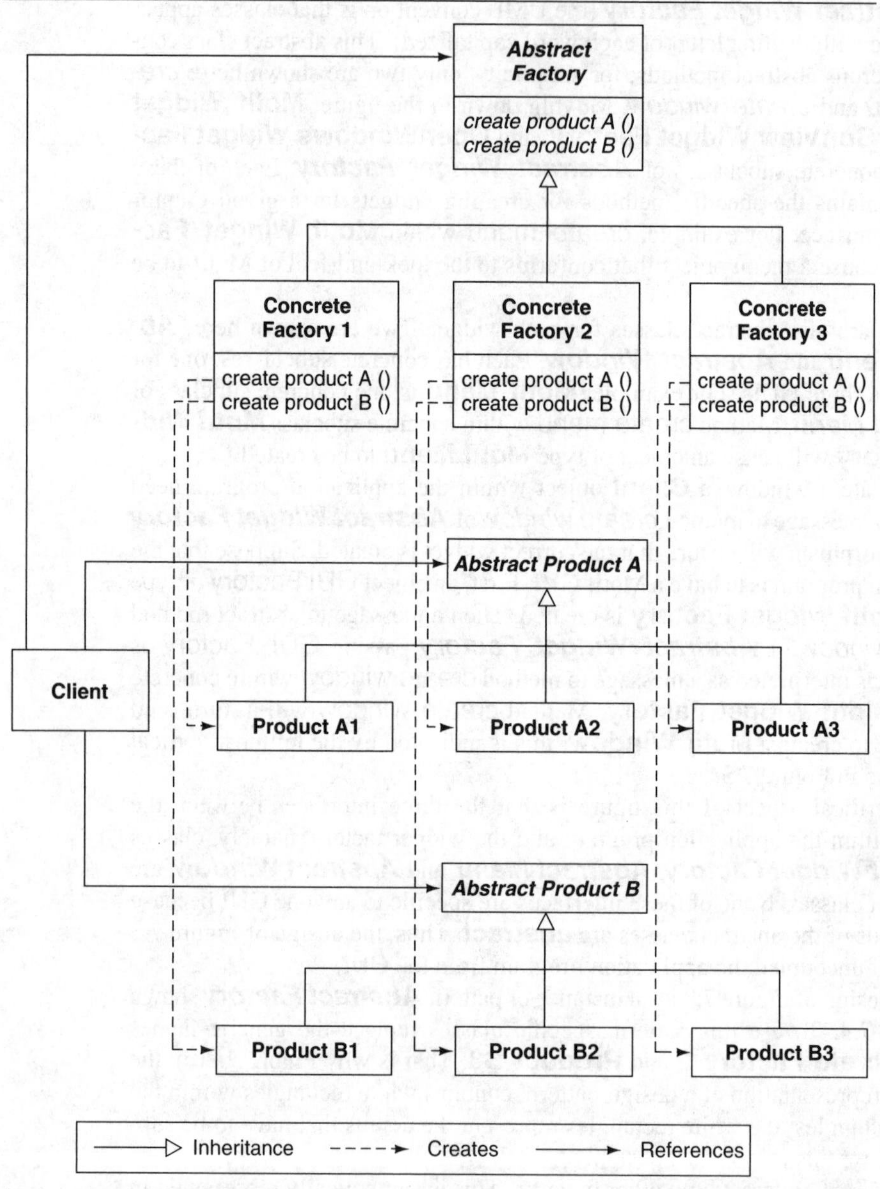

Figure 7.4 Pattern Abstract Factory. Names of abstract classes and their abstract methods are italicized.

7.5.4 SOFTWARE ARCHITECTURE

The architecture of a cathedral might be described as Romanesque, Gothic, or Baroque. Similarly, the architecture of a software product might be described as object-oriented, pipes and filters (UNIX components), or client-server (with a central server providing file storage and computing facilities for a network of client computers). Figure 7.2(d) symbolically depicts an architecture that is comprised of a toolkit, a framework, and three design patterns.

Because it applies to the design of a product as a whole, the field of *software architecture* encompasses a variety of design issues including the organization of the product in terms of its components; product-level control structures; issues of communication and synchronization; databases and data access; the physical distribution of the components; performance; and choice of design alternatives [Shaw and Garlan, 1996]. Thus, software architecture is a considerably more wide-ranging concept than design patterns.

In fact, Shaw and Garlan state [Shaw and Garlan, 1996], "Abstractly, software architecture involves the description of elements from which systems are built, interactions among those elements, *patterns that guide their composition,* and *constraints on those patterns* [emphasis added]." Thus, in addition to the many items listed in the previous paragraph, software architecture includes patterns as a subfield. This is one reason why Figure 7.2(d) shows three design patterns as components of a software architecture.

Software architecture, like object-oriented patterns, is a relatively new field; the subtitle of the first major book on the subject [Shaw and Garlan, 1996] is "Perspectives on an Emerging Discipline." There is active research in this area because reuse at the architecture level would be large scale. Accordingly, the many advantages of design reuse will be even greater if architectural reuse ever becomes feasible.

7.6 REUSE AND MAINTENANCE

The traditional reason for promoting reuse is that it can shorten the development process. For example, a number of major software organizations are trying to halve the time needed to develop a new product, and reuse is a primary strategy in these endeavors. However, as reflected in Figure 1.2, for every $1 spent on developing a product, $2 is spent on maintaining that product. Thus, a second important reason for reuse is to reduce the time and cost of maintaining a product. In fact, reuse has a greater impact on maintenance than on development.

Suppose now that 40 percent of a product consists of components reused from earlier products and that this reuse is evenly distributed across the entire product. That is, 40 percent of the specification document consists of reused components, 40 percent of the design, 40 percent of the code modules, 40 percent of the manuals, and so on. Unfortunately, this does not mean that the time to develop the

Activity	Percentage of Total Cost over Product Lifetime	Percentage Savings over Product Lifetime due to Reuse
Development	33%	9.3%
Maintenance	67	17.9

Figure 7.5 Average percentage cost savings under the assumption that 40 percent of a new product consists of reused components, three-quarters of which are reused unchanged.

product as a whole will be 40 percent less than it would have been without reuse. First, some of the components will have to be changed to tailor them to the new product. Suppose that one-quarter of the reused components are changed. If a component has to be changed, then the documentation for that component will also have to be changed. Also, the changed component will have to be tested. Second, if a code module is reused unchanged, then unit testing of that module is not required. However, integration testing of that module is still needed. Thus, even if 30 percent of a product consists of components reused unchanged and a further 10 percent are reused changed, the time needed to develop the complete product will at best be only about 27 percent less [Schach, 1992]. On average, 33 percent of a software budget is devoted to development. Consequently, if reuse reduces development costs by 27 percent, then the overall cost of that product over its 12- to 15-year lifetime is reduced by only about 9 percent as a consequence of reuse; this is reflected in Figure 7.5.

Similar but lengthier arguments can be applied to the maintenance component of the software process [Schach, 1994]. Under the assumptions of the previous paragraph, the effect of reuse on maintenance is an overall cost saving of about 18 percent, as shown in Figure 7.5. It is clear that the major impact of reuse is on maintenance rather than development. The underlying reason is that reused components are generally well designed, thoroughly tested, and comprehensively documented, thereby simplifying all three types of maintenance.

If the actual reuse rates in a given product are lower (or higher) than what has been assumed in this section, then the benefits of reuse will be different. But the overall result will still be the same, namely, that reuse affects maintenance more than it does development.

7.7 PORTABILITY

The ever-rising cost of software makes it imperative that some means be found for containing costs. One way is to ensure that the product as a whole can easily be adapted to run on a variety of different hardware/operating system combinations. Some of the costs of writing the product may then be recouped by selling versions that will run on other computers. Another reason for writing software that can easily be implemented on other computers is that the client organization may purchase new hardware, and all its software will then have to be converted to run on the new hardware. A product is considered to be *portable* if it is significantly less expensive to adapt the product to run on a new computer than to write a new product from scratch [Mooney, 90].

More precisely, portability may be defined as follows: Suppose a product P is compiled by compiler C and then runs on the *source* computer, namely, hardware configuration H under operating system O. A product P' is needed that functionally is equivalent to P, but must be compiled by compiler C' and run on the *target* computer, namely, hardware configuration H' under operating system O'. If the cost of converting P into P' is significantly less than the cost of coding P' from scratch, then P is said to be *portable.*

For example, a numerical integration package has been implemented on a VAX 10000 running under the VAX/VMS operating system. It is written in FORTRAN and compiled by the VAX FORTRAN compiler. The package is to be ported to a SPARCstation 20 workstation running under the UNIX operating system. The compiler to be used will be the Sun FORTRAN compiler.

Offhand, this would seem to be a trivial task. After all, the package is written in a high-level language. But if the package contains any operating system calls, such as to determine the CPU time used so far, then these require conversion. In addition, VAX FORTRAN and Sun FORTRAN are not identical languages; there are some features that are supported by one and not the other. Overall, the problem of porting software is nontrivial because of incompatibilities between different hardware configurations, operating systems, and compilers. Each of these aspects is now examined in turn.

7.7.1 HARDWARE INCOMPATIBILITIES

Product P currently running on hardware configuration H is to be installed on hardware configuration H'. Superficially, this is simple; copy P from the hard drive of H onto DAT tape, and transfer it to H'. However, this will not work if H' uses a Zip drive for backup; DAT tape cannot be read on a Zip drive.

Suppose now that the problem of physically copying the source code of product P to computer H' has been solved. There is no guarantee that H' can interpret the bit patterns created by H. A number of different character codes exist, the most popular of which are Extended Binary Coded Decimal Interchange Code (EBCDIC) and American Standard Code for Information Interchange (ASCII), the American version of the 7-bit ISO code [Mackenzie, 1980]. If H uses EBCDIC but H' uses ASCII, then H' will treat P as so much garbage. Similarly, data in Macintosh format generally cannot be read by a PC, and vice versa.

Although the original reason for these differences is historical, namely, that researchers working independently for different manufacturers developed different ways of doing the same thing, there are definite economic reasons for perpetuating them. To see this, consider the following imaginary situation. MCM

Computer Manufacturers has sold thousands of its MCM-1 computer. MCM now wishes to design, manufacture, and market a new computer, the MCM-2, that will be more powerful in every way than the MCM-1, but will cost considerably less. Suppose further that the MCM-1 uses ASCII code and has 36-bit words consisting of four 9-bit bytes. Now the chief computer architect of MCM decides that the MCM-2 should employ EBCDIC and have 16-bit words consisting of two 8-bit bytes. The sales force will then have to tell current MCM-1 owners that the MCM-2 is going to cost them $35,000 less than any competitor's equivalent machine, but that it will cost them up to $200,000 to convert existing software and data from MCM-1 format to MCM-2 format. No matter how good the scientific reasons for redesigning the MCM-2, marketing considerations will ensure that the new computer will be compatible with the old one. A salesperson can then point out to an existing MCM-1 owner that not only is the MCM-2 computer $35,000 less expensive than any competitor's machine, but that any customer ill-advised enough to buy from a different manufacturer will be spending $35,000 too much and will also have to pay some $200,000 to convert existing software and data to the format of the non-MCM machine.

Moving from the preceding imaginary situation to the real world, the most successful line of computers to date has been the IBM System/360-370 series [Gifford and Spector, 1987]. The success of this line of computers is due largely to full compatibility between machines; a product that runs on an IBM System/360 Model 30 built in 1964 will run unchanged on an IBM S/390 Model 1C5 built in 1998. However, that same product that runs on the IBM System/360 Model 30 under OS/360 may require considerable modification before it can run on a totally different 1998 machine such as a Sun Ultra 50 under Solaris. Part of the difficulty may be due to hardware incompatibilities. But part may be caused by operating system incompatibilities.

7.7.2 OPERATING SYSTEM INCOMPATIBILITIES

The job control language (JCL) of any two computers are usually vastly different. Some of the difference is syntactic—the command for executing an executable load image might be `@xeq` on one computer, `//xqt` on another, and `.exc` on a third. When porting a product to a different operating system, syntactic differences are relatively straightforward to handle by simply translating commands from the one JCL into the other. But other differences can be more serious. For example, some operating systems support virtual memory. Suppose that a certain operating system allows products to be up to 128 megabytes in size, but the actual area of main memory allocated to a particular product may be only 8 megabytes. What happens is that the user's product is partitioned into pages 256 kilobytes in size, and only 32 of these pages can be in main memory at any one time. The rest of the pages are stored on disk and swapped in and out as needed by the virtual memory operating system. As a result, products can be written without any effective constraints as to size. But if a product that has been successfully implemented under a virtual memory operating system is to be ported to an operating system with physical constraints on product size, the entire product may have to be rewritten and then linked using overlay techniques to ensure that the size limit is not exceeded.

7.7.3 NUMERICAL SOFTWARE INCOMPATIBILITIES

When a product is ported from one machine to another, or even compiled using a different compiler, the results of performing arithmetic may differ. On a 16-bit machine, that is, a computer with a word size of 16 bits, an integer will ordinarily be represented by one word (16 bits), and a double-precision integer by two adjacent words (32 bits). Unfortunately, some language implementations do not include double-precision integers. For example, standard Pascal does not include double-precision integers. Thus, a product that functions perfectly on a compiler/hardware/operating system configuration in which Pascal integers are represented using 32 bits may fail to work correctly when ported to a computer in which integers are represented by only 16 bits. The obvious solution, namely, representing integers larger than 2^{16} by floating-point numbers (**type** real), does not work because integers are represented exactly whereas floating-point numbers are in general only approximated using a mantissa (fraction) and exponent.

This problem can be solved in Ada, because in Ada it is possible to specify the range of an integer type and the precision (number of significant digits) of a floating-point type. The Ada–Europe Portability Working Group has produced a list of further recommendations for ensuring portability. These recommendations are specific to Ada and generally require a detailed understanding of the Ada 83 Reference Manual [ANSI/MIL-STD-1815A, 1983]; the interested reader is referred to [Nissen and Wallis, 1984].

With regard to Java, each of the eight primitive data types has been carefully specified. For example, type **int** is always implemented as a signed 32-bit two's complement integer, and type **float** always occupies 32 bits and satisfies IEEE Standard 754 for floating-point numbers [ANSI/IEEE 754, 1985]. The problem of ensuring that a numerical computation will be correctly performed on every target hardware/operating system therefore cannot arise in Java. (For more insights into the design of Java, see the Just in Case You Wanted to Know box on pages 240–41.) However, where a numerical computation is performed in a language other than Ada or Java, it is important, but often difficult, to ensure that numerical computations will be correctly performed on the target hardware/operating system.

7.7.4 COMPILER INCOMPATIBILITIES

Portability is difficult to achieve if a product is implemented in a language for which few compilers exist. If the product has been implemented in a specialized language such as CLU [Liskov, Snyder, Atkinson, and Schaffert, 1977], it may be necessary to rewrite it in a different language if the target computer does not have a compiler for that language. On the other hand, if a product is implemented in a popular language such as COBOL, FORTRAN, Lisp, Pascal, C, or Java, the

JUST IN CASE YOU WANTED TO KNOW

In 1991 James Gosling of Sun Microsystems developed Java. While he was developing the language, he frequently stared out the window at a large oak tree outside his office. In fact, he did this so often that he decided to name his new language "Oak." However, his choice of name was unacceptable to Sun because it could not be trademarked, and without a trademark Sun would lose control of the language.

After an intensive search for a name that could be trademarked and was easy to remember, Gosling's group came up with "Java." During the eighteenth century, much of the coffee imported into England was grown in Java, the most populous island in the Dutch East Indies (now Indonesia). As a result, "Java" is now a slang word for coffee, the third most popular beverage among software engineers. Unfortunately, the names of the Big Two carbonated cola beverages have already been trademarked.

In order to understand why Gosling designed Java, it is necessary to appreciate the source of the weaknesses that he perceived in C++. And to do that, we have to go back to C, the parent language of C++.

In 1972 the programming language C was developed by Dennis Ritchie at AT&T Bell Laboratories (now Lucent Technologies) for use in systems software. The language was designed to be extremely flexible. For example, it permits arithmetic on pointer variables, that is, on variables used to store memory addresses. From the viewpoint of the average programmer, this poses a distinct danger; the resulting programs can be extremely insecure because control can be passed to anywhere in the computer. Also, C does not embody arrays as such. Instead, a pointer to the address of the beginning of the array is used. As a result, the concept of an out-of-range array subscript is not intrinsic to C. This is a further source of possible insecurity.

These and other insecurities were not a problem at Bell Labs. After all, C was designed by an experienced software engineer for use by other experienced software engineers at Bell Labs. These professionals could be relied upon to use the powerful and flexible features of C in a secure way. A basic philosophy in the design of C was that the person using C knows exactly what he or she is doing. Software failures that have occurred when C is used by less competent or inexperienced programmers should not be blamed on AT&T; there was never any intent that C should be widely employed as a general-purpose programming language as it is today. With the rise of the object-oriented paradigm, a number of object-oriented programming languages based on C were developed, including Object C, Objective C, and C++. The idea behind these languages was to embed object-oriented constructs within C, which by then was a popular programming language. It was argued that it would be easier for programmers to learn a language that was based on a familiar language than to learn a totally new syntax. However, only one of the many C-based object-oriented languages became widely accepted and that was C++, developed by Bjarne Stroustrup also of AT&T Bell Laboratories.

It has been suggested that the reason behind the success of C++ is the enormous financial clout of AT&T. However, if corporate size and financial strength were relevant features in promoting a programming language, today we would all be using PL/I, a language developed and strongly promoted by IBM. The reality is that PL/I, notwithstanding the prestige of IBM, has retreated into obscurity.

The real reason for the success of C++ is that it is a true superset of C. That is, unlike any of the other C-based object-oriented programming languages, virtually any C program is also valid C++. Thus, organizations realized that they could switch from C to C++ without changing any of their existing C software. They could advance from the structured paradigm to the object-oriented paradigm without disruption. A remark that is frequently encountered in the Java literature is "Java is what C++ should have been." The implication is that, if only Stroustrup had been as smart as Gosling, C++ would have turned out to be Java. On the contrary, if C++ had not been a true superset of C, it would have gone the way of all other C-based object-oriented programming languages, that is, it would essentially

continued

concluded

have disappeared. It was only after C++ had taken hold as a popular language that Java was designed in reaction to perceived weaknesses in C++. Java is not a superset of C; for example, Java has no pointer variables. Thus, it would be more accurate to say "Java is what C++ could not possibly have been."

Finally, it is important to realize that Java, like every other programming language, has weaknesses of its own. In addition, there are areas (such as access rules) where C++ is superior to Java [Schach, 1997]. It will be interesting to see, in the coming years, whether C++ will continue to be the predominant object-oriented programming language, or whether it will be supplanted by Java or some other language.

chances are good that a compiler or interpreter for that language can be found for a target computer.

Suppose that a product is written in a popular high-level language such as standard FORTRAN. In theory, there should be no problem in porting the product from one machine to another—after all, standard FORTRAN is standard FORTRAN. Regrettably, that is not the case; in practice, there is no such thing as standard FORTRAN. Even though there is an ISO/IEC FORTRAN standard, known as Fortran 90 [ISO/IEC 1539, 1991], there is no reason for a compiler writer to adhere to it (see the Just in Case You Wanted to Know Box below for more on the name Fortran 90). For example, a decision may be taken to support additional features not usually found in FORTRAN so that the marketing division can then tout a "new, extended FORTRAN compiler." Conversely, a microcomputer compiler may not be a full FORTRAN implementation. Also, if there is a deadline to produce a compiler, management may decide to bring out a less-than-complete implementation, intending to support the full standard in a later revision. Suppose that the compiler on the source computer supports a superset of Fortran 90. Suppose further that the target compiler is an implementation of standard Fortran 90. When a product implemented on that source computer is ported to the target, any portions of the product that make use of nonstandard Fortran 90 constructs from the superset have to be recoded. Thus, to ensure portability, programmers should use only standard FORTRAN language features.

Early COBOL standards were developed by the Conference on Data Systems Languages (CODASYL), a committee of American computer manufacturers and

JUST IN CASE YOU WANTED TO KNOW

Names of programming languages are spelled in uppercase when the name is an acronym. Examples include ALGOL (ALGOrithmic Language), COBOL (COmmercial and Business Oriented Language), and FORTRAN (FORmula TRANslator). Conversely, all other programming languages begin with an uppercase letter and the remaining letters in the name (if any) are in lowercase. Examples include Ada, C, C++, Java, and Pascal. Unfortunately, the FORTRAN Standards Committee decided that, with effect from the 1990 version, the language would thenceforth be spelled "Fortran."

government and private users. Joint Technical Committee JCT1, Subcommittee SC22 of the International Standards Organization (ISO) and the International Electrotechnical Commission (IEC) is now responsible for COBOL standards. Unfortunately, COBOL standards do not promote portability. A COBOL standard has an official life of 5 years, but each successive standard is not necessarily a superset of its predecessor. It is equally worrisome that many features are left to the individual implementer, subsets may be termed *standard COBOL,* and there is no restriction on extending the language to form a superset [Wallis, 1982].

OO-COBOL, the language of the current COBOL draft standard (slated for final approval in 2000), is fully object-oriented [ISO/IEC 1989, 1997]. In contrast, Fortran 90 is merely *object based* [Wegner, 1989]. That is, inheritance and classes are not implemented in Fortran 90. Fortran 90 objects are therefore entities in their own right; they are not instances of classes. It would be worthwhile if the language of the next FORTRAN standard were object-oriented.

There are several different Pascal standards. First came Jensen and Wirth's definition of the language [Jensen and Wirth, 1975]. Then there is the ANSI standard [ANSI/IEEE 770X3.97, 1983] and the ISO standard [ISO-7185, 1980]. Notwithstanding this plethora of standards, subsets and supersets of Pascal abound. For instance, all Pascal standards specify that procedure and function names may be passed as arguments. However, that feature is by no means universally supported by Pascal compilers. Conversely, many supersets of Pascal have been implemented. For example, some implementations of Pascal incorporate nonstandard bit manipulation operations such as bitwise **and** and **or**, perhaps to compete with C. Also, a number of Pascal implementations now include object-oriented extensions to Pascal.

ANSI has approved a standard for the programming language C [ANSI X3.159, 1989]. The standard was approved by ISO in 1990. Most C compilers adhere quite closely to the original language specification [Kernighan and Ritchie, 1978]. The reason for this is that almost all C compiler writers use the standard front end of the portable C compiler, *pcc* [Johnson, 1979], and as a result the language accepted by the vast majority of compilers is identical. C products are, in general, easily ported from one implementation to another. An aid to C portability is the *lint* processor that can be used to determine implementation-dependent features, as well as constructs that may lead to difficulties when the product is ported to a target computer. Unfortunately, *lint* checks only the syntax and the static semantics, and therefore is not foolproof. However, it can be of considerable help in reducing future problems. For example, in C it is legal to assign an integer value to a pointer and vice versa, but this is forbidden by *lint*. In some implementations, the size (number of bits) of an integer and a pointer will be the same, but the sizes may be different on other implementations; this sort of potential future portability problem can be flagged by *lint* and obviated by recoding the offending portions.

The standard for C++ [ISO/IEC 14882, 1998] was unanimously approved by the various national standards committees (including ANSI, the American National Standards Institute) in November 1997. The standard then received final ratification in 1998.

The only truly successful language standard so far has been the Ada 83 standard, embodied in the Ada Reference Manual [ANSI/MIL-STD-1815A, 1983]. (For background information on Ada, see the Just in Case You Wanted to Know box on page 244.) Until the end of 1987, the name "Ada" was a registered trademark of the U.S. Government, Ada Joint Program Office (AJPO). As owner of the trademark, the AJPO stipulated that the name Ada could legally be used only for language implementations that complied exactly with the standard; subsets and supersets were expressly forbidden. A mechanism was set up for validating Ada compilers, and only a compiler that successfully passed the validation process could be called an Ada compiler. Thus the trademark was used as a means of enforcing standards, and hence portability. The Ada 95 standard [ISO/IEC 8652, 1995] has so far proved to be equally successful.

Now that the name Ada is no longer a trademark, enforcement of the standard is being achieved via a different mechanism. There is little or no market for an Ada compiler that has not been validated. Thus there are strong economic forces encouraging Ada compiler developers to have their compilers validated, and hence certified as conforming to the Ada standard. This has applied to compilers for both Ada 83 [ANSI/MIL-STD-1815A, 1983] and Ada 95 [ISO/IEC 8652, 1994].

A validation certificate is for a specific compiler running on specific hardware under a specific operating system; if an organization that has developed an Ada compiler wishes to port the compiler to another hardware and/or operating system configuration, revalidation is necessary. The reference manual for every Ada compiler must incorporate an appendix, namely, Appendix F, in which the implementation-dependent characteristics of that Ada implementation are described. For example, it is possible to suppress type conversion and to treat an argument simply as a bit pattern; an implementation may impose restrictions on the size of such an item. Technically, then, Ada products can be made fully portable, except with regard to features mentioned in Appendix F.

In order for Java to be a totally portable language, it is essential for the language to be standardized and to ensure that the standard is strictly obeyed. Sun Microsystems, like the Ada Joint Program Office is using the legal system to achieve standardization. As mentioned in the Just in Case You Wanted to Know Box on pages 240–41, Sun chose a name for their new language that could be copyrighted. It seems likely that Sun will enforce their copyright and bring legal action against alleged violators. After all, portability is one of the most powerful features of Java. If multiple versions of Java are permitted, the portability of Java will suffer; Java can be truly portable only if every Java program is handled identically by every Java compiler. To try to influence public opinion, in 1997 Sun ran a "Pure Java" advertising campaign.

Version 1.0 of Java was released early in 1997. A series of revised versions have followed in response to comments and criticisms. This process of stepwise refinement of Java will continue. When the language eventually stabilizes, it is likely that a standards organization such as the American National Standards Institute (ANSI) or the International Standards Organization (ISO) will publish a draft standard and elicit comments from all over the world. These comments will then be used to put together the official Java standard.

JUST IN CASE YOU WANTED TO KNOW

During the early 1970s, the U.S. Department of Defense (DoD) became acutely aware of problems with its software. One of the more worrisome issues was that at least 450 different languages were being used in DoD products. A major implication of this proliferation was that maintenance, difficult enough under normal circumstances, was made all but impossible by the need to find competent maintenance programmers for this babel of languages. In addition, tools to support software development and maintenance were rudimentary, mainly because of the enormous cost of buying or building an adequate CASE toolkit for each of those languages.

The situation with regard to embedded software (the software in an embedded computer—see Section 5.4.4) was particularly bad. Each branch of the Armed Forces had its own favorite real-time language; the Army supported TACPOL, the Navy promoted CMS-2, and the choice of the Air Force was JOVIAL. In short, the situation regarding embedded software was bad and, bearing the maintenance implications in mind, could only get worse.

Embedded DoD software tends to be large, namely, on the order of hundreds of thousands or millions of lines of code, to have a lifetime of 10 to 15 years, and to change frequently over that period as requirements change [Fisher, 1976]. In addition, embedded software is almost always subject to space constraints in that the size of the computer embedded within military hardware such as a tank, a drone, or a helicopter is generally restricted. Furthermore, the time constraints of real-time software are ever present. Finally, embedded software must be highly reliable. To put it bluntly, once a ballistic missile has been launched from a nuclear submarine, it is too late to make any changes to its software in the event of a failure of any sort being detected.

In 1975, DoD initiated a worldwide competition to find a common high-order language for all the armed services. Seventeen submissions were received from teams that included academics, industry professionals, and military experts in their ranks; four of those submissions were chosen for further development. To ensure that reviewers would not know the identities of the competing organizations, the language proposals were given the code names Blue, Green, Red, and Yellow. The overall winner was Green, a mainly European team led by Jean Ichbiah of Honeywell Bull, France. That is why the Ada Reference Manual [ANSI/MIL-STD-1815A, 1983] is bound with a green cover. Until recently, issues of *Ada Letters,* a major Ada journal published by the Special Interest Group on Ada of the Association for Computing Machinery (ACM SIGAda), also had a green cover.

But DoD was as unhappy with the name Green as it had been with the earlier name DoD-1. Jack Cooper of the U.S. Navy suggested the name Ada, after Ada, Countess of Lovelace, daughter of the poet Lord Byron. She had written programs for Babbage's Analytic Engine, the first computer, in the first half of the nineteenth century. Although Babbage's design was correct, the Analytic Engine could not be constructed because of the limitations of nineteenth-century technology. The Deputy Secretary of Defense obtained permission from the Countess of Lovelace's heir, the Earl of Lytton, to use the name Ada [Carlson, Druffel, Fisher, and Whitaker, 1980]. That is why the name of the language is written Ada, and not ADA. It is not an acronym; it is named after Ada, Countess of Lovelace, the world's first programmer.

The language was approved by DoD in 1980 and assigned military standard MIL-STD-1815. The number 1815 is significant, being the year of birth of Ada Lovelace. In 1994 a revised version of Ada was approved by the International Organization for Standardization (ISO) and the International Electrotechnical Commission (IEC). Because the standard [ISO/IEC 8652, 1995] was published in 1995, the language is called Ada 95. A number of new features were added to the original version (Ada 83), especially object orientation.

In 1997, on the advice of the National Research Council at the National Academy of Sciences, DoD dropped its stipulation that Ada be used for all its software, requiring Ada only for what it termed "warfighting" software, a term that was rather narrowly defined [AdaIC, 1997]. In view of this change to the Ada mandate, the future of Ada is not as clear as it previously was.

7.8 WHY PORTABILITY?

In the light of the many barriers to porting software, the reader might well wonder if it is worthwhile to port software at all. One argument in favor of portability stated in Section 7.7 is that the cost of software can perhaps be partially recouped by porting the product to a different hardware/operating system configuration. However, selling multiple variants of the software may not be possible. The application may be highly specialized, and no other client may need the software. For instance, a management information system written for one major car rental corporation may simply be inapplicable to the operations of other car rental corporations. Alternatively, the software itself may give the client a competitive advantage, and selling copies of the product would then be tantamount to economic suicide. In the light of all this, is it not a waste of time and money to engineer portability into a product when it is designed?

The answer to this question is an emphatic NO. One major reason why portability is essential is that the life of a software product is generally longer than the life of the hardware for which it was first written. Good software products can have a life of 15 years or more, whereas hardware is frequently changed at least every 4 or 5 years. Thus good software can be implemented, over its lifetime, on three or more different hardware configurations.

One way to solve this problem is to buy upwardly compatible hardware. The only expense is the cost of the hardware; the software will not need to be changed. Nevertheless, in some cases it may be economically more sound to port the product to different hardware entirely. For example, the first version of a product may have been implemented 7 years ago on a mainframe. Although it may be possible to buy a new mainframe on which the product can run without any changes, it may be considerably less expensive to implement multiple copies of the product on a network of personal computers, one on the desk of each user. In this instance, if the software has been written to promote portability, then porting the product to the personal computer network makes good financial sense.

But there are other kinds of software. For example, many software organizations that write software for personal computers make their money by selling multiple copies of "shrink-wrapped software." For instance, the profit on a spreadsheet package is small and cannot possibly cover the cost of development. In order to make a profit, 10,000 (or even 100,000) copies may have to be sold. After this point, additional sales are pure profit. So if the product can be ported to additional types of hardware with ease, even more money can be made.

Of course, as with all software, the product is not just the code; there is also documentation, including the manuals. Porting the spreadsheet package to other hardware means changing the documentation as well. Thus portability also means being able to change the documentation easily to reflect the target configuration, instead of having to write new documentation from scratch. Considerably less training is needed if the familiar existing product is ported to a new computer than if a completely new product were to be written. For this reason, too, portability is to be encouraged.

Techniques to facilitate portability are now described.

7.9 TECHNIQUES FOR ACHIEVING PORTABILITY

One way to try to achieve portability is to forbid programmers to use constructs that might cause problems when ported to another computer. For example, an obvious principle would seem to be: Write all software in a standard version of a high-level programming language. But how then is a portable operating system to be written? After all, it is inconceivable that an operating system could be written without at least some assembler code. Similarly, a compiler has to generate object code for a specific computer. Here, too, it is impossible to avoid all implementation-dependent components.

7.9.1 PORTABLE SYSTEM SOFTWARE

Instead of forbidding all implementation-dependent aspects, which would have the consequence of preventing almost all system software from being written, a better technique is to isolate any necessary implementation-dependent pieces. An example of this technique is the way the UNIX operating system was constructed [Johnson and Ritchie, 1978]. About 9000 lines of the operating system are written in C. The remaining 1000 lines constitute the kernel. The kernel is written in assembler and must be rewritten for each implementation. About 1000 lines of the C code consist of device drivers; this code, too, must be rewritten each time. However, the remaining 8000 lines of C code remain largely unchanged from implementation to implementation.

Another useful technique for increasing the portability of system software is to use levels of abstraction (Section 6.4.1). Consider, for example, graphical display routines for a workstation. A user inserts a command such as drawLine into his or her source code. The source code is compiled and then linked together with graphical display routines. At run-time, drawLine causes the workstation to draw a line on the screen as specified by the user. This can be implemented using two levels of abstraction. The upper level, written in a high-level language, interprets the user's command and calls the appropriate lower-level module to execute that command. If the graphical display routines are ported to a new type of workstation, then no changes need be made to the user's code or to the upper level of the graphical display routines. However, the lower-level modules of the routines will have to be rewritten because they interface with the actual hardware, and the hardware of the new workstation is different from that of the workstation on which the package was previously implemented. This technique has also been successfully used for porting communications software that conforms to the seven levels of abstraction of the ISO-OSI model [Tanenbaum, 1996].

7.9.2 PORTABLE APPLICATION SOFTWARE

With regard to application software, rather than system software such as operating systems and compilers, it is generally possible to write the product in a high-level language. In Section 13.1 it is pointed out that there is frequently no choice with regard to implementation language, but that when it is possible to select a language the choice should be made on the basis of cost–benefit analysis (Section 4.7). One of the factors that must enter into the cost–benefit analysis is the impact on portability.

At every stage in the development of a product, decisions can be made that will result in a more portable resulting product. One potential problem can arise as a consequence of the fact that not all characters are supported by every computer. For example, comments in Pascal can be delimited by { ... } pairs or by (* ... *) pairs. Because some computers do not support brace brackets, it is preferable to use (* ... *) pairs. Also, some compilers distinguish between uppercase and lowercase letters. For such a compiler, variables This_Is_A_Name and this_is_a_name are two different variables. But other compilers treat the two names the same. A product that relies on differences between uppercase letters and lowercase letters can lead to hard-to-discover faults when the product is ported.

Just as there frequently is no choice of programming language, there may also be no choice of operating system. However, if at all possible the operating system under which the product runs should be a popular one. This is an argument in favor of the UNIX operating system. UNIX has been implemented on a wide range of hardware. In addition, UNIX, or more precisely, UNIX-like operating systems, have been implemented on top of mainframe operating systems such as IBM VM/370 and VAX/VMS. For personal computers, the most widely used operating system is Windows. Just as use of a widely implemented programming language will promote portability, so too will use of a widely implemented operating system.

In order to facilitate the moving of software from one UNIX-based system to another, the Portable Operating System Interface for Computer Environments (POSIX) was developed [NIST 151, 1988]. POSIX standardizes the interface between an application program and a UNIX operating system. POSIX has now been implemented on a number of non-UNIX operating systems as well, thus broadening the number of computers to which application software can be ported with little or no problem.

Language standards can play their part in achieving portability. If the coding standards of a development organization stipulate that only standard constructs may be used, then the resulting product is more likely to be portable. To this end, programmers must be provided with a list of nonstandard features supported by the compiler, but whose use is forbidden without prior managerial approval. Like other sensible coding standards, this one can be checked by machine.

Graphical user interfaces (GUI) are similarly becoming portable via the introduction of standard GUI languages. Examples of these include Motif and X11. The standardization of GUI languages is in reaction to the growing importance of GUIs as described in Section 9.3 and the resulting need for portability of human–computer interfaces.

Planning should also be done for potential future numerical incompatibilities. For example, if a product is being developed on 32-bit hardware but there is a possibility that in the future it may have to be ported to an older 16-bit machine, then integers should be kept within the range $\pm 32{,}767$, and the modulus of real numbers should be within the range $\pm 10^{68}$. In addition, no more than six decimal digits of precision should be assumed [Wallis, 1982]. As explained in Section 7.7.3, these problems cannot arise in Ada or Java.

It is also necessary to plan for potential lack of compatibility between the operating system under which the product is being constructed and any future operating systems to which the product may be ported. If at all possible, operating system calls should be localized to one or two modules. In any event, every operating system call must be carefully documented. The documentation standard for operating system calls should assume that the next programmer to read the code will have no familiarity whatsoever with the current operating system, often a reasonable assumption.

Documentation in the form of an installation manual should also be provided to assist with future porting. That manual will point out what parts of the product will have to be changed when porting the product and what parts may have to be changed. In both instances, a careful explanation of what has to be done, and how to do it, must be provided. Finally, lists of changes that will have be made in other manuals, such as the user manual or the operator manual, must also appear in the installation manual.

7.9.3 PORTABLE DATA

The problem of portability of data can be a vexing one. Problems of hardware incompatibilities were pointed out in Section 7.7.1. But even after such problems have been solved, software incompatibilities remain. Suppose that a data file is used by a Pascal or COBOL product on the source computer. If that same product is now ported to another compiler/hardware/operating system configuration, it is unlikely that the data file can be read by the ported product; the format required for Pascal or COBOL data files in the new system will probably be totally different from that in the old system. For instance, the format of an indexed-sequential file is determined by the operating system; a different operating system generally implies a different format. Many files require headers containing information such as the format of the data in that file. The format of a header is almost always unique to the specific compiler and operating system under which that file was created.

But bad as the situation is with regard to porting data files used by popular programming languages, the situation can be far worse when database management systems are used.

The safest way of porting data is to construct an unstructured (sequential) file, which can then be ported with minimal difficulty to the target machine. From this unstructured file, the desired structured file, be it a Pascal file, a COBOL file, or a database, can be reconstructed. Two special conversion routines have to be written, one running on the source machine to convert the original structured file into sequential form and one running on the target machine to reconstruct the structured file from the ported sequential file. Although this solution seems simple enough, the two routines will be nontrivial when conversions between complex database models have to be performed.

7.10 INTEROPERABILITY

Suppose that we wish to create a document that is to be printed on request. The document must contain the annual budgeted expenditure in a number of categories together with the actual year-to-date expenditure in each category. The document must also incorporate a message from the chief financial officer that is regularly updated. One way of achieving this would be to use a spreadsheet tool, such as Lotus 1-2-3, to create the budget and a word processing tool, such as Microsoft Word, to create the document as a whole. Then, each time that the document is requested, the user first updates the spreadsheet to reflect the latest budget figures, then copies the current spreadsheet into the document. Finally, the user updates the chief financial officer's message and prints the document.

One improvement would be to utilize some sort of import/export mechanism whereby a change in the spreadsheet is automatically reflected within the word processor document. But even this is not ideal. Each time the user first has to update the spreadsheet using the spreadsheet tool, and then open the document using the word processing tool. What is needed is a way of integrating the word processing tool and the spreadsheet tool, notwithstanding the fact that the two tools are apparently incompatible products of two different software vendors. The document will then be opened from within the word processing tool as before, and when the user uses the mouse to click on the budget spreadsheet, the spreadsheet tool will be invoked from within the word processor.

This is an example of *interoperability*, which may be defined as the mutual cooperation of object code from different vendors, written in different languages and running on different platforms. For example, consider a nation-wide network of automated teller machines (ATMs). The server is a mainframe computer running COBOL-based database software written by one organization; the clients, the ATMs, are running C++ code written by a different organization. In addition, there is communications software, and security is an essential aspect. All these components have to work together for the ATM network to function successfully.

A number of standards have been put forward to promote interoperability, including OLE/COM/ActiveX and CORBA.

7.10.1 OLE, COM, AND ACTIVEX

The first version of Object Linking and Embedding (OLE) was released in 1990, as part of Windows 3.0. It was designed by Microsoft to support compound documents, such as the spreadsheet within the word processing document described in the previous section. However, it was soon realized that OLE was also a partial solution to the larger problem of interoperability. Microsoft next developed the Component Object Model (COM) as a further step toward achieving the overall goal of interoperability. The term *OLE* was then used to denote anything built using COM-based technology. The full name *Object Linking and Embedding* no longer made sense in this new context, so the name *OLE* was transformed from a three-letter acronym (TLA) into a name in its own right. In 1996, Microsoft started using the term *ActiveX* in connection with its Internet-related technologies. However, the term *ActiveX* soon became all but synonymous with *OLE* in its second meaning of COM-related technology. As a result, the term *OLE* is once again being used in its original sense of a mechanism for supporting compound documents. Finally, DCOM (distributed COM) was released in 1996 to support interoperability on distributed platforms [Chappell, 1996].

The underlying technology supporting interoperability is COM. Suppose that software component Q supplies services to component P, that is, P is a *client* of Q. There are a number of different ways in which P and Q can interact. If P and Q are parts of the same process, P can invoke Q. On the other hand, if P and Q are in different processes running on the same machine, then P and Q can communicate via some form of interprocess communication. But if the different processes are running on different machines in a network, then a remote process call (RPC) can be used. The idea behind COM is to use a common mechanism for all situations in which one component provides services to another component. Every piece of the software is implemented as a COM component (Microsoft terms this an *object*). Each component has one or more interfaces, each of which supports one or more functions (these are termed *methods*). To utilize a COM component, a client calls the COM library, specifying the class of the component (every COM component is an instance of a specific class) and the specific interface of the component. The COM library then instantiates a COM component of that class and returns a pointer to the chosen interface. The client can now invoke a function of that interface.

COM terminology as specified by Microsoft is somewhat confusing in that COM is not yet object oriented. A COM object is indeed an instance of a class, but COM does not support inheritance (Section 6.8). COM is therefore *object based* [Wegner, 1989], but not object oriented. However, future versions of COM (such as COM+, formerly COM3) may well be object oriented.

7.10.2 CORBA

In 1989, the Object Management Group (OMG), a consortium of vendors of object-oriented technology currently numbering over 500, was set up with the aim of developing a common architecture for object-oriented systems. Specifically, the Common Object Request Broker Architecture (CORBA) supports the interoperability of software applications running on different machines within a distributed environment [OMG, 1993]. That is, CORBA supports interoperability across vendors, networks, languages, and operating systems. All OMG standards are recognized by the International Standards Organization (ISO), so CORBA is an international standard architecture for object-oriented systems.

The heart of CORBA is an object request broker (ORB) that allows a client to invoke a method of an object, irrespective of where in the distributed system the object is located. The term *middleware* describes software that supports interoperability, and ORB has been called the "mother of all client/server middleware" [Orfali, Harkey, and Edwards, 1996]. Hewlett-Packard ORB Plus, DEC ObjectBroker, IBM System Object Model, Visigenic ORB, and Iona ORBIX are just a few of the many CORBA implementations currently available.

7.10.3 COMPARING OLE/COM AND CORBA

Superficially, both OLE/COM and CORBA provide equivalent support for interoperability. However, there are numerous significant differences between the two [Mowbray and Zahavi, 1995]. For brevity, we consider just three differences here.

One key difference is a consequence of the fact that OLE/COM is a product of Microsoft, the world's largest computer organization, whereas CORBA is an international standard developed by software professionals from literally hundreds of different computer organizations. As a result, CORBA ORB products are currently implemented on a wider variety of different platforms than OLE/COM. Furthermore, CORBA is defined to be independent of underlying communications mechanisms, whereas OLE/COM's communication mechanism is a proprietary Microsoft product. It is consequently hard to use OLE/COM with legacy software that uses a different communications mechanism.

A second difference relates to integration of shrink-wrapped (COTS) software. Microsoft supplies at least 80 percent of such software. The ease with which Microsoft shrink-wrapped software can be integrated into Microsoft-proprietary OLE/COM is a clear advantage over the more convoluted methods currently needed to integrate shrink-wrapped software into a CORBA-based product.

Third, CORBA has the advantage of simplicity. OLE/COM is one of the most complex Microsoft technologies; the documentation for OLE/COM is nearly 2000 pages in length, and a developer needs to have a detailed understanding of Win32 (the Windows API) as well. Furthermore, developers have indicated that OLE/COM has a steep learning curve. CORBA, on the other hand, is defined in just 178 pages, and the documentation for most CORBA products is between 200 and 300 pages. CORBA training is readily available, and experience has shown that CORBA is generally easy to learn.

CORBA and OLE/COM each have its champions and its detractors. It remains to be seen how interoperability will be implemented in future years.

7.11 FUTURE TRENDS IN INTEROPERABILITY

The current two major interoperability products are OLE/COM (Section 7.10.1) and CORBA (Section 7.10.2). In the past, a number of apparently strong contenders have fallen by the wayside, notably OpenDoc [Mowbray and Zahavi, 1995]. However, many other products are currently available or under development. For example, Fresco is a portable CORBA-based system for compound documents that is available virtually free of charge, as is GNUstep from the Free Software Foundation. A number of organizations, notably Sun and IBM, are jointly developing Java Beans, a fully portable, compact, architecturally neutral, and platform neutral API. Java Beans will support compound documents in Java [Gaskill, 1996].

It has been suggested that CORBA is superior in many ways to OLE/COM [Mowbray and Zahavi, 1995]. Nevertheless, Microsoft is the world's largest computer organization with the power to persuade organizations that OLE/COM (or its successor at time of writing, COM3) is the appropriate standard for achieving interoperability. It is not clear whether CORBA or OLE/COM will become the dominant interoperability mechanism or whether some future product will predominate. Another possibility would be bridges between CORBA and OLE/COM that would allow interoperability between the two competing standards. But whatever direction the industry chooses to follow, interoperability will be easier to achieve in the future than it has been in the past.

CHAPTER REVIEW

Reuse is described in Section 7.1. Impediments to reuse are discussed in Section 7.2. Six reuse case studies are presented in Section 7.3. The impact of objects on productivity is analyzed in Section 7.4. Reuse during the design and implementation phases is the subject of Section 7.5; the topics covered include frameworks, patterns, and software architecture. The impact of reuse on maintenance is discussed in Section 7.6.

Portability is discussed in Section 7.7. Portability can be hampered by incompatibilities caused by hardware (Section 7.7.1), operating systems (Section 7.7.2), numerical software (Section 7.7.3), or compilers (Section 7.7.4). Nevertheless, it is important to try to make all products as portable as possible (Section 7.8). Ways of facilitating portability include using popular high-level languages, isolating the nonportable pieces of a product (Section 7.9.1), and adhering to language standards (Section 7.9.2).

Interoperability is introduced in Section 7.10. OLE, COM, and ActiveX are presented in Section 7.10.1, and CORBA in Section 7.10.2. These items are compared in Section 7.10.3. The chapter concludes with a discussion of future trends in interoperability in Section 7.11.

FOR FURTHER READING

Further information on the reuse case studies in this chapter can be found in [Lanergan and Grasso, 1984], [Matsumoto, 1984, 1987], [Selby, 1989], [Prieto-Díaz, 1991], [Lim, 1994] and [Jézéquel and Meyer, 1997]. A corporate-level software reuse program at Hewlett-Packard is described in [Griss, 1993]. Two pilot studies at Motorola are described in [Joos, 1994]. The management of reuse is described in [Lim, 1998]; some warnings regarding reuse are given in [Tracz, 1988] and [Tracz, 1995]. [Frakes and Fox, 1995] is a report on industry attitudes to reuse. A search scheme for object retrieval and reuse is described in [Isakowitz and Kauffman, 1996]. Reuse issues regarding Ada can be found in [Nissen and Wallis, 1984] and [Gargaro and Pappas, 1987]. Ada reuse case studies are outlined in [Wildblood, 1990] and [Skazinski, 1994]. The cost-effectiveness of reuse is described in [Barnes and Bollinger, 1991] and ways of identifying components for future reuse in [Caldiera and Basili, 1991]. [Meyer, 1996a] analyzes the claim that the object-oriented paradigm promotes reuse; four case studies in reuse and object technology appear in [Fichman and Kemerer, 1997]. Reuse metrics are discussed in [Poulin, 1997]. [Prieto-Díaz, 1993] is a status report on reuse. Further papers on reuse are to be found in [Freeman, 1987], [Biggerstaff and Perlis, 1989], and the September 1994 issue of *IEEE Software.* [Mili, Mili, and Mili, 1995] is a important source on the past and future of reuse.

A good source of information on frameworks is [Lewis et al., 1995b]. Managing reuse of object-oriented frameworks is described in [Sparks, Benner, and Faris, 1996]. A framework for building software is discussed in [Schmid, 1996]. The effect of object-oriented frameworks on developer productivity is discussed in [Moser and Nierstrasz, 1996]. The October 1997 issue of *Communications of the ACM* contains a number of articles on object-oriented frameworks, including [Johnson, 1997].

Design patterns were put forward by Alexander within the context of architecture [Alexander et al., 1977]. The most important work on software design patterns is [Gamma, Helm, Johnson, and Vlissides, 1995]. Analysis patterns are described in [Coad, 1992] and in [Fowler, 1997a]. [Schmidt, 1995] describes the use of design patterns to develop reusable object-oriented communications software. The October 1996 issue of the *Communications of the ACM* is a source of many articles on patterns, including [Cline, 1996] which describes advantages and disadvantages of design patterns. Articles on patterns and architectures are to be found in the January/February 1997 issue of *IEEE Software*. These include [Kerth and Cunningham, 1997], which explains the importance of pattern languages, and [Monroe, Kompanek, Melton, and Garlan, 1997], [Tepfenhart and Cusick, 1997], and [Coplien, 1997], all of which connect architectures, patterns, and objects.

The primary source of information on software architectures is [Shaw and Garlan, 1996]. The interaction of social issues and software architecture appears in [Cockburn, 1996]. Articles on software architecture can be found in the April 1995 issue of *IEEE Transactions on Software Engineering* and also in the November 1995 issue of *IEEE Software,* especially [Shaw, 1995] and [Garlan, Allen, and Ockerbloom, 1995].

Three introductory texts on portability are [Wallis, 1982], [Wolberg, 1983], and [Lecarme and Gart, 1986]. Strategies for achieving portability can be found in [Mooney, 1990]. Portability of C and UNIX is discussed in [Johnson and Ritchie, 1978]. With regard to portability of Ada products, the reader should consult [Nissen and Wallis, 1984].

For an overview of interoperability in general and OLE, CORBA, and ActiveX in particular, consult [Adler, 1995]. A comprehensive source of information on interoperability is [Orfali, Harkey, and Edwards, 1996]. ActiveX and OLE are described in [Brockschmidt, 1994] and [Chappell, 1996]; detailed information is available from the Microsoft home page, www.microsoft.com. CORBA is described in detail in [Mowbray and Zahavi, 1995]. [Leppinen, Pulkkinen, and Rautiainen, 1997] is a case study in integrating Java and CORBA.

PROBLEMS

7.1 Distinguish carefully between reusability, portability, and interoperability.

7.2 A code module is reused, unchanged, in a new product. In what ways does this reuse reduce the overall cost of the product? In what ways is the cost unchanged?

7.3 Suppose that a code module is reused with one change; an addition operation is changed to a subtraction. What impact does this minor change have on the savings of Problem 7.2?

7.4 What is the influence of cohesion on reusability?

7.5 What is the influence of coupling on reusability?

7.6 You have just joined a large organization that manufactures industrial robots. The organization has hundreds of software products in which are embedded some 80,000 different FORTRAN modules. You have been hired to come up with a plan for reusing as many of these modules as possible in future products. What is your proposal?

7.7 Consider an automated library circulation system. Every book has a bar code, and every borrower has a card bearing a bar code. When a borrower wishes to check out a book, the librarian scans the bar code on the book and on the borrower's card, and then enters C at the computer terminal. Similarly, when a book is returned, it is again scanned and the librarian enters R. Librarians can add books (+) to the library collection or remove them (−). Borrowers can go to a terminal and determine all the books in the library by a particular author (the borrower enters A= followed by the author's name), all the books with a specific title (T= followed by the title), or all the books in a particular subject area (S= followed by the subject area). Finally, if a borrower wants a book that is currently checked out, the librarian can place a hold on the book so that when it is returned it will be held for the borrower who requested it (H= followed by the number of the book). Explain how you would ensure a high percentage of reusable modules.

7.8 You are required to build a product for determining whether a bank statement is correct. The data needed include the balance at the beginning of the month; the number, date, and amount of each check; the date and amount of each deposit; and the balance at the end of the month. Explain how you would ensure that as many modules as possible of the product can be reused in future products.

7.9 Consider an automated teller machine (ATM). The user puts a card into a slot and enters a four-digit personal identification number (PIN). If the PIN is incorrect, the card is ejected. Otherwise, the user may perform the following operations on up to four different bank accounts:

(i) Deposit any amount. A receipt is printed showing the date, amount deposited, and account number.

(ii) Withdraw up to $200 in units of $20 (the account may not be overdrawn). In addition to the money, the user is given a receipt showing the date, amount withdrawn, account number, and account balance after the withdrawal.

(iii) Determine account balance. This is displayed on the screen.

(iv) Transfer funds between two accounts. Again, the account from which the funds are transferred must not be overdrawn. The user is given a receipt showing the date, amount transferred, and the two account numbers.

(v) Quit. The card is ejected.

Explain how you would ensure that as many modules as possible of the product can be reused in future products.

7.10 How early in the software life cycle could the developers have caught the fault in the Ariane 5 software (Section 7.6.6)?

7.11 In Section 7.6.2 it is stated that "the Raytheon COBOL program logic structure of the 1970s is a classical precursor of today's object-oriented application framework." What are the implications of this for technology transfer?

7.12 Explain the role played by abstract classes in the design pattern of Figure 7.3.

7.13 Explain how you would ensure that the product that checks whether a bank statement is correct (Problem 7.8) is as portable as possible.

7.14 Explain how you would ensure that the automated library circulation system (Problem 7.7) is as portable as possible.

7.15 Explain how you would ensure that the software for the automated teller machine (ATM) of Problem 7.9 is as portable as possible.

7.16 Your organization is developing a real-time control system for a new type of laser that will be used in cancer therapy. You are in charge of writing two assembler modules. How will you instruct your team to ensure that the resulting code will be as portable as possible?

7.17 You are responsible for porting a 750,000-line COBOL product to your company's new computer. You copy the source code to the new machine, but discover when you try to compile it that every one of the over 15,000 input/output statements has been written in a nonstandard COBOL syntax that the new compiler rejects. What do you do now?

7.18 (Term Project) Suppose that the Air Gourmet product of Appendix A was developed using the structured paradigm. What parts of the product could be reused in future products? Now suppose that the product is using the object-oriented paradigm. What parts of the product could be reused in future products?

7.19 (Readings in Software Engineering) Your instructor will distribute copies of [Schmidt, 1995]. Do you agree with Schmidt that the use of design patterns promotes reuse within object-oriented software?

REFERENCES

[AdaIC, 1997] "DoD to Replace Ada Mandate with Software-Engineering Process," *AdaIC News*, Summer 1997, Ada Information Clearinghouse, Falls Church, VA.

[Adler, 1995] R. M. ADLER, "Emerging Standards for Component Software," *IEEE Computer* **28** (March 1995), pp. 68–77.

[Alexander et al., 1977] C. ALEXANDER, S. ISHIKAWA, M. SILVERSTEIN, M. JACOBSON, I. FIKSDAHL-KING, AND S. ANGEL, *A Pattern Language,* Oxford University Press, New York, 1977.

[Anderson et al., 1995] E. ANDERSON, Z. BAI, C. BISCHOF, J. DEMMEL, J. DONGARRA, J. DU CROZ, A. GREENBAUM, S. HAMMARLING, A. MCKENNEY, S. OSTROUCHOV, AND D. SORENSEN, *LAPACK Users' Guide,* Second Edition, SIAM, Philadelphia, 1995.

[ANSI X3.159, 1989] "The Programming Language C," ANSI X3.159-1989, American National Standards Institute, Inc., 1989.

[ANSI/IEEE 754, 1985] "Standard for Binary Floating Point Arithmetic," ANSI/IEEE 754, American National Standards Institute, Inc., Institute of Electrical and Electronic Engineers, Inc., 1985.

[ANSI/IEEE 770X3.97, 1983] "Pascal Computer Programming Language," ANSI/IEEE 770X3.97-1983, American National Standards Institute, Inc., Institute of Electrical and Electronic Engineers, Inc., 1983.

[ANSI/MIL-STD-1815A, 1983] "Reference Manual for the Ada Programming Language," ANSI/MIL-STD-1815A, American National Standards Institute, Inc., United States Department of Defense, 1983.

[Barnes and Bollinger, 1991] B. H. BARNES AND T. B. BOLLINGER, "Making Reuse Cost-Effective," *IEEE Software* **8** (January 1991), pp. 13–24.

[Biggerstaff and Perlis, 1989] T. J. BIGGERSTAFF AND A. J. PERLIS (Editors), *Software Reusability, Volumes I and II,* ACM Press, New York, 1989.

[Brockschmidt, 1994] K. BROCKSCHMIDT, *Inside OLE2,* Microsoft Press, Redmond, WA, 1994.

[Bruegge, Blythe, Jackson, and Shufelt, 1992] B. BRUEGGE, J. BLYTHE, J. JACKSON, AND J. SHUFELT, "Object-Oriented Modeling with OMT," *Proceedings of the Conference on Object-Oriented Programming, Languages, and Systems, OOPSLA '92, ACM SIGPLAN Notices* **27** (October 1992), pp. 359–76.

[Caldiera and Basili, 1991] G. CALDIERA AND V. R. BASILI, "Identifying and Qualifying Reusable Software Components," *IEEE Computer* **24** (February 1991), pp. 61–70.

[Capper, Colgate, Hunter, and James, 1994] N. P. CAPPER, R. J. COLGATE, J. C. HUNTER, AND M. F. JAMES, "The Impact of Object-Oriented Technology on Software Quality: Three Case Histories," *IBM Systems Journal* **33** (No. 1, 1994), pp. 131–57.

[Carlson, Druffel, Fisher, and Whitaker, 1980] W. E. CARLSON, L. E. DRUFFEL, D. A. FISHER, AND W. A. WHITAKER, "Introducing Ada," *Proceedings of the ACM Annual Conference, ACM 80,* Nashville, TN, 1980, pp. 263–71.

[Chappell, 1996] D. CHAPPELL, *Understanding ActiveX and OLE,* Microsoft Press, Redmond, WA, 1996.

[Cline, 1996] M. P. CLINE, "The Pros and Cons of Adopting and Applying Design Patterns in the Real World," *Communications of the ACM* **39** (October 1996), pp. 47–49.

[Coad, 1992] P. COAD, "Object-Oriented Patterns," *Communications of the ACM* **35** (September 1992), pp. 152–59.

[Cockburn, 1996] A. COCKBURN, "The Interaction of Social Issues and Software Architecture," *Communications of the ACM* **39** (October 1996), pp. 40–46.

[Coplien, 1997] J. O. COPLIEN, "Idioms and Patterns as Architectural Literature," *IEEE Software* **14** (January/February 1997), pp. 36–42.

[Dongarra et al., 1993] J. DONGARRA, R. POZO, AND D. WALKER, "LAPACK++: A Design Overview of Object-Oriented Extensions for High Performance Linear Algebra," *Proceedings of Supercomputing '93,* IEEE Press 1993, pp. 162–71.

[Fichman and Kemerer, 1997] R. G. FICHMAN AND C. F. KEMERER, "Object Technology and Reuse: Lessons from Early Adopters," *IEEE Computer* **30** (October 1997), pp. 47–59.

[Fisher, 1976] D. A. FISHER, "A Common Programming Language for the Department of Defense—Background and Technical Requirements," Report P-1191, Institute for Defense Analyses, Alexandria, VA, 1976.

[Flanagan, 1996] D. FLANAGAN, *Java in a Nutshell,* O'Reilly and Associates, Sebastopol, CA, 1996.

[Fowler, 1997a] M. FOWLER, *Analysis Patterns: Reusable Object Models,* Addison-Wesley, Reading, MA, 1997.

[Frakes and Fox, 1995] W. B. FRAKES AND C. J. FOX, "Sixteen Questions about Software Reuse," *Communications of the ACM* **38** (June 1995), pp. 75–87.

[Freeman, 1987] P. FREEMAN (Editor), *Tutorial: Software Reusability,* IEEE Computer Society Press, Washington, DC, 1987.

[Gamma, Helm, Johnson, and Vlissides, 1995] E. GAMMA, R. HELM, R. JOHNSON, AND J. VLISSIDES, *Design Patterns: Elements of Reusable Object-Oriented Software,* Addison-Wesley, Reading, MA, 1995

[Gargaro and Pappas, 1987] A. GARGARO AND T. L. PAPPAS, "Reusability Issues and Ada," *IEEE Software* **4** (July 1987), pp. 43–51.

[Garlan, Allen, and Ockerbloom, 1995] D. GARLAN, R. ALLEN, AND J. OCKERBLOOM, "Architectural Mismatch: Why Reuse Is So Hard," *IEEE Software* **12** (November 1995), pp. 17–26.

[Gaskill, 1996] B. GASKILL, "OpenDoc, ActiveX, JavaBeans, GNUstep (OpenStep), and Fresco Comparison," www.jagunet.com/~braddock/opendoccomp.html, 12 November, 1996.

[Gifford and Spector, 1987] D. GIFFORD AND A. SPECTOR, "Case Study: IBM's System/360-370 Architecture," *Communications of the ACM* **30** (April 1987), pp. 292–307.

[Griss, 1993] M. L. GRISS, "Software Reuse: From Library to Factory," *IBM Systems Journal* **32** (No. 4, 1993), pp. 548–66.

[Holzner, 1993] S. HOLZNER, *Microsoft Foundation Class Library Programming,* Brady, New York, 1993.

[Isakowitz and Kauffman, 1996] T. ISAKOWITZ AND R. J. KAUFFMAN, *IEEE Transactions on Software Engineering* **22** (June 1996), pp. 407–23.

[ISO-7185, 1980] "Specification for the Computer Programming Language Pascal," ISO-7185, International Standards Organization, Geneva, 1980.

[ISO/IEC 1539, 1991] "Programming Language Fortran," Second Edition, ISO/IEC 1539, International Standards Organization, International Electrotechnical Commission, Geneva, 1991. (Also published as ANSI Standard X3.9-198-1992.)

[ISO/IEC 1989, 1997] "Committee Draft 1.1, Proposed Revision of ISO 1989: 1985, Programming Language COBOL," JCT1/SC22/WG4, International Standards Organization, International Electrotechnical Commission, Geneva, 1997.

[ISO/IEC 8652, 1995] "Programming Language Ada: Language and Standard Libraries," ISO/IEC 8652, International Organization for Standardization, International Electrotechnical Commission, Geneva, 1995.

[ISO/IEC 14882, 1998] "Programming Language C++," ISO/IEC 14882, International Organization for Standardization, International Electrotechnical Commission, Geneva, 1998.

[Jensen and Wirth, 1975] K. JENSEN AND N. WIRTH, *Pascal User Manual and Report,* Second Edition, Springer-Verlag, New York, 1975.

[Jézéquel and Meyer, 1997] J.-M. JÉZÉQUEL AND B. MEYER, "Put It in the Contract: The Lessons of Ariane," *IEEE Computer* **30** (January 1997), pp. 129–30.

[Johnson, 1997] R. E. JOHNSON, "Frameworks = (Components + Patterns)," *Communications of the ACM* **40** (October 1997), pp. 39–42.

[Johnson and Ritchie, 1978] S. C. JOHNSON AND D. M. RITCHIE, "Portability of C Programs and the UNIX System," *Bell System Technical Journal* **57** (No. 6, Part 2, 1978), pp. 2021–48.

[Johnson, 1979] S. C. JOHNSON, "A Tour through the Portable C Compiler," Seventh Edition, UNIX Programmer's Manual, Bell Laboratories, Murray Hill, NJ, January 1979.

[Jones, 1984] T. C. JONES, "Reusability in Programming: A Survey of the State of the Art," *IEEE Transactions on Software Engineering* **SE-10** (September 1984), pp. 488–94.

[Jones, 1996] C. JONES, *Applied Software Measurement,* McGraw-Hill, New York, 1996.

[Joos, 1994] R. JOOS, "Software Reuse at Motorola," *IEEE Software* **11** (September 1994), pp. 42–47.

[Kernighan and Ritchie, 1978] B. W. KERNIGHAN AND D. M. RITCHIE, *The C Programming Language,* Prentice Hall, Englewood Cliffs, NJ, 1978.

[Kerth and Cunningham, 1997] N. L. KERTH AND W. CUNNINGHAM, "Using Patterns to Improve Our Architectural Vision," *IEEE Software* **14** (January/February 1997), pp. 53–59.

[Klatte et al., 1993] R. KLATTE, U. KULISCH, A. WIETHOFF, C. LAWO, AND M. RAUCH, *C-XSC: A C++ Class Library for Extended Scientific Computing,* Springer-Verlag, Heidelberg, New York, 1993.

[Lanergan and Grasso, 1984] R. G. LANERGAN AND C. A. GRASSO, "Software Engineering with Reusable Designs and Code," *IEEE Transactions on Software Engineering* **SE-10** (September 1984), pp. 498–501.

[Langtangen, 1994] H. P. LANGTANGEN, "Getting Started with Finite Element Programming in DIFFPACK," The DiffPack Report Series, SINTEF, Oslo, Norway, October 2, 1994.

[Lecarme and Gart, 1986] O. LECARME AND M. P. GART, *Software Portability,* McGraw-Hill, New York, 1986.

[Leppinen, Pulkkinen, and Rautiainen, 1997] M. LEPPINEN, P. PULKKINEN, AND A. RAUTIAINEN, "Java- and CORBA-Based Network Management," *IEEE Computer* **30** (June 1997), pp. 83–87.

[Lewis et al., 1995b] T. LEWIS, L. ROSENSTEIN, W. PREE, A. WEINAND, E. GAMMA, P. CALDER, G. ANDERT, J. VLISSIDES, AND K. SCHMUCKER, *Object-Oriented Application Frameworks,* Manning, Greenwich, CT, 1995.

[Lim, 1994] W. C. LIM, "Effects of Reuse on Quality, Productivity, and Economics," *IEEE Software* **11** (September 1994). pp. 23–30.

[Lim, 1998] W. C. LIM, *Managing Software Reuse,* Prentice Hall, Upper Saddle River, NJ, 1998.

[Liskov, Snyder, Atkinson, and Schaffert, 1977] B. LISKOV, A. SNYDER, R. ATKINSON, AND C. SCHAFFERT, "Abstraction Mechanisms in CLU," *Communications of the ACM* **20** (August 1977), pp. 564–76.

[Mackenzie, 1980] C. E. MACKENZIE, *Coded Character Sets: History and Development,* Addison-Wesley, Reading, MA, 1980.

[Matsumoto, 1984] Y. MATSUMOTO, "Management of Industrial Software Production," *IEEE Computer* **17** (February 1984), pp. 59–72.

[Matsumoto, 1987] Y. MATSUMOTO, "A Software Factory: An Overall Approach to Software Production," in: *Tutorial: Software Reusability,* P. Freeman (Editor), Computer Society Press, Washington, DC, 1987, pp. 155–78.

[Meyer, 1987] B. MEYER, "Reusability: The Case for Object-Oriented Design," *IEEE Software* **4** (March 1987), pp. 50–64.

[Meyer, 1990] B. MEYER, "Lessons from the Design of the Eiffel Libraries," *Communications of the ACM* **33** (September 1990), pp. 68–88.

[Meyer, 1996a] B. MEYER, "The Reusability Challenge," *IEEE Computer* **29** (February 1996), pp. 76–78.

[Mili, Mili, and Mili, 1995] H. MILI, F. MILI, AND A. MILI, "Reusing Software: Issues and Research Directions," *IEEE Transactions on Software Engineering* **21** (June 1995), pp. 528–62.

[Mione, 1998] A. MIONE, *CDE and Motif, A Practical Primer,* Prentice Hall, Upper Saddle River, NJ, 1998.

[Monroe, Kompanek, Melton, and Garlan, 1997] R. T. MONROE, A. KOMPANEK, R. MELTON, AND D. GARLAN, "Architectural Styles, Design Patterns, and Objects," *IEEE Software* **14** (January/February 1997), pp. 43–52.

[Mooney, 1990] J. D. MOONEY, "Strategies for Supporting Application Portability," *IEEE Computer* **23** (November 1990), pp. 59–70.

[Moser and Nierstrasz, 1996] S. MOSER AND O. NIERSTRASZ, "The Effect of Object-Oriented Frameworks on Developer Productivity," *IEEE Computer* **29** (September 1996), pp. 45–51.

[Mowbray and Zahavi, 1995] T. J. MOWBRAY AND R. ZAHAVI, *The Essential CORBA,* John Wiley & Sons, New York, 1995.

[Musser and Saini, 1996] D. R. MUSSER AND A. SAINI, *STL Tutorial and Reference Guide: C++ Programming with the Standard Template Library,* Addison-Wesley, Reading, MA, 1996.

[Nissen and Wallis, 1984] J. NISSEN AND P. WALLIS (Editors), *Portability and Style in Ada,* Cambridge University Press, Cambridge, UK, 1984.

[NIST 151, 1988] "POSIX: Portable Operating System Interface for Computer Environments," Federal Information Processing Standard 151, National Institute of Standards and Technology, Washington, DC, 1988.

[Norusis, 1982] M. J. NORUSIS, *SPSS Introductory Guide: Basic Statistics and Operations,* McGraw-Hill, New York, 1982.

[OMG, 1993] "The Common Object Request Broker: Architecture and Specification (CORBA) Revision 1.2," OMG TC Document 93.12.43, Object Management Group, Framingham, MA, December 1993.

[OpenWindows, 1993] *Solaris OpenWindows User's Guide/OpenWindows 3.1,* Prentice Hall, Englewood Cliffs, NJ, 1993.

[Orfali, Harkey, and Edwards, 1996] R. ORFALI, D. HARKEY, AND J. EDWARDS, *The Essential Distributed Objects Survival Guide,* John Wiley & Sons, New York, 1996.

[Phillips, 1986] J. PHILLIPS, *The NAG Library: A Beginner's Guide,* Clarendon Press, Oxford, UK, 1986.

[Poulin, 1997] J. S. POULIN, *Measuring Software Reuse: Principles, Practice, and Economic Models,* Addison-Wesley, Reading, MA, 1997.

[Prieto-Díaz, 1991] R. PRIETO-DÍAZ, "Implementing Faceted Classification for Software Reuse," *Communications of the ACM* **34** (May 1991), pp. 88–97.

[Prieto-Díaz, 1993] R. PRIETO-DÍAZ, "Status Report: Software Reusability," *IEEE Software* **10** (May 1993), pp. 61–66.

[Schach, 1992] S. R. SCHACH, *Software Reuse: Past, Present, and Future,* Videotape, 150 mins, US-VHS format. IEEE Computer Society Press, Los Alamitos, CA, November 1992.

[Schach, 1994] S. R. SCHACH, "The Economic Impact of Software Reuse on Maintenance," *Journal of Software Maintenance—Research and Practice* **6** (July/August 1994), pp. 185–96.

[Schach, 1997] S. R. SCHACH, *Software Engineering with Java,* Richard D. Irwin, Chicago, 1997.

[Schmid, 1996] H. A. SCHMID, "Creating Applications from Components: A Manufacturing Framework Design," *IEEE Software* **13** (November/December 1996), pp. 67–75.

[Schmidt, 1995] D. C. SCHMIDT, "Using Design Patterns to Develop Reusable Object-Oriented Communications Software," *Communications of the ACM* **38** (October 1995), pp. 65–74.

[Selby, 1989] R. W. SELBY, "Quantitative Studies of Software Reuse," in: *Software Reusability. Volume II: Applications and Experience,* T. J. Biggerstaff and A. J. Perlis (Editors), ACM Press, New York, 1989, pp. 213–33.

[Shaw, 1995] M. SHAW, "Comparing Architectural Design Styles," *IEEE Software* **12** (November 1995), pp. 27–41.

[Shaw and Garlan, 1996] M. SHAW AND D. GARLAN, *Software Architecture: Perspectives on an Emerging Discipline,* Prentice Hall, Upper Saddle River, NJ, 1996.

[Skazinski, 1994] J. G. SKAZINSKI, "Porting Ada: A Report from the Field," *IEEE Computer* **27** (October 1994), pp. 58–64.

[Sparks, Benner, and Faris, 1996] S. SPARKS, K. BENNER, AND C. FARIS, "Managing Object-Oriented Framework Reuse," *IEEE Computer* **29** (September 1996), pp. 52–61.

[Tanenbaum, 1996] A. S. TANENBAUM, *Computer Networks,* Third Edition, Prentice Hall, Upper Saddle River, NJ, 1996.

[Tepfenhart and Cusick, 1997] W. M. TEPFENHART AND J. J. CUSICK, "A Unified Object Topology," *IEEE Software* **14** (January/February 1997), pp. 31-35.

[Tracz, 1988] W. TRACZ, "Software Reuse Myths," *ACM SIGSOFT Software Engineering Notes* **13** (January 1988), pp. 17–21.

[Tracz, 1994] W. TRACZ, "Software Reuse Myths Revisited," *Proceedings of the 16th International Conference on Software Engineering,* Sorrento, Italy, May 1994, pp. 271–72.

[Tracz, 1995] W. TRACZ, *Confessions of a Used Program Salesman: Institutionalizing Software Reuse,* Addison-Wesley, Reading, MA, 1995.

[Wallis, 1982] P. J. L. WALLIS, *Portable Programming,* John Wiley and Sons, New York, 1982.

[Wegner, 1989] P. WEGNER, "Dimensions of Object-Oriented Modeling," *IEEE Computer* (October 1992), pp. 12–20.

[Wells, 1996] T. D. WELLS, "A Technical Comparison of Borland ObjectWindows 2.0 and Microsoft MFC 2.5," www.it.rit.edu/~tdw/refs/om.htm, February 05, 1996.

[Wildblood, 1990] A. WILDBLOOD, "Ada Reuse: The Promises Ring True," *Defense Science* **9** (April 1990), pp. 38–39.

[Wilson, Rosenstein, and Shafer, 1990] D. A. WILSON, L. S. ROSENSTEIN, AND D. SHAFER, *Programming with MacApp,* Addison-Wesley, Reading, MA, 1990.

[Wolberg, 1983] J. R. WOLBERG, *Conversion of Computer Software,* Prentice Hall, Englewood Cliffs, NJ, 1983.

chapter

8

❖PLANNING AND ESTIMATING

There is no easy solution to the difficulties of constructing a software product. A large software product takes time and resources to put together. And like any other large construction project, careful planning at the beginning of the project is perhaps the single most important factor that distinguishes success from failure. This initial planning, however, is by no means enough. Planning, like testing, must continue throughout the software development and maintenance process. Notwithstanding the need for continual planning, these activities reach a peak after the specifications have been drawn up but before design activities commence. At this point in the process, meaningful duration and cost estimates are computed and a detailed plan for completing the project is produced.

In this chapter we distinguish these two types of planning, the planning that proceeds throughout the project and the intense planning that must be carried out once the specifications are complete.

8.1 PLANNING AND THE SOFTWARE PROCESS

Ideally, we would like to be able to plan the entire software project at the very beginning of the process, and then follow that plan until the target software has finally been delivered to the client. This is impossible, however, because we do not have enough information available during the initial phases to be able to draw up a meaningful plan for the complete project. For example, during the requirements phase, any sort of planning (other than just for the requirements phase itself) will be futile.

Suppose now that the developers have built a rapid prototype (Section 3.3) and the client feels that the rapid prototype indeed encapsulates the key functionality of the target product. It might seem that at this stage it would be possible

❖As explained in the preface, this chapter may be taught in parallel with Part 2. The material of Chapter 8 is required for the software project management plan of the Case Study (Sections 10.15 and 11.10) and of the Term Project (Problem 10.16 and Problems 10.20 through 10.22).

to provide reasonably accurate duration and cost estimates for the project. Unfortunately, that is not true. There is a world of difference between the information at the developers' disposal at the end of the requirements phase and at the end of the specifications phase, analogous to the difference between a rough sketch and a detailed blueprint. By the end of the requirements phase, the developers at best have an informal understanding of what the client needs. In contrast, by the end of the specifications phase, at which time the client signs a document stating precisely what is going to be built, the developers have a detailed appreciation of most (but usually not yet all) aspects of the target product. This is the earliest point in the process at which accurate duration and cost estimates can be determined.

Nevertheless, in some situations an organization may be required to produce duration and cost estimates before the specifications can be drawn up. In the worst case, a client may insist on a bid on the basis of an hour or two of preliminary discussion, even before a rapid prototype has been constructed. Figure 8.1 shows how problematic this can be. Based on a model in [Boehm et al., 1995], it depicts the relative range of cost estimates for the various phases of the life cycle. For example, suppose that when a product passes its acceptance test at the end of the integration phase and is delivered to the client, its cost is found to be $1 million. If a cost estimate had been made midway through the requirements phase, it is

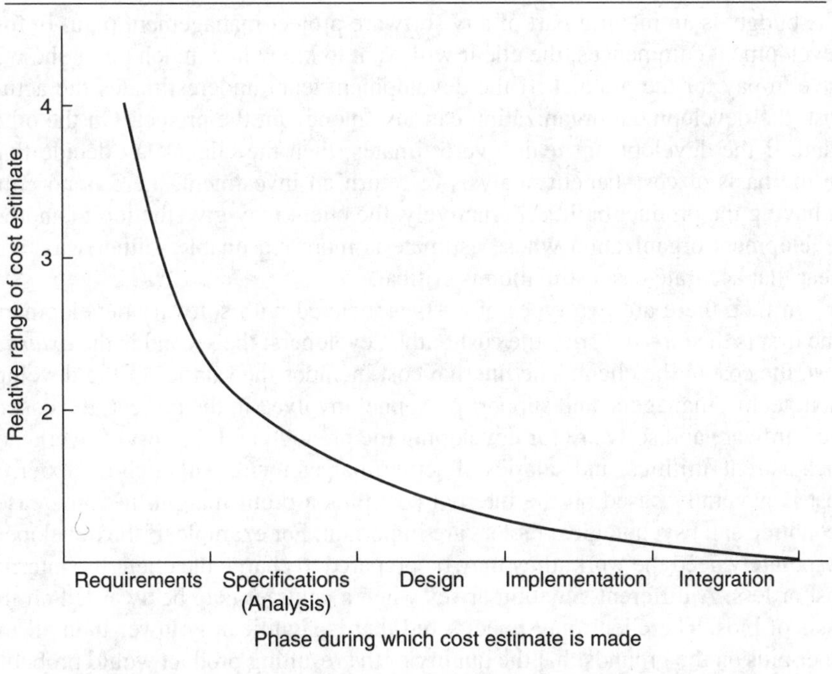

Figure 8.1 Model estimate of relative range of cost estimate for each life-cycle phase.

likely that it would have been somewhere in the range ($0.25 million, $4 million). Similarly, if it had been made midway through the specifications phase the range of likely estimates would have shrunk to ($0.5 million, $2 million). Furthermore, if the cost estimate had been made at the end of the specifications phase, that is, at the earliest possible appropriate time, the result would probably have been in the still relatively wide range of ($0.67 million, $1.5 million). In other words, cost estimation is not an exact science, for reasons given in the next section. The data on which this model is based are old, including five proposals submitted to the U.S. Air Force Electronic Systems Division [Devenny, 1976], and estimation techniques have improved since that time. Nevertheless, the overall shape of the curve in Figure 8.1 has probably not changed overmuch. Consequently, a premature duration or cost estimate, that is, an estimate made before the specifications have been signed off by the client, is likely to be considerably less accurate than an estimate made at the correct time.

We now examine techniques for estimating duration and cost. The assumption throughout the remainder of this chapter is that the specification phase has been completed, that is, meaningful estimating and planning can now be carried out.

8.2 ESTIMATING DURATION AND COST

The budget is an integral part of any software project management plan. Before development commences, the client will want to know how much he or she will have to pay for the product. If the development team underestimates the actual cost, the development organization can lose money on the project. On the other hand, if the development team overestimates, then the client may decide that, on the basis of cost–benefit analysis or return on investment, there is no point in having the product built. Alternatively, the client may give the job to another development organization whose estimate is more reasonable. Either way, it is clear that accurate cost estimation is critical.

In fact, there are two types of costs associated with software development. The first is the *internal cost,* the cost to the developers; the second is the *external cost,* the cost to the client. The internal cost includes the salaries of the development teams, managers, and support personnel involved in the project; the cost of the hardware and software for developing the product; and the cost of overheads such as rent, utilities, and salaries of senior management. Although the external cost is generally based on the internal cost plus a profit margin, in some cases economic and psychological factors are important. For example, if the developers desperately need the work, they may be prepared to charge the client the internal cost or less. A different situation arises when a contract is to be awarded on the basis of bids. The client may reject a bid that is significantly lower than all the other bids on the grounds that the quality of the resulting product would probably also be significantly lower. A development team may therefore try to come up with a bid that will be slightly, but not significantly, lower than what they believe their competitors' bids will be.

Another important part of any plan is estimating the duration of the project. The client will certainly want to know when the finished product will be delivered. If the development organization is unable to keep to its schedule, then at best the organization loses credibility, at worst penalty clauses will be invoked. In all cases, the managers responsible for the software project management plan have a lot of explaining to do. Conversely, if the development organization overestimates the time that will be needed to build the product, then there is a good chance that the client will go elsewhere.

Unfortunately, it is by no means easy to estimate cost and duration requirements accurately. There are just too many variables to be able to get an accurate handle on either cost or duration. One big difficulty is the human factor. Over 30 years ago Sackman and co-workers showed differences of up to 28 to 1 between pairs of programmers [Sackman, Erikson, and Grant, 1968]. It is easy to try to brush off Sackman's results by saying that experienced programmers will always outperform beginners, but Sackman and his colleagues compared matched pairs of programmers. They observed, for example, two programmers with 10 years of experience on similar types of projects and measured the time it took them to perform tasks like coding and debugging. Then they observed, say, two beginners who had been in the profession for the same short length of time and who had similar educational backgrounds. Comparing worst and best performances, they observed differences of 6 to 1 in product size, 8 to 1 in product execution time, 9 to 1 in development time, 18 to 1 in coding time, and 28 to 1 in debugging time. A particularly alarming observation is that the best and worst performances on one product were by two programmers, each of whom had 11 years of experience. Even when the best and worst cases were removed from Sackman's sample, observed differences were still of the order of 5 to 1. On the basis of these results, it is clear that we cannot hope to estimate software cost or duration with any degree of accuracy (unless we have detailed information regarding all the skills of all our employees, which is unusual). It has been argued that, in a large project, differences between individuals will tend to cancel out, but this is perhaps wishful thinking; the presence of one or two very good (or very bad) team members will cause marked deviations from schedules and significantly impact the budget.

Another human factor that can affect estimation is that in a free country there is no way of ensuring that a critical staff member will not resign during the project. Time and money are then spent attempting to fill the vacated position and integrate the replacement into the team, or in reorganizing the remaining team members to compensate for the loss. Either way schedules slip, and estimates come unstuck.

Underlying the cost estimation problem is another issue: How is the size of a product to be measured?

8.2.1 METRICS FOR THE SIZE OF A PRODUCT

The most common metric for the size of a product is the number of lines of code. Two different units are commonly used, namely, lines of code (LOC) and thousand delivered source instructions (KDSI). Many problems are associated with the use of lines of code [van der Poel and Schach, 1983].

First, creation of source code is only a small part of the total software development effort. It seems somewhat far-fetched that the time required for specifying, planning, designing, implementing, integrating, and testing can be expressed solely as a function of the number of lines of code of the final product.

Second, implementing the same product in two different languages will result in versions with different numbers of lines of code. Also, with languages such as Lisp or with many nonprocedural 4GLs, the concept of lines of code is not defined.

Third, it is often not clear exactly how to count lines of code. Should only executable lines of code be counted, or data definitions as well? And should comments be counted? If not, there is a danger that programmers will be reluctant to spend time on what they perceive to be "nonproductive" commenting, but if comments are counted, then there is the opposite danger that programmers will write reams of comments in an attempt to boost their apparent productivity. Also, what about counting job control language statements? Another problem is how changed lines or deleted lines are counted—in the course of enhancing a product to improve its performance, it sometimes happens that the number of lines of code is decreased. Reuse of code (Section 7.1) also complicates line counting; if reused code is modified, how is it counted? And what if code is inherited from a parent class (Section 6.7)? In short, the apparently straightforward metric of lines of code is anything but straightforward to count.

Fourth, not all the code written is delivered to the client. It is not uncommon for half the code to consist of tools needed to support the development effort.

Fifth, suppose that a software developer is using a code generator, such as a report generator, a screen generator, or a graphical user interface (GUI) generator. After a few minutes of design activity on the part of the developer, the tool may generate many thousands of lines of code.

Sixth, the number of lines of code in the final product can be determined only when the product is completely finished. Thus, basing cost estimation on lines of code is doubly dangerous. To start the estimation process, the number of lines of code in the finished product must be estimated. Then, this estimate is used to estimate the cost of the product. Not only is there uncertainty in every costing technique, but if the input to an uncertain cost estimator is itself uncertain, namely, the number of lines of code in a product that has not yet been built, then the reliability of the resulting cost estimate is unlikely to be too high.

Because the number of lines of code is so unreliable, other metrics must be considered. So-called software science [Halstead, 1977; Shen, Conte, and Dunsmore, 1983] proposed a variety of measures of product size. These are derived from the fundamental metrics of software science, namely, the number of operands and operators in the software product and the number of unique operands and unique operators. As with lines of code, these numbers can be determined only after the product has been completed, thus severely reducing the predictive power of the metrics. Also, many studies have cast doubt on the validity of software science [Hamer and Frewin, 1982; Coulter, 1983; Shen, Conte, and Dunsmore, 1983; Shepperd, 1988a; Weyuker, 1988b; Shepperd and Ince, 1994].

An alternative approach to estimating the size of a product is the use of metrics based on measurable quantities that can be determined early in the software process. For example, van der Poel and Schach put forward the FFP metric for cost estimation of medium-scale data-processing products, that is, products that take between 2 and 10 person-years to complete [van der Poel and Schach, 1983]. The three basic structural elements of a data-processing product are its files, flows, and processes; the name FFP is an acronym formed from the initial letters of those three elements. A file is defined as a collection of logically or physically related records that is permanently resident in the product; transaction and temporary files are excluded. A flow is a data interface between the product and the environment such as a screen or a report. A process is a functionally defined logical or arithmetic manipulation of data. Examples include sorting, validating, or updating. Given the number of files Fi, flows Fl, and processes Pr in a product, its size S and cost C are given by

$$S = Fi + Fl + Pr \tag{8.1}$$

$$C = d \times S \tag{8.2}$$

where d is a constant that will vary from organization to organization. Constant d is a measure of the efficiency (productivity) of the software development process within the organization. The size of a product is simply the sum of the number of files, flows, and processes, a quantity that can be determined once the architectural design is complete. The cost is then proportional to the size, the constant of proportionality d being determined by a least-squares fit to cost data relating to products previously developed by that organization. Unlike metrics based on the number of lines of code, the cost can be estimated before coding begins.

The validity and reliability of the FFP metric were demonstrated using a purposive sample that covered a range of medium-scale data-processing applications. Unfortunately, the metric was never extended to include databases, an essential component of many data processing products.

A similar, but independently developed, metric for the size of a product is one developed by Albrecht based on function points [Albrecht, 1979; Albrecht and Gaffney, 1983]. Albrecht's metric is based on the number of input items Inp, output items Out, inquiries Inq, master files Maf, and interfaces Inf. In its simplest form the number of function points FP is given by the equation

$$FP = 4 \times Inp + 5 \times Out + 4 \times Inq + 10 \times Maf + 7 \times Inf \tag{8.3}$$

Because this is a measure of the product's size, it can be used for cost estimation and productivity estimation.

Equation 8.3 is an oversimplification of a three-step calculation. First, each of the components of a product, namely, Inp, Out, Inq, Maf, and Inf, must be classified as simple, average, or complex (see Figure 8.2). Each component is assigned a number of function points depending on its level. For example, an average input is assigned 4 function points, as reflected in equation (8.3), but a simple input is assigned only 3, whereas a complex input is assigned 6 function points. The data needed for this computation appear in Figure 8.2. The function points assigned to each component are then summed, yielding the unadjusted function points (UFP).

	Level of Complexity		
Component	Simple	Average	Complex
Input item	3	4	6
Output item	4	5	7
Inquiry	3	4	6
Master file	7	10	15
Interface	5	7	10

Figure 8.2 Table of function point values.

Second, the technical complexity factor (*TCF*) is computed. This is a measure of the effect of 14 technical factors such as high transaction rates, performance criteria (for example, throughput or response time), and online updating; the complete set of factors is shown in Figure 8.3. Each of these 14 factors is assigned a value from 0 ("not present or no influence") to 5 ("strong influence throughout"). The resulting 14 numbers are summed, yielding the total degree of influence (*DI*). The *TCF* is then given by

$$TCF = 0.65 + 0.01 \times DI \tag{8.4}$$

Because *DI* can vary from 0 to 70, *TCF* will vary from 0.65 to 1.35.

Finally, *FP*, the number of function points, is given by

$$FP = UFP \times TCF \tag{8.5}$$

1. Data communications
2. Distributed data processing
3. Performance criteria
4. Heavily utilized hardware
5. High transaction rates
6. Online data entry
7. End-user efficiency
8. Online updating
9. Complex computations
10. Reusability
11. Ease of installation
12. Ease of operation
13. Portability
14. Maintainability

Figure 8.3 Technical factors for function point computation.

	Assembler Version	Ada Version
Source code size	70 KDSI	25 KDSI
Development costs	$1,043,000	$590,000
KDSI per person-month	0.335	0.211
Cost per source statement	$14.90	$23.60
Function points per person-month	1.65	2.92
Cost per function point	$3,023	$1,170

Figure 8.4 Comparison of assembler and Ada products [Jones, 1987]. (©1987 IEEE.)

Experiments by Albrecht and others [Albrecht, 1979; Albrecht and Gaffney, 1983; Behrens, 1983; Jones, 1987] to measure software productivity rates have shown a better fit using function points than using KDSI. Jones states that he has observed errors in excess of 800 percent counting KDSI, but *only* [emphasis added] 200 percent in counting function points [Jones, 1987], a most revealing remark.

To show the superiority of function points over lines of code, Jones cites the example shown in Figure 8.4 [Jones, 1987]. The same product was coded both in assembler and in Ada and the results compared. First, consider KDSI per person-month. This metric tells us that coding in assembler is apparently 60 percent more efficient than coding in Ada, a fact that is patently false. Third-generation languages like Ada have superseded assembler simply because it is much more efficient to code in a third-generation language. Now consider the second metric, cost per source statement. Note that one Ada statement in this product is equivalent to 2.8 assembler statements. Use of cost per source statement as a measure of efficiency again implies that it is more efficient to code in assembler than in Ada, the statement rejected previously as being nonsense. However, when function points per person-month is taken as the metric of programming efficiency, the superiority of Ada over assembler is clearly reflected.

On the other hand, both function points and the FFP metric of equations (8.1) and (8.2) suffer from the same disadvantage: Product maintenance is often inaccurately measured. When a product is maintained, major changes to the product can be made without changing the number of files, flows, and processes or the number of inputs, outputs, inquiries, master files, and interfaces. Lines of code is no better in this respect. To take an extreme case, it is possible to replace every line of a product by a completely different line without changing the total number of lines of code.

A number of extensions to Albrecht's function points have been proposed. Mk II function points were put forward by Symons in 1987 to provide a more accurate way of computing the unadjusted function points (*UFP*). The software is decomposed into a set of component transactions, each consisting of an input, a process, and an output. The value of *UFP* is then computed from these inputs, processes, and outputs. Mk II function points are widely used all over the world [Boehm, 1997].

Both function points and the FFP metric were designed to estimate the size of data processing applications. *Feature points* were put forward in 1986 as a size estimator for software in which algorithms play a role, such as real-time software, embedded software, and communications software [Jones, 1991]. The relationship between function points and feature points is

$$Feature\ Points = FP - 3 \times Maf + 3 \times Alg \qquad \textbf{(8.6)}$$

where FP is the number of function points computed from equation (8.3), Maf the number of master files, and Alg the number of algorithms (examples of an algorithm include a sort, an interest computation, or a cube root computation). Jones considers feature points still to be experimental; the accuracy of this metric remains to be proven [Jones, 1995].

Another experimental technique is 3D function points, developed by the Boeing Company to simplify function point counting and measure the size of scientific and real-time software more accurately. Unfortunately, neither the ease of use nor the accuracy of 3D function points has thus far been demonstrated [Boehm, 1997].

8.2.2 TECHNIQUES OF COST ESTIMATION

Notwithstanding the difficulties with estimating size, it is essential that software developers simply do the best they can to obtain accurate estimates of both project duration and project cost, while taking into account as many as possible of the factors that can affect their estimates. These include the skill levels of the personnel, the complexity of the project, the size of the project (cost increases with size, but much faster than linearly), familiarity of the development team with the application area, the hardware on which the product is to run, and availability of CASE tools. Another factor is the deadline effect. If a project has to be completed within a certain time, the effort in person-months is greater than if there is no constraint on completion time.

From the preceding list, which is by no means comprehensive, it is clear that estimation is a difficult problem. There are a number of approaches that have been used, with greater or lesser success.

1. Expert Judgment by Analogy In this technique a number of experts are consulted. An expert arrives at an estimate by comparing the target product to completed products with which the expert was actively involved and noting the similarities and differences. For example, an expert may compare the target product to a similar product developed 2 years ago for which the data were input in batch mode, whereas the target product is to have online data capture. Because the organization is familiar with the type of product to be developed, the expert reduces development time and effort by 15 percent. However, the graphical user interface (GUI) is somewhat complex; this will increase time and effort by 25 percent. Finally, the target product has to be developed in a language with which most of the team members are unfamiliar, thus increasing time by 15 percent and effort by 20 percent. Combining these three figures, the expert decides that the target product will take 25 percent more time and 30 percent more effort than the previous one. Thus, because the previous product took 12 months to complete and required 100 person-months, the target product will take 15 months and consume 130 person-months.

Two other experts within the organization compare the same two products. One concludes that the target product will take 13.5 months and 140 person-months. The other comes up with the figures of 16 months and 95 person-months. How can the predictions of these three experts be reconciled? One technique is the Delphi technique; it allows experts to arrive at a consensus without having group meetings, which can have the undesirable side effect of one persuasive member swaying the group. In this technique [Helmer-Hirschberg, 1966] the experts work independently. Each produces an estimate and a rationale for that estimate. These estimates and rationales are then distributed to all the experts, who now produce a second estimate. This process of estimation and distribution continues until the experts can agree within an accepted tolerance. No group meetings take place during the iteration process.

Valuation of real estate is frequently done on the basis of expert judgment by analogy. An appraiser will arrive at a valuation by comparing a house with similar houses that have recently been sold. Suppose that house A is to be valued, house B next door has just been sold for $150,000, and house C on the next street was sold 3 months ago for $165,000. The appraiser may reason as follows: House A has one more bathroom than house B, and the yard is 5,000 square feet larger. House C is approximately the same size as house A, but its roof is in poor condition. On the other hand, House C has a jacuzzi. After careful thought, the appraiser may arrive at a figure of $168,000 for house A.

In the case of software products, expert judgment by analogy is less precise than real estate valuation. Recall that our first software expert claimed that using an unfamiliar language would increase time by 15 percent and effort by 20 percent. Unless the expert has some validated data from which the effect of each and every difference can be determined (a highly unlikely possibility), errors induced by what can only be described as guesses will result in hopelessly incorrect cost estimates. In addition, unless the experts are blessed with total recall (or have kept detailed records), their recollections of completed products may be sufficiently inaccurate as to invalidate their predictions. Finally, experts are human and, therefore, have biases that may affect their predictions. At the same time, the results of estimation by a group of experts should reflect their collective experience; if this is broad enough, the result may well be accurate.

2. Bottom-Up Approach One way of trying to reduce the errors resulting from evaluating a product as a whole is to break the product into smaller components. Estimates of duration and cost are made for each component separately and then combined to provide an overall figure. This approach has the advantage that estimating costs for several smaller components is generally quicker and more accurate than for one large one. In addition, the estimation process is likely to be more detailed than with one large, monolithic product. The disadvantage of this approach is that a product is more than the sum of its components.

With the object-oriented paradigm, the independence of the various classes helps the bottom-up approach. However, interactions among the various objects in the product complicate the estimation process.

3. Algorithmic Cost Estimation Models In this approach, a metric such as function points or the FFP metric is used as input to a model for determining product cost. The estimator computes the value of the metric; duration and cost estimates can then be computed using the model. On the surface an algorithmic cost estimation model is superior to expert opinion, because a human expert is, as pointed out previously, subject to biases and may overlook certain aspects of both the completed and target products. In contrast, an algorithmic cost estimation model is unbiased; every product is treated the same way. The danger with such a model is that its estimates are only as good as the underlying assumptions. For example, underlying the function-point model is the assumption that every aspect of a product is embodied in the five quantities on the right-hand side of equation (8.3) and the 14 technical factors. A further problem is that a significant amount of subjective judgment is often needed in deciding what values to assign to the parameters of the model. For example, it is frequently unclear whether a specific technical factor of the function-point model should be rated a 3 or a 4.

Many algorithmic cost estimation models have been proposed. Some are based on mathematical theories as to how software is developed. For example, underlying the SLIM model [Putnam, 1978] is the assumption that resource consumption during software development obeys a specific distribution; this is described in Section 8.3. Other models are statistically based; large numbers of projects are studied and empirical rules determined from the data. Then there are hybrid models incorporating mathematical equations, statistical modeling, and expert judgment. One hybrid model is the RCA Price S model [Freiman and Park, 1979]. The most important hybrid model is Boehm's COCOMO, which is described in detail in the next section. (See the Just in Case You Wanted to Know box below for a discussion of the acronym COCOMO.)

Just in Case You Wanted to Know

COCOMO is an acronym formed from the first two letters of each word in COnstructive COst MOdel. Any connection with Kokomo, Indiana, is purely homophonic.

The phrase *COCOMO model* should not be used. After all, the "MO" in COCOMO already stands for "model."

8.2.3 INTERMEDIATE COCOMO

COCOMO is actually a series of three models, ranging from a macroestimation model that treats the product as a whole to a microestimation model that treats the product in detail. In this section a description is given of Intermediate COCOMO, which has a middle level of complexity and detail. COCOMO is described in detail in [Boehm, 1981]; an overview is presented in [Boehm, 1984b].

Computing the development time using Intermediate COCOMO is done in two stages. First, a rough estimate of the development effort is provided. Two parameters have to be estimated: the length of the product in KDSI (thousands of delivered source instructions) and the product's development mode, a measure of the intrinsic level of difficulty of developing that product. There are three modes, namely, *organic* (small and straightforward), *semidetached* (medium-sized), and *embedded* (complex).

From these two parameters the *nominal effort* can be computed. For example, if the project is judged to be essentially straightforward (organic), then the nominal effort (in person-months) is given by the equation

$$\text{Nominal effort} = 3.2 \times (\text{KDSI})^{1.05} \text{ person-months} \qquad \textbf{(8.7)}$$

The constants 3.2 and 1.05 are the values that best fitted the data on the organic mode products used by Boehm to develop Intermediate COCOMO.

For example, if the product to be built is organic and is estimated to be 12,000 delivered source statements (12 KDSI), then the nominal effort is

$$3.2 \times (12)^{1.05} = 43 \text{ person-months}$$

(but read the Just in Case You Wanted to Know box on this page for a comment on this value).

Next, this nominal value must be multiplied by 15 *software development effort multipliers*. These multipliers and their values are given in Figure 8.5. Each of these multipliers can have up to six values. For example, the product complexity multiplier is assigned the values 0.70, 0.85, 1.00, 1.15, 1.30, or 1.65 according

JUST IN CASE YOU WANTED TO KNOW

One reaction to the value of the nominal effort might be, "If 43 person-months of effort are needed to produce 12,000 delivered source instructions, then on average each programmer is turning out fewer than 300 lines of code a month—I have written more than that in one night!"

A 300-line product is usually just that: 300 lines of code. In contrast, a maintainable 12,000-line product has to go through all the phases of the life cycle. In other words, the total effort of 43 person-months is shared between many activities, including coding. As reflected in the pie chart of Figure 1.2, module coding is on average only about 15 percent of the total development effort.

Cost Drivers	Rating					
	Very Low	Low	Nominal	High	Very High	Extra High
Product Attributes						
Required software reliability	0.75	0.88	1.00	1.15	1.40	
Database size		0.94	1.00	1.08	1.16	
Product complexity	0.70	0.85	1.00	1.15	1.30	1.65
Computer Attributes						
Execution time constraint			1.00	1.11	1.30	1.66
Main storage constraint			1.00	1.06	1.21	1.56
Virtual machine volatility*		0.87	1.00	1.15	1.30	
Computer turnaround time		0.87	1.00	1.07	1.15	
Personnel Attributes						
Analyst capabilities	1.46	1.19	1.00	0.86	0.71	
Applications experience	1.29	1.13	1.00	0.91	0.82	
Programmer capability	1.42	1.17	1.00	0.86	0.70	
Virtual machine experience*	1.21	1.10	1.00	0.90		
Programming language experience	1.14	1.07	1.00	0.95		
Project Attributes						
Use of modern programming practices	1.24	1.10	1.00	0.91	0.82	
Use of software tools	1.24	1.10	1.00	0.91	0.83	
Required development schedule	1.23	1.08	1.00	1.04	1.10	

*For a given software product, the underlying virtual machine is the complex of hardware and software (operating system, database management system) it calls on to accomplish its task.

Figure 8.5 Intermediate COCOMO software development effort multipliers [Boehm, 1984b]. (©1984 IEEE)

to whether the developers rate the project complexity as very low, low, nominal (average), high, very high, or extra high. As can be seen from Figure 8.5, all 15 multipliers take on the value 1.00 when the corresponding parameter is nominal.

Boehm has provided guidelines to help the developer determine whether the parameter should indeed be rated nominal or whether the rating is lower or higher. For example, consider again the module complexity multiplier. If the control operations of the module essentially consist of a sequence of the constructs of structured programming (such as **if-then-else, do-while, case**), then the complexity is rated *very low.* If these operators are nested, then the rating is *low.* Adding intermodule control and decision tables increases the rating to *nominal.* If the operators are highly nested, with compound predicates, and if there are queues and stacks, then the rating is *high.* The presence of reentrant and recursive coding and fixed-priority interrupt handling pushes the rating to *very high.* Finally, multiple resource scheduling with dynamically changing priorities and microcode-level control ensures that the rating is *extra high.* These ratings apply to control operations. A module also has to be evaluated from the viewpoint of computational operations, device-dependent operations, and data management operations. For details of the criteria for computing each of the 15 multipliers, the reader should refer to [Boehm, 1981].

To see how this works, [Boehm, 1984b] gives the example of microprocessor-based communications processing software for a highly reliable new electronic funds transfer network, with performance, development schedule, and interface requirements. This product fits the description of embedded mode and is estimated to be 10,000 delivered source instructions (10 KDSI) in length, so the nominal development effort is given by

$$\text{Nominal effort} = 2.8 \times (\text{KDSI})^{1.20} \tag{8.8}$$

(Again, the constants 2.8 and 1.20 are the values that best fitted the data on embedded products.) Because the project is estimated to be 10 KDSI in length, the nominal effort is

$$2.8 \times (10)^{1.20} = 44 \text{ person-months}$$

The estimated development effort is obtained by multiplying the nominal effort by the 15 multipliers. The ratings of these multipliers and their values are given in Figure 8.6. Using these values, the product of the multipliers is found to be 1.35, so the estimated effort for the project is

$$1.35 \times 44 = 59 \text{ person-months}$$

This number is then used in additional formulas to determine dollar costs, development schedules, phase and activity distributions, computer costs, annual maintenance costs, and other related items; for details, see [Boehm, 1981]. Intermediate COCOMO is a complete algorithmic cost estimation model, giving the user virtually every conceivable assistance in project planning.

Intermediate COCOMO has been validated with respect to a broad sample of 63 projects covering a wide variety of application areas. The results of applying Intermediate COCOMO to this sample are that the actual values come within 20 percent of the predicted values about 68 percent of the time. Attempts to improve upon this accuracy make little sense because in most organizations the input data for Intermediate COCOMO are generally accurate to within only ± 20 percent. Nevertheless, the accuracy obtained by experienced estimators placed Intermediate COCOMO at the cutting edge of cost estimation research during the 1980s; no other technique was consistently as accurate.

The major problem with Intermediate COCOMO is that its most important input is the number of lines of code in the target product. If this estimate is incorrect, then every single prediction of the model may be incorrect. Because of the possibility that the predictions of Intermediate COCOMO or any other estimation technique may be inaccurate, management must monitor all predictions throughout software development.

Cost Drivers	Situation	Rating	Effort Multiplier
Required software reliability	Serious financial consequences of software fault	High	1.15
Database size	20,000 bytes	Low	0.94
Product complexity	Communications processing	Very high	1.30
Execution time constraint	Will use 70% of available time	High	1.11
Main storage constraint	45K of 64K store (70 %)	High	1.06
Virtual machine volatility	Based on commercial microprocessor hardware	Nominal	1.00
Computer turnaround time	Two hour average turnaround time	Nominal	1.00
Analyst capabilities	Good senior analysts	High	0.86
Applications experience	Three years	Nominal	1.00
Programmer capability	Good senior programmers	High	0.86
Virtual machine experience	Six months	Low	1.10
Programming language experience	Twelve months	Nominal	1.00
Use of modern programming practices	Most techniques in use over one year	High	0.91
Use of software tools	At basic minicomputer tool level	Low	1.10
Required development schedule	Nine months	Nominal	1.00

Figure 8.6 Intermediate COCOMO effort multiplier ratings for microprocessor communications software [Boehm, 1984b]. (©1984 IEEE)

8.2.4 COCOMO II

COCOMO was put forward in 1981. At that time, the only life-cycle model in use was the waterfall model. Most software was run on mainframes. Technologies such as client-server and object-orientation were essentially unknown. Accordingly, COCOMO did not incorporate any of these factors. However, as newer technologies began to become accepted software engineering practice, COCOMO started to become less accurate.

COCOMO II [Boehm et al., 1995] is a major revision of 1981 COCOMO. COCOMO II can handle a wide variety of modern software engineering techniques, including object-orientation; the various life-cycle models described in Chapter 3; rapid prototyping (Section 9.2); fourth-generation languages (Section 13.2); reuse (Section 7.1); and COTS software (Section 2.6.1). COCOMO II is both flexible and sophisticated. Unfortunately, in order to achieve its goal, COCOMO II is also considerably more complex that the original COCOMO. Accordingly, the reader who wishes to utilize COCOMO II should study [Boehm et al., 1995] in detail; only an overview of the major differences between COCOMO II and Intermediate COCOMO is given here.

First, Intermediate COCOMO consists of one overall model based on lines of code (KDSI). On the other hand, COCOMO II consists of three different models. The *application composition model*, based on object points (similar to function points), is applied at the earliest phases when minimal knowledge is available regarding the product to be built. Then, as more knowledge becomes available, the *early design model* is used; this model is based on function points. Finally, when the developers have maximal information, the *post-architecture model* is used. This model uses function points or lines of code (KDSI). The output from Intermediate COCOMO is a cost and size estimate; the output from each of the three models of COCOMO II is a range of cost and size estimates. Thus, if the most likely estimate of the effort is E, then the application composition model returns the range ($0.50E$, $2.0E$), and the post-architecture model returns the range ($0.80E$, $1.25E$). This reflects the increasing accuracy of the progression of models of COCOMO II.

A second difference lies in the effort model underlying COCOMO, namely

$$\text{effort} = a(\text{size})^b \tag{8.8}$$

where a and b are constants. In the case of Intermediate COCOMO there are three different values of the exponent b, depending on whether the mode of the product to be built is organic ($b = 1.05$), semi-detached ($b = 1.12$), or embedded ($b = 1.20$). In COCOMO II, the value of b varies between 1.01 and 1.26, depending on a variety of parameters of the model. These include familiarity with products of that type, process maturity level (Section 2.11), extent of risk resolution (Section 3.6), and degree of team cooperation (Section 4.1).

A third difference is the assumption regarding reuse. In Intermediate COCOMO, it was assumed that the savings due to reuse are directly proportional to the amount of reuse. COCOMO II takes into account that small changes to reused software incur disproportionately large costs (because the code has to be understood in detail even for a small change and because the cost of testing a modified module is relatively large).

Fourth, there are now 17 multiplicative cost drivers, instead of 15 in Intermediate COCOMO. Seven of the cost drivers are new, such as required reusability in future products, annual personnel turnover, and whether the product is being developed at multiple sites.

COCOMO II has been calibrated using 83 projects from a variety of different domains. The model is still too new for there to be many results regarding its accuracy and, in particular, the extent to which it is an improvement over its predecessor, the original (1981) COCOMO.

8.2.5 TRACKING DURATION AND COST ESTIMATES

While the product is being developed, actual development effort must be constantly compared against predictions. For example, suppose that the estimation metric used by the software developers predicted that the specification phase would last 3 months and require 7 person-months of effort. However, 4 months have gone by and 10 person-months of effort have been expended, but the specification document is by no means complete. Deviations of this kind can serve as an early warning that something has gone wrong and that corrective action must be taken. The problem could be that the size of the product was seriously underestimated or that the development team is not as competent as it was thought to be. Whatever the reason, there are going to be serious duration and cost overruns, and management must take appropriate action to minimize the effects.

Careful tracking of predictions must be done throughout the development process, irrespective of the techniques by which the predictions were made. Deviations could be due to metrics that are poor predictors, inefficient software development, a combination of both, or some other reason. The important thing is to detect deviations early and to take immediate corrective action.

Now that metrics for estimating duration and cost have been discussed, the components of the software project management plan are described.

8.3 COMPONENTS OF A SOFTWARE PROJECT MANAGEMENT PLAN

A software project management plan has three main components: the work to be done, the resources with which to do it, and the money to pay for it all. In this section these three ingredients of the plan are discussed. The terminology is taken from [IEEE 1058.1, 1987], which is discussed in greater detail in Section 8.4.

Software development requires *resources.* The major resources required are the people who will develop the software, the hardware on which the software will be run, and the support software such as operating systems, text editors, and version control software (Section 4.12).

Use of resources such as personnel varies with time. Norden has shown [Norden, 1958] that for large projects, the Rayleigh distribution is a good approximation of the way that resource consumption R_c varies with time t, that is

$$R_c = \frac{t}{k^2} e^{-t^2/2k^2} \qquad 0 \le t < \infty \tag{8.9}$$

Parameter k is a constant, the time at which consumption is at its peak, and e = 2.71828 . . . , the base of Naperian logarithms. A typical Rayleigh curve is shown in Figure 8.7. Resource consumption starts small, climbs rapidly to a peak, then decreases at a slower rate. Putnam investigated the applicability of Norden's results to software development and found that personnel and other resource consumption was modeled with some degree of accuracy by the Rayleigh distribution [Putnam, 1978].

It is therefore insufficient in a software plan merely to state that three senior programmers with at least 5 years of experience are required. What is needed is something like the following:

> Three senior programmers with at least 5 years of experience in real-time programming are needed, two to start 3 months after the project commences, the third to start 6 months after that. Two will be phased out when product testing commences, the third when maintenance begins.

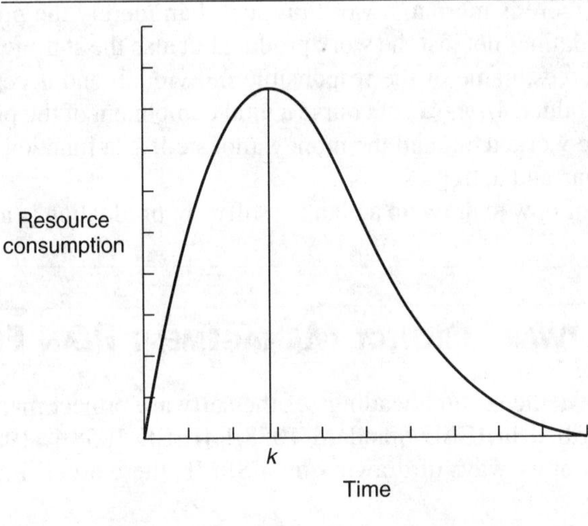

Figure 8.7 Rayleigh curve showing how resource consumption varies with time.

The fact that resource needs depend on time applies not only to personnel but also to computer time, support software, computer hardware, office facilities, and even travel. Thus the software project management plan will be a function of time.

The work to be done falls into two categories. First, there is work that continues throughout the project and does not relate to any specific phase of software development. Such work is termed a *project function.* Examples are project management and quality control. Second, there is work that relates to a specific phase in the development of the product; such work is termed an activity or a task. An *activity* is a major unit of work that has precise beginning and ending dates; consumes *resources,* such as computer time or person-days; and results in *work products* such as a budget, design documents, schedules, source code, or user's manual. An activity, in turn, comprises a set of *tasks,* a task being the smallest unit of work subject to management accountability. There are thus three kinds of work in a software project management plan: project functions that are carried on throughout the project, activities (major units of work), and tasks (minor units of work).

A critical aspect of the plan concerns completion of work products. The date on which a work product is deemed to be completed is termed a *milestone.* In order to determine whether a work product has indeed reached a milestone, it must first pass a series of *reviews* performed by fellow team members, management, and/or the client. A typical milestone is the date on which the design is completed and passes review. Once a work product has been reviewed and agreed upon, it becomes a *baseline* and can be changed only through formal procedures as described in Section 4.13.2.

In reality, there is more to a work product than merely the product itself. A *work package* defines not just the work product but also the staffing requirements, duration, resources, name of the responsible individual, and acceptance criteria for the work product. *Money* is of course a vital component of the plan. A detailed budget must be worked out and the money allocated, as a function of time, to the project functions and activities.

The issue of how to draw up a plan for software production is now addressed.

8.4 SOFTWARE PROJECT MANAGEMENT PLAN FRAMEWORK

Figure 8.8 shows the section headings of the software project management plan (SPMP) prescribed in IEEE Standard 1058.1 [IEEE 1058.1, 1987]. Although there are many other ways of drawing up a SPMP, there are distinct advantages

1. Introduction
   1.1 Project Overview
   1.2 Project Deliverables
   1.3 Evolution of the Software Project Management Plan
   1.4 Reference Materials
   1.5 Definitions and Acronyms
2. Project Organization
   2.1 Process Model
   2.2 Organizational Structure
   2.3 Organizational Boundaries and Interfaces
   2.4 Project Responsibilities
3. Managerial Process
   3.1 Management Objectives and Priorities
   3.2 Assumptions, Dependencies, and Constraints
   3.3 Risk Management
   3.4 Monitoring and Controlling Mechanisms
   3.5 Staffing Plan
4. Technical Process
   4.1 Methods, Tools, and Techniques
   4.2 Software Documentation
   4.3 Project Support Functions
5. Work Packages, Schedule, and Budget
   5.1 Work Packages
   5.2 Dependencies
   5.3 Resources Requirements
   5.4 Budget and Resource Allocation
   5.5 Schedule

Additional Components

Figure 8.8 Components of IEEE software project management plan [IEEE 1058.1, 1987]. (©1987 IEEE.)

to following the IEEE standard. First, it is a standard drawn up by representatives of many major organizations involved in software. There was input from both industry and universities, and the members of the working group and reviewing teams had many years of experience in drawing up project management plans. The standard incorporates this experience. A second advantage is that the IEEE SPMP is designed for use with all types of software products, irrespective of size. It does not impose a specific process model or prescribe specific techniques. The plan is essentially a framework, the contents of which will be tailored by each organization for a particular application area, development team, or technique. By adhering to this framework on an industry-wide basis, the advantages of standardization will accrue. Eventually, all software personnel will become familiar with the IEEE Software Project Management Plan format, and companies will be saved the expense of training new hires.

8.5 IEEE SOFTWARE PROJECT MANAGEMENT PLAN

The plan framework itself is now described in detail. The numbers and headings in the text correspond to the entries in Figure 8.8. The various terms used have been defined in Section 8.3.

1. Introduction. The five subsections of this section of the SPMP provide an overview of the project and of the product to be developed.

1.1. Project Overview. A brief description is given of the project objectives, the product to be delivered, the activities, and their resulting work products. In addition, the milestones are listed, as are the required resources, the master schedule, and master budget.

1.2. Project Deliverables. All the items to be delivered to the client are listed here, together with the delivery dates.

1.3. Evolution of the Software Project Management Plan. No plan can be cast in concrete. The SPMP, like any other plan, requires continual updating in the light of experience and of change within both the client organization and the software development organization. In this section the formal procedures and mechanisms for changing the plan are described.

1.4. Reference Materials. All documents referenced in the SPMP are listed here.

1.5. Definitions and Acronyms. This information ensures that the SPMP will be understood the same way by everyone.

2. Project Organization. The four subsections of the project organization section specify how the product is to be developed, both from the viewpoint of the software process and the organizational structure of the developers.

2.1. Process Model. The process model is specified in terms of the activities such as designing the product or performing product testing, and the project functions such as project management or configuration management. Key aspects here include specification of milestones, baselines, reviews, work products, and deliverables.

2.2. Organizational Structure. The management structure of the development organization is described. It is important to demarcate the lines of authority and responsibility within the organization.

2.3. Organizational Boundaries and Interfaces. No project is constructed in a vacuum. The project members have to interact with the client organization and with other members of their own organization. In addition, subcontractors may be involved in a large project. Administrative and managerial boundaries between the project itself and these other entities must be laid down. In addition, many software development organizations are divided into two types of groups, namely, development groups who work on a single project and support groups who provide support functions, such as configuration management and SQA, on an organizational-wide basis. Administrative and managerial boundaries between the project group and the support groups must also be clearly defined.

2.4. Project Responsibilities. For each project function, such as SQA, and for each activity, such as product testing, the responsible individual must be identified.

3. Managerial Process. The five subsections of this section describe how the project is to be managed.

3.1. Management Objectives and Priorities. The philosophy, goals, and priorities for management are described. The types of items that appear in this subsection of the plan may include frequency and mechanism of reporting; the relative priorities among requirements; schedule and budget for the project; and risk management procedures.

3.2. Assumptions, Dependencies, and Constraints. Any assumptions and constraints in the specification document appear here.

3.3. Risk Management. The various risk factors associated with the project are listed in this subsection, as well as the mechanisms used for tracking these risk factors.

3.4. Monitoring and Controlling Mechanisms. Reporting mechanisms for the project are described in detail, including review and audit mechanisms.

3.5. Staffing Plan. The personnel who will be staffing the project constitute an important resource. The numbers and types of personnel required are listed, together with the durations for which they will be needed.

4. Technical Process. Technical aspects of the project are specified in the three subsections of this section.

4.1. Methods, Tools, and Techniques. Technical aspects of hardware and software are described in detail in this subsection. Items that should be covered include the computing systems (hardware, operating systems, and software) to be used for developing the product, as well as the target systems on which the product will be run. Other necessary aspects include development techniques, testing techniques, team structure, programming language(s), and CASE tools to be employed. In addition, technical standards such as documentation standards and coding standards are included, perhaps by reference to other documents, as well as procedures for developing and modifying work products.

4.2. Software Documentation. This subsection contains the documentation requirements, namely, the milestones, baselines, and reviews for software documentation.

4.3. Project Support Functions. This subsection details plans for the supporting functions such as configuration management and quality assurance, including test plans.

5. Work Packages, Schedule, and Budget. The five subsections of this section emphasize the work packages, their interdependencies, resource requirements, and associated budgeting allocations.

5.1. Work Packages. In this subsection the work packages are specified, with their associated work products broken down into activities and tasks.

5.2. Dependencies. Module coding follows design and precedes integration testing. In general, there will be interdependencies among the work packages and dependencies on external events. In this subsection these dependencies are specified.

5.3. Resource Requirements. To complete the project, a wide variety of resources will be required. Total resources are presented as a function of time.

5.4. Budget and Resource Allocation. The various resources previously listed cost money. Just as the resource needs vary with time, so does the allocation of the budget to the various component resources. The allocation of resources and budget to the various project functions, activities, and tasks is presented.

5.5. Schedule. A detailed schedule is given for each component of the project. This master plan will then be followed; it is hoped that the project will be completed on time and within budget.

Additional Components. For certain projects, additional components may need to appear in the plan. In terms of the IEEE framework, they appear at the end of the plan. Additional components may include subcontractor management plans, security plans, test plans, training plans, hardware procurement plans, installation plans, and the product maintenance plan.

8.6 PLANNING OF TESTING

One component of the SPMP that frequently is overlooked is test planning. Like every other activity of software development, testing must be planned. The SPMP must include resources for testing, and the detailed schedule must explicitly indicate the testing that is to be done during each phase.

Without a test plan, a project can go awry in a number of ways. For example, during product testing (Section 2.6.1), the SQA group must check that every aspect of the specification document, as signed off by the client, has been implemented in the completed product. A good way of assisting the SQA group in this task is to require that the development be traceable. That is, it must be possible to connect each statement in the specification document to a part of the design, and each part of the design must be explicitly reflected in the code. One technique of achieving this is to number each statement in the specification document and ensure that these numbers are reflected in both the design and the resulting code. However, if the test plan does not specify that this is to be done, it is highly unlikely that the design and the code will be labeled appropriately. Consequently, when the product testing is finally performed, it will be extremely difficult for the SQA team to determine that the product is a complete implementation of the specifications. In fact, traceability should start with the requirements phase; each statement in the requirements document (or each portion of the rapid prototype) much be connected to part of the specification document.

One powerful aspect of inspections is the detailed list of faults detected during an inspection. Suppose that a team is inspecting the specifications of a product. As explained in Section 5.2.3, the list of faults is used in two ways. First, the fault statistics from this inspection must be compared with the accumulated averages of fault statistics from previous specification inspections. Deviations from previous norms indicate that there are problems within the project. Second, the fault statistics from the current specification inspection must be carried forward to the design and code inspections of the product. After all, if there are a large number of faults of a particular type, it is possible that not all of them were detected during the inspection of the specifications, and the design and code inspections provide an additional opportunity for locating any remaining faults of this type. However, unless the test plan states that details of all faults have to be carefully recorded, it is unlikely that this task will be done.

One important way of testing code modules is so-called black-box testing (Section 13.7) in which the code is executed with test cases based on the specifications. Members of the SQA team read through the specifications and draw up test cases to check whether the code obeys the specification document. The best time to draw up black-box test cases is at the end of the specification phase, when the details of the specification document are still fresh in the minds of the members of the SQA team that inspected them. However, unless the test plan explicitly states that the black-box test cases are to be selected at this time, in all probability what will happen is that a few black-box test cases will hurriedly be thrown together later. That is, a limited number of test cases will be rapidly assembled only when the pressure starts mounting from the programming team for the SQA group to approve their modules so that they can be integrated into the product as a whole. As a result, the quality of the product as a whole will suffer.

Thus, every test plan must specify what testing is to be performed, when it is to be performed, and how it is to be performed. Such a test plan is an essential part of Section 4.3 of the SPMP. Without it, the quality of the overall product will undoubtedly suffer.

8.7 Planning of Object-Oriented Projects

Suppose the structured paradigm is used. From a conceptual viewpoint the resulting product is generally one large unit, even though it is composed of separate modules. In contrast, use of the object-oriented paradigm results in a product consisting of a number of relatively independent smaller components, namely, the classes at the analysis and architectural design levels of abstraction or the objects at the detailed design and implementation levels. This makes planning considerably easier, in that cost and duration estimates can be computed more easily and more accurately in smaller units. Of course, the estimates must take into account that a product is more than just the sum of its parts. The separate components are not totally independent; they can invoke one another, and these effects must not be overlooked.

Are the techniques for estimating cost and duration described in this chapter applicable to the object-oriented paradigm? COCOMO II (Section 8.2.4) was designed to handle modern software technology, including object orientation, but what about earlier metrics such as function points (Section 8.2.1) and Intermediate

COCOMO (Section 8.2.3)? In the case of Intermediate COCOMO, minor changes to some of the cost multipliers are required [Pittman, 1993]. Other than that, the estimation tools of the structured paradigm appear to work reasonably well on object-oriented projects—provided that there is no reuse. Reuse enters the object-oriented paradigm in two ways: reuse of existing components during development and the deliberate production (during the current project) of components to be reused in future products. Both these forms of reuse affect the estimating process. Reuse during development clearly reduces the cost and duration. Formulas have been published showing the savings as a function of this reuse [Schach, 1994], but these results relate to the structured paradigm. At present, no information is available as to how the cost and duration change when reuse is utilized in the development of an object-oriented product.

We turn now to the goal of reusing parts of the current project. It can take about three times as long to design, implement, test, and document a reusable component compared to a similar nonreusable component [Pittman, 1993]. Cost and duration estimates must be modified to incorporate this additional labor, and the SPMP as a whole must be adjusted to incorporate the effect of the reuse endeavor. Thus, the two reuse activities work in opposite directions. Reuse of existing components reduces the overall effort in developing an object-oriented product, whereas designing components for reuse in future products increases the effort. It is anticipated that, in the long term, the savings due to reuse of classes will outweigh the costs, and there is already some evidence to support this [Lim, 1994].

8.8 TRAINING REQUIREMENTS

When the subject of training is raised in discussions with the client, a common response is "We don't need to worry about training until the product is finished, and then we can train the users." This is a somewhat unfortunate remark, implying as it does that only users require training. In fact, training may also be needed by members of the development team, starting with training in software planning and estimating. When new software development techniques, such as new design techniques or testing procedures, are used training must be provided to every member of the team involved in using the new technique.

Introduction of the object-oriented paradigm has major training consequences. The introduction of hardware or software tools such as workstations or an integrated environment (see Section 14.8) also requires training. Programmers may need training in the operating system of the machine to be used for product development, as well as in the implementation language. Documentation preparation training is frequently overlooked, as evidenced by the poor quality of so much documentation. Computer operators will certainly require some sort of training in order to be able to run the new product; they may also require additional training if new hardware is utilized.

The required training can be obtained in a number of ways. The easiest and least disruptive is in-house training, either by fellow employees or by consultants. Many companies offer a variety of training courses, and colleges often offer training courses in the evenings. Videotape-based courses for self-instruction are another alternative.

Once the training needs have been determined and the training plan drawn up, the plan must be incorporated into the SPMP.

8.9 DOCUMENTATION STANDARDS

The development of a software product is accompanied by a wide variety of documentation. Jones has found that 28 pages of documentation were generated per 1000 instructions (KDSI) for an IBM internal commercial product around 50 KDSI in size, and about 66 pages per KDSI for a commercial software product of the same size. Operating system IMS/360 Version 2.3 was about 166 KDSI in size, and 157 pages of documentation per KDSI were produced. The documentation was of various types, including planning, control, financial, and technical [Jones, 1986a]. In addition to these types of documentation, the source code itself is a form of documentation; comments within the code constitute further documentation.

A considerable portion of the software development effort is absorbed by documentation. A survey of 63 development projects and 25 maintenance projects showed that for every 100 hours spent on activities related to code, 150 hours were spent on activities related to documentation [Boehm, 1981]. For large TRW products, the proportion of time that was devoted to documentation-related activities rose to 200 hours per 100 code-related hours [Boehm et al., 1984].

Standards are needed for every type of documentation. For instance, uniformity in design documentation reduces misunderstandings between team members and aids the SQA group. Although new employees have to be trained in the documentation standards, no further training will be needed when existing employees move from project to project within the organization. From the viewpoint of product maintenance, uniform coding standards assist maintenance programmers in understanding source code. Standardization is even more important for user manuals, because these have to be read by a wide of variety of users, few of whom are computer experts. The IEEE has developed a standard for user manuals (IEEE Standard 1063 for Software User Documentation).

As part of the planning process, standards must be established for all documentation to be produced during software production. These standards are incorporated in the SPMP. Where an existing standard is to be used, such as the IEEE Standard for Software Test Documentation [ANSI/IEEE 829, 1983], the standard is listed in Section 1.4 of the SPMP (Reference Materials). If a standard is specially written for the development effort, then it appears in Section 4.1 (Methods, Tools, and Techniques).

Documentation is an essential aspect of the software production effort. In a very real sense the product *is* the documentation, because without documentation the product cannot be maintained. Planning the documentation effort in every detail, and then ensuring that the plan is adhered to, is a critical component of successful software production.

8.10 CASE Tools for Planning and Estimating

A number of tools are available that automate Intermediate COCOMO and COCOMO II. For speed of computation when the value of a parameter is modified, several implementations of Intermediate COCOMO have been written in spreadsheet languages such as Lotus 1-2-3 or Excel. For developing and updating the plan itself, a word processor is essential.

Management information tools are also useful for planning. For example, suppose that a large software organization has 150 programmers. A scheduling tool can help planners keep track of programmers who have already been assigned to specific tasks and of who is available for the current project.

More general types of management information are also needed. An example of this is critical path management (CPM), otherwise known as program evaluation review techniques (PERT) [Moder, Phillips, and Davis, 1983]. (For background information on PERT, see the Just in Case You Wanted to Know box below).

Just in Case You Wanted to Know

PERT was developed in 1957 by the U.S. Navy to plan and schedule the development of the Polaris missiles. When applied to the missile program, the technique was found to yield overly optimistic results, and the missiles were delivered late. Afterwards it was discovered that the PERT network had many paths that were almost critical. That is, if those estimated durations had been slightly longer, the corresponding activities would have been critical.

When some of the activities on the almost-critical paths had actual durations that were longer than predicted, those paths then became critical. The project managers had concentrated their efforts on ensuring that the original critical activities would be completed on time. The project as a whole was then slowed by the newly critical activities that had not received the same managerial monitoring as the original critical activities.

The solution to this problem is to replace the single value for a predicted duration by an appropriate statistical distribution. Then the PERT network is simulated. For each simulation run, the value of the duration will be a random value selected from the distribution, rather than a fixed value as before. The critical activities flagged in each simulation run are recorded. Any activity that is flagged as critical in a large percentage of the runs is then closely monitored by management; such an activity has a high probability of turning out to be critical in the actual project. This statistical technique yields more accurate predictions than deciding which activities are critical on the basis of a single estimated duration [Deo, 1983].

Many hundreds of activities have to be performed in the course of building a product, such as projecting cash flow or checking that the database manual is an accurate reflection of the structure of the database. Some activities have to precede others; for instance, a module cannot be coded until it has been designed. Other activities can be carried on in parallel. For example, implementation of the various modules can be assigned to different members of the programming team.

Suppose that two activities are started at the same time and can be performed in parallel, but that both have to be completed before proceeding with the project as a whole. If the first takes 12 days, whereas the second needs only 3 days, then the first activity is *critical.* Any delay in the first activity will cause the project as a whole to be delayed. However, the second activity can be delayed up to 9 days without adversely impacting the project; there is a *slack* of 9 days associated with the second activity. When using PERT/CPM, the manager inputs the activities, their estimated durations, and any precedence relations, that is, the activities that have to be completed before a specific activity can be started. The PERT/CPM package will then determine which of the hundreds of activities are critical, and it will also compute the slack for each of the noncritical activities. Most packages also print out a PERT chart showing the precedence relationships between the activities and highlighting the *critical path,* the path through the chart that consists of critical activities only. If any activity on the critical path is delayed, then so is the project as a whole.

A simple PERT chart is shown in Figure 8.9. There are 12 activities and 9 milestones. Starting with milestone A, activities AB, AC, and AD can be started in parallel. Activity FJ cannot be started until both BF and CF are finished. The project as a whole is complete when activities HJ, FJ, and GJ are all

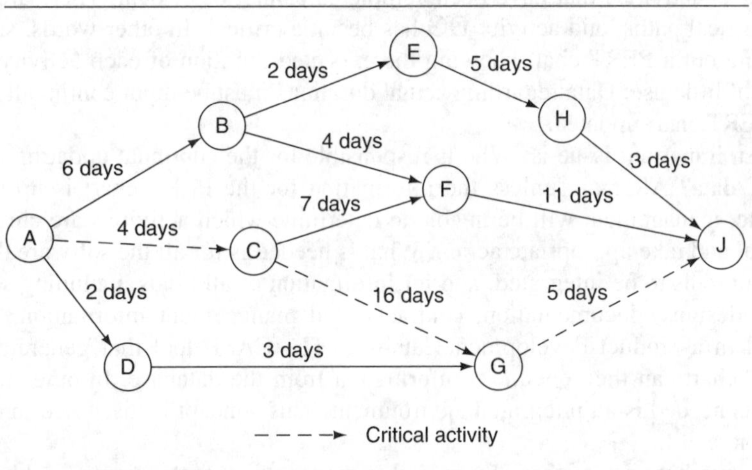

Figure 8.9 PERT chart showing estimated durations of activities and the critical path.

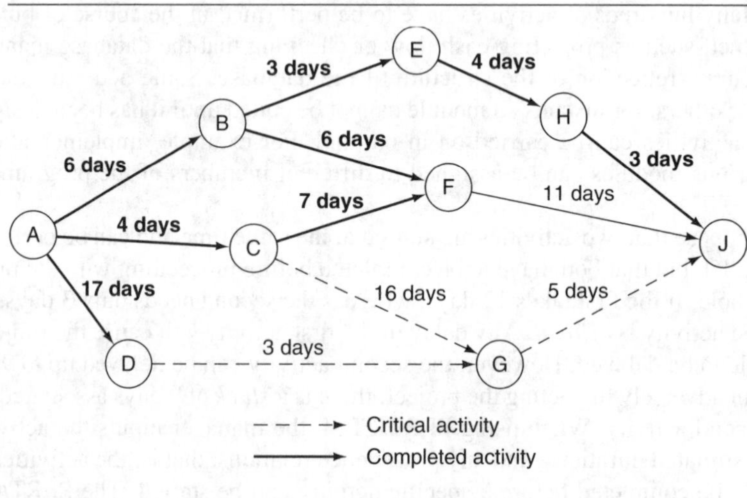

Figure 8.10 Updated PERT chart at day 17. Actual durations of completed activities are in boldface.

complete. Completing the whole project will take at least 25 days. The critical path is ACGJ; if any one of the critical activities, namely, AC, CG, or GJ, is delayed in any way, the project as a whole will be delayed. On the other hand, if activity AD is delayed by up to 15 days, the project as a whole will not be delayed, because there is a slack of 15 days associated with activity AD.

Now suppose that activity AD is in fact delayed by 15 days. The situation at day 17 is shown in Figure 8.10. Actual durations of completed activities are in boldface; activities that have been completed cannot be critical. There are now two critical paths, and activity DG has become critical. In other words, simply printing out a PERT chart showing the expected duration of each activity is in itself of little use. Data regarding actual durations must be input continually, and the PERT chart updated.

An important issue is: Who is responsible for the continual updating of the PERT data? After all, unless the information for the PERT chart is up to the minute, management will be unable to determine which activities are currently critical and take appropriate action. What is needed is for all the software development tools to be integrated, and for information of all kinds, including source code, designs, documentation, contracts, and management information, to be stored in a product development database. The CASE tool that generates the PERT chart can then obtain its information from the database. In other words, what is needed is an integrated environment. This concept is discussed in detail in Chapter 14.

A number of commercially available management tools can be used both to assist with the planning and estimating process and to monitor the development process as a whole. These include MacProject and Microsoft Project.

8.11 TESTING THE SOFTWARE PROJECT MANAGEMENT PLAN

As pointed out at the beginning of this chapter, a fault in the software project management plan can have serious financial implications for the developers. It is critical that the development organization neither overestimate nor underestimate the cost of the project or its duration. For this reason, the entire SPMP must be checked by the SQA group before estimates are given to the client. The best way to test the plan is by means of a plan inspection, similar to the specification inspection described in Section 10.11.

The plan inspection team must review the SPMP in detail, paying particular attention to the cost and duration estimates. To reduce risks even further, irrespective of the metrics used, the duration and cost estimates should be independently computed by a member of the SQA group as soon as the members of the planning team have determined their estimates.

CHAPTER REVIEW

The main theme of this chapter is the importance of planning in the software process (Section 8.1). A vital component of any software project management plan is estimating the duration and the cost (Section 8.2). Several metrics are put forward for estimating the size of a product, including function points (Section 8.2.1). Various metrics for cost estimation are then described, especially Intermediate COCOMO (Section 8.2.3) and COCOMO II (Section 8.2.4). The three major components of a software project management plan, namely, the work to be done, the resources with which to do it, and the money to pay for it, are explained in Section 8.3. One particular SPMP, namely, the IEEE standard, is outlined in Section 8.4 and described in detail in Section 8.5. Next follow sections on planning of testing (Section 8.6); planning of object-oriented projects (Section 8.7); and training requirements and documentation standards, and their implications for the planning process (Sections 8.8 and 8.9). CASE tools for planning and estimating are described in Section 8.10. The chapter concludes with material on testing the software project management plan (Section 8.11).

FOR FURTHER READING

An introduction to software management can be found in [DeMarco, 1986]. A somewhat more advanced text is [Jones, 1986a]. Weinberg's four-volume work [Weinberg, 1992, 1993, 1994, 1997] provides detailed information on many aspects of software management, as does [Whitten, 1995]. Two IEEE Computer Society tutorials, namely, [Reifer, 1986] and [Thayer, 1988], consist of papers that are good sources for more information on software management in general as well as planning in particular. Metrics for managing software projects are discussed in [Weller, 1994].

For management of the object-oriented paradigm, [Pittman, 1993] should be consulted. The effect of object-oriented frameworks (Section 7.5.2) on developer productivity is discussed in [Moser and Nierstrasz, 1996]. The July 1996 issue of *IEEE Software* contains a number of articles on the management of large-scale projects; these include [Charette, 1996], which discusses the risks involved in managing large-scale projects. Another article on risk management is [Gemmer, 1997]. The September 1996 issue of *IEEE Computer* contains articles on management of object-oriented projects. Of particular interest are [Sparks, Benner, and Faris, 1996] and [Williams, 1996].

For further information on IEEE Standard 1058.1 for Software Project Management Plans, the standard itself should be carefully read [IEEE 1058.1, 1987].

Sackman's work is described in [Sackman, Erikson, and Grant, 1968]. A more detailed source is [Sackman, 1970].

Many critical reviews of software science have been published, including [Hamer and Frewin, 1982], [Coulter, 1983], and [Shen, Conte, and Dunsmore, 1983]. A further source of information on software science is [Conte, Dunsmore, and Shen, 1986]; the book also contains analyses of many other metrics, including lines of code, Putnam's SLIM model, Intermediate COCOMO, and function points. Information on function points can also be found in [Albrecht and Gaffney, 1983], [Jones, 1987], and [Low and Jeffrey, 1990]. A careful analysis of function points, as well as suggested improvements, appears in [Symons, 1991]. Other analyses are given in [Jeffrey, Low, and Barnes, 1993] and [Kitchenham and Känsälä, 1993]. [Dreger, 1989] is a detailed description of the use of function points. Suggestions for improving the cost estimation process are found in [Lederer and Prasad, 1992]. The reliability of function points is discussed in [Kemerer and Porter, 1992] and [Kemerer, 1993]. Strengths and weaknesses of function points are presented in [Furey and Kitchenham, 1997]. A comprehensive source of information on all aspects of function points is [Boehm, 1997].

The theoretical justification for Intermediate COCOMO, together with full details for implementing it, appears in [Boehm, 1981]; a shorter version is found in [Boehm, 1984b]. Extensions of Intermediate COCOMO that incorporate reuse (Chapter 7) and rapid prototyping (Section 3.3) appear in [Balda and Gustafson, 1990]. REVIC (Revised Intermediate COCOMO) is intended for use in Department of Defense projects. For example, it estimates the size of the documentation required by a project that conforms to MIL-STD-2167A, the standard for military software development. COCOMO II is described in [Boehm et al., 1995].

Data on the validity of certain metrics, including function points, can be found in [Kemerer, 1987]. [Myers, 1989] provides information on metrics for estimating development time for very large software projects. Approaches to introducing metrics programs within organizations can be found in [Hall and Fenton, 1997].

The status of metrics research and practice is presented in [Pfleeger, Jeffery, Curtis, and Kitchenham, 1997].

An introduction to PERT/CPM can be found in [Wiest and Levy, 1977] and [Moder, Phillips, and Davis, 1983]. Formulae for estimating the numbers of pages of documentation for a given product are given in [Jones, 1994b].

Standards of various types are described in [Branstad and Powell, 1984]. A complete listing of IEEE standards can be obtained from IEEE, 345 East 47th Street, New York, NY 10017.

PROBLEMS

8.1 Why do you think that some cynical software organizations refer to *milestones* as *millstones*? (Hint: Look up the figurative meaning of "millstone" in a dictionary.)

8.2 You are a software engineer at KWV Software Developers. A year ago your manager announced that your next product would comprise 18 files, 59 flows, and 93 processes.

(i) Using the FFP metric, determine its size.

(ii) For KWV Software Developers, the constant d in equation (8.2) has been determined to be $812. What cost estimate did the FFP metric predict?

(iii) The product was recently completed at a cost of $124,000. What does this tell you about the productivity of your development team?

8.3 A target product has 7 simple inputs, 8 average inputs, and 11 complex inputs. There are 5 average outputs, 40 simple inquiries, 12 average master files, and 18 complex interfaces. Determine the unadjusted function points (*UFP*).

8.4 If the total degree of influence for the product of Problem 8.3 is 52, determine the number of function points.

8.5 Why do you think that, despite its drawbacks, lines of code (LOC or KDSI) is so widely used as a metric of product size?

8.6 You are in charge of developing an 83-KDSI embedded product that is nominal except that the database size is rated very high and the use of software tools is low. Using Intermediate COCOMO, what is the estimated effort in person-months?

8.7 You are in charge of developing two 38-KDSI organic-mode products. Both are nominal in every respect except that product P_1 has extra-high complexity and product P_2 has extra-low complexity. To develop the product, you have two teams at your disposal. Team A has very high analyst capability, applications experience, and programmer capability. Team A also has high virtual machine experience and programming language experience. Team B is rated very low on all five attributes.

(i) What is the total effort (in person-months) if team A develops product P_1 and team B develops product P_2?

(ii) What is the total effort (in person-months) if team B develops product P_1 and team A develops product P_2?

(iii) Which of the two preceding staffing assignments makes more sense? Is your intuition backed by the predictions of Intermediate COCOMO?

8.8 You are in charge of developing a 45-KDSI organic-mode product that is nominal in every respect.

(i) Assuming a cost of $8400 per person-month, how much is the project estimated to cost?

(ii) Your entire development team resigns at the start of the project. You are fortunate enough to be able to replace the nominal team with a very highly experienced and capable team, but the cost per person-month will rise to $11,200. How much money do you expect to gain (or lose) as a result of the personnel change?

8.9 You are in charge of developing the software for a product that uses a set of newly developed algorithms to compute the most cost-effective routes for a large trucking company. Using Intermediate COCOMO, you determine that the cost of the product will be $430,000. However, as a check, you ask a member of your team to estimate the effort using function points. She reports that the function point metric predicts a cost of $890,000, more than twice as large as your COCOMO prediction. What do you do now?

8.10 Show that the Rayleigh distribution (equation 8.9) attains its maximum value when $t = k$. Find the corresponding resource consumption.

8.11 A product maintenance plan is considered an "additional component" of an IEEE SPMP. Bearing in mind that every nontrivial product is maintained and that the cost of maintenance is, on average, about twice the cost of developing the product, how can this be justified?

8.12 (Term project) Consider the Air Gourmet project described in Appendix A. Why is not possible to estimate the cost and duration purely on the basis of the information in Appendix A?

8.13 (Readings in Software Engineering) Your instructor will distribute copies of [Boehm et al., 1995]. Are you confident that COCOMO II will adequately estimate the cost and effort of software built using the object-oriented paradigm?

REFERENCES

[Albrecht, 1979] A. J. ALBRECHT, "Measuring Application Development Productivity," *Proceedings of the IBM SHARE/GUIDE Applications Development Symposium*, Monterey, CA, October 1979, pp. 83–92.

[Albrecht and Gaffney, 1983] A. J. ALBRECHT AND J. E. GAFFNEY, JR., "Software Function, Source Lines of Code, and Development Effort Prediction: A Software Science Validation," *IEEE Transactions on Software Engineering* **SE-9** (November 1983), pp. 639–48.

[ANSI/IEEE 829, 1983] "Software Test Documentation," ANSI/IEEE 829-1983, American National Standards Institute, Inc., Institute of Electrical and Electronic Engineers, Inc., 1983.

[Balda and Gustafson, 1990] D. M. BALDA AND D. A. GUSTAFSON, "Cost Estimation Models for the Reuse and Prototype Software Development Life Cycles," *ACM SIGSOFT Software Engineering Notes* **15** (July 1990), pp. 42–50.

[Behrens, 1983] C. A. BEHRENS, "Measuring the Productivity of Computer Systems Development Activities with Function Points," *IEEE Transactions on Software Engineering* **SE-9** (November 1983), pp. 648–52.

[Boehm, 1981] B. W. BOEHM, *Software Engineering Economics,* Prentice Hall, Englewood Cliffs, NJ, 1981.

[Boehm, 1984b] B. W. BOEHM, "Software Engineering Economics," *IEEE Transactions on Software Engineering* **SE-10** (January 1984), pp. 4–21.

[Boehm, 1997] R. BOEHM (Editor), "Function Point FAQ," ourworld.compuserve.com/homepages/softcomp/fpfaq.htm, June 25, 1997.

[Boehm et al., 1984] B. W. BOEHM, M. H. PENEDO, E. D. STUCKLE, R. D. WILLIAMS, AND A. B. PYSTER, "A Software Development Environment for Improving Productivity," *IEEE Computer* **17** (June 1984), pp. 30–44.

[Boehm et al., 1995] B. BOEHM, B. CLARK, E. HOROWITZ, C. WESTLAND, R. MADACHY, AND R. SELBY, "Cost Models for Future Life Cycle Processes," *Annals of Software Engineering,* **1** (1995), pp. 57–94.

[Branstad and Powell, 1984] M. BRANSTAD AND P. B. POWELL, "Software Engineering Project Standards," *IEEE Transactions on Software Engineering* **SE-10** (January 1984), pp. 73–78.

[Charette, 1996] R. N. CHARETTE, "Large-Scale Project Management *Is* Risk Management," *IEEE Software* **13** (July 1996), pp. 110–17.

[Conte, Dunsmore, and Shen, 1986] S. D. CONTE, H. E. DUNSMORE, AND V. Y. SHEN, *Software Engineering Metrics and Models,* Benjamin/Cummings, Menlo Park, CA, 1986.

[Coulter, 1983] N. S. COULTER, "Software Science and Cognitive Psychology," *IEEE Transactions on Software Engineering* **SE-9** (March 1983), pp. 166–71.

[DeMarco, 1986] T. DEMARCO, *Controlling Software Projects: Management, Measurement, and Estimation,* Second Edition, Yourdon Press, Englewood Cliffs, NJ, 1986.

[Deo, 1983] N. DEO, *System Simulation with Digital Computer,* Prentice Hall, Englewood Cliffs, NJ, 1983.

[Devenny, 1976] T. DEVENNY, "An Exploratory Study of Software Cost Estimating at the Electronic Systems Division," Thesis No. GSM/SM/765–4, Air Force Institute of Technology, Dayton, OH, 1976.

[Dreger, 1989] J. B. DREGER, *Function Point Analysis,* Prentice Hall, Englewood Cliffs, NJ, 1989.

[Freiman and Park, 1979] F. R. FREIMAN AND R. E. PARK, "PRICE Software Model—Version 3: An Overview," *Proceedings of the IEEE-PINY Workshop on Quantitative Software Models,* October 1979, pp. 32–41.

[Furey and Kitchenham, 1997] S. FUREY AND B. KITCHENHAM, "Function Points," *IEEE Software* **14** (March/April 1997), pp. 28–32.

[Gemmer, 1997] A. GEMMER, "Risk Management: Moving beyond Process," *IEEE Computer* **30** (May 1997), pp. 33–43.

[Halstead, 1977] M. H. HALSTEAD, *Elements of Software Science,* Elsevier North-Holland, New York, 1977.

[Hall and Fenton, 1997] T. HALL AND N. FENTON, "Implementing Effective Software Metrics Programs," *IEEE Software* **14** (March/April 1997), pp. 55–65.

[Hamer and Frewin, 1982] P. G. HAMER AND G. D. FREWIN, "M. H. Halstead's Software Science—A Critical Examination," *Proceedings of the Sixth International Conference on Software Engineering,* Tokyo, 1982, pp. 197–205.

[Helmer-Hirschberg, 1966] O. HELMER-HIRSCHBERG, *Social Technology,* Basic Books, New York, 1966.

[IEEE 1058.1, 1987] "Standard for Software Project Management Plans," IEEE 1058.1, Institute of Electrical and Electronic Engineers, Inc., 1987.

[Jeffrey, Low, and Barnes, 1993] D. R. JEFFREY, G. C. LOW, AND M. BARNES, "A Comparison of Function Point Counting Techniques," *IEEE Transactions on Software Engineering* **19** (May 1993), pp. 529–32.

[Jones, 1986a] C. JONES, *Programming Productivity,* McGraw-Hill, New York, 1986.

[Jones, 1987] C. JONES, Letter to the Editor, *IEEE Computer* **20** (December 1987), p. 4.

[Jones, 1991] C. JONES, *Applied Software Measurement,* McGraw-Hill, New York, 1991.

[Jones, 1994b] C. JONES, "Cutting the High Cost of Software 'Paperwork'," *IEEE Computer* **27** (October 1994), pp. 79–80.

[Jones, 1995] C. JONES, "What Are Function Points?" www.spr.com/library/funcmet.htm, 1995

[Kemerer, 1987] C. F. KEMERER, "An Empirical Validation of Software Cost Estimation Models," *Communications of the ACM* **30** (May 1987), pp. 416–429.

[Kemerer, 1993] C. F. KEMERER, "Reliability of Function Points Measurement: A Field Experiment," *Communications of the ACM* **36** (February 1993), pp. 85–97.

[Kemerer and Porter, 1992] C. F. KEMERER AND B. S. PORTER, "Improving the Reliability of Function Point Measurement: An Empirical Study," *IEEE Transactions on Software Engineering* **18** (November 1992), pp. 1011–24.

[Kitchenham and Känsälä, 1993] B. KITCHENHAM AND K. KÄNSÄLÄ, "Inter-Item Correlations among Function Points," *Proceedings of the IEEE Fifteenth International Conference on Software Engineering,* Baltimore, MD, May 1993, pp. 477–80.

[Lederer and Prasad, 1992] A. L. LEDERER AND J. PRASAD, "Nine Management Guidelines for Better Cost Estimating," *Communications of the ACM* **35** (February 1992), pp. 51–59.

[Lim, 1994] W. C. LIM, "Effects of Reuse on Quality, Productivity, and Economics," *IEEE Software* **11** (September 1994), pp. 23–30.

[Low and Jeffrey, 1990] G. C. LOW AND D. R. JEFFREY, "Function Points in the Estimation and Evaluation of the Software Process," *IEEE Transactions on Software Engineering* **16** (January 1990), pp. 64–71.

[Moder, Phillips, and Davis, 1983] J. J. MODER, C. R. PHILLIPS, AND E. W. DAVIS, *Project Management with CPM, PERT, and Precedence Diagramming,* Third Edition, Van Nostrand Reinhold, New York, 1983.

[Moser and Nierstrasz, 1996] S. MOSER AND O. NIERSTRASZ, "The Effect of Object-Oriented Frameworks on Developer Productivity," *IEEE Computer* **29** (September 1996), pp. 45–51.

[Myers, 1989] W. MYERS, "Allow Plenty of Time for Large-Scale Software," *IEEE Software* **6** (July 1989), pp. 92–99.

[Norden, 1958] P. V. NORDEN, "Curve Fitting for a Model of Applied Research and Development Scheduling," *IBM Journal of Research and Development* **2** (July 1958), pp. 232–248.

[Pfleeger, Jeffery, Curtis, and Kitchenham, 1997] S. L. PFLEEGER, R. JEFFERY, B. CURTIS, AND B. KITCHENHAM, "Status Report on Software Measurement," *IEEE Software* **14** (March/April 1997), pp. 33–43.

[Pittman, 1993] M. PITTMAN, "Lessons Learned in Managing Object-Oriented Development," *IEEE Software* **10** (January 1993), pp. 43–53.

[Putnam, 1978] L. H. PUTNAM, "A General Empirical Solution to the Macro Software Sizing and Estimating Problem," *IEEE Transactions on Software Engineering* **SE-4** (July 1978), pp. 345–61.

[Reifer, 1986] D. J. REIFER (Editor), *Tutorial: Software Management,* Third Edition, IEEE Computer Society Press, Washington, DC, 1986.

[Sackman, 1970] H. SACKMAN, *Man–Computer Problem Solving: Experimental Evaluation of Time-Sharing and Batch Processing,* Auerbach, Princeton, NJ, 1970.

[Sackman, Erikson, and Grant, 1968] H. SACKMAN, W. J. ERIKSON, AND E. E. GRANT, "Exploratory Experimental Studies Comparing Online and Offline Programming Performance," *Communications of the ACM* **11** (January 1968), pp. 3–11.

[Schach, 1994] S. R. SCHACH, "The Economic Impact of Software Reuse on Maintenance," *Journal of Software Maintenance: Research and Practice* **6** (July/August 1994), pp. 185–96.

[Shen, Conte, and Dunsmore, 1983] V. Y. SHEN, S. D. CONTE, AND H. E. DUNSMORE, "Software Science Revisited: A Critical Analysis of the Theory and Its Empirical Support," *IEEE Transactions on Software Engineering* **SE-9** (March 1983), pp. 155–65.

[Shepperd, 1988a] M. J. SHEPPERD, "An Evaluation of Software Product Metrics," *Information and Software Technology* **30** (No. 3, 1988), pp. 177–88.

[Shepperd and Ince, 1994] M. SHEPPERD AND D. C. INCE, "A Critique of Three Metrics," *Journal of Systems and Software* **26** (September 1994), pp. 197–210.

[Sparks, Benner, and Faris, 1996] S. SPARKS, K. BENNER, AND C. FARIS, "Managing Object-Oriented Framework Reuse," *IEEE Computer* **29** (September 1996), pp. 52–61.

[Symons, 1991] C. R. SYMONS, *Software Sizing and Estimating: Mk II FPA,* John Wiley and Sons, Chichester, UK, 1991.

[Thayer, 1988] R. H. THAYER (Editor), *Tutorial: Software Engineering Management,* IEEE Computer Society Press, Washington, DC, 1988.

[van der Poel and Schach, 1983] K. G. VAN DER POEL AND S. R. SCHACH, "A Software Metric for Cost Estimation and Efficiency Measurement in Data Processing System Development," *Journal of Systems and Software* **3** (September 1983), pp. 187–91.

[Weinberg, 1992] G. M. WEINBERG, *Quality Software Management: Systems Thinking,* Volume 1, Dorset House, New York, 1992.

[Weinberg, 1993] G. M. WEINBERG, *Quality Software Management: First-Order Measurement,* Volume 2, Dorset House, New York, 1993.

[Weinberg, 1994] G. M. WEINBERG, *Quality Software Management: Congruent Action,* Volume 3, Dorset House, New York, 1994

[Weinberg, 1997] G. M. WEINBERG, *Quality Software Management: Anticipating Change,* Volume 4, Dorset House, New York, 1997.

[Weller, 1994] E. F. WELLER, "Using Metrics to Manage Software Projects," *IEEE Computer* **27** (September 1994), pp. 27–34

[Weyuker, 1988b] E. WEYUKER, "Evaluating Software Complexity Measures," *IEEE Trans. on Software Engineering* **14** (September 1988), pp. 1357–65.

[Whitten, 1995] N. M. WHITTEN, *Managing Software Development Projects,* Second Edition, John Wiley and Sons, New York, 1995.

[Wiest and Levy, 1977] J. D. WIEST AND F. K. LEVY, *A Management Guide to PERT/CPM: With GERT/PDM/DCPM and Other Networks,* Second Edition, Prentice Hall, Englewood Cliffs, NJ, 1977.

[Williams, 1996] J. D. WILLIAMS, "Managing Iteration in OO Projects," *IEEE Computer* **29** (September 1996), pp. 39–43.

PART

2

THE PHASES OF THE SOFTWARE LIFE CYCLE

In Part 2 the phases of the software life cycle are described in depth. For each phase, the CASE tools, metrics, and testing techniques appropriate to that phase are also presented.

Chapter 9 is entitled Requirements Phase. The aim of this phase is to determine the client's real needs. One technique for achieving this is rapid prototyping. Various types of rapid prototyping and other requirements analysis techniques are examined.

Once the requirements have been determined, the next phase is to draw up the specifications. This is described in Chapter 10, Specification Phase. Three basic approaches to specifications are presented, namely informal, semiformal, and formal. Instances of each approach are described. Techniques that are described in depth and illustrated by case studies include structured systems analysis, finite state machines, Petri nets, and Z. The chapter concludes with a comparison of the various techniques.

All of the specification techniques in Chapter 10 are from the structured paradigm. Object-oriented specification is described in Chapter 11, Object-Oriented Analysis Phase. This object-oriented specification technique is presented as an alternative to the structured specification techniques of the previous chapter.

In Chapter 12, Design Phase, a variety of different design techniques are compared, including classical techniques like data flow analysis and transaction analysis, as well as object-oriented design. Particular attention is paid to object-oriented design, including case studies. Again, the emphasis is on comparison and contrast.

Implementation issues are discussed in Chapters 13 and 14. Chapter 13 is entitled Implementation Phase. Areas covered include the choice of programming language, fourth-generation languages, good programming practice, and programming standards. The chapter concludes with a detailed discussion of testing techniques and CASE tools for the implementation phase.

The implementation phase and integration phase should be performed in parallel. This is the subject of Chapter 14, Implementation and Integration Phase. There is a description of how this combined phase is carried out. Finally, there is a discussion of CASE environments that support the complete software process.

Part 2 concludes with Chapter 15, Maintenance Phase. Topics covered in this chapter include the importance of maintenance and the challenge of maintenance. The management of maintenance is considered in some detail.

By the end of Part 2, the reader should have a clear understanding of all the phases of the software process, the difficulties associated with each phase, and how to solve those difficulties.

A detailed case study is presented in Part 2. At the end of each chapter, the appropriate phase of the case study is presented. Thus, requirements are presented in Chapter 9, specifications in Chapters 10 and 11, and so on.

Exercises have been set on the case study. Some of those exercises require access to the source code. This can be obtained on the World Wide Web at www.mhhe.com/engcs/compsci/schach.

chapter

9

REQUIREMENTS PHASE

The chances of a product being developed on time and within budget are somewhat slim unless the members of the software development team agree on what the software product will do. The first step in achieving this unanimity is to analyze the client's current situation as precisely as possible. For example, it is inadequate to say: "They need a computer-aided design system because they claim their manual design system is lousy." Unless the development team knows exactly what is wrong with the current manual system, there is a high probability that aspects of the new computerized system will be equally "lousy." Similarly, if a personal computer manufacturer is contemplating development of a new operating system, the first step is to evaluate their current operating system and analyze carefully exactly why it is unsatisfactory. To take an extreme example, it is vital to know whether the problem exists only in the mind of the sales manager who is attempting to blame the operating system for poor sales or whether users of the operating system are thoroughly disenchanted with its functionality and reliability. Only after a clear picture of the present situation has been gained can the team attempt to answer the critical question: What must the new product be able to do? The process of answering this question is carried out during the requirements phase.

A commonly held misconception is that during the requirements phase the developers must determine what software the client *wants*. On the contrary, the real objective of the requirements phase is to determine what software the client *needs*. The problem is that many clients do not know what they need. Furthermore, even if the client has a good idea of what is needed, he or she may have difficulty in accurately conveying these ideas to the developers, because most clients are less computer-literate than the members of the development team.

In 1967, U. S. presidential candidate George Romney put his foot into his mouth one time too many. Calling a press conference, he proceeded to announce: "I know you believe you understood what you think I said, but I am not sure you realize that what you heard is not what I meant!" This excuse applies equally well to the issue of requirements analysis. The developers hear their client's requests, but what they hear is not what the client should be saying.

In Chapter 3 it was pointed out that this communication-based problem can be solved by building a rapid prototype. In this chapter the requirements phase is described in greater detail, and the strengths and weaknesses of various requirements analysis techniques are described.

9.1 REQUIREMENTS ANALYSIS TECHNIQUES

Requirements analysis begins with members of the requirements team meeting with members of the client organization to determine what is needed in the target product. The client usually sets up the initial interviews. Additional interviews may be scheduled during the interview process. Interviews continue until the requirements team is convinced that it has elicited all relevant information from the client and future users of the product.

There are two basic types of interview, namely, structured and unstructured. In a structured interview, specific preplanned close-ended questions are posed. For example, the client might be asked how many salespeople the company employs or how fast a response time is required. In an unstructured interview, open-ended questions are asked to encourage the person being interviewed to speak out. For instance, asking the client why the current product is unsatisfactory may explain many aspects of the client's approach to business. Some of these facts might not have come to light had the interview been more structured.

The interviewer prepares a written report outlining the results of the interview. It is a good idea to give a copy of the report to the people who were interviewed; they may want to clarify statements or add overlooked items.

Another way of eliciting needs is to send a questionnaire to the relevant members of the client organization. This technique is useful when the opinions of, say, hundreds of individuals need to be determined. Furthermore, a carefully thought-out written answer may be more accurate than an immediate verbal response to a question posed by an interviewer. However, an unstructured interview conducted by a methodical interviewer who listens carefully and poses questions that expand on initial responses will usually yield far better information than a thoughtfully worded questionnaire. Because questionnaires are preplanned, there is no way that a question can be posed in response to an answer.

A different way of obtaining information, particularly in a business environment, is to examine the various forms used by the client. For example, a form in a print shop might reflect press number, paper roll size, humidity, ink temperature, paper tension, and so on. The various fields in this form shed light on the flow of print jobs and the relative importance of various phases. Other documents, such as operating procedures and job descriptions, can also be powerful tools for finding out exactly what is done, and how. Comprehensive information regarding how the client currently does business can be extraordinarily helpful in determining the client's needs.

A newer way of obtaining such information is to set up video cameras within the workplace to record exactly what is being done. This technique has been known to backfire because employees may view the cameras as an unwarranted invasion of privacy. It is important that the requirements analysis team have the full cooperation of all employees; if people feel threatened or harassed, it can be extremely difficult to obtain necessary information. The possible risks should be carefully considered before introducing video cameras or, for that matter, taking any other action that has the potential to anger employees.

Scenarios are another technique for requirements analysis. A scenario is a possible way a user can utilize the target product to accomplish some objective. For example, suppose the target product is a weight-loss planner. One possible scenario describes what happens when the dietitian enters the age, gender, height, and other personal data of an obese patient. The product then prints out sample menus for that patient. When this scenario is shown to a future user of the target product, the dietitian quickly points out that the menus would be unsuitable for a patient with special food requirements, such as a diabetic, a vegetarian, or someone who is lactose intolerant. The developers modify the scenario so that the user is asked about special dietary needs before any menus are printed. The use of scenarios enables users to communicate their needs to the requirements analysts.

A scenario can be depicted in a number of ways. One technique is simply to list the actions comprising the scenario; this is done in Chapter 11. Another technique is to set up a storyboard, a series of diagrams depicting the sequence of events. A storyboard can be considered to be a paper prototype [Rettig, 1994], that is, a series of sheets of paper each depicting the relevant screens and the user's response.

Scenarios are useful in a number of different ways. First, they can demonstrate the behavior of the product in a way that is comprehensible to the user. This can result in additional requirements coming to light, as in the weight-loss planner example. Second, because scenarios can be understood by users, the utilization of scenarios can ensure that the client and users play an active role throughout the requirements analysis process. After all, the aim of the requirements analysis phase is to elicit the real needs of the client, and the only source of this information is the client and the users. Third, scenarios (or more precisely, use cases) play an important role in object-oriented analysis. This is discussed in detail in Section 11.5.

The most accurate and powerful requirements analysis technique is rapid prototyping, described in the next section.

9.2 RAPID PROTOTYPING

A rapid prototype is hastily built software that exhibits the key functionality of the target product. For example, a product that helps to manage an apartment complex must incorporate an input screen that allows the user to enter details of a new tenant and print an occupancy report for each month. These aspects will be incorporated in the rapid prototype. However, error-checking capabilities, file-updating routines, and complex tax computations will probably not be included. The key point is that a rapid prototype reflects the functionality that the client sees such as input screens and reports, but omits "hidden" aspects such as file updating. (For a different way of looking at rapid prototypes, see the Just in Case You Wanted to Know box on page 304.)

JUST IN CASE YOU WANTED TO KNOW

The idea of constructing models to show key aspects of a product goes back a long time. For example, a 1618 painting by Domenico Cresti (known as "Il Passignano") shows Michelangelo presenting a wooden model of his design for St. Peter's (in Rome) to Pope Paul IV. Architectural models could be huge; a model of an earlier design proposal for St. Peter's by the architect Bramante is more than 20 feet long on each side.

Architectural models were used for a number of different purposes. First, as depicted in the Cresti painting (now hanging in Casa Buonarroti in Florence), models were used to try to interest a client in funding a project. This is analogous to the use of a rapid prototype to determine the client's real needs. Second, in an age before architectural drawings, the model showed the builder the structure of the building and indicated to the stone masons how the building was to be decorated. This is similar to the way we now build a rapid prototype of the user interface, as described in Section 9.3.

It is not a good idea, however, to draw too close a parallel between such architectural models and software rapid prototypes. Rapid prototypes are used during the requirements phase to elicit the client's needs. Unlike architectural models, they are not used to represent either the architectural design or the detailed design; the design is produced two phases later, that is, during the design phase.

The client and intended users of the product now experiment with the rapid prototype, with members of the development team watching and taking notes. Based on their hands-on experience, users tells the developers how the rapid prototype satisfies their needs and, more importantly, identify the areas that need improvement. The developers change the rapid prototype until both sides are convinced that the needs of the client are accurately encapsulated in the rapid prototype. The rapid prototype is then used as the basis for drawing up the specifications.

An important aspect of the rapid prototyping model is embodied in the word *rapid*. The whole idea is to build the rapid prototype as quickly as possible. After all, the purpose of the rapid prototype is to provide the client with an understanding of the product, and the sooner, the better. It does not matter if the rapid prototype hardly works, if it crashes every few minutes, or if the screen layouts are less than perfect. The purpose of the rapid prototype is to enable the client and the developers to agree as quickly as possible on what the product is to do. Thus any imperfections in the rapid prototype may be ignored, provided that they do not seriously impair the functionality of the rapid prototype and thereby give a misleading impression of how the product will behave.

A second major aspect of the rapid prototyping model is that the rapid prototype must be built for change. If the first version of the rapid prototype is not what the client needs, then the prototype must be transformed rapidly into a second version that, it is hoped, will better satisfy the client's requirements. In order to achieve rapid development throughout the rapid prototyping process, fourth-generation languages (4GL) and interpreted languages, such as Smalltalk, Prolog, Lisp, and Java are used for rapid prototyping purposes. The UNIX shell programming language is being used more and more for constructing rapid prototypes because it is an interpreted language that is supported by the UNIX Programmer's Workbench, a powerful and comprehensive set of CASE tools. Another popular technique is to use hypertext. Concerns have been expressed about the maintainability of certain interpreted languages, but from the viewpoint of classic rapid prototyping this is irrelevant. All that counts is: Can a given language be used to produce a rapid prototype? And can the rapid prototype be changed quickly? If the answer to both questions is yes, then that language is probably a good candidate for rapid prototyping.

Turning now to the use of rapid prototyping in conjunction with the object-oriented paradigm, three very different object-oriented projects carried out by IBM showed significant improvements compared to projects using the structured paradigm [Capper, Colgate, Hunter, and James, 1994]. One of the recommendations that resulted from these projects is that it is important to build a rapid prototype as early as possible in the object-oriented life cycle.

Rapid prototyping is also particularly effective when developing the user interface to a product. This use is discussed in the next section.

9.3 HUMAN FACTORS

It is important that both the client and the future users of the product interact with the rapid prototype of the user interface. Encouraging users to experiment with the human–computer interface (HCI) greatly reduces the risk that the finished product will have to be altered. In particular, this experimentation will help achieve user friendliness, a vital objective for all software products.

The term *user friendliness* refers to the ease with which human beings can communicate with the software product. If users have difficulty in learning how to use a product, or find the screens confusing or irritating, then they will either not use the product or use it incorrectly. To try to eliminate this problem, menu-driven products were introduced. Instead of having to enter a command such as Perform computation or Print service rate report, the user merely has to select from a set of possible responses, such as

1. Perform computation
2. Print service rate report
3. Select view to be graphed

In this example, the user enters 1, 2, or 3 in order to invoke the corresponding command.

Nowadays, instead of simply displaying lines of text, HCIs employ graphics. Windows, icons, and pull-down menus are components of a graphical user interface (GUI). Because of the plethora of windowing systems, standards such as X Window have evolved. Also, "point and click" selection is becoming the norm. The user moves a mouse (that is, a hand-held pointing device) to move the screen cursor to the desired response ("point"), and pushes a mouse button ("click") to select the response.

However, even when the target product employs modern technology, the designers must never forget that the product is to be used by human beings. In other words, the HCI designers must consider *human factors* such as size of letters, capitalization, color, line length, and the number of lines on the screen.

Another example of human factors applies to the above menu. If the user chooses option 3, Select view to be graphed, then another menu will appear with another list of choices. Unless a menu-driven system is thoughtfully designed, there is the danger that the users will encounter a lengthy sequence of menus to achieve even a relatively simple operation. This delay can anger users, sometimes causing them to make inappropriate menu selections. Also, the HCI must allow the user to change a previous selection without having to return to the top-level menu. This problem can exist even when a GUI is used because many graphical user interfaces are essentially a series of menus displayed in an attractive screen format.

Sometimes it is impossible for a single user interface to cater to all users. For example, if a product is to be used by both computer professionals and high-school dropouts with no previous computer experience, then it is preferable that two different sets of HCIs be designed, each carefully tailored to the skill level and psychological profile of its intended users. This technique can be extended by incorporating sets of user interfaces requiring varied levels of sophistication. If the product deduces that the user would be more comfortable with a less sophisticated user interface, perhaps because the user is making frequent mistakes or is continually invoking help facilities, then the user is automatically shown screens that are more appropriate to his or her current skill level. But as the user becomes more familiar with the product, streamlined screens that provide less information are displayed, leading to speedier completion. This automated approach reduces user frustration and leads to increased productivity [Schach and Wood, 1986].

Many benefits can accrue when human factors are taken into account during the design of an HCI, including reduced learning times and lower error rates. Although help facilities must always be provided, they will be utilized less with a carefully designed HCI. This, too, will increase productivity. Uniformity of HCI appearance across a product or group of products can result in users intuitively knowing how to use a screen that they have never seen before because it is similar to other screens with which they are familiar. Designers of Macintosh software have taken this principle into account; this is one of the many reasons that software for the Macintosh is generally so user friendly.

It has been suggested that simple common sense is all that is needed to design a user-friendly HCI. Whether or not this charge is true, it is essential that a rapid prototype of the HCI of every product be constructed. Intended users of the product can experiment with the rapid prototype of the HCI and inform the designers whether the target product will indeed be user friendly, that is, whether the designers have taken the necessary human factors into account.

In the next two sections, superficially attractive but dangerous variants of the rapid prototyping model are discussed.

9.4 RAPID PROTOTYPING AS A SPECIFICATION TECHNIQUE

The conventional form of the rapid prototyping model, as described in Section 3.3 and depicted in Figure 3.3, is reproduced here as Figure 9.1. (Again, the implementation and integration steps will generally be performed in parallel.) The rapid prototype is used solely as a means to determine the client's needs accurately and is discarded after the client signs off on the specifications. That is, rapid

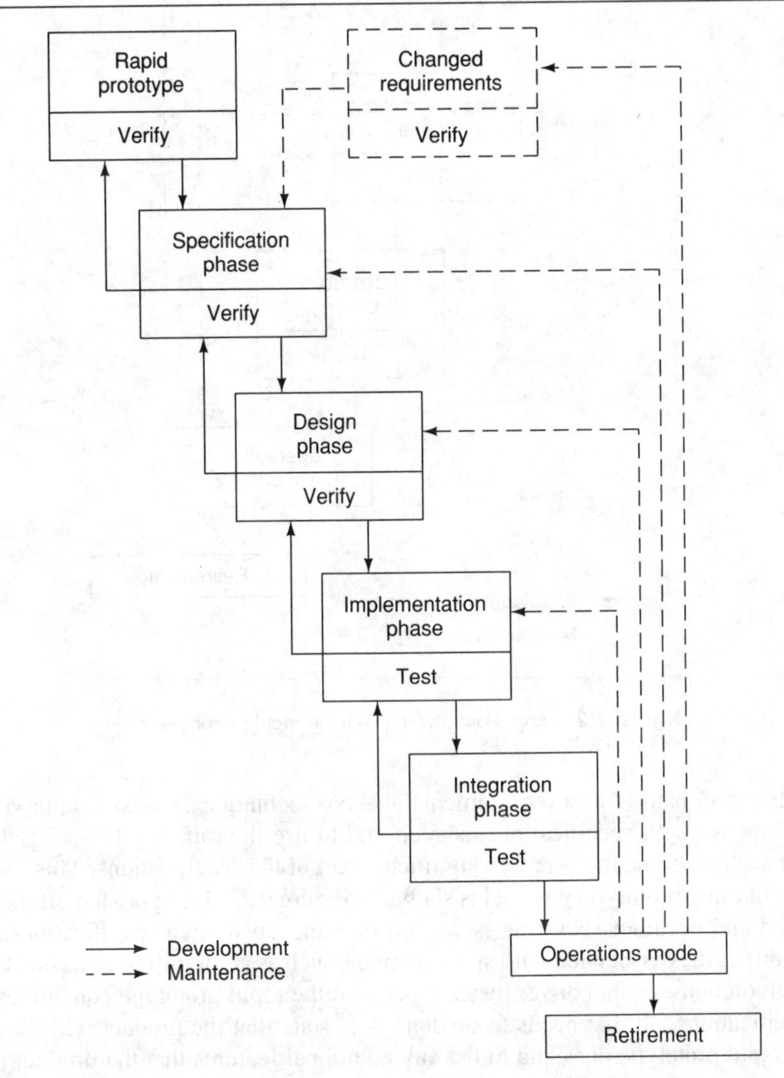

Figure 9.1 Rapid prototyping model.

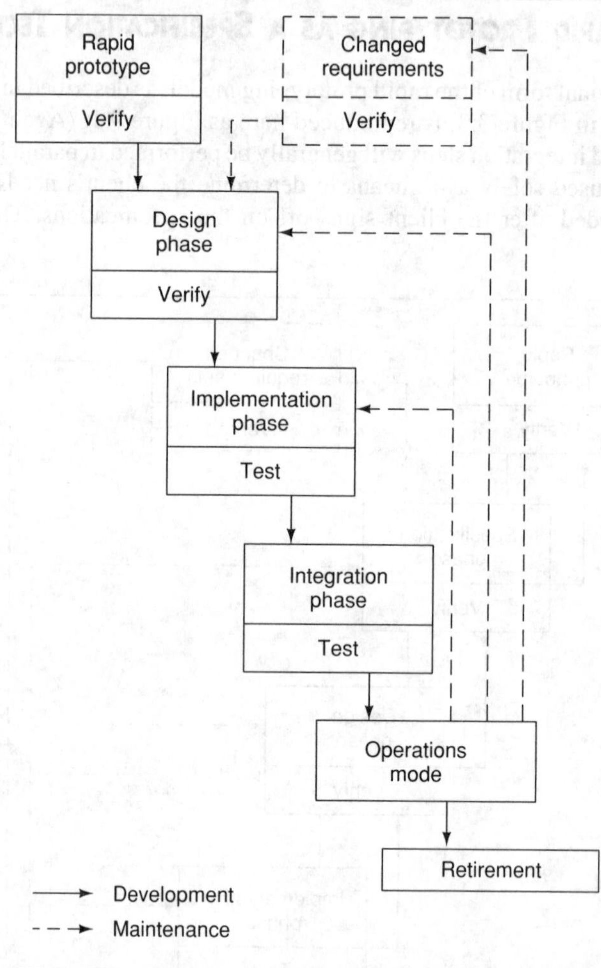

Figure 9.2 Rapid prototyping with the rapid prototype serving as specifications.

prototyping is used as a requirements analysis technique. A second approach is to dispense with specifications as such and to use the rapid prototype itself either as the specifications or as a significant part of the specifications. This second type of rapid prototyping model is shown in Figure 9.2. This approach offers both speed and accuracy. No time is wasted drawing up written specifications, and the difficulties associated with specifications, such as ambiguities, omissions, and contradictions, cannot arise. Instead, because the rapid prototype constitutes the specifications, all that needs to be done is to state that the product will do what the rapid prototype does and to list any additional features that the product must support, such as file updating, security, and error handling.

This version of the rapid prototyping model can have a major drawback. If there is a disagreement as to whether the developers have satisfactorily discharged their obligations, it is unlikely that a rapid prototype will stand as a legal statement of a contract between developer and client. For this reason, using the rapid prototype as the sole specification should never be done, not even if the software is developed internally (that is, when the client and developers are members of the same organization). After all, it is unlikely that the head of the investment management division of a bank will take the data processing division to court. Nevertheless, disagreements between client and developers can arise just as easily within an organization. Thus, in order to protect themselves, software developers should not use the rapid prototype as the specifications even when software is developed internally.

A second reason that the rapid prototype should not take the place of written specifications is potential problems with maintenance. Because there are no written specifications, during the maintenance phase the current specifications are simply the current version of the product, and changes to the specifications must be made in terms of the functionality of the current version of the product. As described in Chapter 15, maintenance is challenging even when all the documentation is available and up-to-date. If there are no specifications, maintenance can rapidly become a nightmare. The problem is particularly acute in the case of enhancement, where changes in requirements have to be implemented. It can be exceedingly difficult to change the design documents to reflect the new specifications because, in the absence of written specifications, the maintenance team will not have a clear statement of the current specifications.

For both these reasons, the rapid prototype should simply be used as a requirements analysis technique, that is, as a means of determining the client's real needs. Thereafter, written specification documents should be produced using the rapid prototype as a basis.

9.5 REUSING THE RAPID PROTOTYPE

In both versions of the rapid prototyping model discussed previously, the rapid prototype is discarded early in the software process. An alternate, but generally unwise, way of proceeding is to develop and refine the rapid prototype until it becomes the product. This is shown in Figure 9.3. In theory, this approach should lead to fast software development; after all, instead of throwing away the code constituting the rapid prototype along with the knowledge built into it, the rapid prototype is converted into the final product. However, in practice the process is very similar to the build-and-fix approach of Figure 3.1. Thus, as with the build-and-fix model, the first problem with this form of the rapid prototyping model follows from the fact that, in the course of refining the rapid prototype, changes have to be made to a working product. This is an expensive way to proceed, as shown in Figure 1.5. A different problem is that a primary objective when constructing a rapid prototype is speed of building. A rapid prototype is (correctly) hurriedly put together, rather than carefully specified, designed,

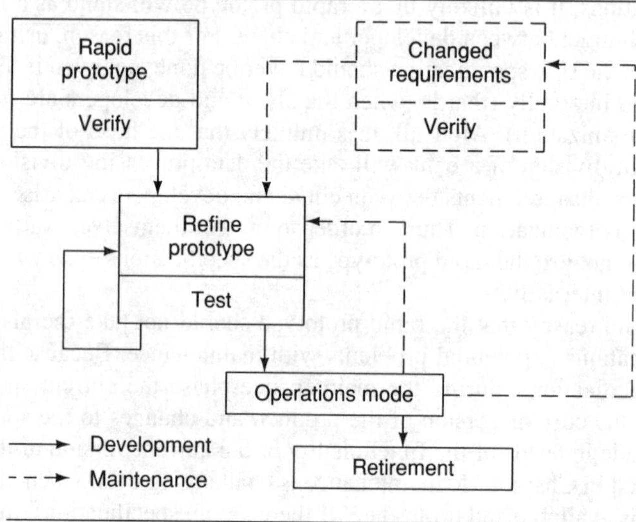

Figure 9.3 Unwise version of rapid prototyping model.

and then implemented. In the absence of specification and design documents, the resulting code is difficult and expensive to maintain. It might seem wasteful to construct a rapid prototype and then to throw it away and design the product from scratch, but it is far cheaper in both the short term and the long term to do this rather than try to convert a rapid prototype into production quality software [Brooks, 1975].

Another reason for discarding the rapid prototype is the issue of performance, particularly of real-time systems. In order to ensure that time constraints are met, it is necessary to design the product carefully. In contrast, a rapid prototype is constructed so as to display key functionality to the client; performance issues are not handled. As a result, if an attempt is made to refine a rapid prototype into a delivered product, it is unlikely that response times and other timing constraints will be met.

One way of ensuring that the rapid prototype is thrown away and that the product is properly designed and implemented is to build the rapid prototype in a different language from that of the product. For example, the client may specify that the product must be written in C++. If the rapid prototype is implemented in hypertext, for example, it will have to be discarded. First, the rapid prototype is implemented in hypertext and refined until the client is satisfied that it does everything, or almost everything, that the target product is to do. Next, the product is designed, relying on the knowledge and skills acquired in constructing the rapid prototype. Finally, the design is implemented in C++, and the tested product handed over to the client in the usual way.

Nevertheless, there is one instance when it is permissible to refine a rapid prototype or, more specifically, portions of the rapid prototype. When portions of the rapid prototype are computer-generated, then those portions may be used in the final product. For example, user interfaces are often a key aspect of a rapid prototype (Section 9.3). When CASE tools such as screen generators and report generators (Section 4.10) have been utilized to generate the user interfaces, then those portions of the rapid prototype may indeed be used as part of production quality software.

The desire not to "waste" the rapid prototype has resulted in a modified version of the rapid prototyping model being adopted by some organizations. Here, management decides *before* the rapid prototype is built that portions may be utilized in the final product, provided that those portions pass the same quality assurance tests as other software components. Thus, after the rapid prototype is complete, those sections that the developers wish to continue to use must pass design and code inspections. This approach goes beyond rapid prototyping. For example, components that are of sufficiently high quality to pass design and code inspections are not usually found in a rapid prototype. Furthermore, design documents are not part of classic rapid prototyping. Nevertheless, this hybrid approach is attractive to some organizations hoping to recover some of the time and money invested in the rapid prototype. However, in order to ensure that the quality of the code is sufficiently high, the rapid prototype will have to be built somewhat more slowly than is customary for a "rapid" prototype.

9.6 OTHER USES OF RAPID PROTOTYPING

A different use of rapid prototyping is as a means of arriving at consensus where there is disagreement as to the client's requirements. The author was once called in to advise a committee of six top executives of a major corporation with regard to the development of a management information system (MIS) [Blair, Murphy, Schach, and McDonald, 1988]. A requirement of the product was that one-page reports had to be printed at the end of each month incorporating month-by-month information for a full year. Each member of the committee then insisted that every one-page report had to incorporate data from his or her specific area of responsibility. Because there were six areas in all, this was clearly impossible. The solution was to construct a rapid prototype. Within 4 person-days a working product was constructed; it computed the relevant quantities and printed a one-page report incorporating what the author felt was the most important management information. The rapid prototype was partially acceptable to the management team; the necessary changes were made rapidly; and within 4 weeks the complete operational quality product was in place. Without rapid prototyping, consensus would not have been reached as quickly and as amicably. In fact, it is possible that no consensus at all could have been achieved, and the product would never have been developed.

Management implications of the rapid prototyping model are now considered.

9.7 MANAGEMENT IMPLICATIONS OF THE RAPID PROTOTYPING MODEL

One difficulty with rapid prototyping is that the ease with which changes can generally be made to a rapid prototype may encourage the client to request all sorts of major changes to the delivered operational-quality version of the product. Furthermore, the client may expect the changes to be implemented as rapidly as were changes to the rapid prototype. This was the author's experience with the MIS described previously. A related challenge is having to explain to the client that the rapid prototype is not of operational quality and that the client will have to wait for the operational quality version, despite the fact that the rapid prototype appears to do everything needed. Before rapid prototyping is used, it is essential that the managers responsible for developing the product discuss these and related issues with the client.

As with the introduction of any new technology, before an organization introduces the rapid prototyping model it is vital that management be aware of the advantages and disadvantages of rapid prototyping. In all fairness, although the case for rapid prototyping is a strong one, it has not yet been proved beyond all doubt. For example, a frequently quoted experiment is that of Boehm, Gray, and Seewaldt who compared seven different versions of a product [Boehm, Gray, and Seewaldt, 1984]. Four versions were specified and three were prototyped with the rapid prototype serving as the specifications. The results were that rapid prototyping and specifying yielded products with roughly equivalent performance, but the prototyped versions contained about 40 percent less code and required about 45 percent less effort. The reason was that the specification teams had no compunctions about adding bells and whistles to the specification document. On the other hand, the rapid prototypers realized that they would have to build every feature into the rapid prototype and were, therefore, reluctant to incorporate any functionality that did not seem to be essential. With on average 40 percent less code, it is not surprising that the prototyped versions were rated somewhat lower on functionality and robustness. But interestingly enough, they were rated higher on ease of use and ease of learning. Finally, specifying produced more coherent designs and software that was easier to integrate.

One important point about this experiment was that it was conducted on seven teams of graduate students, three two-member teams and four three-member teams. The project was only 10 weeks in duration, and no maintenance of the product was performed. In other words, the experiment is not typical of real products with respect to number of participants, team size, project size, or software process. It is therefore perhaps unwise to accept Boehm's results as a blanket endorsement for rapid prototyping. Instead, they should be taken as indications of the comparative strengths and weaknesses of rapid prototyping when compared to specifying. In addition to the weaknesses pointed out previously, Boehm and his collaborators found that prototyped products are harder to integrate than specified products. Ease of integration is important for large-scale products, especially

C^4I (command, control, communications, computers, and intelligence) software. This is a further reason to use the rapid prototyping model depicted in Figure 9.1, where rapid prototyping is employed as a requirements analysis technique, and not to use the model of Figure 9.2 where rapid prototyping takes the place of specifying.

Two aspects of rapid prototyping must be taken into account by any manager. In Section 9.5 it was pointed out that it is short-sighted to turn a rapid prototype into the final product; the rapid prototype should be used solely as a means of accurately determining the client's requirements. A second important issue is that under some circumstances rapid prototyping can take the place of the specifications phase; it can *never* replace the design phase. A team can certainly use the information and experience gained from the rapid prototype as a guide to fashioning a good design; however, because the rapid prototype is rapidly thrown together, it is unlikely that a good rapid prototype will have a good design.

A more fundamental issue is that managing the rapid prototyping model requires a major change in outlook for a manager who is accustomed to managing only the waterfall model. The concept underlying the waterfall model is to do things correctly the first time. Certainly the waterfall model incorporates a number of feedback loops if the team does not accomplish this goal (and the goal is seldom, if ever, reached). However, the ideal for the waterfall model team is to perform each phase of the development process one time only. In contrast, a rapid prototype is specifically built to be changed frequently and then thrown away. This concept is diametrically opposed to the approach to which the average manager is accustomed. The rapid prototyping approach of taking several iterations to get it right is probably a more realistic approach than the first-time-right waterfall model expectation, and this logic may help convince a manager to change to the rapid prototyping model.

Another aspect of the rapid prototyping model that requires a different approach on the part of the manager is the increased interaction between the client and the developers, particularly the rapid prototyping team. In the waterfall model, interaction between client and developers is essentially restricted to a series of interviews between the requirements team and the client and his or her employees. When rapid prototyping is used, there is almost continual interaction between the rapid prototyping team and the client's team until the rapid prototype has been accepted.

9.8 EXPERIENCES WITH RAPID PROTOTYPING

Gordon and Bieman have analyzed 39 published and unpublished case studies that use rapid prototyping [Gordon and Bieman, 1995]. Of these 33 were considered successes, 3 were considered failures, and 3 were not rated. Gordon and Bieman have pointed out that studies of unsuccessful cases are rarely published. Consequently, they do not claim that their analysis reflects a high success rate as a consequence of rapid prototyping. Their work is rather a report on a number of commercial software projects in which rapid prototyping was used with some success.

Not all the case studies, as published, reflected every issue of interest. For example, comments on ease of use appeared in only 17 of the case studies. In all 17 instances, improved ease of use of the delivered product as a consequence of rapid prototyping was reported; none of the other 22 case studies claimed that the product was harder to use. Thus, although the data are incomplete and specific topics may not be explicitly mentioned, it is possible to draw some conclusions.

All the case studies that commented on user participation reported enthusiastic user participation early in the process. It was also found that rapid prototyping meets client needs. There was less unanimity in other issues. For example, four sources reported that rapid prototyping resulted in smaller delivered products, and one reported increased code size. Many case studies mentioned that fewer unnecessary features were implemented with rapid prototyping, but two reported an increase in such features.

Choice of language for rapid prototyping does not appear to be of critical importance. A total of 26 different languages were used in the 39 case studies. The most popular languages were Lisp (4 instances) and Smalltalk (3 instances).

The most controversial part of the results relates to whether or not the rapid prototype should be discarded. It is difficult to reach definite conclusions on this issue because of the wide variety of software processes that were used. In some cases, the rapid prototype as a whole was successively refined until it became the final product. In others, only part of the rapid prototype was retained and the rest was discarded. In one instance, a design phase was required for each iteration of the rapid prototype. For some of the case studies, management specified in advance that the rapid prototype would be retained and refined. Twenty-two of the cases studied specifically recommended retaining and refining all or part of the rapid prototype, and eight insisted that it be discarded. It has been suggested that retaining the rapid prototype is particularly important for large products. Of the 39 case studies, 7 were considered large (over 100,000 lines of code), and all 7 recommended retaining all or part of the rapid prototype. In view of the generally held belief that rapid prototypes for large products should be discarded, further research needs to be conducted in this area. In particular, it is important to know whether the modified rapid prototyping model described at the end of Section 9.5 was followed. That is, did management decide *before* the rapid prototypes were built that portions might be utilized in the final product and that the parts that the developers wished to retain first had to pass design and code inspections?

Some tentative conclusions can be drawn from this work. The first is that rapid prototyping is a viable technique that can lead to successful software development. At the same time, there are a number of possible risks. If the rapid prototype is retained, there is a danger that the resulting product will be badly designed, hard to maintain, and perform poorly; these risks appear to grow in proportion to the size of the product. However, the risks can be reduced. One way is to use the modified version of rapid prototyping described in Section 9.5.

There is a difference between reporting on case studies and conducting controlled experiments. But bearing in mind that controlled experimentation in software engineering can be extremely difficult, one alternative is to learn from the experiences of others.

Joint application design is considered next.

9.9 JOINT APPLICATION DESIGN (JAD)

When rapid prototyping is used for the requirements phase, the role of the members of the client organization is largely restricted to responding to actions of the developers. In contrast, joint application design (JAD) is an extended form of rapid prototyping in which the client organization plays a more active role. Notwithstanding the name joint application *design*, JAD is a technique for the requirements and specification phases in which members of the development and client organizations work as a team and take joint responsibility for the result.

A joint team, consisting of representatives of both the development organization and the client organization, discusses the needs of the client. The team designs the screens and reports, builds the rapid prototype, and draws up the specification document. The client organization takes an active, rather than reactive, role in the first two phases of the software process.

As a consequence of team synergy, productivity increases of between 20 percent and 60 percent have been reported [Gibson and Jackson, 1987]. An important proviso for the success of this technique is that the JAD team leader should not have a vested interest in the success of the project. The aim of the team leader should be to obtain consensus without having a specific interest in the decisions [Gane, 1989]; the leader must therefore be a skilled facilitator.

9.10 COMPARISON OF REQUIREMENTS ANALYSIS TECHNIQUES

The primary requirements analysis technique is interviewing (Section 9.1). To illustrate this, suppose that the requirements analysis team decides at the start of the project to build a rapid prototype. Before the first iteration of the rapid prototype can be built, however, it is necessary for the team to interview the relevant client personnel. The more thorough these interviews, the greater is the probability that this first iteration will accurately reflect the client's needs. On the other hand, simply throwing together a rapid prototype and then going through a lengthy refinement process will not be time- or cost-effective.

Interviewing is also required if the forms technique is used (Section 9.1). Careful perusal of forms, reports, and job descriptions can be extremely useful. However, the only way to be sure of the accuracy of the information gleaned from this process is to interview the relevant members of the client organization. Finally, if JAD is used (Section 9.9), the developers on the joint client-developer team have to interview the client members in order to start the process, just as when rapid prototyping is used.

Consequently, as claimed at the beginning of this section, interviewing is indeed the primary requirements analysis technique. On the other hand, it was pointed out in Section 9.1 that rapid prototyping is the most accurate requirements analysis technique. Rapid prototyping results in the construction of a working model of the product and is more likely to meet the client's real needs than other techniques.

It is apparent that any combination of requirements techniques must include interviewing. In addition, unless rapid prototyping or a related technique such as JAD is utilized, there is a significant risk that the requirements analysis phase will not be adequately performed and that the client's needs will not be completely met by the target product.

9.11 TESTING DURING THE REQUIREMENTS PHASE

Although the aim of the requirements phase is to establish the client's real needs, usually the client will not be the primary user of the target product. It is therefore essential to give the users the opportunity to experiment with the rapid prototype and to suggest changes that, when approved by the client, will be implemented in the delivered version of the software product.

Thus the role of the software quality assurance (SQA) group during the rapid prototyping phase is to ensure that the relevant individuals in the client organization have the opportunity to interact with the rapid prototype and to make sure that their suggestions actually reach the client or, perhaps, a committee of client managers responsible for analyzing the suggestions of the users.

9.12 CASE TOOLS FOR THE REQUIREMENTS PHASE

Interpreted languages generally serve as good media for rapid prototyping. Because interpreted languages do not need to be compiled or linked, the development of the rapid prototype is faster. Also, minor changes requested by the client can often be implemented while the rapid prototype is being demonstrated. Interpreted languages are, in general, less efficient to execute than compiled languages, and difficulties with maintenance have been associated with some interpreted languages. However, neither of these issues is relevant within the context of rapid prototyping. The key point is that a rapid prototype is rapidly put together and then discarded, and most interpreted languages are ideal for this purpose.

Further efficiency can be gained by using CASE tools associated with the rapid prototyping language. For example, Smalltalk has an environment that assists the user with a variety of tools and speeds up the rapid prototyping process. The Interlisp environment is a similar product that assists Lisp programmers. Java is a fully portable interpreted language. There are many Java environments currently on the market, and more are expected in the future. As previously mentioned, the UNIX shell programming language is popular for constructing rapid prototypes. Hypertext is another important and widely used rapid prototyping language. If it has been decided that the rapid prototype will be discarded (as described in Section 9.8), then hypertext has a further advantage. It is almost inconceivable that the delivered product will be written in hypertext, so use of hypertext virtually guarantees that the rapid prototype will be discarded.

With regard to rapid prototyping of user interfaces, two popular CASE tools are Demo II and Guide. Hypertext is especially useful for rapid prototyping of user interfaces. Examples of hypertext CASE tools are Hypercard and Hypertalk.

A recent trend is the widespread use of a fourth-generation language (4GL) such as Oracle, PowerBuilder, and SQL, for rapid prototyping (4GLs are discussed in Section 13.2). There are a number of reasons for this. First, a design goal of every 4GL is that fewer statements are needed to achieve the same functionality than with a third-generation language like COBOL, Ada, or Java. Thus the rapid prototype is likely to be delivered more rapidly when a 4GL is used. Second, many 4GLs are interpreted. This speeds up rapid prototyping, as explained at the beginning of this section. Third, many 4GLs are supported by powerful CASE tools, thus speeding up the rapid prototyping process even more.

On the other hand, the use of a 4GL for rapid prototyping can have an inherent disadvantage. The CASE environment in which a 4GL is embedded is frequently part of a larger set of tools to be used for the complete software process. The software process that is usually recommended by a 4GL supplier is to build the rapid prototype and then to refine it successively until it becomes the final product. After all, the supplier frequently does not care if the software process degenerates into the build-and-fix model; unfortunately, the sole aim of many 4GL suppliers is to ensure that development organizations purchase their product, a single CASE environment which can handle all aspects of a project.

Suppose that a software development manager has just paid tens if not hundreds of thousands of dollars for a CASE environment that will support every phase of the software process. It is certainly not easy to convince that manager to spend still more money on a workbench for a different language to be used for rapid prototyping in order to ensure that rapid prototypes can be discarded. The manager may well retort that he or she has purchased a perfectly good rapid prototyping tool as part of the new environment and is now being asked to throw away money buying an unnecessary additional rapid prototyping tool so that rapid prototypes can be thrown away. The manager must be shown that the cost of a rapid prototyping tool or workbench is small compared to the potentially huge expense of trying to convert a rapid prototype into production quality software and then attempting to maintain that product.

9.13 METRICS FOR THE REQUIREMENTS PHASE

Bearing in mind that software quality and reliability are not important when building a rapid prototype, measures such as defect rates or mean time between failures are less meaningful within the context of rapid prototyping than in later phases. What is important is how rapidly the rapid prototyping team determines the client's real needs. So a useful metric during this phase is a measure of requirements volatility. Keeping a record of how frequently the requirements change during the requirements phase gives management a way of determining the rate at which the rapid prototyping team converges on the actual requirements of the product. This metric has the further advantage that it can be applied to any requirements analysis technique, such as interviewing or scenarios.

Another measure of how well the requirements team is doing its job is the number of requirements that change during the rest of the software development process. If a large number of requirements have to be changed during the specification, design, and subsequent phases, then it is clear that the way that the team carries out the requirements phase should be thoroughly analyzed. Again, this metric is applicable not just to rapid prototyping, but also to all the other techniques described in Section 9.1.

A useful metric when rapid prototyping is used is the number of times each feature of the rapid prototype is tried when the client and users experiment with the rapid prototype. For example, if every user selects Screen J from the menu at least once but no one ever chooses Screen B, then the development team should ask the client about those two screens. Specifically, the developers need to know whether Screen J is so important that the design should minimize execution time for that screen and whether Screen B even needs to be included in the product. If so, then at least one user should experiment with Screen B; it is vital that all screens should meet the users' needs.

9.14 OSBERT OGLESBY CASE STUDY: REQUIREMENTS PHASE

Osbert Oglesby is a noted art dealer. He specializes in buying and selling French Impressionist paintings, but he will buy any piece of art if he thinks he can make a profit when he sells it in his gallery, *Les Objets d'Orient*.

Lately, however, Osbert has been losing money. After having carefully analyzed his business records, he concludes that he has been overpaying for paintings. He decides that he needs a software product, running on a portable computer, that he can use to determine the maximum price he should pay for a painting. (Osbert plans to take the computer when he views a painting in a client's home or office.) The input to the program is the painting classification (masterpiece, masterwork,[1]

[1] A masterwork is an inferior work by an artist who previously or subsequently has painted a masterpiece.

or other), together with the data needed to compute the price for that classification of painting.

Osbert commissions a software engineer to devise an algorithm for determining the maximum price he should pay for a painting. Here is the algorithm:

- A masterpiece: Scan auction records for the most similar work by the same artist. Use the auction purchase price of the most similar work as the base price. (For the definition of similarity, see below.) The maximum purchase price is found by adding 8.5 percent to the base price, compounded annually, for each year since that auction.
- A masterwork: First, compute the maximum purchase price as if it were a masterpiece by the same artist. Then, if the picture was painted in the 20th century, multiply this figure by 0.25, otherwise multiply it by $(20-c)/(21-c)$, where c is the century in which the work was painted $(12 < c < 20)$.
- Other: Measure the dimensions of the canvas. The maximum purchasing price is then given by the formula F_*A, where F is a constant for that artist (fashionability coefficient) and A is the area of the canvas in square centimeters. If there is no fashionability coefficient for that artist, Osbert will not buy the painting.

In the case of masterpieces and masterworks, the coefficient of similarity between two paintings is computed as follows:

Score 1 for a match on medium, otherwise 0.

Score 1 for a match on subject, otherwise 0.

Add these two numbers, multiply by the area of the smaller of the two paintings, and divide by the area of the larger of the two.

The resulting number is the coefficient of similarity.

If the coefficient of similarity between the painting under consideration and the paintings in the file of auction data is zero, then Osbert will not buy that masterwork or masterpiece.

The program must include a file of artists and their corresponding F values. The value of F can vary from month to month, depending on the current fashionability of an artist, so the file must be implemented to allow Osbert to perform regular updates. The program must also include a file containing data on auction sales of masterpieces. This file will include the name of artist, title of painting, date of painting, date of auction (assumed to be in the twentieth century), sale price, and type of work. The type of work consists of three components, namely, medium (oil, watercolor, or other), dimensions (height and width), and subject (portrait, still-life, landscape, or other). This file is updated regularly by an outside source and is never modified by Osbert.

For each painting he has bought since introducing his scheme, Osbert needs to record the following:

Description of painting

First name of artist (20 characters, followed by ? if there is uncertainty)
Last name of artist (20 characters, followed by ? if there is uncertainty)
Title of work (40 characters, followed by ? if there is uncertainty)
Date of work (yyyy, followed by ? if there is uncertainty)
Classification (masterpiece, masterwork, other)
Height (cm)
Width (cm)
Medium (oil, watercolor, other)
Subject (portrait, still-life, landscape, other)

Date of purchase (mm/dd/yy)
Name of seller (30 characters)
Address of seller (40 characters)
Maximum purchase price determined by algorithm
Actual purchase price
Target selling price (2.15 times the purchase price)
If the piece has been sold then add:

Date of sale (mm/dd/yy)
Name of buyer (30 characters)
Address of buyer (40 characters)
Actual selling price

Question marks in the first four fields are to be ignored when determining similarity. They should be included, however, in the three reports described below. All three reports are to be generated on demand and must incorporate sales and purchases during the past year. That is to say, Osbert wishes a report generated at any time on April 6, 1998, to cover the period from April 7, 1997, through April 6, 1998. The product should pause after every 20 lines of text to allow Osbert to view each report one screen at a time.

A report is needed to display all the paintings purchased during the past year. The output should be in the following order: classification type, purchase date, artist's last name, painting title, suggested maximum purchase price, and actual purchase price. Any painting purchased for more than the maximum purchase price computed by the algorithm must be flagged (by placing an asterisk before the classification type). This report must be sorted by classification and by date of purchase within classification. The average ratio of the actual purchase price to the algorithm's suggested maximum purchase price for all the paintings in the report should be displayed at the end of the report.

A second report should display the paintings that have been sold during the past year. The output should be in the following order: classification type, sale date, artist's last name, painting title, target selling price, and actual selling price.

Any painting sold at a price of 5 percent or more below the target selling price must be flagged. This report must be sorted by classification and by date of sale within classification. The average ratio of the actual selling price to the target selling price for all of the paintings in the report should be displayed at the end of the report.

Finally, Osbert is keen to detect new trends in the art market as soon as possible. He is particularly interested in determining when higher prices than expected are consistently paid for a particular artist's work, so that he can buy up paintings by that artist before others notice the trend. He therefore requires a report that shows artists whose works have been sold at a price that has exceeded the target selling price in every instance during the past year. For an artist to appear in this report, at least two of his or her works must have been sold in that period. The names of the relevant artists (if any) should be in alphabetical order. Each name should appear on one line of the screen. The various works sold must appear on successive lines, in order of date of sale. For each work, the date of sale, classification type, painting title, target selling price, and actual selling price must appear, in that order.

9.15 Osbert Oglesby Case Study: Rapid Prototype

Notwithstanding the care taken when interviewing Osbert Oglesby and his staff to determine their requirements accurately, the only way to be sure that the final product will indeed meet the real needs of the client is to build a rapid prototype. Unfortunately, the only language available to the developers is Java. Thus, both the rapid prototype and the production-quality version will have to be written in that language. Java is a good language for rapid prototyping because it is interpreted. Nevertheless, a better choice would have been an interpreted language other than Java; this would guarantee that the rapid prototype would be discarded once the users' requirements have been determined.

The rapid prototype is available at www.mhhe.com/engcs/compsci/schach. The code is straightforward. Nevertheless, three aspects need to be discussed. First, up to 10 gallery records are stored in array gallery_records (Figure 9.4). In the delivered product, a data structure that allows for a variable number of gallery records is needed. For example, a file or a dynamic data structure could be used. In the rapid prototype, however, an array is used because it is easy and quick to implement, and the rapid prototype can be tested with a small number of gallery records. Analogously, up to 7 auction records are stored in array auctionRecords (Figure 9.4).

The second important aspect of the rapid prototype is that it is unfinished. For example, the only report that can be printed is for sold paintings, not for bought paintings or current fashions. Also, the rapid prototype contains a complete routine to determine whether or not to buy a masterpiece. However, method buyMasterwork is a stub, that is, a dummy method consisting of an interface but with no body; it just displays a message when invoked (Figure 9.5). Omitting

```
class Painting
{
    String              firstName;
    String              lastName;
    ...
} // class Painting

class Auction
{
    Painting            description = new Painting ();
    Date                auctionDate;
    float               salePrice;
} // class Auction

class gallery
{
    String              classification;
    Painting            description = new Painting ();
    ...
} // class Gallery

class OsbertPrototype
{
    public static final int    NUM_GALLERY_RECORDS = 10;
    public static final int    NUM_AUCTION_RECORDS =  7;

    public Gallery      galleryRecords[] = new Gallery[NUM_GALLERY_RECORDS];

    public Auction      auctionRecords[] = new Auction[NUM_AUCTION_RECORDS];

    public void initializeAuctionRecords ()
    //
    // initializeAuctionRecords initializes the auction records
    {
        auctionRecords[0]                              = new Auction ();
        auctionRecords[0].description.firstName        = "Leonardo";
        auctionRecords[0].description.lastName         = "da Vinci";
        auctionRecords[0].description.title            = "Ceiling Painting";
        auctionRecords[0].description.paintingDate     = "1530";
        auctionRecords[0].description.height           = (float) 482.5;
        auctionRecords[0].description.width            = (float) 530.9;
        auctionRecords[0].description.medium           = "oil";
        auctionRecords[0].description.subject          = "other";
        auctionRecords[0].auctionDate                  = convertDate ("11/20/1970");
        auctionRecords[0].salePrice                    = (float) 43.4;
        ...
```

Figure 9.4 Portion of rapid prototype of Osbert Oglesby product: arrays for gallery records and auction records.

```
public void buyMasterwork ()
//
// buyMasterwork allows user to buy masterwork
{
    ...
    clearScreen ();
    System.out.println ("This option is not implemented in the prototype.");
    System.out.println ("\n\n Press <ENTER> to continue");
    ...
} // buyMasterwork
```

Figure 9.5 Rapid prototype of Osbert Oglesby product: portion of method **buyMasterwork**.

the body of this function speeds up development of the rapid prototype without significantly detracting from its functionality. After all, the only difference between the maximum purchase price for a masterwork and for a masterpiece is the multiplier that changes with the century. Thus, if the complete functionality for masterpieces is implemented in the rapid prototype, there is probably no need to do the same for masterworks.

Finally, the user interface of the rapid prototype is menu-driven; a portion is shown in Figure 9.6. This is certainly not as elegant as a graphical user interface (GUI). However, it does have two advantages. First, the emphasis in rapid prototyping is on speed. Unless a powerful GUI generator is available, it is usually quicker to code a simple menu-driven user interface. Second, a GUI is often hardware/operating system dependent. If the delivered product is implemented on a hardware/operating system platform that is significantly different from that on which the rapid prototype was run, then the GUI may have to be

```
cleanScreen ();
System.out.println ("\t   MAIN MENU");
System.out.println ("\t Osbert Oglesby — Collector of Fine Art\n");
System.out.println ("\t   1. Buy a Painting");
System.out.println ("\t   2. Sell a Painting");
System.out.println ("\t   3. Produce a Report");
System.out.println ("\t   4. Quit");
```

Figure 9.6 Rapid prototype of Osbert Oglesby product: portion of method **mainMenu**.

reimplemented from scratch, consuming additional cost and additional time. For both these reasons, it is often better to build a rapid prototype with a simple textual user interface. Decisions regarding more elaborate user interfaces can be made later in the life cycle.

9.16 OBJECT-ORIENTED REQUIREMENTS?

Nothing in this chapter appertains to the object-oriented paradigm. It certainly is reasonable to ask why this is so. After all, the title of this book is *Classical and Object-Oriented Software Engineering*, and lack of material on object-oriented requirements appears to be a serious omission.

The answer is that there is no such thing as "object-oriented requirements," nor should there be such a thing. The aim of the requirements phase is to determine the client's needs, that is, what the functionality of the target system should be. The requirements phase has nothing to do with how the system is to be built. Thus, it is meaningless to refer to the classical paradigm or the object-oriented paradigm within the context of the requirements phase, just as it is meaningless to refer to a classical or object-oriented user manual. The user manual describes the steps to be followed by the user when running the software product and has nothing to do with how the product has been built. In the same way, the requirements phase results in a statement of what the product is to do; the way that the product will be built does not enter into it.

Having stated categorically that there is no such thing as object-oriented requirements, it should nevertheless be mentioned that there is one way that the object-oriented paradigm can enter into the requirements phase. Suppose that, as has been strongly recommended in this chapter, the requirements phase for a specific project includes the building of a rapid prototype. As a consequence of writing the code for the rapid prototype, the development team will acquire insights into the problem domain, including ideas as to what might constitute a class within the target software. That is, even if the rapid prototype has been written in a classical language like C, COBOL, or Lisp, the team will become aware of the fundamental building blocks of the product to be constructed. Then, in the next phase, object-oriented analysis (OOA), this information can be of assistance in the first step of OOA, namely, extracting the classes (see Section 11.4). Other than this, the object-oriented paradigm does not play a role in the requirements phase.

CHAPTER REVIEW

The chapter begins with a description of requirements analysis techniques (Section 9.1). A careful definition is given of rapid prototyping (Section 9.2). The importance of taking human factors into account when designing user interfaces is discussed in Section 9.3. The use of rapid prototyping as a specification technique is discouraged in Section 9.4. The issue of reusing a rapid prototype is discussed in Section 9.5. In Section 9.6 other uses of rapid prototyping are discussed. Management implications of the rapid prototyping model appear in Section 9.7. Experiences with rapid prototyping are discussed in Section 9.8. In Section 9.9 joint application design (JAD) is described. Other techniques of requirements analysis are compared in Section 9.10. Next are presented ways of checking the rapid prototype (Section 9.11), CASE tools for the requirements phase (Section 9.12), and metrics for the requirements phase (Section 9.13). The chapter concludes with the Osbert Oglesby Case Study (Sections 9.14 and 9.15), and a discussion of whether there is such a thing as object-oriented requirements (Section 9.16).

FOR FURTHER READING

Books on requirements analysis include [Gause and Weinberg, 1990] and [Davis, 1993]. [Thayer and Dorfman, 1990] is a collection of papers on requirements analysis. The strengths of paper prototypes are discussed in [Rettig, 1994]. Articles on the requirements phase appear in the May 1995 issue of the *Communications of the ACM* and in the March 1996 issue of *IEEE Software*. The use of cost-benefit analysis in prioritizing requirements is described in [Karlsson and Ryan, 1997].

For an introduction to rapid prototyping, suggested books include [Lantz, 1985], [Connell and Shafer, 1989], and [Gane, 1989]. A graphical tool for rapid prototyping of real-time systems appears in [Coomber and Childs, 1990]. Articles on rapid prototyping include [Luqi, 1989]. The role of computer-aided prototyping is assessed in [Luqi and Royce, 1992]. In addition to the experiment on prototyping by Boehm and his co-workers [Boehm, Gray, and Seewaldt, 1984], another experiment on rapid prototyping is described in [Alavi, 1984].

The February 1995 issue of *IEEE Computer* contains a number of different articles on rapid prototyping. Sources of information on joint application design (JAD) include [Gane, 1989] and [Wood and Silver, 1994]. The report on the use of rapid prototyping in 39 commercial products is an extremely useful source of information [Gordon and Bieman, 1995]. [Lichter, Schneider-Hufschmidt, and Züllighoven, 1994] gives details of five industrial software projects in which prototyping played a major role. JAD is one version of rapid application development (RAD); there are a variety of articles on RAD in the September 1995 issue of *IEEE Software*.

Human factors are discussed in [Dix, Finlay, Abowd, and Beale, 1993], [Browne, 1994], and [Preece, 1994]. [Nielsen, 1993] describes how user interaction with a user interface can significantly improve usability. [Myers and Rosson, 1992] point out that up to half of the total software effort can be devoted to portions of the product that are related to the user interface.

Articles on user interface design can be found in the April 1993 issue of *Communications of the ACM* and the July/August 1997 issue of *IEEE Software*. [Gentner and Grudin, 1996] analyzes models underlying user-interface design. The proceedings of the Annual Conference on Human Factors in Computer Systems (sponsored by ACM SIGCHI) are a valuable source of information on wide-ranging aspects of human factors.

PROBLEMS

9.1 You have just joined Bach Brothers Software as a software manager. Bach Brothers has been developing word processing software for years using the waterfall model, usually with some success. On the basis of your experience, you think that the rapid prototyping model is a far superior way of developing software. Write a report addressed to the vice-president for software development explaining why you believe that the organization should switch to the rapid prototyping model. Remember that vice-presidents do not like reports that are more than one page in length.

9.2 You are the vice-president for software development of Bach Brothers. Reply to the report of Problem 9.1.

9.3 Of the programming languages available to you, which should not be used for rapid prototyping? Give reasons for your answer.

9.4 Describe a project in which rapid prototyping is unlikely to be of much assistance to the development team.

9.5 In Section 9.3 it is stated that rapid prototyping is particularly effective when developing the user interface. Under what circumstances is there an equally effective alternative way to determine the client's needs in this regard?

9.6 Under what circumstances does it make sense to refine a rapid prototype?

9.7 What is the result if a rapid prototype is not constructed rapidly?

9.8 Should rapid prototyping be used if the product is to be developed using the object-oriented paradigm?

9.9 (Term Project) Construct a rapid prototype for the Air Gourmet project in Appendix A. Use the software and hardware specified by your instructor.

9.10 (Case Study) Starting with the requirements of Section 9.14, construct a rapid prototype in an interpreted language such as Java, Lisp, Smalltalk, or UNIX shell language.

9.11 (Case Study) The rapid prototype of Section 9.15 is written in C and the production-quality version is also to be written in Java. How would you prevent the rapid prototype from being refined into the delivered version of the product?

9.12 (Case Study) If the software is available to you, add a graphical user interface (GUI) to the rapid prototype of Section 9.15.

9.13 (Case Study) In the rapid prototype of Section 9.15, arrays of records is used for storing auction records and gallery records. The code includes a comment to the effect that, in the actual implementation, dynamic data structures are needed because the number of such records is not known. Was this a good decision on the part of the rapid prototyping team? To support your answer, recode the rapid prototype using a dynamic data structure.

9.14 (Case Study) A number of the routines of the rapid prototype of Section 9.15 are empty. For example, the routines to print reports for bought paintings or current fashions have not been coded. Was this a good decision on the part of the rapid prototyping team? To support your answer, complete the bodies of the empty routines.

9.15 (Readings in Software Engineering) Your instructor will distribute copies of [Karlsson and Ryan, 1997]. The spiral model is a risk-based life-cycle model. How could Karlsson and Ryan's approach be extended to a complete life-cycle model based on cost–benefit analysis?

REFERENCES

[Alavi, 1984] M. ALAVI, "An Assessment of the Prototyping Approach to Information Systems Development," *Communications of the ACM* **27** (June 1984), pp. 556–63.

[Blair, Murphy, Schach, and McDonald, 1988] J. A. BLAIR, L. C. MURPHY, S. R. SCHACH, AND C. W. MCDONALD, "Rapid Prototyping, Bottom-Up Design, and Reusable Modules: A Case Study," *ACM Mid-Southeast Summer Meeting*, Nashville, TN, May 1988.

[Boehm, Gray, and Seewaldt, 1984] B. W. BOEHM, T. E. GRAY, AND T. SEEWALDT, "Prototyping versus Specifying: A Multi-Project Experiment," *IEEE Transactions on Software Engineering* **SE-10** (May 1984), pp. 290–303.

[Brooks, 1975] F. P. BROOKS, JR., *The Mythical Man-Month: Essays on Software Engineering*, Addison-Wesley, Reading, MA, 1975. Twentieth Anniversary Edition, Addison-Wesley, Reading, MA, 1995.

[Browne, 1994] D. BROWNE, *STUDIO: STructured User-interface Design for Interaction Optimization*, Prentice Hall, Englewood Cliffs, NJ, 1994.

[Capper, Colgate, Hunter, and James, 1994] N. P. CAPPER, R. J. COLGATE, J. C. HUNTER, AND M. F. JAMES, "The Impact of Object-Oriented Technology on Software Quality: Three Case Histories," *IBM Systems Journal* **33** (No. 1, 1994), pp. 131–57.

[Connell and Shafer, 1989] J. L. CONNELL AND L. SHAFER, *Structured Rapid Prototyping: An Evolutionary Approach to Software Development*, Yourdon Press, Englewood Cliffs, NJ, 1989.

[Coomber and Childs, 1990] C. J. COOMBER AND R. E. CHILDS, "A Graphical Tool for the Prototyping of Real-Time Systems," *ACM SIGSOFT Software Engineering Notes* **15** (April 1990), pp. 70–82.

[Davis, 1993] A. M. DAVIS, "Software Requirements: Objects, Functions, and States," Revised Edition, Prentice Hall, Englewood Cliffs, NJ, 1993.

[Dix, Finlay, Abowd, and Beale, 1993] A. DIX, J. FINLAY, G. ABOWD, AND R. BEALE, *Human-Computer Interaction*, Prentice Hall, Englewood Cliffs , NJ, 1993.

[Gane, 1989] C. GANE, *Rapid System Development: Using Structured Techniques and Relational Technology*, Prentice Hall, Englewood Cliffs , NJ, 1989.

[Gause and Weinberg, 1990] D. GAUSE AND G. WEINBERG, *Are Your Lights On? How to Figure out What the Problem Really Is*, Dorset House, New York, 1990.

[Gentner and Grudin, 1996] D. R. GENTNER AND J. GRUDIN, "Design Models for Computer-Human Interfaces," *IEEE Computer* **29** (June 1996), pp. 28–35.

[Gibson and Jackson, 1987] C. F. GIBSON AND B. B. JACKSON, *The Information Imperative: Managing the Impact of Information Technology on Business and People*, Lexington Books, Lexington, MA, 1987.

[Gordon and Bieman, 1995] V. S. GORDON AND J. M. BIEMAN, "Rapid Prototyping Lessons Learned," *IEEE Software* **12** (January 1995), pp. 85–95.

[Karlsson and Ryan, 1997] J. KARLSSON AND K. RYAN, "A Cost-Value Approach for Prioritizing Requirements," *IEEE Software* **14** (September/October 1997), pp. 67–74.

[Lantz, 1985] K. E. LANTZ, *The Prototyping Methodology*, Prentice Hall, Englewood Cliffs, NJ, 1985.

[Lichter, Schneider-Hufschmidt, and Züllighoven, 1994] H. LICHTER, M. SCHNEIDER-HUFSCHMIDT, AND H. ZÜLLIGHOVEN, "Prototyping in Industrial Software Projects—Bridging the Gap between Theory and Practice," *IEEE Transactions on Software Engineering* **20** (November 1994), pp. 825–32.

[Luqi, 1989] LUQI, "Software Evolution through Rapid Prototyping," *IEEE Computer* **22** (May 1989), pp. 13–25.

[Luqi and Royce, 1992] LUQI AND W. ROYCE, "Status Report: Computer-Aided Prototyping," *IEEE Software* **9** (November 1992), pp. 77–81.

[Myers and Rosson, 1992] B. A. MYERS AND M. B. ROSSON, "Survey on User Interface Programming," *Proceedings of ACM SIGCHI Conference on Human Factors in Computing Systems*, Monterey, CA, May 1992, pp. 195–202.

[Nielsen, 1993] J. NIELSEN, "Iterative User-Interface Design," *IEEE Computer* **26** (November 1993), pp. 32–41.

[Preece, 1994] J. PREECE, *Human-Computer Interaction*, Addison-Wesley, Reading, MA, 1994.

[Rettig, 1994] M. RETTIG, "Prototyping for Tiny Fingers," *Communications of the ACM* **37** (April 1994), pp. 21–27.

[Schach and Wood, 1986] S. R. SCHACH AND P. T. WOOD, "An Almost Path-Free Very High-Level Interactive Data Manipulation Language for a Microcomputer-Based Database System," *Software–Practice and Experience* **16** (March 1986), pp. 243–68.

[Thayer and Dorfman, 1990] R. THAYER AND M. DORFMAN, *Tutorial: System and Software Requirements Engineering*, IEEE Computer Society Press, Los Alamitos, CA, 1990.

[Wood and Silver, 1994] J. WOOD AND D. SILVER, *Joint Application Design: How to Design Quality Software in 40% Less Time*, Second Edition, John Wiley and Sons, 1994.

chapter

10

SPECIFICATION PHASE

A specification document must satisfy two mutually contradictory requirements. On the one hand, it is important that this document be clear and intelligible to the client, who is probably not a computer specialist. After all, the client is paying for the product, and unless the client believes that he or she really understands what the new product will be like, there is a good chance that the client will either decide not to authorize the development of the product or will ask some other software organization to build it.

On the other hand, the specification document must be complete and detailed because it is virtually the sole source of information available to the design team for drawing up the design. Even if the client agrees that all needs have been accurately determined during the requirements phase, if the specification document contains faults such as omissions, contradictions, and ambiguities, the inevitable result will be faults in the design that will be carried over into the implementation. What is needed, therefore, are techniques for representing the target product in a format that is sufficiently nontechnical to be intelligible to the client, yet at the same time precise enough to result in a fault-free product being delivered to the client at the end of the development cycle. These specification techniques are the subject of this and the next chapter. The emphasis in this chapter is on structured specification techniques, whereas Chapter 11 is devoted to object-oriented analysis.

10.1 THE SPECIFICATION DOCUMENT

Virtually every specification document incorporates constraints that the product has to satisfy. There is almost always a deadline specified for delivering the product. Another common stipulation is "The product shall be installed in such a way that it can run in parallel with the existing product" until the client is satisfied that the new product indeed satisfies every aspect of the specification document. Other constraints might include portability, namely, that the product be constructed to run on other hardware under the same operating system or perhaps run under a variety of different operating systems. Reliability may be another constraint. If the product has to monitor patients in an intensive care unit, then it is of paramount importance that it should be fully operational 24 hours a day. Rapid response time may be another requirement; a typical constraint in this category might be "95 percent of all queries of Type 4 shall be answered within 0.25 seconds." Many response-time constraints have to be expressed in probabilistic terms because the response time depends on the current load on the computer. In contrast, so-called hard real-time constraints are expressed in absolute terms. For instance, it is useless to develop software that informs a warplane pilot of an incoming missile within 0.25 seconds only 95 percent of the time—the product must meet the constraint 100 percent of the time.

A vital component of the specification document is the set of acceptance criteria. It is important from the viewpoint of both the client and the developer to spell out a series of tests that can later be used to prove that the product does indeed satisfy its specifications and that the developer's job is done. Some of the acceptance criteria may be restatements of the constraints, whereas others will address different issues. For example, the client might supply the developer with a description of the data that the product will handle. An appropriate acceptance criterion would then be that the product correctly processes data of this type and filters out nonconforming (that is, erroneous) data.

The specification document is a contract between client and developer. It specifies precisely what the product must do and the constraints on the product. Once the development team fully understands the problem, possible solution strategies can be suggested. A *solution strategy* is a general approach to building the product. For example, one possible solution strategy for a product would be to use an online database; another would be to use conventional flat files and to extract the required information using overnight batch runs. When determining solution strategies it is often a good idea to come up with strategies without worrying about the constraints in the specification document. Then the various solution strategies can be evaluated in the light of the constraints and necessary modifications can be made. There are a number of ways of determining whether a specific solution strategy will satisfy the client's constraints. An obvious one is prototyping, which can be a good technique for resolving issues relating to user interfaces and timing constraints, as previously discussed in Section 3.6. Other techniques for determining whether constraints will be satisfied include simulation [Banks, Carson, and Nelson, 1995] and analytic network modeling [Jain, 1991].

During this process a number of solution strategies will be put forward and then discarded. It is important that a written record be kept of all discarded strategies and the reasons they were rejected. This will assist the development team if they are ever called upon to justify their chosen strategy. But more importantly, there is an ever-present danger during the maintenance phase that the process of enhancement will be accompanied by an attempt to come up with a new and unwise solution strategy. Having a record of why certain strategies were rejected during development can be extremely helpful during maintenance.

By this point the development team will have determined one or more possible solution strategies that satisfy the constraints. A two-stage decision now has to be made. First, whether the client should be advised to computerize, and if so, which of the viable solution strategies should be adopted. The answer to the first question can best be decided on the basis of cost–benefit analysis (Section 4.7). Second, if the client decides to proceed with the project, then the client must inform the development team as to the optimization criterion to be used, such as minimizing the total cost to the client or maximizing the return on investment. The developers will then advise the client as to which of the viable solution strategies will best satisfy the optimization criterion.

10.2 INFORMAL SPECIFICATIONS

In many development projects, the specification document consists of page after page of English, or some other natural language such as French or Xhosa. A typical paragraph of such a specification document reads:

> BV.4.2.5. If the sales for the current month are below the target sales, then a report is to be printed, unless the difference between target sales and actual sales is less than half of the difference between target sales and actual sales in the previous month or if the difference between target sales and actual sales for the current month is under 5 percent.

The background leading up to that paragraph is as follows. The management of a retail chain sets a target sales figure for each shop for each month, and if a shop does not meet this target, then a report is to be printed. Consider the following scenario: Suppose that the January sales target for one particular shop is $100,000, but actual sales are only $64,000, that is, 36 percent below target. In this case, a report must be printed. Now suppose further that the February target figure is $120,000 and that actual sales are only $100,000, 16.7 percent below target. Although sales are below the target figure, the percentage difference for February, namely, 16.7 percent, is less than half of the previous month's percentage difference, namely, 36 percent; management believes that an improvement has been made, and no report is to be printed. Next suppose that in March the target is again $100,000 but the shop makes $98,000, only 2 percent below target. Because the percentage difference is small, less than 5 percent, no report should be printed.

Careful rereading of the preceding specification paragraph shows some divergence from what the retail chain's management actually requested. Paragraph BV.4.2.5 speaks of the "difference between target sales and actual sales"; percentage difference is not mentioned. The difference in January was $36,000 and in February it was $20,000. The percentage difference, which is what management wanted, dropped from 36 percent in January to 16.7 percent in February, less than half of the January percentage difference. However, the actual difference dropped from $36,000 to $20,000, which is greater than half of $36,000. So if the development team had faithfully implemented the specification document, the report would have been printed, which is not what management wanted. Then the last clause speaks of a "difference ... [of] 5 percent." What is meant, of course, is a percentage difference of 5 percent, only the word percentage does not occur anywhere in the paragraph.

There are thus a number of faults in the specification document. First, the wishes of the client have been ignored. Second, there is ambiguity—should the last clause read "percentage difference . . . [of] 5 percent," or "difference . . . [of] $5,000," or something else entirely? In addition, the style is poor. What the paragraph says is "If something happens, print a report. However, if something else happens, don't print it. And if a third thing happens, don't print it either." It would have been much clearer if the specifications had simply stated when the report is to be printed. All in all, paragraph BV.4.2.5 is not a very good example of how to write a specification document.

In fact, paragraph BV.4.2.5 is fictitious, but it is, unfortunately, typical of too many specification documents. The reader may think that the example is unfair and that this sort of problem cannot arise if specifications are written with care by professional specification writers. To refute this charge, the case study of Chapter 5 is resumed below.

10.2.1 CASE STUDY: TEXT PROCESSING

Recall from Section 5.5.2 that in 1969 Naur published a paper on correctness proving [Naur, 1969]. He illustrated his technique by means of a text-processing problem. Using his technique, Naur constructed an ALGOL 60 procedure to solve the problem and informally proved the correctness of his procedure. A reviewer of Naur's paper pointed out one fault in the procedure [Leavenworth, 1970]. London then detected three additional faults in Naur's procedure and presented a corrected version of the procedure and proved its correctness formally [London, 1971]. Goodenough and Gerhart then found three further faults that London had not detected [Goodenough and Gerhart, 1975]. Of the total of seven faults collectively detected by the reviewer, London, and Goodenough and Gerhart, two can be considered as specification faults. For example, Naur's specifications do not state what happens if the input includes two successive adjacent breaks (blank or newline characters). For this reason, Goodenough and Gerhart then produced a new set of specifications. Their specifications were about four times longer than Naur's, which are given in Section 5.5.2.

In 1985 Meyer wrote an article on formal specification techniques [Meyer, 1985]. The main thrust of his article is that specifications written in a natural language such as English tend to have contradictions, ambiguities, and omissions. He recommended using mathematical terminology to express specifications formally. Meyer detected some 12 faults in Goodenough and Gerhart's specifications and then developed a set of mathematical specifications to correct all the problems. Meyer then paraphrased his mathematical specifications and constructed English specifications. In the author's opinion, Meyer's English specifications contain a fault. Meyer points out in his paper that if the maximum number of characters per line is, say, 10, and the input is, for instance, WHO WHAT WHEN, then, in terms of both Naur's and Goodenough and Gerhart's specifications, there are two equally valid outputs, namely, WHO WHAT on the first line and WHEN on the second, or WHO on the first line and WHAT WHEN on the second. In fact, Meyer's paraphrased English specifications also contain this ambiguity.

The key point is that Goodenough and Gerhart's specifications were constructed with the greatest of care. After all, the reason they were constructed was to correct Naur's specifications. Furthermore, Goodenough and Gerhart's paper went through two versions, the first of which was published in the proceedings of a refereed conference and the second in a refereed journal [Goodenough and Gerhart, 1975]. Finally, both Goodenough and Gerhart are experts in software engineering in general, and specifications in particular. Thus, if two experts with as much time as they needed carefully produced specifications in which Meyer detected 12 faults, what chance does an ordinary computer professional working under time pressure have of producing a fault-free specification document? Worse still, the text-processing problem can be coded in 25 or 30 lines, whereas real-world products can consist of hundreds of thousands or even millions of lines of source code.

It is clear that natural language is not a good way of specifying a product. In this chapter better alternatives are described. The order in which the specification techniques are presented is from the informal to the more formal.

10.3 STRUCTURED SYSTEMS ANALYSIS

The use of graphics to specify software was an important technique of the 1970s. Three techniques making uses of graphics became particularly popular, namely, those of DeMarco [DeMarco, 1978], Gane and Sarsen [Gane and Sarsen, 1979], and Yourdon and Constantine [Yourdon and Constantine, 1979]. The three techniques are all equally good and are essentially equivalent. Gane and Sarsen's approach is presented here because their notation is currently probably the most widely used in the industry.

As an aid to understanding the technique, consider the following example.

10.3.1 SALLY'S SOFTWARE SHOP

Sally's Software Shop buys software from various suppliers and sells it to the public. Sally stocks popular software packages and orders others as required. Sally extends credit to institutions, corporations, and some individuals. Sally's Software Shop is doing well, with a monthly turnover of 300 packages at an average retail cost of $250 each. Despite her business success, Sally has been advised to computerize. Should she?

The question, as stated, is inadequate. It should read: Which, if any, business functions, namely, accounts payable, accounts receivable, and inventory, should be computerized? Even this is not enough—is the system to be batch or online? Is there to be an in-house computer or is outsourcing to be used? But even if the question is refined further, it still misses the fundamental issue: What is Sally's objective in computerizing her business?

Only when Sally's objectives are known can the analysis continue. For example, if she wishes to computerize simply because she sells software, then she needs an in-house system with a variety of sound and light effects that ostentatiously shows off the possibilities of a computer. On the other hand, if she uses her business to launder "hot" money, then she needs a product that keeps four or five different sets of books and does not have an audit trail.

This example assumes that Sally wishes to computerize "in order to make more money." This does not help very much, but it is clear that cost–benefit analysis can determine whether or not to computerize each (or any) of the three sections of her business.

The main danger of many standard approaches is that one is tempted to come up with the solution first, for example, a Lime III computer with a 4-Gigabyte hard disk and a laser printer, and find out what the problem is later! In contrast, Gane and Sarsen use a nine-step technique to analyze the client's needs [Gane and Sarsen, 1979]. An important point is that stepwise refinement is used in many of those nine steps; this will be indicated as the technique is demonstrated.

Having determined Sally's requirements, the first step in the structured systems analysis is to determine the *logical data flow,* as opposed to the physical data flow (that is, *what* happens, as opposed to *how* it happens). This is done by drawing a data flow diagram (DFD). The DFD uses the four basic symbols shown in Figure 10.1. (The notation of Gane and Sarsen is similar, but not identical, to that of DeMarco [DeMarco, 1978] and that of Yourdon and Constantine [Yourdon and Constantine, 1979].)

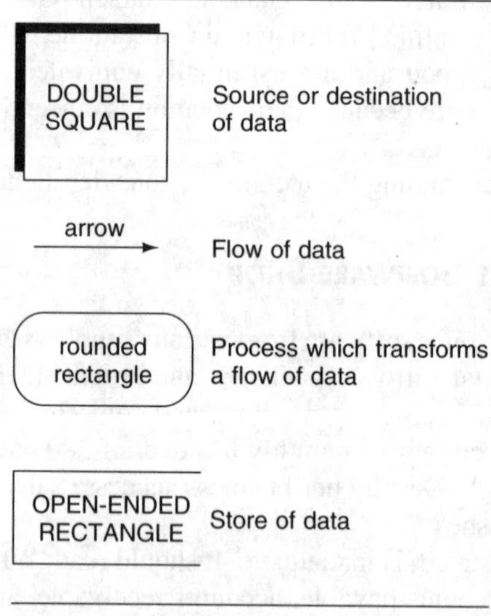

Figure 10.1 Symbols of Gane and Sarsen's structured systems analysis.

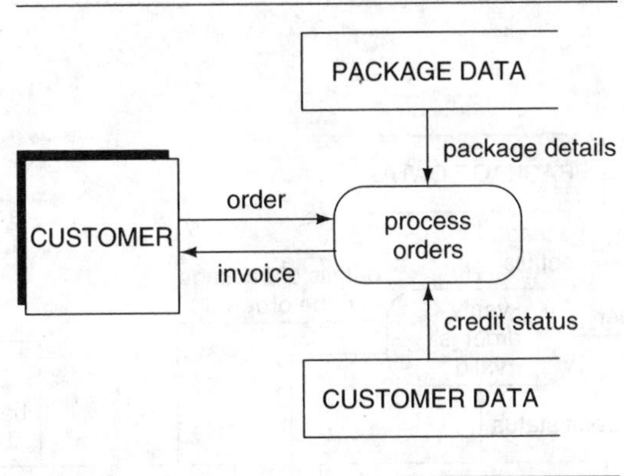

Figure 10.2 Data flow diagram: first refinement.

Step 1. Draw the DFD The DFD for any nontrivial product is likely to be large. The DFD is a pictorial representation of all aspects of the logical data flow and as such is guaranteed to contain considerably more than 7 ± 2 elements. For this reason, the DFD must be developed by stepwise refinement (Section 4.6). Returning to the example, the first refinement is shown in Figure 10.2.

This diagram of *logical data flow* can have many interpretations. Two possible implementations are as follows:

Implementation 1. Data store PACKAGE DATA consists of some 900 boxes containing diskettes displayed on shelves, as well as a number of catalogs in a desk drawer. Data store CUSTOMER DATA is a collection of 5 × 7 cards held together by a rubber band, plus a list of customers whose payments are overdue. Process (action) process orders is Sally looking for the appropriate package on the shelves, if necessary looking it up in a catalog, then finding the correct 5 × 7 card and checking that the customer's name is not on the list of defaulters. This implementation is totally manual and corresponds to the way Sally currently conducts her business.

Implementation 2. Data stores PACKAGE DATA and CUSTOMER DATA are computer files and process orders is Sally entering the customer's name and the name of the package at a terminal. This implementation corresponds to a fully computerized solution with all information available online.

The DFD of Figure 10.2 represents not only the preceding two implementations, but also literally an infinity of other possibilities. The key point is that the DFD represents a flow of information—the actual package that Sally's customer wants is not important to the flow.

The DFD is now refined stepwise. The second refinement is depicted in Figure 10.3. Now when the customer requests a package that Sally does not have on hand, details of that package are placed in the data store PENDING ORDERS, which might be a computer file, but at this stage could equally well be a manila folder. Data store PENDING ORDERS is scanned daily, by the computer or by Sally, and if there are sufficient orders for one supplier, then a batched

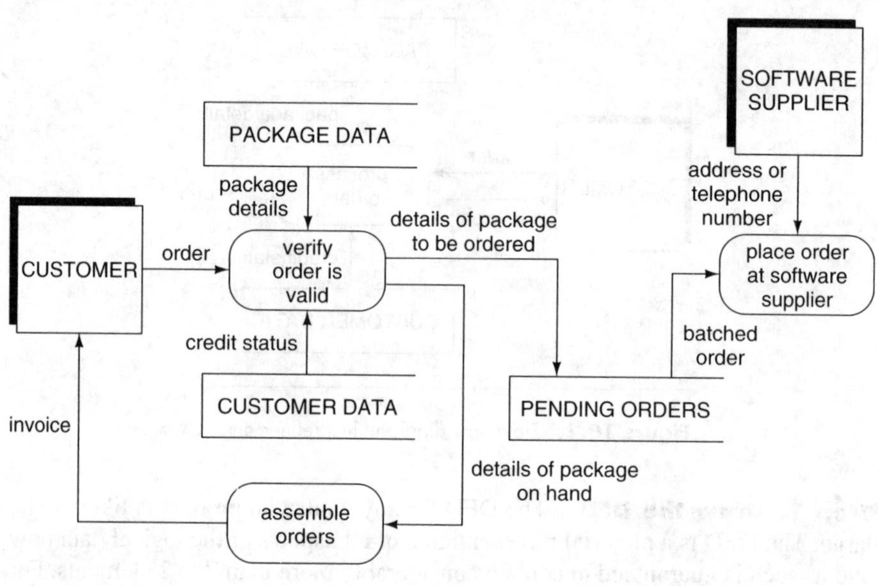

Figure 10.3 Data flow diagram: second refinement.

order is placed. Also, if an order has been waiting for 5 working days, it is ordered, regardless of how many packages are waiting to be ordered from the relevant supplier. This DFD does not show the logical flow of data when the software package arrives from the supplier, nor does it show financial functions such as accounts payable and accounts receivable. These will be added in the third refinement.

Only a portion of the third refinement is shown in Figure 10.4 because the DFD is starting to become large. The rest of the DFD relates to accounts payable and to the software suppliers. The final DFD will be larger still, stretching over perhaps six pages. But it will be easily understood by Sally who will sign it off, confirming that it is an accurate representation of the logical flow of data in her business.

Of course, for a larger product the DFD will be larger. After a certain point it becomes impractical to have just one DFD, and a hierarchy of DFDs is needed. A single box at one level is expanded into a complete DFD at a lower level. A difficulty with this approach frequently arises as a consequence of the positioning of sources and destinations of data. For instance, a particular process p may be reflected at level L and expanded at level L+1. The correct place for the sources and destinations of data for process p is level L+1, because that is where they are used. But a client, even one who is experienced in reading a DFD, frequently cannot understand the DFD at level L because the sources and destinations of data relating to process p appear to be missing. In order to prevent this confusion, it is sometimes advisable to draw the correct DFD and then modify it by moving

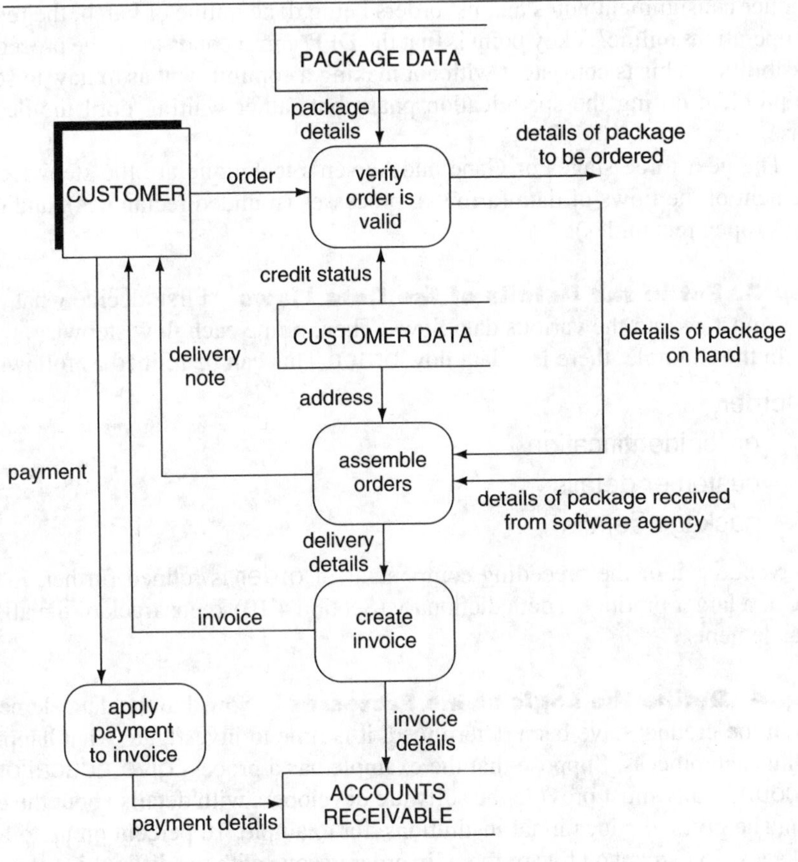

Figure 10.4 Data flow diagram: part of third refinement.

sources and destinations of data one or more levels up so that the client will not be confused.

Step 2. Decide What Sections to Computerize and How (Batch or Online) The choice of what to automate often depends on how much the client is prepared to spend. Obviously, it would be nice to automate the entire operation, but the cost of this may be prohibitive. In order to determine which sections to automate, cost–benefit analysis is applied to the various possible strategies for computerizing each section. For example, for each section of the DFD a decision has to be made as to whether that group of operations should be performed in batch or online. With large volumes to process and tight controls required, batch processing is often the answer, but with small volumes and an in-house computer, online processing appears to be better. Returning to the example, one alternative is to automate accounts payable in batch and to perform validation of orders online. A second alternative is to automate everything, with the editing of the software supplier consignment notes against orders being done online or batch, the rest of the operations online. A key point is that the DFD corresponds to all the preceding possibilities. This is consistent with not making a commitment as to how to solve the problem during the specification phase but rather waiting until the design phase.

The next three stages of Gane and Sarsen's technique are the stepwise refinement of the flows of data (arrows), processes (rounded rectangles), and data stores (open rectangles).

Step 3. Put in the Details of the Data Flows First, decide what data items must go into the various data flows. Then, refine each flow stepwise.

In the example, there is a data flow order. This can be refined as follows:

order:
  order identification
  customer details
  package details

Next, each of the preceding components of order is refined further. In the case of a larger product, a data dictionary (Section 4.10) keeps track of the all the data elements.

Step 4. Define the Logic of the Processes Now that the data elements within the product have been determined, it is time to investigate what happens within each process. Suppose that the example has a process give educational discount. Sally must provide the software developers with details about the discount she gives to educational institutions, for example, 10 percent on up to four packages, 15 percent on five or more. In order to cope with the difficulties of natural language specification documents, this should be translated from English into a decision tree. Such a tree is shown in Figure 10.5.

A decision tree makes it easy to check that all possibilities have been taken into account, especially in more complex cases. An example is shown in Figure 10.6. From Figure 10.6 it is immediately obvious that the cost to an alumnus

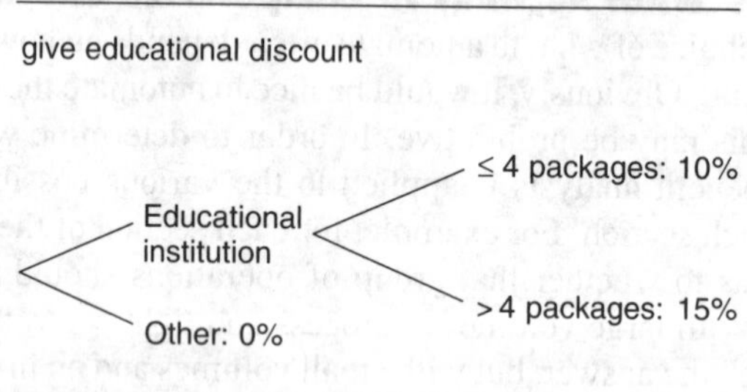

Figure 10.5 Decision tree depicting Sally's Software Shop educational discount policy.

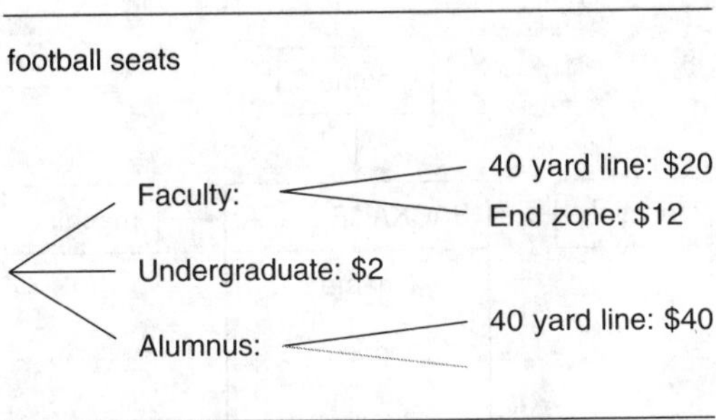

Figure 10.6 Decision tree describing seating prices for college football games.

of a seat behind the end zone has not been specified. Another good way of representing processes is with decision tables [Pollack, Hicks, and Harrison, 1971]. Decision tables have an advantage over decision trees in that CASE tools exist that allow the contents of a decision table to be entered automatically into a computer, thereby obviating the need to code that part of the product.

Step 5. Define the Data Stores At this stage it is necessary to define the exact contents of each store and its representation (format). Thus, if the product is to be implemented in COBOL, this information must be provided down to the **pic** level; if Ada is to be used, the **digits** or **delta** must be specified. In addition, it is necessary to specify where immediate access is required.

The issue of immediate access depends on what queries are going to be put to the product. For example, suppose that in the example it is decided to validate orders online. A customer may order a package by name ("Do you have Lotus 1-2-3 in stock?"), by function ("What accounting packages do you have?"), or by machine ("Do you have anything new for the 686?"), but rarely by price ("What do you have for $149.50?"). Thus immediate access to PACKAGE DATA is required by name, function, and machine. This is depicted in the data immediate-access diagram (DIAD) of Figure 10.7.

Step 6. Define the Physical Resources Now that the developers know what is required online and the representation (format) of each element, a decision can be made regarding blocking factors. In addition, for each file the following can be specified: file name; organization (sequential, indexed, etc.); storage medium; and records, down to the field level. If a database management system (DBMS) is to be used, then the relevant information for each table is specified here.

Step 7. Determine the Input/Output Specifications The input forms must be specified, at least with respect to components, if not detailed layout. Input screens must similarly be determined. The printed output must also be specified, where possible in detail, otherwise just estimated length.

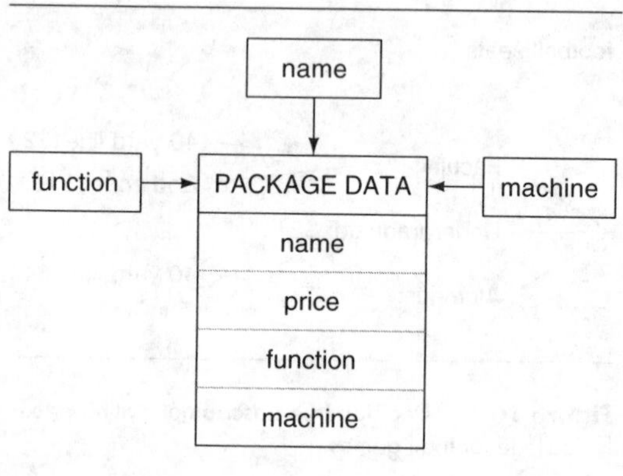

Figure 10.7 Data immediate-access diagram (DIAD) for PACKAGE DATA.

Step 8. Perform Sizing Now it is necessary to compute the numerical data that will be used in step 9 to determine the hardware requirements. This includes the volume of input (daily or hourly), the frequency of each printed report and its deadline, the size and number of records of each type that are to pass between the CPU and mass storage, and the size of each file.

Step 9. Determine the Hardware Requirements From the sizing information on the disk files determined in step 8, mass storage requirements can be computed. In addition, mass storage requirements for back-up purposes can also be determined. From knowledge of input volumes, the needs in this area can be found. Because the number of lines and frequency of printed reports is known, output devices can be specified. If the client already has hardware, it can be determined whether this hardware will be adequate or if additional hardware will have to be purchased. On the other hand, if the client does not have suitable hardware, a recommendation can be made as to what should be acquired, and whether it should be purchased or leased.

Determining the hardware requirements is the ninth and final step of Gane and Sarsen's specification technique, and the example is therefore concluded. After approval by the client, the resulting specification document is handed to the design team, and the software process continues.

Despite its many strengths, Gane and Sarsen's technique does not provide the answer to every question. For example, it cannot be used to determine response times. The number of input/output channels can at best be roughly gauged. Also, CPU size and timing cannot be estimated with any degree of accuracy. These are distinct drawbacks of Gane and Sarsen's technique and, to be fair, virtually every other technique for either specification or design. Nonetheless, at the end of the specification phase, hardware decisions have to be made, whether or not accurate information is available. This situation is considerably better than what was done in the past; before methodical approaches to specifying were put forward, decisions regarding hardware were made right at the beginning of the software development process. Gane and Sarsen's technique has led to major improvements in the ways that products are specified, and the fact that Gane and Sarsen and the authors of most competing techniques essentially ignore time as a variable should not detract from the advantages that these techniques have brought to the software industry.

10.4 OTHER SEMIFORMAL TECHNIQUES

Gane and Sarsen's technique is clearly more formal than writing a specification in a natural language. At the same time, it is less formal than many of the techniques presented in the following discussion, such as Petri nets (Section 10.7) and Z (Section 10.8). Dart and her co-workers classify specification and design techniques as informal, semiformal, or formal [Dart, Ellison, Feiler, and Habermann, 1987]. In terms of this classification Gane and Sarsen's structured systems analysis is a semiformal technique, whereas the other two techniques mentioned in this paragraph are formal techniques.

Structured systems analysis is widely used; there is a good chance that the reader may be employed by an organization that uses structured systems analysis or some variant of it. However, there are many other good semiformal techniques; see, for example, the proceedings of the various International Workshops on Software Specification and Design. Because of space limitations, all that will be given here is a brief description of a few well-known techniques.

PSL/PSA [Teichroew and Hershey, 1977] is a computer-aided technique for specifying information processing products. The name comes from the two components of the technique, namely, the problem statement language (PSL) that is used to describe the product, and the problem statement analyzer (PSA) that enters the PSL description into a database and produces reports on request. PSL/PSA is widely used, particularly for documenting products.

SADT [Ross, 1985] consists of two interrelated components, a box-and-arrow diagramming language termed structural analysis (SA) and a design technique (DT)—hence the name SADT. Stepwise refinement underlies SADT to a greater extent than with Gane and Sarsen's technique; a conscious effort has been made to adhere to Miller's law. As Ross puts it, "Everything worth saying, about anything worth saying something about, must be expressed in six or fewer pieces" [Ross, 1985]. SADT has been used successfully in specifying a wide variety of products, especially complex, large-scale projects. Like many other similar semiformal techniques, its applicability to real-time systems is less clear.

On the other hand, SREM (software requirements engineering method, pronounced "shrem") was explicitly designed for specifying the conditions under which certain actions are to occur [Alford, 1985]. For this reason SREM has been particularly useful for specifying real-time systems and has been extended to distributed systems. SREM consists of a number of components. RSL is a specification language. REVS is a set of tools that perform a variety of specification-related tasks such as translating the RSL specifications into an automated database, automatically checking for data flow consistency (ensuring that no data item is used before it has been assigned a value), and generating simulators from the specifications that can be used to ensure that the specifications are correct. In addition, SREM has a design technique named DCDS, distributed computing design system.

The power of SREM comes from the fact that the model underlying the whole technique is a finite state machine (FSM), described in Section 10.6. As a result of this formal model underlying SREM, it is possible to perform the consistency checking mentioned previously and also to verify that performance constraints on the product as a whole can be met, given the performance of individual components. SREM has been used by the U.S. Air Force to specify two C^3I (command, control, communications, and intelligence) systems [Scheffer, Stone, and Rzepka, 1985]. Although SREM proved to be of great use in the specification phase, it appears that the REVS tools employed later in the development cycle were considered to be less useful.

10.5 ENTITY-RELATIONSHIP MODELING

The emphasis in structured systems analysis is on the actions, rather than the data, of the product to be built. It is certainly true that the data of the product are also modeled, but the data are secondary to the actions. In contrast, entity-relationship modeling (ERM) is a semiformal data-oriented technique for specifying a product. It is widely used for specifying databases. In that application area, the emphasis is on the data. Of course, actions are needed to access the data, and the database must be organized in such a way as to minimize access times. Nevertheless, the actions that are performed on the data are less significant.

Entity-relationship modeling is not a new technique; it is has been widely used since 1976 [Chen, 1976; 1983]. Now it is undergoing a new lease of life, because entity-relationship modeling is one element of object-oriented analysis, described in detail in Chapter 11.

A simple entity-relationship diagram is shown in Figure 10.8. This diagram models the relationships between authors, autobiographies, and readers. There are three entities, namely, Author, Autobiography, and Reader. The top relationship, namely, writes, reflects the fact that an author writes an autobiography. This is a one-to-many relationship, because one author can write more than one autobiography; this is reflected by the 1 next to Author and the n next to Autobiography. The entity-relationship diagram also shows two relationships between Autobiography and Reader. Both are one-to-many relationships. The relationship on the left models the fact that a reader may have read many autobiographies. Similarly, as shown on the right, a reader may own many autobiographies. Two separate relationships are shown because a reader can read an autobiography without owning it, and a reader can buy an autobiography but not read it.

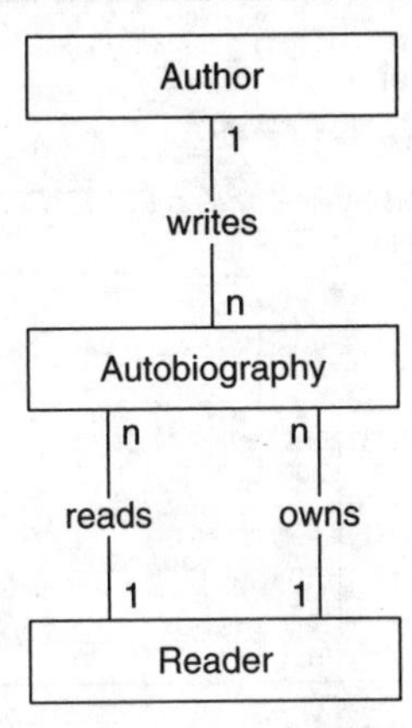

Figure 10.8 Simple entity-relationship diagram.

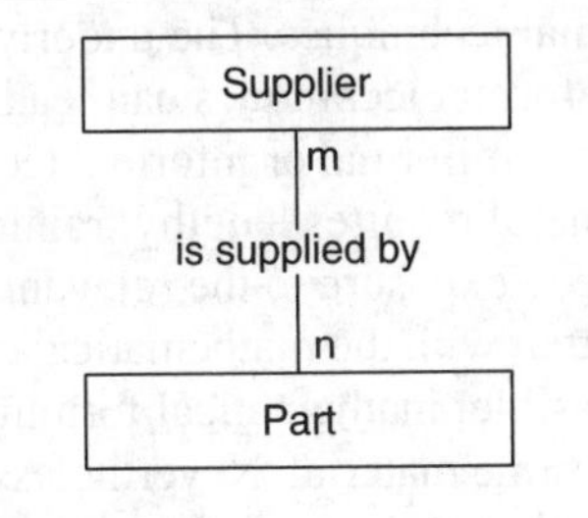

Figure 10.9 Many-to-many entity-relationship diagram.

The next example is taken from the domain of suppliers and the parts they supply. Figure 10.9 shows a many-to-many relationship between parts and suppliers. That is, one supplier supplies many parts and, conversely, a specific part can be obtained from many suppliers. This many-to-many relationship is reflected by the m next to entity Supplier and the n next to entity Part.

More complex relationships are also possible. For example, as shown in Figure 10.10, a Part may in turn be viewed as consisting of a number of component Parts. Also, many-to-many-to-many relationships are possible. Consider the three entities Supplier, Part, and Project shown in that figure. A particular part may be supplied by several suppliers depending on the project. Also, the various parts supplied for a specific project may come from different suppliers. A many-to-many-to-many relationship is necessary to model such a situation accurately.

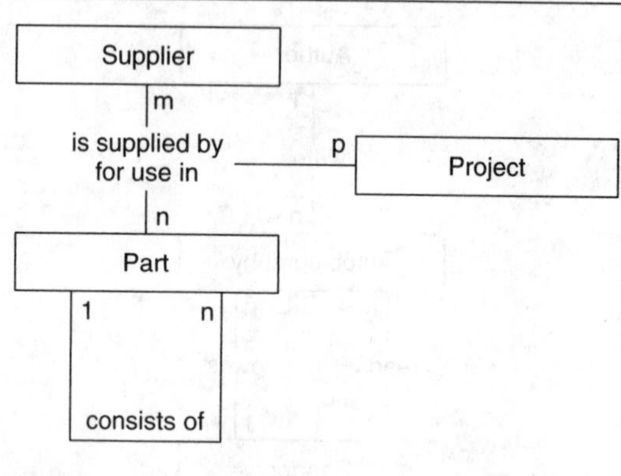

Figure 10.10 More complex entity-relationship diagram.

Entity-relationship modeling is discussed further in the following chapter, which describes object-oriented analysis, another semiformal technique. The next topic of this chapter is formal techniques. The underlying theme of the next four sections is that employing formal techniques can lead to more precise specifications than are possible with semiformal or informal techniques. However, the use of formal techniques in general requires lengthy training, and software engineers using formal techniques need exposure to the relevant mathematics. The following sections have been written with the mathematical content kept to a minimum. Furthermore, wherever possible, mathematical formulations are preceded by informal presentations of the same material. Nevertheless, the level of Sections 10.6 through 10.9 is higher than that of the rest of the book.

10.6 FINITE STATE MACHINES

Consider the following example, originally formulated by the M202 team at the Open University, U.K. [Brady, 1977]. A safe has a combination lock that can be in one of three positions, labeled 1, 2, and 3. The dial can be turned left or right (L or R). Thus at any time there are six possible dial movements, namely, 1L, 1R, 2L, 2R, 3L, and 3R. The combination to the safe is 1L, 3R, 2L; any other dial movement will cause the alarm to go off. The situation is depicted in Figure 10.11. There is one initial state, namely, Safe Locked. If the input is 1L, then the next state is A, but if any other dial movement, 1R, say, or 3L, is made, then the next state is Sound Alarm, one of the two final states. If the correct combination is chosen, then the sequence of transitions is from Safe Locked to A to B to Safe Unlocked, the other final state. What is shown in Figure 10.11 is a state transition diagram (STD) of a finite state machine (FSM). It is not necessary to depict a STD graphically; the same information is shown in tabular form in

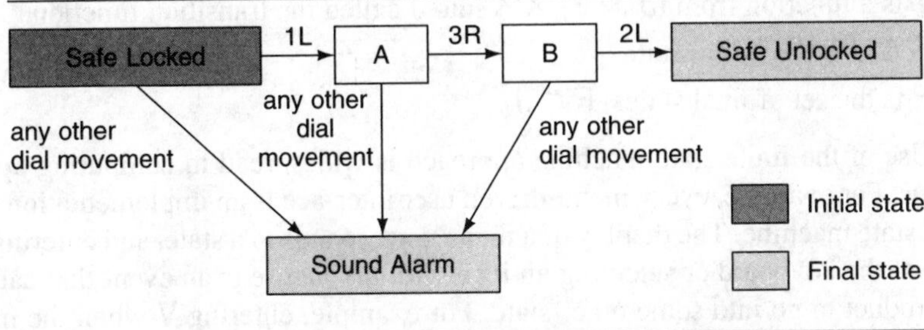

Figure 10.11 Finite state machine representation of combination safe.

Table of Next States

Dial movement \ Current state	Safe locked	A	B
1L	A	Sound Alarm	Sound Alarm
1R	Sound Alarm	Sound Alarm	Sound Alarm
2L	Sound Alarm	Sound Alarm	Safe Unlocked
2R	Sound Alarm	Sound Alarm	Sound Alarm
3L	Sound Alarm	Sound Alarm	Sound Alarm
3R	Sound Alarm	B	Sound Alarm

Figure 10.12 Transition table for finite state machine.

Figure 10.12. For each state other than the two final states, the transition to the next state is indicated, depending on the way the dial is moved.

A finite state machine consists of five parts: a set of states J, a set of inputs K, the transition function T that specifies the next state given the current state and the current input, the initial state S, and the set of final states F. In the case of the combination lock on the safe:

The set of states J is {Safe Locked, A, B, Safe Unlocked, Sound Alarm}.
The set of inputs K is {1L, 1R, 2L, 2R, 3L, 3R}.
The transition function T is depicted in tabular form in Figure 10.12.
The initial state S is Safe Locked.
The set of final states F is {Safe Unlocked, Sound Alarm}.

In more formal terms, a finite state machine is a 5-tuple (J, K, T, S, F), where

J is a finite, nonempty set of states.
K is a finite, nonempty set of inputs.

T is a function from $(J \sim F) \times K$ into J called the transition function.

$S \in J$ is the initial state.

F is the set of final states, $F \subseteq J$.

Use of the finite state machine approach is widespread in computing applications. For example, every menu-driven user interface is an implementation of a finite state machine. The display of a menu corresponds to a state, and entering an input at the keyboard or selecting an icon with the mouse is an event that causes the product to go into some other state. For example, entering V when the main menu appears on the screen might cause a volumetric analysis to be performed on the current data set. A new menu then appears, and the user may enter G, P, or R. Selecting G causes the results of the calculation to be graphed, P causes them to be printed, and R causes a return to the main menu. Each transition has the form

current state [menu] and **event** [option selected] $\Longrightarrow$ **next state** **(10.1)**

For the purposes of specifying a product, a useful extension of FSMs is to add a sixth component to the preceding 5-tuple, namely, a set of predicates P, where each predicate is a function of the global state Y of the product [Kampen, 1987]. More formally, the transition function T is now a function from $(J \sim F) \times K \times P$ into J. Transition rules now have the form

current state and **event** and **predicate** $\Longrightarrow$ **next state** **(10.2)**

Finite state machines are a powerful formalism for specifying a product that can be modeled in terms of states and transitions between states. To see how this formalism works in practice, the technique will now be applied to a modified version of the so-called elevator problem; see the Just in Case You Wanted to Know box on page 347 for background information on the elevator problem.

10.6.1 ELEVATOR PROBLEM: FINITE STATE MACHINES

The problem concerns the logic required to move n elevators between floors according to the following constraints:

Constraint 1: Each elevator has a set of m buttons, one for each floor. These illuminate when pressed and cause the elevator to visit the corresponding floor. The illumination is canceled when the corresponding floor is visited by the elevator.

Constraint 2: Each floor, except the first floor and top floor, has two buttons, one to request an up-elevator and one to request a down-elevator. These buttons illuminate when pressed. The illumination is canceled when an elevator visits the floor and then moves in the desired direction.

Constraint 3: When an elevator has no requests, it remains at its current floor with its doors closed.

The product will now be specified using an extended finite state machine [Kampen, 1987]. There are two sets of buttons in the problem. In each of the

JUST IN CASE YOU WANTED TO KNOW

The elevator problem is a truly classic problem of software engineering. It first appeared in print in 1968 in Don Knuth's landmark book, *The Art of Computer Programming, Volume I, Fundamental Algorithms,* pages 280-295 [Knuth, 1968]. It is based on the single elevator in the mathematics building at the California Institute of Technology. The example was used to illustrate co-routines in the mythical language MIX.

By the mid 1980s, the elevator problem had been generalized to n elevators; in addition, specific properties of the solution had to be proved, for example, that an elevator would eventually arrive within a finite time. It was now *the* problem for researchers working in the area of formal specification languages, and any proposed formal specification language had to work for the elevator problem.

The problem attained broader prominence in 1986 when it was published in *ACM SIGSOFT Software Engineering Notes* in the Call for Papers for the Fourth International Workshop on Software Specification and Design [IWSSD, 1986]. The elevator problem was one of five problems that were to be used as examples by researchers in their submissions to the conference, held in Monterey, California, in May 1987. In the form in which it appeared in the Call for Papers, it was termed the *lift problem* and was attributed to N. [Neil] Davis of STC-IDEC [a division of Standard Telecommunications and Cable, in Stevenage, United Kingdom].

Since then, the problem has attained even wider prominence and has been used to demonstrate an extensive variety of techniques within software engineering in general, not just formal specification languages. It is used in this book to illustrate every technique because, as the reader will soon discover, the problem is by no means as simple as it looks!

---

n elevators there is a set of m buttons, one for each floor. Because these n × m buttons are inside the elevators, they will be referred to as *elevator buttons.* Then, on each floor there are two buttons, one to request an up-elevator, one to request a down-elevator. These will be referred to as *floor buttons.*

The state transition diagram (STD) for an elevator button is shown in Figure 10.13. Let EB(e, f) denote the button in elevator e that is pressed to request floor f. EB(e, f) can be in two states, namely, with the button on (illuminated) or off. More precisely, the states are

EBON(e, f): Elevator Button (e, f) ON **(10.3)**
EBOFF(e, f): Elevator Button (e, f) OFF

If the button is on and the elevator arrives at floor f, then the button is turned off. Conversely, if the button is off and it is pressed, then the button comes on.

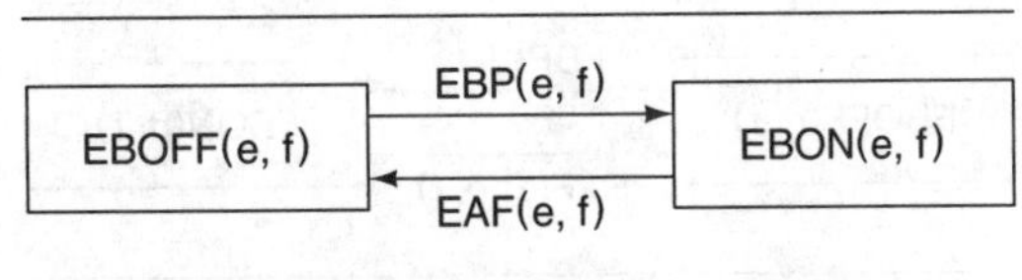

Figure 10.13 STD for elevator button [Kampen, 1987]. (©1987 IEEE)

There are thus two events involved, namely

EBP(e, f): Elevator Button (e, f) Pressed **(10.4)**
EAF(e, f): Elevator e Arrives at Floor f

In order to define the state transition rules connecting these events and states, a predicate V(e, f) is needed. (A predicate is a condition that is either true or false.)

V(e, f): Elevator e is Visiting (stopped at) floor f **(10.5)**

Now the formal transition rules can be stated. If elevator button (e, f) is off [current state] and elevator button (e, f) is pressed [event] and elevator e is not visiting floor f [predicate], then the button is turned on. In the format of transition rule (10.2) this becomes

EBOFF(e, f) and EBP(e, f) and not V(e, f) $\Longrightarrow$ EBON(e, f) **(10.6)**

If the elevator is currently visiting floor f, nothing happens. In Kampen's formalism, events that do not trigger a transition may indeed occur, but if they do then they are ignored.

Conversely, if the elevator arrives at floor f and the button is on, then it is turned off. This is expressed as

EBON(e, f) and EAF(e, f) $\Longrightarrow$ EBOFF(e, f) **(10.7)**

Now the floor buttons are considered. FB(d, f) denotes the button on floor f that requests an elevator traveling in direction d. The STD for floor button FB(d, f) is shown in Figure 10.14. More precisely, the states are

FBON(d, f): Floor Button (d, f) ON **(10.8)**
FBOFF(d, f): Floor Button (d, f) OFF

If the button is on and an elevator arrives at floor f traveling in the correct direction d, then the button is turned off. Conversely, if the button is off and it is pressed, then the button comes on. Again there are two events involved, namely

FBP(d, f): Floor Button (d, f) Pressed **(10.9)**
EAF(1..n, f): Elevator 1 or . . . or n Arrives at Floor f

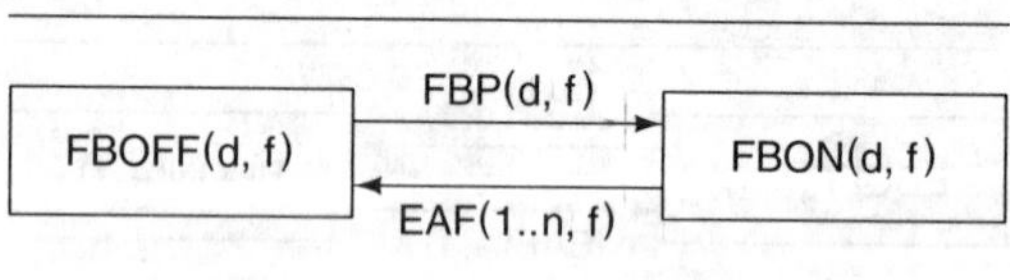

Figure 10.14 STD for floor button [Kampen, 1987]. (©1987 IEEE)

Note the use of 1..n to denote disjunction. Throughout this section an expression such as P(a, 1..n, b) denotes

P(a, 1, b) or P(a, 2, b) or... or P(a, n, b) **(10.10)**

In order to define the state transition rules connecting these events and states, a predicate is again needed. In this case it is S(d, e, f), which is defined as follows:

S(d, e, f): Elevator e is visiting floor f and the direction in which it is about to move is either up (d = U), down (d = D), or no requests are pending (d = N) **(10.11)**

This predicate is actually a state. In fact, the formalism allows both events and states to be treated as predicates.

Using S(d, e, f) the formal transition rules are then

FBOFF(d, f) and FBP(d, f) and not S(d, 1..n, f) **(10.12)**
$\Longrightarrow$ FBON(d, f),
FBON(d, f) and EAF(1..n, f) and S(d, 1..n, f)
$\Longrightarrow$ FBOFF(d, f),d = U or D

That is, if the floor button at floor f for motion in direction d is off and the button is pushed and none of the elevators are currently visiting floor f about to move in direction d, then the floor button is turned on. Conversely, if the button is on and at least one of the elevators arrives at floor f, and the elevator is about to move in direction d, then the button is turned off. The notation 1..n in S(d, 1..n, f) and EAF(1..n, f) was defined in definition (10.10). The predicate V(e, f) of definition (10.5) can be defined in terms of S(d, e, f) as follows:

V(e, f) = S(U, e, f) or S(D, e, f) or S(N, e, f) **(10.13)**

The states of the elevator button and floor button were straightforward to define. Turning now to the elevators, complications arise. The state of an elevator essentially consists of a number of component substates. Kampen identifies several, such as the elevator slowing and stopping, the door opening, the door open with a timer running, or the door closing after a timeout [Kampen, 1987]. He makes the reasonable assumption that the elevator controller (the mechanism that directs the motion of the elevator) initiates a state such as S(d, e, f) and that the controller then moves the elevator through the substates. Three elevator states can now be defined, one of which, S(d, e, f), was defined in definition (10.11), but is included here for completeness.

M(d, e, f): Elevator e is Moving in direction d (floor f is next) **(10.14)**
S(d, e, f): Elevator e is Stopped (d-bound) at floor f
W(e, f): Elevator e is Waiting at floor f (door closed)

These states are shown in Figure 10.15. Note that the three stopped states S(U, e, f), S(N, e, f), and S(D, e, f) have been grouped into one larger state in order to simplify the diagram and to reduce the overall number of states.

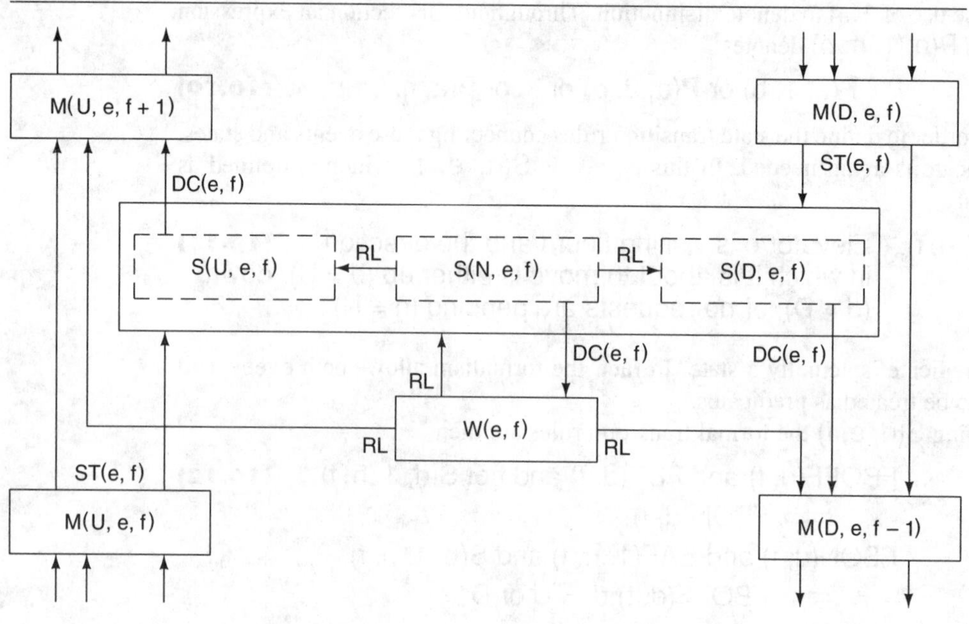

Figure 10.15 STD for elevator [Kampen, 1987]. (©1987 IEEE)

The events that can trigger state transitions are: DC(e, f), the closing of the door of elevator e at floor f; ST(e, f), which occurs when the sensor on the elevator is triggered as it nears floor f and the elevator controller must decide whether or not to stop the elevator at that floor; and RL, which occurs whenever an elevator button or a floor button is pressed and enters its ON state.

$$
\begin{aligned}
&\text{DC(e, f):} && \text{Door Closed for elevator e, at floor f} \\
&\text{ST(e, f):} && \text{Sensor Triggered as elevator e nears floor f} \\
&\text{RL:} && \text{Request Logged (button pressed)}
\end{aligned} \tag{10.15}
$$

These events are indicated in Figure 10.15.

Finally, the state transition rules for an elevator can be presented. They can be deduced from Figure 10.15, but in some cases additional predicates are necessary. To be more precise, Figure 10.15 is nondeterministic; among other reasons, the predicates are necessary to make the STD deterministic. The interested reader should consult [Kampen, 1987] for the complete set of rules; for the sake of brevity, the only rules presented here are those which declare what happens when the door closes. The elevator moves up, down, or enters a wait state, depending on the current state.

$$
\begin{aligned}
&\text{S(U, e, f) and DC(e, f)} \Longrightarrow \text{M(U, e, f + 1)} \\
&\text{S(D, e, f) and DC(e, f)} \Longrightarrow \text{M(D, e, f} - 1) \\
&\text{S(N, e, f) and DC(e, f)} \Longrightarrow \text{W(e, f)}
\end{aligned} \tag{10.16}
$$

The first rule states that if elevator e is in state S(U, e, f), that is, stopped at floor f about to go up, and the doors close, then the elevator will move up toward the next floor. The second and third rules correspond to the cases of the elevator about to go down or with no requests pending.

The format of these rules reflects the power of finite state machines for specifying complex products. Instead of having to list a complex set of preconditions that have to hold for the product to do something and then having to list all the conditions that hold after the product has done it, the specifications take the simple form

current state and **event** and **predicate** $\Longrightarrow$ **next state**

This type of specification is easy to write down, easy to validate, and easy to convert into a design and into code. In fact, it is straightforward to construct a CASE tool that will translate a finite state machine (FSM) specification directly into source code. Maintenance is then achieved by replay. That is, if new states and/or events are needed, the specifications are modified and a new version of the product generated directly from the new specifications.

The FSM approach is more precise than the graphical technique of Gane and Sarsen presented in Section 10.3.1, but it is almost as easy to understand. It has a drawback in that for large systems the number of (**state**, **event**, **predicate**) triples can grow rapidly. Also, like Gane and Sarsen's technique, timing considerations are not handled in Kampen's formalism.

These problems can be solved using statecharts, an extension of FSMs [Harel et al., 1990]. Statecharts are extremely powerful and are supported by a CASE workbench, Statemate. The approach has been successfully used for a number of large real-time systems.

Another formal technique that can handle timing issues is Petri nets.

10.7 PETRI NETS

A major difficulty with specifying concurrent systems is coping with timing. This difficulty can manifest itself in many different ways, such as synchronization problems, race conditions, and deadlock [Silberschatz and Galvin, 1998]. Although it is true that timing problems can arise as a consequence of a poor design or a faulty implementation, such designs and implementations are often the consequence of poor specifications. If the specifications are not properly drawn up, there is a very real risk that the corresponding design and implementation will be inadequate. One powerful technique for specifying systems with potential timing problems is Petri nets. A further advantage of this technique is that it can be used for the design as well.

Petri nets were invented by Carl Adam Petri [Petri, 1962]. Originally of interest only to automata theorists, Petri nets have found wide applicability in computer

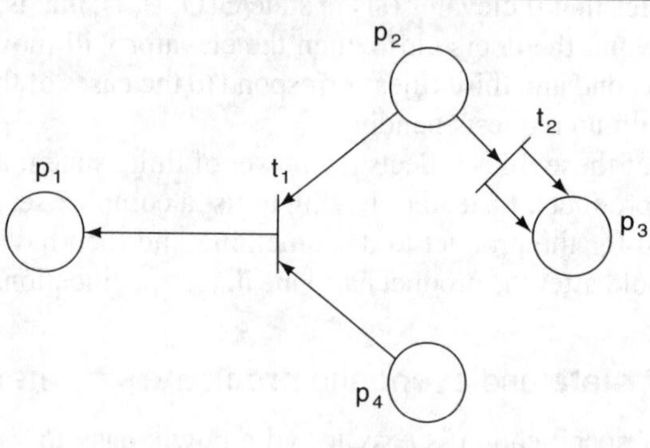

Figure 10.16 Petri net.

science, being used in such fields as performance evaluation, operating systems, and software engineering. In particular, Petri nets have proved to be useful for describing concurrent interrelated activities. But before the use of Petri nets for specifications can be demonstrated, a brief introduction to Petri nets is given for those readers who may be unfamiliar with them.

A Petri net consists of four parts: a set of places P, a set of transitions T, an input function I, and an output function O. Consider the Petri net shown in Figure 10.16.

The set of places P is $\{p_1, p_2, p_3, p_4\}$.

The set of transitions T is $\{t_1, t_2\}$.

The input functions for the two transitions, represented by the arrows from places to transitions, are

$$I(t_1) = \{p_2, p_4\}$$
$$I(t_2) = \{p_2\}$$

The output functions for the two transitions, represented by the arrows from transitions to places, are

$$O(t_1) = \{p_1\}$$
$$O(t_2) = \{p_3, p_3\}$$

Note the duplication of p_3; there are two arrows from t_2 to p_3.

More formally [Peterson, 1981], a Petri net structure is a 4-tuple C = (P, T, I, O).

$P = \{p_1, p_2, \ldots, p_n\}$ is a finite set of *places*, $n \geq 0$.

$T = \{t_1, t_2, \ldots, t_m\}$ is a finite set of transitions, $m \geq 0$, with P and T disjoint.

$I : T \longrightarrow P^{\infty}$ is the *input* function, a mapping from transitions to bags of places.

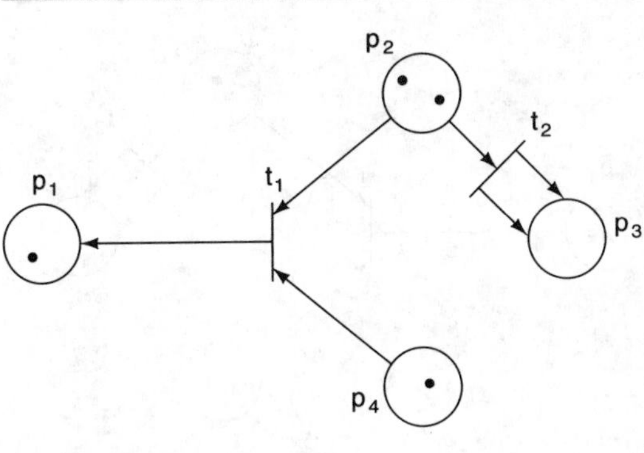

Figure 10.17 Marked Petri net.

$O: T \longrightarrow P^{\infty}$ is the *output* function, a mapping from transitions to bags of places. (A *bag*, or *multiset*, is a generalization of a set that allows for multiple instances of an element.)

A *marking* of a Petri net is an assignment of *tokens* to that Petri net. In Figure 10.17 there are four tokens, one in p_1, two in p_2, none in p_3, and one in p_4. The marking can be represented by the vector $(1, 2, 0, 1)$. Transition t_1 is enabled (ready to fire), because there are tokens in p_2 and in p_4; in general, a transition is enabled if each of its input places has as many tokens in it as there are arcs from the place to that transition. If t_1 were to fire, one token would be removed from p_2 and one from p_4, and one new token would be placed in p_1. The number of tokens is not conserved—two tokens are removed, but only one new one is placed in p_1. In Figure 10.17, transition t_2 is also enabled, because there are tokens in p_2. If t_2 were to fire, one token would be removed from p_2, and two new tokens would be placed in p_3.

Petri nets are nondeterministic; that is, if more than one transition is able to fire, then any one of them may be fired. Figure 10.17 has marking $(1, 2, 0, 1)$; both t_1 and t_2 are enabled. Suppose that t_1 fires. The resulting marking $(2, 1, 0, 0)$ is shown in Figure 10.18 where only t_2 is enabled. It fires, the enabling token is removed from p_2, and two new tokens are placed in p_3. The marking is now $(2, 0, 2, 0)$ as shown in Figure 10.19.

More formally [Peterson, 1981], a marking M of a Petri net $C = (P, T, I, O)$ is a function from the set of places P to the set of nonnegative integers.

$$M: P \longrightarrow \{0, 1, 2, \ldots\}$$

A marked Petri net is then a 5-tuple (P, T, I, O, M).

An important extension to a Petri net is an inhibitor arc. Referring to Figure 10.20, the inhibitor arc is marked by a small circle rather than an arrowhead. Transition t_1 is enabled because there is a token in p_3 but no token in p_2. In general, a transition is enabled if there is at least one token on each of its

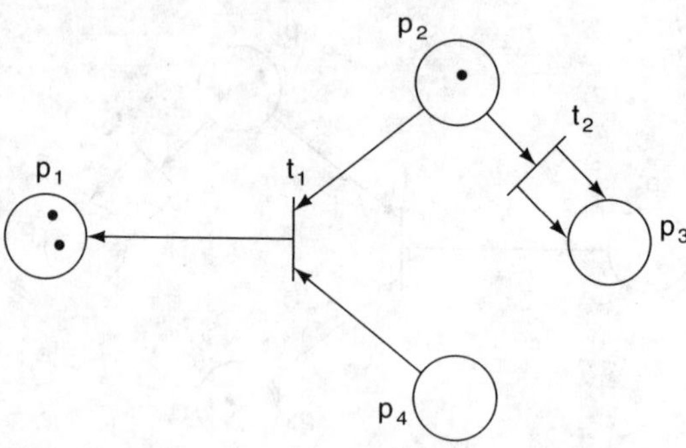

Figure 10.18 Petri net of Figure 10.17 after firing transition t_1.

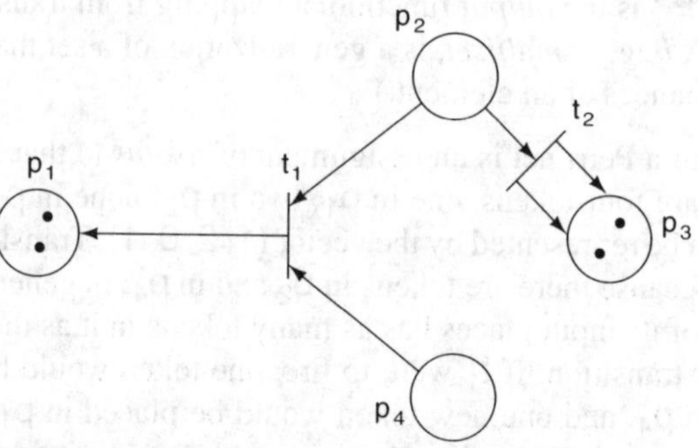

Figure 10.19 Petri net of Figure 10.18 after firing transition t_2.

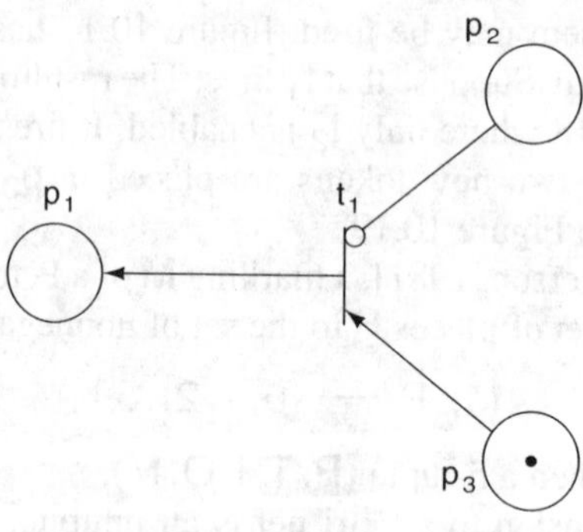

Figure 10.20 Petri net with inhibitor arc.

(normal) input arcs and no tokens on any of its inhibitor input arcs. This extension will be used in a Petri net specification of the elevator problem presented in Section 10.6.1 [Guha, Lang, and Bassiouni, 1987].

10.7.1 ELEVATOR PROBLEM: PETRI NETS

Recall that an n elevator system is to be installed in a building with m floors. In this Petri net specification each floor in the building will be represented by a place F_f, $1 \leq f \leq m$, in the Petri net; an elevator is represented by a token. A token in F_f denotes that an elevator is at floor f.

First constraint Each elevator has a set of m buttons, one for each floor. These illuminate when pressed and cause the elevator to visit the corresponding floor. The illumination is canceled when the corresponding floor is visited by the elevator.

To incorporate this into the specification, additional places are needed. The elevator button for floor f is represented in the Petri net by place EB_f, $1 \leq f \leq m$. More precisely, because there are n elevators, the place should be denoted $EB_{f,e}$ with $1 \leq f \leq m, 1 \leq e \leq n$. But for the sake of simplicity of notation, the subscript e representing the elevator will be suppressed. A token in EB_f denotes that the elevator button for floor f is illuminated. Because the button must be illuminated the first time the button is pressed and subsequent button presses must be ignored, this is specified using a Petri net as shown in Figure 10.21. First, suppose that button EB_f is not illuminated. There is accordingly no token in place and hence, because of the presence of the inhibitor arc, transition EB_f pressed is enabled. The button is now pressed. The transition fires and a new token is placed in EB_f as shown in Figure 10.21. Now, no matter how many times the button is pressed, the combination of the inhibitor arc and the presence of the token means that transition EB_f pressed cannot be enabled. Therefore, there can never be more than one token in place EB_f. Suppose that the elevator is to travel

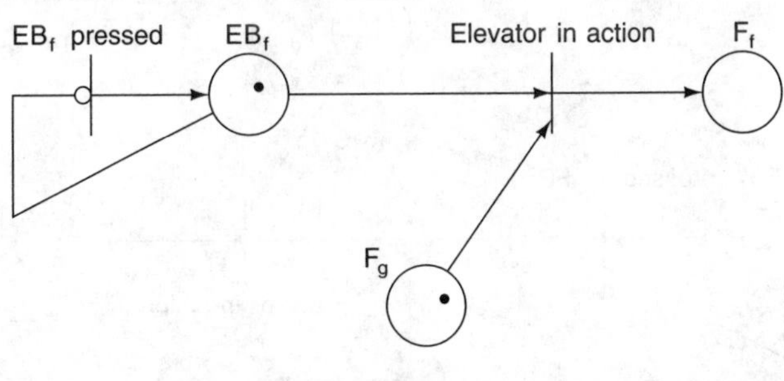

Figure 10.21 Petri net representation of an elevator button [Guha, Lang, and Bassiouni, 1987]. (©1987 IEEE)

from floor g to floor f. Because the elevator is at floor g, a token is in place F_g, as shown in Figure 10.21. Transition Elevator in action is enabled and then fires. The tokens in EB_f and F_g are removed, thereby turning off button EB_f, and a new token appears in F_f; the firing of this transition brings the elevator from floor g to floor f.

This motion from floor g to floor f cannot take place instantaneously. To handle this and similar issues, such as the fact that it is physically impossible for a button to illuminate at the very instant it is pressed, timing must be added to the Petri net model. That is, in classical Petri net theory transitions are instantaneous. In practical situations such as the elevator problem, timed Petri nets [Coolahan and Roussopoulos, 1983] are needed in order to be able to associate a nonzero time with a transition.

Second constraint Each floor, except the first floor and top floor, has two buttons, one to request an up-elevator and one to request a down-elevator. These buttons illuminate when pressed. The illumination is canceled when an elevator visits the floor and then moves in the desired direction.

The floor buttons are represented by places FB_f^u and FB_f^d representing the buttons for requesting up- and down-elevators, respectively. More precisely, floor 1 has a button FB_1^u, floor m has a button FB_m^d, and the intermediate floors each have two buttons, FB_f^u and FB_f^d, $1 < f < m$. The situation when an elevator reaches floor f from floor g with one or both buttons illuminated is shown in Figure 10.22. In fact, that figure needs further refinement because, if both the

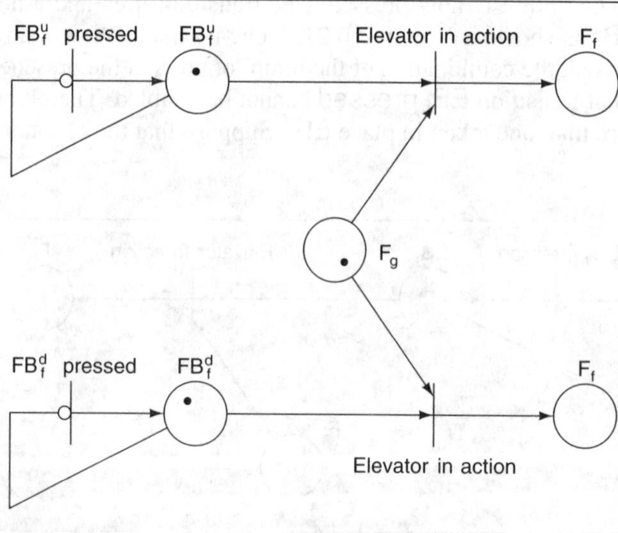

Figure 10.22 Petri net representation of floor buttons [Guha, Lang, and Bassiouni, 1987]. (© 1987 IEEE)

buttons are illuminated, one is turned off on a nondeterministic basis. To ensure that the correct button is turned off requires a Petri net model that is too complicated to present here; see, for example, [Ghezzi and Mandrioli, 1987].

Third constraint When an elevator has no requests, it remains at its current floor with its doors closed.

This is easily achieved: If there are no requests, no Elevator in action transition is enabled.

Not only can Petri nets be used to represent the specifications, they can be used for the design as well [Guha, Lang, and Bassiouni, 1987]. Even at this stage of the development of the product, it is clear that Petri nets possess the expressive power necessary for specifying the synchronization aspects of concurrent systems.

10.8 Z

A formal specifications language that is gaining widely in popularity is Z [Spivey, 1992]. (For the correct pronunciation of the name Z, see the Just in Case You Wanted to Know box below.) Use of Z requires knowledge of set theory, functions, and discrete mathematics, including first-order logic. Even for users with the necessary background (and this includes most computer science majors), Z is initially difficult to learn because, in addition to the usual set theoretic and logic symbols like $\exists$, $\supset$, and $\Longrightarrow$, it also uses many unusual special symbols, such as $\oplus$, $\lhd$, $\mapsto$, and $\twoheadrightarrow\!\!\!\!\!\!\rightarrowtail$.

Just in Case You Wanted to Know

The name Z was given to the formal specification language by its inventor Jean-Raymond Abrial in honor of the great set theorist Ernst Friedrich Ferdinand Zermelo (1871–1953). Because it was developed at Oxford University [Abrial, 1980], the name Z is properly pronounced "zed" because that is the way that the British pronounce the 26th letter of the alphabet.

Lately, however, there are moves afoot to acknowledge that Z is named after a German mathematician, and to pronounce it the German way, namely, "tzet." In response, Francophiles and Francophones point out that Abrial is a Frenchman, and that the letter Z is pronounced "zed" in French, too.

The one pronunciation that is totally unacceptable is American-style, that is, "zee." The reason is that Z (pronounced "zee") is the name of an American fourth-generation language (see Section 13.2). However, we cannot trademark a single letter of the alphabet. Furthermore, we are all free to pronounce the letter Z the way we wish. Nevertheless, within the programming language context, the pronunciation "zee" refers to the 4GL, not the formal specification language.

Watch this space for the next round in the Z pronunciation wars!

For insight into how Z is used to specify a product, the elevator problem of Section 10.6.1 is now considered again.

10.8.1 ELEVATOR PROBLEM: Z

In its simplest form, a Z specification consists of four sections, namely:

1. Given sets, data types, and constants
2. State definition
3. Initial state
4. Operations

Each of these sections is now examined in turn.

1. Given Sets A Z specification begins with a list of *given sets,* that is, sets that need not be defined in detail. The names of any such sets appear in brackets. For the elevator problem, the given set will be called Button, the set of all buttons. The Z specification therefore begins:

[Button]

2. State Definition A Z specification consists of a number of schemata. Each schema consists of a group of variable declarations together with a list of predicates that constrain the possible values of the variables. The format of a schema *S* is shown in Figure 10.23.

In the case of the elevator problem, there are four subsets of Button, namely, the floor buttons, the elevator buttons, buttons (the set of all buttons in the elevator problem), and pushed, the set of those buttons that have been pushed (and are therefore on). Figure 10.24 depicts schema *Button_State.* The symbol **P** denotes the power set (the set of all subsets of a given set). The constraints, that is, the statements below the horizontal line, state that the set of floor_buttons and elevator_buttons are disjoint, and that together they constitute the set of buttons. (The sets floor_buttons and elevator_buttons are not needed in what follows; they are included in Figure 10.24 only to demonstrate the power of Z.)

```
──── S ──────────────
 declarations
─────────────────────
 predicates
─────────────────────
```

Figure 10.23 Format of Z schema *S.*

Button_State	
floor_buttons, elevator_buttons	: **P** Button
buttons	: **P** Button
pushed	: **P** Button
floor_buttons ∩ elevator_buttons = ∅	
floor_buttons ∪ elevator_buttons = buttons	

Figure 10.24 Z schema *Button_State.*

3. Initial State The *abstract initial state* describes the state when the system is first turned on. The abstract initial state for the elevator problem is:

$$\textit{Button\_Init} \mathrel{\hat{=}} [\text{Button\_State}' \mid \text{pushed}' = \varnothing]$$

This is a *vertical schema definition,* as opposed to a *horizontal schema definition* such as Figure 10.24. The vertical schema states that when the elevator system is first turned on, the set pushed is initially empty, that is, all the buttons are off.

4. Operations If a button is pushed for the first time, then that button is turned on. The button is added to the set pushed. This is depicted in the schema of Figure 10.25 in which operation *Push_Button* is defined. The Δ in the first line of the schema denotes that this operation changes the state of *Button_State.* The operation has one input variable, namely, button?. As in various other languages (such as CSP [Hoare, 1985]), the question mark ? denotes an input variable, whereas an exclamation mark ! denotes an output variable.

The predicate part of an operation consists of a group of preconditions that must hold before the operation is invoked and postconditions that must hold after the operation has completed execution. Provided the preconditions are met, the

Push_Button
Δ*Button_State*
button?: Button
(button? ∈ buttons)∧
(((button? ∉ pushed) ∧ (pushed′ = pushed ∪ {button?})) ∨
((button? ∉ pushed) ∧ (pushed′ = pushed)))

Figure 10.25 Z specification of operation *Push_Button.*

postconditions will hold after completing execution. However, if the operation is invoked without the preconditions being satisfied, unspecified (and therefore unpredictable) results can occur.

The first precondition of Figure 10.25 states that button? must be a member of buttons, the set of all buttons in this elevator system. If the second precondition, namely, button? $\notin$ pushed, is met (that is, if the button is not on), then the set of pushed buttons is updated to include button?. In Z the new value of a variable is denoted by a prime ($'$). Thus, the postcondition says that after operation *Push_Button* has been performed, button? must be added to the set pushed. There is no need to turn on the button explicitly; it is sufficient that button? is now an element of pushed.

The other possibility is that a button that has already been pushed is pushed again. Because button? $\in$ pushed, the third precondition holds[1] and, as required, nothing happens. This is indicated by the statement pushed$'$ = pushed; the new state of pushed is the same as the old state.

Now suppose an elevator arrives at a floor. If the corresponding floor button is on, then it must be turned off, and similarly for the corresponding elevator button. That is, if button? is an element of pushed, then it must be removed from the set, as shown in Figure 10.26. (The symbol \ denotes set difference). However, if a button is not on, then set pushed is unchanged.

The solution presented in this section is an oversimplification in that it does not distinguish between up and down floor buttons. Nevertheless, it gives an indication of how Z can be used to specify the behavior of the buttons in the elevator problem.

10.8.2 ANALYSIS OF Z

Z has been used successfully in a wide variety of projects, including CASE tools [Hall, 1990], a real-time kernel [Spivey, 1990], and an oscilloscope [Delisle and

```
——————— Floor_Arrival ———————
ΔButton_State
button?: Button
——————————————————————————————
(button? ∈ buttons)∧
(((button? ∈ pushed) ∧ (pushed′ = pushed \ {button?})) ∨
((button? ∉ pushed) ∧ (pushed′ = pushed)))
——————————————————————————————
```

Figure 10.26 Z specification of operation *Floor_Arrival*.

[1] Without the third precondition, the specification would not state what is to happen if a button that has already been pushed is pushed again. The results would then be unspecified.

Garlan, 1990]. Z has also been used to specify large portions of a new release of CICS, the IBM transaction-processing system [Nix and Collins, 1988].

These successes are perhaps somewhat surprising in view of the fact that, even for the simplified version of the elevator problem, it is clear that Z is not straightforward to use. First, there is the problem caused by the notation; a new user has to learn the set of symbols and their meanings before being able to read Z specifications, let alone write them. Second, not every software engineer necessarily has the required training in mathematics to be able to use Z (although recent graduates of almost all computer science programs either know enough mathematics to use Z, or could learn what they still need to know without much difficulty).

Z is perhaps the most widely used formal language of its type. Why is this, and why has Z been so successful, especially on large-scale projects? A number of different reasons have been put forward.

First, it has been found that it is easy to find faults in specifications written in Z, especially during inspections of the specifications themselves and inspections of designs or code against the formal specifications [Nix and Collins, 1988; Hall, 1990].

Second, writing Z specifications requires the specifier to be extremely precise; as a result of this need for exactness, there appear to be fewer ambiguities, contradictions, and omissions than with informal specifications.

Third, the fact that Z is a formal language allows developers to prove specifications correct when necessary. Thus, although some organizations rarely do any correctness proving of Z, such proofs have been done, even for such practical specifications as the CICS storage manager [Woodcock, 1989].

Fourth, it has been suggested that software professionals with only high-school mathematics can be taught in a relatively short period of time to write Z specifications [Hall, 1990]. Clearly such individuals cannot prove the resulting specifications to be correct, but then formal specifications do not necessarily always have to be proved to be correct.

Fifth, the use of Z has decreased the cost of software development. There is no doubt that more time has to be spent on the specifications themselves than when informal techniques are used, but the overall time for the complete development process is decreased.

Sixth, the problem that the client cannot understand specifications written in Z has been solved in a number of ways, including rewriting the specifications in natural language. It has been found that the resulting natural language specifications are clearer than informal specifications constructed from scratch. (This was also the experience with Meyer's English paraphrase of his formal specification for Naur's text-processing problem, described in Section 10.2.1.)

The bottom line is that, notwithstanding the arguments to the contrary, Z has been successfully used in the software industry for a number of large-scale projects. Although it is true that the vast majority of specifications continue to be written in languages considerably less formal than Z, there is a growing global trend toward the use of formal specifications. The use of such formal specifications has traditionally been largely a European practice. However, more and more organizations in the United States are employing formal specifications of one sort or another. The extent to which Z and similar languages will be used in the future remains to be seen.

10.9 OTHER FORMAL TECHNIQUES

Many other formal techniques have been proposed. These techniques are extremely varied. For example, Anna [Luckham and von Henke, 1985] is a formal specification language for Ada. Some formal techniques are knowledge-based such as Gist [Balzer, 1985]. Gist was designed so that users can describe processes in a way that is as close as possible to the way that we think about processes. This was to be achieved by formalizing the constructs used in natural languages. In practice, Gist specifications are as hard to read as most other formal specifications, so much so that a paraphraser from Gist to English has been written.

Vienna definition method (VDM) [Jones, 1986b; Bjørner, 1987] is a technique based on denotational semantics [Gordon, 1979]. VDM can be applied not just to the specifications, but also to the design and implementation. VDM has been successfully used in a number of projects, most spectacularly in the Dansk Datamatik Center development of the DDC Ada Compiler System [Oest, 1986].

A different way of looking at specifications is to view them in terms of sequences of events, where an event is either a simple action or a communication that transfers data into or out of the system. For example, in the elevator problem, one event consists of pushing the elevator button for floor f on elevator e and its resulting illumination. Another event is elevator e leaving floor f in the downward direction and the canceling of the illumination of the corresponding floor button. The language Communicating Sequential Processes (CSP) invented by Hoare is based on the idea of describing the behavior of a system in terms of such events [Hoare, 1985]. In CSP, a process is described in terms of the sequences of events in which the process will engage with its environment. Processes interact with each other by sending messages to one another. CSP allows processes to be combined in a wide variety of ways, such as sequentially, in parallel, or interleaved nondeterministically.

The power of CSP lies in the fact that CSP specifications are executable [Delisle and Schwartz, 1987] and, as a result, can be checked for internal consistency. In addition, CSP provides a framework for going from specifications to design to implementation by a sequence of steps that preserve validity. In other words, if the specifications are correct and if the transformations are correctly performed, then the design and implementation will be correct as well. Going from design to implementation is particularly straightforward if the implementation language is Ada.

However, CSP also has its disadvantages. In particular, like Z it is not an easy language to learn. An attempt was made to include a CSP specification for the elevator problem in this book [Schwartz and Delisle, 1987]. But the quantity of essential preliminary material and the level of detail of explanation needed to describe each CSP statement adequately were simply too great to permit inclusion in a book as general as this one. The relationship between the power of a specification language and its degree of difficulty of use is expanded in the next section.

10.10 COMPARISON OF SPECIFICATION TECHNIQUES

The main lesson of this chapter is that every development organization has to decide what type of specification language is appropriate for the product about to be developed. An informal technique is easy to learn, but does not have the power of a semiformal or formal technique. Conversely, each formal technique supports a variety of features that may include executability, correctness proving, or transformability to design and implementation through a series of correctness-preserving steps. Although it is generally true that the more formal the technique the greater its power, it is also generally true that formal techniques can be difficult to learn and use. Also, a formal specification can be difficult for the client to understand. In other words, there is a trade-off between ease of use and the power of a specification language.

In some circumstances, the choice of specification language type is easy. For example, if the vast majority of the members of the development team do not have any training in computer science, then it is virtually impossible to use anything other than an informal or semiformal specification technique. Conversely, where a mission-critical real-time system is being built in a research laboratory, the power of a formal specification technique will almost certainly be required.

An additional complicating factor is that many of the newer formal techniques have not been tested under practical conditions. There is a considerable risk involved in using such a technique. Large sums of money will be needed to pay for training the relevant members of the development team, and more money will be spent while the team adjusts from using the language in the classroom to using it on the actual project. It may well happen that the language's supporting software tools do not work properly, as happened with SREM [Scheffer, Stone, and Rzepka, 1985], with the resulting additional expense and time slippage. But if everything works, and if the software project management plan takes into account the additional time and money needed when a new technology is used on a nontrivial project for the first time, huge gains are possible.

Which specification technique should be used for a specific project? It depends on the project, the development team, the management team, and on myriad other factors, such as the client insisting that a specific method be used (or not be

Specification Method	Category	Strengths	Weaknesses
Natural language (Section 10.2)	Informal	Easy to learn Easy to use Easy for client to understand	Imprecise Specifications can be ambiguous, contradictory, and/or incomplete
Entity-relationship modeling (Section 10.5) PSL/PSA (Section 10.4) SADT (Section 10.4) SREM (Section 10.4) Structured systems analysis (Section 10.3)	Semiformal	Can be understood by client More precise than informal methods	Not as precise as formal methods Generally cannot handle timing
Anna (Section 10.9) CSP (Section 10.9) Extended finite state machines (Section 10.6) Gist (Section 10.9) Petri nets (Section 10.7) VDM (Section 10.9) Z (Section 10.8)	Formal	Extremely precise Can reduce specification faults Can reduce development cost and effort Can support correctness proving	Hard for team to learn Hard to use Almost impossible for most clients to understand

Figure 10.27 Summary of the specification methods discussed in this chapter and the section in which each is described.

used). As with so many other aspects of software engineering, trade-offs have to be made. Unfortunately, there is no simple rule for deciding which specification technique to use.

Figure 10.27 is a summary of the ideas of this section.

10.11 TESTING DURING THE SPECIFICATION PHASE

During the specification phase the functionality of the proposed product is precisely expressed in the specification document. It is vital to verify that the specification document is correct. One way to do this is by means of a walkthrough of the specification document (Section 5.2.1).

A more powerful mechanism for detecting faults in specification documents is an inspection (Section 5.2.3). A team of inspectors reviews the specifications against a checklist. Typical items on a specification inspection checklist include: Have the required hardware resources been specified? Have the acceptance criteria been specified?

Inspections were first suggested by Fagan in the context of testing the design and the code [Fagan, 1976]. Fagan's work is described in detail in Section 5.2.3.

However, inspections have also proved to be of considerable use in the testing of specifications. For example, Doolan used inspections to validate the specifications of a product that, when built, consisted of over 2 million lines of FORTRAN [Doolan, 1992]. From data on the cost of fixing faults in the product, he was able to deduce that each hour invested in inspections saved 30 hours of execution-based fault detection and correction.

When a specification has been drawn up using a formal technique, other testing techniques can be applied. For example, correctness-proving methods (Section 5.5) can be employed. Even if formal proofs are not performed, informal proof techniques such as those used in Section 5.5.1 can be an extremely useful way of highlighting specification faults. In fact, the product and its proof should be developed in parallel. In this way, faults will be quickly detected.

10.12 CASE TOOLS FOR THE SPECIFICATION PHASE

Two classes of CASE tools are particularly helpful during the specification phase. The first is a graphical tool. Whether a product is represented using data flow diagrams (DFD), Petri nets, entity-relationship diagrams, or any of the many other representations omitted from this book simply for reasons of space, drawing the entire product by hand is a lengthy process. In addition, making substantial changes can result in having to redraw everything from scratch. Having a drawing tool is therefore a great time-saver. Tools of this type exist for the specification techniques described in this chapter, as well as for many other graphical representations for specifications. A second tool that is needed during this phase is a data dictionary. As mentioned in Section 4.10, this is a tool that stores the name and representation (format) of every component of every data item in the product, including data flows and their components, data stores and their components, and processes and their internal variables. Again, there is a wide selection of data dictionaries running on a variety of hardware.

What really is needed is not a separate graphical tool and a separate data dictionary. Instead, the two tools should be integrated, so that any change made to a data component is automatically reflected in the corresponding part of the specification. There are many examples of this type of tool; some of the more popular are Analyst/Designer, Software through Pictures, and System Architect. Furthermore, many such tools also incorporate an automatic consistency checker that ensures consistency between the specification document and the corresponding design document. For example, it is possible to check that every item in the specification document is carried forward to the design document, and that everything mentioned in the design has been declared in the data dictionary.

A specification technique is unlikely to receive widespread acceptance unless there is a tool-rich CASE environment supporting that technique. For example, SREM (Section 10.4) would probably be used far more widely today had REVS, its associated CASE tool set, performed better in the U.S. Air Force tests

[Scheffer, Stone, and Rzepka, 1985]. It is not easy to specify a system correctly, even for experienced software professionals. It is only reasonable to provide specifiers with a set of state-of-the-art CASE tools to assist them in every way possible.

10.13 METRICS FOR THE SPECIFICATION PHASE

As with all other phases, during the specification phase it is necessary to measure the five fundamental metrics, namely, size, cost, duration, effort, and quality. One measure of the size of a specification is the number of pages in the specification document. If the same technique is used for specifying a number of products, then differences in specification size may be significant predictors of the effort that will be needed to build the various products.

Turning to quality, a vital aspect of specification inspections is the record of fault statistics. Noting the number of faults of each type found during an inspection is thus an integral part of the inspection process. Also, the rate at which faults are detected can give a measure of the efficiency of the inspection process.

Metrics for predicting the size of the target product include the number of items in the data dictionary. Several different counts should be taken, including the number of files, data items, processes, and so on. This information can give management a preliminary estimate regarding the effort that will be required to build the product. It is important to note that this information will be tentative at best. After all, during the design phase a process in a DFD may be broken down into a number of different modules. Conversely, a number of processes may together constitute a single module. Nevertheless, metrics derived from the data dictionary can give management an early clue as to the eventual size of the target product.

10.14 OSBERT OGLESBY CASE STUDY: STRUCTURED SYSTEMS ANALYSIS

As a consequence of the careful interviews followed by the building of a rapid prototype in the requirements phase, the Gane and Sarsen structured systems analysis process is straightforward. The data flow diagram is shown in Figure 10.28. The remainder of the structured systems analysis appears in Appendix D.

The organization and presentation of the material in Appendix D is such that the client can rapidly understand exactly what is going to be built. However, a major factor in achieving that understanding is the fact that the client was able to experiment with the rapid prototype during the requirements phase.

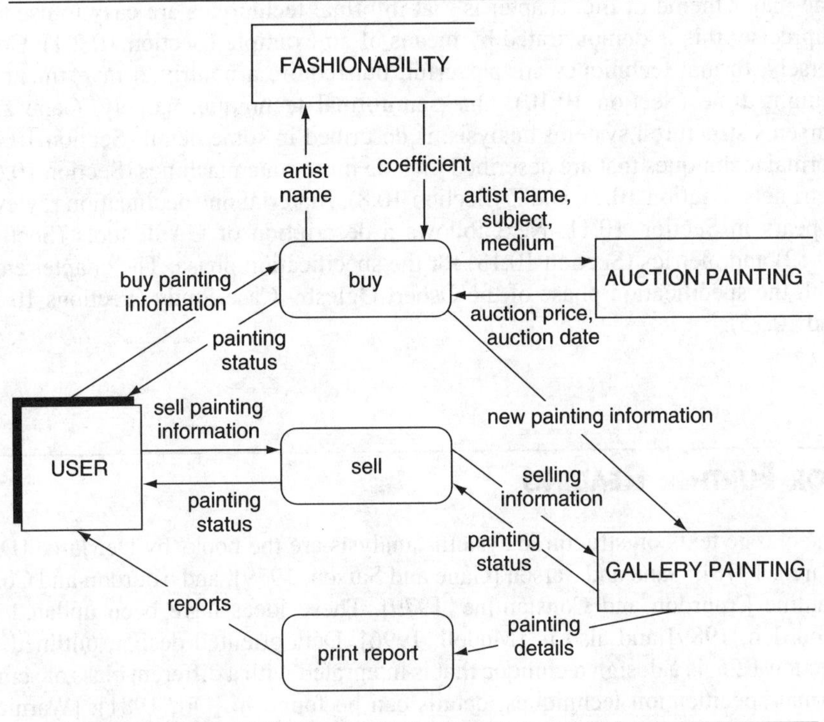

Figure 10.28 Data flow diagram for Osbert Oglesby case study.

10.15 OSBERT OGLESBY CASE STUDY: SOFTWARE PROJECT MANAGEMENT PLAN

Now that the specifications are complete, the software project management plan (SPMP) is drawn up, including estimates of cost and duration (see Chapter 8). Appendix F contains a software project management plan (SPMP) for development of the Osbert Oglesby product by a small (three-person) software organization. The Instructor's Manual for the First Edition of *Software Engineering* (available from McGraw-Hill) contains a SPMP for a project developed by a large software organization. Both types of plan fit the IEEE SPMP format (Section 8.5) equally well, further evidence of its broad range of applicability.

CHAPTER REVIEW

Specifications (Section 10.1) can be expressed informally (Section 10.2), semiformally (Sections 10.3 through 10.5), or formally (Sections 10.6 through 10.9).

The major theme of this chapter is that informal techniques are easy to use but imprecise; this is demonstrated by means of an example (Section 10.2.1). Conversely, formal techniques are powerful, but require a nontrivial investment in training time (Section 10.10). One semiformal technique, namely, Gane and Sarsen's structured systems analysis, is described in some detail (Section 10.3). Formal techniques that are described include finite state machines (Section 10.6), Petri nets (Section 10.7), and Z (Section 10.8). Material on specification reviews appears in Section 10.11. Next follows a description of CASE tools (Section 10.12) and metrics (Section 10.13) for the specification phase. The chapter ends with the specification phase of the Osbert Oglesby Case Study (Sections 10.14 and 10.15).

For Further Reading

The classic texts on structured systems analysis are the books by DeMarco [DeMarco, 1978], Gane and Sarsen [Gane and Sarsen, 1979], and Yourdon and Constantine [Yourdon and Constantine, 1979]. These ideas have been updated in [Yourdon, 1989] and also in [Modell, 1996]. Data-oriented design, outlined in Section 12.5, is a design technique that is integrated with a different class of semiformal specification techniques; details can be found in [Orr, 1981], [Warnier, 1981], and [Jackson, 1983]. SADT is described in [Ross, 1985], and PSL/PSA is described in [Teichroew and Hershey, 1977]. Two sources of information on SREM are [Alford, 1985] and [Scheffer, Stone, and Rzepka, 1985].

Six formal techniques are described in [Wing, 1990]. An outstanding collection of papers on formal techniques can be found in the September 1990 issues of *IEEE Transactions on Software Engineering, IEEE Computer, IEEE Software,* and *ACM SIGSOFT Software Engineering Notes.* Of particular interest is [Hall, 1990]; the paper should be read in its entirety. [Bowen and Hinchey, 1995b] is a sequel to Hall's seminal article, and [Bowen and Hinchey, 1995a] is a list of guidelines for use of formal techniques. Additional articles on formal techniques can be found in the February 1995 issue of *IEEE Transactions on Software Engineering.* Lessons learned from applying formal specifications in industry are discussed in [Larsen, Fitzgerald, and Brookes, 1996] and [Pfleeger and Hatton, 1997]. A variety of opinions on formal methods can be found in [Saiedian et al., 1996].

An early reference to the finite state machine approach is [Naur, 1964] where it is unfortunately referred to as the Turing machine approach. The finite state machine approach is described in [Ferrentino and Mills, 1977] and [Linger, 1980]. An FSM model for real-time systems is given in [Chandrasekharan, Dasarathy, and Kishimoto, 1985]. A graphical tool for FSMs is described in [Jacob, 1985], and the use of FSMs in specifying the interaction between humans and computers is found in [Wasserman, 1985]. Statecharts are a powerful extension of FSMs;

they are described in [Harel, 1987] and [Harel et al., 1990]. Object-oriented extensions of Statecharts appear in [Coleman, Hayes, and Bear, 1992] and in [Harel and Gery, 1997].

[Peterson, 1981] is an excellent introduction to Petri nets and their applications. The use of Petri nets in prototyping is described in [Bruno and Marchetto, 1986]. Timed Petri nets are described in [Coolahan and Roussopoulos, 1983].

With regard to Z, [Spivey, 1988] and [Diller, 1990] are good introductory texts. For the reference manual with full details about the specification language, see [Spivey, 1992]. Using the results of an experiment in reading Z specifications, [Finney, 1996] questions whether Z specifications are as easy to read as has been claimed by some Z proponents.

Specification of real-time systems is discussed in the September 1992 issue of *IEEE Transactions on Software Engineering*. The specification of distributed systems is described in [Kramer, 1994]. The proceedings of the International Workshops on Software Specification and Design are a preeminent source for research ideas regarding specifications.

PROBLEMS[2]

10.1 Why should the following constraints not appear in a specification document:

(i) The product must significantly reduce the echo in recordings made in a large auditorium.

(ii) The spectral analysis component must be set up at a reasonable cost.

10.2 Consider the following recipe for grilled pockwester.

Ingredients:

1 large onion
1 can of frozen orange juice
Freshly squeezed juice of 1 lemon
1/2 cup bread crumbs
Flour
Milk
3 medium-sized shallots
2 medium-sized eggplants
1 fresh pockwester
1/2 cup Pouilly Fuissé

[2] Problem 10.16 (Term Project) and Problems 10.20 through 10.22 (Case Study) can be done either at the end of Chapter 10 or Chapter 11.

1 garlic
Parmesan cheese
4 free-range eggs

The night before, take one lemon, squeeze it, strain the juice, and freeze it. Take one large onion and three shallots, dice them, and grill them in a skillet. When clouds of black smoke start to come off, add 2 cups of fresh orange juice. Stir vigorously. Slice the lemon into paper-thin slices and add to the mixture. In the meantime, coat the mushrooms in flour, dip them in milk, and then shake them up in a paper bag with the bread crumbs. In a saucepan, heat 1/2 cup of Pouilly Fuissé. When it reaches 170°, add the sugar and continue to heat. When the sugar has caramelized, add the mushrooms. Blend the mixture for 10 minutes or until all lumps have been removed. Add the eggs. Now take the pockwester, and kill it by sprinkling it with frobs. Skin the pockwester, break it into bite-sized chunks, and add it to the mixture. Bring to a boil and simmer, uncovered. The eggs should previously have been vigorously stirred with a wire whisk for 5 minutes. When the pockwester is soft to the touch, place it on a serving platter, sprinkle with Parmesan cheese, and broil for not more than 4 minutes.

Determine the ambiguities, omissions, and contradictions in the preceding specification. (For the record, a pockwester is an imaginary sort of fish and "frobs" is slang for generic hors d'oeuvres.)

10.3 Correct the specification paragraph of Section 10.2 to reflect the client's wishes more accurately.

10.4 Use mathematical formulas to represent the specification paragraph of Section 10.2. Compare your answer with your answer to Problem 10.3.

10.5 Write a precise English specification for the product to determine whether a bank statement is correct (Problem 7.8).

10.6 Draw a data flow diagram for the specification you drew up for Problem 10.5. Ensure that your DFD simply reflects the flow of data and that no assumptions regarding computerization have been made.

10.7 Consider the automated library circulation system of Problem 7.7. Write down precise specifications for the library circulation system.

10.8 Draw a data flow diagram showing the operation of the library circulation system of Problem 7.7.

10.9 Complete the specification document for the library circulation system of Problem 7.7 using Gane and Sarsen's technique. Where data have not been specified (for example, the total number of books checked in/out each day), make your own assumptions, but make sure that they are clearly indicated.

10.10 A fixed-point binary number consists of an optional sign followed by one or more bits, followed by a binary point, followed by one or more bits. Examples of floating-point binary numbers include 11010.1010, −0.000001, and +1101101.0.

More formally, this can be expressed as:

⟨fixed-point binary⟩ ::= [⟨sign⟩]⟨bitstring⟩⟨binary point⟩⟨bitstring⟩
⟨sign⟩ ::= + | −
⟨bitstring⟩ ::= ⟨bit⟩[⟨bitstring⟩]
⟨binary point⟩ ::= .
⟨bit⟩ ::= 0 | 1

(The notation [...] denotes an optional item, and a | b denotes a or b.) Specify a finite state machine that will take as input a string of characters and determine whether or not that string constitutes a valid fixed-point binary number.

10.11 Use the finite state machine approach to specify the library circulation system of Problem 7.7.

10.12 Show how your solution to Problem 10.11 can be used to design and implement a menu-driven product for the library circulation system of Problem 7.7

10.13 Use a Petri net to specify the circulation of a single book through the library of Problem 7.7. Include operations H, C, and R in your specification.

10.14 You are a software engineer working for a large company that specializes in computerizing library systems. Your manager asks you to specify the complete library circulation system of Problem 7.7 using Z. What is your reaction?

10.15 (Term Project) Using the technique specified by your instructor, draw up a specification document for the Air Gourmet product described in Appendix A.

10.16 (Term Project) Draw up a software project management plan for the Air Gourmet product described in Appendix A.

10.17 (Case Study) Draw up the requirements of the Osbert Oglesby product using the finite state machine approach.

10.18 (Case Study) Use the Petri net technique to specify the states through which a single painting in the Osbert Oglesby product passes.

10.19 (Case Study) Specify a portion of the Osbert Oglesby product using the Z constructs of Section 10.8.

10.20 (Case Study) The SPMP of Appendix F is for a small software engineering organization consisting of 3 software engineers. Modify the plan so that it is appropriate for a medium-sized organization with between 50 and 100 software engineers.

10.21 (Case Study) Now modify the SPMP so that it is appropriate for a large organization with over 1000 software engineers.

10.22 (Case Study) In what way would the SPMP of Appendix F have to be modified if the Osbert Oglesby product had to be completed in only 8 weeks?

10.23 (Readings in Software Engineering) Your instructor will distribute copies of [Bowen and Hinchey, 1995b]. Do you agree with Bowen and Hinchey's position, or do you feel that some of the "seven myths" are at least partially true? Justify your answer.

REFERENCES

[Abrial, 1980] J.-R. ABRIAL, "The Specification Language Z: Syntax and Semantics," Oxford University Computing Laboratory, Programming Research Group, Oxford, UK, April 1980.

[Alford, 1985] M. ALFORD, "SREM at the Age of Eight; The Distributed Computing Design System," *IEEE Computer* **18** (April 1985), pp. 36–46.

[Balzer, 1985] R. BALZER, "A 15 Year Perspective on Automatic Programming," *IEEE Transactions on Software Engineering* **SE-11** (November 1985), pp. 1257–68.

[Banks, Carson, and Nelson, 1995] J. BANKS, J. S. CARSON, AND B. L. NELSON, *Discrete-event System Simulation,* Second Edition, Prentice Hall, Upper Saddle River, NJ, 1995.

[Bjørner, 1987] D. BJØRNER, "On the Use of Formal Methods in Software Development," *Proceedings of the Ninth International Conference on Software Engineering,* Monterey, CA, March 1987, pp. 17–29.

[Bowen and Hinchey, 1995a] J. P. BOWEN AND M. G. HINCHEY, "Ten Commandments of Formal Methods," *IEEE Computer* **28** (April 1995), pp. 56–63.

[Bowen and Hinchey, 1995b] J. P. BOWEN AND M. G. HINCHEY, "Seven More Myths of Formal Methods," *IEEE Software* **12** (July 1995), pp. 34–41.

[Brady, 1977] J. M. Brady, *The Theory of Computer Science,* Chapman and Hall, London, 1977.

[Bruno and Marchetto, 1986] G. Bruno and G. Marchetto, "Process-Translatable Petri Nets for the Rapid Prototyping of Process Control Systems," *IEEE Transactions on Software Engineering* **SE-12** (February 1986), pp. 346–57.

[Chandrasekharan, Dasarathy, and Kishimoto, 1985] M. CHANDRASEKHARAN, B. DASARATHY, AND Z. KISHIMOTO, "Requirements-Based Testing of Real-Time Systems: Modeling for Testability," *IEEE Computer* **18** (April 1985), pp. 71–80.

[Chen, 1976] P. CHEN, "The Entity-Relationship Model—Towards a Unified View of Data," *ACM Transactions on Database Systems* **1** (March 1976), pp. 9–36.

[Chen, 1983] P. P.-S. CHEN, "ER—A Historical Perspective and Future Directions," in: *Entity Relationship Approach to Software Engineering,* C. G. Davis (Editor), North-Holland, Amsterdam, 1983.

[Coleman, Hayes, and Bear, 1992] D. COLEMAN, F. HAYES, AND S. BEAR, "Introducing Objectcharts or How to Use Statecharts in Object-Oriented Design," *IEEE Transactions on Software Engineering* **18** (January 1992), pp. 9–18.

[Coolahan and Roussopoulos, 1983] J. E. COOLAHAN, JR., AND N. ROUSSOPOULOS, "Timing Requirements for Time-Driven Systems Using Augmented Petri Nets," *IEEE Transactions on Software Engineering* **SE-9** (September 1983), pp. 603–16.

[Dart, Ellison, Feiler, and Habermann, 1987] S. A. DART, R. J. ELLISON, P. H. FEILER, AND A. N. HABERMANN, "Software Development Environments," *IEEE Computer* **20** (November 1987), pp. 18–28.

[Delisle and Garlan, 1990] N. DELISLE AND D. GARLAN, "A Formal Description of an Oscilloscope," *IEEE Software* **7** (September 1990), pp. 29–36.

[Delisle and Schwartz, 1987] N. DELISLE AND M. SCHWARTZ, "A Programming Environment for CSP," *Proceedings of the Second ACM SIGSOFT/SIGPLAN Software Engineering Symposium on Practical Software Development Environments, ACM SIGPLAN Notices* **22** (January 1987), pp. 34–41.

[DeMarco, 1978] T. DEMARCO, *Structured Analysis and System Specification,* Yourdon Press, New York, 1978.

[Diller, 1990] A. DILLER, *Z: An Introduction to Formal Methods,* John Wiley and Sons, Chichester, UK, 1990.

[Doolan, 1992] E. P. DOOLAN, "Experience with Fagan's Inspection Method," *Software—Practice and Experience* **22** (February 1992), pp. 173–82.

[Fagan, 1976] M. E. FAGAN, "Design and Code Inspections to Reduce Errors in Program Development," *IBM Systems Journal* **15** (No. 3, 1976), pp. 182–211.

[Ferrentino and Mills, 1977] A. B. FERRENTINO AND H. D. MILLS, "State Machines and Their Semantics in Software Engineering," *Proceedings of the First International Computer Software and Applications Conference, COMPSAC '77,* Chicago, 1977, pp. 242–51.

[Finney, 1996] K. FINNEY, "Mathematical Notation in Formal Specification: Too Difficult for the Masses?" *IEEE Transactions on Software Engineering* **22** (1996), pp. 158–59.

[Gane and Sarsen, 1979] C. GANE AND T. SARSEN, *Structured Systems Analysis: Tools and Techniques,* Prentice Hall, Englewood Cliffs, NJ, 1979.

[Ghezzi and Mandrioli, 1987] C. GHEZZI AND D. MANDRIOLI, "On Eclecticism in Specifications: A Case Study Centered around Petri Nets," *Proceedings of the Fourth International Workshop on Software Specification and Design,* Monterey, CA, 1987, pp. 216–24.

[Goodenough and Gerhart, 1975] J. B. GOODENOUGH AND S. L. GERHART, "Toward a Theory of Test Data Selection," *Proceedings of the Third International Conference on Reliable Software,* Los Angeles, 1975, pp. 493–510. Also published in: *IEEE Transactions on Software Engineering* **SE-1** (June 1975), pp. 156–73. Revised version: J. B. Goodenough, and S. L. Gerhart, "Toward a Theory of Test Data Selection: Data Selection Criteria," in: *Current Trends in Programming Methodology, Volume 2,* R. T. Yeh (Editor), Prentice Hall, Englewood Cliffs, NJ, 1977, pp. 44–79.

[Gordon, 1979] M. J. C. GORDON, *The Denotational Description of Programming Languages: An Introduction,* Springer-Verlag, New York, 1979.

[Guha, Lang, and Bassiouni, 1987] R. K. GUHA, S. D. LANG, AND M. BASSIOUNI, "Software Specification and Design Using Petri Nets," *Proceedings of the Fourth International Workshop on Software Specification and Design,* Monterey, CA, April 1987, pp. 225–30.

[Hall, 1990] A. HALL, "Seven Myths of Formal Methods," *IEEE Software* **7** (September 1990), pp. 11–19.

[Harel, 1987] D. HAREL, "Statecharts: A Visual Formalism for Complex Systems," *Science of Computer Programming* **8** (June 1987), pp. 231–74.

[Harel and Gery, 1997] D. HAREL AND E. GERY, "Executable Object Modeling with Statecharts," *IEEE Computer* **30** (July 1997), pp. 31–42.

[Harel et al., 1990] D. HAREL, H. LACHOVER, A. NAAMAD, A. PNUELI, M. POLITI, R. SHERMAN, A. SHTULL-TRAURING, AND M. TRAKHTENBROT, "STATEMATE: A Working Environment for the Development of Complex Reactive Systems," *IEEE Transactions on Software Engineering* **16** (April 1990), pp. 403–14.

[Hoare, 1985] C. A. R. HOARE, *Communicating Sequential Processes,* Prentice Hall International, Englewood Cliffs, NJ, 1985.

[IWSSD, 1986] Call for Papers, Fourth International Workshop on Software Specification and Design, *ACM SIGSOFT Software Engineering Notes* **11** (April 1986), pp. 94–96.

[Jackson, 1983] M. A. JACKSON, *System Development,* Prentice Hall, Englewood Cliffs, NJ, 1983.

[Jacob, 1985] R. J. K. JACOB, "A State Transition Diagram Language for Visual Programming," *IEEE Computer* **18** (August 1985), pp. 51–59.

[Jain, 1991] R. JAIN, *The Art of Computer Systems Performance Analysis: Techniques for Experimental Design, Measurement, Simulation, and Modeling,* John Wiley and Sons, New York, 1991.

[Jones, 1986b] C. B. JONES, *Systematic Software Development Using VDM,* Prentice Hall, Englewood Cliffs, NJ, 1986.

[Kampen, 1987] G. R. KAMPEN, "An Eclectic Approach to Specification," *Proceedings of the Fourth International Workshop on Software Specification and Design,* Monterey, CA, April 1987, pp. 178–82.

[Knuth, 1968] D. E. KNUTH, *The Art of Computer Programming, Volume I, Fundamental Algorithms,* Addison-Wesley, Reading, MA, 1968.

[Kramer, 1994] J. KRAMER, "Distributed Software Engineering," *Proceedings of the 16th International Conference on Software Engineering,* Sorrento, Italy, May 1994, pp. 253–63.

[Larsen, Fitzgerald, and Brookes, 1996] P. G. LARSEN, J. FITZGERALD, AND T. BROOKES, "Applying Formal Specification in Industry," *IEEE Software* **13** (May 1996), pp. 48–56.

[Leavenworth, 1970] B. LEAVENWORTH, Review #19420, *Computing Reviews* **11** (July 1970), pp. 396–97.

[Linger, 1980] R. C. LINGER, "The Management of Software Engineering. Part III. Software Design Practices," *IBM Systems Journal* **19** (No. 4, 1980), pp. 432–50.

[London, 1971] R. L. LONDON, "Software Reliability through Proving Programs Correct," *Proceedings of the IEEE International Symposium on Fault-Tolerant Computing,* March 1971.

[Luckham and von Henke, 1985] D. C. LUCKHAM AND F. W. VON HENKE, "An Overview of Anna, a Specification Language for Ada," *IEEE Software* **2** (March 1985), pp. 9–22.

[Meyer, 1985] B. MEYER, "On Formalism in Specifications," *IEEE Software* **2** (January 1985), pp. 6–26.

[Modell, 1996] M. E. MODELL, *A Professional's Guide to Systems Analysis,* Second Edition, McGraw-Hill, 1996.

[Naur, 1964] P. NAUR, "The Design of the GIER ALGOL Compiler," in: *Annual Review in Automatic Programming, Volume 4,* Pergamon Press, Oxford, UK, 1964, pp. 49–85.

[Naur, 1969] P. NAUR, "Programming by Action Clusters," *BIT* 9 (No. 3, 1969), pp. 250–58.

[Nix and Collins, 1988] C. J. NIX AND B. P. COLLINS, "The Use of Software Engineering, Including the Z Notation, in the Development of CICS," *Quality Assurance* **14** (September 1988), pp. 103–10.

[Oest, 1986] O. N. OEST, "VDM from Research to Practice," *Proceedings of the IFIP Congress, Information Processing '86,* 1986, pp. 527–33.

[Orr, 1981] K. ORR, *Structured Requirements Definition,* Ken Orr and Associates, Inc., Topeka, KS, 1981.

[Peterson, 1981] J. L. PETERSON, *Petri Net Theory and the Modeling of Systems,* Prentice Hall, Englewood Cliffs, NJ, 1981.

[Petri, 1962] C. A. PETRI, "Kommunikation mit Automaten," Ph.D. Dissertation, University of Bonn, Germany, 1962. (In German.)

[Pfleeger and Hatton, 1997] S. L. PFLEEGER AND L. HATTON, "Investigating the Influence of Formal Methods," *IEEE Computer* **30** (February 1997), pp. 33–43.

[Pollack, Hicks, and Harrison, 1971] S. L. POLLACK, H. T. HICKS, JR., AND W. J. HARRISON, *Decision Tables: Theory and Practice,* Wiley-Interscience, New York, 1971.

[Ross, 1985] D. T. ROSS, "Applications and Extensions of SADT," *IEEE Computer* **18** (April 1985), pp. 25–34.

[Saiedian et al., 1996] H. SAIEDIAN, J. P. BOWEN, R. W. BUTLER, D. L. DILL, R. L. GLASS, D. GRIES, A. HALL, M. G. HINCHEY, C. M. HOLLOWAY, D. JACKSON, C. B. JONES, M. J. LUTZ, D. L. PARNAS, J. RUSHBY, J. WING, AND P. ZAVE, "An Invitation to Formal Methods," *IEEE Computer* **29** (April 1996), pp. 16–30.

[Scheffer, Stone, and Rzepka, 1985] P. A. SCHEFFER, A. H. STONE, III, AND W. E. RZEPKA, "A Case Study of SREM," *IEEE Computer* **18** (April 1985), pp. 47–54.

[Schwartz and Delisle, 1987] M. D. SCHWARTZ AND N. M. DELISLE, "Specifying a Lift Control System with CSP," *Proceedings of the Fourth International Workshop on Software Specification and Design,* Monterey, CA, April 1987, pp. 21–27.

[Silberschatz and Galvin, 1998] A. SILBERSCHATZ AND P. B. GALVIN, *Operating System Concepts,* Fifth Edition, Addison-Wesley, Reading, MA, 1998.

[Smith, Kotik, and Westfold, 1985] D. R. SMITH, G. B. KOTIK, AND S. J. WESTFOLD, "Research on Knowledge-Based Software Environments at the Kestrel Institute," *IEEE Transactions on Software Engineering* **SE-11** (November 1985), pp. 1278–95.

[Spivey, 1988] J. M. SPIVEY, *Understanding Z: A Specification Language and Its Informal Semantics,* Cambridge University Press, Cambridge, UK, 1988.

[Spivey, 1990] J. M. SPIVEY, "Specifying a Real-Time Kernel," *IEEE Software* **7** (September 1990), pp. 21–28.

[Spivey, 1992] J. M. SPIVEY, *The Z Notation: A Reference Manual,* Prentice Hall, New York, 1992.

[Teichroew and Hershey, 1977] D. TEICHROEW AND E. A. HERSHEY, III, "PSL/PSA: A Computer-Aided Technique for Structured Documentation and Analysis of Information Processing Systems," *IEEE Transactions on Software Engineering* **SE-3** (January 1977), pp. 41–48.

[Warnier, 1981] J. D. WARNIER, *Logical Construction of Systems,* Van Nostrand Reinhold, New York, 1981.

[Wasserman, 1985] A. I. WASSERMAN, "Extending State Transition Diagrams for the Specification of Human-Computer Interaction," *IEEE Transactions on Software Engineering* **SE-11** (August 1985), pp. 699–713.

[Wing, 1990] J. WING, "A Specifier's Introduction to Formal Methods," *IEEE Computer* **23** (September 1990), pp. 8–24.

[Woodcock, 1989] J. WOODCOCK, "Calculating Properties of Z Specifications," *ACM SIGSOFT Software Engineering Notes* **14** (July 1989), pp. 43–54.

[Yourdon, 1989] E. YOURDON, *Modern Structured Analysis,* Yourdon Press, Englewood Cliffs, NJ, 1989.

[Yourdon and Constantine, 1979] E. YOURDON AND L. L. CONSTANTINE, *Structured Design: Fundamentals of a Discipline of Computer Program and Systems Design,* Prentice Hall, Englewood Cliffs, NJ, 1979.

chapter

11

OBJECT-ORIENTED ANALYSIS PHASE

The specification phase is sometimes called the "analysis phase." That is why the object-oriented counterpart of the classical specification phase is called the "object-oriented analysis phase." This chapter can thus be viewed as the object-oriented counterpart of Sections 10.3 through 10.8.

As mentioned in Chapter 1, the object-oriented paradigm was introduced in reaction to perceived shortcomings in the structured paradigm. Many small- and medium-scale software projects made use of the structured paradigm with great success. However, the structured paradigm seemed to be less successful when applied to the larger software products that were starting to become more common toward the end of the 1980s.

11.1 OBJECT-ORIENTED VERSUS STRUCTURED PARADIGM

There are two ways of looking at every structured software product. One way is to consider just the data, including local and global variables, parameters, dynamic data structures, files, and so on. Another way of viewing a product is to consider just the actions performed on the data, that is, the procedures and the functions. In terms of this division of software into data and actions, the structured techniques essentially fall into two groups. Action-oriented techniques primarily consider the actions of the product. The data are then of secondary importance and are considered only after the actions of the product have been analyzed in depth. Conversely, data-oriented techniques stress the data of the product; the actions are examined only within the framework of the data.

An example of an action-oriented structured technique is the finite state machine (Section 10.6). Here the emphasis is on the actions; data are considerably less important to an FSM. Structured systems analysis (Section 10.3) is another example of an action-oriented technique. It is true that a data flow diagram shows both data and actions. However, the purpose of a data flow diagram is to show all the various actions that are performed by the product; the data are secondary to the actions. There are also data-oriented structured techniques such as Jackson system development (JSD) [Jackson, 1983] in which the structure of the data is determined first and is then used to determine the structure of the actions that operate on the data. In other words, the structure of the actions conforms to the structure of the data. Another example of a data-oriented structured technique is entity-relationship modeling (ERM), described in Section 10.5.

A fundamental weakness of both data- and action-oriented approaches is that data and action are two sides of the same coin; a data item cannot change unless an action is performed on it, and actions without associated data are equally meaningless. Therefore, techniques that give equal weight to data and to actions are needed. It should not come as a surprise that the object-oriented techniques do this. After all, an object comprises both data and actions. Recall from Chapter 6 that an object is an instance of an abstract data type (or more precisely, of a class). It therefore incorporates both data and the actions that are performed on those data. The data of an object are variously called *attributes, state variables, instance variables, fields,* or *data members*. The actions are called *methods* or *member functions*. But irrespective of the terminology used for data and actions, both are present in objects as equal partners. Similarly, in all the object-oriented techniques, data and actions are considered to be of the same importance, and neither takes precedence over the other.

It is inaccurate to claim that data and actions are considered simultaneously in the techniques of the object-oriented paradigm. From the material on stepwise refinement (Section 4.6), it is clear that there are times when data have to be stressed, and times when actions are more critical. Overall, however, data and actions are given equal importance during the phases of the object-oriented paradigm.

Many reasons are given in Chapters 1 and 6 as to why the object-oriented paradigm is superior to the structured paradigm. Underlying all these reasons is the fact that a well-designed object, that is, an object with high cohesion and low coupling, models all aspects of one physical entity. The details of how this is implemented are hidden; the only communication with an object is via messages sent to that object. As a result, objects are essentially independent units with a well-defined interface. Consequently, they are easily and safely maintainable; the chance of a regression fault is reduced. Furthermore, objects are reusable, and this reusability is enhanced by the property of inheritance. Turning now to development using objects, it is safer to construct a large-scale product by combining these fundamental building blocks of software than to use the structured paradigm. Because objects are essentially independent components of a product, development of the product, as well as management of that development, is easier, and hence less likely to induce faults.

All these aspects of the superiority of the object-oriented paradigm raise a question: If the structured paradigm is so inferior to the object-oriented paradigm, why has the structured paradigm had so many successes? This can be explained by realizing that the structured paradigm was adopted at a time when software engineering was not widely practiced. Instead, software was simply "written."

For managers, the most important thing was for programmers to churn out lines of code. Little more than lip service was paid to the requirements and specification (*systems analysis*) of a product, and design was almost never performed. The build-and-fix model (Section 3.1) was typical of the techniques of the 1970s. Thus, use of the structured paradigm exposed the majority of software developers to methodical techniques for the first time. Small wonder, then, that the structured techniques led to major improvements in the software industry worldwide. However, as software products grew in size, inadequacies of the structured techniques started to become apparent, and the object-oriented paradigm was proposed as a better alternative.

This, in turn, leads to another question: How do we know for certain that the object-oriented paradigm is superior to all other present-day techniques? There are no data available that prove beyond all doubt that object-oriented technology is better than anything else currently available, and it is hard to imagine how such data could be obtained. The best that we can do is to rely on the experiences of organizations that have adopted the object-oriented paradigm. Although not all reports are favorable, the majority (if not the overwhelming majority) attest that using the object-oriented paradigm is a wise decision.

For example, IBM has reported on three totally different projects that were developed using object-oriented technology [Capper, Colgate, Hunter, and James, 1994]. In almost every respect, the object-oriented paradigm greatly outperformed the structured paradigm. Specifically, there were major decreases in the number of faults detected, there were far fewer change requests during both development and maintenance that were not the result of unforeseeable business changes, and both adaptive and perfective maintainability increased significantly. There was also an improvement in usability, though not as large as the previous four improvements, and no meaningful difference in performance.

One final question: Is it not possible that someday there will be something better than the object-oriented paradigm? Even its strongest proponents do not claim that the object-oriented paradigm is the ultimate answer to all software engineering problems. Furthermore, today's software engineers are looking beyond objects to the next major breakthrough. After all, there are few fields of human endeavor in which the techniques of the past are superior to anything that is being put forward today. Present-day techniques, such as the object-oriented paradigm, are equally likely to be superseded by the techniques of the future. The important lesson is that, based on today's knowledge, the object-oriented techniques appear to be the best.

11.2 OBJECT-ORIENTED ANALYSIS

Object-oriented analysis (OOA) is a semiformal specification technique for the object-oriented paradigm. In Chapter 10 it was pointed out that there are a number of different techniques for structured systems analysis, all essentially equivalent.

Similarly, there are currently well over 50 different techniques for performing OOA, and new techniques are put forward on a regular basis. Again, all the techniques are largely equivalent. The "For Further Reading" section of this chapter includes references to a wide variety of techniques, as well as to published comparisons of different techniques.

Because object-oriented analysis is a semiformal technique, an intrinsic part of every technique for OOA is the graphical notation associated with that technique. Thus, learning to use a specific technique also requires learning the relevant graphical notation. This has changed with the publication of the Unified Modeling Language (UML). In this book UML is used for representing both the object-oriented analysis and the object-oriented design. For more information on UML, see the Just in Case You Wanted to Know Box below.

OOA consists of three steps:

1. Use-case modeling. Determine how the various results are computed by the product (without regard to sequencing). Present this information in the form of a *use-case diagram* and associated scenarios. (A scenario, described in Section 9.1, is an instance of a use case.) This step, sometimes referred to as *functional modeling,* is largely action oriented.

JUST IN CASE YOU WANTED TO KNOW

Currently, the most popular object-oriented analysis and design methodologies are Object Modeling Technique (OMT) [Rumbaugh, et al., 1991] and Booch's technique [Booch, 1994]. OMT was developed by Jim Rumbaugh and his team at the General Electric Research and Development Center in Schenectady, NY, whereas Grady Booch developed his methodology at Rational, Inc., in Santa Clara, CA. As explained in the text, all object-oriented analysis (OOA) techniques are essentially equivalent. Object-oriented design (OOD) techniques are also largely equivalent to one another, so the differences between OMT and Booch's methodology are small. Nevertheless, there was always a friendly rivalry between supporters of the two camps.

This changed in October, 1994 when Rumbaugh joined Booch at Rational. The two methodologists immediately began to develop what they termed the Unified Methodology (UM) based on a combination of their techniques. When the first version of their work was published, it was pointed out that what they had developed was not a methodology, but merely a notation for representing an object-oriented software product. The name "Unified Methodology" was quickly changed to *Unified Modeling Language* (UML).

In 1995 they were joined at Rational by Ivar Jacobson, a pioneer of object-oriented software engineering. Jacobson had developed his methodology, Object-Oriented Software Engineering (OOSE) [Jacobson, Christerson, Jonsson, and Overgaard, 1992] in Sweden, starting in 1967. OOSE is based on use cases (see Section 11.4). Version 1.0 of UML [UML, 1997] reflects the combined work of Booch, Rumbaugh, and Jacobson, sometimes collectively referred to as "The Three Amigos."

At the time of writing, no specific techniques or methodologies have been attached to UML by the team at Rational. UML remains a common notation that can be used by any modeling technique and, thus, with any methodology.

2. Class modeling. Determine the classes and their attributes. Then, determine the interrelationships between the classes. Present this information in the form of a diagram somewhat similar to an entity-relationship diagram (Section 10.5), termed the *class diagram.* (Some authors refer to this diagram as the *class model.*) This step is purely data-oriented.

3. Dynamic modeling. Determine the actions performed by or to each class or subclass. Present this information in the form of a diagram somewhat similar to a finite state machine (Section 10.6), termed the *state diagram.* This step is purely action-oriented.

In practice, the three steps are not performed purely sequentially. A change in one diagram will trigger corresponding revisions of the other two diagrams. Thus, the three steps of OOA are effectively performed in parallel. This makes sense in view of the fact that, in the object-oriented paradigm, neither data (Step 2) nor actions (Steps 1 and 3) take precedence over the other.

OOA should certainly not be viewed as a combination of two of the structured specification techniques of the previous chapter, namely, entity-relationship modeling (ERM) and finite state machines (FSM). On the contrary, OOA is a modeling technique that makes use of diagrams for specifying the results of the three modeling steps. Instead of inventing totally new ways of displaying this information, it makes sense to employ notations based on widely used structured techniques.

Another way of looking at this is to appreciate that the aim of OOA, like that of all other specification techniques, is to specify the target product to be built. Two critical aspects of that product are its data and its actions. OOA uses a variety of modeling techniques in order to understand the data, the actions, and the interplay between data and actions. During the course of the analysis, the knowledge gained about the product is represented in different ways, each reflecting a different aspect of the target product. The diagrams are continually updated as a more thorough perception of the system being modeled is achieved. By the end of the OOA phase, the combined views provide an overall understanding of the product that would be difficult to achieve if only one modeling technique were employed.

11.3 ELEVATOR PROBLEM: OBJECT-ORIENTED ANALYSIS

The steps of OOA are described by means of an example, namely, the elevator problem first described in Chapter 10. For ease of reference, the problem is repeated here.

A product is to be installed to control n elevators in a building with m floors. The problem concerns the logic required to move elevators between floors according to the following constraints:

Constraint 1: Each elevator has a set of m buttons, one for each floor. These illuminate when pressed and cause the elevator to visit the corresponding floor.

The illumination is canceled when the corresponding floor is visited by the elevator.

Constraint 2: Each floor, except the first floor and top floor, has two buttons, one to request an up-elevator and one to request a down-elevator. These buttons illuminate when pressed. The illumination is canceled when an elevator visits the floor and then moves in the desired direction.

Constraint 3: When an elevator has no requests, it remains at its current floor with its doors closed.

The first step in OOA is to model the use cases.

11.4 USE-CASE MODELING

A use case describes the functionality of the product to be constructed. It provides a generic description of the overall functionality; scenarios are then specific instantiations of the use case, just as objects are instantiations of a class. A use case is concerned with the overall interaction between the classes of the software product and the actors (users) of the product. A scenario is one particular set of interactions between specific objects and users.

A UML representation of the use case for the elevator problem is shown in Figure 11.1. The only interactions possible between users and classes is a user pressing an elevator button to summon an elevator or a user pressing a floor button to request the elevator to stop at a specific floor. Within this generic description of the overall functionality we can extract a vast number of different scenarios, each representing one specific set of interactions. For example, Figure 11.2 depicts a normal scenario, that is, a set of interactions between users and elevators that corresponds to the way that we understand elevators should be used. In contrast, Figure 11.3 is an abnormal scenario. It depicts what happens when a user presses the Up button at floor 3 but actually wants to go to floor 1. (UML provides

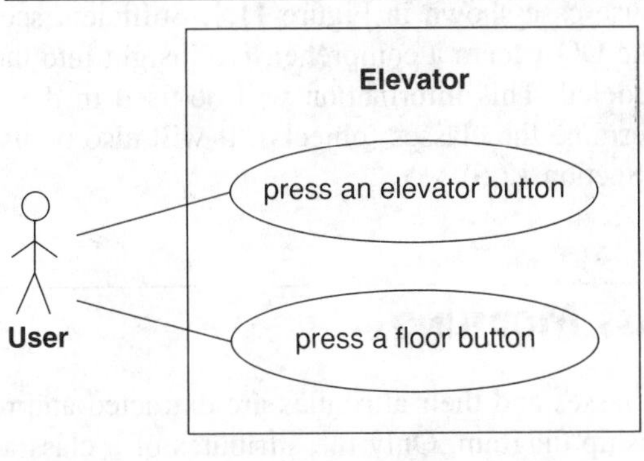

Figure 11.1 Use case for elevator problem.

1. User A presses Up floor button at floor 3 to request elevator. User A wishes to go to floor 7.
2. Up floor button is turned on.
3. An elevator arrives at floor 3. It contains User B who has entered the elevator at floor 1 and pressed the elevator button for floor 9.
4. Up floor button is turned off.
5. Elevator doors open.

   User A enters elevator.
6. User A presses elevator button for floor 7.
7. Floor 7 elevator button is turned on.
8. Elevator doors close.
9. Elevator travels to floor 7.
10. Floor 7 elevator button is turned off.
11. Elevator doors open to allow User A to exit elevator.
12. Timer starts.

    User A exits.
13. Elevator doors close after timeout.
14. Elevator proceeds to floor 9 with User B.

Figure 11.2 A normal scenario.

two types of diagrams for representing scenarios, namely, sequence diagrams and collaboration diagrams. However, these diagrams are more useful for object-oriented design than object-oriented analysis, so the discussion of these diagrams is deferred until Section 12.7.)

The scenarios of Figures 11.2 and 11.3, plus innumerable others, are specific instances of the use case shown in Figure 11.1. Sufficient scenarios should be studied to give the OOA team a comprehensive insight into the behavior of the system being modeled. This information will be used in the next phase, class modeling, to determine the classes (objects). It will also be used in the object-oriented design (Section 12.6).

11.5 CLASS MODELING

In this step, the classes and their attributes are extracted and represented using an entity-relationship diagram. Only the attributes of a class are determined at this time, not the methods; the latter are assigned to the classes during the object-oriented design (OOD) phase.

1. User A presses Up floor button at floor 3 to request elevator. User A wishes to go to floor 1.
2. Up floor button is turned on.
3. An elevator arrives at floor 3. It contains User B who has entered the elevator at floor 1 and pressed the elevator button for floor 9.
4. Up floor button is turned off.
5. Elevator doors open.

   User A enters elevator.
6. User A presses elevator button for floor 1.
7. Floor 1 elevator button is turned on.
8. Elevator doors close after timeout.
9. Elevator travels to floor 9.
10. Floor 9 elevator button is turned off.
11. Elevator doors open to allow User B to exit elevator.
12. Timer starts.

    User B exits.
13. Elevator doors close after timeout.
14. Elevator proceeds to floor 1 with User A.

Figure 11.3 An abnormal scenario.

A characteristic of the whole object-oriented paradigm is that the various steps are rarely easy to carry out. Fortunately, the resulting benefits of using objects make the effort worthwhile. So it should not come as a surprise that the very first part of class modeling, namely, extracting classes and their attributes, is usually difficult to get right the first time.

One method of determining the classes is to deduce them from the use cases. That is, the developers carefully study all the scenarios, both normal and abnormal, and identify the items that play a role in the use cases. From just the scenarios of Figures 11.2 and 11.3, candidate classes are elevator buttons, floor buttons, elevators, doors, and timers. As we will see, these candidate classes are extremely close to the actual classes extracted during class modeling. In general, however, there will be many scenarios and, consequently, a large number of potential classes. An inexperienced developer may be tempted to infer too many candidate classes from the scenarios. This will have a deleterious effect on the class modeling because it is easier to add a new class than to remove a candidate class that should not have been included.

Another approach to determining the classes that also is effective when the developers have domain expertise is CRC cards (Section 11.5.2). However, if the developers have little or no experience in the application domain then it is advisable to use noun extraction, described in the next section.

11.5.1 NOUN EXTRACTION

For developers without domain expertise, a good way to proceed is to use the following three-stage process to extract candidate classes and then to refine the solution.

Stage 1. Concise Problem Definition. Define the product as briefly and concisely as possible, preferably in a single sentence. In the case of the elevator problem, one possible way of doing this is

> Buttons in elevators and on the floors control the motion of n elevators in a building with m floors.

Stage 2. Informal Strategy. In order to come up with an informal strategy for solving the problem, the constraints must be taken into account. The three constraints of the elevator problem appear at the end of the previous section. Now the informal strategy can be expressed, preferably in a single paragraph. One possible paragraph for the elevator problem is

> Buttons in elevators and on the floors control the movement of n elevators in a building with m floors. Buttons illuminate when pressed to request the elevator to stop at a specific floor; the illumination is canceled when the request has been satisfied. When an elevator has no requests, it remains at its current floor with its doors closed.

Stage 3. Formalize the Strategy. Identify the nouns in the informal strategy (excluding those that lie outside the problem boundary), and then use these nouns as candidate classes. The informal strategy is now reproduced, but this time with the nouns identified printed in a different typeface.

> Buttons in elevators and on the floors control the movement of n elevators in a building with m floors. Buttons illuminate when pressed to request an elevator to stop at a specific floor; the illumination is canceled when the request has been satisfied. When an elevator has no requests, it remains at its current floor with its doors closed.

There are eight different nouns, namely, button, elevator, floor, movement, building, illumination, request, and door. Three of these nouns, namely, floor, building, and door, lie outside the problem boundary and may therefore be ignored. Three of the remaining nouns, namely, movement, illumination, and request, are abstract nouns. That is, they "identify ideas or quantities that have no physical existence" [World Book Encyclopedia, 1996]. It is a useful rule of thumb that abstract nouns rarely end up corresponding to

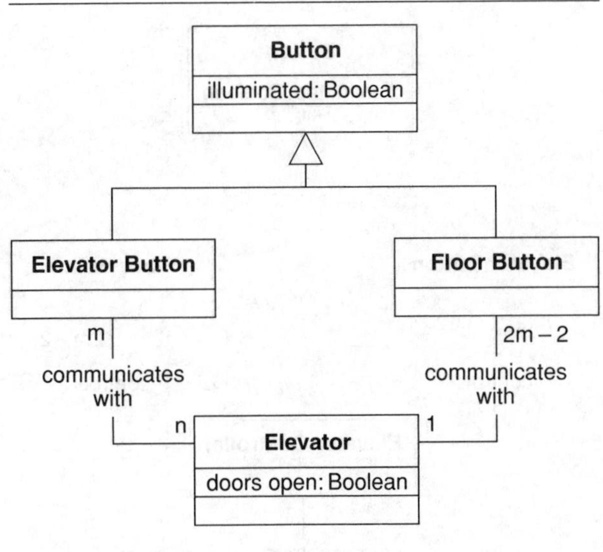

Figure 11.4 First iteration of class diagram.

classes. Instead, they frequently are attributes of classes. For example, illumination turns out to be an attribute of button. Other abstract nouns (for example request) turn out to be extraneous to the problem description. This leaves two candidate classes, namely, **Elevator** and **Button**. (The UML convention is to use boldface for classes and to capitalize the initial letter of the name of a class.)

The problem specifies two types of button, so two subclasses of **Button** will be defined, namely, **Elevator Button** and **Floor Button**. The resulting class diagram is shown in Figure 11.4. There are two base classes, namely, **Elevator**, with attribute doors open, and **Button**, with attribute illuminated. The figure also shows that **Elevator Button** and **Floor Button** are subclasses of **Button**; the open triangle denotes inheritance in UML.

This is not a good beginning. In a real elevator, the buttons do not directly communicate with the elevators; there must be some sort of elevator controller, if only to decide which elevator to dispatch in response to a particular request. However, the problem statement makes no mention of a controller, so it was not selected as a class. In other words, the technique for finding candidate classes provides a starting point, but certainly should not be relied upon to do more than that.

Adding the controller yields Figure 11.5. This certainly makes more sense. In addition, the fact that all three relationships (or, more precisely, associations—see Section 6.7) are now one-to-many may make the design and implementation easier. It therefore seems reasonable to go on to Step 3 at this point, bearing in mind that it is possible to return to class modeling at any time. However, before proceeding with the dynamic modeling, a different technique for class modeling is considered.

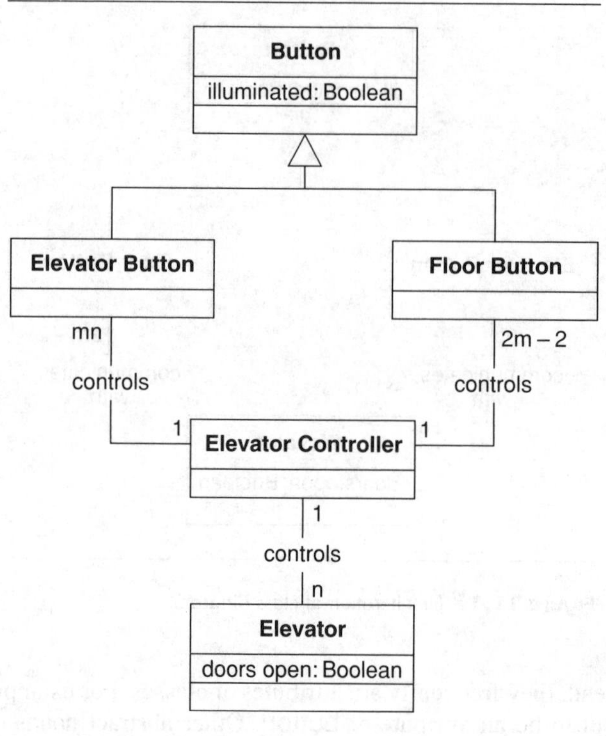

Figure 11.5 Second iteration of class diagram.

11.5.2 CRC CARDS

For a number of years, class-responsibility-collaboration (CRC) cards have been utilized during the object-oriented analysis phase [Wirfs-Brock, Wilkerson, and Wiener, 1990]. For each class, the software development team fills in a card showing the name of the class, the functionality of that class (responsibility), and a list of the other classes it invokes in order to achieve that functionality (collaboration).

This approach has subsequently been extended. First, a CRC card often explicitly contains the attributes and methods of the class, rather than just its "responsibility" expressed in some natural language. Second, the technology has changed. Instead of using cards, some organizations put the names of the classes on Post-it notes that they then move around on a white board; lines are drawn between the Post-it notes to denote collaboration. Nowadays the whole process can be automated; CASE tools like System Architect include modules for creating and updating CRC "cards" on the screen.

The strength of CRC cards is that, when utilized by a team, the interaction between the members can highlight missing or incorrect items in a class, whether attributes or methods. Also, relationships between classes are clarified when CRC cards are used. One especially powerful technique is to distribute the cards among

JUST IN CASE YOU WANTED TO KNOW

How do we find the number of days between February 21, 1996, and August 10, 1998? Such subtractions are needed in many financial computations, such as calculating an interest payment or determining the present value of a future cash flow. The usual way this is done is to convert each date into an integer, the number of days since a specified starting date. The problem is that we cannot agree what starting date to use.

Astronomers use Julian Days, the number of days since noon GMT on January 1, 4713 BCE. This system was invented in 1582 by Joseph Scaliger, who named it for his father, Julius Caesar Scaliger. (If you really have to know why January 1, 4713 BCE, was chosen, consult [Alburger, 1996].)

A Lilian date is the number of days since October 15, 1582, the first day of the Gregorian calendar introduced by Pope Gregory XIII. Lilian dates are named for Luigi Lilio, a leading proponent of the Gregorian calendar reform. Lilio was responsible for deriving many of the algorithms of the Gregorian calendar, including the rule for leap years.

Turning to software, ANSI COBOL 85 intrinsic functions use January 1, 1601 as the starting date for integer dates. Almost all spreadsheets, however, use January 1, 1900, following the lead of Lotus 1-2-3.

the team members who then act out the responsibilities of their classes. Thus, someone might say, "I am the **Date** class and my responsibility is to create new date objects." Another team member might then interject that he or she needs additional functionality from the **Date** class, such as converting a date from the conventional format to an integer, the number of days from January 1, 1990, so that finding the number of days between any two dates can easily be computed by subtracting the corresponding two integers (see the Just in Case You Wanted to Know Box above). Thus, acting out the responsibilities of CRC cards is an effective means of verifying that the class diagram is complete and correct.

A weakness of CRC cards is that this approach is generally not a good way of finding the classes unless the team members have considerable experience in the relevant domain. On the other hand, once the developers have already determined many of the classes and have a good idea of their responsibilities and collaborations, then CRC cards can be an excellent way of completing the process and making sure that everything is correct.

11.6 DYNAMIC MODELING

The aim of dynamic modeling is to produce a state diagram, a description of the target product similar to a finite state model, for each class. First consider class **Elevator Controller**. For simplicity, only one elevator is considered. The relevant state diagram for the **Elevator Controller** is shown in Figure 11.6. The notation is somewhat similar to that of the finite state machines of Section 10.6, but there is a significant difference. An FSM as presented in Chapter 10 is an example of a formal technique. The state transition diagram (STD) themselves are not a complete representation of the product to be built. Instead, the model consists of a set of transition rules of the form given in Equation (10.2), namely

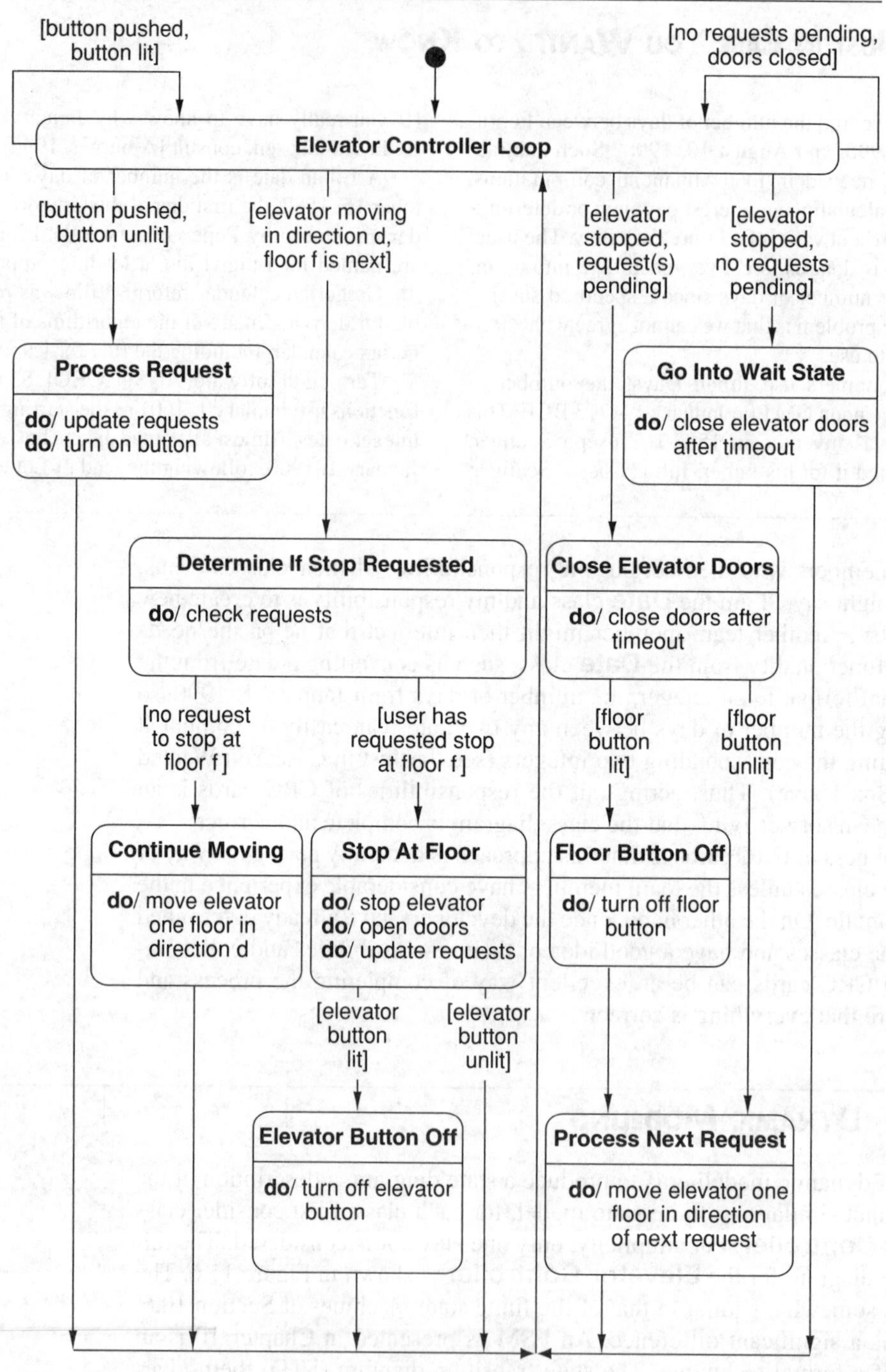

Figure 11.6 State diagram for **Elevator Controller** class.

current state and **event** and **predicate** ⇒ **next state**

Formality is achieved by presenting the model in the form of a set of mathematical rules.

In contrast, the representation of a UML state diagram is somewhat less formal. The three aspects of a state machine, namely, state, event, and predicate, are distributed over the UML diagram. For example, state **Go into Wait State** is entered if the present state is **Elevator Control Loop** and the predicate elevator stopped, no requests pending holds. (UML predicates or "guards" appear in brackets, as shown in Figure 11.6). When the state has been entered, the UML reserved word **do** indicates that action close elevator doors after timeout is to be carried out. Current versions of OOA are semiformal (graphical) techniques, and the intrinsic lack of formality of the state diagram is accordingly not a problem. However, when the object-oriented paradigm matures, it is likely that more formal versions will be developed and that the corresponding dynamic models will be somewhat closer to finite state machines.

To see the equivalence of the state diagram of Figure 11.6 and the STDs of Figures 10.13 through 10.15, consider various scenarios. For example, consider the first part of the scenario of Figure 11.2. First, User A presses the Up floor button at floor 3. If the floor button is not on, then according to both Figure 10.14 and the leftmost path of Figure 11.6, the button is turned on as required. In the case of the state diagram, the next state is **Elevator Controller Loop.**

Next, the elevator nears floor 3. In Figure 10.15, the elevator goes into state S(U, 3), that is, it stops at floor 3, about to go up. (Because the simplifying assumption has been made that there is only one elevator, the argument e in Figure 10.15 is suppressed here.) From Figure 10.14, when the elevator arrives, the floor button is turned off. Now (Figure 10.15) the doors close, and the elevator starts to move toward floor 4.

Returning to the state diagram of Figure 11.6, consider what happens when the elevator nears floor 3. Because the elevator is in motion, the next state entered is **Determine If Stop Requested**. The requests are checked and, because User A has requested the elevator to stop there, the next state is **Stop At Floor**. The elevator stops at floor 3 and the doors are opened. The elevator button for floor 3 has not been pressed, so state **Elevator Controller Loop** is next.

User A enters and presses the elevator button for floor 7. Thus, the next state is **Process Request**, followed again by **Elevator Controller Loop**. The elevator has stopped and there are two requests pending, so state **Close Elevator Doors** is next and the doors are closed after a timeout. The floor button at floor 3 was pressed by User A, so **Floor Button Off** is the following state, and the floor button is turned off. State **Process Next Request** is next, and the elevator starts to move towards floor 4. The relevant aspects of the corresponding diagrams are clearly equivalent with respect to this scenario; the reader may wish to consider other possible scenarios as well.

The state diagrams for the other classes are relatively straightforward and are therefore left as an exercise (Problem 11.1).

CLASS
Elevator Controller
RESPONSIBILITY
1. Turn on elevator button
2. Turn off elevator button
3. Turn on floor button
4. Turn off floor button
5. Open elevator doors
6. Close elevator doors
7. Move elevator one floor up
8. Move elevator one floor down
COLLABORATION
1. Class **Elevator Button**
2. Class **Floor Button**
3. Class **Elevator**

Figure 11.7 First iteration of CRC card for class **Elevator Controller**.

11.7 TESTING DURING THE OBJECT-ORIENTED ANALYSIS PHASE

At this point, the three models of the object-oriented analysis process seem to be complete. The next step is to review the OOA to date. One component of this review, as suggested in Section 11.5.2, is to use CRC cards.

Accordingly, CRC cards are filled in for each of the classes, namely **Button**, **Elevator Button**, **Floor Button**, **Elevator**, and **Elevator Controller**. The CRC card for **Elevator Controller**, shown in Figure 11.7, is deduced from the class diagram of Figure 11.5 and the state diagram of Figure 11.6.

The CRC card highlights two major problems with the OOA. First consider responsibility 1. Turn on elevator button. This command is totally out of place in the object-oriented paradigm. From the viewpoint of responsibility-driven design (Section 1.6), objects of class **Elevator Button** are responsible for turning themselves on or off. Also, from the viewpoint of information hiding (Section 6.6), the **Elevator Controller** should not have the knowledge of the internals of **Elevator Button** needed to be able to turn a button on. The correct responsibility is: send a message to **Elevator Button** to turn itself on. Similar changes are needed to responsibilities 2, 3, 4, 7 and 8 in Figure 11.7.

The second problem is that a class has been overlooked. Consider the responsibility 5. Open elevator doors. The key concept here is the notion of *state*. The attributes of a class are sometimes termed *state variables*. The reason for

JUST IN CASE YOU WANTED TO KNOW

Some years ago, I was on the 10th floor of a building, waiting impatiently for an elevator. The doors opened, I started to step forward—only there was no elevator there. What saved me was the total blackness that I saw as I was about to step into the elevator shaft, and I instinctively realized that something was wrong.

Perhaps if that elevator control system had been developed using the object-oriented paradigm, the inappropriate opening of the doors on the 10th floor might have been avoided.

this terminology is that in most object-oriented implementations the state of the product is determined by the values of the attributes of the various component objects. The state diagram has many features in common with a finite state machine. Accordingly, it is not surprising that the concept of state plays an important role in the object-oriented paradigm. This concept can be used to help determine whether an item should be modeled as a class. If the item in question possesses a state that will be changed during execution of the implementation, then it should probably be modeled as a class. It is clear that the doors of the elevator possess a state (open or closed), and that **Elevator Doors** is therefore a missing class.

There is another reason why **Elevator Doors** should be a class. The object-oriented paradigm allows state to be hidden within an object, and hence protected from unauthorized change. If there is an **Elevator Doors** object, the only way that the doors of the elevator can be opened or shut is by sending a message to that **Elevator Doors** object. Serious accidents can be caused by opening or closing the doors of an elevator at the wrong time; see the Just in Case You Wanted to Know Box above. Thus, for certain types of products, safety considerations should be added to the other advantages of objects listed in Chapters 6 and 7.

The corrected class diagram is shown in Figure 11.8. The figure also reflects two additional classes. Class **Elevator Application** will be required for method main. Also, during the detailed design, various utility routines will almost certainly be needed; these will be assigned to class **Elevator Utilities**. (Recall that Java is a pure object-oriented language and hence there are no procedures or functions. Instead, all data and actions have to be fields of classes.)

Having modified the class diagram, the use-case and state diagrams must now be reexamined to see if they, too, need further refinement. The use-case diagram is clearly still adequate. However, the set of state diagrams must be extended to include the additional class. The CRC cards must also be modified and then rechecked; the corrected CRC card for the **Elevator Controller** class is shown in Figure 11.9. Even after all these changes have been made and checked, it may still be necessary during the object-oriented design phase to return to the object-oriented analysis and revise one or more of the diagrams.

As pointed out in Section 10.1, the specification document is a contract between client and developers. Accordingly, after the OOA is complete, a more conventional specification document has to be drawn up; one alternative is to use a format similar to that of Appendix D. Once approved, the specification document is handed to the design team together with the various UML diagrams.

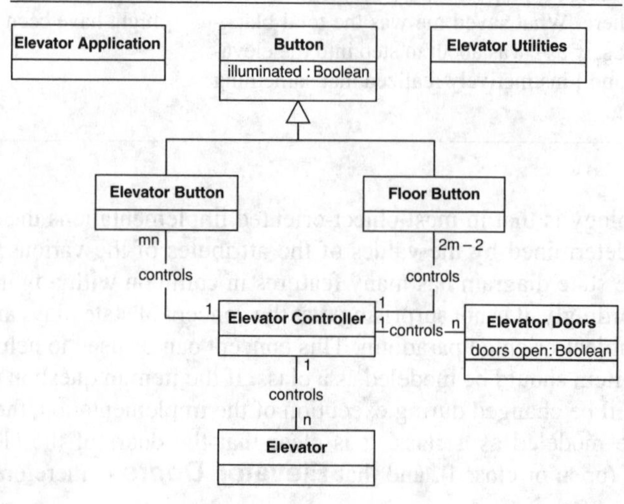

Figure 11.8 Third iteration of class diagram.

CLASS **Elevator Controller**
RESPONSIBILITY
1. Send message to **Elevator Button** to turn on button 2. Send message to **Elevator Button** to turn off button 3. Send message to **Floor Button** to turn on button 4. Send message to **Floor Button** to turn off button 5. Send message to **Elevator Doors** to open doors 6. Send message to **Elevator Doors** to close doors 7. Send message to **Elevator** to move one floor up 8. Send message to **Elevator** to move one floor down
COLLABORATION
1. Subclass **Elevator Button** 2. Subclass **Floor Button** 3. Class **Elevator Doors** 4. Class **Elevator**

Figure 11.9 Second iteration of CRC card for class **Elevator Controller**.

11.8 CASE TOOLS FOR THE OBJECT-ORIENTED ANALYSIS PHASE

Bearing in mind the role played by diagrams in object-oriented analysis, it is not surprising that a number of different CASE tools have been developed for supporting object-oriented analysis. In its basic form, such a tool is essentially a drawing tool that makes it easy to perform each of the modeling steps. More importantly, it is far simpler to modify a diagram that has been constructed with a drawing tool than to attempt to change a hand-drawn figure. Thus, a CASE tool of this type supports the graphical aspects of object-oriented analysis. In addition, some tools of this type not only draw all the relevant diagrams, but CRC cards as well. A strength of these tools is that a change to the underlying model is automatically reflected in all the affected diagrams.

On the other hand, some CASE tools support not just object-oriented analysis, but a considerable portion of the rest of the object-oriented life cycle as well. Furthermore, many of these tools support a variety of notations, including OMT [Rumbaugh et al., 1991]), Booch's technique [Booch, 1994], as well as UML [UML, 1997]. Examples of such tools include Rose and Software through Pictures.

11.9 OSBERT OGLESBY CASE STUDY: OBJECT-ORIENTED ANALYSIS

OOA consists of three steps: use-case modeling, class modeling, and dynamic modeling. These steps are carried out iteratively, starting with the first step, *use-case modeling*.

The use-case diagram is shown in Figure 11.10. It shows the three kinds of functionality of the Osbert Oglesby product, namely, buying a painting, selling a painting, and printing a report. (Because the fashionability coefficient is used in computing a buying price, updating a fashionability coefficient is considered part of buying.)

Normal and exceptional scenarios are now needed for each of the three kinds of functionality of the use-case diagram. For example, buying a painting consists of buying a masterpiece, a masterwork, or other. Similarly, printing a report consists of printing a report of paintings sold, paintings bought, or fashionability trends. Scenarios are needed for each possibility. One approach is to show normal and abnormal scenarios; one of each for the elevator problem is shown in Figures 11.2 and 11.3. For the Osbert Oglesby problem we use a slightly different formalism, namely, an expanded scenario that reflects possible alternatives. Figure 11.11 is an expanded scenario for buying a masterpiece. The remaining scenarios are equally straightforward so, for the sake of brevity, they are omitted here (but see Problem 11.9).

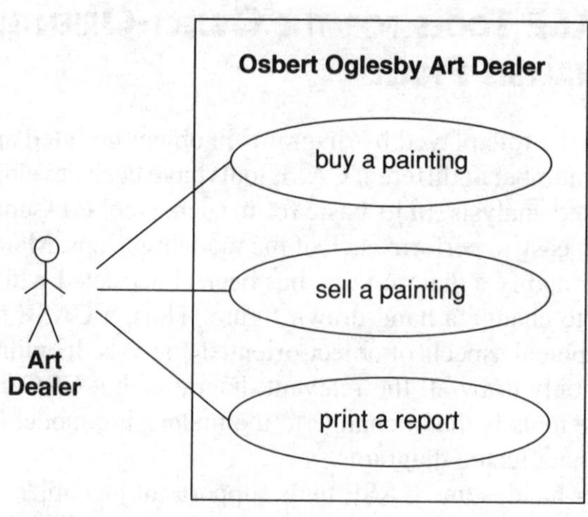

Figure 11.10 Use-case diagram for Osbert Oglesby product.

	Art dealer wishes to buy a masterpiece.
1.	Dealer enters description of painting.
2.	Product scans auction records for price and year of sale of most similar work by same artist.
3.	Product computes maximum purchase price by adding 8.5%, compounded annually, for each year since that auction.
	Dealer makes bid below maximum purchase price. Bid is accepted by seller.
4.	Dealer enters sales information (name and address of seller, purchase price).
	Possible Alternatives
A.	There is no similar painting in auction file by that artist.
B.	Seller turns down bid.

Figure 11.11 Expanded scenario for buying a masterpiece.

The second step is *class modeling*. The aim of this step is to extract the classes, find their attributes, and determine their interrelationships. Here we use the noun extraction method of Section 11.5.1. Stage 1 is to define the product as briefly and concisely as possible, preferably in a single sentence. In the case of Osbert Oglesby, one possible way of doing this is

> A computerized system is needed to improve the decision-making process for purchasing works of art.

In Stage 2, an informal strategy is drawn up, preferably in a single paragraph. One possible such paragraph is

> Reports are to be generated in order to improve the efficacy of the decision-making process for purchasing works of art. The reports contain buying and selling information about paintings which are classified as masterpieces, masterworks, and other.

In Stage 3 the nouns are extracted from this paragraph, yielding

> Reports are to be generated in order to improve the efficacy of the decision-making process for purchasing works of art. The reports contain buying and selling information about paintings, which are classified as masterpieces, masterworks, and other.

The nouns are report, efficacy, process, work of art, buying, selling, information, painting, masterpiece, masterwork, and other. Efficacy, process and information are abstract nouns and are therefore unlikely to be classes. Buying and selling will probably be methods of some class. Report may turn out to be a class. However, because it is usually easier to add a class than to delete one, it is probably better to set it aside for now. Work of art is clearly a synonym for painting. This leaves four candidate classes, namely, **Painting**, **Masterpiece**, **Masterwork**, and **Other**. The resulting first iteration of the class diagram is shown in Figure 11.12. The figure reflects that the base class is **Painting**, and the other three classes are subclasses of that base class.

Rereading the algorithm for determining the maximum price that Osbert will pay for a painting, it is clear that a number of aspects of the case study have been overlooked. The informal strategy has ignored auction records and fashionability coefficients. Two other classes are needed to rectify this, namely, **Auctioned Painting** and **Fashionability**. These two new classes are fundamentally different in nature; an **Auctioned Painting** is a painting, whereas a **Fashionability** coefficient relates to an artist. Another problem is that, from the viewpoint of the algorithm, class **Masterwork** should be a subclass of **Masterpiece**. A second iteration of the class diagram incorporating these changes is shown in Figure 11.13.

The base class remains **Painting**. However, now there are two subclasses of a **Painting**, a **Gallery Painting** (that is, a painting purchased by the gallery and possibly subsequently resold), and an **Auctioned Painting**. The algorithm for computing the maximum price for a painting of type **Other** requires the fashionability coefficient of the artist. Thus, there is an association between class **Other** and class **Fashionability**; it is labeled uses in Figure 11.13. (The association relation is explained in Section 6.7.)

Why was the first iteration of the class diagram so wrong? The informal strategy (that is, the one-paragraph description of what the product should do) did not incorporate the details of the pricing algorithm. After all, the Osbert Oglesby case study appears to be a straightforward data processing application, so it is unreasonable to expect that the computational details of an algorithm would have a major impact on the class diagram. The informal strategy therefore appropriately

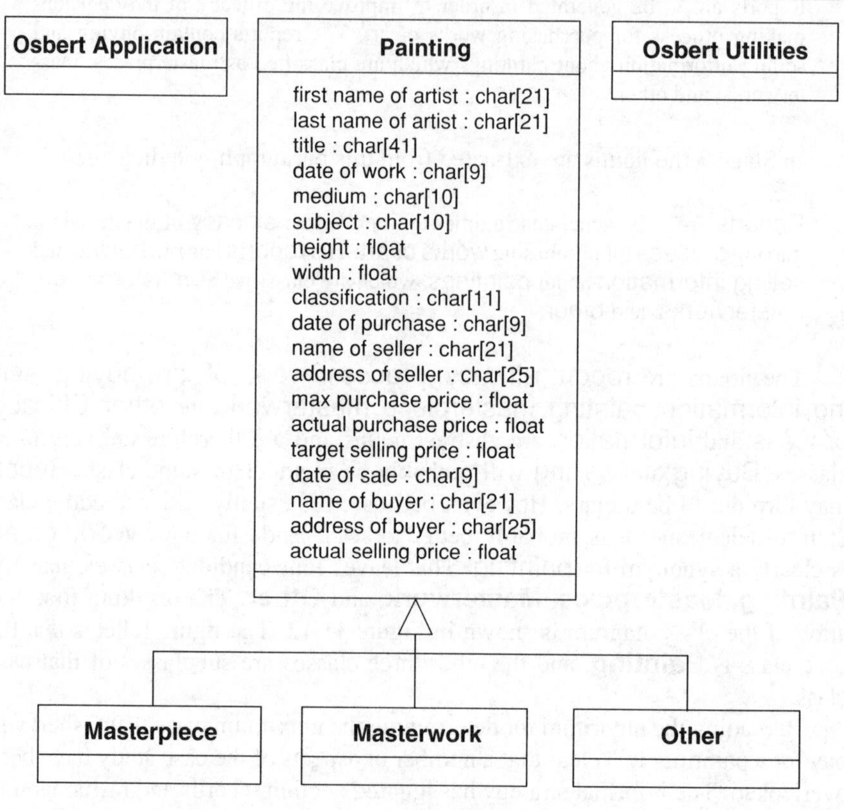

Figure 11.12 First iteration of class diagram for Osbert Oglesby Case Study.

excluded the details of the algorithm. Unfortunately, the algorithmic details turned out to be critical to the class diagram, so the first iteration of the class diagram was far from correct. Once again, the iterative nature of the object-oriented paradigm has been demonstrated.

Now suppose that the candidate classes had been deduced from the scenarios of the use case instead of employing the noun-extraction method. If, as typified by Figure 11.11, separate scenarios had been drawn up for each of the three types of paintings (masterpiece, masterwork, and other), then the need to include algorithmic details would have been apparent. However, if through lack of experience the developers had instead included just one overall buying scenario that stated that Product computes maximum purchase price using given algorithm, then the result would have been the same as with noun extraction.

The third step in object-oriented analysis is *dynamic modeling*. All the possible scenarios are reflected in the state diagram of Figure 11.14 for the complete product. Strictly speaking, a state diagram appertains to a class, not the product

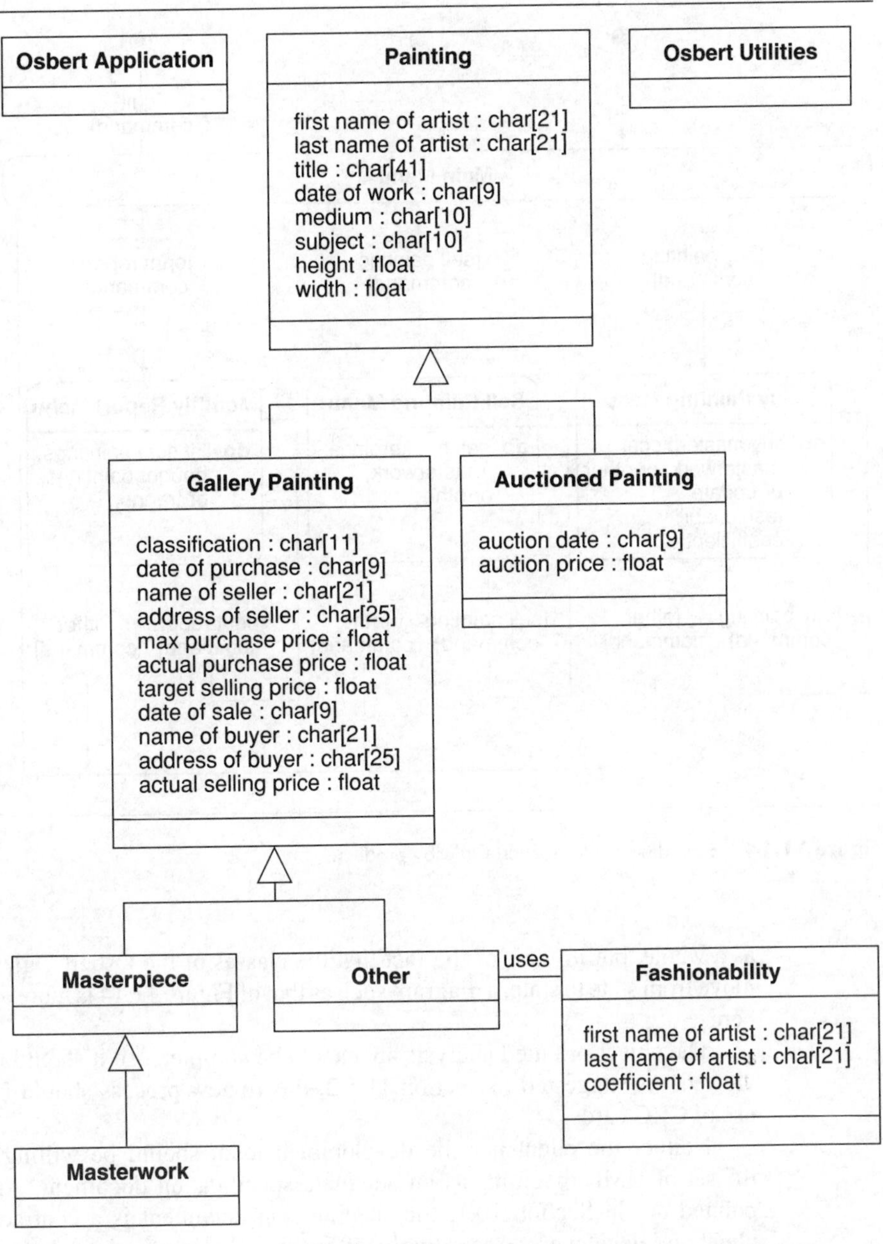

Figure 11.13 Second iteration of class diagram for Osbert Oglesby Case Study.

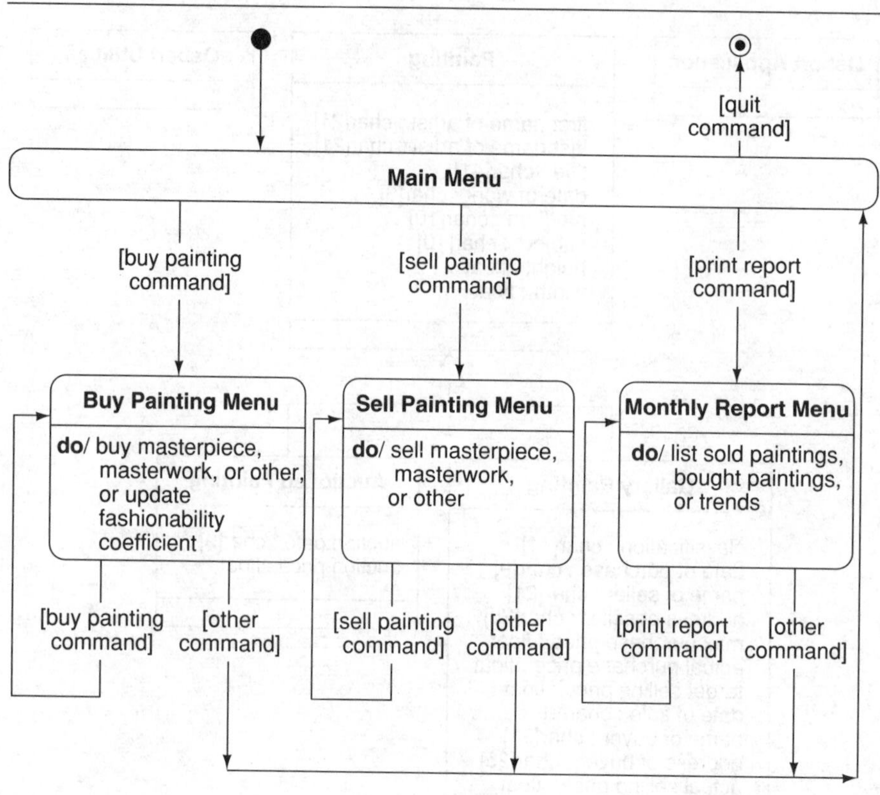

Figure 11.14 State diagram for Osbert Oglesby product.

as a whole, but in view of the fact that the classes of the Osbert Oglesby do not move from state to state, a diagram such as that of Figure 11.14 is more appropriate here.

The object-oriented analysis appears to be complete, so it should now be reviewed. As suggested in Section 11.5.2, this review process should include the use of CRC cards.

Neither the client nor the development team should be willing to accept the set of UML diagrams as an adequate specification document. After all, as pointed out in Section 10.1, the specification document is a contract between client and developers. Accordingly, after the OOA is complete, a more conventional specification document has to be drawn up. Because that document would be so similar to the material of Appendix D, it is omitted from this case study for brevity.

As with the structured paradigm (Section 10.15), at this point the software project management plan is drawn up.

11.10 Osbert Oglesby Case Study: Software Project Management Plan

Appendix F contains a software project management plan (SPMP) for development of the Osbert Oglesby product by a small (three-person) software organization. As explained in Section 10.15, the Instructor's Manual for the First Edition of *Software Engineering* (available from McGraw-Hill) contains a SPMP for a project developed by a large software organization. Both types of plan fit the IEEE SPMP format equally well, further evidence of its broad range of applicability.

Chapter Review

The object-oriented and structured paradigms are compared (Section 11.1). Then, object-oriented analysis is described (Section 11.2) and demonstrated by means of a case study (Section 11.3). Next, the three steps of the object-oriented analysis phase are described, namely, use-case modeling (Section 11.4), class modeling (Section 11.5), and dynamic modeling (Section 11.6). CASE tools for object-oriented analysis are discussed in Section 11.8. The chapter concludes with the Osbert Oglesby case study (Sections 11.9 and 11.10).

For Further Reading

Books describing different versions of object-oriented analysis include [Coad and Yourdon, 1991a], [Rumbaugh et al., 1991], [Jacobson, Christerson, Jonsson, and Overgaard, 1992], [Martin and Odell, 1992], [Shlaer and Mellor, 1988, 1992], and [Booch, 1994]. As mentioned in the chapter, these techniques (and others not listed here) are basically similar. In addition to object-oriented analysis techniques of this type, Fusion [Coleman et al., 1994] is a second-generation OOA technique, a combination (or fusion) of a number of first-generation techniques, including OMT [Rumbaugh et al., 1991], and Objectory [Jacobson, Christerson, Jonsson, and Overgaard, 1992]. ROOM is an object-oriented technique for real-time software [Selic, Gullekson, and Ward, 1995]. Further information on real-time object-oriented technology can be found in [Awad, Kuusela, and Ziegler, 1996].

Full details regarding UML can be found at www.rational.com. Introductions to UML 1.0 include [Lee and Tepfenhart, 1997] and [Fowler, 1997b].

CRC cards were first put forward in [Beck and Cunningham, 1989]. [Wirfs-Brock, Wilkerson, and Wiener, 1990] is a good source of information on CRC cards.

The September 1992 issue of the *Communications of the ACM* contains a number of articles on object-oriented analysis. A number of comparisons of object-oriented analysis techniques have been published, including [de Champeaux and Faure, 1992], [Monarchi and Puhr, 1992], and [Embley, Jackson, and Woodfield, 1995]. A comparison of both object-oriented and structured analysis techniques appears in [Fichman and Kemerer, 1992]. [Capper, Colgate, Hunter, and James, 1994] describes three projects that use the object-oriented paradigm and explains the ways that the object-oriented paradigm has proved to be superior to the structured approach.

Management of iteration in object-oriented projects is described in [Williams, 1996]. Statecharts (Section 10.6.1) have been extended to the object-oriented paradigm; this is described in [Coleman, Hayes, and Bear, 1992] and [Harel and Gery, 1997]. The reuse of specifications in the object-oriented paradigm is described in [Bellinzona, Fugini, and Pernici, 1995]. [Kazman, Abowd, Bass, and Clements, 1996] proposes the use of scenarios to assist with object-oriented analysis.

PROBLEMS[1]

11.1 Complete the elevator problem case study by developing state diagrams for the other classes shown in Figure 11.8.

11.2 Use object-oriented analysis to specify the automated library circulation system of Problem 7.7.

11.3 Why cannot the finite state machine formalism of Chapter 10 be used unchanged in object-oriented analysis?

11.4 Use object-oriented analysis to specify the software for controlling the ATM of Problem 7.9. There is no need to consider the details of the constituent hardware components such as the card reader, printer, and cash dispenser. Instead, simply assume that when the ATM sends commands to those components, they are correctly executed.

11.5 What is the latest point in the object-oriented analysis process in which classes can be introduced without adversely affecting the project?

11.6 What is the earliest point in the object-oriented paradigm in which classes can meaningfully be introduced?

11.7 Is it possible to represent the dynamic model using a formalism other than the state diagram described in this chapter? Explain your answer.

11.8 Why do you think that the attributes of the classes but not the methods are determined during object-oriented analysis?

[1] Problem 10.16 (Term Project) and Problems 10.20 through 10.22 (Case Study) can be done at the end of either Chapter 10 or Chapter 11.

11.9 Develop the remaining scenarios for the Osbert Oglesby use case.

11.10 (Term Project) Use object-oriented analysis to specify the Air Gourmet product described in Appendix A.

11.11 (Case Study) Add class **Report** to the object-oriented analysis of the Osbert Oglesby case study. Is this an improvement or an unnecessary complication?

11.12 (Case Study) Determine what happens when object-oriented analysis starts with class modeling. Start with the class diagram of Figure 11.12 and complete the object-oriented analysis process.

11.13 (Case Study) Compare and contrast the structured systems analysis of Appendix D with the object-oriented analysis of Section 11.9.

11.14 (Readings in Software Engineering) Your instructor will distribute copies of [Williams, 1996]. If you were in charge of an object-oriented development project, would you be comfortable managing the iterative aspects?

REFERENCES

[Alburger, 1996] T. ALBURGER, "The Origin of Julian Days," intranet.on.ca/~rbirchal/draco/julian_d.html, April 24, 1996.

[Awad, Kuusela, and Ziegler, 1996] M. AWAD, J. KUUSELA, AND J. ZIEGLER, *Object-Oriented Technology for Real-Time Systems*, Prentice Hall, Upper Saddle River, NJ, 1996.

[Beck and Cunningham, 1989] K. BECK AND W. CUNNINGHAM, "A Laboratory for Teaching Object-Oriented Thinking," *Proceedings of OOPSLA '89, ACM SIGPLAN Notices* **24** (October 1989), pp. 1–6.

[Bellinzona, Fugini, and Pernici, 1995] R. BELLINZONA, M. G. FUGINI, AND B. PERNICI, "Reusing Specifications in OO Applications ," *IEEE Software* **12** (March 1995), pp. 656–75.

[Booch, 1994] G. BOOCH, *Object-Oriented Analysis and Design with Applications, Second Edition*, Benjamin/Cummings, Redwood City, CA, 1994.

[Capper, Colgate, Hunter, and James, 1994] N. P. CAPPER, R. J. COLGATE, J. C. HUNTER, AND M. F. JAMES, "The Impact of Object-Oriented Technology on Software Quality: Three Case Histories," *IBM Systems Journal* **33** (No. 1, 1994), pp. 131–57.

[Coad and Yourdon, 1991a] P. COAD AND E. YOURDON, *Object-Oriented Analysis, Second Edition*, Yourdon Press, Englewood Cliffs, NJ, 1991.

[Coleman et al., 1994] D. COLEMAN, P. ARNOLD, S. BODOFF, C. DOLLIN, H. GILCHRIST, F. HAYES, AND P. JEREMAES, *Object-Oriented Development: The Fusion Method*, Prentice Hall, Englewood Cliffs, NJ, 1994.

[Coleman, Hayes, and Bear, 1992] D. COLEMAN, F. HAYES, AND S. BEAR, "Introducing Objectcharts or How to Use Statecharts in Object-Oriented Design," *IEEE Transactions on Software Engineering* **18** (January, 1992), pp. 9–18.

[de Champeaux and Faure, 1992] D. DE CHAMPEAUX AND P. FAURE, "A Comparative Study of Object-Oriented Analysis Methods," *Journal of Object-Oriented Programming* **5** (March/April 1992), pp. 21–33.

[Embley, Jackson, and Woodfield, 1995] D. W. EMBLEY, R. B. JACKSON, AND S. N. WOODFIELD, "OO Systems Analysis: Is It or Isn't It?" *IEEE Software* **12** (July 1995), pp. 18–33.

[Fichman and Kemerer, 1992] R. G. FICHMAN AND C. F. KEMERER, "Object-Oriented and Conventional Analysis and Design Methodologies: Comparison and Critique," *IEEE Computer* **25** (October 1992), pp. 22–39.

[Fowler, 1997b] M. FOWLER WITH K. SCOTT, *UML Distilled*, Addison-Wesley, Reading, MA, 1997.

[Harel and Gery, 1997] D. HAREL AND E. GERY, "Executable Object Modeling with Statecharts," *IEEE Computer* **30** (July 1997), pp. 31–42.

[Jackson, 1983] M. A. JACKSON, *System Development*, Prentice Hall, Englewood Cliffs, NJ, 1983.

[Jacobson, Christerson, Jonsson, and Overgaard, 1992] I. JACOBSON, M. CHRISTERSON, P. JONSSON, AND G. OVERGAARD, *Object-Oriented Software Engineering: A Use Case Driven Approach*, ACM Press, New York, 1992.

[Kazman, Abowd, Bass, and Clements, 1996] R. KAZMAN, G. ABOWD, L. BASS, AND P. CLEMENTS, "Scenario-Based Analysis of Software Architecture," *IEEE Software* **13** (November/December 1996), pp. 47–55.

[Lee and Tepfenhart, 1997] R. C. LEE AND W. M. TEPFENHART, *UML: A Practical Guide to Object-Oriented Development*, Prentice Hall, Upper Saddle River, NJ, 1997.

[Martin and Odell, 1992] J. MARTIN AND J. J. ODELL, *Object-Oriented Analysis and Design*, Prentice Hall, Englewood Cliffs, NJ, 1992.

[Monarchi and Puhr, 1992] D. E. MONARCHI AND G. I. PUHR, "A Research Typology for Object-Oriented Analysis and Design," *Communications of the ACM* **35** (September 1992), pp. 35–47.

[Rumbaugh et al., 1991] J. RUMBAUGH, M. BLAHA, W. PREMERLANI, F. EDDY, AND W. LORENSEN, *Object-Oriented Modeling and Design*, Prentice Hall, Englewood Cliffs, NJ, 1991.

[Selic, Gullekson, and Ward, 1995] B. SELIC, G. GULLEKSON, AND P. T. WARD, *Real-Time Object-Oriented Modeling*, John Wiley and Sons, New York, 1995.

[Shlaer and Mellor, 1988] S. SHLAER AND S. MELLOR, *Object-Oriented Systems Analysis: Modeling the World in Data*, Yourdon Press, Englewood Cliffs, NJ, 1988.

[Shlaer and Mellor, 1992] S. SHLAER AND S. MELLOR, *Object Lifecycles: Modeling the World in States*, Yourdon Press, Englewood Cliffs, NJ, 1992.

[UML, 1997] UML Notation Guide, Version 1.0, www.rational.com/uml/start/notation_guide.html, 13 January 1997.

[Williams, 1996] J. D. WILLIAMS, "Managing Iteration in OO Projects," *IEEE Computer* **29** (September 1996), pp. 39–43.

[Wirfs-Brock, Wilkerson, and Wiener, 1990] R. WIRFS-BROCK, B. WILKERSON, AND L. WIENER, *Designing Object-Oriented Software*, Prentice Hall, Englewood Cliffs, NJ, 1990.

[World Book Encyclopedia, 1996] *World Book Encyclopedia,* World Book-Childcraft International, Inc., Chicago, 1996, Volume 14: N–O, p. 552–53.

chapter

12

DESIGN PHASE

Over the past 30 or so years, literally hundreds of design techniques have been put forward. Some are variations of existing techniques, others are radically different from anything previously proposed. A few design techniques have been used by tens of thousands of software engineers, many have been used only by their authors. Some design strategies, particularly those developed by academics, have a firm theoretical basis. Others, including many drawn up by academics, are more pragmatic in nature; they were put forward because their authors found that they worked well in practice. Most design techniques are manual, but automation is increasingly becoming an important aspect of design, if only to assist in management of documentation.

Notwithstanding this plethora of design techniques, there is a certain underlying pattern. A major theme of this book is that two essential aspects of a product are its actions and the data on which the actions operate. Thus, the two basic ways of designing a product are action-oriented design and data-oriented design. In *action-oriented design*, the emphasis is on the actions. An example is data flow analysis (Section 12.3), where the objective is to design modules with high cohesion (Section 6.2). In *data-oriented design*, the data are considered first. For example, in Jackson's technique (Section 12.5) the structure of the data is determined first. Then the procedures are designed to conform to the structure of the data.

A weakness of action-oriented design techniques is that they concentrate on the actions; the data are only of secondary importance. Data-oriented design techniques similarly emphasize the data, to the detriment of the actions. The solution is to use object-oriented techniques, which give equal weight to actions and data. In this chapter action- and data-oriented designs are described first, and then object-oriented design is described. Just as an object incorporates both action and data, so object-oriented design combines features of action-oriented and data-oriented design. Thus, a basic understanding of action- and data-oriented design is needed to get a full understanding of object-oriented design.

Before specific design techniques are examined, some general remarks must be made regarding the design phase.

12.1 DESIGN AND ABSTRACTION

The software design phase consists of three activities: architectural design, detailed design, and design testing. The input to the design process is the specification document, a description of *what* the product is to do. The output is the design document, a description of *how* the product is to achieve this.

During *architectural design* (also known as *general design, logical design,* or *high-level design*), a modular decomposition of the product is developed. That is, the specifications are carefully analyzed, and a module structure that has the desired functionality is produced. The output from this activity is a list of the modules and a description of how they are to be interconnected. From the viewpoint of abstraction, during architectural design the existence of certain modules is assumed; the design is then developed in terms of those modules. When the object-oriented paradigm is used, as explained in Section 1.6, part of the architectural design is performed during the object-oriented analysis phase (Chapter 11). This is because the first step in OOA is to determine the classes. Because a class is a type of module, some of the modular decomposition has been performed during the analysis phase.

The next activity is *detailed design*, also known as *modular design, physical design,* or *low-level design*, during which each module is designed in detail. For example, specific algorithms are selected and data structures are chosen. Again from the viewpoint of abstraction, during this activity the fact that the modules are to be interconnected to form a complete product is ignored.

This two-stage process is typical of abstraction as described in Chapter 6. First, the top level (the overall product) is designed in terms of modules that do not yet exist. Then each module in turn is designed, without regard to its being a component of the complete product.

It was stated previously that the design phase has three activities and that the third activity is testing. The word *activity* was used, rather than *stage* or *step*, to emphasize that testing is an integral part of design, just as it is an integral part of the entire software development and maintenance process. Testing is not something that is performed only after the architectural design and detailed design have been completed.

A variety of different design techniques are now described, first action-oriented techniques, then data-oriented techniques, and finally object-oriented techniques.

12.2 ACTION-ORIENTED DESIGN

In Sections 6.2 and 6.3 a theoretical case was made for decomposing a product into modules with high cohesion and low coupling. A description is now given of two practical techniques for achieving this design objective, namely, data flow analysis (Section 12.3) and transaction analysis (Section 12.4). In theory, data flow analysis can be applied whenever the specifications can be represented by a data flow diagram (DFD) and because (at least in theory) every product can be represented by a DFD, data flow analysis is accordingly universally applicable. In practice, however, there are a number of situations where there are more appropriate design techniques, specifically for designing products where the flow of data is secondary to other considerations. Examples where other design techniques are indicated include rule-based systems (expert systems), databases, and transaction processing products. (Transaction analysis, described in Section 12.4, is a good way of decomposing transaction processing products into modules.)

12.3 DATA FLOW ANALYSIS

Data flow analysis (DFA) is a design technique for achieving modules with high cohesion. It can be used in conjunction with most specification techniques. Here DFA will be presented in conjunction with structured systems analysis (Section 10.3). The input to the technique is a data flow diagram (DFD). A key point is that once the DFD has been completed, the software designer has precise and complete information regarding the input to and output from every module.

Consider the flow of data in the product represented by the DFD of Figure 12.1. The product is somehow transforming input into output. At some point in the DFD the input ceases to be input and becomes some sort of internal data. Then, at some further point, these internal data take on the quality of output. This is shown in more detail in Figure 12.2. The point at which the input loses the quality of being input and simply becomes internal data operated on by the product is termed the *point of highest abstraction of input*. The point of highest abstraction of output is similarly the first point in the flow of data at which the output can be identified as such, rather than as some sort of internal data.

Using the points of highest abstraction of input and output, the product is decomposed into three modules, namely, the input module, transform module,

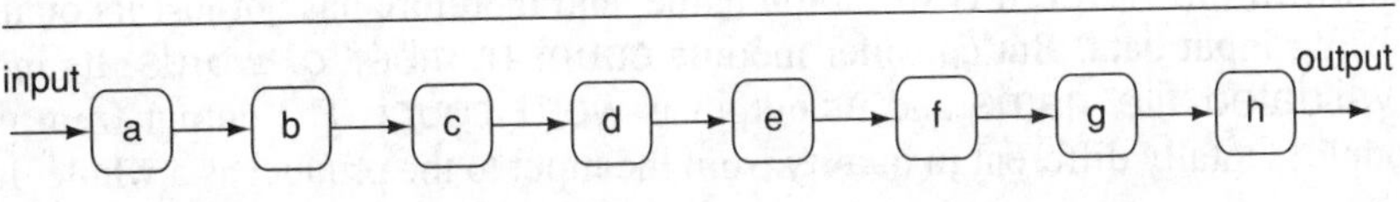

Figure 12.1 Data flow diagram showing flow of data and actions of product.

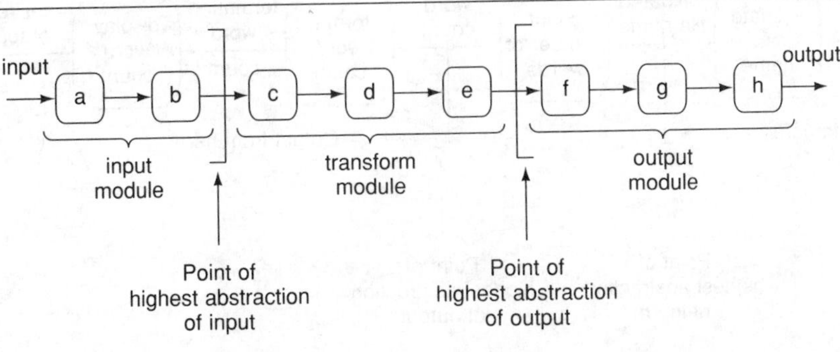

Figure 12.2 Points of highest abstraction of input and output.

and output module. Now each module is taken in turn, its points of highest abstraction found, and the module is decomposed again. This procedure is continued stepwise until each module performs a single action, that is, the design consists of modules with high cohesion. Thus stepwise refinement, the foundation of so many other software engineering techniques, also underlies data flow analysis.

In fairness it should be pointed out that minor modifications might have to be made to the decomposition in order to achieve the lowest possible coupling. Data flow analysis is a way of achieving high cohesion. The aim of composite/structured design is high cohesion but also low coupling. In order to achieve the latter it is sometimes necessary to make minor modifications to the design. For example, because DFA does not take coupling into account, control coupling may inadvertently arise in a design constructed using DFA. In such a case, all that is needed is to modify the two modules involved so that data, and not control, are passed between them.

12.3.1 DATA FLOW ANALYSIS EXAMPLE

Consider the problem of designing a product which takes as input a file name and returns the number of words in that file, similarly to the UNIX wc utility.

Figure 12.3 depicts the data flow diagram. There are five modules. Module read file name reads the name of the file that is then validated by validate file name. The validated name is passed to count number of words that does precisely that. The word count is passed on to format word count, and the formatted word count is finally passed to display word count for output.

Examining the data flow, the initial input is file name. When this becomes validated file name it is still a file name, and therefore has not lost its quality of being input data. But consider module count number of words. Its input is validated file name and its output is word count. The output from this module is totally different in quality from the input to the product as a whole. It is

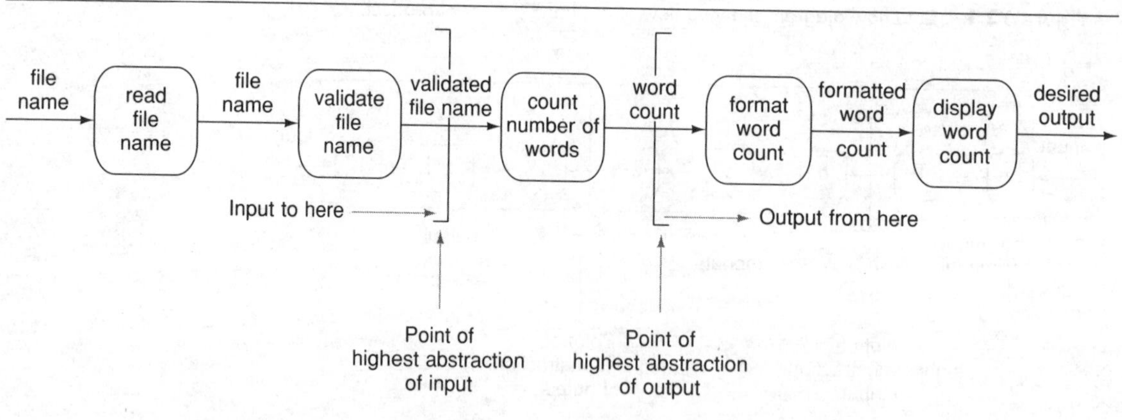

Figure 12.3 Data flow diagram: first refinement.

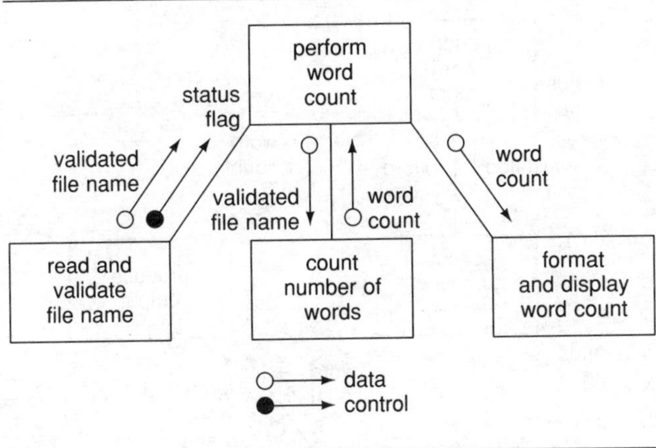

Figure 12.4 Structure chart: first refinement.

clear that the point of highest abstraction of input is as indicated on Figure 12.3. Similarly, even though the output from count number of words undergoes some sort of formatting, it is essentially *output* from the time it emerges from module count number of words. The point of highest abstraction of output is therefore as shown in Figure 12.3.

The result of decomposing the product using these two points of highest abstraction is shown in the structure chart of Figure 12.4. Figure 12.4 also reveals that the data flow diagram of Figure 12.3 is somewhat too simplistic. The DFD does not show the logical flow corresponding to what happens if the file specified by the user does not exist. Module read and validate file name must return a status flag to perform word count. If the name is invalid, then it is ignored by perform word count and an error message of some sort is printed. But if the name is valid it is passed on to count number of words. In general, wherever there is a conditional data flow, there needs to be a corresponding control flow.

In Figure 12.4 there are two modules with communicational cohesion, namely, read and validate file name and format and display word count. These must be decomposed further. The final result is shown in Figure 12.5. All eight modules have functional cohesion, and there is either data coupling or no coupling between them.

Now that the architectural design has been completed, the next step is the detailed design. Here data structures are chosen and algorithms selected. The detailed design of each module is then handed to the programmers for implementation. Just as with virtually every other phase of software production, time constraints usually require that the implementation be done by a team, rather than having a single programmer responsible for coding all the modules. For this reason, the detailed design of each module must be presented so it can be understood without reference to any other module. The detailed design of four of the eight modules appears in Figure 12.6; the other four modules will be presented in a different format.

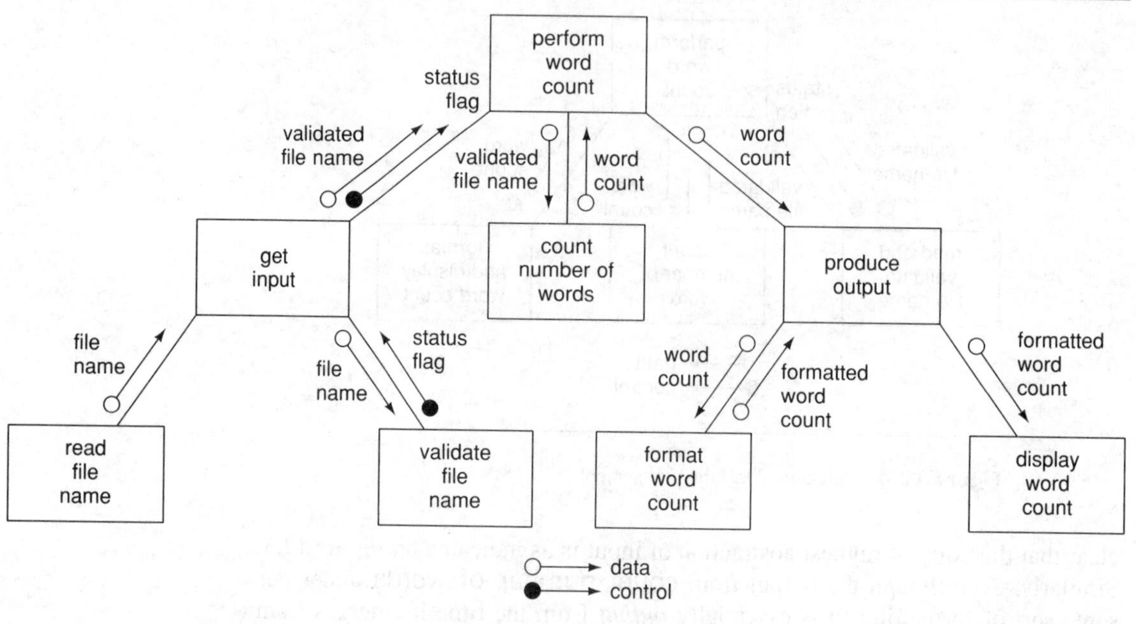

Figure 12.5 Structure chart: second refinement.

Module name	read file name
Return type	String
Input parameters	none
Output parameters	none
Error messages	none
Files accessed	none
Files changed	none
Modules called	none
Narrative	The product is invoked by the user by means of the command string word count <file name> Using an operating system call, this module accesses the contents of the command string that was input by the user, extracts <file name> and returns it as the value of the module.

Figure 12.6 Detailed design of four modules of example.

Module name	validate file name
Return type	boolean
Input parameters	file name : String
Output parameters	none
Error messages	none
Files accessed	none
Files changed	none
Modules called	none
Narrative	This module makes an operating system call to determine whether file file name exists. The module returns **true** if the file exists and **false** otherwise.

Module name	count number of words
Return type	integer
Input parameters	validated file name : String
Output parameters	none
Error messages	none
Files accessed	none
Files changed	none
Modules called	none
Narrative	This module determines whether validated file name is a text file, that is, divided into lines of characters. If so, the module returns the number of words in the text file. Otherwise, the module returns −1.

Module name	produce output
Return type	**void**
Input parameters	word count : integer
Output parameters	none
Error messages	none
Files accessed	none
Files changed	none
Modules called	format word count arguments: word count : integer formatted word count : String display word count arguments: formatted word count : String
Narrative	This module takes the integer word count passed to it by the calling module and calls format word count to have that integer formatted according to the specifications. Then it calls display word count to have the line printed.

Figure 12.6 Detailed design of four modules of example (continued).

```
void perform word count ()
{
  String          validated file name;
  int             word count;

  if (get input (validated file name) is false)
    print "error 1: file does not exist";
  else
  {
    set word count equal to count number of words (validated file name);
    if (word count is equal to −1)
      print "error 2: file is not a text file";
    else
      produce output (word count);
  }
}

boolean get input (String validated file name)
{
  String          file name;

  file name = read file name ();
  if (validate file name (file name) is true)
  {
    set validated file name equal to file name;
    return true;
  }
  else
    return false;
}

void display word count (String formatted word count)
{
  print formatted word count, left justified;
}

String format word count (int word count);
{
  return "File contains" word count "words";
}
```

Figure 12.7 PDL (pseudocode) representation of detailed design of four methods of example.

The design of Figure 12.6 is programming language-independent. However, if management has decided on an implementation language before the detailed design is started, the use of a program description language (PDL) for representing the detailed design is an attractive alternative (pseudocode is an earlier name for PDL). PDL essentially consists of comments connected by the control statements of the chosen implementation language. Figure 12.7 shows a detailed design for the remaining four modules of the product written in a PDL with the flavor of Java. A PDL has the advantage that it is generally clear and concise, and the implementation step usually consists merely of translating the comments into the

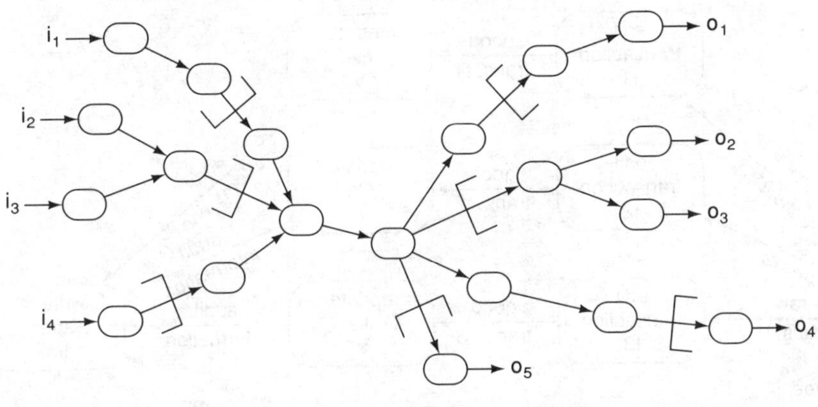

Figure 12.8 Data flow diagram with multiple input and output streams.

relevant programming language. The disadvantage is that there is sometimes a tendency for the designers to go into too much detail and to produce a complete code implementation of a module rather than a PDL detailed design.

After it has been fully documented and successfully tested, the detailed design is handed over to the implementation team for coding. The product then proceeds through the remaining phases of the software process.

12.3.2 EXTENSIONS

The reader may well feel that this example is somewhat artificial in that the data flow diagram (Figure 12.3) has only one input stream and one output stream. To see what happens in more complex situations, consider Figure 12.8. Now there are four input streams and five output streams, a situation that corresponds more closely to reality.

When there are multiple input and output streams, the way to proceed is to find the point of highest abstraction of input for each input stream and the point of highest abstraction of output for each output stream. Use these points to decompose the given data flow diagram into modules with fewer input/output streams than the original. Continue in this way until each resulting module has high cohesion. Finally, determine the coupling between each pair of modules and make any necessary adjustments.

12.4 TRANSACTION ANALYSIS

A *transaction* is an operation from the viewpoint of the user of the product, such as "process a request" or "print a list of today's orders." Data flow analysis is

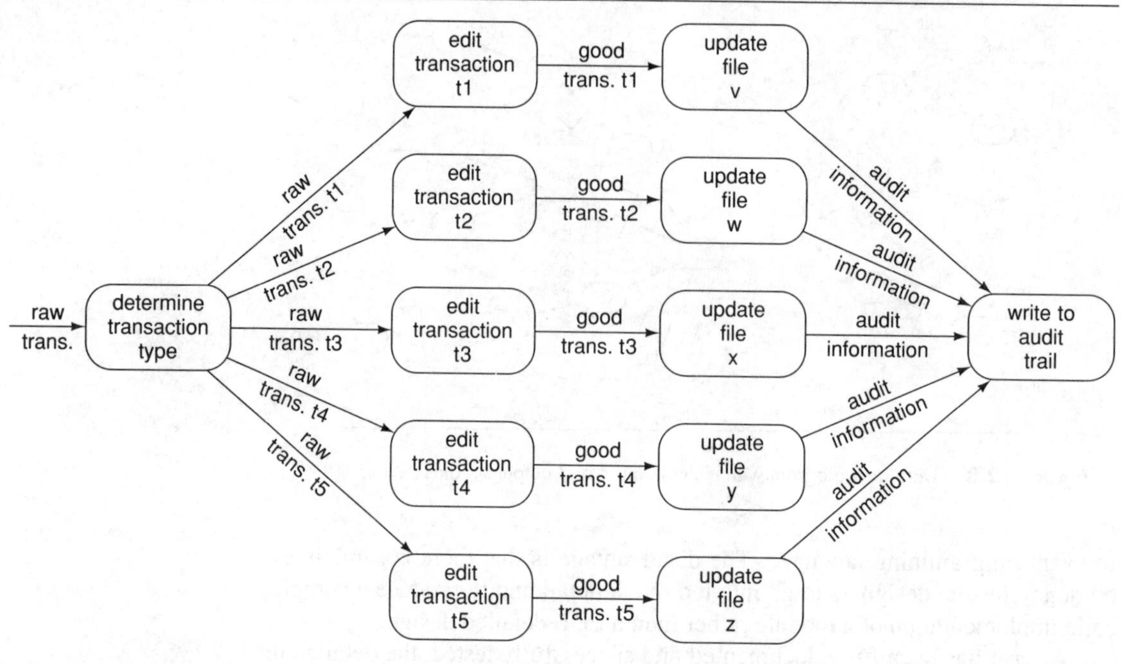

Figure 12.9 Typical transaction-processing system.

inappropriate for the transaction-processing type of product in which a number of related actions, similar in outline but differing in detail, must be performed. A typical example is the software controlling an automated teller machine (ATM). The customer inserts a magnetized card into a slot, keys in a password, and then performs actions such as deposit to a checking, savings, or credit card account; withdraw from an account; or determine the balance in an account. This type of product is depicted in Figure 12.9. A good way to design such a product is to break it up into two pieces, the analyzer and the dispatcher. The analyzer determines the transaction type and passes this information to the dispatcher, which then performs the transaction.

A poor design of this type is shown in Figure 12.10 which has two modules with logical cohesion, namely, edit any transaction and update any file. On the other hand, it seems a waste of effort to have five very similar edit modules and five very similar update modules. The solution is software reuse (Section 7.1): A basic edit module should be designed, coded, documented, and tested and then instantiated five times. Each version will be slightly different, but the differences will be small enough to make this approach worthwhile. Similarly, a basic update module can be instantiated five times and slightly modified to cater to the five different update types. The resulting design will have high cohesion and low coupling.

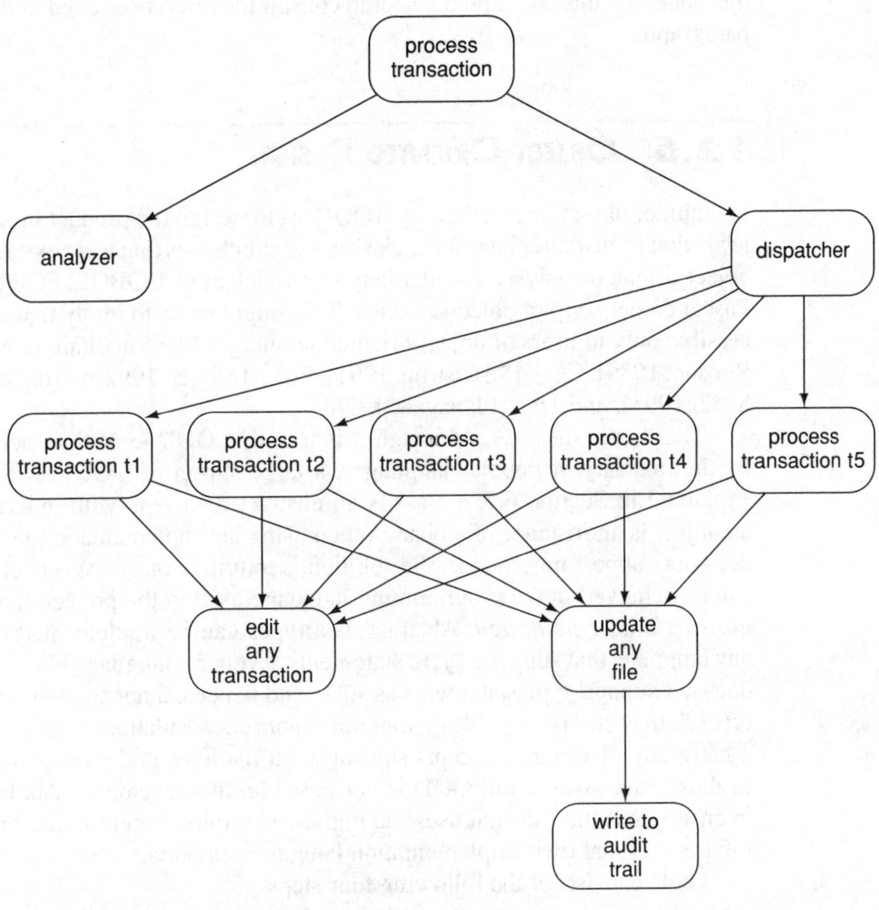

Figure 12.10 Poor design of transaction-processing system.

12.5 DATA-ORIENTED DESIGN

The basic principle behind data-oriented design is to design the product according to the structure of the data on which it is to operate. There are a number of data-oriented techniques of this type; the most well-known are those of Michael Jackson [Jackson, 1975; 1983], Warnier [Warnier, 1976; 1981] and Orr [Orr, 1981]. The three techniques share many similarities.

Data-oriented design has never been as popular as action-oriented design and, with the rise of the object-oriented paradigm, has largely fallen out of fashion. For reasons of space, data-oriented design is therefore not discussed further in this book; the interested reader should consult the references cited in the previous paragraph.

12.6 OBJECT-ORIENTED DESIGN

The aim of object-oriented design (OOD) is to design the product in terms of objects, that is, instantiations of the classes and subclasses that were extracted during object-oriented analysis. Popular languages such as C, COBOL, FORTRAN, and Pascal do not support objects as such. This might seem to imply that OOD is accessible only to users of object-oriented languages like Smalltalk [Goldberg and Robson, 1989], C++ [Stroustrup, 1991], Eiffel [Meyer, 1992b], Ada 95 [ISO/IEC 8652, 1995], and Java [Flanagan, 1996].

That is not the case. Although it is true that OOD as such is not supported by the majority of popular languages, a large subset of OOD can be used. As explained in Section 6.7, a class is an abstract data type with inheritance, and an object is an instance of a class. When using an implementation language that does not support inheritance, the solution is to utilize those aspects of OOD that can be achieved in the programming language used in the project, that is, to use *abstract data type design*. Abstract data types can be implemented in virtually any language that supports **type** statements. Even in a language like COBOL that does not support type statements as such, and hence cannot support abstract data types, it may still be possible to implement data encapsulation. Figure 6.27 depicts a hierarchy of design concepts starting with modules and ending with objects. In those cases where full OOD is not possible, the developers should endeavor to ensure that their design uses the highest possible concept in the hierarchy of Figure 6.27 that their implementation language supports.

OOD consists of the following four steps:

1. Construct interaction diagrams for each scenario.
2. Construct the detailed class diagram.
3. Design the product in terms of clients of objects.
4. Proceed to the detailed design.

OOD is now illustrated by means of an example. As before, the elevator problem will be presented, with just one elevator for simplicity. By using the same example, the reader is able to compare different approaches without having to worry about the ramifications of the problem itself.

12.7 ELEVATOR PROBLEM: OBJECT-ORIENTED DESIGN

Step 1. Construct Interaction Diagrams for Each Scenario. UML supports two types of interaction diagrams, namely, sequence diagrams and collaboration diagrams. Both diagrams show the same thing, namely, objects and the messages passed between them. However, the emphasis in the two diagrams is different. Sequence diagrams emphasize the explicit chronological sequence of messages. Sequence diagrams are therefore useful in situations where the order in which events occur is important. Collaboration diagrams emphasize the relationship between objects and are thus a powerful tool for understanding the structure of the software product.

Consider the scenario of Figure 11.2, reproduced here as Figure 12.11. In the corresponding sequence diagram of Figure 12.12, the users and objects are represented by vertical lines. In UML, an instance of a class (an object) is represented by the underlined name of the class in lowercase.

Time goes from top to bottom. Thus, the first action is that User A presses the Up floor button. This is represented by the horizontal line from User A to the elevator controller labeled 1. press floor button. The elevator controller then sends a message to the relevant floor button to turn on the light. This is represented by the horizontal line from the elevator controller to floor button marked 2. turn on light. The third item in the scenario is that the elevator arrives at floor 3. This is modeled by iterating the message sent by the elevator controller to the elevator to move up one floor; this repetition is denoted by the asterisk in 3.* move up one floor. The rest of the sequence diagram is similar.

The collaboration diagram for the same scenario is shown in Figure 12.13. Unlike the sequence diagram, the collaboration diagram clearly shows the central role played by elevator controller. In fact, every message in the scenario is

1. User A presses Up floor button at floor 3 to request elevator. User A wishes to go to floor 7.
2. Up floor button is turned on.
3. An elevator arrives at floor 3. It contains User B who has entered the elevator at floor 1 and pressed the elevator button for floor 9.
4. Up floor button is turned off.
5. Elevator doors open.

   User A enters elevator.
6. User A presses elevator button for floor 7.
7. Floor 7 elevator button is turned on.
8. Elevator doors close.
9. Elevator travels to floor 7.
10. Floor 7 elevator button is turned off.
11. Elevator doors open to allow User A to exit elevator.
12. Timer starts.

    User A exits.
13. Elevator doors close after timeout.
14. Elevator proceeds to floor 9 with User B.

Figure 12.11 Normal scenario of Figure 11.2.

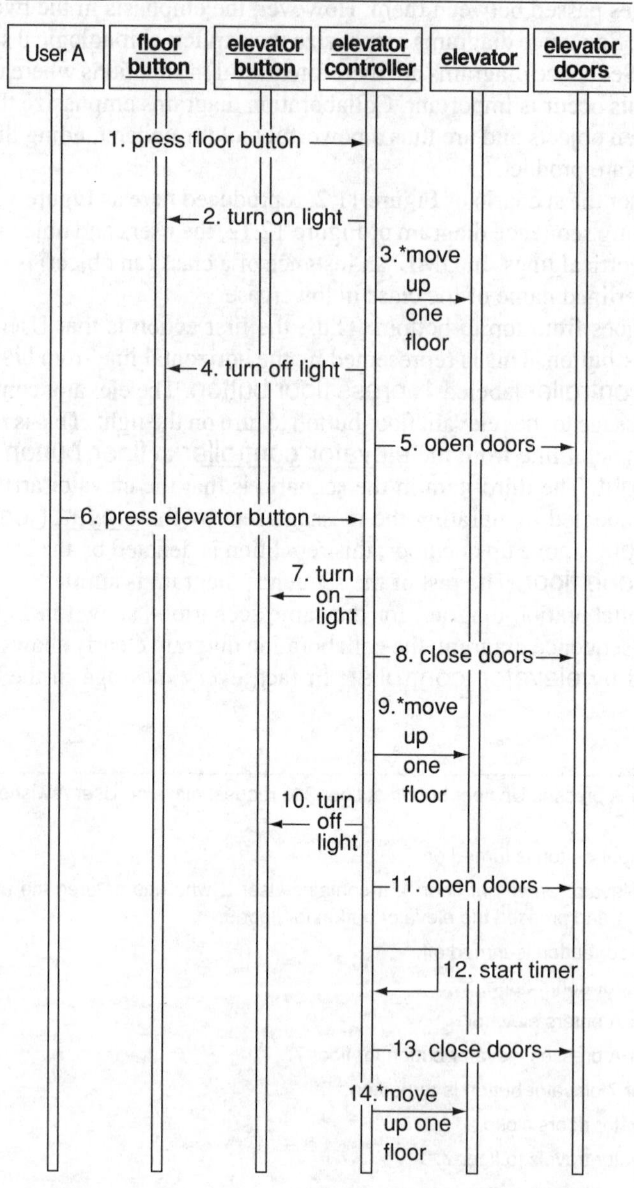

Figure 12.12 Sequence diagram for scenario of Figure 12.11.

either sent to or from elevator controller. On the other hand, the timing information of the sequence diagram of Figure 12.12 is obscured in the collaboration diagram of Figure 12.13, even though both diagrams contain exactly the same information. The lesson is that in every project the design team must decide which of the two interaction diagrams is more appropriate; in some cases, both will be

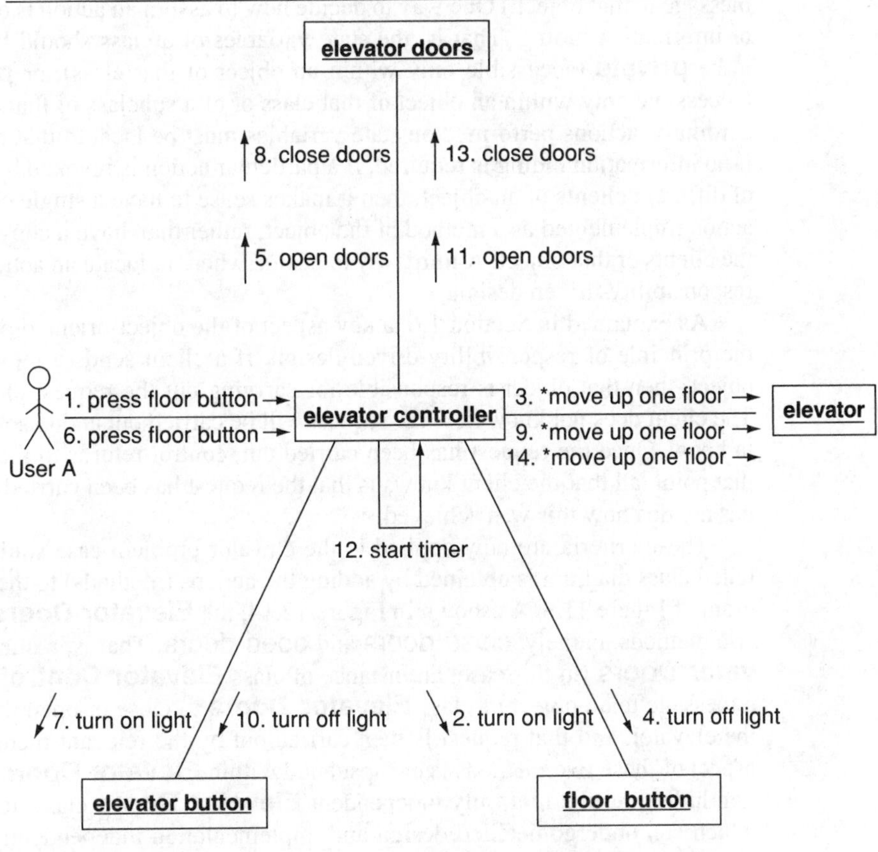

Figure 12.13 Collaboration diagram for scenario of Figure 12.11.

needed. In fact, if software is developed using a CASE tool for OOA and OOD, the tool can generate either diagram on demand. This enables the team to choose the appropriate interaction diagram literally on the spur of the moment.

Step 2. Construct the Detailed Class Diagram. The class diagram of the OOA phase (Section 11.5) depicts the classes and their attributes, but not their actions ("methods"). The methods are inserted into the detailed class diagram of the OOD phase.

Determination of all the actions of the product is performed by examining the interaction diagrams of all the scenarios. This is straightforward. The problem is to determine how to decide which actions should be associated with each class.

An action can be assigned either to a class or to a client that sends a message to an object of that class. (A client of an object is a program unit that sends a message to that object.) One way to decide how to assign an action is on the basis of information hiding. That is, the state variables of a class should be declared to be **private** (accessible only within an object of that class), or **protected** (accessible only within an object of that class or of a subclass of that class). Accordingly, actions performed on state variables must be local to that class. Even if no information hiding is required, if a particular action is invoked by a number of different clients of an object, then it makes sense to have a single copy of that action implemented as a method of the object, rather than have a copy in each of the clients of that object. A third way to decide where to locate an action is to use responsibility-driven design.

As explained in Section 1.6, a key aspect of the object-oriented paradigm is the principle of responsibility-driven design. If a client sends a message to an object, then that object is responsible for carrying out the request of the client. The client does not know how the request will be carried out and is not permitted to know. Once the request has been carried out, control returns to the client. At that point, all that the client knows is that the request has been carried out; it still has no idea how this was achieved.

These criteria are now applied to the elevator problem case study. The detailed class diagram is obtained by adding the actions (methods) to the class diagram of Figure 11.8. As shown in Figure 12.14, the **Elevator Doors** class has two methods, namely, close doors and open doors. That is, a client of **Elevator Doors** (in this case, an instance of class **Elevator Controller**) sends a message to an object of class **Elevator Doors** to close or open the doors of the elevator, and that request is then carried out by the relevant method. Every aspect of those two methods is encapsulated within **Elevator Doors**. Information hiding results in a truly independent **Elevator Doors** class, instances of which can undergo detailed design and implementation independently, and can be reused later in other products.

Class **Elevator** also has two methods, namely, move one floor down and move one floor up. There is no need for an explicit instruction to cause an elevator to stop. If neither of its two methods is invoked, then the elevator cannot move; there is no other way to change the state of an elevator other than by invoking one of its methods.

Elevator Button and **Floor Button** both have two methods, namely, turn button off and turn button on. The reasoning here is similar to that in the case of **Elevator Doors**. First, the principle of responsibility-driven design requires that the buttons themselves have full control over whether they are on or off. Second, the principle of information hiding requires the internal state of a button to be hidden. The actions that turn an elevator button on or off must therefore be local to class **Elevator Button**, and similarly for class **Floor Button**. To make use of polymorphism and dynamic binding, methods turn button on and turn button off must be declared to be **virtual** in base class **Button** for the reasons stated in Section 6.8. At run time, the message turn button on will cause the correct version of turn button on to be invoked.

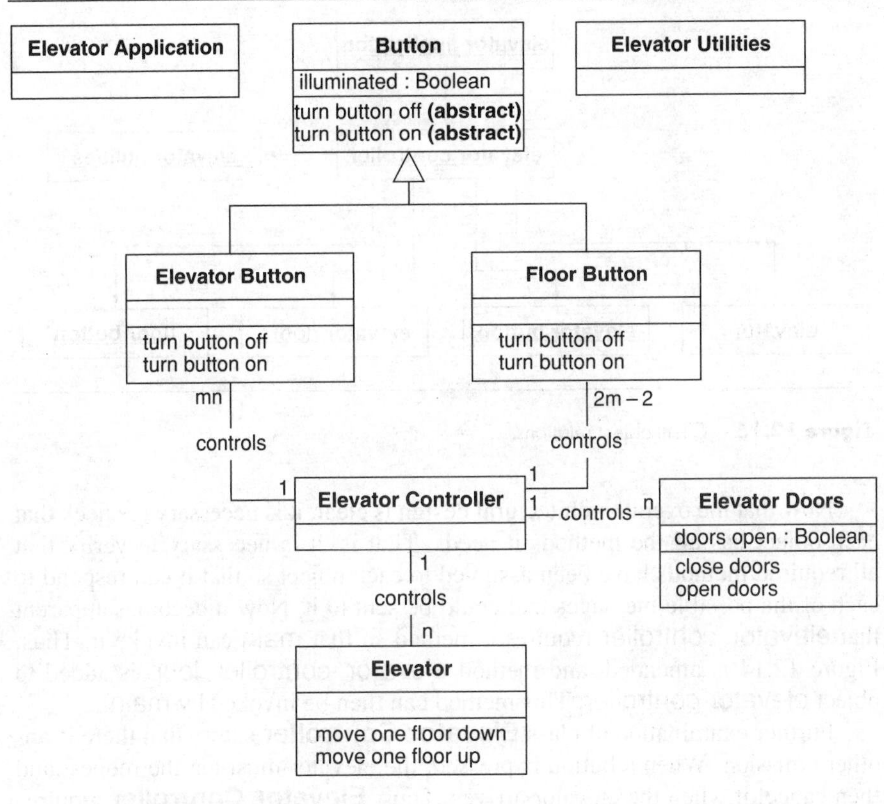

Figure 12.14 Detailed class diagram. (Additional state variables and methods will be added later to Elevator Controller.)

Finally, class **Elevator Controller** does not have any methods at all. This implies that there is no way to invoke an instance of an **Elevator Controller**. This will be corrected during the next step.

Step 3. Design the Product in Terms of Clients of Objects. An object C that sends a message to object O is a client of O. The detailed class diagram (Figure 12.14) is utilized to draw a diagram showing the clients of each object (Figure 12.15). A message that could be sent from client C to object O is represented by an arrow from C to O. Any object that is not a client of some other object then needs to be initiated, usually by the main program. In the elevator problem case study, an object of class **Elevator Controller** sends messages to objects of the other four classes. Thus, in order to start the product, function main must invoke object <u>elevator controller</u>. This form of architecture is not uncommon when the object-oriented paradigm is used, namely, a simple main program that essentially starts things off; the objects themselves take over from then on.

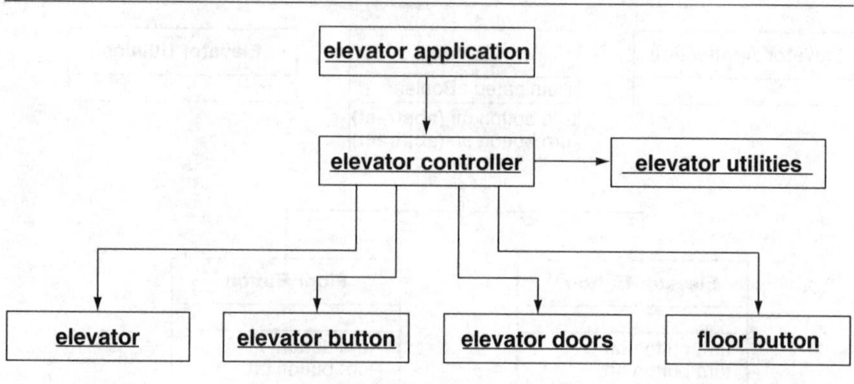

Figure 12.15 Client-object relations.

Now that the overall architectural design is clear, it is necessary to check that each object has all the methods it needs. That is, it is necessary to verify that all required methods have been assigned to each object so that it can respond to each of the possible messages that could be sent to it. Now it becomes apparent that elevator controller requires a method so that main can invoke it. Thus, Figure 12.14 is amended, and method elevator controller loop is added to object elevator controller. This method can then be invoked by main.

Further examination of class **Elevator Controller** shows that there is another omission. When a button is pressed, the elevator must log the request and then cancel it when the elevator arrives. Thus, **Elevator Controller** requires state variable requests and methods log request, update requests, and request is pending. These, too, must be added to the detailed class diagram of Figure 12.14.

Step 4. Detailed Design A detailed design is now developed for main and all the classes. Any suitable technique may be used, such as stepwise refinement as described in Chapter 4. The detailed design of method elevator controller loop is shown in Figure 12.16. Here PDL (pseudocode) is used, but a tabular representation (such as that of Figure 12.6) can be equally effective.

12.8 FORMAL TECHNIQUES FOR DETAILED DESIGN

One technique for detailed design has already been presented. In Section 4.6 a description of stepwise refinement was given. It was then applied to detailed design using flowcharts. In addition to stepwise refinement, formal techniques can also be used to advantage in detailed design. In Chapter 5 it was suggested that implementing a complete product and then proving it correct could be counterproductive. However, developing the proof and the detailed design in parallel,

```
void elevator control loop (void)
{
  do
  {
    if (a button has been pressed)
      if (button is not on)
      {
        button.turn button on;
        log request;
      }
    else if (elevator is moving up)
    {
      if (there is no request to stop at floor f)
        elevator.move one floor up;
      else
      {
        stop elevator by not sending a message to move;
        elevator doors.open doors;
        if (elevator button is on)
          elevator button.turn button off;
        update requests;
      }
    }
    else if (elevator is moving down)
      [similar to up case]
    else if (elevator is stopped and request is pending)
    {
      elevator doors.close doors;
      if (floor button is on)
        floor button.turn button off;
      determine direction of next request;
      elevator.move one floor up/down;
    }
    else if (elevator is at rest and not (request is pending))
      elevator doors.close doors;
    else
      there are no requests, elevator is stopped with elevator doors closed, so do nothing;
  }
}
```

Figure 12.16 Detailed design of method elevator control loop.

and carefully testing the code as well, is quite a different matter. Formal techniques at the detailed design phase can greatly assist in three ways. First, the state of the art in correctness proving is such that, although it cannot generally be applied to a product as a whole, it can be applied to module-sized pieces of a product. Second, developing a proof together with the detailed design should lead to a design with fewer faults than if correctness proofs were not used. Third, if the same programmer is responsible for both the detailed design and the implementation, as is often the case, then that programmer will feel confident that the detailed design is correct. This positive attitude toward the design should lead to fewer faults in the code.

12.9 REAL-TIME DESIGN TECHNIQUES

As explained in Section 5.4.4, real-time software is characterized by hard time constraints, that is, time constraints of such a nature that if a constraint is not met, information is lost. In particular, each input must be processed before the next input arrives. An example of such a system is a computer-controlled nuclear reactor. Inputs such as the temperature of the core and the level of the water in the reactor chamber are continually being sent to the computer that reads the value of each input and performs the necessary processing before the next input arrives. Another example is a computer-controlled intensive care unit. There are two types of patient data: routine information such as heart rate, temperature, and blood pressure of each patient, and emergency information when the system deduces that the condition of a patient has become critical. When such emergencies occur, the software must be able to process both the routine inputs as well as the emergency-related inputs from one or more patients.

A characteristic of many real-time systems is that they are implemented on distributed hardware. For example, software controlling a fighter aircraft may be implemented on five computers, one to handle navigation, another the weapons system, a third for electronic countermeasures, a fourth to control the flight hardware such as wing flaps and engines, and the fifth to propose tactics in combat. Because hardware is not totally reliable, there may be additional back-up computers that automatically replace a malfunctioning unit. Not only does the design of such a system have major communications implications, but timing issues, over and above those of the type described in the previous paragraph, arise as a consequence of the distributed nature of the system. For example, it can happen under combat conditions that the tactical computer might suggest that the pilot should climb, whereas the weapons computer recommends that the pilot go into a dive so that a particular weapon may be launched under optimal conditions. However, the human pilot decides to move the stick to the right, thereby sending a signal to the flight hardware computer to make the necessary adjustments so that the plane banks in the indicated direction. All this information must be carefully managed in such a way that the actual motion of the plane takes precedence in every way over suggested maneuvers. Furthermore, the actual motion must be relayed to the tactical and weapons computers so that new suggestions can be formulated in the light of actual, rather than suggested, conditions.

A further difficulty with real-time systems is the problem of synchronization. Suppose that a real-time system is to be implemented on distributed hardware. Situations such as deadlock (or deadly embrace) can arise when two actions each have exclusive use of a data item and each then requests exclusive use of the other's data item in addition. Of course, deadlock does not occur only in real-time systems implemented on distributed hardware. But it is particularly troublesome in real-time systems where there is no control over the order or timing of the inputs, and the situation can be complicated by the distributed nature of the hardware. In addition to deadlock, other synchronization problems are also possible, including race conditions; for details, the reader may refer to [Silberschatz and Galvin, 1998] or other operating systems textbooks.

From these examples it is clear that the major difficulty with regard to the design of real-time systems is ensuring that the timing constraints are met by the design. That is, the design technique should provide a mechanism for checking that, when implemented, the design will be able to read and process incoming data at the required rate. Furthermore, it should be possible to show that synchronization issues in the design have also been correctly addressed.

Since the beginning of the computer age, advances in hardware technology have outstripped, in almost every respect, advances in software technology. Thus, although the hardware exists to handle every aspect of the real-time systems described previously, software design technology has lagged considerably behind. In some areas of real-time software engineering, major progress has been made. For instance, many of the specification techniques of Chapters 10 and 11 can be used to specify real-time systems. Unfortunately, software design has not reached the same level of sophistication. Great strides are indeed being made, but the state of the art is not yet comparable to what has been achieved with regard to specification techniques. Because almost any design technique for real-time systems is preferable to no technique at all, a number of real-time design techniques are being used in practice. But there is still a long way to go before it will be possible to design real-time systems such as those described previously and be certain that, before the system has been implemented, every real-time constraint will be met and that synchronization problems cannot arise.

Most real-time design techniques are extensions of nonreal-time techniques to the real-time domain. For example, structured development for real-time systems (SDRTS) [Ward and Mellor, 1985] is essentially an extension of structured systems analysis (Section 10.3), data flow analysis (Section 12.3), and transaction analysis (Section 12.4) to real-time software. The development technique includes a component for real-time design. Another extension of the same group of techniques to the real-time domain is design approach for real-time systems (DARTS) [Gomaa, 1986]. Software cost reduction (SCR) [Kmielcik et al., 1984] is a real-time design technique based on the concept of information hiding [Parnas, 1971; 1972a; 1972b]. Other techniques in this class are described in [Hatley and Pirbhai, 1987] and [Levi and Agrawala, 1990].

As stated previously, it is unfortunate that the state-of-the-art of real-time design is not as advanced as one would wish. Nevertheless, strenuous efforts are underway to improve the situation as described, for example, in [Stankovic, 1997].

12.10 TESTING DURING THE DESIGN PHASE

The goal of testing at the design phase is to verify that the specifications have been accurately and completely incorporated into the design, as well as to ensure the correctness of the design itself. For example, the design must not have any logic faults, and all interfaces must be correctly defined. It is important that any faults in the design be detected before coding commences, otherwise the cost of fixing the faults will be considerably higher, as reflected in Figure 1.5. Detection of design faults can be achieved by means of design inspections, as well as design walkthroughs. Design inspections are discussed in the remainder of this section, but the remarks are equally applicable to design walkthroughs.

A design inspection is similar to the inspection at the specification phase except that representatives of the client organization are not usually present at a design inspection. This is a consequence of the fact that nontechnical individuals generally find design documents harder to understand than specification documents.

When the product is transaction-oriented (Section 12.4), the design inspection should reflect this fact [Beizer, 1990]. Inspections that will include all possible transaction types should be scheduled. The reviewer should relate each transaction in the design to the specification, showing how the transaction arises from the specification document. For example, if the application is an automated teller machine (ATM) product, a transaction will correspond to each operation that the customer performs, such as to deposit to or withdraw from a credit card account. In other instances, the correspondence between specifications and transactions will not necessarily be one-to-one. In a traffic-light control system, for example, if an automobile driving over a sensor pad results in the system deciding to change a particular light from red to green in 15 seconds then further impulses from that sensor pad may be ignored. Conversely, in order to speed traffic flow, a single impulse may cause a whole series of lights to be changed from red to green.

Restricting reviews to transaction-driven inspections will not detect cases where the designers have overlooked instances of transactions required by the specifications. To take an extreme example, the specifications for the traffic-light controller may stipulate that between 11:00 p.m. and 6:00 a.m. all lights are to flash orange in one direction and red in the other direction. If the designers overlooked this stipulation, then clock-generated transactions at 11:00 p.m. and 6:00 a.m. would not be included in the design, and if these transactions were overlooked, they could not be tested in a design inspection based on transactions. Thus, it is not adequate just to schedule design inspections that are transaction-driven; specification-driven inspections are also essential to ensure that no statement in the specification document has been either overlooked or misinterpreted.

12.11 CASE TOOLS FOR THE DESIGN PHASE

As stated in the previous section, a critical aspect of the design phase is testing that the design document accurately incorporates all aspects of the specification document. What therefore is needed is a CASE tool that can be used both for the specification document and the design document, a so-called *front-end* or *upperCASE* tool (as opposed to a *back-end* or *lowerCASE* tool, which assists with the implementation, integration, and maintenance phases).

There are a number of upperCASE tools on the market. Some of the more popular ones include Analyst/Designer, Software through Pictures, and System Architect. UpperCASE tools are generally built around a data dictionary. The CASE tool can check that every field of every record in the dictionary is mentioned somewhere in the design document or that every item in the design document is reflected in the data flow diagram. In addition, many upperCASE tools incorporate a consistency checker that uses the data dictionary to determine that every item in the design has been declared in the specifications and conversely that every item in the specifications appears in the design.

Furthermore, many upperCASE tools also incorporate screen and report generators. That is, the client can specify what items are to appear in a report or on an input screen and where and how each item is to appear. Because full details regarding every item are in the dictionary, the CASE tool can then easily generate the code for printing the report or displaying the input screen according to the client's wishes. Some upperCASE products also incorporate management tools for estimating and planning.

With regard to object-oriented design, OMTool, Rose, and Software through Pictures provide support for this phase within the context of the complete object-oriented life cycle.

12.12 METRICS FOR THE DESIGN PHASE

A variety of metrics can be used to describe aspects of the design. For example, the number of modules is a crude measure of the size of the target product. Module cohesion and coupling are measures of the quality of the design, as are fault statistics. As with all other types of inspection, it is vital to keep a record of the number and type of design faults detected during a design inspection. This information is used during code inspections of the product, and also in design inspections of subsequent products.

The cyclomatic complexity *M* of a detailed design is the number of binary decisions (predicates) plus 1 [McCabe, 1976] or equivalently, the number of branches in the module. It has been suggested that cyclomatic complexity is a metric of design quality, the lower the value of *M*, the better. An advantage of this metric is that it is easy to compute. However, it has an inherent problem. Cyclomatic complexity is a measure purely of the control complexity; the data complexity is ignored. That is, *M* does not measure the complexity of a module that is data-driven, such as by the values in a table. For example, suppose that a designer is unaware of C++ library function `toascii` and designs a module from scratch that reads a character input by the user and returns the corresponding ASCII code (an integer between 0 and 127). One way of designing this is by means of a 128-way branch to be implemented by means of a **switch** statement. A second way is to have an array containing the 128 characters in ASCII code order, utilizing a loop to compare the character input by the user with each element of the array of characters; the loop is exited when a match is obtained. The current value of the loop variable is then the corresponding ASCII code. The two designs are equivalent in functionality but have cyclomatic complexities of 128 and 1, respectively.

When the structured paradigm is used, a related class of metrics for the design phase is based on representing the architectural design as a directed graph with the modules represented by nodes and the flows between modules (procedure and function calls) represented by arcs. The *fan-in* of a module can then be defined as the number of flows into the module plus the number of global data structures accessed by the module. The *fan-out* is similarly the number of flows out of the module plus the number of global data structures updated by the module. A measure of complexity of the module is then given by $length \times (fan\text{-}in \times fan\text{-}out)^2$ [Henry and Kafura, 1981], where *length* is a measure of the size of the module (Section 8.2.1). The fact that the definitions of *fan-in* and *fan-out* incorporate global data means that this metric has a data-dependent component. Nevertheless, experiments have shown that this metric is no better a measure of complexity than simpler metrics such as cyclomatic complexity [Kitchenham, Pickard, and Linkman, 1990; Shepperd, 1990]. Currently, the most successful design metric for the classical paradigm is CDM, described in Section 6.3.7.

The issue of design metrics is even more complicated when the object-oriented paradigm is used. For example, the cyclomatic complexity of a class is usually low, because many classes typically include a large number of small, straightforward methods (member functions). Furthermore, as previously pointed out, cyclomatic complexity ignores data complexity. Because data and actions are equal partners within the object-oriented paradigm, cyclomatic complexity overlooks a major component that could contribute towards the complexity of an object. Thus, metrics for classes that incorporate cyclomatic complexity are generally of little use.

A number of object-oriented design metrics have been put forward, for example, in [Chidamber and Kemerer, 1994]. These and other metrics have been questioned on both theoretical and experimental grounds [Binkley and Schach, 1996; 1997; 1998]. At the time of writing, the most accurate object-oriented design metric is again CDM.

12.13 OSBERT OGLESBY CASE STUDY: OBJECT-ORIENTED DESIGN

As described in Section 12.6, object-oriented design consists of four steps. First, interaction diagrams (sequence and collaboration diagrams) are constructed for each scenario. Second, the actions ("methods") of the classes are determined and the detailed class diagram constructed. Third, the product is designed in terms of objects and their clients. Fourth, the detailed design is produced.

	Art dealer wishes to buy a masterpiece.
1.	Dealer enters description of painting.
2.	Product scans auction records for price and year of sale of most similar work by same artist.
3.	Product computes maximum purchase price by adding 8.5%, compounded annually, for each year since that auction.
4.	Product reports maximum purchase price to dealer.
	Dealer makes bid below maximum purchase price. Bid is accepted by seller.
5.	Dealer enters sales information (name and address of seller, purchase price).

Figure 12.17 A normal scenario.

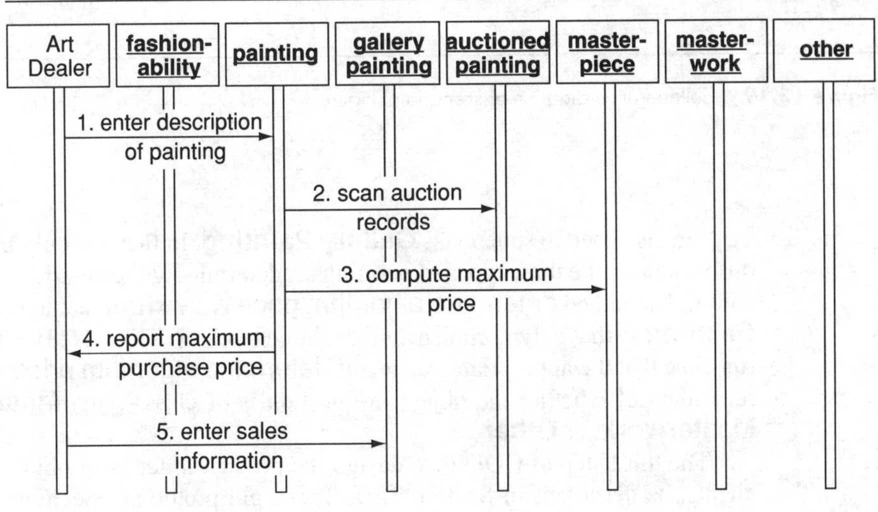

Figure 12.18 Sequence diagram of scenario of Figure 12.17.

The process is best performed iteratively. In the case of the Osbert Oglesby case study, the sequence diagram and collaboration diagram corresponding to the scenario of Figure 11.11 (reproduced as Figure 12.17) appear in Figures 12.18 and 12.19, respectively.

The difficulty in the second step is in deciding how to assign the various methods to the classes. The resulting detailed class diagram, that is, the class diagram of Figure 11.11 with the methods added, appears in Figure 12.20. Methods that are identical for all three types of paintings, such as add new painting and

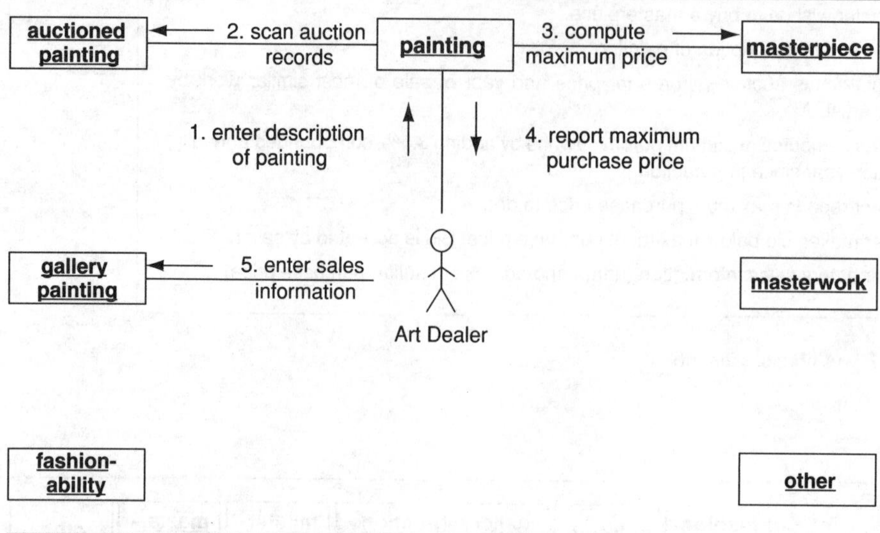

Figure 12.19 Collaboration diagram of scenario of Figure 12.17.

buy, are assigned to superclass **Gallery Painting**. In fact, the only method that differs among the three types of paintings is determining the algorithm price. Accordingly, method **determine algorithm price** is a **virtual** method of **Gallery Painting** so that polymorphism and dynamic binding (Section 6.8) will ensure at run-time that the appropriate version of **determine algorithm price** is invoked, regardless of whether the object in question is of class (type) **Masterpiece**, **Masterwork**, or **Other**.

The third step of OOD is to design the product in terms of objects and their clients, as described in Section 12.7. The rapid prototype (Section 9.15) indicates that a design in terms of a hierarchy of menus would be feasible. The main menu allows the user to select whether to print a report, buy a painting, or sell a painting. If the user chooses to print a report, the print submenu appears, and similarly, appears if the user chooses to buy or sell a painting. Each of the three submenu modules then sends a message to an object of type **Gallery Painting**. The final version of the client-object relations is shown in Figure 12.21.

Finally, the detailed design is performed. For the sake of brevity, only a small portion of the detailed design is shown in Figure 12.22; the complete detailed design appears in Appendix G.

The design must now be checked. However, if no faults are found, it is quite likely that the design will change again, perhaps radically, when the Osbert Oglesby product is implemented and integrated.

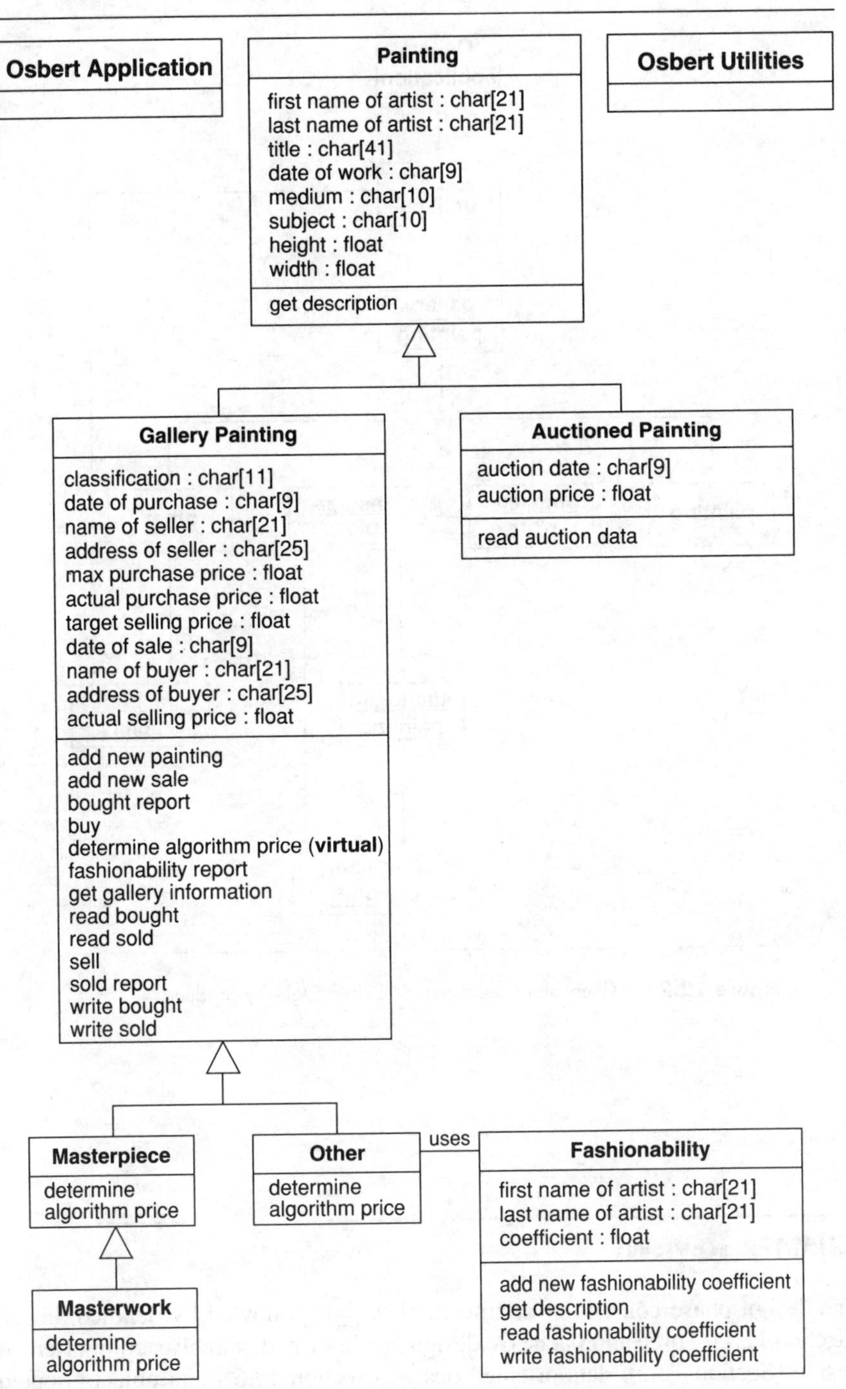

Figure 12.20 Detailed class diagram for Osbert Oglesby product.

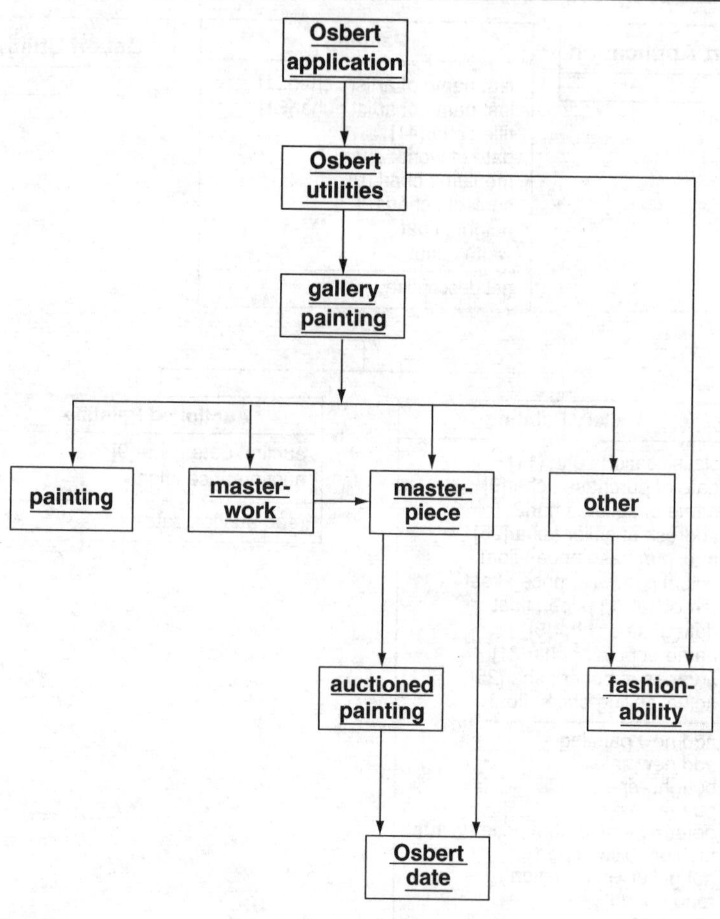

Figure 12.21 Client-object relations for Osbert Oglesby product.

CHAPTER REVIEW

The design phase consists of architectural design, followed by detailed design (Section 12.1). Three approaches to design are described, namely, action-oriented design (Section 12.2), data-oriented design (Section 12.5), and object-oriented design (Section 12.6). Two instances of action-oriented design are described,

Class name	GalleryPaintingClass
Method name	buy
Modifiers, type	**public void**
Arguments	none
Error messages	none
Files accessed	gallery.dat
Files changed	none
Methods called	getDescription, readBought, addNewPainting, determineAlgorithmPrice, getGalleryInformation
Narrative	This method first retrieves information from the user concerning the painting to be purchased. If the painting does not already exist in the gallery, the maximum buying price for the painting is given. The user is then requested to enter additional purchase information before the painting is actually inserted into the gallery via a call to addNewPainting.

Class name	OtherClass
Method name	determineAlgorithmPrice
Modifiers, type	**public void**
Arguments	none
Error messages	none
Files accessed	fash.dat
Files changed	none
Methods called	readFash
Narrative	Determines the maximum price to be offered for an "other" piece of work. This operation is performed by first finding the appropriate fashionability coefficient from fash.dat. The maximum price is then computed as the area of the painting object multiplied by the fashionability coefficient.

Class name	OsbertDate
Method name	parse
Modifiers, type	**public static long**
Arguments	String
Error messages	none
Files accessed	none
Files changed	none
Methods called	none
Narrative	Parses an input string from the form mm/dd/yy into a long integer via a call to computeLongDate.

Figure 12.22 Portion of detailed design of Osbert Oglesby product.

namely, data flow analysis (Section 12.3) and transaction analysis (Section 12.4). Techniques for detailed design are put forward in Section 12.8. Real-time system design is described in Section 12.9. In Section 12.10, design inspections are discussed. CASE tools and metrics for the design phase are presented in Sections 12.11 and 12.12, respectively. The chapter concludes with the object-oriented design of the Osbert Oglesby case study (Section 12.13).

FOR FURTHER READING

A useful overall source on design techniques is [Freeman and Wasserman, 1983]. The tutorial covers a wide variety of techniques, including many of those described in this chapter. [Yau and Tsai, 1986] is a survey of design techniques that cites over 80 references to a broad variety of approaches to design. A wide variety of design techniques can also be found in the February 1986 issue of *IEEE Transactions on Software Engineering*.

Data flow analysis and transaction analysis are described in books such as [Gane and Sarsen, 1979] and [Yourdon and Constantine, 1979]. Related techniques are found in [Martin and McClure, 1985]. Jackson's technique is described in [Jackson, 1975] and [Jackson, 1983]; other excellent sources are the work of Cameron, Jackson's associate [Cameron, 1986; 1988], and [King, 1988]. For readers interested in Warnier's work, the original sources are [Warnier, 1976] and [Warnier, 1981]. Orr's approach can be found in [Orr, 1981] and [Hansen, 1983].

Turning now to object-oriented design, information can be obtained from [Wirfs-Brock, Wilkerson, and Wiener, 1990], [Coad and Yourdon, 1991b], [Jacobson, Christerson, Jonsson, and Overgaard, 1992], [Martin and Odell, 1992], [Rumbaugh et al., 1991], [Shlaer and Mellor, 1992], and [Booch, 1994]. Comparisons of a variety of techniques for object-oriented design appear in [Monarchi and Puhr, 1992] and [Walker, 1992]. A comparison of both object-oriented and structured design techniques appears in [Fichman and Kemerer, 1992].

Formal design techniques are described in [Hoare, 1987].

With regard to reviews during the design process, useful checklists for inspections can be found in [Fagan, 1976], [Perry, 1983], and [Dunn, 1984]. The original paper on design inspections is [Fagan, 1976]; detailed information can be obtained from that paper. Later advances in review techniques are described in [Fagan, 1986]. A newer approach to design reviews is presented in [Parnas and Weiss, 1987]. The use of walkthroughs to test user interface design is described in [Bias, 1991].

With regard to real-time design, specific techniques are to be found in [Ward and Mellor, 1985], [Gomaa, 1986], [Hatley and Pirbhai, 1987], [Faulk and Parnas, 1988], [Levi and Agrawala, 1990], and [Cooling, 1997]. A comparison of four real-time design techniques is found in [Kelly and Sherif, 1992]. The

September 1992 issue of *IEEE Software* contains a number of articles on the design of real-time systems, as does the June 1995 issue of *IEEE Computer*. The design of distributed systems is described in [Kramer, 1994].

Metrics for the design phase are described in [Henry and Kafura, 1981], [Brandl, 1990], [Henry and Selig, 1990], and [Zage and Zage, 1993]. Metrics for object-oriented design are discussed in [Chidamber and Kemerer, 1994] and in [Binkley and Schach, 1996].

The proceedings of the International Workshops on Software Specification and Design are a comprehensive source for information on design techniques.

PROBLEMS

12.1 Starting with the DFD for Problem 10.6, use data flow analysis to design a product for determining whether a bank statement is correct.

12.2 Use transaction analysis to design the software to control an ATM (Problem 7.9). At this stage omit error-handling capabilities.

12.3 Now take your design for Problem 12.2 and add modules to perform error handling. Carefully examine the resulting design and determine the cohesion and coupling of the modules. Be on the lookout for situations such as that depicted in Figure 12.10.

12.4 Two different techniques for depicting a detailed design are presented in Section 12.3.1 (Figures 12.6 and 12.7). Compare and contrast the two techniques.

12.5 Starting with your data flow diagram for the automated library circulation system (Problem 10.8), design the circulation system using data flow analysis.

12.6 Repeat Problem 12.5 using transaction analysis. Which of the two techniques did you find to be more appropriate?

12.7 Starting with your specifications for the automated library circulation system (Problem 10.9), design the library system using object-oriented design.

12.8 Design the ATM software (Problem 7.9) using object-oriented design.

12.9 (Term Project) Starting with your specifications of Problem 10.15 or 11.10, design the Air Gourmet product (Appendix A). Use the design technique specified by your instructor.

12.10 (Case Study) Redesign the Osbert Oglesby product using data flow analysis.

12.11 (Case Study) Redesign the Osbert Oglesby product using transaction analysis.

12.12 (Case Study) The detailed design of Appendix G is represented in tabular form. Represent the design using a PDL (pseudocode) of your choice. Which representation is superior? Give reasons for your answer.

12.13 (Readings in Software Engineering) Your instructor will distribute copies of [Binkley and Schach, 1996]. Are you surprised that 14 of the 16 design quality metrics performed worse than chance?

REFERENCES

[Beizer, 1990] B. BEIZER, *Software Testing Techniques,* Second Edition, Van Nostrand Reinhold, New York, 1990.

[Bias, 1991] R. BIAS, "Walkthroughs: Efficient Collaborative Testing," *IEEE Software* **8** (September 1991), pp. 94–95.

[Binkley and Schach, 1996] A. B. BINKLEY AND S. R. SCHACH, "A Comparison of Sixteen Quality Metrics for Object-Oriented Design," *Information Processing Letters*, Vol. 57, No. 6 (June 1996), pp. 271–75.

[Binkley and Schach, 1997] A. B. BINKLEY AND S. R. SCHACH, "Toward a Unified Approach to Object-Oriented Coupling," *Proceedings of the 35th Annual ACM Southeast Conference*, Murfreesboro, TN, April 2–4, 1997, pp. 91–97.

[Binkley and Schach, 1998] A. B. BINKLEY AND S. R. SCHACH, "Validation of the Coupling Dependency Metric as a Predictor of Run-Time Failures and Maintenance Measures," *Proceedings of the Twentieth International Conference on Software Engineering*, Kyoto, Japan, April 1998, pp. 452–55.

[Booch, 1994] G. BOOCH, *Object-Oriented Analysis and Design with Applications, Second Edition*, Benjamin/Cummings, Redwood City, CA, 1994.

[Brandl, 1990] D. L. BRANDL, "Quality Measures in Design: Finding Problems before Coding," *ACM SIGSOFT Software Engineering Notes* **15** (January 1990), pp. 68–72.

[Cameron, 1986] J. R. CAMERON, "An Overview of JSD," *IEEE Transactions on Software Engineering* **SE-12** (February 1986), pp. 222–40.

[Cameron, 1988] J. CAMERON, *JSP & JSD—The Jackson Approach to Software Development,* Second Edition, IEEE Computer Society Press, Washington, DC, 1988.

[Chidamber and Kemerer, 1994] S. R. CHIDAMBER AND C. F. KEMERER, "A Metrics Suite for Object Oriented Design," *IEEE Transactions on Software Engineering* **20** (June 1994), pp. 476–93.

[Coad and Yourdon, 1991b] P. COAD AND E. YOURDON, *Object-Oriented Design*, Yourdon Press, Englewood Cliffs, NJ, 1991.

[Cooling, 1997] J. E. COOLING, *Real-Time Software Systems: An Introduction*, Van Nostrand Reinhold, New York, 1997.

[Dunn, 1984] R. H. DUNN, *Software Defect Removal*, McGraw-Hill, New York, 1984.

[Fagan, 1976] M. E. FAGAN, "Design and Code Inspections to Reduce Errors in Program Development," *IBM Systems Journal* **15** (No. 3, 1976), pp. 182–211.

[Fagan, 1986] M. E. FAGAN, "Advances in Software Inspections," *IEEE Transactions on Software Engineering* **SE-12** (July 1986), pp. 744–51.

[Faulk and Parnas, 1988] S. R. FAULK AND D. L. PARNAS, "On Synchronization in Hard-Real-Time Systems," *Communications of the ACM* **31** (March 1988), pp. 274–87.

[Fichman and Kemerer, 1992] R. G. FICHMAN AND C. F. KEMERER, "Object-Oriented and Conventional Analysis and Design Methodologies: Comparison and Critique," *IEEE Computer* **25** (October 1992), pp. 22–39.

[Flanagan, 1996] D. FLANAGAN, *Java in a Nutshell*, O'Reilly and Associates, Sebastopol, CA, 1996.

[Freeman and Wasserman, 1983] P. FREEMAN AND A. J. WASSERMAN (Editor), *Tutorial: Software Design Techniques,* Fourth Edition, IEEE Computer Society Press, Washington, DC, 1983.

[Gane and Sarsen, 1979] C. GANE AND T. SARSEN, *Structured Systems Analysis: Tools and Techniques*, Prentice Hall, Englewood Cliffs, NJ, 1979.

[Goldberg and Robson, 1989] A. GOLDBERG AND D. ROBSON, *Smalltalk-80: The Language*, Addison-Wesley, Reading, MA, 1989.

[Gomaa, 1986] H. GOMAA, "Software Development of Real-Time Systems," *Communications of the ACM* **29** (July 1986), pp. 657–68.

[Hansen, 1983] K. HANSEN, *Data Structured Program Design*, Ken Orr and Associates, Topeka, KS, 1983.

[Hatley and Pirbhai, 1987] D. J. HATLEY AND I. A. PIRBHAI, *Strategies for Real-Time System Specification*, Dorset House, New York, 1987.

[Henry and Kafura, 1981] S. M. HENRY AND D. KAFURA, "Software Structure Metrics Based on Information Flow," *IEEE Transactions on Software Engineering* **SE-7** (September 1981), pp. 510–18.

[Henry and Selig, 1990] S. HENRY AND C. SELIG, "Predicting Source-Code Complexity at the Design Stage," *IEEE Software* **7** (March 1990), pp. 36–44.

[Hoare, 1987] C. A. R. HOARE, "An Overview of Some Formal Methods for Program Design," *IEEE Computer* **20** (September 1987), pp. 85–91.

[ISO/IEC 8652, 1995] "Programming Language Ada: Language and Standard Libraries," ISO/IEC 8652, International Organization for Standardization, International Electrotechnical Commission, 1995.

[Jackson, 1975] M. A. JACKSON, *Principles of Program Design*, Academic Press, New York, 1975.

[Jackson, 1983] M. A. JACKSON, *System Development,* Prentice Hall, Englewood Cliffs, NJ, 1983.

[Jacobson, Christerson, Jonsson, and Overgaard, 1992] I. JACOBSON, M. CHRISTERSON, P. JONSSON, AND G. OVERGAARD, *Object-Oriented Software Engineering: A Use Case Driven Approach*, ACM Press, New York, 1992.

[Kelly and Sherif, 1992] J. C. KELLY AND J. S. SHERIF, "A Comparison of Four Design Methods for Real-Time Software Development," *Information and Software Technology* **34** (February 1992), pp. 74–82.

[King, 1988] D. KING, *Creating Effective Software: Computer Program Design Using the Jackson Methodology*, Prentice Hall, Englewood Cliffs, NJ, 1988.

[Kitchenham, Pickard, and Linkman, 1990] B. A. KITCHENHAM, L. M. PICKARD, AND S. J. LINKMAN, "An Evaluation of Some Design Metrics," *Software Engineering Journal* **5** (January 1990), pp. 50–58.

[Kmielcik et al., 1984] J. KMIELCIK ET AL., "SCR Methodology User's Manual," Grumman Aerospace Corporation, Report SRSR-A6-84-002, 1984.

[Kramer, 1994] J. KRAMER, "Distributed Software Engineering," *Proceedings of the 16th International Conference on Software Engineering*, Sorrento, Italy, May 1994, pp. 253–63.

[Levi and Agrawala, 1990] S.-T. LEVI and A. K. AGRAWALA, *Real Time System Design*, McGraw-Hill, New York, 1990.

[Martin and McClure, 1985] J. P. MARTIN AND C. MCCLURE, *Diagramming Techniques for Analysts and Programmers,* Prentice Hall, Englewood Cliffs, NJ, 1985.

[Martin and Odell, 1992] J. MARTIN AND J. J. ODELL, *Object-Oriented Analysis and Design*, Prentice Hall, Englewood Cliffs, NJ, 1992.

[McCabe, 1976] T. J. MCCABE, "A Complexity Measure," *IEEE Transactions on Software Engineering* **SE-2** (December 1976), pp. 308–20.

[Meyer, 1992b] B. MEYER, *Eiffel: The Language*, Prentice Hall, New York, 1992.

[Monarchi and Puhr, 1992] D. E. MONARCHI AND G. I. PUHR, "A Research Typology for Object-Oriented Analysis and Design," *Communications of the ACM* **35** (September 1992), pp. 35–47.

[Orr, 1981] K. ORR, *Structured Requirements Definition*, Ken Orr and Associates, Inc., Topeka, KS, 1981.

[Parnas, 1971] D. L. PARNAS, "Information Distribution Aspects of Design Methodology," *Proceedings of the IFIP Congress*, Ljubljana, Yugoslavia, 1971, pp. 339–44.

[Parnas, 1972a] D. L. PARNAS, "A Technique for Software Module Specification with Examples," *Communications of the ACM* **15** (May 1972), pp. 330–36.

[Parnas, 1972b] D. L. PARNAS, "On the Criteria to Be Used in Decomposing Systems into Modules," *Communications of the ACM* **15** (December 1972), pp. 1053–58.

[Parnas and Weiss, 1987] D. L. PARNAS AND D. M. WEISS, "Active Design Reviews: Principles and Practices," *Journal of Systems and Software* **7** (December 1987), pp. 259–65.

[Perry, 1983] W. E. PERRY, *A Structured Approach to Systems Testing*, Prentice Hall, Englewood Cliffs, NJ, 1983.

[Rumbaugh et al., 1991] J. RUMBAUGH, M. BLAHA, W. PREMERLANI, F. EDDY, AND W. LORENSEN, *Object-Oriented Modeling and Design*, Prentice Hall, Englewood Cliffs, NJ, 1991.

[Shepperd, 1990] M. SHEPPERD, "Design Metrics: An Empirical Analysis," *Software Engineering Journal* **5** (January 1990), pp. 3–10.

[Shlaer and Mellor, 1992] S. SHLAER AND S. MELLOR, *Object Lifecycles: Modeling the World in States,* Yourdon Press, Englewood Cliffs, NJ, 1992.

[Silberschatz and Galvin, 1998] A. SILBERSCHATZ AND P. B. GALVIN, *Operating System Concepts,* Fifth Edition, Addison-Wesley, Reading, MA, 1998.

[Stankovic, 1997] J. A. STANKOVIC, "Real-Time and Embedded Systems," in: *The Computer Science and Engineering Handbook,* A. B. Tucker, Jr. (Editor-in-Chief), CRC Press, Boca Raton, FL, pp. 1709–24.

[Stroustrup, 1991] B. STROUSTRUP, *The C++ Programming Language*, Second Edition, Addison-Wesley, Reading, MA, 1991.

[Walker, 1992] I. J. WALKER, "Requirements of an Object-Oriented Design Method," *Software Engineering Journal* **7** (March 1992), pp. 102–13.

[Ward and Mellor, 1985] P. T. WARD AND S. MELLOR, *Structured Development for Real-Time Systems. Volumes 1, 2 and 3,* Yourdon Press, New York, 1985.

[Warnier, 1976] J. D. WARNIER, *Logical Construction of Programs*, Van Nostrand Reinhold, New York, 1976.

[Warnier, 1981] J. D. WARNIER, *Logical Construction of Systems*, Van Nostrand Reinhold, New York, 1981.

[Wirfs-Brock, Wilkerson, and Wiener, 1990] R. WIRFS-BROCK, B. WILKERSON, AND L. WIENER, *Designing Object-Oriented Software*, Prentice Hall, Englewood Cliffs, NJ, 1990.

[Yau and Tsai, 1986] S. S. YAU AND J. J.-P. TSAI, "A Survey of Software Design Techniques," *IEEE Transactions on Software Engineering* **SE-12** (June 1986), pp. 713–21.

[Yourdon and Constantine, 1979] E. YOURDON AND L. L. CONSTANTINE, *Structured Design: Fundamentals of a Discipline of Computer Program and Systems Design*, Prentice Hall, Englewood Cliffs, NJ, 1979.

[Zage and Zage, 1993] W. M. ZAGE AND D. M. ZAGE, "Evaluating Design Metrics on Large-Scale Software," *IEEE Software* **10** (July 1993), pp. 75–81.

chapter

13

IMPLEMENTATION PHASE

Implementation is the process of translating the detailed design into code. When this is done by a single individual, the process is relatively well understood. But most real-life products today are too large to be implemented by one programmer within the given time constraints. Instead, the product is implemented by a team, all working at the same time on different components of the product. This is termed *programming-in-the-many*. Issues associated with programming-in-the-many are examined in this chapter.

13.1 CHOICE OF PROGRAMMING LANGUAGE

In most cases, the issue of which programming language to choose for the implementation simply does not arise. Suppose the client wants a product to be written in, say, FORTRAN. It may be the case that, in the opinion of the development team, FORTRAN is entirely unsuitable for the product. Such an opinion is irrelevant to the client. Management of the development organization has only two choices: Implement the product in FORTRAN or turn down the job.

Similarly, if the product has to be implemented on a specific computer, and the only language available on that computer is assembler, then again there is no choice. If no other language is available, either because no compiler has yet been written for any high-level language on that computer or because management is not prepared to pay for a new C++ compiler for the stipulated computer, then it is again clear that the issue of choice of programming language is not relevant.

A more interesting question is: A contract specifies that the product is to be implemented in "the most suitable" programming language. What language should be chosen? In order to answer this question, consider the following scenario. QQQ Corporation has been writing COBOL products for over 25 years. The entire 200-member software staff of QQQ, from the most junior programmer to the vice-president for software, have COBOL expertise. Why on earth should the most suitable programming language be anything but COBOL? The introduction of a new language, C++ for example, would mean having to hire new programmers, or, at the very least, existing staff would have to be intensively retrained. Having invested all that money and effort in C++ training, management might well decide that future products should also be written in C++. Nevertheless, all the existing COBOL products would still have to be maintained. There would then be two classes of programmers, COBOL maintenance programmers and C++ programmers writing the new applications. Quite undeservedly, maintenance is almost always considered to be an inferior activity to developing new applications, so there would be distinct unhappiness among the ranks of the COBOL programmers. This unhappiness would be compounded by the fact that C++ programmers are usually paid more than COBOL programmers because C++ programmers are in short supply. Although QQQ has excellent development tools for COBOL, a C++ compiler would have to be purchased, as well as appropriate C++ CASE tools. Additional hardware may have to be purchased or leased to run this new software. Perhaps most serious of all, QQQ has accumulated hundreds of person-years of COBOL expertise, the kind of expertise that can be gained only through hands-on experience, such as what to do when a certain cryptic error message appears on the screen, or how to handle the quirks of the compiler. In brief, it would seem that "the most suitable" programming language could only be COBOL—any other choice would be financially suicidal, either from the viewpoint of the costs involved, or as a consequence of plummeting staff morale leading to poor quality code.

And yet, the most suitable programming language for QQQ Corporation's latest project may indeed be some language other than COBOL. Notwithstanding its position as the world's most widely used programming language (see the Just in Case You Wanted to Know box on page 439), COBOL is suited for only one class of software products—data-processing applications. But if QQQ Corporation has software needs outside this class, then COBOL rapidly loses its attractiveness. For example, if QQQ wishes to construct a knowledge-based product using artificial intelligence (AI) techniques, then an AI language such as Lisp could be used, but COBOL is totally unsuitable for AI applications. If large-scale communications software is to be built, perhaps because QQQ requires satellite links to hundreds of branch offices all over the world, then a language such as C++ would prove to be far more suitable than COBOL. If QQQ is to go into the business of writing systems software such as operating systems, compilers, and linkers, then COBOL is very definitely unsuitable. And if QQQ Corporation has decided to go into defense contracting, the U.S. Department of Defense directive regarding the use of Ada for embedded, real-time weapons systems precludes the use of COBOL in this area (in the unlikely event of a misguided QQQ manager actually thinking that COBOL can be used for real-time embedded software).

The issue of which programming language to use can often be decided by using cost–benefit analysis (Section 4.7). That is, management must compute a dollar cost of an implementation in COBOL as well as the dollar benefits, present and future, of using COBOL. This computation must be repeated for every

JUST IN CASE YOU WANTED TO KNOW

Far more code has been written in COBOL than in all other programming languages put together. The major reason COBOL is the most widely used language stems from the fact that COBOL is a product of the U.S. Department of Defense (DoD). Developed under the direction of the late Rear-Admiral Grace Murray Hopper, COBOL was approved by DoD in 1960. Thereafter, DoD would not buy hardware for running data processing applications unless that hardware had a COBOL compiler [Sammet, 1978]. DoD was, and still is, the world's largest purchaser of computer hardware, and in the 1960s a considerable proportion of DoD software was written for data processing purposes. As a result, COBOL compilers were written as a matter of urgency for virtually every computer. This widespread availability of COBOL, at a time when the only alternative language was usually assembler, resulted in COBOL becoming the world's most popular programming language.

Languages such as C, C++, Java, and 4GLs are undoubtedly growing in popularity for new applications. Nevertheless, maintenance is still the major software activity, and this maintenance is being performed on existing COBOL software. In short, DoD put its stamp onto the world's software via its first major programming language, COBOL.

Another reason for the popularity of COBOL is that COBOL is frequently the best language for implementing a data-processing product. In particular, COBOL is generally the language of choice when money is involved. Financial books have to balance, so rounding errors cannot be allowed to creep in. Thus, all computations have to be performed using integer arithmetic. COBOL supports integer arithmetic on very large numbers (that is, billions of dollars). In addition, COBOL can also handle very small numbers, namely, fractions of a cent. Banking regulations require interest computations to be calculated to at least four decimal places of a cent, and COBOL can do this arithmetic with ease as well. Finally, COBOL probably has the best formatting, sorting, and report generation facilities of any third-generation language (Section 13.2). All these reasons have made COBOL an excellent choice for implementing a data-processing product.

As mentioned in Section 7.7.4 the upcoming COBOL Language Standard is for an object-oriented language. This standard will surely further boost the popularity of COBOL.

language under consideration. The language with the largest expected gain, that is, the difference between estimated benefits and estimated costs, is then the appropriate implementation language. Another way of deciding which programming language to select is to use risk analysis. For each language under consideration a list is made of the potential risks and ways of resolving them. The language for which the overall risk is the smallest is then selected.

Currently, there is pressure on software organizations to develop new software in an object-oriented language—any object-oriented language! The question that arises is: Which is the appropriate object-oriented language? Ten years ago, there was really only one choice, namely, Smalltalk. Today, however, the majority of object-oriented software is being written in C++. There are a number of reasons for this. One is the widespread availability of C++ compilers. In fact, many C++ compilers simply translate the source code from C++ into C, and then invoke the C compiler. Thus, any computer with a C compiler can essentially handle C++.

But the real explanation for the popularity of C++ is its apparent similarity to C. This is unfortunate, in that a number of managers view C++ simply as a superset of C and, therefore, conclude that any programmer who knows C can quickly pick up the additional pieces. It is indeed true that, from just a syntactical viewpoint, C++ is essentially a superset of C. After all, virtually any C program can be compiled using a C++ compiler. Conceptually, however, C++ is totally different from C. C is a product of the structured paradigm, whereas C++ is for the object-oriented paradigm. Using C++ makes sense only if object-oriented techniques have been used and if the product is organized around objects and classes, not modules.

Thus, before an organization adopts C++, it is essential that the relevant software professionals be trained in the object-oriented paradigm. It is particularly important that the information of Chapter 6 be taught. Unless it is clear to all involved, and particularly to management, that the object-oriented paradigm is a different way of developing software and what the precise differences are, then all that will happen is that the structured paradigm will continue to be used, but with the code written in C++ rather than C. When organizations are disappointed with the results of switching from C to C++, a major contributory factor is a lack of education in the object-oriented paradigm.

Now suppose that an organization decides to adopt Java. In that case it is not possible to move gradually from the structured paradigm to the object-oriented paradigm. Java is a pure object-oriented programming language; it does not support the functions and procedures of the structured paradigm. Unlike a hybrid object-oriented language such as C++, Java programmers have to use the object-oriented paradigm (and only the object-oriented paradigm) from the very beginning. Because of the necessity of an abrupt transition from the one paradigm to the other, education and training is even more important when adopting Java (or other pure object-oriented language such as Smalltalk) than if the organization were to switch to a hybrid object-oriented language like C++ or OO-COBOL.

What about implementation in a fourth-generation language? This issue is addressed in the next section.

13.2 FOURTH GENERATION LANGUAGES

The first computers had neither interpreters nor compilers. They were programmed in binary, either hard-wired with plug boards or by setting switches. Such a binary machine code was a *first-generation language*. The *second-generation languages* were assemblers, developed in the late 1940s and early 1950s. Instead of having to program in binary, instructions could be expressed in symbolic notation such as

```
mov    $17, next
```

```
for every surveyor
  if rating is excellent
    add 6500 to salary
```

Figure 13.1 Nonprocedural fourth-generation language.

In general, each assembler instruction is translated into one machine code instruction. Thus, although assembler was easier to write than machine code and easier for maintenance programmers to comprehend, the assembler source code was still the same length as the machine code.

The idea behind a *third-generation language* (or high-level language) such as FORTRAN, ALGOL 60, or COBOL is that one statement of a high-level language is compiled to as many as 5 or 10 machine code instructions (this is another example of abstraction; see Section 6.4.1). High-level language code is thus considerably shorter than the equivalent assembler code. It is also simpler to understand and, therefore, easier to maintain than assembler code. The fact that the high-level language code may not be quite as efficient as the equivalent assembler code is generally a small price to pay for ease in maintenance.

This concept was taken further in the late 1970s. A major objective in the design of a *fourth-generation language* (4GL) is that each 4GL statement should be equivalent to 30, or even 50, machine code instructions. Products written in a 4GL such as Focus or Natural would then be shorter, and hence quicker to develop and easier to maintain.

It is difficult to program in machine code. It is somewhat easier to program in assembler, and easier still to use a high-level language. A second major design objective of a 4GL is ease in programming. In particular, many 4GLs are *nonprocedural* (see the Just in Case You Wanted to Know box below for an insight into this term). For example, consider the command shown in Figure 13.1. It is up to the compiler of the 4GL to translate this nonprocedural instruction into a sequence of machine code instructions that can be executed procedurally.

JUST IN CASE YOU WANTED TO KNOW

Some years ago I hailed a cab outside Grand Central Station in New York City, and said to the driver, "Please take me to Lincoln Center." This was a *nonprocedural* request because I expressed the desired result, but I left it to the driver to decide how to achieve that result. It turned out that the driver was an immigrant from Central Europe who had been in America less than two days and who knew virtually nothing about the geography of New York City or the English language. As a result, I quickly replaced my nonprocedural request by a *procedural* request of the form, "Straight, straight. Take a right at the next light. I said right. Right, here, yes, right! Now straight. Slow down, please. I said slow down. For heaven's sake, slow down!" and so on, until we finally reached Lincoln Center.

Success stories abound from organizations that have switched to a 4GL. A few that previously have used COBOL have reported a 10-fold increase in productivity through use of a 4GL. Many organizations have found that their productivity has indeed increased through use of a 4GL, but not spectacularly so. Other organizations have tried a 4GL and have been bitterly disappointed with the results.

One reason for this inconsistency is that it is unlikely that one 4GL will be appropriate for all products. On the contrary, it is important to select the correct 4GL for the specific product. For example, Playtex used IBM's Application Development Facility (ADF) and reported an 80 to 1 productivity increase over COBOL. Notwithstanding this impressive result, Playtex subsequently used COBOL for products that were deemed by management to be less well suited to ADF [Martin, 1985].

A second reason for these inconsistent results is that many 4GLs are supported by powerful CASE workbenches and environments (Section 4.10). A CASE workbench or environment can be both a strength and a weakness. As explained in Section 2.11, it is inadvisable to introduce large-scale CASE within an organization with a low maturity level. The reason is that the purpose of a CASE workbench or environment is to support the software process. An organization at level 1 does not have a software process in place. If CASE is now introduced as part of the transition to a 4GL, the result will be to impose a process onto an organization that is not ready for any sort of process. The usual consequences are at best unsatisfactory and can be disastrous. In fact, a number of reported 4GL failures can be ascribed to the effects of the associated CASE environment rather than to the 4GL itself.

The attitudes of 43 organizations to 4GLs is reported in [Guimaraes, 1985]. It was found that use of a 4GL reduced user frustration because the data-processing department was able to respond more quickly when a user needed information to be extracted from the organization's database. However, there were also a number of problems. Some 4GLs proved to be slow and inefficient, with long response times. One product consumed 60 percent of the CPU cycles on an IBM 4331, while supporting at most 12 concurrent users. Overall, the 28 organizations that had been using 4GLs for over 3 years felt that the benefits outweighed the costs.

No one 4GL dominates the software market. Instead, there are literally hundreds of 4GLs; some of them, including DB2, Oracle, PowerBuilder, and SQL, have sizable user groups. This widespread proliferation of 4GLs is further evidence that care has to be taken in selecting the correct 4GL. Of course, few organizations can afford to support more than one 4GL. Once a 4GL has been chosen and used, the organization must either use that 4GL for subsequent products or fall back on the language that was used before the 4GL was introduced.

Notwithstanding the potential productivity gain, there is also the potential danger of using a 4GL the wrong way. In many organizations there is currently a large backlog of products to be developed and a long list of maintenance tasks to be performed. A design objective of many 4GLs is *end-user programming*, that is, programming by the person who will use the product. For example, before the advent of 4GLs the investment manager of an insurance company would ask the data-processing manager for a product that would display certain information regarding the bond portfolio. The investment manager would then wait a year or so for the data-processing group to find the time to develop the product. It was intended that a 4GL would be so simple to use that the investment manager, previously untrained in programming, would be able to write the desired product. End-user programming was intended to help reduce the development backlog, leaving the professionals to maintain existing products.

In practice, end-user programming can be dangerous. First, consider the situation when all product development is performed by computer professionals. Computer professionals are trained to mistrust computer output. After all, probably less than 1 percent of all output during product development is correct. On the other hand, the user is told to trust all computer output, because a product should not be delivered to the user until it is fault-free. Now consider the situation when end-user programming is encouraged. When a user who is inexperienced in programming writes code with a user-friendly, nonprocedural 4GL, the natural tendency is for that user to believe the output. After all, for years the user has been instructed to trust computer output. As a result, many business decisions have been based on data generated by hopelessly incorrect end-user code. In some cases the user-friendliness of certain 4GLs has led to financial catastrophes.

Another potential danger lies in the fact that, in some organizations, users have been allowed to write 4GL products that update the organization's database. A programming error made by a user may eventually result in the corruption of the entire database. The lesson is clear: Programming by inexperienced or inadequately trained users can be exceedingly dangerous, if not fatal, to the financial health of a corporation.

The ultimate choice of a 4GL will be made by management. In making such a decision, management should be guided by the many success stories resulting from the use of a 4GL. At the same time, management should also carefully analyze the failures caused by using an inappropriate 4GL, by premature introduction of a CASE environment, or by poor management of the development process. For example, a common cause of failure is neglecting to train the development team thoroughly in all aspects of the 4GL, including relational database theory [Date, 1994] where appropriate. Management should study both the successes and failures in the specific application area and learn from past mistakes. Choosing the correct 4GL can mean the difference between a major success and dismal failure.

Having decided on the implementation language, the next issue is how software engineering principles can lead to better quality code.

13.3 GOOD PROGRAMMING PRACTICE

Many recommendations on good coding style are language-specific. For example, suggestions regarding use of COBOL 88-level entries or parentheses in Lisp are of little interest to programmers implementing a product in Java. The reader who is actively involved in implementation is urged to read one of the many books, such as those by Henry Ledgard, on good programming practice for the specific language in which the product is being implemented. Some recommendations regarding language-independent good programming practice are now given.

Use of Consistent and Meaningful Variable Names As stated in Chapter 1, on average two-thirds of a software budget is devoted to maintenance. This implies that the programmer developing a module is merely the first of many other programmers who will work on that module. It is counterproductive for a programmer to give names to variables that are meaningful to only that programmer; within the context of software engineering, the term *meaningful* means "meaningful from the viewpoint of future maintenance programmers."

This point is illustrated by events at a small software production organization in Johannesburg, South Africa, in the late 1970s. The organization consisted of two programming teams. Team A was made up of émigrés from Mozambique. They were of Portuguese extraction, and their native language was Portuguese. Their code was well written. Variable names were meaningful, but unfortunately only to a speaker of Portuguese. Team B comprised Israeli immigrants whose native language was Hebrew. Their code was equally well written, and the names they chose for their variables were equally meaningful—but only to a speaker of Hebrew. One fine day, team A resigned en masse, together with the team leader. Team B was totally unable to maintain any of the excellent code that team A had written, because they could not speak a word of Portuguese. The variable names, meaningful as they were to Portuguese speakers, were incomprehensible to the Israelis whose linguistic abilities were restricted to Hebrew and English. The owner of the software organization was unable to hire enough Portuguese-speaking programmers to replace team A, and the company soon went into bankruptcy, under the weight of numerous lawsuits from disgruntled customers whose code was now essentially unmaintainable. The situation could so easily have been avoided. The head of the company should have insisted from the start that all variable names be in English, the language understood by every South African computer professional. Variable names would then have been meaningful to any maintenance programmer.

In addition to the use of meaningful variable names, it is equally essential that variable names be consistent. For example, the following four variables are declared in a module: averageFreq, frequencyMaximum, minFr, and frqncyTotl. A maintenance programmer who is trying to understand the code has to know if freq, frequency, fr, and frqncy all refer to the same thing. If yes, then the identical word should be used, preferably frequency, although freq or frqncy are marginally acceptable; fr is not. But if one or more variable names refer to a different quantity, then a totally different name, such as rate, should be used. Conversely, do not use two different names to denote the identical concept; for example, average and mean should not both be used in the same program.

A second aspect of consistency is the ordering of the components of variable names. For example, if one variable is named frequencyMaximum, then the name minimumFrequency would be confusing; it should be frequencyMinimum. Thus, in order to make the code clear and unambiguous for future maintenance programmers, the four variables listed previously should be named frequencyAverage, frequencyMaximum, frequencyMinimum, and frequencyTotal, respectively. Alternatively, the frequency component can appear at the end of all four variable names, yielding the variable names averageFrequency, maximumFrequency, minimumFrequency, and totalFrequency. It clearly does not matter which of the two sets is chosen; what is important is that all the names be from the one set or from the other.

A number of different naming conventions have been put forward that are intended to make it easier to understand the code. The idea is that the name of a variable should incorporate type information. For example, ptrChTmp might denote a temporary variable (Tmp) of type pointer (ptr) to an character (Ch). The best-known of such schemes are the Hungarian Naming Conventions [Klunder, 1988]. (If you want to know why they are called Hungarian, see the Just in Case You Wanted to Know box below.) One drawback of many of such schemes is that the effectiveness of code inspections (Section 13.9) can be reduced when participants are unable to pronounce the names of variables. It is extremely frustrating to have to spell out variable names, letter by letter.

The Issue of Self-Documenting Code When asked why their code contains no comments whatsoever, programmers often reply, "I write self-documenting code." The implication is that their variable names are so carefully chosen and their code so exquisitely crafted that there is no need for any comments. Self-documenting code does exist, but it is exceedingly rare. Instead, the usual scenario is that the programmer appreciates every nuance of the code at the time the module is written. It is conceivable that the programmer uses the same style for every module, and that in 5 years' time the code will still be crystal clear in every respect to the original programmer. Unfortunately, this is irrelevant. The important point is whether the module can be understood easily and unambiguously by all the other programmers who will have to read the code, starting with the SQA group and including a number of different maintenance

JUST IN CASE YOU WANTED TO KNOW

There are two explanations for the term *Hungarian Naming Conventions*. First, they were invented by Charles Simonyi, who was born in Hungary. Second, it is generally agreed that, to the uninitiated, programs with variable names conforming to the conventions are about as easy to read as Hungarian. Nevertheless, organizations (such as Microsoft) that use them claim that they enhance code readability for those with experience in the Hungarian Naming Conventions.

programmers. The problem becomes more acute in the light of the unfortunate practice of assigning maintenance tasks to inexperienced programmers and not supervising them closely. The undocumented code of the module may be only partially comprehensible to an experienced programmer. How much worse, then, is the situation when the maintenance programmer is inexperienced.

To see the sort of problems that can arise, consider the variable xCoordinateOfPositionOfRobotArm. Such a variable name is undoubtedly self-documenting in every sense of the word, but few programmers are prepared to use a 31-character variable name, especially if that name is used frequently. Instead, a shorter name is used, xCoord, for example. The reasoning behind this is that if the entire module deals with the movement of the arm of a robot, xCoord can refer only to the x-coordinate of the position of the arm of the robot. Although that argument holds water within the context of the development process, it is not necessarily true for maintenance. The maintenance programmer may not have sufficient knowledge of the product as a whole to realize that, within this module, xCoord refers to the arm of the robot or may not have the necessary documentation to understand the workings of the module. The way to avoid this sort of problem is to insist that every variable name be explained at the beginning of the module, in the *prologue comments*. If this rule is followed, the maintenance programmer will quickly understand that the variable xCoord is used for the x-coordinate of the position of the robot arm.

Prologue comments are mandatory in every single module. The minimum information that must be provided at the top of every module is: module name; a brief description of what the module does; programmer's name; date module was coded; date module was approved and by whom; module arguments; list of variable names, preferably in alphabetical order, and their uses; names of files accessed by this module, if any; names of files changed by this module, if any; module input/output, if any; error-handling capabilities; name of file containing test data, to be used later for regression testing; list of modifications made, their dates, and who approved them; and known faults, if any.

Even if a module is clearly written, it is unreasonable to expect someone to have to read every line in order to understand what the module does and how it does it. Prologue comments make it easy for others to understand the key points. Only a member of the SQA group or a maintenance programmer who is modifying a specific module should be expected to have to read every line of that module.

In addition to prologue comments, inline comments should be inserted into the code to assist maintenance programmers in understanding that code. It has been suggested that inline comments should be used only when the code is written in a nonobvious way or makes use of some subtle aspect of the language. On the contrary, confusing code should be rewritten in a clearer way. Inline comments are a means of helping maintenance programmers and should not be used to promote or excuse poor programming practice.

Use of Parameters There are very few genuine constants, that is, variables whose values will *never* change. For instance, satellite photographs have caused changes to be made in submarine navigation systems incorporating the latitude and longitude of Pearl Harbor, Hawaii, in order to reflect more accurate geographic data regarding the exact location of Pearl Harbor. To take another example, sales tax is not a genuine constant; legislators tend to change the sales tax rate from time to time. Suppose that the sales tax rate is currently 6.0 percent. If the value 6.0 has been hard coded in a number of modules of a product, then changing the product is a major exercise, with the likely outcome of one or two instances of the "constant" 6.0 being overlooked and perhaps changing an unrelated 6.0 by mistake. A better solution is a declaration such as

```
public static final float salesTaxRate = (float) 6.0;
```

Then, wherever the value of the sales tax rate is needed, the constant salesTaxRate should be used and not the number 6.0. If the sales tax rate changes, then only the line containing the value of salesTaxRate need be altered using an editor. Better still, the value of the sales tax rate should be read in from a parameter file at the beginning of the run. All such apparent constants should be treated as parameters. If a value should change for any reason, this change can then be implemented quickly and effectively.

Code Layout for Increased Readability It is relatively simple to make a module easy to read. For example, no more than one statement should appear on a line, even though many programming languages permit more than one. Indentation is perhaps the most important technique for increasing readability. Just imagine how difficult it would be to read the code examples in Chapter 6 if indentation had not been used to assist in understanding the code. In Java, indentation can be used to connect corresponding {...} pairs. It also shows which statements belong in a given block. In fact, correct indentation is too important to be left to human beings. Instead, as described in Section 4.11, CASE tools should be used to ensure that indentation is done correctly.

Another useful aid is blank lines. Methods should be separated by blank lines; in addition, it is often helpful to break up large blocks of code with blank lines. The extra "white space" makes the code easier to read and, hence, comprehend.

Nested if Statements Consider the following example. A map consists of two squares, as shown in Figure 13.2. It is required to write code to determine whether a point on the Earth's surface lies in map square 1 or map square 2, or is not on the map at all. The solution of Figure 13.3 is so badly formatted that it is incomprehensible. A properly formatted version appears in Figure 13.4. Notwithstanding this, the combination of **if-if** and **if-else-if** constructs is so complex that it is difficult to check whether the code fragment is correct. This is fixed in Figure 13.5.

When faced with complex code containing the **if-if** construct, one way to simplify it is to make use of the fact that the **if-if** combination

```
if <condition 1>
if <condition 2>
```

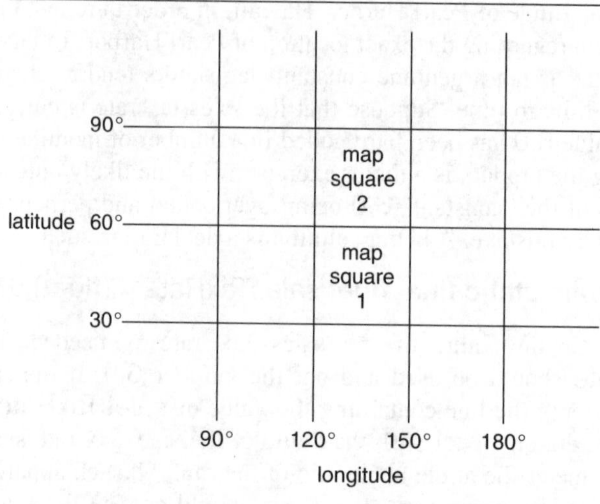

Figure 13.2 Coordinates for map.

```
if (latitude > 30 && longitude > 120) { if (latitude <= 60 && longitude <= 150)
mapSquareNo = 1; else if (latitude <= 90 && longitude <= 150) mapSquareNo =
2 else System.out.println("Not on the map"); } else System.out.println("Not on the
map");
```

Figure 13.3 Badly formatted nested **if** statements.

```
if (latitude > 30 && longitude > 120)
{
  if (latitude <= 60 && longitude <= 150)
    mapSquareNo = 1;
  else if (latitude <= 90 && longitude <= 150)
      mapSquareNo = 2;
    else
      System.out.println("Not on the map");
}
else
  System.out.println("Not on the map");
```

Figure 13.4 Well-formatted, but badly constructed, nested **if** statements.

```
if (longitude > 120 && longitude <= 150 && latitude > 30 && latitude <= 60)
  mapSquareNo = 1;
else if (longitude > 120 && longitude <= 150 && latitude > 60 && latitude <= 90)
    mapSquareNo = 2;
  else
    System.out.println("Not on the map");
```

Figure 13.5 Acceptably nested **if** statements.

is equivalent to the single condition

if <*condition* 1> **and** <*condition* 2>

provided that <*condition* 2> is defined even if <*condition* 1> does not hold. For example, <*condition* 1> might check that a pointer is not null and, if so, then <*condition* 2> can use that pointer. (This problem does not arise in Java or C++. The && operator is defined such that if <*condition* 1> is false, then <*condition* 2> is not evaluated.)

Another problem with the **if-if** construct is that nesting **if** statements too deeply leads to code that can be difficult to read. As a rule of thumb, **if** statements nested to a depth greater than three is poor programming practice and should be avoided.

13.4 CODING STANDARDS

Coding standards can be both a blessing and a curse. It was pointed out in Section 6.2.1 that modules with coincidental cohesion generally arise as a consequence of rules such as: Every module will consist of between 35 and 50 executable statements. Instead of stating a rule in such a dogmatic fashion, a better formulation is: Programmers should consult their managers before constructing a module with fewer than 35 or more than 50 executable statements. The point is that no coding standard can ever be applicable under all possible circumstances.

Coding standards imposed from above tend to be ignored. As mentioned previously, a useful rule of thumb is that **if** statements should not be nested to a depth greater than three. If programmers are shown examples of unreadable code resulting from nesting **if** statements too deeply, then it is likely that they will conform to such a regulation. But they are unlikely to adhere to a list of coding rules imposed on them without discussion or explanation. Furthermore, such standards are likely to lead to friction between programmers and their managers.

In addition, unless a coding standard can be checked by machine, it is either going to waste a lot of the SQA group's time, or it will simply be ignored by the programmers and SQA group alike. On the other hand, consider the following rules:

- Nesting of **if** statements should not exceed a depth of three, except with prior approval from the team leader.
- Modules should consist of between 35 and 50 statements, except with prior approval from the team leader.
- The use of **goto** statements should be avoided. However, with prior approval from the team leader, a forward **goto** may be used for error handling.

Such rules may be checked by machine, provided that some mechanism is set up for capturing the data relating to permission to deviate from the standard.

Some organizations have strict standards regarding names of modules and variables. One COBOL software organization has laid down highly restrictive coding standards. For example, if a subprogram is named, say, sub-23, then its sections are numbered a01-sub-23 through a99-sub-23, and paragraphs within section a34-sub-23 are named b01-a34-sub-23 through b99-a34-sub-23. There are special naming conventions for error-handling paragraphs, paragraphs that perform input, paragraphs that perform output, and the exit-program paragraph. In addition, there are even more complex rules for naming variables. Such artificial names are meaningful only to someone who has been forced to learn the standard.

The aim of coding standards is to make maintenance easier. However, if the effect of a standard is to make the life of software developers difficult, then such a standard should be modified, even in the middle of a project. Overly restrictive coding standards are counterproductive in that the quality of software production must inevitably suffer if programmers have to develop software within such a framework. On the other hand, standards such as those listed previously regarding nesting of **if** statements, module size, and **goto** statements, coupled with a mechanism for deviating from those standards, can lead to improved software quality, which is, after all, a major goal of software engineering.

13.5 MODULE REUSE

Reuse was presented in detail in Chapter 7. In fact, the material on reuse could have appeared virtually anywhere in this book, because components from all phases of the software process are reused, including portions of specifications, contracts, plans, designs, and modules. That is why the material on reuse was put into the first part of the book, rather than tying it to one or other specific phase. In particular, it was important that the material on reuse not be presented in this chapter in order to underline the fact that, even though reuse of modules is by far the most common form of reuse, more than just modules can be reused.

Testing during the implementation phase is examined next.

13.6 MODULE TEST CASE SELECTION

As explained in Chapter 6, an object is a specific type of module. Thus in this chapter, as in the rest of the book, whatever holds for a module in general also applies to objects in particular. In addition, however, there are issues that are specific to objects. In this and the following sections, testing issues that are specific to objects are highlighted within the context of the testing of modules in general.

As pointed out in Section 5.6, modules undergo two types of testing, namely, informal testing performed by the programmer while developing the module and methodical testing carried out by the SQA group after the programmer is satisfied that the module appears to function correctly. It is this methodical testing that is described in the following discussion. There are in turn two basic types of methodical testing, namely, nonexecution-based testing in which the module is reviewed by a team and execution-based testing in which the module is run against test cases. Techniques for selecting these test cases are now described.

The worst way to test a module is to use haphazard test data. The tester sits in front of the keyboard, and whenever the module requests input, the tester responds with arbitrary data. As will be shown, there is never time to test more than the tiniest fraction of all possible tests cases, which can easily number many more than 10^{100}. The few test cases that can be run, perhaps of the order of 1000, are too valuable to waste on haphazard data. Worse, there is a tendency when the machine solicits input to respond more than once with the same data, thus wasting even more test cases. It is clear that test cases must be constructed systematically.

13.6.1 TESTING TO SPECIFICATIONS VERSUS TESTING TO CODE

There are two basic ways of systematically constructing test data to test a module. The first is to *test to specifications*. This technique is also called *black-box*, *structural*, *data-driven*, *functional*, or *input/output-driven* testing. In this approach, the code itself is ignored; the only information used in drawing up test cases is the specification document. The other extreme is to *test to code* and to ignore the specification document when selecting test cases. Other names for this technique are *glass-box*, *white-box*, *behavioral*, *logic-driven*, or *path-oriented* testing (for an explanation of why there are so many different terms, see the Just in Case You Wanted to Know box on page 452).

We now consider the feasibility of each of these two techniques, starting with testing to specifications.

13.6.2 FEASIBILITY OF TESTING TO SPECIFICATIONS

Consider the following example. Suppose that the specifications for a certain data processing product state that five types of commission and seven types of discount must be incorporated. Testing every possible combination of just commission and discount requires 35 test cases. It is no use saying that commission and

JUST IN CASE YOU WANTED TO KNOW

It is reasonable to ask why there are so many different names for the same testing concept. The reason is that, as so often happens in software engineering, the same concept was discovered, independently, by a number of different researchers, each of whom invented his or her own terminology. By the time the software engineering community realized that these were different names for the identical concept, it was too late—the diverse names had crept into our software engineering vocabulary.

In this book, I use the terminology *black-box testing* and *glass-box testing*. These terms are particularly descriptive. When we test to specifications, we treat the code as a totally opaque black box. Conversely, when we test to code, we need to be able to see inside the box; hence the term *glass-box testing*. I avoid the term *white-box* testing because it is somewhat confusing. After all, a box that has been painted white is just as opaque as one that is painted black!

discount are computed in two entirely separate modules and hence may be tested independently—in black-box testing the product is treated as a black box, and its internal structure is therefore completely irrelevant.

In this example, there are only two factors, namely, commission and discount, taking on five and seven different values, respectively. In any realistic product there will be hundreds, if not thousands, of different factors. Even if there are only 20 factors, each taking on only 4 different values, then a total of 4^{20} or 1.1×10^{12} different test cases have to be examined.

To see the implications of over a trillion test cases, consider how long it would take to test them all. If a team of programmers could be found who could generate, run, and examine test cases at an average rate of one every 30 seconds, then it would take more than a million years to test the product exhaustively.

Thus, exhaustive testing to specifications is impossible in practice because of the combinatorial explosion. There are simply too many test cases to consider. Testing to code is therefore now examined.

13.6.3 FEASIBILITY OF TESTING TO CODE

The most common form of testing to code requires that each path through the module must be executed at least once. To see the infeasibility of this, consider the flowchart depicted in Figure 13.6. Despite the fact that the flowchart appears to be almost trivial, there are over 10^{12} different paths through the flowchart. There are five possible paths through the central group of six shaded boxes, and the total number of possible paths through the flowchart is therefore

$$5^1 + 5^2 + 5^3 + \ldots + 5^{18} = 4.77 \times 10^{12} \qquad \textbf{(13.1)}$$

If there can be this many paths through a simple flowchart containing a single loop, it is not difficult to imagine the total number of different paths in a module of reasonable size and complexity, let alone in a large module with many

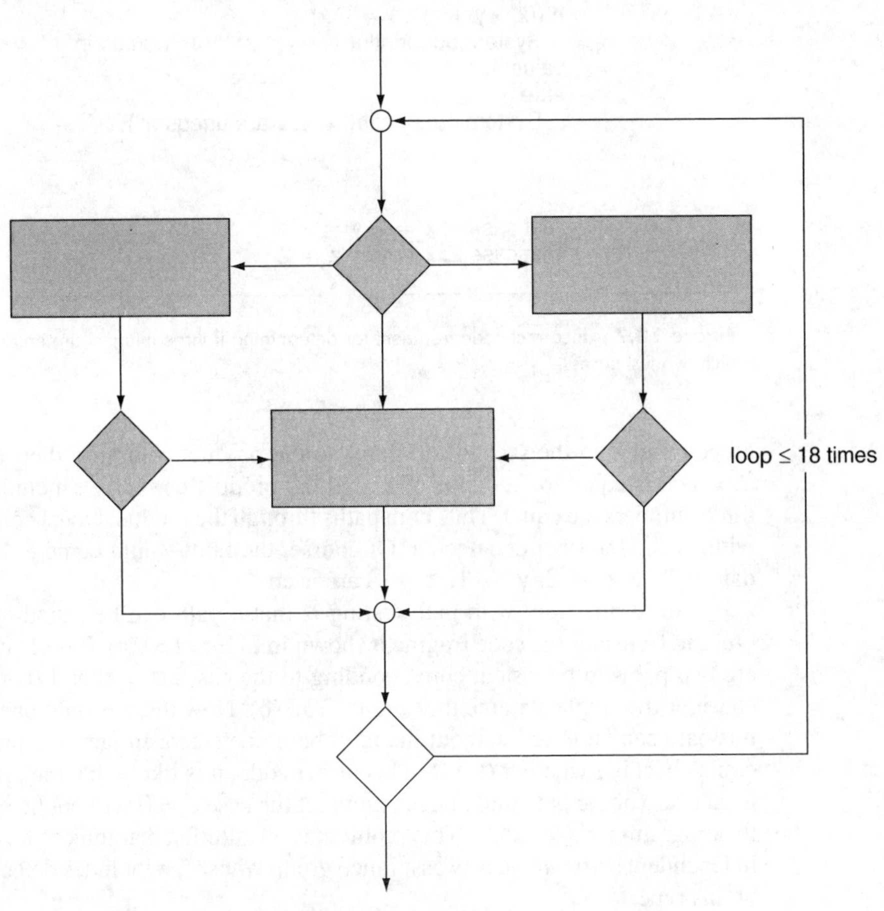

Figure 13.6 Flowchart with over 10^{12} possible paths.

loops. In short, the huge number of possible paths renders exhaustive testing to code as infeasible as exhaustive testing to specifications.

There are additional reasons why testing to code is problematic. Testing to code requires the tester to exercise every path. It is possible to exercise every path without detecting every fault in the product, that is, testing to code is not reliable. To see this, consider the code fragment shown in Figure 13.7 [Myers, 1976]. The fragment was written to test the equality of three integers, x, y, and z, using the totally fallacious assumption that if the average of three numbers is equal to the first number then the three numbers are equal. Two test cases are also shown in Figure 13.7. In the first test case the value of the average of the three numbers is 6/3 or 2, which is not equal to 1. The product therefore correctly informs the tester that x, y, and z are unequal. The integers x, y, and z are

```
if ((x + y + z) / 3 = = x)
   System.out.println("x,  y,  z  are  equal  in
value");
else
   System.out.println("x, y, z are unequal");


Test case 1: x = 1, y = 2, z = 3
Test case 2: x = y = z = 2
```

Figure 13.7 Incorrect code fragment for determining if three integers are equal, together with two test cases.

all equal to 2 in the second test case, so the product computes their average as 2, which is equal to the value of x, and the product correctly concludes that the three numbers are equal. Thus both paths through the product have been exercised without the fault being detected. Of course, the fault would come to light if test data such as x = 2, y = 1, z = 3 are used.

A third difficulty with path testing is that a path can be tested only if it is present. Consider the code fragment shown in Figure 13.8(a). It is clear that there are two paths to be tested, corresponding to the cases d = 0 and d ≠ 0. Next, consider the single statement of Figure 13.8(b). Now there is only one path, and this path can be tested without the fault being detected. In fact, if a programmer omits checking whether d = 0 in his or her code, it is likely that the programmer is unaware of the potential danger, and that the case d = 0 will not be included in the programmer's test data. This problem is an additional argument for having an independent software quality assurance group whose job includes detecting faults of this type.

These examples show conclusively that the criterion "exercise all paths in the product" is not *reliable,* as there exist products for which some data exercising a given path will detect a fault and different data exercising the same path will not.

```
if (d == 0)
   zeroDivisionRoutine ();
else
   x = n / d;
```

(a)

```
x = n / d;
```

(b)

Figure 13.8 Two code fragments for computing a quotient.

However, path-oriented testing is *valid*, because it does not inherently preclude selecting test data that might reveal the fault.

Because of the combinatorial explosion, neither exhaustive testing to specifications nor exhaustive testing to code is feasible. A compromise is needed, using techniques that will highlight as many faults as possible, while accepting that there is no way to guarantee that all faults have been detected. A reasonable way to proceed is to use black-box test cases first (testing to specifications) and then develop additional test cases using glass-box techniques (testing to code).

13.7 BLACK-BOX MODULE-TESTING TECHNIQUES

Exhaustive black-box testing generally requires literally billions and billions of test cases. The art of testing is to devise a small, manageable set of test cases so as to maximize the chances of detecting a fault while minimizing the chances of wasting a test case by having the same fault detected by more than one test case. Every test case must be chosen to detect a previously undetected fault. One such black-box technique is equivalence testing combined with boundary value analysis.

13.7.1 EQUIVALENCE TESTING AND BOUNDARY VALUE ANALYSIS

Suppose the specifications for a database product state that the product must be able to handle any number of records from 1 through 16,383 ($2^{14} - 1$). If the product can handle 34 records and 14,870 records, then the chances are good that it will work fine for, say, 8252 records. In fact, the chances of detecting a fault, if present, are likely to be equally good if any test case from 1 through 16,383 records is selected. Conversely, if the product works correctly for any one test case in the range from 1 through 16,383, then it will probably work for any other test case in the range. The range from 1 through 16,383 constitutes an *equivalence class,* that is, a set of test cases such that any one member of the class is as good a test case as any other member of the class. To be more precise, the specified range of numbers of records that the product must be able to handle defines three equivalence classes:

Equivalence class 1: Less than 1 record.

Equivalence class 2: From 1 through 16,383 records.

Equivalence class 3: More than 16,383 records.

Testing the database product using the technique of equivalence classes then requires that one test case from each equivalence class be selected. The test case from equivalence class 2 should be handled correctly, whereas error messages should be printed for the test cases from class 1 and class 3.

A successful test case is one that detects a previously undetected fault. In order to maximize the chances of finding such a fault, a high-payoff technique is *boundary value analysis*. Experience has shown that when a test case that is on or just to one side of the boundary of an equivalence class is selected, the probability of detecting a fault increases. Thus, when testing the database product, seven test cases should be selected:

Test case 1:	0 records	Member of equivalence class 1 and adjacent to boundary value
Test case 2:	1 record	Boundary value
Test case 3:	2 records	Adjacent to boundary value
Test case 4:	723 records	Member of equivalence class 2
Test case 5:	16,382 records	Adjacent to boundary value
Test case 6:	16,383 records	Boundary value
Test case 7:	16,384 records	Member of equivalence class 3 and adjacent to boundary value

The preceding example applies to the input specifications. An equally powerful technique is to examine the output specifications. For example, in 1998 the minimum Social Security (OASDI) deduction from any one paycheck permitted by the tax code was $0.00, and the maximum was $3,887.40, the latter corresponding to gross earnings of $62,700. Thus, when testing a payroll product, the test cases for the Social Security deduction from paychecks should include input data that are expected to result in deductions of exactly $0.00 and $3,887.40. In addition, test data should be set up that might result in deductions of less than $0.00 or more than $3,887.40.

In general, for each range (R_1, R_2) listed in either the input or the output specifications, five test cases should be selected, corresponding to values less than R_1, equal to R_1, greater than R_1 but less than R_2, equal to R_2, and greater than R_2. Where it is specified that an item has to be a member of a certain set (for example, the input must be a letter), two equivalence classes must be tested, namely, a member of the specified set and a nonmember of the set. Where the specifications lay down a precise value (for example, the response must be followed by a # sign), then there are again two equivalence classes, namely, the specified value and anything else.

The use of equivalence classes, together with boundary value analysis, to test both the input specifications and the output specifications is a valuable technique for generating a relatively small set of test data with the potential of uncovering a number of faults that might well remain hidden if less powerful techniques for test data selection were used.

13.7.2 FUNCTIONAL TESTING

An alternative form of black-box testing is to base the test data on the functionality of the module. In *functional testing* [Howden, 1987], each item of functionality or *function* implemented in the module is identified. Typical functions in a module for a computerized warehouse product might be get next database record or determine whether quantity on hand is below the reorder point. In a weapons control system, a module might include the function compute trajectory. In a module of an operating system, one function might be determine whether file is empty.

After determining all the functions of the module, test data are devised to test each function separately. Now the functional testing is taken a step further. If the module consists of a hierarchy of lower-level functions, connected together by the control structures of structured programming, then functional testing proceeds recursively. For example, if a higher-level function is of the form

```
<higher-level function>  ::=  if <conditional expression>
                                   <lower-level function 1>;
                               else                                (13.2)
                                   <lower-level function 2>;
```

then, because *<conditional expression>*, *<lower-level function* 1>, and *<lower-level function* 2> have been subjected to functional testing, *<higher-level function>* can be tested using branch coverage, a glass-box technique described in Section 13.8.1. Note that this form of structural testing is a hybrid technique—the lower-level functions are tested using a black-box technique, but the higher-level functions are tested using a glass-box technique.

In practice, however, higher-level functions are not constructed in such a structured fashion from lower-level functions. Instead, the lower-level functions are usually intertwined in some way. To determine faults in this situation, *functional analysis* is required, a somewhat complex procedure; for details, see [Howden, 1987]. A further complicating factor is that functionality frequently does not coincide with module boundaries. Thus the distinction between module testing and integration testing becomes blurred; one module cannot be tested without, at the same time, testing the other modules whose functionality it uses. This problem also arises in the object-oriented paradigm when a method of one object sends a message to (invokes) a method of a different object.

The random interrelationships between modules from the viewpoint of functional testing may have unacceptable consequences for management. For example, milestones and deadlines can become somewhat ill-defined, making it difficult to determine the status of the product with respect to the software project management plan.

13.8 GLASS-BOX MODULE-TESTING TECHNIQUES

In glass-box techniques, test cases are selected on the basis of examination of the code, rather than the specifications. There are a number of different forms of glass-box testing, including statement, branch, and path coverage.

13.8.1 STRUCTURAL TESTING: STATEMENT, BRANCH, AND PATH COVERAGE

The simplest form of glass-box testing is *statement coverage*, that is, running a series of test cases during which every statement is executed at least once. To keep track of which statements are still to be executed, a CASE tool keeps a record of how many times each statement has been executed over the series of tests. A weakness of this approach is that there is no guarantee that all outcomes of branches are properly tested. To see this, consider the code fragment of Figure 13.9. The programmer has made a mistake; the compound conditional `s > 1 && t == 0` should have read `s > 1 || t == 0`. The test data shown in the figure allow the statement `x = 9` to be executed without the fault being highlighted.

An improvement over statement coverage is *branch coverage*, that is, running a series of tests to ensure that all branches are tested at least once. Again, a tool is usually needed to help the tester keep track of which branches have or have not been tested; *btool* and General Coverage Tool (GCT) are examples of branch coverage tools for C programs. Techniques such as statement or branch coverage are termed *structural tests*.

The most powerful form of structural testing is *path coverage*, that is, testing all paths. As shown previously, the number of paths in a product with loops can be very large indeed. As a result, researchers have been investigating ways of reducing the number of paths to be examined while still being able to uncover more faults than would be possible using branch coverage. One criterion for selecting paths is to restrict test cases to linear code sequences [Woodward, Hedley, and Hennell, 1980]. To do this, first identify the set of points *L* from which control flow may jump. The set *L* includes entry and exit points, and branch statements such as an **if** statement or a **goto** statement. Then linear code sequences are those paths that begin at an element of *L* and end at an element of *L*. The technique has been successful in that it has uncovered many faults without having to test every path.

Another way of reducing the number of paths to test is *all-definition-use-path coverage* [Rapps and Weyuker, 1985]. In this technique, each occurrence of a variable `qqq`, say, in the source code is labeled either as a *definition* of the variable, such as `qqq = 1` or `read (qqq)`, or as a *use* of the variable, such as `y = qqq + 3` or `if (qqq < 9) errorB ()`. All paths between the definition of a variable and the use of that definition are now identified, nowadays by means of an automatic tool. Finally, a test case is set up for each such path. All-definition-

```
if (s > 1 && t == 0)
  x = 9;

Test case:   s = 2, t = 0.
```

Figure 13.9 Code fragment with test data.

use-path coverage is an excellent test technique in that large numbers of faults are frequently detected by relatively few test cases. However, all-definition-use-path coverage does have the disadvantage that the upper bound on the number of paths is 2^d, where d is the number of decision statements (branches) in the product. Examples can be constructed exhibiting the upper bound. However, it has been shown that for real products, as opposed to artificial examples, this upper bound is not reached, and the actual number of paths is proportional to d [Weyuker, 1988a]. In other words, the number of test cases needed for all-definition-use-path coverage is generally much smaller than the theoretical upper bound. Thus all-definition-use-path coverage is a practical test case selection technique.

When using structural testing, the situation can arise in which the tester simply cannot come up with a test case that will exercise a specific statement, branch, or path. What may have happened is that there is an infeasible path ("dead code") in the module, that is, a path that cannot possibly be executed for any input data. Figure 13.10 shows two examples of infeasible paths. In Figure 13.10(a) the programmer has omitted a minus sign. If k is less than 2, then k cannot possibly be greater than 3, so the statement x = x * k cannot be reached. Similarly, in Figure 13.10(b), j is never less than 0, so the statement total = total + value[j] can never be reached; the programmer had intended the test to be j < 10, but made a typing error. A tester using statement coverage would soon realize that neither statement could be reached, and the faults would be found.

13.8.2 COMPLEXITY METRICS

The quality assurance viewpoint provides another approach to glass-box testing. Suppose that a manager is told that module m1 is more complex than module

```
if (k < 2)
{
  if (k > 3)            [should be: k > -3]
         ↑

     x = x * k;
}
```

(a)

```
for (j = 0; j < 0; j++)   [should be: j < 10]
                ↑

  total = total + value[j];
```

(b)

Figure 13.10 Two examples of infeasible paths.

m2. Irrespective of the precise way in which the term *complex* is defined, the manager will intuitively believe that m1 is likely to have more faults than m2. Following this idea, computer scientists have developed a number of metrics of software complexity as an aid in determining which modules are most likely to have faults. If the complexity of a module is found to be unreasonably high, a manager may direct that the module be redesigned and reimplemented on the grounds that it will probably be less costly and faster to start from scratch than to attempt to debug a fault-prone module.

A simple metric for predicting numbers of faults is lines of code. The underlying assumption is that there is a constant probability p that a line of code contains a fault. Thus, if a tester believes that, on average, a line of code has a 2 percent chance of containing a fault, and the module under test is 100 lines long, then this implies that the module is expected to contain two faults, and a module that is twice as long is likely to have four faults. Basili and Hutchens as well as Takahashi and Kamayachi showed that the number of faults is indeed related to the size of the product as a whole [Basili and Hutchens, 1983; Takahashi and Kamayachi, 1985].

Attempts have been made to find more sophisticated predictors of faults based on measures of product complexity. A typical contender is McCabe's measure of cyclomatic complexity, namely, the number of binary decisions (predicates) plus 1 [McCabe, 1976]. As described in Section 12.12, the cyclomatic complexity is essentially the number of branches in the module. Accordingly, cyclomatic complexity can be used as a metric for the number of test cases needed for branch coverage of a module. This is the basis for so-called structured testing [McCabe, 1983].

McCabe's metric can be computed almost as easily as lines of code. In some cases it has been shown to be a good metric for predicting faults; the higher the value of M, the greater the chance that a module contains a fault. For example, Walsh analyzed 276 modules in the Aegis system, a shipboard combat system [Walsh, 1979]. Walsh measured the cyclomatic complexity M and found that 23 percent of the modules with M greater than or equal to 10 had 53 percent of the faults detected. In addition, the modules with M greater than or equal to 10 had 21 percent more faults per line of code than the modules with smaller M values. However, the validity of McCabe's metric has been seriously questioned both on theoretical grounds and on the basis of the many different experiments cited in [Shepperd, 1988b] and [Shepperd and Ince, 1994].

Halstead's software science metrics [Halstead, 1977] have also been used for fault prediction. Two of the four basic elements of software science are n_1, the number of distinct operators in the module and n_2, the number of distinct operands. Typical operators include $+$, $*$, **if**, **goto**; operands are user-defined variables or constants. The other two basic elements are N_1, the total number of operators and N_2, the total number of operands. The code fragment of Figure 13.10(a) is reproduced in Figure 13.11. From the latter figure it can be seen that the code fragment has 10 distinct operators and 4 distinct operands. The total number of operators and operands are 13 and 7, respectively. These four basic elements then serve as input for fault prediction metrics [Ottenstein, 1979].

```
if (k < 2)
{
  if (k > 3)
    x = x * k;
}
```

Distinct operators:
if (<) { > = * ; }

Distinct operands:
k 2 3 x

Number of distinct operators $n_1 = 10$
Number of distinct operands $n_2 = 4$
Total number of operators $N_1 = 13$
Total number of operands $N_2 = 7$

Figure 13.11 Software science metrics applied to code fragment of Figure 13.10(a).

Musa, Iannino, and Okumoto have analyzed the data available on fault densities [Musa, Iannino, and Okumoto, 1987]. They concluded that most complexity metrics, including Halstead's and McCabe's, show a high correlation with the number of lines of code, or more precisely, the number of deliverable, executable source instructions. In other words, when researchers measure what they believe to be the complexity of a module or product, the result they obtain may largely be a reflection of the number of lines of code, a measure that correlates strongly with the number of faults. In addition, complexity metrics provide little improvement over lines of code for predicting fault rates. These conclusions are supported by Basili and Hutchens and also by Gremillion and by Shepperd [Basili and Hutchens, 1983; Gremillion, 1984; Shepperd, 1988b]. Other problems with complexity are discussed in [Shepperd, 1988a; Weyuker, 1988b; Shepperd and Ince, 1994]. Furthermore, there are problems when applying Halstead's metrics to modern languages such as Java or C++; for example, is a constructor an operator or an operand?

Using lines of code to predict fault rates seems to contradict the many arguments and experimental results negating the validity of that metric [van der Poel and Schach, 1983; Jones, 1986a] as described in Section 8.2.1. In fact, there is no contradiction. The work of Jones and others is within the context of software productivity, and in that area there is no question that lines of code is a poor metric. The results of Basili and others referenced in the previous paragraph relate specifically to fault rates and have nothing to do with productivity. Thus, when performing module testing, the larger modules should indeed be given special attention, whether from the viewpoint of test cases or walkthroughs and inspections.

13.9 CODE WALKTHROUGHS AND INSPECTIONS

In Section 5.2 a strong case was made for the use of walkthroughs and inspections. The same arguments hold equally well for code walkthroughs and code inspections. In brief, the fault-detecting power of these two nonexecution-based techniques leads to rapid, thorough, and early fault detection. The additional time required for code walkthroughs or code inspections is more than repaid by increased productivity due to the presence of fewer faults at the integration phase. Furthermore, code inspections have led to a reduction of up to 95% in corrective maintenance costs [Crossman, 1982].

Another reason why code inspections should be performed is that the alternative, execution-based testing (test cases), can be extremely expensive in two ways. First, it is time consuming. Second, inspections lead to detection and correction of faults earlier in the life cycle than with execution-based testing. As reflected in Figure 1.5, the earlier a fault is detected and corrected, the less it costs. An extreme case of the high cost of running test cases is that 80% of the budget for the software of the NASA Apollo Program was consumed by testing [Dunn, 1984].

Further arguments in favor of walkthroughs and inspections are given in the next section.

13.10 COMPARISON OF MODULE-TESTING TECHNIQUES

A number of studies have compared strategies for module testing. Myers compared black-box testing, a combination of black-box and glass-box testing, and three-person code walkthroughs [Myers, 1978a]. The experiment was performed using 59 highly experienced programmers testing the same product. All three techniques were equally effective in finding faults, but code walkthroughs proved to be less cost-effective than the other two techniques. Hwang compared black-box testing, glass-box testing, and code reading by one person [Hwang, 1981]. All three techniques were found to be equally effective, with each technique having its own strengths and weaknesses.

A major experiment was conducted by Basili and Selby [Basili and Selby, 1987]. The techniques compared were the same as in Hwang's experiment, namely, black-box testing, glass-box testing, and one-person code reading. The subjects were 32 professional programmers and 42 advanced students. Each tested three products, using each testing technique once. Fractional factorial design [Basili and Weiss, 1984] was used to compensate for the fact that the products were tested in different ways by different participants; no participant tested the same product in more than one way. Different results were obtained from the two groups of participants. The professional programmers detected more faults with code reading than the other two techniques, and the fault detection rate was faster. Two groups of advanced students participated. In one group there was no significant difference among the three techniques; in the other, code reading and black-box testing were equally good, and both outperformed glass-box testing. However, the rate at which students detected faults was the same for all techniques. Overall, code reading led to the detection of more interface faults than did the other two techniques, whereas black-box testing was most successful at finding control faults. The main conclusion that can be drawn from this experiment is that code inspection is at least as successful at detecting faults as glass-box and black-box testing.

A development technique that makes good use of this conclusion is the Cleanroom software development technique.

13.11 CLEANROOM

The Cleanroom technique [Cobb and Mills, 1990; Dyer, 1992; Linger, 1994] is a combination of a number of different software development techniques, including an incremental life-cycle model (Section 3.4), formal techniques for specification and design, and nonexecution-based module-testing techniques such as code reading [Mills, Dyer, and Linger, 1987; Selby, Basili, and Baker, 1987] and code walkthroughs and inspections (Section 13.9). A critical aspect of Cleanroom is that a module is not compiled until it has passed an inspection. That is, a module should be compiled only after nonexecution-based testing has been successfully accomplished.

The technique has had a number of great successes. For example, a prototype automated documentation system was developed for the U. S. Naval Underwater Systems Center using Cleanroom [Trammel, Binder, and Snyder, 1992]. Altogether 18 faults were detected while the design underwent "functional verification," a review process in which correctness-proving techniques are employed (Section 5.5). Informal proofs such as the one presented in Section 5.5.1 were used as much as possible; full mathematical proofs were developed only when participants were unsure of the correctness of the portion of the design being inspected. Another 19 faults were detected during walkthroughs of the 1820 lines of FoxBASE code; when the code was then compiled, there were no compilation errors. Furthermore, there were no failures at execution time. This is an additional indication of the power of nonexecution-based testing techniques.

These are certainly impressive results. However, as has been pointed out, results that apply to small-scale software products cannot necessarily be scaled up to large-scale software. In the case of Cleanroom, however, results for larger products are also impressive. The relevant metric is the *testing fault rate*, that is, the total number of faults detected per KLOC (thousand lines of code). This is a relatively common metric in the software industry. However, there is a critical difference in the way this metric is computed when Cleanroom is used as opposed to traditional development techniques.

As pointed out in Section 5.6, when traditional development techniques are used, a module is tested informally by its programmer while it is being developed and thereafter it is tested methodically by the SQA group. Faults detected by the programmer while developing the code are not recorded. However, from the time the module leaves the private workspace of the programmer and is handed over to the SQA group for execution-based and nonexecution-based testing, a tally is kept of the number of faults detected. In contrast, when Cleanroom is used, "testing faults" are counted from the time of compilation. Fault counting then continues through execution-based testing. In other words, when traditional development techniques are used, faults detected informally by the programmer do not count towards the testing fault rate. When Cleanroom is used, faults detected during the inspections and other nonexecution-based testing procedures that precede compilation are certainly recorded, but they do not count towards the testing fault rate.

A report on 17 Cleanroom products appears in [Linger, 1994]. For example, Cleanroom was used to develop the 350,000-line Ericsson Telecom OS32 operating system. The product was developed in 18 months by a team of 70. The testing fault rate was only 1.0 faults per KLOC. Another product was the prototype automated documentation system described above; the testing fault rate was 0.0 faults per KLOC for the 1820-line program. The 17 products together total nearly 1 million lines of code. The weighted average testing fault rate was 2.3 faults per KLOC, which Linger describes as a remarkable quality achievement. That praise is certainly not an exaggeration.

13.12 POTENTIAL PROBLEMS WHEN TESTING OBJECTS

One of the many reasons put forward for using the object-oriented paradigm is that it reduces the need for testing. Reuse via inheritance is a major strength of the paradigm; once a class has been tested, the argument goes, there is no need to retest it. Furthermore, new methods defined within a subclass of such a tested class have to be tested, but inherited methods need no further testing.

In fact, both these claims are only partially true. In addition, the testing of objects poses certain problems that are specific to object orientation. These issues are discussed in detail in this section.

To begin, it is necessary to clarify an issue regarding the testing of classes and of objects. As explained in Section 6.7, a class is an abstract data type that supports inheritance, and an object is an instance of a class. That is, a class has no concrete realization, whereas an object is a physical piece of code executing within a specific environment. Thus it is impossible to perform execution-based testing on a class; only nonexecution-based testing, such as an inspection, can be done.

Information hiding and the fact that many methods consist of relatively few lines of code can have a significant impact on testing. First consider a product developed using the structured paradigm. Nowadays, such a product generally consists of modules of roughly 50 executable instructions. The interface between a module and the rest of the product is the argument list. There are arguments of two kinds, namely, input arguments that are supplied to the module when it is invoked and output arguments that are returned by the module when it returns control to the calling module. Testing a module consists of supplying values to the input arguments and invoking the module and then comparing the values of the output arguments to the predicted results of the test.

In contrast, a "typical" object will contain perhaps 30 methods, many of which are relatively small, frequently just two or three executable statements [Wilde, Matthews and Huitt, 1993]. These methods do not return a value to the caller, but rather they change the state of the object. That is, these methods modify attributes (state variables) of the object. The difficulty here is that, in order to test that the change of state has in fact been correctly performed, it is necessary to send additional messages to the object. For example, consider the bank account object described in Section 1.6. The effect of method deposit is to increase the value of state variable account balance. However, as a consequence of information hiding, the only way to test whether a particular deposit action has been correctly executed is to invoke method determine balance both before and after invoking method deposit and see how the bank balance changes.

The situation is worse if the object does not include methods that can be invoked to determine the values of all the state variables. One alternative is to include additional methods for this purpose and then use conditional compilation to ensure that they are not available other than for testing purposes (in C++, this is achieved using #ifdef). The test plan (Section 8.6) should stipulate that the value of every state variable should be accessible during testing. In order to satisfy this requirement, additional methods that return the values of the state variables may have to be added to the relevant classes during the design phase. As a result, it will be possible to test the effect of invoking a specific method of an object by querying the value of the applicable state variable.

Surprisingly enough, an inherited method may still have to be tested. That is, even if a method has been adequately tested, the same method may still require thorough testing when inherited, unchanged, by a subclass. To see this latter point, consider the class hierarchy shown in Figure 13.12. Two methods are defined in base class **RootedTree**, namely, displayNodeContents and printRoutine, where method displayNodeContents uses method printRoutine.

Next consider subclass **BinaryTree**. This subclass inherits method printRoutine from its base class **RootedTree**. In addition, a new method displayNodeContents is defined that overrides the method defined in **RootedTree**. This new method still uses printRoutine. In Java notation, **BinaryTree**.displayNodeContents uses **RootedTree**.printRoutine.

Now consider subclass **BalancedBinaryTree**. This subclass inherits method displayNodeContents from its superclass **BinaryTree**. However, a new method printRoutine is defined that overrides the one defined in **RootedTree**. When displayNodeContents uses printRoutine within the context of **BalancedBinaryTree**, the scope rules of Java specify that the local version of printRoutine is to be used. Again in Java notation, when method **Binary-**

```
class RootedTree
{
   ...
   void displayNodeContents (Node a);
   void printRoutine (Node b);
//
// method displayNodeContents uses method printRoutine
//
   ...
}

class BinaryTree extends RootedTree
{
   ...
   void displayNodeContents (Node a);
//
// method displayNodeContents defined in this class uses
// method printRoutine inherited from class RootedTree
//
   ...
}

class BalancedBinaryTree extends BinaryTree
{
   ...
   void printRoutine (Node b);
//
// method displayNodeContents (inherited from BinaryTree) uses this
// local version of printRoutine within class BalancedBinaryTree
//
   ...
}
```

Figure 13.12 Tree hierarchy.

Tree.displayNodeContents is invoked within the lexical scope of **BalancedBinaryTree**, it uses method **BalancedBinaryTree**.printRoutine.

Thus, the actual code (method printRoutine) that is executed when displayNodeContents is invoked within instantiations of **BinaryTree**, is different from what is executed when displayNodeContents is invoked within instantiations of **BalancedBinaryTree**. This holds notwithstanding the fact that method displayNodeContents itself is inherited, unchanged, by **BalancedBinaryTree** from **BinaryTree**. Thus, even if method displayNodeContents has been thoroughly tested within a **BinaryTree** object, the method has to be retested from scratch when reused within a **BalancedBinaryTree** environment. To make matters even more complex, there are theoretical reasons why it needs to be retested with different test cases [Perry and Kaiser, 1990].

It must immediately be pointed out that these complications are not a reason to abandon the object-oriented paradigm. First, they arise only through the interaction of methods (displayNodeContents and printRoutine in the example). Second, it is possible to determine when this retesting is needed [Harrold, McGregor, and Fitzpatrick, 1992]. Thus, suppose an instantiation of a class has been thoroughly tested. Any new or redefined methods of a subclass then need to be tested, together with methods that are flagged for retesting because of their interaction with other methods. In short, then, the claim that use of the object-oriented paradigm reduces the need for testing is largely true.

Some management implications of module testing are now considered.

13.13 MANAGEMENT ASPECTS OF MODULE TESTING

An important decision that must be made during the development of every module is how much time, and therefore money, to spend on testing that module. As with so many other economic issues in software engineering, cost–benefit analysis (Section 4.7) can play a useful role. For example, the decision as to whether or not the cost of correctness proving exceeds the benefit of the assurance that a specific product satisfies its specifications can be decided on the basis of cost–benefit analysis. Cost–benefit analysis can also be used to compare the cost of running additional test cases against the cost of failure of the delivered product caused by inadequate testing.

There is another approach for determining whether testing of a specific module should continue or whether it is likely that virtually all the faults have been removed. The techniques of reliability analysis can be used to provide statistical estimates of how many faults are still remaining. A variety of different techniques have been proposed for determining statistical estimates of the number of remaining faults. The basic idea underlying these techniques is the following. Suppose that a module is tested for 1 week. On Monday 23 faults are found, and 7 more on Tuesday. On Wednesday 5 more faults are found, 2 on Thursday, and 0 on Friday. Because the rate of fault detection is steadily decreasing from 23 faults per day to none, it seems likely that most faults have been found, and testing of that module could well be halted. Determining the probability that there are no more faults in the code requires a level of mathematical statistics beyond that required for readers of this book. Details are therefore not given here; the reader who is interested in reliability analysis should consult [Shooman, 1983] or [Grady, 1992]. An example of how statistical-based testing can be used is given in Section 14.17.

13.14 WHEN TO REWRITE RATHER THAN DEBUG A MODULE

When a member of the SQA group detects a failure (erroneous output), the module must, as stated previously, be returned to the original programmer for debugging,

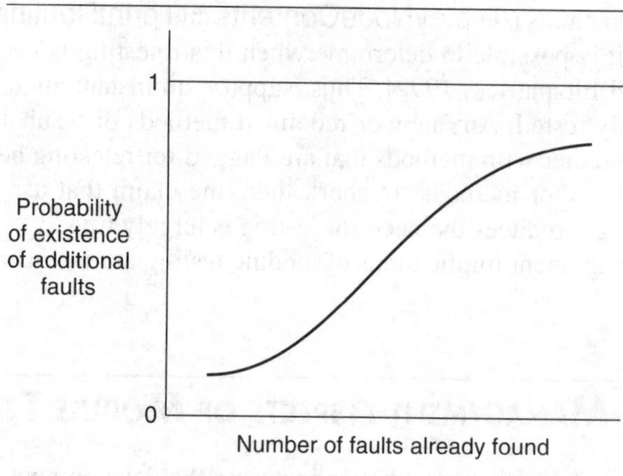

Figure 13.13 Graph showing that probability that there are faults still to be found is proportional to number of faults already detected.

that is, detection of the fault and correction of the code. There will be occasions when it is preferable for the module to be thrown away and redesigned and recoded from scratch, either by the original programmer or by another, possibly more senior, member of the development team. To see why this may be necessary, consider Figure 13.13. The graph shows the apparently nonsensical fact that the probability of the existence of more faults in a module is proportional to the number of faults already found in that module [Myers, 1979]. To see why this should be so, consider two modules, m1 and m2. Suppose that both modules are approximately the same length, and that both have been tested for the same number of hours. Suppose further that only two faults were detected in m1, but that 48 faults were detected in m2. It is likely that more faults remain to be rooted out of m2 than out of m1. Furthermore, additional testing and debugging of m2 is likely to be a lengthy process, and there will always be the suspicion that m2 is still not perfect. In both the short run and the long run, it is preferable to discard m2, redesign it, and then recode it.

The distribution of faults in modules is certainly not uniform. Myers cites the example of faults found by users in OS/370 [Myers, 1979]. It was found that 47 percent of the faults were associated with only 4 percent of the modules. An earlier study by Endres regarding internal tests of DOS/VS (Release 28) at IBM Laboratories, Böblingen, Germany, showed similar nonuniformity [Endres, 1975]. Of the total of 512 faults detected in 202 modules, only 1 fault was detected in each of 112 of the modules. On the other hand, there were modules with 14, 15, 19, and 28 faults, respectively. Endres points out that the latter three modules were three of the largest modules in the product, each comprising over 3000 lines of DOS macro assembler language. But the module with 14 faults was a relatively small module that was previously known to be very unstable. This type of module is a prime candidate for being discarded and recoded.

Just in Case You Wanted to Know

The discussion regarding the maximum permitted number of faults detected during development of a module means precisely that: the maximum number permitted *during development*. The maximum permitted number of faults detected after the product has been delivered to the client should be *zero* for all modules of all products. That is, it should be the aim of every software engineer to deliver fault-free code to the client.

The way for management to cope with this sort of situation is to predetermine the maximum number of faults that will be permitted during development of a given module; when that maximum is reached the module must be thrown away, then redesigned and recoded, preferably by an experienced software professional. This maximum will vary from application area to application area and from module to module. After all, the maximum permitted number of faults detected in a module that reads in a record from a database and checks the validity of the part number should be far smaller than the number of faults in a complex module from a tank weapons control system that must coordinate data from a variety of sensors and direct the aim of the main gun toward the intended target. One way to decide on the maximum fault figure for a specific module is to examine fault data on similar modules that have required corrective maintenance. But whatever estimation technique is used, management must ensure that the module is scrapped if that figure is exceeded (but see the Just in Case You Wanted to Know box above).

13.15 CASE Tools for the Implementation Phase

CASE tools for the implementation phase were discussed in some detail in Section 4.11. For reasons of space, that material is not repeated here.

13.16 Osbert Oglesby Case Study: Black-Box Test Cases

Figure 13.14 contains sample black-box test cases for the Osbert Oglesby case study; the complete set appears in Appendix H. The test cases are of two types, namely, those based on equivalence classes and boundary value analysis and those based on functional testing.

Turning initially to equivalence classes and boundary value analysis, the first set of cases is to test whether the product will detect an error if the first name

Equivalence Classes and Boundary Value Analysis:

Painting data:

Equivalence classes for first name and last name

1. First character not alphabetic	Error
2. < 1 character	Error
3. 1 character	Acceptable
4. Between 1 and 21 characters	Acceptable
5. 21 characters	Acceptable
6. > 21 characters	Acceptable (truncated to 21 characters)

Equivalence classes for title

1. < 1 character	Error
2. 1 character	Acceptable
3. Between 1 and 41 characters	Acceptable
4. 41 characters	Acceptable
5. > 41 characters	Acceptable (truncated to 41 characters)

Functional Analysis:

The functions outlined in the specifications document are used to create test cases.

1. Buy a masterpiece where the artist cannot be found in the auction records.
2. Buy a masterpiece where the artist can be found in the auction records.
3. Buy a masterwork where the artist cannot be found in the auction records.
4. Buy a masterwork where the artist can be found in the auction records.
5. Update the fashionability coefficients of several artists.
6. Buy an "other" type of painting where the artist cannot be found in the fashion records.
7. Buy an "other" type of painting where the artist can be found in the fashion records.
8. Buy a painting where the purchase price is less than the price suggested by the algorithm.
9. Buy a painting where the purchase price is equal to the price suggested by the algorithm.
10. Buy a painting where the purchase price is greater than the price suggested by the algorithm.
11. Sell a painting where the selling price is less than the target price.
12. Sell a painting where the selling price is equal to the target price.
13. Sell a painting where the selling price is greater than the target price.
14. For one or more artists, sell at least two paintings where every painting is sold over the target price (to be used in test case 17).
15. Display report of bought paintings.
16. Display report of sold paintings.
17. Display report of fashionability trends.

In addition to these direct tests, it is necessary to perform the following further tests:

18. Attempt to buy a painting that is already in the gallery.
19. Attempt to sell a painting that does not exist in the gallery.
20. Attempt to sell a painting that has already been sold.

Figure 13.14 Sample black-box test cases for Osbert Oglesby product.

of an artist does not begin with an alphabetic character. This generates two test cases, corresponding to an initial nonalphabetic character (should be flagged as an input error), or a name with an alphabetic initial character (acceptable). The next set of five test cases checks that a first name of an artist consists of between 1 and 21 characters, and that a name longer than 21 characters is truncated to 21 characters. The same set of test cases are set up for the last name of an artist.

Similar test cases check other statements in the specifications; the full set appears in Appendix H.

Turning now to functional testing, 17 functions are listed in the specification document, as reflected in Figure 13.14. An additional 3 test cases correspond to misuses of these functions.

It is important to be aware that these test cases could have been developed as soon as the specifications were complete; the only reason that they appear here is that test case selection is a topic of this chapter, rather than an earlier chapter. A major component of every test plan should be a stipulation that black-box test cases be drawn up as soon as possible (Section 8.6). If a contract has been signed for the project as a whole, then this will be as soon as the specification document has been approved. Otherwise, the contract for completing the product is signed once the client has agreed to the duration and cost estimates, that is, at the end of the specifications phase. The black-box test cases can then be drawn up, for use by the SQA group during the implementation and integration phase.

CHAPTER REVIEW

In this chapter various issues relating to the implementation of a product by a team are presented. These include choice of programming language (Section 13.1). The issue of fourth-generation languages is discussed in some detail in Section 13.2. Good programming practice is described in Section 13.3, and the need for practical coding standards is presented in Section 13.4. Then, comments are made regarding reuse of modules (Section 13.5). Test cases must be selected systematically (Section 13.6). Various black-box, glass-box, and nonexecution-based testing techniques are described (Sections 13.7, 13.8, and 13.9, respectively) and then compared (Section 13.10). The Cleanroom technique is described in Section 13.11. The testing of objects is presented in Section 13.12. This is followed by a discussion of the managerial implications of module testing (Section 13.13). Then there is a discussion of when to rewrite rather than debug a module (Section 13.14). CASE tools for the implementation phase are mentioned next (Section 13.15). Finally (Section 13.16), black-box test cases for the Osbert Oglesby Case Study are presented.

FOR FURTHER READING

A wide-ranging source of information on 4GLs is [Martin, 1985]. Two opposing views on 4GLs can be found in [Cobb, 1985] and [Grant, 1985]. Contrasting productivity results with specific 4GLs are reported in [Misra and Jalics, 1988] and [Verner and Tate, 1988]. The attitudes of 43 organizations to 4GLs are reported in

[Guimaraes, 1985]. [Klepper and Bock, 1995] describes how McDonnell Douglas obtained higher productivity with 4GLs than with 3GLs.

Excellent books on good programming practice include [Kernighan and Plauger, 1974], [Ledgard, 1975], [Bentley, 1986], and [McConnell, 1993].

Probably the most important early work on execution-based testing is [Myers, 1979]. A comprehensive source of information on testing in general is [Beizer, 1990]. Issues in test case selection are discussed in [Petschenik, 1985]. Functional testing is described in [Howden, 1987]; structural techniques are compared in [Clarke, Podgurski, Richardson, and Zeil, 1989]. Black-box testing is described in detail in [Beizer, 1995]. The relationship between the various coverage measures of structural testing and software quality is discussed in [Horgan, London, and Lyu, 1994]. A formal approach to glass-box testing is described in [Stocks and Carrington, 1996].

Cleanroom is described in [Cobb and Mills, 1990], [Dyer, 1992], and [Linger, 1994]. The use of Cleanroom during the maintenance phase is presented in [Sherer, Kouchakdjian, and Arnold, 1996].

Statistical techniques are described in [Shooman, 1983] and also in [Goel, 1985]. A good introduction to software reliability is [Musa and Everett, 1990]. In addition, the proceedings of the annual International Symposium on Software Reliability Engineering contain a wide variety of articles on software reliability. Reliability is also discussed in articles in the May 1995 issue of *IEEE Software* and the November 1996 issue of *IEEE Computer*.

The proceedings of the International Symposia on Software Testing and Analysis cover a particularly broad range of testing issues.

A survey of different approaches to the testing of objects can be found in [Turner, 1994]. Two important papers on the subject are [Perry and Kaiser, 1990] and [Harrold, McGregor, and Fitzpatrick, 1992]. [Beizer, 1995], mentioned above, also covers black-box testing of object-oriented software. The September 1994 issue of the *Communications of the ACM* contains a number of articles on the testing of object-oriented software.

With regard to metrics for the implementation phase, articles questioning the validity of software science include [Coulter, 1983], [Conte, Dunsmore, and Shen, 1986], [Musa, Iannino, and Okumoto, 1987], [Shepperd, 1988b], [Weyuker, 1988b], and [Shepperd and Ince, 1994]. McCabe's cyclomatic complexity was first presented in [McCabe, 1976]. Extensions of the metric to the design phase appear in [McCabe and Butler, 1989]. Criticisms of cyclomatic complexity can be found in [Shepperd, 1988a], [Weyuker, 1988b], and [Shepperd and Ince, 1994]. Metrics for managing code inspections are described in [Barnard and Price, 1994].

PROBLEMS

13.1 Your instructor has asked you to implement the Osbert Oglesby product (Appendix A). Which language would you choose for implementing the product, and why? Of the various languages available to you, list their benefits and their costs. Do not attempt to attach dollar values to your answers.

13.2 Repeat Problem 13.1 for the elevator problem (Section 10.6).

13.3 Repeat Problem 13.1 for the automated library circulation system (Problem 7.7).

13.4 Repeat Problem 13.1 for the product that determines whether a bank statement is correct (Problem 7.8).

13.5 Repeat Problem 13.1 for the automated teller machine (Problem 7.9).

13.6 Add prologue comments to a module that you have recently written.

13.7 How do coding standards for a one-person software production company differ from those in organizations with 300 software professionals?

13.8 How do coding standards for a software company that develops and maintains software for intensive-care units differ from those in an organization that develops and maintains accounting products?

13.9 Set up black-box test cases for Naur's text-processing problem (Section 5.5.2). For each test case, state what is being tested and the expected outcome of that test case.

13.10 Using your product for Problem 5.15 (or code distributed by your instructor), set up statement coverage test cases. For each test case, state what is being tested and the expected outcome of that test case.

13.11 Repeat Problem 13.10 for branch coverage.

13.12 Repeat Problem 13.10 for all-definition-use-path coverage.

13.13 Repeat Problem 13.10 for path coverage.

13.14 Repeat Problem 13.10 for linear code sequences.

13.15 Draw a flowchart of your product for Problem 5.15 (or code distributed by your instructor). Determine its cyclomatic complexity. If you are unable to determine the number of branches, consider the flowchart as a directed graph. Determine the number of edges e, nodes n, and connected components c. (Each method constitutes a connected component.) The cyclomatic complexity V is then given by [McCabe, 1976]

$$V = e - n + 2c$$

13.16 Determine Halstead's four basic metrics for the code fragment of Figure 13.10(b).

13.17 You are the owner and sole employee of One-Person Software Company. You have bought the programming toolkit described in Section 4.11. List its five capabilities in order of importance to you, giving reasons.

13.18 You are now the vice-president for software technology of Very Big Software Company; there are 17,500 employees in your organization. How do you rank the capabilities of the programming toolkit described in Section 4.11? Explain any differences between your answer to this problem and the previous one.

13.19 As SQA manager for a software development organization, you are responsible for determining the maximum number of faults that may be found in a given module during testing. If this maximum is exceeded, then the module must be redesigned and recoded. What criteria would you use to determine the maximum for a given module?

13.20 (Term Project) Draw up black-box test cases for the product you specified in Problem 10.15 or 11.10. For each test case, state what is being tested and the expected outcome of that test case.

13.21 (Case Study) Obtain a copy of the Java implementation of the Osbert Oglesby Case Study described in Section 14.13. Draw up statement coverage test cases for the product. For each test case, state what is being tested and the expected outcome of that test case.

13.22 (Case Study) Repeat Problem 13.21 for branch coverage.

13.23 (Case Study) Repeat Problem 13.21 for all-definition-use-path coverage.

13.24 (Case Study) Repeat Problem 13.21 for path coverage.

13.25 (Case Study) Repeat Problem 13.21 for linear code sequences.

13.26 (Readings in Software Engineering) Your instructor will distribute copies of [Sherer, Kouchakdjian, and Arnold, 1996]. Do you believe that Cleanroom is applicable to the maintenance phase?

REFERENCES

[Apple, 1984] *Macintosh Pascal User's Guide,* Apple Computer, Inc., Cupertino, CA, 1984.

[Aron, 1983] J. D. ARON, *The Program Development Process. Part II. The Programming Team*, Addison-Wesley, Reading, MA, 1983.

[Baker, 1972] F. T. BAKER, "Chief Programmer Team Management of Production Programming," *IBM Systems Journal* **11** (No. 1, 1972), pp. 56–73.

[Barnard and Price, 1994] J. BARNARD AND A. PRICE, "Managing Code Inspection Information," *IEEE Software* **11** (March 1994), pp. 59–69.

[Basili and Hutchens, 1983] V. R. BASILI AND D. H. HUTCHENS, "An Empirical Study of a Syntactic Complexity Family," *IEEE Transactions on Software Engineering* **SE-9** (November 1983), pp. 664–72.

[Basili and Selby, 1987] V. R. BASILI AND R. W. SELBY, "Comparing the Effectiveness of Software Testing Strategies," *IEEE Transactions on Software Engineering* **SE-13** (December 1987), pp. 1278–96.

[Basili and Weiss, 1984] V. R. BASILI AND D. M. WEISS, "A Methodology for Collecting Valid Software Engineering Data," *IEEE Transactions on Software Engineering* **SE-10** (November 1984), pp. 728–38.

[Beizer, 1990] B. BEIZER, *Software Testing Techniques*, Second Edition, Van Nostrand Reinhold, New York, 1990.

[Beizer, 1995] B. BEIZER, *Black-Box Testing: Techniques for Functional Testing of Software and Systems*, John Wiley and Sons, New York, 1995.

[Bentley, 1986] J. BENTLEY, *Programming Pearls*, Addison-Wesley, Reading, MA, 1986.

[Brooks, 1975] F. P. BROOKS, JR., *The Mythical Man-Month: Essays in Software Engineering*, Addison-Wesley, Reading, MA, 1975. Twentieth Anniversary Edition, Addison-Wesley, Reading, MA, 1995.

[Clarke, Podgurski, Richardson, and Zeil, 1989] L. A. CLARKE, A. PODGURSKI, D. J. RICHARDSON, AND S. J. ZEIL, "A Formal Evaluation of Data Flow Path Selection Criteria," *IEEE Transactions on Software Engineering* **15** (November 1989), pp. 1318–32.

[Cobb, 1985] R. H. COBB, "In Praise of 4GLs," *Datamation* **31** (July 15, 1985), pp. 90–96.

[Cobb and Mills, 1990] R. H. COBB AND H. D. MILLS, "Engineering Software under Statistical Quality Control," *IEEE Software* **7** (November 1990), pp. 44–54.

[Conte, Dunsmore, and Shen, 1986] S. D. CONTE, H. E. DUNSMORE, AND V. Y. SHEN, *Software Engineering Metrics and Models*, Benjamin/Cummings, Menlo Park, CA, 1986.

[Coulter, 1983] N. S. COULTER, "Software Science and Cognitive Psychology," *IEEE Transactions on Software Engineering* **SE-9** (March 1983), pp. 166–71.

[Crossman, 1982] T. D. CROSSMAN, "Inspection Teams, Are They Worth It?" *Proceedings of the Second National Symposium on EDP Quality Assurance,* Chicago, November 1982.

[Date, 1994] C. J. DATE, *An Introduction to Database Systems,* Sixth Edition, Addison-Wesley, Reading, MA, 1994.

[Dunn, 1984] R. H. DUNN, *Software Defect Removal,* McGraw-Hill, New York, 1984.

[Dyer, 1992] M. DYER, *The Cleanroom Approach to Quality Software Development,* John Wiley and Sons, New York, 1992.

[Endres, 1975] A. ENDRES, "An Analysis of Errors and their Causes in System Programs," *IEEE Transactions on Software Engineering* **SE-1** (June 1975), pp. 140–49.

[Garcia-Molina, Germano, and Kohler, 1984] H. GARCIA-MOLINA, F. GERMANO, JR, AND W. H. KOHLER, "Debugging a Distributed Computer System," *IEEE Transactions on Software Engineering* **SE-10** (March 1984), pp. 210–19.

[Goel, 1985] A. L. GOEL, "Software Reliability Models: Assumptions, Limitations, and Applicability," *IEEE Transactions on Software Engineering* **SE-11** (December 1985), pp. 1411–23.

[Grady, 1992] R. B. GRADY, *Practical Software Metrics for Project Management and Process Improvement,* Prentice Hall, Englewood Cliffs, NJ, 1992.

[Grant, 1985] F. J. GRANT, "The Downside of 4GLs," *Datamation* **31** (July 15, 1985), pp. 99–104.

[Gremillion, 1984] L. L. GREMILLION, "Determinants of Program Repair Maintenance Requirements," *Communications of the ACM* **27** (August 1984), pp. 826–32.

[Guimaraes, 1985] T. GUIMARAES, "A Study of Application Program Development Techniques," *Communications of the ACM* **28** (May 1985), pp. 494–99.

[Halstead, 1977] M. H. HALSTEAD, *Elements of Software Science*, Elsevier North-Holland, New York, 1977.

[Harrold, McGregor, and Fitzpatrick, 1992] M. J. HARROLD, J. D. MCGREGOR, AND K. J. FITZPATRICK, "Incremental Testing of Object-Oriented Class Structures," *Proceedings of the 14th International Conference on Software Engineering,* Melbourne, Australia, May 1992, pp. 68–80.

[Horgan, London, and Lyu, 1994] J. R. HORGAN, S. LONDON, AND M. R. LYU, "Achieving Software Quality with Testing Coverage Measures," *IEEE Computer* **27** (1994), pp. 60–69.

[Howden, 1987] W. E. HOWDEN, *Functional Program Testing and Analysis*, McGraw-Hill, New York, 1987.

[Hwang, 1981] S.-S. V. HWANG, "An Empirical Study in Functional Testing, Structural Testing, and Code Reading Inspection," Scholarly Paper 362, Department of Computer Science, University of Maryland, College Park, MD, 1981.

[Jones, 1986a] C. JONES, *Programming Productivity*, McGraw-Hill, New York, 1986.

[Kernighan and Plauger, 1974] B. W. KERNIGHAN AND P. J. PLAUGER, *The Elements of Programming Style*, McGraw-Hill, New York, 1974.

[Klepper and Bock, 1995] R. KLEPPER AND D. BOCK, "Third and Fourth Generation Productivity Differences," *Communications of the ACM* **38** (September, 1995), pp. 69–79.

[Klunder, 1988] D. KLUNDER, "Hungarian Naming Conventions," Technical Report, Microsoft Corporation, Redmond, WA, January 1988.

[Ledgard, 1975] H. LEDGARD, *Programming Proverbs,* Hayden Books, Rochelle Park, NJ, 1975.

[Linger, 1994] R. C. LINGER, "Cleanroom Process Model," *IEEE Software* **11** (March 1994), pp. 50–58.

[Martin, 1985] J. MARTIN, *Fourth-Generation Languages, Volumes I, II, and III,* Prentice Hall, Englewood Cliffs, NJ, 1985.

[McCabe, 1976] T. J. MCCABE, "A Complexity Measure," *IEEE Transactions on Software Engineering* **SE-2** (December 1976), pp. 308–20.

[McCabe, 1983] T. J. MCCABE, *Structural Testing*, IEEE Computer Society Press, Los Angeles, 1983.

[McCabe and Butler, 1989] T. J. MCCABE AND C. W. BUTLER, "Design Complexity Measurement and Testing," *Communications of the ACM* **32** (December 1989), pp. 1415–25.

[McConnell, 1993] S. MCCONNELL, *Code Complete: A Practical Handbook of Software Construction,* Microsoft Press, Redmond, WA, 1993.

[Mills, Dyer, and Linger, 1987] H. D. MILLS, M. DYER, AND R. C. LINGER, "Cleanroom Software Engineering," *IEEE Software* **4** (September 1987), pp. 19–25.

[Misra and Jalics, 1988] S. K. MISRA AND P. J. JALICS, "Third-Generation versus Fourth-Generation Software Development," *IEEE Software* **5** (July 1988), pp. 8–14.

[Musa and Everett, 1990] J. D. MUSA AND W. W. EVERETT, "Software-Reliability Engineering: Technology for the 1990s," *IEEE Software* **7** (November 1990), pp. 36–43.

[Musa, Iannino, and Okumoto, 1987] J. D. MUSA, A. IANNINO, AND K. OKUMOTO, *Software Reliability: Measurement, Prediction, Application*, McGraw-Hill, New York, 1987.

[Myers, 1976] G. J. MYERS, *Software Reliability: Principles and Practices*, Wiley-Interscience, New York, 1976.

[Myers, 1978a] G. J. MYERS, "A Controlled Experiment in Program Testing and Code Walkthroughs/Inspections," *Communications of the ACM* **21** (September 1978), pp. 760–68.

[Myers, 1979] G. J. MYERS, *The Art of Software Testing*, John Wiley and Sons, New York, 1979.

[Ottenstein, 1979] L. M. OTTENSTEIN, "Quantitative Estimates of Debugging Requirements," *IEEE Transactions on Software Engineering* **SE-5** (September 1979), pp. 504–14.

[Perry and Kaiser, 1990] D. E. PERRY AND G. E. KAISER, "Adequate Testing and Object-Oriented Programming," *Journal of Object-Oriented Programming* **2** (January/February 1990), pp. 13–19.

[Petschenik, 1985] N. H. PETSCHENIK, "Practical Priorities in System Testing," *IEEE Software* **2** (September 1985), pp. 18–23.

[Rapps and Weyuker, 1985] S. RAPPS AND E. J. WEYUKER, "Selecting Software Test Data Using Data Flow Information," *IEEE Transactions on Software Engineering* **SE-11** (April 1985), pp. 367–75.

[Sammet, 1978] J. E. SAMMET, "The Early History of COBOL," *Proceedings of the History of Programming Languages Conference*, Los Angeles, 1978, pp. 199–276.

[Selby, Basili, and Baker, 1987] R. W. SELBY, V. R. BASILI, AND F. T. BAKER, "Cleanroom Software Development: An Empirical Evaluation," *IEEE Transactions on Software Engineering* **SE-13** (September 1987), pp. 1027–37.

[Shepperd, 1988a] M. J. SHEPPERD, "An Evaluation of Software Product Metrics," *Information and Software Technology* **30** (No. 3, 1988), pp. 177–88.

[Shepperd, 1988b] M. SHEPPERD, "A Critique of Cyclomatic Complexity as a Software Metric," *Software Engineering Journal* **3** (March 1988), pp. 30–36.

[Shepperd and Ince, 1994] M. SHEPPERD AND D. C. INCE, "A Critique of Three Metrics," *Journal of Systems and Software* **26** (September 1994), pp. 197–210.

[Sherer, Kouchakdjian, and Arnold, 1996] S. W. SHERER, A. KOUCHAKDJIAN, AND P. G. ARNOLD, "Experience Using Cleanroom Software Engineering," *IEEE Software* **13** (May 1996), pp. 69–76.

[Shooman, 1983] M. L. SHOOMAN, *Software Engineering: Design, Reliability, and Management*, McGraw-Hill, New York, 1983.

[Stocks and Carrington, 1996] P. STOCKS AND D. CARRINGTON, "A Framework for Specification-Based Testing," *IEEE Transactions on Software Engineering* **22** (November 1996), pp. 777–93.

[Takahashi and Kamayachi, 1985] M. TAKAHASHI AND Y. KAMAYACHI, "An Empirical Study of a Model for Program Error Prediction," *Proceedings of the Eighth International Conference on Software Engineering*, London, 1985, pp. 330–36.

[Trammel, Binder, and Snyder, 1992] C. J. TRAMMEL, L. H. BINDER, AND C. E. SNYDER, "The Automated Production Control Documentation System: A Case Study in Cleanroom Software Engineering," *ACM Transactions on Software Engineering and Methodology* **1** (January 1992), pp. 81–94.

[Turner, 1994] C. D. TURNER, "State-Based Testing: A New Method for the Testing of Object-Oriented Programs," Ph.D. Thesis, Computer Science Division, University of Durham, Durham, UK, November, 1994.

[van der Poel and Schach, 1983] K. G. VAN DER POEL AND S. R. SCHACH, "A Software Metric for Cost Estimation and Efficiency Measurement in Data Processing System Development," *Journal of Systems and Software* **3** (September 1983), pp. 187–91.

[Verner and Tate, 1988] J. VERNER AND G. TATE, "Estimating Size and Effort in Fourth-Generation Development," *IEEE Software* **5** (July 1988), pp. 15–22.

[Walsh, 1979] T. J. WALSH, "A Software Reliability Study Using a Complexity Measure," *Proceedings of the AFIPS National Computer Conference*, New York, 1979, pp. 761–68.

[Weinberg, 1971] G. M. WEINBERG, *The Psychology of Computer Programming*, Van Nostrand Reinhold, New York, 1971.

[Weyuker, 1988a] E. J. WEYUKER, "An Empirical Study of the Complexity of Data Flow Testing," *Proceedings of the Second Workshop on Software Testing, Verification, and Analysis*, Banff, Canada, July 1988, pp. 188–95.

[Weyuker, 1988b] E. WEYUKER, "Evaluating Software Complexity Measures," *IEEE Trans. on Software Engineering* **14** (September 1988), pp. 1357–65.

[Wilde, Matthews, and Huitt, 1993] N. WILDE, P. MATTHEWS, AND R. HUITT, "Maintaining Object-Oriented Software," *IEEE Software* **10** (January 1993), pp. 75–80.

[Woodward, Hedley, and Hennell, 1980] M. R. WOODWARD, D. HEDLEY, AND M. A. HENNELL, "Experience with Path Analysis and Testing of Programs," *IEEE Transactions on Software Engineering* **SE-6** (May 1980), pp. 278–86.

chapter

14

IMPLEMENTATION AND INTEGRATION PHASE

Up to now, implementation and integration have been treated as two separate and independent phases. In the approach that has been presented, each module (or object) is implemented by a member of the programming team and tested by SQA. Then, during the integration phase the modules are put together and tested as a whole. In fact, this is not a good way to develop software. Instead, the implementation and integration phases should be carried out in parallel. This parallel approach is the subject of this chapter.

In both the title and the body of this chapter we refer to the "implementation and integration phase." Strictly speaking, there is no such thing. Implementation and integration are two different activities, as distinct as design and planning. Nevertheless, from now on we use the term *implementation and integration phase* to describe the activities that are performed when the implementation phase and the integration phase are carried out in parallel.

The basic concepts of integration and of integration testing are now introduced, followed by a description of how object-oriented products are implemented and integrated.

14.1 IMPLEMENTATION AND INTEGRATION

Consider the product depicted in Figure 14.1. One approach in developing the product is to code and test each module separately, link all 13 modules together, and test the product as a whole. There are two difficulties with this approach. First, consider module a. It cannot be tested on its own, because it calls modules b, c, and d. Thus in order to test module a, modules b, c, and d must be coded as stubs. In its simplest form, a stub is an empty module. A more effective stub prints a message such as module displayRadarPattern called. Best of all, a stub should return values corresponding to preplanned test cases.

Now consider module h. To test it on its own requires a driver, a module that calls it one or more times, if possible checking the values returned by the module under test. Similarly, testing module d requires a driver and two stubs. Thus one

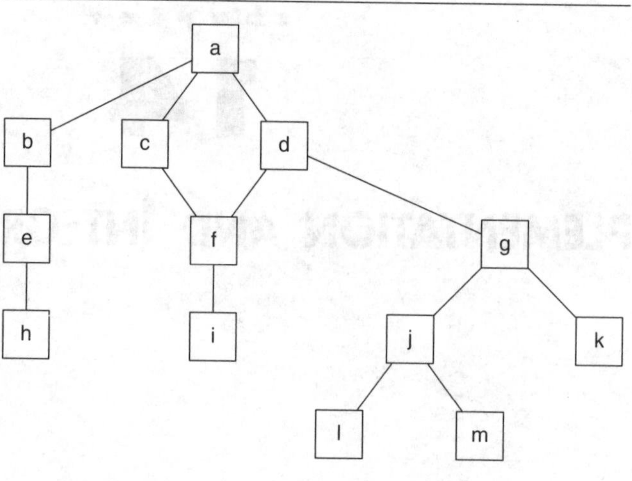

Figure 14.1 Typical module interconnection diagram.

problem that arises with separate implementation and integration is that effort has to be put into constructing stubs and drivers, all of which are thrown away after module testing is completed.

The second, and much more important, difficulty that arises when the implementation phase is completed before integration starts is lack of fault isolation. If the product as a whole is tested against a specific test case and the product fails, then the fault could lie in any of the 13 modules or 13 interfaces. In a large product with, say, 103 modules and 108 interfaces, there are no fewer than 211 places where the fault might lie.

The solution to both these difficulties is to combine module and integration testing.

14.1.1 Top-Down Implementation and Integration

In top-down implementation and integration, if module mAbove calls module mBelow, then mAbove is implemented and integrated before mBelow. Suppose that the product shown in Figure 14.1 is implemented and integrated top-down. One possible top-down ordering is a, b, c, d, e, f, g, h, i, j, k, l, and m. First, module a is coded and tested with b, c, and d implemented as stubs. Now stub b is expanded into module b, linked to module a, and tested with module e implemented as a stub. Implementation and integration proceeds in this way until all the modules have been integrated into the product. Another possible top-down ordering is a, b, e, h, c, d, f, i, g, j, k, l, and m. With this latter ordering, portions of the implementation and integration can proceed in parallel in the following way. After a has been coded and tested, one programmer can use module a to implement and integrate b, e, and h, while another programmer can use a to work in parallel on c, d, f, and i. Once d and f are completed, a third programmer can start work on g, j, k, l, and m.

Suppose that module a by itself executes correctly on a specific test case. However, when the same test data are submitted after b has been coded and integrated into the product, now consisting of modules a and b linked together, the test fails. The fault can be in one of two places, namely, in module b or the interface between modules a and b. In general, whenever a module mNew is added to what has been tested so far and a previously successful test case fails, the fault almost certainly will lie either in mNew or in the interface(s) between mNew and the rest of the product. Thus top-down implementation and integration supports fault isolation.

Another strength of top-down implementation and integration is that major design flaws show up early. The modules of a product can be divided in two groups, *logic modules* and *operational modules.* Logic modules essentially incorporate the decision-making flow of control aspects of the product. The logic modules are generally those situated close to the root in the module interconnection diagram. For example, in Figure 14.1 it is reasonable to expect modules a, b, c, d, and perhaps g and j to be logic modules. The operational modules, on the other hand, perform the actual operations of the product. For example, a operational module may be named getLineFromTerminal or measureTemperatureOfReactorCore. The operational modules are generally found in the lower levels, close to the leaves, of the module interconnection diagram. In Figure 14.1, modules e, f, h, i, k, l, and m turn out to be operational modules.

It is always important to code and test the logic modules before coding and testing the operational modules. This will ensure that any major design faults will show up early. Suppose that the whole product is completed before a major fault is detected. Large parts of the product will have to be rewritten, especially the logic modules that embody the flow of control. Many of the operational modules will probably be reusable in the rebuilt product; for example, a module like getLineFromTerminal or measureTemperatureOfReactorCore will be needed no matter how the product is restructured. However, the way the operational modules will be interconnected to the other modules in the product may have to be changed, resulting in unnecessary work. Thus the earlier a design fault is detected, the quicker and less costly it will be to correct the product and get back on the development schedule. The order in which modules are implemented and integrated using the top-down strategy essentially ensures that logic modules are indeed implemented and integrated before operational modules, because logic modules are almost always the ancestors of operational modules in the module interconnection diagram. This is a major strength of top-down implementation and integration.

Nevertheless, top-down implementation and integration has a disadvantage, namely, potentially reusable modules may not be adequately tested. Reuse of a module that is thought, incorrectly, to have been thoroughly tested is likely to be less cost-effective than writing that module from scratch, because the assumption that a module is correct can lead to wrong conclusions when the product fails.

Instead of suspecting the insufficiently tested module, the tester may think that the fault lies elsewhere, resulting in a waste of effort.

Logic modules are likely to be somewhat problem-specific, and hence unusable in another context. However, operational modules, particularly if they have informational or functional cohesion (Section 6.2), are probably reusable in future products and, therefore, require thorough testing. Unfortunately, the operational modules are generally the lower-level modules in the module interconnection diagram and hence are not tested as frequently as the upper-level modules. For example, if there are 184 modules, the root module will be tested 184 times, whereas the last module to be integrated into the product will be tested only once. Top-down implementation and integration makes reuse a risky undertaking as a consequence of inadequate testing of operational modules.

The situation is exacerbated if the product is well designed; in fact, the better the design, the less thoroughly the modules are likely to be tested. To see this, consider a module computeSquareRoot. This module takes two arguments, a floating-point number x whose square root is to be determined and an errorFlag that is set to true if x is negative. Suppose further that computeSquareRoot is called by module m3, and that m3 contains the statement

```
if (x >= 0)
    y = computeSquareRoot (x, errorFlag); cr
```

In other words, computeSquareRoot is never called unless the value of x is nonnegative, and therefore the module can never be tested with negative values of x to see if it functions correctly. The type of design where the calling module includes a safety check of this kind is referred to as *defensive programming*. As a result of defensive programming, subordinate operational modules are unlikely to be thoroughly tested if implemented and integrated top-down. An alternative to defensive programming is the use of responsibility-driven design (Section 1.6). Here, the necessary safety checks are built into the called module, rather than the caller. Another approach is the use of assertions in the called module (Section 5.5.3).

14.1.2 BOTTOM-UP IMPLEMENTATION AND INTEGRATION

In bottom-up implementation and integration, if module mAbove calls module mBelow, then mBelow is implemented and integrated before mAbove. Returning to Figure 14.1, one possible bottom-up ordering is l, m, h, i, j, k, e, f, g, b, c, d, and a. In order to have the product coded by a team, a better bottom-up ordering is as follows: h, e, and b are given to one programmer and i, f, and c to another. The third programmer starts with l, m, j, k, and g, then implements d and integrates his or her work with the work of the second programmer. Finally, when b, c, and d have been successfully integrated, a can be implemented and integrated.

The operational modules are thus thoroughly tested when a bottom-up strategy is used. In addition, the testing is done with the aid of drivers, rather than by fault-shielding, defensively programmed calling modules. Although bottom-up implementation and integration solves the major difficulty of top-down implementation and integration and shares with top-down implementation and integration the advantage of fault isolation, it unfortunately has a difficulty of its own. Specifically, major design faults will be detected late in the integration phase. The logic modules are integrated last, and hence if there is a major design fault, it will be picked up at the end of the integration process with the resulting huge cost of redesigning and recoding large portions of the product.

Thus both top-down and bottom-up implementation and integration have their strengths and their weaknesses. The solution for product development is to combine the two strategies in such a way as to make use of their strengths and minimize their weaknesses. This leads to the idea of sandwich implementation and integration.

14.1.3 SANDWICH IMPLEMENTATION AND INTEGRATION

Consider the module interconnection diagram shown in Figure 14.2. Six of the modules, namely, a, b, c, d, g, and j, are logic modules, and therefore should be

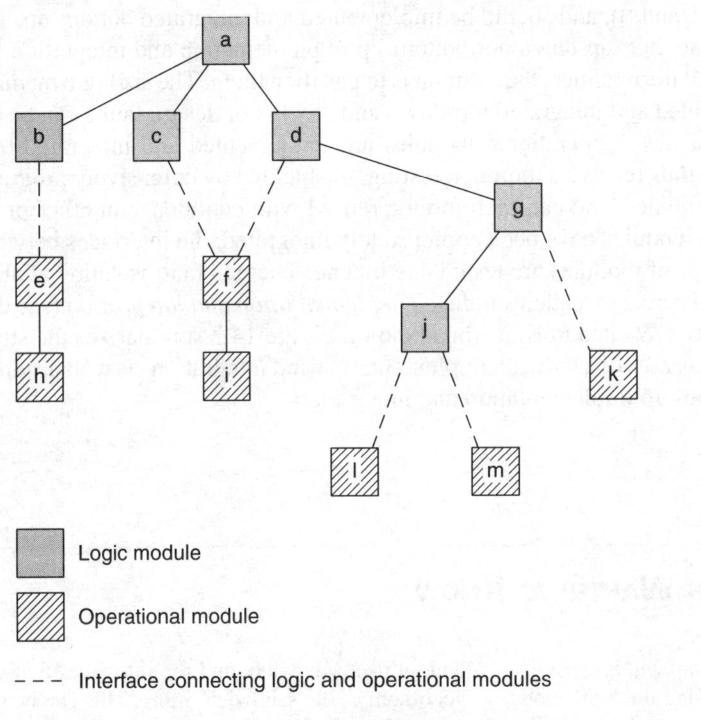

Figure 14.2 Product of Figure 14.1 developed using sandwich implementation and integration.

Approach	Strengths	Weaknesses
Implementation, then integration (Section 14.1)	—	No fault isolation Major design faults show up late
Top-down implementation and integration (Section 14.1.1)	Fault isolation Major design faults show up early	Potentially reusable modules are not adequately tested
Bottom-up implementation and integration (Section 14.1.2)	Fault isolation Potentially reusable modules are adequately tested	Major design faults show up late
Sandwich implementation and integration (Section 14.1.3)	Fault isolation Major design faults show up early Potentially reusable modules are adequately tested	—

Figure 14.3 Summary of implementation and integration approaches and the section in which each is described.

implemented and integrated top-down. Seven are operational modules, namely, e, f, h, i, k, l, and m, and should be implemented and integrated bottom-up. That is, because neither top-down nor bottom-up implementation and integration is suitable for all the modules, the solution is to partition them. The six logic modules are implemented and integrated top-down and any major design faults can be caught early. The seven operational modules are implemented and integrated bottom-up. They thus receive a thorough testing, unshielded by defensively programmed calling modules, and can therefore be reused with confidence in other products. When all modules have been appropriately integrated, the interfaces between the two groups of modules are tested one by one. There is fault isolation at all times during this process, called *sandwich implementation and integration* (see the Just in Case You Wanted to Know box below). Figure 14.3 summarizes the strengths and weaknesses of sandwich implementation and integration, as well as top-down and bottom-up implementation and integration.

JUST IN CASE YOU WANTED TO KNOW

The term *sandwich implementation and integration* [Myers, 1979] comes from viewing the logic modules and the operational modules as the top and the bottom of a sandwich, and the interfaces that connect them as the sandwich filling. This can be seen (sort of!) in Figure 14.2.

14.1.4 Implementation and Integration of Object-Oriented Products

Objects can be implemented and integrated either bottom-up or top-down. If top-down implementation and integration is chosen, stubs are used for each method in the same way as with classical modules.

If bottom-up implementation and integration is used, the objects that do not send any messages to other objects are implemented and integrated first. Then, the objects that send messages to those objects are implemented and integrated, and so on, until all the objects in the product have been implemented and integrated. (This process must be modified if there is recursion.)

Because both top-down and bottom-up implementation and integration are supported, sandwich implementation and integration can also be used. If the product is implemented in a hybrid object-oriented language like C++, the objects often correspond to operational modules of the classical paradigm and are therefore implemented and integrated bottom-up. Many of the modules that are not objects are logic modules. These are implemented and integrated in a top-down manner. Other modules are operational, so they are implemented and integrated bottom-up. Finally, all the non-object modules are integrated with the objects.

Even when the product is implemented using a pure object-oriented language like Java, class methods (sometimes referred to as "static methods") such as `main` and utility methods are usually similar in structure to logic modules of the structured paradigm. Thus, class methods are also implemented top-down and then integrated with the other objects. In other words, when performing implementation and integration of an object-oriented product, variants of sandwich implementation and integration are used.

14.1.5 Management Issues during the Implementation and Integration Phase

A problem for management is discovering, at integration time, that pieces of the modules simply do not fit together. For example, suppose that programmer 1 coded object `o1`, and programmer 2 coded object `o2`. In the version of the design documentation used by programmer 1, object `o1` sends a message to object `o2` passing four arguments, but the version of the design documentation used by programmer 2 states clearly that only three arguments are passed to `o2`. A problem like this can arise when a change is made to only one copy of the design document, without informing all members of the development group. Both programmers know that they are in the right; neither is prepared to compromise, because the programmer who gives in will have to recode large portions of the product.

In order to solve these and similar problems of incompatibility, the entire integration process should be run by the SQA group. Furthermore, as with testing during other phases, the SQA group has the most to lose if the integration testing is improperly performed. The SQA group is therefore the most likely to ensure that the testing is performed thoroughly. Thus the manager of the SQA group should have responsibility for all aspects of integration testing. He or she must decide which modules will be implemented and integrated top-down and which will be implemented and integrated bottom-up and will assign the integration-testing tasks to the appropriate individuals. The SQA group, which will have drawn up the integration test plan in the SPMP, is responsible for implementing that plan.

At the end of the integration phase all the modules will have been tested and combined into a single product.

14.2 TESTING DURING THE IMPLEMENTATION AND INTEGRATION PHASE

There are a number of different types of testing that have to be performed during the implementation and integration phase. First, each new module must be tested when it is added to what has already been integrated. The key points here are to test the new module as described in Chapter 13 and to check that the rest of the partial product continues to behave as it did before the new module was integrated into it.

When the product has a graphical user interface (GUI), special issues can arise with regard to integration testing. These are described in the next section.

14.3 INTEGRATION TESTING OF GRAPHICAL USER INTERFACES

Testing a product can usually be simplified by storing the input data for a test case in a file. The product is then executed, and the relevant data submitted to it. With the aid of a relatively rudimentary CASE tool, the whole process can be automated; that is, a set of test cases is set up, together with the expected outcome of each case. The CASE tool runs each test case in turn, compares the actual results with the expected results, and reports to the user on each case. The test cases are then stored, so that they can be used for regression testing whenever the product is modified.

However, when a product incorporates a graphical user interface (GUI), this approach does not work. Specifically, test data for pulling down a menu or clicking on a mouse button cannot be stored in a file in the same way as conventional test data. At the same time, it is both time-consuming and boring to test a GUI manually. The solution to this problem is to use a special CASE tool. Test cases are written in the form of scripts, using a special script language. A script is a machine-readable version of a manual GUI test case. Once the required scripts have been set up, automated testing proceeds as if there were no GUI. There are a number of CASE tools available that support the testing of GUIs, including QAPartner and XRunner.

When the integration process is complete, the product as a whole is tested; this is termed *product testing*. When the developers are confident about the correctness of every aspect of the product, it is handed over to the client for *acceptance testing*. These latter two forms of testing are now described in more detail.

14.4 PRODUCT TESTING

The fact that the last module has been successfully integrated into the product does not mean that the task of the developers is complete. The SQA group must still perform a number of testing tasks in order to be certain that the product will be successful. There are two main types of software, COTS (shrink-wrapped) software (Section 2.6.1), and custom software. The aim when developing COTS software is to ensure that the product is sold to as many buyers as possible. Thus, when all the modules of COTS software have been successfully integrated, the product is handed over the the SQA group for product testing. The aim of COTS product testing is to ensure that the product as a whole is free of faults. When the product testing is complete, the product then undergoes alpha and beta testing, as described in Section 2.6.1. That is, preliminary versions are shipped to selected prospective buyers of the product in order to get feedback, particularly regarding residual faults overlooked by the SQA team.

Custom software, on the other hand, undergoes a somewhat different type of product testing. The SQA group performs a number of testing tasks in order to be certain that the product will not fail its acceptance test, the final hurdle that the custom software development team must overcome. The failure of a product to pass its acceptance test is almost always a poor reflection of the management capabilities of the development organization. The client may conclude that the developers are incompetent, which all but guarantees that the client will do everything in his or her power to avoid employing those developers again. Worse, the client may believe that the developers are dishonest and deliberately handed over substandard software in order to finish the contract and be paid as quickly as possible. If the client genuinely believes this and tells other potential clients, then the developers have a major public relations problem on their hands. It is up to the SQA group to make sure that the product passes the acceptance test with flying colors.

To ensure a successful acceptance test, the SQA group must perform product testing. This essentially consists of tests that the SQA group believes will closely approximate the forthcoming acceptance tests. First, black-box test cases for the product as a whole must be run. Up to now, test cases have been set up on a module-by-module or object-by-object basis, ensuring that each module or object individually satisfies its specifications. Second, the robustness of the product as a whole must be tested. Again, the robustness of individual modules and objects was tested during integration, but now product-wide robustness is the issue for which test cases must be set up and run. In addition, the product must be subjected to *stress testing*, that is, making sure that it behaves correctly when operating under a peak load, such as all terminals trying to log on at the same time or customers operating all the automated teller machines simultaneously. The product must also be subjected to *volume testing*, for example, making sure that it can handle large input files. Third, the SQA group must check that the product satisfies all its constraints. For example, if the specifications state that the response time for 95 percent of queries when the product is working under full load must be under 3 seconds, then it is the responsibility of the SQA group to verify that this is indeed the case. There is no question that the client will check constraints during acceptance testing, and if the product fails to meet a major constraint, the development organization will lose a considerable amount of credibility. Similarly, storage constraints and security constraints must be checked. Fourth, the SQA group must review all documentation that is to be handed over to the client together with the code. The SQA group must check that the documentation conforms to the standards laid down in the SPMP. In addition, the documentation must be verified against the product. For instance, the SQA group has to determine that the user manual indeed reflects the correct way of using the product and that the product will function as specified in the user manual.

Scenarios (Section 11.4) can be useful in the product testing of object-oriented software. The product as a whole is inspected on a scenario-by-scenario basis to ensure that the behavior of the product is precisely as specified. It is true that scenario checking is also useful during design inspections, as well as inspections of individual modules and objects. However, many scenarios, especially the critical ones, cross module and object boundaries, so it is only during product testing that scenario checking achieves its fullest potential.

Once the SQA group assures management that the product can handle anything the acceptance testers can throw at it, the product (that is, the code plus all the documentation) is handed over to the client organization for acceptance testing.

14.5 ACCEPTANCE TESTING

The purpose of acceptance testing is for the client to determine whether the product indeed satisfies its specifications as claimed by the developer. Acceptance testing is done either by the client organization, by the SQA group in the presence of client representatives, or by an independent SQA group hired by the client for this purpose. Acceptance testing naturally includes correctness testing, but in addition it is necessary to test performance and robustness. The four major components of acceptance testing, namely, testing correctness, robustness, performance, and documentation, are exactly what is done by the developer during product testing; this is not surprising, because product testing is a rehearsal for the acceptance test.

A key aspect of acceptance testing is that it must be performed on actual data, rather than on test data. No matter how well test cases are set up, by their very nature they are artificial. More importantly, test data should be a true reflection of the corresponding actual data, but in practice this is not always the case. For example, the member of the specification team responsible for characterizing the actual data may perform this task incorrectly. Alternatively, even if the data are correctly specified, the SQA group member who use that data specification may misunderstand it or misinterpret it. The resulting test cases will not be a true reflection of the actual data, leading to an inadequately tested product. For these reasons, acceptance testing must be performed on actual data. Furthermore, because the development team endeavors to ensure that the product testing will duplicate every aspect of the acceptance testing, as much of the product testing as possible should also be performed on actual data.

When a new product is to replace an existing product, the specification document will almost always include a clause to the effect that the new product must be installed to run in parallel with the existing product. The reason is that there is a very real possibility that the new product may be faulty in some way. The existing product works correctly, but is inadequate in some respects. If the existing product is replaced by a new product that works incorrectly, then the client is in trouble. Therefore, both products must run in parallel until the client is satisfied that the new product can take over the functions of the existing product. Successful parallel running concludes acceptance testing, and the existing product can be retired.

When the product has passed its acceptance test, the task of the developers is complete. Any changes now made to that product constitute maintenance.

14.6 CASE TOOLS FOR THE IMPLEMENTATION AND INTEGRATION PHASE

CASE tools to support implementation were described in some detail in Chapter 4. For the integration component of the implementation and integration phase, version control tools, build tools, and configuration management tools are needed (Chapter 4). The reason is that modules under test are continually changing as a consequence of faults being detected and corrected, and these CASE tools are essential in order to be sure that the appropriate version of each module is compiled and linked. As previously mentioned, the three major UNIX version control tools are *sccs* (source code control system) [Rochkind, 1975], *rcs* (revision control system) [Tichy, 1985], and *cvs* (concurrent versions system) [Loukides and Oram, 1997]. Commercially available configuration control workbenches include CCC and Aide-de-Camp.

In each chapter so far, CASE tools and workbenches specific to that phase have been described. Now that all phases of the development process have been described, it is appropriate to consider CASE tools for the process as a whole.

14.7 CASE Tools for the Complete Software Process

There is a natural progression within CASE. As described in Section 4.10, the simplest CASE device is a single *tool* such as an online interface checker or a build tool. Next, tools can be combined, leading to a *workbench* that can support one or two activities within the software process, such as configuration control or coding. However, such a workbench will not necessarily provide management information even for the limited portion of the software process to which it is applicable, let alone for the project as a whole. Finally, an *environment* provides computer-aided support for most, if not all, of the process.

Ideally, every software development organization should utilize an environment. But the cost of an environment can be large—not just the package itself but also the hardware on which to run it. For a smaller organization, a workbench, or perhaps just a set of tools, may suffice. But if at all possible, an integrated environment should be utilized to support the development and maintenance effort.

14.8 Integrated Environments

The most common meaning of the word *integrated* within the CASE context is in terms of *user interface integration*. That is, all the tools in the environment share a common user interface. The idea behind this is that if all the tools have the same visual appearance, the user of one tool should have little difficulty in learning and using another tool in the environment. This has been successfully achieved on the Macintosh, where most applications have a similar "look and feel." Although this is the usual meaning, there are other types of integration as well.

14.8.1 Process Integration

Process integration refers to the fact that the environment supports one specific software process. A subset of this class of environment is the *technique-based environment* (but see the Just in Case You Wanted to Know box on page 491). An environment of this type supports a specific technique for developing software, rather than a complete process. Environments exist for a variety of the techniques discussed in this book, such as Gane and Sarsen's structured systems analysis (Section 10.3), Jackson's system development (Section 12.5), and Petri

JUST IN CASE YOU WANTED TO KNOW

In the literature, technique-based environments are usually called "method-based environments." The rise of the object-oriented paradigm gave the word *method* a second meaning (in the software engineering context). The original meaning was a technique or an approach; this is how the word is used in the phrase "method-based environment." The object-oriented meaning, as explained in Section 6.7, is an action within an object or class. Unfortunately, it is sometimes not totally clear from the context which of the two meanings is intended!

Accordingly, I have used the word *method* exclusively in the object-oriented paradigm sense. Otherwise, I have employed the term *technique* or *approach*. For example, that is why the term *formal method* never appears in Chapter 10. Instead, I have used the term *formal technique*. Similarly, in this chapter, I have used the term *technique-based environments*.

nets (Section 10.7). The majority of these environments provide graphical support for the specification and design phases, and incorporate a data dictionary. Some consistency checking is usually provided. Support for managing the development process is frequently incorporated into the environment. There are many commercially available environments of this type, including Analyst/Designer and Statemate. Analyst/Designer is specific to Yourdon's methodology [Yourdon, 1989], and Statemate supports Statecharts [Harel et al, 1990]. With regard to object-oriented methodologies, Rose supports Booch's methodology [Booch, 1994]. In addition, some older environments have been extended to support the object-oriented paradigm; Software through Pictures is an example of this type. Almost all object-oriented environments now support UML as well as the methodology that they originally supported.

The emphasis in most technique-based environments is on the support and formalization of the manual processes for software development laid down by the technique. That is, these environments force users to utilize the technique step by step in the way intended by its author, while assisting the user by providing graphical tools, a data dictionary, and consistency checking. This computerized framework is a strength of technique-based environments in that users are forced to use a specific technique and to use it correctly. But it can also be a weakness. Unless the software process of the organization incorporates this specific technique, use of a technique-based environment can be counterproductive.

14.8.2 TOOL INTEGRATION

The term *tool integration* means that all the tools communicate via the same data format. For example, in the UNIX Programmer's Workbench, the UNIX pipe formalism assumes that all data are in the form of an ASCII stream. It is thus easy to combine two tools by directing the output stream from one tool to the input stream of the other tool.

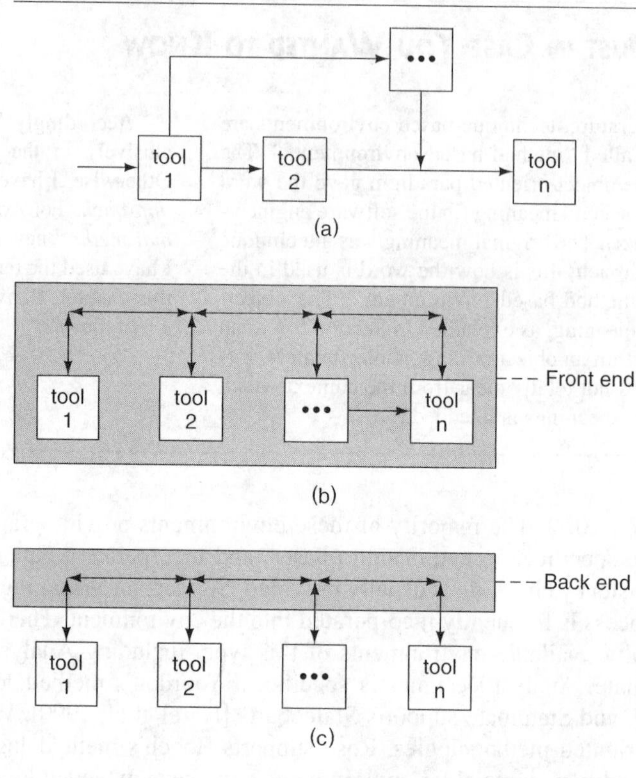

Figure 14.4 Representation of (a) stream, (b) front-end, and (c) back-end tool integration.

There are a number of different ways of achieving tool integration and each results in a different type of environment. The simplest is data stream tool integration.

Data Stream Tool Integration Consider the UNIX Programmer's Workbench. The input to and output from each individual tool is an ASCII stream, and integration is effected by passing a data stream from one tool to another. This is depicted in Figure 14.4(a).

Front-End Tool Integration A second form of tool integration is via a common front end into which all the tools are embedded, as shown in Figure 14.4(b). A commercially available environment of this type of front end is SoftBench [Riehle, 1991]. Communication between tools is now more than just a data stream; with SoftBench, a tool may send a message to another tool when it wants that tool to perform an action. For example, SoftBench may cause electronic mail to be sent to a specific manager if a test fails. More precisely, if a test fails, the testing tool sends a message to the mail tool telling it to inform the manager as to which test failed. It is possible to impose a wide variety of processes by specifying the messages to be sent when particular events occur. SoftBench is essentially a metaCASE tool, that is, a CASE tool that operates on CASE tools.

With front-end tool integration, each tool continues to store information the way that it does in stand-alone fashion, that is, if it were not integrated into the front end. In order to achieve integration, the front end may have to transform the way data are stored by one tool so that information can be used by a different tool. This is a possible drawback of front-end integration.

Historically, computer manufacturers have built their products so that their customers are essentially "married" to that company. It has not been uncommon for company A to design its operating system for total incompatibility with software made by company B. In contrast, Hewlett-Packard, a major hardware and software manufacturer, designed SoftBench to accept a wide variety of other manufacturers' tools. Even more surprising, SoftBench is available on hardware platforms from a number of different manufacturers.

There are several reasons why many software manufacturers are now building products that can interface with competitors' products. The first is that if a software organization is successfully using CASE tool CT, say, with great success, then that organization will want to continue to use CT. A product like SoftBench will allow the software developer to use CT in conjunction with other tools that, up to now, have not been accessible because of interfacing problems. The software developer may therefore purchase SoftBench and boost productivity even further by using CT together with new tools. A second reason is that some clients do not like to be tied to one manufacturer, and a framework such as SoftBench allows a client to use CASE tools from a variety of different manufacturers. In addition, if a CASE tool from one manufacturer proves to be disappointing, there may well be a better tool from another manufacturer that can be substituted for it within the SoftBench framework. The third reason is that software manufacturers have realized that building an environment is a major undertaking. The cost of developing an environment can be literally tens of millions of dollars. Furthermore, there is a considerable risk involved in developing an environment. For example, after perhaps $25 million has been spent, a competing product may be marketed 6 months before the environment is due to be completed. Thus, from the viewpoint of risk management, it may make more sense for a computer manufacturer to develop a CASE framework that runs on that manufacturer's hardware and that allows a wide variety of competitors' CASE tools to be integrated. Another example of this approach is described below.

Back-End Tool Integration A third type of tool integration is achieved by using a common back end, the software project database. This is depicted in Figure 14.4(c). All tools are then interfaced with this database, sometimes called a repository or encyclopedia. Integrated CASE tools then modify the common data stored in the repository. The key to the success of such a scheme is that the manufacturer of the repository must carefully define the interface between the repository and the tools that are to be integrated into it.

The first major example of this class of tool integration was AD/Cycle [Mercurio, Meyers, Nisbet, and Radin, 1990], which was both a software development process (AD stands for application development) and the associated repository. AD/Cycle was a product of IBM, in conjunction with a large number of IBM business partners, that is, CASE tool manufacturers who would ensure that their products would be compatible in every way with the AD/Cycle repository. This is another example of a major computer manufacturer deliberately building a CASE product in a way that encourages its erstwhile competitors to become collaborators in constructing an environment. Unfortunately, despite a major effort, AD/Cycle was never completed.

14.8.3 Other Forms of Integration

Team integration refers to the fact that the CASE environment promotes effective team coordination and communication. Another objective is *management integration*. Here, the environment supports management of the process. In particular, reports are generated directly from the software project database containing management information, together with all versions of all modules, classes, contracts, plans, test cases, and the myriad other components of a software project. In other words, reports are generated from objective data, rather than synthesized subjectively by project managers.

In practice, not all these laudable objectives have been achieved. In most commercially available environments, tool integration is all that is available; user interface integration is becoming more widespread. Nevertheless, team integration, management integration, and especially process integration are important future goals toward which environment designers are striving.

14.9 Environments for Business Applications

An important class of environments is used for building business-oriented products. The emphasis is on ease of use, achieved in a number of ways. In particular, the environment incorporates a number of standard screens, and these can be endlessly modified via a user-friendly GUI generator. One popular feature of such environments is a code generator. The lowest level of abstraction of a product is then the detailed design. The detailed design is the input to a code generator that automatically generates code in a language such as COBOL, C, C++, or Java. This automatically generated code is then compiled; no "programming" of any kind is performed on it.

Languages for specifying the detailed design could well be the programming languages of the future. The level of abstraction of programming languages rose from the physical machine level of first- and second-generation languages to the abstract machine level of third- and fourth-generation languages. Today, the level of abstraction of environments of this type is the detailed design level, a portable level. In Section 13.2 it was stated that one of the objectives in using a fourth-generation language (4GL) is shorter code, and hence quicker development and easier maintenance. The use of code generators takes these goals even further, in that the programmer has to provide fewer details to a code generator than to an interpreter or compiler for a 4GL.Thus, it is expected that use of business-oriented environments that support code generators will increase productivity.

There are a number of environments of this type currently available, including Powerhouse, Foundation, and the Bachman Product Set. Bearing in mind the size of the market for business-oriented CASE environments, it is likely that many more environments of this type will be developed in future years.

14.10 PUBLIC TOOL INFRASTRUCTURES

The European Strategic Programme for Research in Information Technology (ESPRIT) has developed an infrastructure for supporting CASE tools. Despite its name, the Portable Common Tool Environment (PCTE) [Thomas, 1989; Long and Morris, 1993] is *not* an environment. Instead, it is an infrastructure that provides the services needed by CASE tools, in much the same way that UNIX provides the operating system services needed by user products. (The word *Common* in PCTE is in the sense of "public" or "not copyrighted.")

PCTE is starting to gain widespread acceptance. For example, in 1990 the European Computer Manufacturers Association (ECMA) adopted PCTE as ECMA Standard 149. Subsequently, the C and Ada interfaces to PCTE have also been adopted as ECMA standards. In addition, PCTE has been submitted for international standardization. Implementations of PCTE include those of Emeraude and IBM.

The hope is that, in the future, many CASE tools will conform to the PCTE standard and that PCTE itself will be implemented on a wide variety of computers. A tool that conforms to PCTE will be able to run on any computer that supports PCTE. Accordingly, this should result in the widespread availability of a broad range of CASE tools. This, in turn, should lead to better software processes and hence to better quality software.

14.11 POTENTIAL PROBLEMS WITH ENVIRONMENTS

No one environment is ideal for all products and all organizations, any more than one programming language can be considered to be "the best." Every environment has its strengths and its weaknesses, and choosing an inappropriate environment can be worse than using no environment at all. For example, as explained in

Section 14.8.1, a technique-based environment essentially automates a manual process. If an organization chooses to use an environment that enforces a technique that is inappropriate for that organization as a whole, or for a current software product under development, then use of that CASE environment will be counterproductive.

A worse situation occurs when an organization chooses to ignore the advice of Section 4.15, namely, that the use of a CASE environment should be firmly avoided until the organization has attained CMM level 3 (see Section 2.11). Of course, every organization should use CASE tools, and there is generally little harm in using a workbench. However, an environment imposes an automated software process on an organization that uses it. If there is a good process being used, that is, the organization is at level 3 or higher, then use of the environment will assist in all aspects of software production by automating that process. But if the organization is at the crisis-driven level 1, or even at level 2, then there is no process as such in place. Automation of this nonexistent process, that is, the introduction of a CASE environment (as opposed to a CASE tool or CASE workbench), can lead only to chaos.

14.12 METRICS FOR THE IMPLEMENTATION AND INTEGRATION PHASE

A number of different complexity metrics for the implementation and integration phase are discussed in Section 13.8.2, including lines of code, McCabe's cyclomatic complexity, and the CDM metric.

From a testing viewpoint, relevant metrics include the total number of test cases and the number of test cases that resulted in a failure. The usual fault statistics must be maintained for code inspections. The total number of faults is important, because if the number of faults detected in a module or object exceeds a predetermined maximum, then that module or object must be redesigned and recoded, as discussed in Section 13.14. But in addition, detailed statistics need to be kept regarding the types of faults detected. Typical fault types include misunderstanding the design, lack of initialization, and inconsistent use of variables. The fault data can then be incorporated into the checklists used during code inspections of future products.

A powerful set of metrics for the implementation and integration phase is associated with statistical-based testing (Section 13.13). To see how these metrics work, we consider one, namely, the zero-failure technique. This is a technique for determining how long to continue testing a product. The underlying idea is that the longer a product is tested without a single failure being observed, the greater the likelihood that the product is free of faults. The technique specifies how long the product must be tested without a single failure in order for the developers to be confident that the product is fault-free. Under the reasonable assumption that the chance of a failure occurring decreases exponentially as testing proceeds, the number of test hours required without a single failure occurring is given by the formula [Brettschneider, 1989]

$$\frac{\ln\left(\dfrac{f_{target}}{0.5 + f_{target}}\right)}{\ln\left(\dfrac{0.5 + f_{target}}{f_{total} + f_{target}}\right)} \times t_h \qquad \textbf{(14.1)}$$

where f_{target} is the target projected number of failures, f_{total} is the total number of failures detected so far, t_h denotes the total number of test hours up to the last failure, and ln denotes logarithm to base *e*.

For example, suppose that a product is 50,000 lines of code in length, and the contract stipulates not more than 0.02 failures per thousand lines of delivered code. This implies 1 delivered failure, so $f_{target} = 1$. Suppose further that the product has so far been tested for 400 hours. During this time, a total of 20 failures has been detected, and the product has run for 50 hours since the last failure occurred. This means that $f_{total} = 20$, and $t_h = 400 - 50 = 350$ hours. Substituting these figures into Equation (14.1) yields

$$\frac{\ln\left(\dfrac{1}{0.5 + 1}\right)}{\ln\left(\dfrac{0.5 + 1}{20 + 1}\right)} \times 350 = 54 \text{ hours}$$

The product has already run failure-free for 50 hours, so a further 4 hours of testing are required. Of course, if a failure is detected during these last 4 hours, additional failure-free execution is required for a time that is again determined from Equation (14.1).

14.13 OSBERT OGLESBY CASE STUDY: IMPLEMENTATION AND INTEGRATION PHASE

A complete Java implementation of the Osbert Oglesby Case Study can be downloaded from www.mhhe.com/engcs/compsci/schach.

The implementation can be considered to be a direct translation of the detailed design (Appendix G) into code. That is, the designers presented the programming team with a well-thought-out design that merely required implementation in Java. The programmers have included a variety of comments to aid the maintenance programmers. The implementation was tested against the black-box test cases of Appendix H, as well as the white-box test cases of Problems 13.21 through 13.25.

The next chapter describes the many difficulties of maintenance and suggests ways to simplify the task of maintenance.

CHAPTER REVIEW

Implementation and integration activities must be carried out in parallel (Section 14.1). Top-down, bottom-up, and sandwich implementation and integration are described and compared (Sections 14.1.1 through 14.1.3). Implementation and integration of object-oriented products is discussed in Section 14.1.4. Various types of testing must be carried out during the implementation and integration phase (Section 14.2), including product testing (Section 14.4) and acceptance testing (Section 14.5). Special problems can be posed by the integration testing of graphical user interfaces (Section 14.3). In Section 14.6, CASE tools for the implementation and integration phase are discussed; CASE tools for the complete process are discussed in Section 14.7. The issue of integrated CASE tools is discussed in Section 14.8. Environments for business applications are presented in Section 14.9. Section 14.10 is devoted to public tool infrastructures. Next, there is a comparison of environment types (Section 14.11) and a description of metrics for the implementation and integration phase (Section 14.12). The chapter concludes with the Osbert Oglesby Case Study (Section 14.13).

FOR FURTHER READING

Selection of test data for integration testing appears in [Harrold and Soffa, 1991]. [Munoz, 1988] describes an approach to product testing. It is important to know how long it will be cost effective to continue testing a product; solutions to this problem are described in [Brettschneider, 1989] and in [Sherer, 1991]. The testing of large-scale products is described in [House and Newman, 1989].

A good starting point for information about CASE environments is [Barstow, Shrobe, and Sandewall, 1984]. There are many technique-based environments, including Software through Pictures [Wasserman and Pircher, 1987]. Information on integrated CASE tools can be found in the March 1992 issue of *IEEE Software*, and especially [Brown and McDermid, 1992] and [Chen and Norman, 1992]. An earlier article on data stream tool integration is [Reiss, 1990]. [Mercurio, Meyers, Nisbet, and Radin, 1990] provides an overview of AD/Cycle.

Every 2 or 3 years, ACM SIGSOFT and SIGPLAN sponsor a Symposium on Practical Software Development Environments. The proceedings provide information on a broad spectrum of toolkits and environments. Also useful are the proceedings of the annual International Workshops on Computer-Aided Software Engineering. Further papers on environments can be found in special issues of various journals, including the May 1992 issue of *IEEE Software*.

With regard to the object-oriented paradigm, [Jorgensen and Erickson, 1994] describes the integration testing of object-oriented software. The September 1994 issue of *Communications of the ACM* contains a number of articles on testing object-oriented software.

An overview of PCTE can be found in [Thomas, 1989]. [Long and Morris, 1993] contains a number of information sources on PCTE.

PROBLEMS

14.1 Explain the difference between logic modules and operational modules.

14.2 Defensive programming is good software engineering practice. At the same time, it can prevent operational modules from being tested thoroughly enough for reuse purposes. How can this apparent contradiction be resolved?

14.3 What are the similarities between product testing and acceptance testing? What are the major differences?

14.4 What is the role of SQA during the implementation and integration phase?

14.5 You are the owner and sole employee of One-Person Software Company. You decide that in order to be competitive, you must buy CASE tools. You therefore apply for a bank loan for $15,000. Your bank manager asks you for a statement not more than one page in length (and preferably shorter) explaining in lay terms why you need CASE tools. Write the statement.

14.6 The newly appointed vice-president for software development of Olde Fashioned Software Corporation has hired you to help her change the way the company develops software. There are 650 employees, all writing COBOL code without the assistance of any CASE tools. Write a memo to the vice-president stating what sort of CASE equipment the company should purchase. Carefully justify your choice.

14.7 You and a friend decide to start Personal Computer Software Programs Are Us, developing software for personal computers on personal computers. Then a distant cousin dies, leaving you $1 million on condition that you spend the money on a business-oriented environment and the hardware needed to run it and that you keep the environment for at least 5 years. What do you do, and why?

14.8 You are a computer science professor at an excellent small liberal arts college. Programming assignments for computer science courses are done on a network of 35 personal computers. The dean asks you whether to use the limited software budget to buy CASE tools, bearing in mind that, unless some sort of site license can be obtained, 35 copies of every CASE tool will have to be purchased. What do you advise?

14.9 You have just been elected mayor of a major city. You discover that no CASE tools are being used to develop software for the city. What do you do?

14.10 (Term Project) Implement and integrate the Air Gourmet product (Appendix A) in Java. Remember to utilize the black-box test cases you developed in Problem 13.20 for testing your code.

14.11 (Case Study) Starting with the detailed design of Appendix G, code the Osbert Oglesby Case Study in an object-oriented language other than Java.

14.12 (Case Study) Recode the Osbert Oglesby Case Study (Appendix I) in pure C, without any C++ features. Although C does not support inheritance, object-based concepts such as encapsulation and information hiding can easily be achieved. How would you implement polymorphism and dynamic binding?

14.13 (Case Study) To what extent is the documentation of the code of the implementation of Section 14.13 inadequate? Make any necessary additions.

14.14 (Readings in Software Engineering) Your instructor will distribute copies of [Jorgensen and Erickson, 1994]. What do you view as the major differences between object-oriented integration and classical integration?

REFERENCES

[Barstow, Shrobe, and Sandewall, 1984] D. R. BARSTOW, H. E. SHROBE, AND E. SANDEWALL (Editors), *Interactive Programming Environments*, McGraw-Hill, New York, 1984.

[Booch, 1994] G. BOOCH, *Object-Oriented Analysis and Design with Applications, Second Edition*, Benjamin/Cummings, Redwood City, CA, 1994.

[Brettschneider, 1989] R. BRETTSCHNEIDER, "Is Your Software Ready for Release?" *IEEE Software* **6** (July 1989), pp. 100, 102, and 108.

[Brown and McDermid, 1992] A. W. BROWN AND J. A. MCDERMID, "Learning from IPSE's Mistakes," *IEEE Software* **9** (March 1992), pp. 23–29.

[Chen and Norman, 1992] M. CHEN AND R. J. NORMAN, "A Framework for Integrated CASE," *IEEE Software* **8** (March 1992), pp. 18–22.

[Fuggetta, 1993] A. FUGGETTA, "A Classification of CASE Technology," *IEEE Computer* **26** (December 1993), pp. 25–38.

[Harel et al., 1990] D. HAREL, H. LACHOVER, A. NAAMAD, A. PNUELI, M. POLITI, R. SHERMAN, A. SHTULL-TRAURING, AND M. TRAKHTENBROT, "STATEMATE: A Working Environment for the Development of Complex Reactive Systems," *IEEE Transactions on Software Engineering* **16** (April 1990), pp. 403–14.

[Harrold and Soffa, 1991] M. J. HARROLD AND M. L. SOFFA, "Selecting and Using Data for Integration Testing," *IEEE Software* **8** (1991), pp. 58–65.

[House and Newman, 1989] D. E. HOUSE AND W. F. NEWMAN, "Testing Large Software Products," *ACM SIGSOFT Software Engineering Notes* **14** (April 1989), pp. 71–78.

[Jorgensen and Erickson, 1994] P. C. JORGENSEN AND C. ERICKSON, "Object-Oriented Integration Testing," *Communications of the ACM* **37** (September 1994), pp. 30–38.

[Long and Morris, 1993] F. LONG AND E. MORRIS, "An Overview of PCTE: A Basis for a Portable Common Tool Environment," Technical Report CMU/SEI–93–TR–1, Software Engineering Institute, Carnegie Mellon University, Pittsburgh, January 1993.

[Loukides and Oram, 1997] M. K. LOUKIDES AND A. ORAM, *Programming with GNU Software*, O'Reilly and Associates, Sebastopol, CA, 1997.

[Mercurio, Meyers, Nisbet, and Radin, 1990] V. J. MERCURIO, B. F. MEYERS, A. M. NISBET, AND G. RADIN, "AD/Cycle Strategy and Architecture," *IBM Systems Journal* **29** (No. 2, 1990), pp. 170–88.

[Meyer, 1992a] B. MEYER, "Applying 'Design by Contract'," *IEEE Computer* **25** (October 1992), pp. 40–51.

[Myers, 1979] G. J. MYERS, *The Art of Software Testing*, John Wiley and Sons, New York, 1979.

[Munoz, 1988] C. U. MUNOZ, "An Approach to Software Product Testing," *IEEE Transactions on Software Engineering* **14** (November 1988), pp. 1589–96.

[Reiss, 1990] S. P. REISS, "Connecting Tools Using Message Passing in the Field Environment," *IEEE Software* **7** (July 1990), pp. 57–66.

[Riehle, 1991] R. RIEHLE, "A Space for CASE," *HP Professional* **5** (July 1991), pp. 40–47.

[Rochkind, 1975] M. J. ROCHKIND, "The Source Code Control System," *IEEE Transactions on Software Engineering* **SE-1** (October 1975), pp. 255–65.

[Rumbaugh et al., 1991] J. RUMBAUGH, M. BLAHA, W. PREMERLANI, F. EDDY, AND W. LORENSEN, *Object-Oriented Modeling and Design*, Prentice Hall, Englewood Cliffs, NJ, 1991.

[Sherer, 1991] S. A. SHERER, "A Cost-Effective Approach to Testing," *IEEE Software* **8** (March 1991), pp. 34–40.

[Thomas, 1989] I. THOMAS, "PCTE Interfaces: Supporting Tools in Software Engineering Environments," *IEEE Software* **6** (November 1989), pp. 15–23.

[Tichy, 1985] W. F. TICHY, "RCS—A System for Version Control," *Software—Practice and Experience* **15** (July 1985), pp. 637–54.

[Wasserman and Pircher, 1987] A. I. WASSERMAN AND P. A. PIRCHER, "A Graphical, Extensible Integrated Environment for Software Development," *Proceedings of the Second ACM SIGSOFT/SIGPLAN Software Engineering Symposium on Practical Software Development Environments, ACM SIGPLAN Notices* **22** (January 1987), pp. 131–42.

[Yourdon, 1989] E. YOURDON, *Modern Structured Analysis*, Yourdon Press, Englewood Cliffs, NJ, 1989.

chapter

15

MAINTENANCE PHASE

Once the product has passed its acceptance test, it is handed over to the client. Any changes after the client has accepted the product constitute maintenance. Because the product consists of more than just the source code, any changes to the documentation, manuals, or any other component of the product are also examples of maintenance. Some computer scientists prefer to use the term *evolution* rather than maintenance to indicate that a product evolves in time. In fact, there are those who view the entire software life cycle, from beginning to end, as an evolutionary process.

A major theme of this book is the vital importance of maintenance. The reader might therefore be surprised that this is a relatively short chapter. The reason is that maintainability has to be built into a product from the very beginning and must not be compromised at any time during the development process. Thus, in a very real sense, the previous chapters have been devoted to the subject of maintenance. What is described in this chapter is how to ensure that maintainability is not compromised during the maintenance process itself.

15.1 WHY MAINTENANCE IS NECESSARY

There are three main reasons for making changes to a product after it has been delivered to the client. The first reason is to correct any residual faults, whether specification faults, design faults, coding faults, documentation faults, or any other type of faults. This is termed *corrective maintenance*. Surprisingly enough, a study of 69 organizations showed that maintenance programmers spend only 17.5 percent of their time on corrective maintenance [Lientz, Swanson, and Tompkins, 1978]. This is depicted in the pie chart of Figure 15.1. Most of their time, namely, 60.5 percent, was spent on the second type of maintenance, *perfective maintenance*. Here, changes are made to the code to improve the effectiveness of the product. For instance, the client may wish to have additional functionality added or might request that the product be modified so that it runs faster. Improving the maintainability of a product is another example of perfective maintenance. The

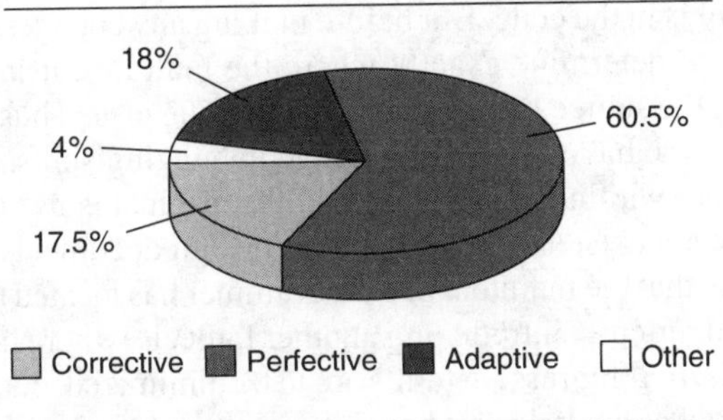

Figure 15.1 Percentage of time devoted to each of the types of maintenance.

third reason for changing a product is *adaptive maintenance*, changes made to the product in order to react to changes in the environment in which the product operates. For example, a product will almost certainly have to be modified if it is ported to a new compiler, operating system, and/or hardware. If there is a change to the tax code, then a product that prepares tax returns has to be modified accordingly. When the U.S. Postal Service introduced nine-digit ZIP codes in 1981, products that had allowed for only five-digit ZIP codes had to be changed. Adaptive maintenance is thus not requested by a client; instead, it is externally imposed on the client. The study showed that 18 percent of software maintenance was adaptive in nature. The remaining 4 percent of maintenance time was devoted to other types of maintenance that did not fall into the other three categories.

15.2 WHAT IS REQUIRED OF MAINTENANCE PROGRAMMERS

During the software life cycle, more time is spent on maintenance than on any other phase. In fact, on average, 67 percent of the total cost of a product can be attributed to maintenance, as shown in Figure 1.2. But many organizations, even today, assign the task of maintenance to beginners and to less competent programmers, leaving the "glamorous" job of product development to better or more experienced programmers.

In fact, maintenance is the most difficult of all aspects of software production. A major reason is that maintenance incorporates aspects of all the other phases of the software process. Consider what happens when a fault report is handed to a maintenance programmer. A fault report is filed if, in the opinion of the user, the product is not working as specified in the user manual. There are a number of possible causes. First, there could be nothing wrong at all; perhaps the user has either misunderstood the user manual or is using the product incorrectly. Alternatively, if the fault does lie in the product, it might simply be that the user manual has been badly worded, and that there is nothing wrong with the code itself. Usually, however, the fault is in the code. But before making any changes, the maintenance programmer has to determine exactly where the fault lies, using the fault report filed by the user, the source code—and often nothing else. Thus the maintenance programmer needs to have far above average debugging skills, because the fault could lie anywhere within the product. And the original cause of the fault might lie in the by now nonexistent specification or design documents.

Now suppose that the maintenance programmer has located the fault and must fix it without inadvertently introducing another fault elsewhere in the product, that is, a *regression fault*. If regression faults are to be minimized, detailed documentation for the product as a whole and for each individual module must be available. However, software professionals are notorious for their dislike of paperwork of all kinds, especially documentation, and it is quite common for the documentation to be incomplete, faulty, or totally missing. In these cases the maintenance programmer has to be able to deduce from the source code itself, the only valid form of documentation available, all the information needed to avoid introducing a regression fault.

Having determined the probable fault, and tried to correct it, the maintenance programmer must now test that the modification works correctly and that no regression faults have in fact been introduced. In order to check the modification itself, the maintenance programmer must construct special test cases; checking for regression faults is done using the set of test data stored precisely for the purpose of performing regression testing (Section 2.7.1). Then the test cases constructed for the purpose of checking the modification must be added to the set of stored test cases to be used for future regression testing of the modified product. In addition, if changes to the specification and/or design had to be made in order to correct the fault, then these changes must also be checked. Expertise in testing is therefore an additional prerequisite for maintenance. Finally, it is essential that the maintenance programmer document every change. The preceding discussion relates to corrective maintenance. For that task, the maintenance programmer must first and foremost be a superb diagnostician to be able to determine if there is a fault, and if so, an expert technician to be able to fix it.

However, the major maintenance tasks are adaptive and perfective maintenance. To perform these, the maintenance programmer must go through the phases of requirements, specification, design, and implementation and integration, taking the existing product as the starting point. For some types of changes, additional modules have to be designed and implemented. In other cases, changes to the design and implementation of existing modules are needed. Thus, whereas specifications are frequently produced by specification experts, designs by design experts, and code by programming experts, the maintenance programmer has to be an expert in all three areas. Perfective and adaptive maintenance are adversely affected by a lack of adequate documentation, just as corrective maintenance is. Furthermore, the ability to design suitable test cases and the ability to write good documentation are needed for perfective and adaptive maintenance, just as they are needed for corrective maintenance. Thus none of the forms of maintenance is a task for a less experienced programmer unless a top-rank computer professional supervises the process.

From the preceding discussion, it is clear that maintenance programmers have to possess almost every technical skill that a software professional could have. But what does he or she get in return? Maintenance is a thankless task in every way. Maintainers deal with dissatisfied users; if the user were happy with the product it would not need maintenance. Furthermore, the user's problems have frequently been caused by the individuals who developed the product, not the maintainer. The code itself may be badly written, adding to the frustrations of the maintainer. Finally, maintenance is looked down on by many software developers who consider development to be a glamorous job and maintenance to be drudge work fit only for junior programmers or incompetents.

Maintenance can be likened to after-sales service. The product has been delivered to the client. But now there is client dissatisfaction, either because the product does not work correctly, or because it does not do everything that the client currently wants, or because the circumstances for which the product was built have changed in some way. Unless the software organization provides the client with good maintenance service, the client will take his or her future product development business elsewhere. When the client and software group are part of the same organization, and hence are inextricably tied from the viewpoint of future work, a dissatisfied client may use every means, fair or foul, to discredit the software group. This, in turn, leads to an erosion of confidence, from both outside and inside the software group, and to resignations and dismissals. It is important for every software organization to keep its clients happy by providing excellent maintenance service.

For product after product, maintenance is the most challenging phase of software production—and frequently the most thankless.

How can this situation be changed? Managers must restrict maintenance tasks to programmers with all the skills needed to perform maintenance. They must make it known that only top computer professionals merit maintenance assignments in their organization and pay them accordingly. If management believes that maintenance is a challenge and that good maintenance is critical for the success of the organization, attitudes toward maintenance will slowly improve.

Some of the problems that maintenance programmers face are now highlighted in a case study.

15.3 MAINTENANCE CASE STUDY

In countries with centralized economies, the government controls the distribution and marketing of agricultural products. In one such country, temperate fruits such as peaches, apples, and pears were the responsibility of the Temperate Fruit Committee (TFC). One day, the chairman of the TFC asked a government computer consultant to computerize the operations of the TFC. The chairman informed the consultant that there are exactly seven temperate fruits, namely, apples, apricots, cherries, nectarines, peaches, pears, and plums. The database was to be designed for those seven fruits, no more and no less. After all, that was the way that the world was, and the consultant was not to waste time and money allowing for any sort of expandability.

The product was duly delivered to the TFC. About a year later, the chairman summoned the maintenance programmer responsible for the product. "What do you know about kiwi fruit?" asked the chairman. "Nothing," replied the mystified programmer. "Well," said the chairman, "it seems that kiwi fruit is a temperate fruit that has just started to be grown in our country, and the TFC is responsible for it. Please change the product accordingly."

The maintenance programmer discovered that the consultant fortunately had not carried out the chairman's original instructions to the letter. The good practice of allowing for some sort of future expansion was too ingrained, and the consultant had provided a number of unused fields in the relevant database records. By slightly rearranging certain items, the maintenance programmer was able to incorporate kiwi fruit, the eighth temperate fruit, into the product.

Another year went by, and the product functioned well. Then the maintenance programmer was again called to the chairman's office. The chairman was in a good mood. He jovially informed the programmer that the government had reorganized the distribution and marketing of agricultural products. His committee was now responsible for all fruit produced in that country, not just temperate fruit, and so the product now had to be modified to incorporate the 26 additional kinds of fruit on the list he handed to the maintenance programmer. The programmer protested, pointing out that this change would take almost as long as rewriting the product from scratch. "Nonsense," replied the chairman. "You had no trouble adding kiwi fruit. Just do the same thing another 26 times!"

There are a number of important lessons to be learned from this. First, the problem with the product, namely, no provision for expansion, was caused by the developer, not the maintainer. The developer made the mistake of obeying the chairman's instruction regarding future expandability of the product, but it was the maintenance programmer who suffered the consequences. In fact, unless he reads this book, the consultant who developed the original product may never realize that his product was anything but a success. This is one of the more annoying aspects of maintenance, in that the maintainer is responsible for fixing other people's mistakes. The person who caused the problem either has other duties or has left the organization, but the maintenance programmer is left holding the baby. Second, the client frequently does not understand that maintenance can be difficult, or in some instances, all but impossible. The problem is exacerbated when the maintenance programmer has successfully carried out previous perfective and adaptive maintenance tasks, but now suddenly protests that a new assignment cannot be done, even though superficially it seems no different from what has been done before with little difficulty. Third, all software development activities must be carried out with an eye on future maintenance. If the consultant had designed the product for an arbitrary number of different kinds of fruit, there would have been no difficulty in incorporating first the kiwi fruit and then the 26 other kinds of fruit. As has been stated many times, maintenance is a vital phase of software production, and the one which consumes the most resources. During product development, it is essential that the development team never forget about the maintenance programmer who will be responsible for the product once it has been installed.

15.4 MANAGEMENT OF MAINTENANCE

Issues regarding management of maintenance are now considered.

15.4.1 FAULT REPORTS

The first thing that is needed when maintaining a product is to set up a mechanism for changing the product. With regard to corrective maintenance, that is, removing residual faults, if the product appears to be functioning incorrectly, then a *fault report* should be filed by the user. This must include enough information to enable the maintenance programmer to recreate the problem, which will usually be some sort of software failure.

Ideally, every fault reported by a user should be fixed immediately. In practice, programming organizations are usually understaffed, and there is a backlog of work, both development and maintenance. If the fault is critical, such as if a payroll product crashes the day before payday or overpays employees or underpays them, then immediate corrective action will have to be taken. Otherwise, each fault report must at least receive an immediate preliminary investigation.

The maintenance programmer should first consult the fault report file. This contains all reported faults that have not yet been fixed, together with suggestions for working around them, that is, ways for the user to bypass the portion of the product that apparently is responsible for the failure, until such time as the fault can be fixed. If the fault has previously been reported, any information in the fault report file should be given to the user. But if what the user has reported appears to be a new fault, then the maintenance programmer should study the problem and attempt to find the cause and a way to fix it. In addition, an attempt should be made to find a way to work around the problem, because it may take 6 or 9 months before someone can be assigned to make the necessary changes to the software. In the light of the serious shortage of programmers, and in particular, programmers who are good enough to perform maintenance, suggesting a way to live with the fault until it can be solved is often the only way to deal with fault reports that are not true emergencies.

The maintenance programmer's conclusions should then be added to the fault report file, together with any supporting documentation such as listings, designs, and manuals used to arrive at those conclusions. The manager in charge of maintenance should consult the file regularly, prioritizing the various fixes. The file should also contain the client's requests for perfective and adaptive maintenance. The next modification to be made to the product will then be the one with the highest priority. However, it is not a good idea for a new release to address more than one of corrective, perfective, or adaptive maintenance. This should be taken into account when planning maintenance tasks.

When copies of a product have been distributed to a variety of sites, copies of fault reports must be circulated to all users of the product, together with an estimate of when each fault can be fixed. Then if the same failure occurs at another site, the user can consult the relevant fault report to determine if it is possible to work around the fault and when it will be fixed. It would of course be preferable to fix every fault immediately and then distribute a new version of the product to all sites. Given the current worldwide shortage of good programmers and the realities of software maintenance, distributing fault reports is probably the best that can be done.

There is another reason why faults are usually not fixed immediately. It is almost always cheaper to make a number of changes, test them all, change the documentation, and then install the new version than it is to perform each change separately, test it, document it, install the new version, and then repeat the entire cycle for the next change. This is particularly true if every new version has to be installed on a significant number of computers (such as a large number of clients in a client-server network), or when the software is running on a variety of different sites. As a result, organizations prefer to accumulate noncritical maintenance tasks and then implement the changes as a group.

15.4.2 AUTHORIZING CHANGES TO THE PRODUCT

Once a decision has been made to perform corrective maintenance, a maintenance programmer will be assigned the task of determining the fault that caused the failure and then repairing it. After the code has been changed, the fix must be tested, as must the product as a whole (regression testing). Then the documentation must be updated to reflect the changes. In particular, a detailed description of what was changed, why it was changed, by whom, and when, must be added to the prologue comments of any changed module. If necessary, design and/or specification documents also have to be changed. A similar set of steps is followed when performing perfective or adaptive maintenance; the only real difference is that perfective and adaptive maintenance are initiated by a change in requirements rather than by a fault report.

At this point all that would seem to be needed would be to distribute the new version to the users. But what if the maintenance programmer has not tested the fix adequately? Before the product is distributed, it must be subjected to SQA performed by an independent group, that is, the members of the maintenance SQA group must not report to the same manager as the maintenance programmer; it is important that SQA remain managerially independent (Section 5.1.2).

Reasons were given previously as to why maintenance is difficult. For those same reasons, maintenance is also fault-prone. Testing during the maintenance phase is both difficult and time-consuming, and the SQA group should not underestimate the implications of software maintenance with regard to testing. Once the new version has been approved by SQA, it can be distributed.

Another area in which management must ensure that procedures are carefully followed is when the technique of baselines and private copies (Section 4.13.2) is used. Suppose that a programmer wishes to change class **TaxProvision**. The programmer freezes the relevant module and makes copies of all other modules that will be needed to perform the required maintenance task; often this will be all the other modules in the product. The programmer makes the necessary changes to **TaxProvision**, tests them, and the new revision of **TaxProvision** incorporating the changes is installed in the baseline. But when the modified product is delivered to the user, it immediately crashes. What went wrong is that the maintenance programmer tested the modified version of **TaxProvision** using his or her private workspace copies, that is, the copies of the other modules that were in the baseline at the time that maintenance of **TaxProvision** was started. In the meantime, certain other modules were updated by other maintenance programmers working on the same product. The lesson is clear: Before installing a module, it must be tested using the current baseline versions of all the other modules and not the programmer's private versions. This is a further reason for stipulating independent SQA—members of the SQA group simply do not have access to programmers' private workspaces.

15.4.3 ENSURING MAINTAINABILITY

Maintenance is not a one-time effort. A well-written product will go through a series of versions over its lifetime. As a result, it is necessary to plan for maintenance during the entire software process. During the design phase, for example, information hiding techniques (Section 6.6) should be employed; during implementation, variable names should be selected that will be meaningful to future maintenance programmers (Section 13.3). Documentation should be complete and correct, and reflect the current version of every component module of the product.

During the maintenance phase, it is important not to compromise the maintainability that has been built into the product from the very beginning. In other words, just as software development personnel should always be conscious of the inevitable maintenance that will occur, so software maintenance personnel should always be conscious of the equally inevitable future maintenance. The principles established for maintainability during development are equally applicable to the maintenance phase itself.

15.4.4 PROBLEM OF REPEATED MAINTENANCE

One of the more frustrating difficulties of product development is the moving target problem (Section 3.4.1). What can happen is that as fast as the developer constructs the product, the client changes the requirements. Not only is this frustrating to the development team, but the frequent changes can result in a poorly constructed product. In addition, such changes add to the cost of the product. In theory, the way to cope with this is to start by constructing a rapid prototype. Then it does not matter how often the client changes the requirements. Once the client is finally satisfied, the specifications are approved and the product itself is constructed. In practice, there is nothing to stop the client from changing the requirements the day after he or she has finally approved them. The main advantage to prototyping in this situation is that, by presenting the client with a working model, it *may* reduce the number and the frequency of the changes. But if the client is willing to pay the price, nothing can be done to prevent the requirements being changed every Monday and Thursday.

The problem is exacerbated during the maintenance phase. The more a completed product is changed, the more it will deviate from its original design, and the more difficult it will become to make further changes. Under repeated maintenance the documentation is likely to become even less reliable than usual, and the regression testing files may not be up to date. If still more maintenance has to be done, the product as a whole may first have to be completely rewritten using the current version as a prototype.

The problem of the moving target is clearly a management problem. In theory, if management is sufficiently firm with the client and explains the problem at the beginning of the project, then the requirements can be frozen from the time the prototype has been accepted until the product is delivered. Again, after each request for perfective maintenance, the requirements can be frozen for, say, 3 months or 1 year. In practice, it does not work that way. For example, if the client happens to be the president of the corporation and the development organization is the information systems division of that corporation, then the president can indeed order changes every Monday and Thursday, and they will be implemented. The old proverb, "he who pays the piper calls the tune," is unfortunately only too relevant in this situation. Perhaps the best that the vice-president for information systems can do is to try to explain to the president the effect on the product of repeated maintenance, and then simply have the complete product rewritten whenever further maintenance would be hazardous to the integrity of the product.

Trying to discourage additional maintenance by ensuring that the requested changes are implemented slowly only has the effect of the relevant personnel being replaced by others who are prepared to do the job faster. In short, if the person who requests the repeated changes has sufficient clout, then there is no solution to the problem of the moving target.

15.5 MAINTENANCE OF OBJECT-ORIENTED SOFTWARE

One of the reasons put forward for using the object-oriented paradigm is that it promotes maintenance. After all, an object is an independent unit of a program. More specifically, a well-designed object exhibits conceptual independence, otherwise known as encapsulation (Section 6.4). Every aspect of the product that relates to the portion of the real world modeled by that object is localized to the object itself. In addition, objects exhibit physical independence; information hiding is employed to ensure that implementation details are not visible outside that object (Section 6.6). The only form of communication permitted is the sending of a message to the object to carry out a specific method.

As a consequence, the argument goes, it will be easy to maintain an object for two reasons. First, conceptual independence means it will be easy to determine which part of a product must be changed in order to achieve a specific maintenance goal, be it enhancement or corrective maintenance. Second, information hiding ensures that a change made to an object will have no impact outside that object, and hence the number of regression faults will be greatly reduced.

In practice, however, the situation is not quite this idyllic. In fact, there are three obstacles that are specific to the maintenance of object-oriented software. One of the problems can be solved through use of appropriate CASE tools, but the others are less tractable. First, consider the Java class hierarchy shown in Figure 15.2. Method **displayNode** is defined in class **UndirectedTree**,

```
class UndirectedTree
{
  ...
  void displayNode (Node a);
  ...
} // class UndirectedTree

class DirectedTree extends UndirectedTree
{
  ...
} // class DirectedTree

class RootedTree extends DirectedTree
{
  ...
  void displayNode (Node a);
  ...
} // class RootedTree

class BinaryTree extends RootedTree
{
  ...
} // class BinaryTree

class BalancedBinaryTree extends BinaryTree
{
  Node      hhh;
  displayNode (hhh);
} // class BalancedBinaryTree
```

Figure 15.2 Class hierarchy.

inherited by class **DirectedTree**, and then redefined in class **RootedTree**. It is this redefined version that is inherited by class **BinaryTree** and class **BalancedBinaryTree** and is utilized in class **BalancedBinaryTree**. Thus, a maintenance programmer has to study the complete inheritance hierarchy to understand class **BalancedBinaryTree**.

Worse, the hierarchy may not be displayed in the linear fashion of Figure 15.2, but will generally be spread over the entire product. Thus, in order to understand what displayNode does in class **BalancedBinaryTree**, the maintenance programmer may have to peruse a major proportion of the product. This is a far cry from the "independent" object described at the beginning of this section.

The solution to this problem is straightforward, namely, the use of an appropriate CASE tool. Just as a Java compiler can resolve precisely the version of displayNode within instances of class **BalancedBinaryTree**, so a programming workbench can provide a "flattened" version of a class, that is, a definition of the class with all features inherited directly or indirectly appearing explicitly, with any renaming or redefinition incorporated. Thus, the flattened form of class **BalancedBinaryTree** of Figure 15.2 includes the definition of displayNode from class **RootedTree**. CASE tools for flattening are not restricted to Java. For example, Eiffel incorporates the command **flat** for this purpose [Meyer, 1990].

The second obstacle to the maintenance of a product implemented using an object-oriented language is less easy to solve. It arises as a consequence of polymorphism and dynamic binding; these concepts were explained in Section 6.8. An example was given in that section, namely, a base class named **FileClass**, together with three subclasses, namely, **DiskFileClass**, **TapeFileClass**, and **DisketteFileClass**. This is shown in Figure 6.30, reproduced here for convenience as Figure 15.3. In base class **FileClass**, a dummy (**virtual**) method open is declared. Then, a specific implementation of the method appears in each of the three subclasses; each of the methods is given the identical name, that is, open, as shown in Figure 15.3(b). Suppose that myFile is declared to be an object, an instance of **FileClass**, and that the code to be maintained contains the message myFile.open (). As a consequence of polymorphism and dynamic binding, at run-time myFile could be a member of any of the three derived classes of **FileClass**, that is a disk file, a tape file, or a diskette file. Once the run-time system has determined in which derived class it is, the appropriate version of open is invoked.

This can have adverse consequences for maintenance. If a maintenance programmer encounters the call myFile.open () in the code then, in order to understand that part of the product, he or she has to consider what would happen if myFile were an instance of each of the three subclasses. A CASE tool cannot help here because, in general, there is no way to resolve dynamic binding issues using static methods. The only way to determine which of a number of dynamic bindings actually occurs in a particular set of circumstances is to trace through the code, either by running it on a computer or tracing through it manually. Polymorphism and dynamic binding are indeed extremely powerful aspects

tools that assist by creating visual displays of the structure of the product include Battlemap, Teamwork, and Bachman Reengineering Product Set.

Maintenance is difficult and frustrating. The very least that management can do is to provide the maintenance team with the tools that are needed for efficient and effective product maintenance.

15.10 METRICS FOR THE MAINTENANCE PHASE

The activities of the maintenance phase are essentially specification, design, implementation, integration, testing, and documentation. Thus the metrics that measure these activities are equally applicable to the maintenance phase. For example, the complexity metrics of Section 13.8.2 are relevant to maintenance in that a module with high complexity is a likely candidate for inducing a regression fault. Particular care must therefore be taken in modifying such a module.

In addition, metrics specific to the maintenance phase include measures relating to software fault reports, such as the total number of faults reported, as well as classifications of those faults by severity and by fault type. In addition, information regarding the current status of the fault reports is needed. For example, there is a considerable difference between having 13 critical faults reported and fixed during 1999 and having only 3 critical faults reported during that year but with none of them fixed.

15.11 OSBERT OGLESBY CASE STUDY: MAINTENANCE

A major challenge currently facing the information technology industry is that, unless corrective action is taken, many software products will fail on January 1, 2000. In the 1960s, when computers first started to be used on a widespread basis, hardware was far more expensive than it is today. As a result, the vast majority of software of that vintage represented a date using only the last two digits for a year; the leading 19 was understood. The problem with this scheme is that the year 00 is interpreted as 1900, not 2000.

When hardware became cheaper in the 1970s and 1980s, few managers saw any point in spending large sums of money rewriting existing software with 4-digit dates. After all, by the time the year 2000 arrived, it would be someone else's problem. As a result, legacy software remained year-2000 noncompliant. Now that the third millennium is imminent, organizations are being forced to work against the clock to fix their software; there is no way to postpone the looming deadline.

The Osbert Oglesby product has been developed as specified in Section 10.14 or Section 11.9. Osbert now notices that, as required, dates of sale, dates of purchase, and auction dates are in the format mm/dd/yy. The product therefore suffers from what has been termed the *millennium bug* or *Y2K problem*, and will have to be fixed before January 01, 2000. In addition, the algorithm for computing the price of a masterwork will break down when applied to a 21st century masterwork. These changes will have to be made before the end of 1999; they are left as an exercise (Problem 15.11).

******

The Third Edition of this book concluded with a Just in Case You Wanted to Know box that described possible future directions for software engineering. It was suggested that, in the 21st century, formal techniques might attain widespread acceptance, or that software might be built by reusing hundreds of standard "software chips." In this edition, the final Just in Case You Wanted to Know box below goes back into the past.

CHAPTER REVIEW

Maintenance is an important and challenging software activity (Sections 15.1 and 15.2). This is illustrated by means of the case study of Section 15.3. Issues relating to the management of maintenance are described (Section 15.4), including the problem of repeated maintenance (Section 15.4.4). The maintenance of object-oriented software is discussed in Section 15.5. The skills that a maintenance programmer needs are the same as those of a developer; the difference is that a developer can specialize in one aspect of the software process, whereas the maintainer must be an expert in all aspects of software production (Section 15.6). A description of reverse engineering is given in Section 15.7. Next follows a description of testing during the maintenance phase (Section 15.8) and CASE tools for maintenance (Section 15.9). Finally, metrics for the maintenance phase are discussed in Section 15.10.

JUST IN CASE YOU WANTED TO KNOW

In his *Meditations* (Book Three, Entry 11), the Roman Emperor Marcus Aurelius (121–180) wrote:

> "When an object presents itself to your perception, make a mental definition or at least an outline of it, so as to discern its essential character, to pierce beyond its separate attributes to a distinct view of the naked whole, and to identify for yourself both the object itself and the elements of which it is composed, and into which it will again be resolved."

It is hard to come up with a better concise description of object-oriented analysis than the above sentence, written more than 1800 years ago by Marcus Aurelius.

FOR FURTHER READING

Sources of information on maintenance in general include [Lientz and Swanson, 1980], [Glass and Noiseux, 1981], [Babich, 1986], and [Parikh, 1988]. [Schneidewind, 1987] is an excellent overview of the subject. [Basili, 1990] presents an interesting view of maintenance as a reuse process.

Ways of reducing the cost of maintenance are described in [Guimaraes, 1983]. The impact of the use of objects on maintenance is described in [Henry and Humphrey, 1990] and [Mancl and Havanas, 1990]. Useful material on maintenance can be found in [Longstreet, 1990]. Regression testing is analyzed in [Rothermel and Harrold, 1996]; predicting its cost-effectiveness is described in [Rosenblum and Weyuker, 1997]. Planning of reengineering is covered in [Sneed, 1995], one of the many articles on reengineering in the January 1995 issue of *IEEE Software*. Costs and benefits of reengineering are discussed in [Adolph, 1996]. [Charette, Adams, and White, 1997] describes risk management within the framework of maintenance. [von Mayrhauser and Vana, 1997] describes various mechanisms of program comprehension for maintenance of large-scale products. The proceedings of the annual Conference on Software Maintenance are a broadly based source of information on all aspects of maintenance.

The maintenance of object-oriented products is described in [Lejter, Meyers, and Reiss, 1992] and [Wilde, Matthews, and Huitt, 1993]. The use of metrics within the context of maintainability is discussed in [Banker, Datar, Kemerer, and Zwieg, 1993], [Coleman, Ash, Lowther, and Oman, 1994], and [Henry, Henry, Kafura, and Matheson, 1994].

Papers on software maintenance appear in the December 1992 issue of *IEEE Transactions on Software Engineering*, and the May 1994 issue of *Communications of the ACM*.

PROBLEMS

15.1 Why do you think that the mistake is frequently made of considering software maintenance to be inferior to software development?

15.2 Consider a product that determines whether a computer is virus-free. Describe why such a product is likely to have multiple variations of many of its modules. What are the implications for maintenance? How can the resulting problems be solved?

15.3 Repeat Problem 15.2 for the automated library circulation system of Problem 7.7.

15.4 Repeat Problem 15.2 for the product of Problem 7.8 that checks whether a bank statement is correct.

15.5 Repeat Problem 15.2 for the automated teller machine (ATM) of Problem 7.9.

15.6 You are the manager in charge of maintenance in a large software organization. What qualities do you look for when hiring new employees?

15.7 What are the implications of maintenance for a one-person software production organization?

15.8 You have been asked to build a computerized fault report file. What sort of data would you store in the file? What sort of queries could be answered by your tool? What sort of queries could *not* be answered by your tool?

15.9 You receive a memo from the vice-president for software maintenance of Olde Fashioned Software Corporation (Problem 14.6) pointing out that for the foreseeable future Olde Fashioned will have to maintain tens of millions of lines of COBOL code and asking your advice with regard to CASE tools for such maintenance. What do you reply?

15.10 (Term Project) Suppose that the Air Gourmet product has been developed as specified in Appendix A. Now Air Gourmet wishes to use four digits for flight numbers. What changes need to be made to the product?

15.11 (Case Study) Correct the Java implementation of Section 14.13 so that it is year-2000 compliant.

15.12 (Case Study) Improve the aesthetic appearance of all the reports in the Java implementation of Section 14.13 by adjusting the alignment of the various components.

15.13 (Case Study) Replace the menu-driven input routines in the Java implementation of Section 14.13 with a graphical user interface (GUI).

15.14 (Readings in Software Engineering) Your instructor will distribute copies of [Charette, Adams, and White, 1997]. Do you agree with their view of the importance of risk management within the maintenance phase? Give reasons for your answer.

REFERENCES

[Adolph, 1996] W. S. ADOLPH, "Cash Cow in the Tar Pit: Reengineering a Legacy System," *IEEE Software* **13** (May 1996), pp. 41–47.

[Babich, 1986] W. A. BABICH, *Software Configuration Management: Coordination for Team Productivity*, Addison-Wesley, Reading, MA, 1986.

[Banker, Datar, Kemerer, and Zwieg, 1993] R. D. BANKER, S. M. DATAR, C. F. KEMERER, AND D. ZWIEG, "Software Complexity and Maintenance Costs," *Communications of the ACM* **36** (November 1993), pp. 81–94.

[Basili, 1990] V. R. BASILI, "Viewing Maintenance as Reuse-Oriented Software Development," *IEEE Software* **7** (January 1990), pp. 19–25.

[Charette, Adams, and White, 1997] R. N. CHARETTE, K. MACG. ADAMS, AND M. B. WHITE, "Managing Risk in Software Maintenance," *IEEE Software* **14** (May/June, 1997), pp. 43–50.

[Coleman, Ash, Lowther, and Oman, 1994] D. COLEMAN, D. ASH, B. LOWTHER, AND P. OMAN, "Using Metrics to Evaluate Software System Maintainability," *IEEE Computer* **27** (August 1994), pp. 44–49.

[Glass and Noiseux, 1981] R. L. GLASS AND R. A. NOISEUX, *Software Maintenance Guidebook*, Prentice Hall, Englewood Cliffs, NJ, 1981.

[Guimaraes, 1983] T. GUIMARAES, "Managing Application Program Maintenance Expenditures," *Communications of the ACM* **26** (October 1983), pp. 739–46.

[Henry and Humphrey, 1990] S. M. HENRY AND M. HUMPHREY, "A Controlled Experiment to Evaluate Maintainability of Object-Oriented Software," *Proceedings of the IEEE Conference on Software Maintenance,* San Diego, CA, November 1990, pp. 258–65.

[Henry, Henry, Kafura, and Matheson, 1994] J. HENRY, S. HENRY, D. KAFURA, AND L. MATHESON, "Improving Software Maintenance at Martin Marietta," *IEEE Software* **11** (July 1994), pp. 67–75.

[Lientz and Swanson, 1980] B. P. LIENTZ AND E. B. SWANSON, *Software Maintenance Management: A Study of the Maintenance of Computer Applications Software in 487 Data Processing Organizations,* Addison-Wesley, Reading, MA, 1980.

[Lientz, Swanson, and Tompkins, 1978] B. P. LIENTZ, E. B. SWANSON, AND G. E. TOMPKINS, "Characteristics of Application Software Maintenance," *Communications of the ACM* **21** (June 1978), pp. 466–71.

[Lejter, Meyers, and Reiss, 1992] M. LEJTER, S. MEYERS, AND S. P. REISS, "Support for Maintaining Object-Oriented Programs," *IEEE Transactions on Software Engineering* **18** (December 1992), pp. 1045–52.

[Longstreet, 1990] D. H. LONGSTREET (Editor), *Software Maintenance and Computers*, IEEE Computer Society Press, Los Alamitos, CA, 1990.

[Loukides and Oram, 1997] M. K. LOUKIDES AND A. ORAM, *Programming with GNU Software*, O'Reilly and Associates, Sebastopol, CA, 1997.

[Mancl and Havanas, 1990] D. MANCL AND W. HAVANAS, "A Study of the Impact of C++ on Software Maintenance," *Proceedings of the IEEE Conference on Software Maintenance,* San Diego, CA, November 1990, pp. 63–69.

[Meyer, 1990] B. MEYER, "Lessons from the Design of the Eiffel Libraries," *Communications of the ACM* **33** (September 1990), pp. 68–88.

[Parikh, 1988] G. PARIKH (Editor), *Techniques of Program and System Maintenance*, Second Edition, QED Information Services, Wellesley, MA, 1988.

[Rochkind, 1975] M. J. ROCHKIND, "The Source Code Control System," *IEEE Transactions on Software Engineering* **SE-1** (October 1975), pp. 255–65.

[Rosenblum and Weyuker, 1997] D. S. ROSENBLUM AND E. J. WEYUKER, "Using Coverage Information to Predict the Cost-Effectiveness of Regression Testing Strategies," *IEEE Transactions on Software Engineering* **23** (March 1997), pp. 146–56.

[Rothermel and Harrold, 1996] G. ROTHERMEL AND M. J. HARROLD, "Analyzing Regression Test Selection Techniques," *IEEE Transactions on Software Engineering* **22** (August 1996), pp. 529–51.

[Schneidewind, 1987] N. F. SCHNEIDEWIND, "The State of Software Maintenance," *IEEE Transactions on Software Engineering* **SE-13** (March 1987), pp. 303–10.

[Sneed, 1995] H. M. SNEED, "Planning the Reengineering of Legacy Systems," *IEEE Software* **12** (January 1995), pp. 24–34.

[Tichy, 1985] W. F. TICHY, "RCS—A System for Version Control," *Software—Practice and Experience* **15** (July 1985), pp. 637–54.

[von Mayrhauser and Vana, 1997] A. VON MAYRHAUSER AND A. M. VANA, "Identification of Dynamic Comprehension Processes during Large Scale Maintenance," *IEEE Transactions on Software Engineering* **22** (June 1996), pp. 424–37.

[Wilde, Matthews, and Huitt, 1993] N. WILDE, P. MATTHEWS, AND R. HUITT, "Maintaining Object-Oriented Software," *IEEE Software* **10** (January 1993), pp. 75–80.

APPENDIX

A

AIR GOURMET

Many airline passengers have dietary requirements, and the majority of airlines will endeavor to provide food that meets their needs. For example, given sufficient notice, most airlines will serve vegetarian, vegan, sea food, Kosher, or Halaal meals, as well as diabetic, low-fat, low-cholesterol, low-protein, low-calorie, or low-sodium meals. A child's meal can almost always be ordered. Some airlines will supply lactose-free meals. Flight attendants are provided with a list of the passengers who have requested *special meals* and their seat numbers; the special meals are then served at the same time as the regular meals.

Like almost all business decisions, there is a trade-off involved in providing these special meals. The benefits include increased passenger volume and passenger goodwill; after all, if an airline does not provide special meals it will lose passengers to airlines that provide them. On the other hand, there are significant costs involved in providing special meals. First, the ingredients that go into special meals can cost more than those of regular meals. Second, because relatively few special meals are served, there can be no savings via bulk purchases. Third, almost no airlines prepare special meals in their own kitchens. Instead, they contract with outside caterers to provide special meals, which increases the cost still further. Fourth, each special meal has to be transported from a central kitchen to the airport where the relevant flight originates; there are significant handling and paperwork costs involved in this process. Fifth, it frequently happens that a special meal is not consumed by its intended recipient. For example, if a passenger changes his or her flight plans at the last minute or if a connecting flight arrives late, the meal will have been loaded on the original flight for which it was ordered. Sixth, even if a special meal has been ordered well in advance, due to human error it is sometimes not loaded aboard the correct aircraft. Overall, however, most airlines have found that the benefits of providing special meals far outweigh the costs.

Air Gourmet has always prided itself on the high standard of the food it serves in the air, even on those shorter flights where its competitors currently provide at most just a small bag of tasteless peanuts. Up to now, Air Gourmet's profitability has been assured by a steady supply of air travelers willing to pay a slightly higher air fare in order to enjoy gourmet fare in the air. Lately, however, Air Gourmet's profit margins have been shrinking, and its executives are looking for ways to cut expenses. The high cost of providing special meals, combined with anecdotal evidence suggesting that only a small fraction of special meals reach the passengers who ordered them, have made special meals a tempting target for the Air Gourmet bean counters.

Before taking any action, however, Air Gourmet management wants to obtain reliable data concerning the success or failure of the special meals program. Also, because the special meals are provided by outside caterers, some Air Gourmet executives suspect that these special meals may not meet the high standards of the regular Air Gourmet food that is subject to quality control in the Air Gourmet kitchens. A passenger satisfaction survey must therefore be conducted to determine the perceived quality of special meals. Also, Air Gourmet executives need to know what percentage of special meals are not loaded on the correct aircraft.

As with most other airlines that serve special meals, 24 hours before each scheduled flight the database of the Air Gourmet reservation system is scanned for special meal requests. Reports are generated so that the caterers can ensure that the special meals are transported to the relevant aircraft on time. Then, just after each takeoff a report for the flight attendants is printed onboard the aircraft. This report contains the reservation identifier, name, and seat number of each passenger onboard that flight who has ordered a special meal, and the type of that meal. (Passengers are required to show some form of identification before boarding a flight. Thus, the flight computer has the information needed to print this report.)

In order to obtain the information requested by management regarding special meals, certain modifications will have to be made to the Air Gourmet software. First, each time a special meal is ordered, the following information must be recorded: the reservation identifier; flight number, date, and time; passenger name and address; and type of special meal ordered. This information will be used by the new software that is to be written in order to analyze the special meals data. Second, the list of special meals printed onboard the aircraft will include a column of squares. Flight attendants will shade in the square if the relevant meal has been loaded onboard the aircraft. After the flight, the list will be scanned. If the square has been shaded, a postcard bearing the reservation identifier will be mailed to the passenger asking him or her to rate the meal on a scale of 1 (unacceptable) through 5 (superlative). When the postcard is returned, it, too, will be scanned and the reservation identifier and response recorded for later reporting.

There are thus three separate sequential stages for the special meals analysis software: the additional records generated 24 hours before departure, the scanned lists, and the scanned postcards. The formats of the recorded data elements are as follows [optional fields are in brackets]:

Reservation identifier (6 uppercase letters)

Flight number (3 digits, right justified and zero filled)

Flight date (9 characters: 2-digit day, 3-uppercase-letter month, 4-digit year)

Seat number (3 digits, right justified and zero filled, followed by an uppercase letter)

Passenger name:

- First name (up to 15 characters)
- [Middle initial (1 character)]
- Last name (up to 15 characters)
- [Suffix (up to 5 characters)]

Passenger address:

First line of address (up to 25 characters)

[Second line of address (up to 25 characters)]

City (up to 14 characters)

[State, province, or region (up to 14 characters)]

[Postal code (up to 10 letters, digits, hyphens, and blanks)]

Country (up to 20 characters)

Special meal type (child, diabetic, Halaal, Kosher, lactose free, low calorie, low cholesterol, low fat, low protein, low sodium, sea food, vegan, vegetarian)

Was the passenger onboard the flight? (1 character)

Was the special meal loaded on the plane? (1 character)

Perceived meal quality (1 through 5)

The new software must input information from the database and then allow the user to select from the following four reports. For each report, the start date and end date for that report must be obtained from the user.

1. For each special meal type and for the special meals program as a whole:

   Percentage of special meals that were loaded as specified;

   Percentage of passengers who were onboard the flight for which they ordered a special meal;

   Percentage of passengers who were onboard the flight for which they ordered a special meal but whose meal was not loaded.

The Customer Relations Department requires the following reports:

2. The name and address of every passenger whose special meal was not loaded more than once within the time period of the report and the dates of occurrence.
3. The name and address of every passenger who felt that the quality of his or her special meal was less than superlative (5 on the scale), the date of occurrence, and the meal type.

The outside caterer who provides the low-sodium meals has her own quality control program. To assist her, the following report is also required:

4. For each low-sodium meal served, the flight number and date, and perceived meal quality.

Air Gourmet management is greatly concerned about the risks of modifying their existing computer system to incorporate this additional functionality. Also, management is reluctant to purchase the various scanners until the new product is complete. Accordingly, they would like a keyboard-driven, stand-alone product to be constructed that will enter reservations; check in passengers; scan lists of special meals printed onboard (this is to be simulated by keyboard input); scan postcards (also keyboard input); and produce the various reports.

APPENDIX

B

SOFTWARE ENGINEERING RESOURCES

There are two good ways to get more information on software engineering topics, namely by reading journals and conference proceedings, and via the Internet and World Wide Web.

There are journals dedicated exclusively to software engineering, such as *IEEE Transactions on Software Engineering*. There are also journals of a more general nature, such as *Communications of the ACM*, in which significant articles on software engineering are published. For reasons of space, only a selection of journals of both classes appears below. The journals have been chosen on a subjective basis, namely, those which the author has found to be the most useful.

ACM Computing Surveys
ACM Guide to the Computing Literature
ACM SIGAda Ada Letters
ACM SIGCHI Bulletin
ACM SIGPLAN Notices
ACM SIGSOFT Software Engineering Notes
ACM Transactions on Computer Systems
ACM Transactions on Programming Languages and Systems
ACM Transactions on Software Engineering and Methodology
Communications of the ACM
Computer Journal
Computing Reviews
IBM Journal of Research and Development
IBM Systems Journal
IEEE Computer
IEEE Software
IEEE Transactions on Computers

IEEE Transactions on Software Engineering
Journal of Object-Oriented Programming
Journal of Software Maintenance: Research and Practice
Journal of Systems and Software
Software Engineering Journal
Software—Practice and Experience

In addition, there are many conferences whose proceedings contain important articles on software engineering topics. Again, a subjective selection appears below. Most of the conferences are commonly referred to by their acronym or name of sponsoring organization; these appear in parentheses.

ACM SIGPLAN Annual Conference (SIGPLAN)
ACM SIGSOFT Symposium on the Foundations of Software Engineering (FSE)
Conference on Object-Oriented Programming Systems, Languages, and Applications (OOPSLA)
Conference on Software Maintenance (CSM)
Human Factors in Computing Systems (CHI)
International Computer Software and Applications Conference (COMPSAC)
International Conference on Software Engineering (ICSE)
International Conference on Software Reuse (ICSR)
International Software Architecture Workshop (ISAW)
International Software Process Workshop (ISP)
International Symposium on Software Testing and Analysis (ISSTA)
International Workshop on Software Configuration Management (SCM)
International Workshop on Software Specification and Design (IWSSD)

The Internet is another valuable source of information on software engineering. With regard to Usenet newsgroups, the following two have been consistently useful to the author:

comp.object
comp.software-eng

Other newsgroups that sometimes have items that the author finds relevant include the following:

comp.lang.ada
comp.lang.c++.moderated
comp.lang.java.programming
comp.risk
comp.software.config-mgmt

comp.software.measurement
comp.software.testing
comp.specification
comp.specification.z

New newsgroups are continually being formed, so the reader should scan the list of available groups to see if something worthwhile has been formed since the time of writing.

In addition, the World Wide Web Virtual Library for Software Engineering can be found at ricis.cl.uh.edu/virt-lib/soft-eng.html. An especially valuable source is the Software Engineering Institute at Carnegie-Mellon University, www.sei.cmu.edu.

APPENDIX

C

OSBERT OGLESBY CASE STUDY: RAPID PROTOTYPE

The rapid prototype for the Osbert Oglesby case study is available on the World Wide Web at www.mhhe.com/engcs/compsci/schach.

APPENDIX

D

OSBERT OGLESBY CASE STUDY: STRUCTURED SYSTEMS ANALYSIS

Step 1. Draw the Data Flow Diagram: See Figure 10.28.

Step 2. Decide What Sections to Computerize and How: Because the client will be using the product on a portable computer in order to decide on prospective purchases at remote sites, the complete product should be computerized and operate online.

Step 3. Put in the Details of the Data Flows:

buy painting information
- first name of artist (21 characters)
- last name of artist (21 characters)
- title (41 characters)
- date of work (9 characters)
- medium (10 characters)
- subject (10 characters)
- height (4 + 2 digits)
- width (4 + 2 digits)
- classification (11 characters)

new painting information
- buy painting information (see above)
- date of purchase (9 characters)
- name of seller (21 characters)
- address of seller (25 characters)
- maximum purchase price (3 + 2 digits)
- actual purchase price (3 + 2 digits)

sell painting information
- first name of artist (21 characters)
- last name of artist (21 characters)
- title (41 characters)

selling information
  sell painting information (see above)
  target selling price (3 + 2 digits)
  date of sale (9 characters)
  name of buyer (21 characters)
  address of buyer (25 characters)
  actual selling price (3 + 2 digits)

painting details
  last name of artist (21 characters)
  title (41 characters)
  classification (11 characters)
  date of purchase (9 characters)
  maximum purchase price (3 + 2 digits)
  actual purchase price (3 + 2 digits)
  target selling price (3 + 2 digits)
  date of sale (9 characters)
  actual selling price (3 + 2 digits)

painting status
  status (6 characters)

reports
  painting details (see above)

report type
  type (7 characters)

Step 4. Define the Logic of the Processes:

buy

If painting already purchased, print error message,
else
  compute maximum purchase price.
  If maximum purchase price > 0
    Get purchase information.
    Add new painting to GALLERY PAINTING.

sell

Get selling information.
If painting not already purchased, print error message,
else
  add new sale information to GALLERY PAINTING.

print report

For each GALLERY PAINTING item that has been processed over the past year,
  if the item satisfies the conditions of report type, print item information.

Step 5. Define the Data Stores:

AUCTION PAINTING
- first name of artist (21 characters)
- last name of artist (21 characters)
- title (41 characters)
- date of work (9 characters)
- medium (10 characters)
- subject (10 characters)
- height (4 + 2 digits)
- width (4 + 2 digits)
- auction date (9 characters)
- auction price (3 + 2 digits)

FASHIONABILITY
- first name of artist (21 characters)
- last name of artist (21 characters)
- coefficient (4 + 2 digits)

GALLERY PAINTING
- first name of artist (21 characters)
- last name of artist (21 characters)
- title (41 characters)
- date of work (9 characters)
- medium (10 characters)
- subject (10 characters)
- height (4 + 2 digits)
- width (4 + 2 digits)
- classification (11 characters)
- date of purchase (9 characters)
- name of seller (21 characters)
- address of seller (25 characters)
- maximum purchase price (3 + 2 digits)
- actual purchase price (3 + 2 digits)
- target selling price (3 + 2 digits)
- date of sale (9 characters)
- name of buyer (21 characters)
- address of buyer (25 characters)
- actual selling price (3 + 2 digits)

All files are sequential, and hence there is no DIAD.

Step 6. Define the Physical Resources:

AUCTION PAINTING
- Sequential file
- Stored on disk

FASHIONABILITY
- Sequential file
- Stored on disk

GALLERY PAINTING
  Sequential file
  Stored on disk

Step 7. Determine the Input/Output Specifications: Input screens will be designed for the following processes:

get gallery description, buy painting, sell painting, update fashionability coefficient

The following reports will be displayed:

list of bought paintings, list of sold paintings, current fashion trends

The screens and reports of the rapid prototype will be used as a basis for the above.

Step 8. Perform Sizing: Approximately 4 megabytes of storage are needed for the software. Each gallery painting item will require approximately 500 bytes of storage. Thus, approximately 0.5 megabytes of secondary storage are needed for every 1000 paintings stored in on the hard disk.

Step 9. Determine the Hardware Requirements:

Portable computer with hard disk, running UNIX.

Zip drive for backup.

Laser printer for printing reports.

Modem for downloading auction data.

APPENDIX

E

Osbert Oglesby Case Study: Object-Oriented Analysis

The complete object-oriented analysis for the Osbert Oglesby case study appears in Section 11.9.

APPENDIX F

OSBERT OGLESBY CASE STUDY: SOFTWARE PROJECT MANAGEMENT PLAN

The solution presented here is an SPMP for development of the Osbert Oglesby product by a small software organization consisting of three individuals, namely Pat, the owner of the company, and two software engineers, Rob and Mary.

1. Introduction.

1.1. Project Overview. The objective of this project is to develop a software product that will assist Osbert Oglesby, Art Dealer (OOAD) in making decisions regarding the purchase of paintings to be displayed and sold in his gallery. The product will allow the client to buy and sell masterpieces, masterworks, and other paintings. The product will perform the required calculations and record-keeping on these paintings, and produce reports listing bought paintings, sold paintings, and current fashion trends.

The time, budget, and personnel requirements are as follows:

Requirements phase (1 week, two team members, $1690)

Object-oriented analysis phase (1 week, two team members, $1690)

Planning phase (1 week, two team members, $1690)

Design phase (2 weeks, two team members, $3380)

Implementation phase (3 weeks, three team members, $7605)

Integration phase (2 weeks, three team members, $5070)

[*The implementation and integration phases will be combined, as described in Chapter 14.*]

The total development time is 10 weeks and the total internal cost is $21,125.

1.2. Project Deliverables. The complete source code with user and operations manuals will be delivered 10 weeks after the project commences. The client will be responsible for acquiring the recommended hardware and system software by the time the product is delivered.

1.3. Evolution of the SPMP. All changes in the SPMP must be agreed to by Pat before they are implemented. All changes should be documented in order to keep the SPMP correct and up to date.

1.4. Reference materials. Our company coding, documentation, and testing standards.

1.5. Definitions and Acronyms.

OOAD—Osbert Oglesby, Art Dealer; Mr. Oglesby is our client.
SPMP—software project management plan.

2. Project Organization.

2.1. Process Model. The software life-cycle model to be used is the waterfall model with rapid prototyping. The specifications were written by Rob and Mary, and verified by the client at meetings between Pat and the client. The design task will be shared between Rob and Mary, and Pat will check the overall design. Coding will also be performed by Rob and Mary. Rob and Mary will test each other's code and Pat will conduct integration testing. Extensive testing will then be performed by all three. The time required for all these activities is outlined in the Introduction.

2.2. Organizational Structure. The development team consists of Pat (owner), Rob, and Mary (software engineers).

2.3. Organizational Boundaries and Interfaces. All the work on this project will be performed by Pat, Rob, and Mary. Pat will meet weekly with the client to report progress and discuss possible changes and modifications. Any major changes which will affect the milestones or the budget will have to be approved by Pat, and documented. There will be no outside SQA personnel involved. The benefits of having someone other than the individual who carried out the development task do the testing will be accomplished by each person testing another person's work products.

2.4. Project Responsibilities. Each member is responsible for the quality of the module he or she codes. Pat will handle the class definitions and report modules, Rob will write the modules to handle bought paintings, and Mary will code the modules that handle sold paintings. Pat will oversee module integration and overall quality of the product and will liaise with the client.

3. Managerial Process.

3.1. Managerial Objectives and Priorities. The overall objective is to deliver a fault-free product on time and within budget. If this cannot be achieved, priority is given to completing the routines needed to buy paintings; reports have the lowest priority.

The three team members will work separately on their assigned modules. Pat's role will be to monitor the daily progress of the other two, oversee integration, be responsible for overall quality, and interact with the client. Team members will meet at the end of each day and discuss problems and progress. Formal meetings with the client will be held at the end of each week to report progress and determine if any changes need to be made. Pat will ensure that schedule and budget requirements are met. Risk management will also be Pat's responsibility.

Minimizing faults and maximizing user-friendliness will be Pat's priorities. Pat is also responsible for all documentation and has to ensure that it is up to date.

3.2. Assumptions, Dependencies and Constraints. Acceptance criteria are listed in the specification document. In addition:

The deadline must be met.

The budget constraints must be met.

The product must be reliable.

The architecture must be open so that additional modules may be added later.

The product must conform to the client's hardware.

The product must be user-friendly.

3.3. Risk Management. The risk factors and the tracking mechanisms are as follows:

There is no existing software with which the new product can be compared. Accordingly, it will not be possible to run the product in parallel with an existing one. Therefore, the product should be subjected to extensive testing.

The client is assumed to be inexperienced with computers. Therefore, special attention should be paid to the specification phase and communication with the client. The product has to be made as user-friendly as possible.

There is always the possibility of a major design fault, so extensive testing will be performed during the design phase. Also, each of the team members will initially test his or her own code and then test the code of another member. Pat will be responsible for integration testing.

The product must meet the specified storage requirements and response times. This should not be a major problem because of the small size of the product, but it will be monitored by Pat throughout development.

There is a slim chance of hardware failure, in which case another machine will be leased. If there is a fault in the compiler, it will be replaced. These are covered in the warranties received from the hardware and compiler suppliers.

3.4. Monitoring and Controlling Mechanisms. Pat will be responsible for all review and auditing. This will be accomplished through daily meetings with the team members. At each meeting, Rob and Mary will present the day's progress and problems. Pat will determine whether they are progressing as expected, and whether they are following the specifications and the SPMP. Any major problems faced by the team members will immediately be reported to Pat.

3.5. Staffing Plan. Pat is needed for the entire 10 weeks, for the first 5 weeks only in a managerial capacity and the second 5 weeks as both manager and programmer. Rob and Mary are needed for the entire 10 weeks.

4. Technical Process.

4.1. Methods, Tools, and Techniques. The waterfall model with rapid prototyping will be used. The rapid prototype was written in Java. The specifications were drawn up using object-oriented analysis. Object-oriented design will be used. Source code will be written in Java and run under UNIX on a personal computer. Documentation and coding will be performed in accordance with company standards.

4.2. Software Documentation. Software documentation will follow company standards. Reviews of documentation will be conducted by Pat at the completion of each phase of the process model. This will ensure that all the documentation for a particular phase has been completed by the time the next phase is started.

4.3. Project Support Functions. Quality assurance will be performed as described in section 2.1.

5. Work Packages, Schedule, and Budget.

5.1. Work Packages. The items involved, masterpieces, masterworks, and other types of paintings, are to be bought and sold. More specifically, routines are needed to store information about bought and sold paintings, while assisting the client in arriving at a maximum purchase price and a target selling price for each type of painting. In addition, reports listing bought paintings, sold paintings, and fashion trends are to be produced. The methods for each of the classes will be created independently. The team members will be in constant communication; this should ensure that the classes are compatible.

5.2. Dependencies. As specified in the process model. Specifically, no phase will be started until the work products of the previous phase have been approved by Pat.

5.3. Resource Requirements. Three personal computers running under UNIX, together with standard UNIX tools.

5.4. Budget and Resource Allocation. The budget for each phase is as follows:

Requirements phase:	$ 1690
Object-oriented analysis phase:	1690
Planning phase:	1690
Object-oriented design phase:	3380
Implementation phase:	7605
Integration phase:	5070
Total :	$21,125

5.5. Schedule.

Week 1:	Met with client, determined requirements. Produced rapid prototype. Client and users approved rapid prototype.
Week 2:	Wrote specification document. Inspected specification document, approved by client.
Week 3:	Produced SPMP, inspected SPMP.
Weeks 4, 5:	Object-oriented design document, object-oriented design inspection, detailed design document, detailed design inspection.
Weeks 6, 7, 8:	Implementation and inspection of each module, module testing and documentation.
Weeks 9, 10:	Integration of each module, inspection of individual modules, product testing, documentation check.

Additional Components.

Security: A password will be needed to use the product.

Training: Training will be performed by Pat at time of delivery. Because the product is straightforward to use, 1 day is sufficient for training. Pat will answer questions at no cost for the first year of use.

Product Maintenance: Corrective maintenance will be performed by the team at no cost for a period of 12 months. A separate contract will be drawn up regarding enhancement.

APPENDIX

G

OSBERT OGLESBY CASE STUDY: DESIGN

The architectural (object-oriented) design appears in Section 12.13, together with a small sample of the detailed design.

The complete detailed design is given below. To assist the reader, the methods of the Osbert Oglesby product are listed alphabetically by class name and by method name within class name. There are 37 methods in all, one of which is abstract.

Class name	AuctionedPaintingClass
Method name	readAuctionData
Modifiers, type	**public void**
Arguments	RandomAccessFile
Error messages	none
Files accessed	none
Files changed	none
Methods called	none
Narrative	Reads an auction object from the file specified as the input parameter.

Class name	FashionabilityClass
Method name	addNewFash
Modifiers, type	**public void**
Arguments	none
Error messages	none
Files accessed	fash.dat, fash.tmp
Files changed	fash.dat, fash.tmp
Methods called	getFashDescription, readFash, writeFash
Narrative	Inserts a fashion object in alphabetical order (by artist name) into file fash.tmp. File fash.dat is then deleted, and file fash.tmp is renamed fash.dat.

Class name	FashionabilityClass
Method name	getFashDescription
Modifiers, type	**public void**
Arguments	none
Error messages	none
Files accessed	none
Files changed	none
Methods called	none
Narrative	Retrieves fashionability description information (i.e., attributes firstName, lastName, coefficient).

Class name	FashionabilityClass
Method name	readFash
Modifiers, type	**public void**
Arguments	RandomAccessFile
Error messages	none
Files accessed	none
Files changed	none
Methods called	none
Narrative	Reads a fashion object from the file specified as the input parameter.

Class name	FashionabilityClass
Method name	writeFash
Modifiers, type	**public void**
Arguments	RandomAccessFile
Error messages	none
Files accessed	none
Files changed	none
Methods called	none
Narrative	Writes a fashion object to the file specified as the input parameter.

Class name	GalleryPaintingClass
Method name	addNewPainting
Modifiers, type	**public void**
Arguments	none
Error messages	none
Files accessed	gallery.dat, gallery.tmp
Files changed	gallery.dat, gallery.tmp
Methods called	readBought, writeBought
Narrative	Inserts a new gallery painting in alphabetical order into gallery.tmp. File gallery.dat is then deleted, and file gallery.tmp is renamed gallery.dat.

Class name	GalleryPaintingClass
Method name	addNewSale
Modifiers, type	**public void**
Arguments	none
Error messages	none
Files accessed	sold.dat, sold.tmp
Files changed	sold.dat, sold.tmp
Methods called	readSold, writeSold
Narrative	Inserts a sold painting in alphabetical order into sold.tmp. File sold.dat is then deleted, and file sold.tmp is renamed to sold.dat.

Class name	GalleryPaintingClass
Method name	boughtReport
Modifiers, type	**public void**
Arguments	none
Error messages	If no paintings have been bought in the past year.
Files accessed	gallery.dat
Files changed	none
Methods called	readBought
Narrative	Produces bought report by reading gallery.dat and displaying every gallery object that has been bought during the past year.

Class name	GalleryPaintingClass
Method name	buy
Modifiers, type	**public void**
Arguments	none
Error messages	none
Files accessed	gallery.dat
Files changed	none
Methods called	getDescription, readBought, addNewPainting, determineAlgorithmPrice, getGalleryInformation
Narrative	This method first retrieves information from the user concerning the painting to be purchased. If the painting does not already exist in the gallery, the maximum buying price for the painting is given. The user is then requested to enter additional purchase information before the painting is actually inserted into the gallery via a call to addNewPainting.

Class name	GalleryPaintingClass
Method name	determineAlgorithmPrice
Modifiers, type	**protected void**
Arguments	none
Error messages	none
Files accessed	none
Files changed	none
Methods called	none
Narrative	This **abstract** method is instantiated in the subclasses MasterpieceClass, MasterworkClass, and OtherClass

Class name	GalleryPaintingClass
Method name	getGalleryInformation
Modifiers, type	**public void**
Arguments	none
Error messages	none
Files accessed	none
Files changed	none
Methods called	none
Narrative	Retrieves additional information concerning a gallery object (i.e., attributes purchaseDate, sellerName, sellerAddress, purchasePrice, targetPrice).

Class name	GalleryPaintingClass
Method name	readBought
Modifiers, type	**public void**
Arguments	RandomAccessFile
Error messages	none
Files accessed	none
Files changed	none
Methods called	none
Narrative	Reads a gallery object (which has been bought) from the file specified as the input parameter.

Class name	GalleryPaintingClass
Method name	readSold
Modifiers, type	**public void**
Arguments	RandomAccessFile
Error messages	none
Files accessed	none
Files changed	none
Methods called	none
Narrative	Reads a gallery object (which has been sold) from the file specified as the input parameter.

Class name	GalleryPaintingClass
Method name	sell
Modifiers, type	**public void**
Arguments	none
Error messages	If the painting to be sold has already been sold.
Files accessed	sold.dat, gallery.dat
Files changed	none
Methods called	readSold, readBought, addNewSale, OsbertUtilities.addArtist
Narrative	This method first retrieves information from the user concerning which gallery painting is to be sold. Then, a check is made to see if the painting exists in the gallery, and if it has already been sold. If not, the user is then requested to enter the sale information before the painting is actually inserted via a call to addNewSale. After recording a valid sale, the artist name is also added to the file containing artist names via a call to OsbertUtilities.addArtist

Class name	GalleryPaintingClass
Method name	sellReport
Modifiers, type	**public void**
Arguments	none
Error messages	If no paintings have been sold in the past year.
Files accessed	sold.dat
Files changed	none
Methods called	readSold
Narrative	Produces sold report by reading paintings from sold.dat and displaying every gallery object that has been sold over the past year.

Class name	GalleryPaintingClass
Method name	trendsReport
Modifiers, type	**public void**
Arguments	none
Error messages	If no artists qualify for this report.
Files accessed	artist.dat, sold.dat
Files changed	none
Methods called	overTarget, readSold
Narrative	Produces a fashion report by reading every artist (from artist.dat) whose paintings have been sold (from sold.dat). For each artist, all of whose works (a minimum of two) have sold higher than the target price over the past year, the artist's name and each painting sold over the past year is displayed.

Class name	GalleryPaintingClass
Method name	writeBought
Modifiers, type	**public void**
Arguments	RandomAccessFile
Error messages	none
Files accessed	none
Files changed	none
Methods called	none
Narrative	Writes a gallery object (which has been bought) to the file specified as the input parameter.

Class name	GalleryPaintingClass
Method name	writeSold
Modifiers, type	**public void**
Arguments	RandomAccessFile
Error messages	none
Files accessed	none
Files changed	none
Methods called	none
Narrative	Writes a gallery object (which has been sold) to the file specified as the input parameter.

Class name	MasterpieceClass
Method name	determineAlgorithmPrice
Modifiers, type	**public void**
Arguments	none
Error messages	none
Files accessed	auction.dat
Files changed	none
Methods called	readAuctionData
Narrative	Determines the maximum price to be offered for a masterpiece. File auction.dat is scanned for the most similar work by the artist represented by the masterpiece object. The maximum base price is the purchase price of the most similar record in auction.dat. The final maximum price is found by adding 8.5%, compounded annually, to the base price for each year since the auction sale date of the most similar auction record.

Class name	MasterworkClass
Method name	determineAlgorithmPrice
Modifiers, type	**public void**
Arguments	none
Error messages	none
Files accessed	none
Files changed	none
Methods called	MasterpieceClass.determineAlgorithmPrice
Narrative	Determines the maximum price to be offered for a masterwork. First, the maximum base price is determined as if the masterwork were a masterpiece. The final maximum price is the base price multiplied by 0.25 if the item was painted in the twentieth century. For any other century, the base price is multiplied by (20 − c) / (21 − c), where c is the century in which the masterwork was painted.

Class name	OsbertApplication
Method name	main
Modifiers, type	**public static void**
Arguments	String[]
Error messages	none
Files accessed	none
Files changed	none
Methods called	OsbertUtlities.displayMainMenu
Narrative	Drives entire product by calling OsbertUtilities.displayMainMenu to solicit the user's choice.

Class name	OsbertDate
Method name	computeLongDate
Modifiers, type	**public static long**
Arguments	**int, int, int**
Error messages	none
Files accessed	none
Files changed	none
Methods called	none
Narrative	Takes three parameters as input (day, month, year) and returns a long integer whose digits represent the date in the form mmddyy (for example, 09/25/72 would return the long integer 92572).

Class name	OsbertDate
Method name	compareTo
Modifiers, type	**public int**
Arguments	Date
Error messages	none
Files accessed	none
Files changed	none
Methods called	none
Narrative	Compares the current OsbertDate to a Java Date. Returns −1 if the current date comes before the input parameter, 0 if they are the same date, or 1 otherwise.

Class name	OsbertDate
Method name	compareTo
Modifiers, type	**public int**
Arguments	OsbertDate
Error messages	none
Files accessed	none
Files changed	none
Methods called	none
Narrative	Compares two OsbertDates. Returns −1 if the current date comes before the input parameter, 0 if they are the same date, or 1 otherwise.

Class name	OsbertDate
Method name	parse
Modifiers, type	**public static long**
Arguments	String
Error messages	none
Files accessed	none
Files changed	none
Methods called	none
Narrative	Parses an input string from the form mm/dd/yy into a long integer via a call to computeLongDate.

Class name	OsbertDate
Method name	toLongString
Modifiers, type	**public** String
Arguments	none
Error messages	none
Files accessed	none
Files changed	none
Methods called	none
Narrative	Returns a string in long form (i.e., 09/25/72 would return September 25, 1972).

Class name	OsbertDate
Method name	toString
Modifiers, type	**public** String
Arguments	none
Error messages	none
Files accessed	none
Files changed	none
Methods called	none
Narrative	Returns a string representing the date in the form mm/dd/yy. Includes a question mark at the end of the string if the date is questionable.

Class name	OsbertUtilities
Method name	addArtist
Modifiers, type	**public static void**
Arguments	String, String
Error messages	none
Files accessed	artist.dat, artist.tmp
Files changed	artist.dat, artist.tmp
Methods called	none
Narrative	Inserts an artist name (represented by the input strings) in alphabetical order into artist.tmp. File artist.dat is then deleted, and file artist.tmp is renamed artist.dat.

Class name	OsbertUtilities
Method name	clearScreen
Modifiers, type	**public static void**
Arguments	none
Error messages	none
Files accessed	none
Files changed	none
Methods called	none
Narrative	Clears the screen by emitting a sequence of carriage returns.

Class name	OsbertUtilities
Method name	displayBuyPaintingMenu
Modifiers, type	**public static void**
Arguments	none
Error messages	If an invalid choice is made.
Files accessed	none
Files changed	none
Methods called	buy, addNewFash
Narrative	Displays buy painting menu, offering the user the choice of buying a masterpiece, masterwork, or other work, or updating the fashionability coefficients. The user may also choose to return to the main menu.

Class name	OsbertUtilities
Method name	displayMainMenu
Modifiers, type	**public static void**
Arguments	none
Error messages	If an invalid choice is made.
Files accessed	none
Files changed	none
Methods called	displayBuyPaintingMenu, displayReportMenu, sell
Narrative	Displays main menu that drives the product, offering the user the choice of buying a painting, selling a painting, or producing a report. The user may also choose to quit.

Class name	OsbertUtilities
Method name	displayReportMenu
Modifiers, type	**public static void**
Arguments	none
Error messages	If an invalid choice is made.
Files accessed	none
Files changed	none
Methods called	boughtReport, sellReport, trendsReport
Narrative	Displays report menu, offering the user the choice of bought paintings report, sold paintings report, and fashion trends report. The user may also choose to return to the main menu.

Class name	OsbertUtilities
Method name	overTarget
Modifiers, type	**public static boolean**
Arguments	String, String
Error messages	none
Files accessed	sold.dat
Files changed	none
Methods called	readSold
Narrative	This method determines if an artist (represented by the input strings) has had all of his/her paintings sold over the target price during the past year and that at least two paintings have been sold over the past year. Returns true if all paintings (two or more) sold over target, and false otherwise.

Class name	OsbertUtilities
Method name	removeDollarSign
Modifiers, type	**public static** String
Arguments	String
Error messages	none
Files accessed	none
Files changed	none
Methods called	none
Narrative	Removes all dollar signs from the input string and then returns the resulting string.

Class name	OsbertUtilities
Method name	removeQuestionMarks
Modifiers, type	**public static** String
Arguments	String
Error messages	none
Files accessed	none
Files changed	none
Methods called	none
Narrative	Removes all question marks from the input string and then returns the resulting string.

Class name	OtherClass
Method name	determineAlgorithmPrice
Modifiers, type	**public void**
Arguments	none
Error messages	none
Files accessed	fash.dat
Files changed	none
Methods called	readFash
Narrative	Determines the maximum price to be offered for an "other" piece of work. This operation is performed by first finding the appropriate fashionability coefficient from fash.dat. The maximum price is then computed as the area of the painting object multiplied by the fashionability coefficient.

Class name	PaintingClass
Method name	getDescription
Modifiers, type	**public void**
Arguments	none
Error messages	If the medium or subject of the entered painting is invalid.
Files accessed	none
Files changed	none
Methods called	none
Narrative	Retrieves information concerning a painting object (i.e., attributes firstName, lastName, title, paintingDate, height, width, medium, subject).

APPENDIX

OSBERT OGLESBY CASE STUDY: BLACK-BOX TEST CASES

Using boundary value analysis and functional analysis, the following black-box test cases have been created for the Osbert Oglesby product.

Equivalence Classes and Boundary Value Analysis:

Painting data:

Equivalence classes for first name and last name

1.	First character not alphabetic	Error
2.	< 1 character	Error
3.	1 character	Acceptable
4.	Between 1 and 21 characters	Acceptable
5.	21 characters	Acceptable
6.	> 21 characters	Acceptable (truncated to 21 characters)

Equivalence classes for title

1.	< 1 character	Error
2.	1 character	Acceptable
3.	Between 1 and 41 characters	Acceptable
4.	41 characters	Acceptable
5.	> 41 characters	Acceptable (truncated to 41 characters)

Equivalence classes for painting date

1.	Valid date of the form mm/dd/yy	Acceptable
2.	Missing "/" in proper location	Error

3. Missing leading zero (e.g., 6/16/94 instead of 06/16/94) — Error
4. Month component < 1 — Error
5. Month component > 12 — Error
6. Day component < 1 — Error
7. Day component > 31 — Error
8. Year component < 0 — Error
9. Year component > 99 — Error

(Additional tests could be made to check that the number of days is valid for the corresponding month; for example, the month of February should not have 31 days).

Equivalence classes for medium

1. "oil" — Acceptable
2. "watercolor" — Acceptable
3. "other" — Acceptable
4. Any other string — Error (invalid value)

Equivalence classes for subject

1. "portrait" — Acceptable
2. "still-life" — Acceptable
3. "landscape" — Acceptable
4. "other" — Acceptable
5. Any other string — Error (invalid value)

Equivalence classes for height and width

1. < 0.00 — Error
2. 0.00 — Error
3. 0.01 — Acceptable
4. 0.01 and 9999.99 — Acceptable
5. 10000.00 — Error
6. > 10000.00 — Error
7. Characters instead of integers — Error (not a number)

Gallery data:

(Attributes classification, purchase date, sale date, algorithm price, and target price are determined by the system, and are not entered by the user.)

Equivalence classes for seller name and buyer name

1. First character not alphabetic — Error

2. < 1 character — Error
3. 1 character — Acceptable
4. Between 1 and 21 characters — Acceptable
5. 21 characters — Acceptable
6. > 21 characters — Acceptable (truncated to 21 characters)

Equivalence classes for **seller address** and **buyer address**

1. < 1 character — Error
2. 1 character — Acceptable
3. Between 1 and 25 characters — Acceptable
4. 25 characters — Acceptable
5. > 25 characters — Acceptable (truncated to 25 characters)

Equivalence classes for **purchase price** and **selling price**

1. < 0.00 — Error
2. 0.00 — Acceptable
3. 0.01 — Acceptable
4. Between 0.01 and 999.99 — Acceptable
5. 1000.00 — Error
6. > 1000.00 — Error
7. Characters instead of integers — Error (not a number)

Fashionability data:

Equivalence classes for **first name** and **last name**

1. First character not alphabetic — Error
2. < 1 character — Error
3. 1 character — Acceptable
4. Between 1 and 21 characters — Acceptable
5. 21 characters — Acceptable
6. > 21 characters — Acceptable (truncated to 21 characters)

Equivalence classes for **coefficient**

1. < 0.00 — Error
2. 0.00 — Error
3. 0.01 — Acceptable
4. 0.01 and 9999.99 — Acceptable

5. 10000.00	Error
6. > 10000.00	Error
7. Characters instead of integers	Error (not a number)

Functional Analysis:

The functions outlined in the specifications document are used to create test cases.

1. Buy a masterpiece where the artist cannot be found in the auction records.
2. Buy a masterpiece where the artist can be found in the auction records.
3. Buy a masterwork where the artist cannot be found in the auction records.
4. Buy a masterwork where the artist can be found in the auction records.
5. Update the fashionability coefficients of several artists.
6. Buy an "other" type of painting where the artist cannot be found in the fashion records.
7. Buy an "other" type of painting where the artist can be found in the fashion records.
8. Buy a painting where the purchase price is less than the price suggested by the algorithm.
9. Buy a painting where the purchase price is equal to the price suggested by the algorithm.
10. Buy a painting where the purchase price is greater than the price suggested by the algorithm.
11. Sell a painting where the selling price is less than the target price.
12. Sell a painting where the selling price is equal to the target price.
13. Sell a painting where the selling price is greater than the target price.
14. For one or more artists, sell at least two paintings where every painting is sold over the target price (to be used in test case 17).
15. Display report of bought paintings.
16. Display report of sold paintings.
17. Display report of fashionability trends.

In addition to these direct tests, it is necessary to perform the following additional tests:

18. Attempt to buy a painting that is already in the gallery.
19. Attempt to sell a painting that does not exist in the gallery.
20. Attempt to sell a painting that has already been sold.

APPENDIX

I

Osbert Oglesby Case Study: Complete Source Code

The complete Java source code for the Osbert Oglesby case study is available on the World Wide Web at www.mhhe.com/engcs/compsci/schach.

BIBLIOGRAPHY

The chapter number in parentheses denotes the chapter in which the item has been referenced.

[Abrial, 1980] J.-R. ABRIAL, "The Specification Language Z: Syntax and Semantics," Oxford University Computing Laboratory, Programming Research Group, Oxford, UK, April 1980. (Chapter 10)

[Ackerman, Buchwald, and Lewski, 1989] A. F. ACKERMAN, L. S. BUCHWALD, AND F. H. LEWSKI, "Software Inspections: An Effective Verification Process," *IEEE Software* **6** (May 1989), pp. 31–36. (Chapter 5)

[AdaIC, 1997] "DoD to Replace Ada Mandate with Software-Engineering Process," *AdaIC News,* Summer 1997, Ada Information Clearinghouse, Falls Church, VA. (Chapter 7)

[Adler, 1995] R. M. ADLER, "Emerging Standards for Component Software," *IEEE Computer* **28** (March 1995), pp. 68–77. (Chapter 7)

[Adolph, 1996] W. S. ADOLPH, "Cash Cow in the Tar Pit: Reengineering a Legacy System," *IEEE Software* **13** (May 1996), pp. 41–47. (Chapter 15)

[Alavi, 1984] M. ALAVI, "An Assessment of the Prototyping Approach to Information Systems Development," *Communications of the ACM* **27** (June 1984), pp. 556–63. (Chapter 9)

[Albrecht, 1979] A. J. ALBRECHT, "Measuring Application Development Productivity," *Proceedings of the IBM SHARE/GUIDE Applications Development Symposium,* Monterey, CA, October 1979, pp. 83–92. (Chapter 8)

[Albrecht and Gaffney, 1983] A. J. ALBRECHT AND J. E. GAFFNEY, JR., "Software Function, Source Lines of Code, and Development Effort Prediction: A Software Science Validation," *IEEE Transactions on Software Engineering* **SE-9** (November 1983), pp. 639–48. (Chapter 8)

[Alburger, 1996] T. ALBURGER, "The Origin of Julian Days," http://intranet.on.ca/~rbirchal/draco/julian_d.html, April 24, 1996. (Chapter 11)

[Alexander et al., 1977] C. ALEXANDER, S. ISHIKAWA, M. SILVERSTEIN, M. JACOBSON, I. FIKSDAHL-KING, AND S. ANGEL, *A Pattern Language,* Oxford University Press, New York, 1977. (Chapter 7)

[Alford, 1985] M. ALFORD, "SREM at the Age of Eight; The Distributed Computing Design System," *IEEE Computer* **18** (April 1985), pp. 36–46. (Chapter 10)

[Anderson et al., 1995] E. ANDERSON, Z. BAI, C. BISCHOF, J. DEMMEL, J. DONGARRA, J. DU CROZ, A. GREENBAUM, S. HAMMARLING, A. MCKENNEY, S. OSTROUCHOV, AND D. SORENSEN, *LAPACK Users' Guide,* Second Edition, SIAM, Philadelphia, 1995. (Chapter 7)

[ANSI X3.159, 1989] "The Programming Language C," ANSI X3.159-1989, American National Standards Institute, Inc., 1989. (Chapter 7)

[ANSI/IEEE 754, 1985] "Standard for Binary Floating Point Arithmetic," ANSI/IEEE 754, American National Standards Institute, Inc., Institute of Electrical and Electronic Engineers, Inc., 1985. (Chapter 7)

[ANSI/IEEE 770X3.97, 1983] "Pascal Computer Programming Language," ANSI/IEEE 770X3.97-1983, American National Standards Institute, Inc., Institute of Electrical and Electronic Engineers, Inc., 1983. (Chapter 7)

[ANSI/IEEE 829, 1983] "Software Test Documentation," ANSI/IEEE 829-1983, American National Standards Institute, Inc., Institute of Electrical and Electronic Engineers, Inc., 1983. (Chapter 8)

[ANSI/MIL-STD-1815A, 1983] "Reference Manual for the Ada Programming Language," ANSI/MIL-STD-1815A, American National Standards Institute, Inc., United States Department of Defense, 1983. (Chapter 7)

[Apple, 1984] *Macintosh Pascal User's Guide,* Apple Computer, Inc., Cupertino, CA, 1984. (Chapter 4)

[Aron, 1983] J. D. Aron, *The Program Development Process. Part II. The Programming Team,* Addison-Wesley, Reading, MA, 1983. (Chapters 4 and 13)

[Arthur, 1997] L. J. Arthur, "Quantum Improvements in Software System Quality," *Communications of the ACM* **40** (June 1997), pp. 46–52. (Chapter 5)

[Awad, Kuusela, and Ziegler, 1996] M. Awad, J. Kuusela, and J. Ziegler, *Object-Oriented Technology for Real-Time Systems,* Prentice Hall, Upper Saddle River, NJ, 1996. (Chapter 11)

[Baber, 1987] R. L. Baber, *The Spine of Software: Designing Provably Correct Software: Theory and Practice,* John Wiley and Sons, New York, 1987. (Chapter 5)

[Babich, 1986] W. A. Babich, *Software Configuration Management: Coordination for Team Productivity,* Addison-Wesley, Reading, MA, 1986. (Chapters 4 and 15)

[Baker, 1972] F. T. Baker, "Chief Programmer Team Management of Production Programming," *IBM Systems Journal* **11** (No. 1, 1972), pp. 56–73. (Chapters 4 and 13)

[Balda and Gustafson, 1990] D. M. Balda and D. A. Gustafson, "Cost Estimation Models for the Reuse and Prototype Software Development Life Cycles," *ACM SIGSOFT Software Engineering Notes* **15** (July 1990), pp. 42–50. (Chapter 8)

[Balzer, 1985] R. Balzer, "A 15 Year Perspective on Automatic Programming," *IEEE Transactions on Software Engineering* **SE-11** (November 1985), pp. 1257–68. (Chapter 10)

[Bamberger, 1997] J. Bamberger, "Essence of the Capability Maturity Model," *IEEE Computer* **30** (June 1997), pp. 112–14. (Chapter 2)

[Bamford and Deibler, 1993a] R. C. Bamford and W. J. Deibler, II, "Comparing, Contrasting ISO 9001 and the SEI Capability Maturity Model," *IEEE Computer* **26** (October 1993), pp. 68–70. (Chapter 2)

[Bamford and Deibler, 1993b] R. C. Bamford and W. J. Deibler, II, "A Detailed Comparison of the SEI Software Maturity Levels and Technology Stages to the Requirements for ISO 9001 Registration," Software Systems Quality Consulting, San Jose, CA, 1993. (Chapter 2)

[Banker, Datar, Kemerer, and Zwieg, 1993] R. D. Banker, S. M. Datar, C. F. Kemerer, and D. Zwieg, "Software Complexity and Maintenance Costs," *Communications of the ACM* **36** (November 1993), pp. 81–94. (Chapter 15)

[Banks, Carson, and Nelson, 1995] J. Banks, J. S. Carson, and B. L. Nelson, *Discrete-event System Simulation,* Second Edition, Prentice Hall, Upper Saddle River, NJ, 1995. (Chapter 10)

[Barnard and Price, 1994] J. Barnard and A. Price, "Managing Code Inspection Information," *IEEE Software* **11** (March 1994), pp. 59–69. (Chapter 13)

[Barnes and Bollinger, 1991] B. H. Barnes and T. B. Bollinger, "Making Reuse Cost-Effective," *IEEE Software* **8** (January 1991), pp. 13–24. (Chapter 7)

[Barstow, Shrobe, and Sandewall, 1984] D. R. Barstow, H. E. Shrobe, and E. Sandewall (Editors), *Interactive Programming Environments,* McGraw-Hill, New York, 1984. (Chapter 14)

[Basili, 1990] V. R. Basili, "Viewing Maintenance as Reuse-Oriented Software Development," *IEEE Software* **7** (January 1990), pp. 19–25. (Chapter 15)

[Basili and Hutchens, 1983] V. R. Basili and D. H. Hutchens, "An Empirical Study of a Syntactic Complexity Family," *IEEE Transactions on Software Engineering* **SE-9** (November 1983), pp. 664–72. (Chapter 13)

[Basili and Selby, 1987] V. R. Basili and R. W. Selby, "Comparing the Effectiveness of Software Testing Strategies," *IEEE Transactions on Software Engineering* **SE-13** (December 1987), pp. 1278–96. (Chapter 13)

[Basili and Weiss, 1984] V. R. Basili and D. M. Weiss, "A Methodology for Collecting Valid Software Engineering Data," *IEEE Transactions on Software Engineering* **SE-10** (November 1984), pp. 728–38. (Chapter 13)

[Basili et al., 1995] V. Basili, M. Zelkowitz, F. McGarry, J. Page, S. Waligora, and R. Pajerski, "SEL's Software Process-Improvement Program," *IEEE Software* **12** (November 1995), pp. 83–87. (Chapter 2)

[Beck and Cunningham, 1989] K. Beck and W. Cunningham, "A Laboratory for Teaching Object-Oriented Thinking," *Proceedings of OOPSLA '89, ACM SIGPLAN Notices* **24** (October 1989), pp. 1–6. (Chapter 11)

[Behrens, 1983] C. A. Behrens, "Measuring the Productivity of Computer Systems Development Activities with Function Points," *IEEE Transactions on Software Engineering* **SE-9** (November 1983), pp. 648–52. (Chapter 8)

[Beizer, 1990] B. Beizer, *Software Testing Techniques,* Second Edition, Van Nostrand Reinhold, New York, 1990. (Chapters 2, 5, 12 and 13)

[Beizer, 1995] B. Beizer, *Black-Box Testing: Techniques for Functional Testing of Software and Systems,* John Wiley and Sons, New York, 1995. (Chapter 13)

[Bellinzona, Fugini, and Pernici, 1995] R. Bellinzona, M. G. Fugini, and B. Pernici, "Reusing Specifications in OO Applications," *IEEE Software* **12** (March 1995), pp. 656–75. (Chapter 11)

[Bentley, 1986] J. Bentley, *Programming Pearls,* Addison-Wesley, Reading, MA, 1986. (Chapter 13)

[Berard, 1993] E. V. Berard, *Essays on Object-Oriented Software Engineering, Volume I,* Prentice Hall, Englewood Cliffs, NJ, 1993. (Chapter 3)

[Berry, 1978] D. M. Berry, Personal communication, 1978. (Chapter 6)

[Berry, 1985] D. M. Berry, "On the Application of Ada and Its Tools to the Information Hiding Decomposition Methodology for the Design of Software Systems," in: *Methodologies for Computer System Design,* W. K. Giloi and B. D. Shriver (Editors), Elsevier North-Holland, Amsterdam, 1985, pp. 308–21. (Chapter 6)

[Berry and Wing, 1985] D. M. Berry and J. M. Wing, "Specifying and Prototyping: Some Thoughts on Why They Are Successful," in: *Formal Methods and Software Development, Proceedings of the International Joint Conference on Theory and Practice of Software Development, Volume 2,* Springer-Verlag, Berlin, 1985, pp. 117–28. (Chapter 5)

[Bersoff and Davis, 1991] E. H. Bersoff and A. M. Davis, "Impacts of Life Cycle Models on Software Configuration Management," *Communications of the ACM* **34** (August 1991), pp. 104–18. (Chapter 4)

[Berzins, Gray, and Naumann, 1986] V. Berzins, M. Gray, and D. Naumann, "Abstraction-Based Software Developments," *Communications of the ACM* **29** (May 1986), pp. 402–15. (Chapter 6)

[Bhandari et al., 1994] I. Bhandari, M. J. Halliday, J. Chaar, R. Chillarege, K. Jones, J. S. Atkinson, C. Lepori-Costello, P. Y. Jasper, E. D. Tarver, C. C. Lewis, and M. Yonezawa, "In-Process Improvement through Defect Data Interpretation," *IBM Systems Journal* **33** (No. 1, 1994), pp. 182–214. (Chapter 1)

[Bias, 1991] R. Bias, "Walkthroughs: Efficient Collaborative Testing," *IEEE Software* **8** (September 1991), pp. 94–95. (Chapter 12)

[Biggerstaff and Perlis, 1989] T. J. Biggerstaff and A. J. Perlis (Editors), *Software Reusability, Volumes I and II,* ACM Press, New York, 1989. (Chapter 7)

[Binkley and Schach, 1996] A. B. Binkley and S. R. Schach, "A Comparison of Sixteen Quality Metrics for Object-Oriented Design," *Information Processing Letters,* Vol. 57, No. 6 (June 1996), pp. 271–75. (Chapters 6 and 12)

[Binkley and Schach, 1997] A. B. Binkley and S. R. Schach, "Toward a Unified Approach to Object-Oriented Coupling," *Proceedings of the 35th Annual ACM Southeast Conference,* Murfreesboro, TN, April 2–4, 1997, pp. 91–97. (Chapters 6 and 12)

[Binkley and Schach, 1998] A. B. Binkley and S. R. Schach, "Validation of the Coupling Dependency Metric as a Predictor of Run-Time Failures and Maintenance Measures," *Proceedings of the Twentieth International Conference on Software Engineering,* Kyoto, Japan, April 1998, pp. 452–55. (Chapters 6 and 12)

[Bishop, 1994] M. Bishop, Usenet posting <2p8pab$rv0@source.asset.com> on comp.software-eng, April 22, 1994. (Chapter 2)

[Bjørner, 1987] D. Bjørner, "On the Use of Formal Methods in Software Development," *Proceedings of the Ninth International Conference on Software Engineering,* Monterey, CA, March 1987, pp. 17–29. (Chapter 10)

[Blaha, Premerlani, and Rumbaugh, 1988] M. R. BLAHA, W. J. PREMERLANI, AND J. E. RUMBAUGH, "Relational Database Design Using an Object-Oriented Methodology," *Communications of the ACM* **31** (April 1988), pp. 414–27. (Chapter 6)

[Blair, Murphy, Schach, and McDonald, 1988] J. A. BLAIR, L. C. MURPHY, S. R. SCHACH, AND C. W. MCDONALD, "Rapid Prototyping, Bottom-Up Design, and Reusable Modules: A Case Study," *ACM Mid-Southeast Summer Meeting,* Nashville, TN, May 1988. (Chapter 9)

[Boehm, 1976] B. W. BOEHM, "Software Engineering," *IEEE Transactions on Computers* **C-25** (December 1976), pp. 1226–41. (Chapters 1 and 2)

[Boehm, 1979] B. W. BOEHM, "Software Engineering, R & D Trends and Defense Needs," in: *Research Directions in Software Technology,* P. Wegner (Editor), The MIT Press, Cambridge, MA, 1979. (Chapter 1)

[Boehm, 1980] B. W. BOEHM, "Developing Small-Scale Application Software Products: Some Experimental Results," *Proceedings of the Eighth IFIP World Computer Congress,* October 1980, pp. 321–26. (Chapter 1)

[Boehm, 1981] B. W. BOEHM, *Software Engineering Economics,* Prentice Hall, Englewood Cliffs, NJ, 1981. (Chapters 1, 3, and 8)

[Boehm, 1984a] B. W. BOEHM, "Verifying and Validating Software Requirements and Design Specifications," *IEEE Software* **1** (January 1984), pp. 75–88. (Chapter 5)

[Boehm, 1984b] B. W. BOEHM, "Software Engineering Economics," *IEEE Transactions on Software Engineering* **SE-10** (January 1984), pp. 4–21. (Chapter 8)

[Boehm, 1988] B. W. BOEHM, "A Spiral Model of Software Development and Enhancement," *IEEE Computer* **21** (May 1988), pp. 61–72. (Chapter 3)

[Boehm, 1991] B. W. BOEHM, "Software Risk Management: Principles and Practices," *IEEE Software* **8** (January 1991), pp. 32–41. (Chapter 3)

[Boehm, 1997] R. BOEHM (Editor), "Function Point FAQ," http://ourworld.compuserve.com/homepages/softcomp/fpfaq.htm, June 25, 1997. (Chapter 8)

[Boehm and Papaccio, 1988] B. W. BOEHM AND P. N. PAPACCIO, "Understanding and Controlling Software Costs," *IEEE Transactions on Software Engineering* **14** (October 1988), pp. 1462–77. (Chapters 1 and 2)

[Boehm et al., 1984] B. W. BOEHM, M. H. PENEDO, E. D. STUCKLE, R. D. WILLIAMS, AND A. B. PYSTER, "A Software Development Environment for Improving Productivity," *IEEE Computer* **17** (June 1984), pp. 30–44. (Chapters 3 and 8)

[Boehm et al., 1995] B. BOEHM, B. CLARK, E. HOROWITZ, C. WESTLAND, R. MADACHY, AND R. SELBY, "Cost Models for Future Life Cycle Processes," *Annals of Software Engineering,* **1** (1995), pp. 57–94. (Chapter 8)

[Boehm, Gray, and Seewaldt, 1984] B. W. BOEHM, T. E. GRAY, AND T. SEEWALDT, "Prototyping Versus Specifying: A Multi-Project Experiment," *IEEE Transactions on Software Engineering* **SE-10** (May 1984), pp. 290–303. (Chapter 9)

[Bollinger and McGowan, 1991] T. BOLLINGER AND C. MCGOWAN, "A Critical Look at Software Capability Evaluations," *IEEE Software* **8** (July 1991), pp. 25–41. (Chapter 2)

[Bologna, Quirk, and Taylor, 1985] S. BOLOGNA, W. J. QUIRK, AND J. R. TAYLOR, "Simulation and System Validation," in: *Verification and Validation of Real-Time Software,* W. J. Quirk (Editor), Springer-Verlag, Berlin, 1985, pp. 179–201. (Chapter 5)

[Boloix and Robillard, 1995] G. BOLOIX AND P. N. ROBILLARD, "A Software System Evaluation Framework," *IEEE Computer* **28** (December 1995), pp. 17–26. (Chapter 5)

[Booch, 1994] G. BOOCH, *Object-Oriented Analysis and Design with Applications,* Second Edition, Benjamin/Cummings, Redwood City, CA, 1994. (Chapters 3, 11, 12, and 14)

[Bowen and Hinchey, 1995a] J. P. BOWEN AND M. G. HINCHEY, "Ten Commandments of Formal Methods," *IEEE Computer* **28** (April 1995), pp. 56–63. (Chapter 10)

[Bowen and Hinchey, 1995b] J. P. BOWEN AND M. G. HINCHEY, "Seven More Myths of Formal Methods," *IEEE Software* **12** (July 1995), pp. 34–41. (Chapter 10)

[Brady, 1977] J. M. Brady, *The Theory of Computer Science,* Chapman and Hall, London, 1977. (Chapter 10)

[Brandl, 1990] D. L. Brandl, "Quality Measures in Design: Finding Problems before Coding," *ACM SIGSOFT Software Engineering Notes* **15** (January 1990), pp. 68–72. (Chapter 12)

[Branstad and Powell, 1984] M. Branstad and P. B. Powell, "Software Engineering Project Standards," *IEEE Transactions on Software Engineering* **SE-10** (January 1984), pp. 73–78. (Chapter 8)

[Brettschneider, 1989] R. Brettschneider, "Is Your Software Ready for Release?" *IEEE Software* **6** (July 1989), pp. 100, 102, and 108. (Chapter 14)

[Brockschmidt, 1994] K. Brockschmidt, *Inside OLE2,* Microsoft Press, Redmond, WA, 1994. (Chapter 7)

[Brodman and Johnson, 1996] J. G. Brodman and D. Johnson, "Return on Investment from Software Process Improvement as Measured by U.S. Industry," *CrossTalk* **9** (April 1996), pp. 23–28. (Chapter 2)

[Brooks, 1975] F. P. Brooks, Jr., *The Mythical Man-Month: Essays in Software Engineering,* Addison-Wesley, Reading, MA, 1975. *Twentieth Anniversary Edition,* Addison-Wesley, Reading, MA, 1995. (Chapter 1, 2, 4, 9, and 13)

[Brown and McDermid, 1992] A. W. Brown and J. A. McDermid, "Learning from IPSE's Mistakes," *IEEE Software* **9** (March 1992), pp. 23–29. (Chapter 14)

[Browne, 1994] D. Browne, *STUDIO: STructured User-interface Design for Interaction Optimization,* Prentice Hall, Englewood Cliffs, NJ, 1994. (Chapter 9)

[Bruegge, Blythe, Jackson, and Shufelt, 1992] B. Bruegge, J. Blythe, J. Jackson, and J. Shufelt, "Object-Oriented Modeling with OMT," *Proceedings of the Conference on Object-Oriented Programming, Languages, and Systems, OOPSLA '92, ACM SIGPLAN Notices* **27** (October 1992), pp. 359–76. (Chapters 6 and 7)

[Bruno and Marchetto, 1986] G. Bruno and G. Marchetto, "Process-Translatable Petri Nets for the Rapid Prototyping of Process Control Systems," *IEEE Transactions on Software Engineering* **SE-12** (February 1986), pp. 346–57. (Chapter 10)

[Budd, 1991] T. A. Budd, *An Introduction to Object-Oriented Programming,* Addison-Wesley, Reading, MA, 1991. (Chapter 1)

[Bush, 1990] M. Bush, "Improving Software Quality: The Use of Formal Inspections at the Jet Propulsion Laboratory," *Proceedings of the 12th International Conference on Software Engineering,* Nice, France, March 1990, pp. 196–99. (Chapter 5)

[Caldiera and Basili, 1991] G. Caldiera and V. R. Basili, "Identifying and Qualifying Reusable Software Components," *IEEE Computer* **24** (February 1991), pp. 61–70. (Chapter 7)

[Cameron, 1986] J. R. Cameron, "An Overview of JSD," *IEEE Transactions on Software Engineering* **SE-12** (February 1986), pp. 222–40. (Chapter 12)

[Cameron, 1988] J. Cameron, *JSP & JSD—The Jackson Approach to Software Development,* Second Edition, IEEE Computer Society Press, Washington, DC, 1988. (Chapter 12)

[Capper, Colgate, Hunter, and James, 1994] N. P. Capper, R. J. Colgate, J. C. Hunter, and M. F. James, "The Impact of Object-Oriented Technology on Software Quality: Three Case Histories," *IBM Systems Journal* **33** (No. 1, 1994), pp. 131–57. (Chapters 1, 6, 7, 9, and 11)

[Card, McGarry, and Page, 1987] D. N. Card, F. E. McGarry, and G. T. Page, "Evaluating Software Engineering Technologies," *IEEE Transactions on Software Engineering* **SE-13** (July 1987), pp. 845–51. (Chapters 1 and 2)

[Carlson, Druffel, Fisher, and Whitaker, 1980] W. E. Carlson, L. E. Druffel, D. A. Fisher, and W. A. Whitaker, "Introducing Ada," *Proceedings of the ACM Annual Conference, ACM 80,* Nashville, TN, 1980, pp. 263–71. (Chapter 7)

[Chandrasekharan, Dasarathy, and Kishimoto, 1985] M. Chandrasekharan, B. Dasarathy, and Z. Kishimoto, "Requirements-Based Testing of Real-Time Systems: Modeling for Testability," *IEEE Computer* **18** (April 1985), pp. 71–80. (Chapter 10)

[Chappell, 1996] D. CHAPPELL, *Understanding ActiveX and OLE,* Microsoft Press, Redmond, WA, 1996. (Chapter 7)

[Charette, 1996] R. N. CHARETTE, "Large-Scale Project Management *Is* Risk Management," *IEEE Software* **13** (July 1996), pp. 110–17. (Chapter 8)

[Charette, Adams, and White, 1997] R. N. CHARETTE, K. MACG. ADAMS, AND M. B. WHITE, "Managing Risk in Software Maintenance," *IEEE Software* **14** (May/June, 1997), pp. 43–50. (Chapter 15)

[Chen, 1976] P. CHEN, "The Entity-Relationship Model—Towards a Unified View of Data," *ACM Transactions on Database Systems* **1** (March 1976), pp. 9–36. (Chapter 10)

[Chen, 1983] P. P.-S. CHEN, "ER—A Historical Perspective and Future Directions," in: *Entity Relationship Approach to Software Engineering,* C. G. Davis (Editor), North-Holland, Amsterdam, 1983. (Chapter 10)

[Chen and Norman, 1992] M. CHEN AND R. J. NORMAN, "A Framework for Integrated CASE," *IEEE Software* **8** (March 1992), pp. 18–22. (Chapter 14)

[Chidamber and Kemerer, 1994] S. R. CHIDAMBER AND C. F. KEMERER, "A Metrics Suite for Object Oriented Design," *IEEE Transactions on Software Engineering* **20** (June 1994), pp. 476–93. (Chapters 6 and 12)

[Chmura and Crockett, 1995] A. CHMURA AND H. D. CROCKETT, "What's the Proper Role for CASE Tools?" *IEEE Software* **12** (March 1995), pp. 18–20. (Chapter 4)

[Chow, 1985] T. S. CHOW (Editor), *Tutorial: Software Quality Assurance: A Practical Approach,* IEEE Computer Society Press, Washington, DC, 1985. (Chapter 5)

[Clarke, Podgurski, Richardson, and Zeil, 1989] L. A. CLARKE, A. PODGURSKI, D. J. RICHARDSON, AND S. J. ZEIL, "A Formal Evaluation of Data Flow Path Selection Criteria," *IEEE Transactions on Software Engineering* **15** (November 1989), pp. 1318–32. (Chapter 13)

[Cline, 1996] M. P. CLINE, "The Pros and Cons of Adopting and Applying Design Patterns in the Real World," *Communications of the ACM* **39** (October 1996), pp. 47–49. (Chapter 7)

[Coad, 1992] P. COAD, "Object-Oriented Patterns," *Communications of the ACM* **35** (September 1992), pp. 152–59. (Chapter 7)

[Coad and Yourdon, 1991a] P. COAD AND E. YOURDON, *Object-Oriented Analysis,* Second Edition, Yourdon Press, Englewood Cliffs, NJ, 1991. (Chapters 3 and 11)

[Coad and Yourdon, 1991b] P. COAD AND E. YOURDON, *Object-Oriented Design,* Yourdon Press, Englewood Cliffs, NJ, 1991. (Chapter 12)

[Cobb, 1985] R. H. COBB, "In Praise of 4GLs," *Datamation* **31** (July 15, 1985), pp. 90–96. (Chapter 13)

[Cobb and Mills, 1990] R. H. COBB AND H. D. MILLS, "Engineering Software under Statistical Quality Control," *IEEE Software* **7** (November 1990), pp. 44–54. (Chapter 13)

[Cockburn, 1996] A. COCKBURN, "The Interaction of Social Issues and Software Architecture," *Communications of the ACM* **39** (October 1996), pp. 40–46. (Chapter 7)

[Coleman, Ash, Lowther, and Oman, 1994] D. COLEMAN, D. ASH, B. LOWTHER, AND P. OMAN, "Using Metrics to Evaluate Software System Maintainability," *IEEE Computer* **27** (August 1994), pp. 44–49. (Chapters 1 and 15)

[Coleman et al., 1994] D. COLEMAN, P. ARNOLD, S. BODOFF, C. DOLLIN, H. GILCHRIST, F. HAYES, AND P. JEREMAES, *Object-Oriented Development: The Fusion Method,* Prentice Hall, Englewood Cliffs, NJ, 1994. (Chapter 11)

[Coleman, Hayes, and Bear, 1992] D. COLEMAN, F. HAYES, AND S. BEAR, "Introducing Objectcharts or How to Use Statecharts in Object-Oriented Design," *IEEE Transactions on Software Engineering* **18** (January 1992), pp. 9–18. (Chapters 10 and 11)

[Connell and Shafer, 1989] J. L. CONNELL AND L. SHAFER, *Structured Rapid Prototyping: An Evolutionary Approach to Software Development,* Yourdon Press, Englewood Cliffs, NJ, 1989. (Chapters 3 and 9)

[Conte, Dunsmore, and Shen, 1986] S. D. CONTE, H. E. DUNSMORE, AND V. Y. SHEN, *Software Engineering Metrics and Models,* Benjamin/Cummings, Menlo Park, CA, 1986. (Chapters 4, 8, and 13)

[Coolahan and Roussopoulos, 1983] J. E. COOLAHAN, JR., AND N. ROUSSOPOULOS, "Timing Requirements for Time-Driven Systems Using Augmented Petri Nets," *IEEE Transactions on Software Engineering* **SE-9** (September 1983), pp. 603–16. (Chapter 10)

[Cooling, 1997] J. E. COOLING, *Real-Time Software Systems: An Introduction,* Van Nostrand Reinhold, New York, 1997. (Chapter 12)

[Coomber and Childs, 1990] C. J. COOMBER AND R. E. CHILDS, "A Graphical Tool for the Prototyping of Real-Time Systems," *ACM SIGSOFT Software Engineering Notes* **15** (April 1990), pp. 70–82. (Chapter 9)

[Coplien, 1997] J. O. COPLIEN, "Idioms and Patterns as Architectural Literature," *IEEE Software* **14** (January/February 1997), pp. 36–42. (Chapter 7)

[Côté, Bourque, Oligny, and Rivard, 1988] V. CÔTÉ, P. BOURQUE, S. OLIGNY, AND N. RIVARD, "Software Metrics: An Overview of Recent Results," *Journal of Systems and Software* **8** (March 1988), pp. 121–31. (Chapter 4)

[Coulter, 1983] N. S. COULTER, "Software Science and Cognitive Psychology," *IEEE Transactions on Software Engineering* **SE-9** (March 1983), pp. 166–71. (Chapters 4, 8, and 13)

[Cox, 1986] B. J. COX, Object-Oriented Programming: *An Evolutionary Approach,* Addison-Wesley, Reading, MA, 1986. (Chapter 6)

[Cox, 1990] B. J. COX, "There *Is* a Silver Bullet," *Byte* **15** (October 1990), pp. 209–18. (Chapter 2)

[Crossman, 1982] T. D. CROSSMAN, "Inspection Teams, Are They Worth It?" *Proceedings of the Second National Symposium on EDP Quality Assurance,* Chicago, November 1982. (Chapter 13)

[Currit, Dyer, and Mills, 1986] P. A. CURRIT, M. DYER, AND H. D. MILLS, "Certifying the Reliability of Software," *IEEE Transactions on Software Engineering* **SE-12** (January 1986), pp. 3–11. (Chapter 3)

[Cusamano and Selby, 1995] M. A. CUSAMANO AND R. W. SELBY, *Microsoft Secrets: How the World's Most Powerful Software Company Creates Technology, Shapes Markets, and Manages People,* The Free Press/Simon and Schuster, New York, 1995. (Chapters 3 and 4)

[Cusamano and Selby, 1997] M. A. CUSAMANO AND R. W. SELBY, "How Microsoft Builds Software," *Communications of the ACM* **40** (June 1997), pp. 53–61. (Chapters 3 and 4)

[Daly, 1977] E. B. DALY, "Management of Software Development," *IEEE Transactions on Software Engineering* **SE-3** (May 1977), pp. 229–42. (Chapter 1)

[Dahl and Nygaard, 1966] O.-J. DAHL AND K. NYGAARD, "SIMULA—An ALGOL-Based Simulation Language," *Communications of the ACM* **9** (September, 1966), pp. 671–78. (Chapter 6)

[Dahl, Dijkstra, and Hoare, 1972] O.-J. DAHL, E. W. DIJKSTRA, AND C. A. R. HOARE, *Structured Programming,* Academic Press, New York, 1972. (Chapter 5)

[Dahl, Myrhaug, and Nygaard, 1973] O.-J. DAHL, B. MYRHAUG, AND K. NYGAARD, *SIMULA begin,* Auerbach, Philadelphia, 1973. (Chapter 6)

[Dart, Ellison, Feiler, and Habermann, 1987] S. A. DART, R. J. ELLISON, P. H. FEILER, AND A. N. HABERMANN, "Software Development Environments," *IEEE Computer* **20** (November 1987), pp. 18–28. (Chapter 10)

[Dasarathy, 1985] B. DASARATHY, "Timing Constraints of Real-Time Systems: Constructs for Expressing Them, Methods of Validating Them," *IEEE Transactions on Software Engineering* **SE-11** (January 1985), pp. 80–86. (Chapter 5)

[Dasgupta and Pearce, 1972] A. K. DASGUPTA AND D. W. PEARCE, *Cost–Benefit Analysis,* Macmillan, London, 1972. (Chapter 4)

[Date, 1994] C. J. DATE, *An Introduction to Database Systems,* Sixth Edition, Addison-Wesley, Reading, MA, 1994. (Chapter 13)

[Davis, 1993] A. M. DAVIS, *Software Requirements: Objects, Functions, and States,* Revised Edition, Prentice Hall, Englewood Cliffs, NJ, 1993. (Chapter 9)

[Davis, Bersoff, and Comer, 1988] A. M. DAVIS, E. H. BERSOFF, AND E. R. COMER, "A Strategy for Comparing Alternative Software Development Life Cycle Models," *IEEE Transactions on Software Engineering* **14** (October 1988), pp. 1453–61. (Chapter 3)

[Dawood, 1994] M. DAWOOD, "It's Time for ISO 9000," *CrossTalk* (March 1994) pp. 26–28. (Chapter 2)

[de Champeaux and Faure, 1992] D. DE CHAMPEAUX AND P. FAURE, "A Comparative Study of Object-Oriented Analysis Methods," *Journal of Object-Oriented Programming* **5** (March/April 1992), pp. 21–33. (Chapter 11)

[Delisle and Garlan, 1990] N. DELISLE AND D. GARLAN, "A Formal Description of an Oscilloscope," *IEEE Software* **7** (September 1990), pp. 29–36. (Chapter 10)

[Delisle and Schwartz, 1987] N. DELISLE AND M. SCHWARTZ, "A Programming Environment for CSP," *Proceedings of the Second ACM SIGSOFT/SIGPLAN Software Engineering Symposium on Practical Software Development Environments, ACM SIGPLAN Notices* **22** (January 1987), pp. 34–41. (Chapter 10)

[DeMarco, 1978] T. DEMARCO, *Structured Analysis and System Specification,* Yourdon Press, New York, 1978. (Chapter 10)

[DeMarco, 1986] T. DEMARCO, *Controlling Software Projects: Management, Measurement, and Estimation,* Second Edition, Yourdon Press, Englewood Cliffs, NJ, 1986. (Chapter 8)

[DeMarco and Lister, 1987] T. DEMARCO AND T. LISTER, *Peopleware: Productive Projects and Teams,* Dorset House, New York, 1987. (Chapters 1 and 4)

[DeMarco and Lister, 1989] T. DEMARCO AND T. LISTER, "Software Development: The State of the Art vs. State of the Practice," *Proceedings of the 11th International Conference on Software Engineering,* Pittsburgh, May 1989, pp. 271–75. (Chapters 1 and 2)

[DeMillo, Lipton, and Perlis, 1979] R. A. DEMILLO, R. J. LIPTON, AND A. J. PERLIS, "Social Processes and Proofs of Theorems and Programs," *Communications of the ACM* **22** (May 1979), pp. 271–80. (Chapter 5)

[DeMillo, Lipton, and Sayward, 1978] R. A. DEMILLO, R. J. LIPTON, AND F. G. SAYWARD, "Hints on Test Data Selection: Help for the Practicing Programmer," *IEEE Computer* **11** (April 1978), pp. 34–43. (Chapter 5)

[Deming, 1986] W. E. DEMING, *Out of the Crisis,* MIT Center for Advanced Engineering Study, Cambridge, MA, 1986. (Chapter 2)

[Deo, 1983] N. DEO, *System Simulation with Digital Computer,* Prentice Hall, Englewood Cliffs, NJ, 1983. (Chapter 8)

[DeRemer and Kron, 1976] F. DEREMER AND H. H. KRON, "Programming-in-the-Large versus Programming-in-the-Small," *IEEE Transactions on Software Engineering* **SE-2** (June 1976), pp. 80–86. (Chapter 4)

[Devenny, 1976] T. DEVENNY, "An Exploratory Study of Software Cost Estimating at the Electronic Systems Division," Thesis No. GSM/SM/765–4, Air Force Institute of Technology, Dayton, OH, 1976. (Chapter 8)

[Diaz and Sligo, 1997] M. DIAZ AND J. SLIGO, "How Software Process Improvement Helped Motorola," *IEEE Software* **14** (September/October 1997), pp. 75–81. (Chapter 2)

[Dijkstra, 1968a] E. W. DIJKSTRA, "A Constructive Approach to the Problem of Program Correctness," *BIT* **8** (No. 3, 1968), pp. 174–86. (Chapter 5)

[Dijkstra, 1968b] E. W. DIJKSTRA, "The Structure of the 'THE' Multiprogramming System," *Communications of the ACM* **11** (May 1968), pp. 341–46. (Chapter 6)

[Dijkstra, 1972] E. W. DIJKSTRA, "The Humble Programmer," *Communications of the ACM* **15** (October 1972), pp. 859–66. (Chapter 5)

[Dijkstra, 1976] E. W. DIJKSTRA, *A Discipline of Programming,* Prentice Hall, Englewood Cliffs, NJ, 1976. (Chapters 4 and 5)

[Diller, 1990] A. DILLER, *Z: An Introduction to Formal Methods,* John Wiley and Sons, Chichester, UK, 1990. (Chapter 10)

[Dion, 1993] R. DION, "Process Improvement and the Corporate Balance Sheet," *IEEE Software* **10** (July 1993), pp. 28–35. (Chapter 2)

[Dix, Finlay, Abowd, and Beale, 1993] A. DIX, J. FINLAY, G. ABOWD, AND R. BEALE, *Human-Computer Interaction,* Prentice Hall, Englewood Cliffs, NJ, 1993. (Chapter 9)

[DoD, 1987] "Report of the Defense Science Board Task Force on Military Software," Office of the Under Secretary of Defense for Acquisition, Washington, DC, September 1987. (Chapter 2)

[Dongarra et al., 1993] J. DONGARRA, R. POZO, AND D. WALKER, "LAPACK++: A Design Overview of Object-Oriented Extensions for High Performance Linear Algebra," *Proceedings of*

Supercomputing '93, IEEE Press 1993, pp. 162–71. (Chapter 7)

[Doolan, 1992] E. P. DOOLAN, "Experience with Fagan's Inspection Method," *Software—Practice and Experience* **22** (February 1992), pp. 173–82. (Chapters 5 and 10)

[Dooley and Schach, 1985] J. W. M. DOOLEY AND S. R. SCHACH, "FLOW: A Software Development Environment Using Diagrams," *Journal of Systems and Software* **5** (August 1985), pp. 203–19. (Chapter 4)

[Dorling and Simms, 1991] A. DORLING AND P. SIMMS, "ImproveIT," Ministry of Defence, London, UK, June 1991. (Chapter 2)

[Dreger, 1989] J. B. DREGER, *Function Point Analysis,* Prentice Hall, Englewood Cliffs, NJ, 1989. (Chapter 8)

[Dunn, 1984] R. H. DUNN, *Software Defect Removal,* McGraw-Hill, New York, 1984. (Chapters 5, 12, and 13)

[Dunn and Ullman, 1982] R. DUNN AND R. ULLMAN, *Quality Assurance for Computer Software,* McGraw-Hill, New York, 1982. (Chapter 5)

[Dyer, 1992] M. DYER, *The Cleanroom Approach to Quality Software Development,* John Wiley and Sons, New York, 1992. (Chapters 5 and 13)

[El-Rewini et al., 1995] H. EL-REWINI, S. HAMILTON, Y.-P. SHAN, R. EARLE, S. MCGAUGHEY, A. HELAL, R. BADRACHALAM, A. CHIEN, A. GRIMSHAW, B. LEE, A. WADE, D. MORSE, A. ELMAGRAMID, E. PITOURA, R. BINDER, AND P. WEGNER, "Object Technology," *IEEE Computer* **28** (October 1995), pp. 58–72. (Chapters 1 and 6)

[Elshoff, 1976] J. L. ELSHOFF, "An Analysis of Some Commercial PL/I Programs," *IEEE Transactions on Software Engineering* **SE-2** (June 1976), 113–20. (Chapter 1)

[Embley, Jackson, and Woodfield, 1995] D. W. EMBLEY, R. B. JACKSON, AND S. N. WOODFIELD, "OO Systems Analysis: Is It or Isn't It?" *IEEE Software* **12** (July 1995), pp. 18–33. (Chapter 11)

[Endres, 1975] A. ENDRES, "An Analysis of Errors and their Causes in System Programs," *IEEE Transactions on Software Engineering* **SE-1** (June 1975), pp. 140–49. (Chapter 13)

[Fagan, 1974] M. E. FAGAN, "Design and Code Inspections and Process Control in the Development of Programs," Technical Report IBM-SSD TR 21.572, IBM Corporation, December 1974. (Chapter 1)

[Fagan, 1976] M. E. FAGAN, "Design and Code Inspections to Reduce Errors in Program Development," *IBM Systems Journal* **15** (No. 3, 1976), pp. 182–211. (Chapters 5, 10, and 12)

[Fagan, 1986] M. E. FAGAN, "Advances in Software Inspections," *IEEE Transactions on Software Engineering* **SE-12** (July 1986), pp. 744–51. (Chapters 5 and 12)

[Faulk and Parnas, 1988] S. R. FAULK AND D. L. PARNAS, "On Synchronization in Hard-Real-Time Systems," *Communications of the ACM* **31** (March 1988), pp. 274–87. (Chapter 12)

[Fayad, Tsai, and Fulghum, 1996] M. E. FAYAD, W.-T. TSAI, AND M. L. FULGHUM, "Transition to Object-Oriented Software Development," *Communications of the ACM* **39** (February, 1996), pp. 108–121. (Chapter 6)

[Feldman, 1979] S. I. FELDMAN, "Make—A Program for Maintaining Computer Programs," *Software—Practice and Experience* **9** (April 1979), pp. 225–65. (Chapter 4)

[Feldman, 1981] M. B. FELDMAN, "Data Abstraction, Structured Programming, and the Practicing Programmer," *Software—Practice and Experience* **11** (July 1981), pp. 697–710. (Chapter 6)

[Fenton and Pfleeger, 1997] N. E. FENTON AND S. L. PFLEEGER, *Software Metrics : A Rigorous and Practical Approach,* Second Edition, IEEE Computer Society, Los Alamitos, CA, 1997. (Chapter 4)

[Ferguson et al., 1997] P. FERGUSON, W. S. HUMPHREY, S. KHAJENOORI, S. MACKE, AND A. MATVYA, "Results of Applying the Personal Software Process," *IEEE Computer* **30** (May 1997), pp. 24–31. (Chapter 2)

[Ferrentino and Mills, 1977] A. B. FERRENTINO AND H. D. MILLS, "State Machines and Their Semantics in Software Engineering," *Proceedings of the First International Computer Software and Applications Conference, COMPSAC '77,* Chicago, 1977, pp. 242–51. (Chapter 10)

[Fichman and Kemerer, 1992] R. G. FICHMAN AND C. F. KEMERER, "Object-Oriented and Conventional Analysis and Design Methodologies: Comparison and Critique," *IEEE Computer* **25** (October 1992), pp. 22–39. (Chapters 11 and 12)

[Fichman and Kemerer, 1997] R. G. FICHMAN AND C. F. KEMERER, "Object Technology and Reuse: Lessons from Early Adopters," *IEEE Computer* **30** (October 1997), pp. 47–59. (Chapters 1 and 7)

[Finney, 1996] K. FINNEY, "Mathematical Notation in Formal Specification: Too Difficult for the Masses?" *IEEE Transactions on Software Engineering* **22** (1996), pp. 158–59. (Chapter 10)

[Fisher, 1976] D. A. FISHER, "A Common Programming Language for the Department of Defense—Background and Technical Requirements," Report P-1191, Institute for Defense Analyses, Alexandria, VA, 1976. (Chapter 7)

[Flanagan, 1996] D. FLANAGAN, *Java in a Nutshell,* O'Reilly and Associates, Sebastopol, CA, 1996. (Chapters 6, 7, and 12)

[Fowler, 1986] P. J. FOWLER, "In-Process Inspections of Workproducts at AT&T," *AT&T Technical Journal* **65** (March/April 1986), pp. 102–12. (Chapter 5)

[Fowler, 1997a] M. FOWLER, *Analysis Patterns: Reusable Object Models,* Addison-Wesley, Reading, MA, 1997. (Chapter 7)

[Fowler, 1997b] M. FOWLER WITH K. SCOTT, *UML Distilled,* Addison-Wesley, Reading, MA, 1997. (Chapter 11)

[Frakes and Fox, 1995] W. B. FRAKES AND C. J. FOX, "Sixteen Questions about Software Reuse," *Communications of the ACM* **38** (June 1995), pp. 75–87. (Chapter 7)

[Freeman, 1987] P. FREEMAN (Editor), *Tutorial: Software Reusability,* IEEE Computer Society Press, Washington, DC, 1987. (Chapter 7)

[Freeman and Wasserman, 1983] P. FREEMAN AND A. J. WASSERMAN (Editors), *Tutorial: Software Design Techniques,* Fourth Edition, IEEE Computer Society Press, Washington, DC, 1983. (Chapter 12)

[Freiman and Park, 1979] F. R. FREIMAN AND R. E. PARK, "PRICE Software Model—Version 3: An Overview," *Proceedings of the IEEE-PINY Workshop on Quantitative Software Models,* October 1979, pp. 32–41. (Chapter 8)

[Fuggetta, 1993] A. FUGGETTA, "A Classification of CASE Technology," *IEEE Computer* **26** (December 1993), pp. 25–38. (Chapters 4 and 14)

[Fuggetta and Picco, 1994] A. FUGGETTA AND G. P. PICCO, "An Annotated Bibliography on Software Process Improvement," *ACM SIGSOFT Software Engineering Notes* **19** (July 1995), pp. 66–68. (Chapter 2)

[Furey and Kitchenham, 1997] S. FUREY AND B. KITCHENHAM, "Function Points," *IEEE Software* **14** (March/April 1997), pp. 28–32. (Chapter 8)

[Gamma, Helm, Johnson, and Vlissides, 1995] E. GAMMA, R. HELM, R. JOHNSON, AND J. VLISSIDES, *Design Patterns: Elements of Reusable Object-Oriented Software,* Addison-Wesley, Reading, MA, 1995. (Chapter 7)

[Gane, 1989] C. GANE, *Rapid System Development: Using Structured Techniques and Relational Technology,* Prentice Hall, Englewood Cliffs, NJ, 1989. (Chapters 3 and 9)

[Gane and Sarsen, 1979] C. GANE AND T. SARSEN, *Structured Systems Analysis: Tools and Techniques,* Prentice Hall, Englewood Cliffs, NJ, 1979. (Chapters 10 and 12)

[Garcia-Molina, Germano, and Kohler, 1984] H. GARCIA-MOLINA, F. GERMANO, JR., AND W. H. KOHLER, "Debugging a Distributed Computer System," *IEEE Transactions on Software Engineering* **SE-10** (March 1984), pp. 210–19. (Chapters 5 and 13)

[Gargaro and Pappas, 1987] A. GARGARO AND T. L. PAPPAS, "Reusability Issues and Ada," *IEEE Software* **4** (July 1987), pp. 43–51. (Chapter 7)

[Garlan, Allen, and Ockerbloom, 1995] D. GARLAN, R. ALLEN, AND J. OCKERBLOOM, "Architectural Mismatch: Why Reuse is So Hard," *IEEE Software* **12** (November 1995), pp. 17–26. (Chapter 7)

[Garman, 1981] J. R. GARMAN, "The 'Bug' Heard 'Round the World," *ACM SIGSOFT Software Engineering Notes* **6** (October 1981), pp. 3–10. (Chapter 5)

[Gaskill, 1996] B. GASKILL, "OpenDoc, ActiveX, JavaBeans, GNUstep (OpenStep), and Fresco Comparison," www.jagunet.com/~braddock/opendoccomp.html, 12 November, 1996. (Chapter 7)

[Gause and Weinberg, 1990] D. GAUSE AND G. WEINBERG, *Are Your Lights On? How to Figure Out*

What the Problem Really Is, Dorset House, New York, 1990. (Chapter 9)

[Gelperin and Hetzel, 1988] D. GELPERIN AND B. HETZEL, "The Growth of Software Testing," *Communications of the ACM* **31** (June 1988), pp. 687–95. (Chapter 5)

[Gemmer, 1997] A. GEMMER, "Risk Management: Moving beyond Process," *IEEE Computer* **30** (May 1997), pp. 33–43. (Chapter 8)

[Gentner and Grudin, 1996] D. R. GENTNER AND J. GRUDIN, "Design Models for Computer-Human Interfaces," *IEEE Computer* **29** (June 1996), pp. 28–35. (Chapter 9)

[Ghezzi and Mandrioli, 1987] C. GHEZZI AND D. MANDRIOLI, "On Eclecticism in Specifications: A Case Study Centered around Petri Nets," *Proceedings of the Fourth International Workshop on Software Specification and Design,* Monterey, CA, 1987, pp. 216–24. (Chapter 10)

[Gibbs, 1994] W. W. GIBBS, "Software's Chronic Crisis," *Scientific American* **271** (September 1994), pp. 86–95. (Chapter 1)

[Gibson and Jackson, 1987] C. F. GIBSON AND B. B. JACKSON, *The Information Imperative: Managing the Impact of Information Technology on Business and People,* Lexington Books, Lexington, MA, 1987. (Chapter 9)

[Gifford and Spector, 1987] D. GIFFORD AND A. SPECTOR, "Case Study: IBM's System/360-370 Architecture," *Communications of the ACM* **30** (April 1987), pp. 292–307. (Chapter 7)

[Gilb, 1988] T. GILB, *Principles of Software Engineering Management,* Addison-Wesley, Wokingham, UK, 1988. (Chapter 3)

[Glass, 1982] R. L. GLASS, "Real-Time Checkout: The 'Source Error First' Approach," *Software—Practice and Experience* **12** (January 1982), pp. 77–83. (Chapter 5)

[Glass, 1983] R. L. GLASS (EDITOR), *Real-Time Software,* Prentice Hall, Englewood Cliffs, NJ, 1983. (Chapter 5)

[Glass and Noiseux, 1981] R. L. GLASS AND R. A. NOISEUX, *Software Maintenance Guidebook,* Prentice Hall, Englewood Cliffs, NJ, 1981. (Chapter 15)

[Goel, 1985] A. L. GOEL, "Software Reliability Models: Assumptions, Limitations, and Applicability," *IEEE Transactions on Software Engineering* **SE-11** (December 1985), pp. 1411–23. (Chapter 13)

[Goldberg, 1986] R. GOLDBERG, "Software Engineering: An Emerging Discipline," *IBM Systems Journal* **25** (No. 3/4, 1986), pp. 334–53. (Chapters 1 and 2)

[Goldberg and Robson, 1989] A. GOLDBERG AND D. ROBSON, *Smalltalk-80: The Language,* Addison-Wesley, Reading, MA, 1989. (Chapters 6 and 12)

[Gomaa, 1986] H. GOMAA, "Software Development of Real-Time Systems," *Communications of the ACM* **29** (July 1986), pp. 657–68. (Chapter 12)

[Goodenough, 1979] J. B. GOODENOUGH, "A Survey of Program Testing Issues," in: *Research Directions in Software Technology,* P. Wegner (Editor), The MIT Press, Cambridge, MA, 1979, pp. 316–40. (Chapter 5)

[Goodenough and Gerhart, 1975] J. B. GOODENOUGH AND S. L. GERHART, "Toward a Theory of Test Data Selection," *Proceedings of the Third International Conference on Reliable Software,* Los Angeles, 1975, pp. 493–510. Also published in: *IEEE Transactions on Software Engineering* **SE-1** (June 1975), pp. 156–73. Revised version: J. B. Goodenough, and S. L. Gerhart, "Toward a Theory of Test Data Selection: Data Selection Criteria," in: *Current Trends in Programming Methodology, Volume 2,* R. T. Yeh (Editor), Prentice Hall, Englewood Cliffs, NJ, 1977, pp. 44–79. (Chapters 5 and 10)

[Gordon, 1979] M. J. C. GORDON, *The Denotational Description of Programming Languages: An Introduction,* Springer-Verlag, New York, 1979. (Chapter 10)

[Gordon and Bieman, 1995] V. S. GORDON AND J. M. BIEMAN, "Rapid Prototyping Lessons Learned," *IEEE Software* **12** (January 1995), pp. 85–95. (Chapter 9)

[Grady, 1992] R. B. GRADY, *Practical Software Metrics for Project Management and Process Improvement,* Prentice Hall, Englewood Cliffs, NJ, 1992. (Chapters 4 and 13)

[Grady, 1994] R. B. GRADY, "Successfully Applying Software Metrics," *IEEE Computer* **27** (September 1994), pp. 18–25. (Chapter 1)

[Grant, 1985] F. J. GRANT, "The Downside of 4GLs," *Datamation* **31** (July 15, 1985), pp. 99–104. (Chapter 13)

[Gremillion, 1984] L. L. GREMILLION, "Determinants of Program Repair Maintenance Requirements," *Communications of the ACM* **27** (August 1984), pp. 826–32. (Chapter 13)

[Griss, 1993] M. L. GRISS, "Software Reuse: From Library to Factory," *IBM Systems Journal* **32** (No. 4, 1993), pp. 548–66. (Chapter 7)

[Guha, Lang, and Bassiouni, 1987] R. K. GUHA, S. D. LANG, AND M. BASSIOUNI, "Software Specification and Design Using Petri Nets," *Proceedings of the Fourth International Workshop on Software Specification and Design,* Monterey, CA, April 1987, pp. 225–30. (Chapter 10)

[Guimaraes, 1983] T. GUIMARAES, "Managing Application Program Maintenance Expenditures," *Communications of the ACM* **26** (October 1983), pp. 739–46. (Chapter 15)

[Guimaraes, 1985] T. GUIMARAES, "A Study of Application Program Development Techniques," *Communications of the ACM* **28** (May 1985), pp. 494–99. (Chapter 13)

[Guinan, Cooprider, and Sawyer, 1997] P. J. GUINAN, J. G. COOPRIDER, AND S. SAWYER, "The Effective Use of Automated Application Development Tools," *IBM Systems Journal* **36** (No. 1, 1997). pp. 124–39. (Chapter 4)

[Guttag, 1977] J. GUTTAG, "Abstract Data Types and the Development of Data Structures," *Communications of the ACM* **20** (June 1977), pp. 396–404. (Chapter 6)

[Haley, 1996] T. J. HALEY, "Raytheon's Experience in Software Process Improvement," *IEEE Software* **13** (November 1996), pp. 33–41. (Chapter 2)

[Hall, 1990] A. HALL, "Seven Myths of Formal Methods," *IEEE Software* **7** (September 1990), pp. 11–19. (Chapter 10)

[Hall and Fenton, 1997] T. HALL AND N. FENTON, "Implementing Effective Software Metrics Programs," *IEEE Software* **14** (March/April 1997), pp. 55–65. (Chapter 8)

[Halstead, 1977] M. H. HALSTEAD, *Elements of Software Science,* Elsevier North-Holland, New York, 1977. (Chapters 8 and 13)

[Hamer and Frewin, 1982] P. G. HAMER AND G. D. FREWIN, "M. H. Halstead's Software Science—A Critical Examination," *Proceedings of the Sixth International Conference on Software Engineering,* Tokyo, 1982, pp. 197–205. (Chapter 8)

[Hansen, 1983] K. HANSEN, *Data Structured Program Design,* Ken Orr and Associates, Topeka, KS, 1983. (Chapter 12)

[Harel, 1987] D. HAREL, "Statecharts: A Visual Formalism for Complex Systems," *Science of Computer Programming* **8** (June 1987), pp. 231–74. (Chapter 10)

[Harel, 1992] D. HAREL, "Biting the Silver Bullet," *IEEE Computer* **25** (January 1992), pp. 8–24. (Chapter 2)

[Harel and Gery, 1997] D. HAREL AND E. GERY, "Executable Object Modeling with Statecharts," *IEEE Computer* **30** (July 1997), pp. 31–42. (Chapters 10 and 11)

[Harel et al., 1990] D. HAREL, H. LACHOVER, A. NAAMAD, A. PNUELI, M. POLITI, R. SHERMAN, A. SHTULL-TRAURING, AND M. TRAKHTENBROT, "STATEMATE: A Working Environment for the Development of Complex Reactive Systems," *IEEE Transactions on Software Engineering* **16** (April 1990), pp. 403–14. (Chapters 10 and 14)

[Harrold and Soffa, 1991] M. J. HARROLD AND M. L. SOFFA, "Selecting and Using Data for Integration Testing," *IEEE Software* **8** (1991), pp. 58–65. (Chapter 14)

[Harrold, McGregor, and Fitzpatrick, 1992] M. J. HARROLD, J. D. MCGREGOR, AND K. J. FITZPATRICK, "Incremental Testing of Object-Oriented Class Structures," *Proceedings of the 14th International Conference on Software Engineering,* Melbourne, Australia, May 1992, pp. 68–80. (Chapter 13)

[Hatley and Pirbhai, 1987] D. J. HATLEY AND I. A. PIRBHAI, *Strategies for Real-Time System Specification,* Dorset House, New York, 1987. (Chapter 12)

[Helmer-Hirschberg, 1966] O. HELMER-HIRSCHBERG, *Social Technology,* Basic Books, New York, 1966. (Chapter 8)

[Henderson-Sellers, 1996] B. HENDERSON-SELLERS, *Object-Oriented Metrics: Measures of*

Complexity, Prentice Hall, Upper Saddle River, NJ, 1996. (Chapters 4 and 6)

[Henderson-Sellers and Edwards, 1990] B. Henderson-Sellers and J. M. Edwards, "The Object-Oriented Systems Life Cycle," *Communications of the ACM* **33** (September 1990), pp. 142–59. (Chapter 3)

[Henry and Humphrey, 1990] S. M. Henry and M. Humphrey, "A Controlled Experiment to Evaluate Maintainability of Object-Oriented Software," *Proceedings of the IEEE Conference on Software Maintenance,* San Diego, CA, November 1990, pp. 258–65. (Chapter 15)

[Henry and Kafura, 1981] S. M. Henry and D. Kafura, "Software Structure Metrics Based on Information Flow," *IEEE Transactions on Software Engineering* **SE-7** (September 1981), pp. 510–18. (Chapter 12)

[Henry and Selig, 1990] S. Henry and C. Selig, "Predicting Source-Code Complexity at the Design Stage," *IEEE Software* **7** (March 1990), pp. 36–44. (Chapter 12)

[Henry, Henry, Kafura, and Matheson, 1994] J. Henry, S. Henry, D. Kafura, and L. Matheson, "Improving Software Maintenance at Martin Marietta," *IEEE Software* **11** (July 1994), pp. 67–75. (Chapter 15)

[Herbsleb et al., 1994] J. Herbsleb, A. Carleton, J. Rozum, J. Siegel, and D. Zubrow, "Benefits of CMM-Based Software Process Improvement: Initial Results," Technical Report CMU/SEI-94-TR-13, Software Engineering Institute, Carnegie Mellon University, August 1994. (Chapter 2)

[Herbsleb et al., 1997] J. Herbsleb, D. Zubrow, D. Goldenson, W. Hayes, and M. Paulk, "Software Quality and the Capability Maturity Model," *Communications of the ACM* **40** (June 1997), pp. 30–40. (Chapters 2 and 5)

[Hetzel, 1988] W. Hetzel, *The Complete Guide to Software Testing,* Second Edition, QED Information Systems, Wellesley, MA, 1988. (Chapter 5)

[Hicks and Card, 1994] M. Hicks and D. Card, "Tales of Process Improvement," *IEEE Software* **11** (January 1994), pp. 114–15. (Chapter 2)

[Hoare, 1969] C. A. R. Hoare, "An Axiomatic Basis for Computer Programming," *Communications of the ACM* **12** (October 1969), pp. 576–83. (Chapter 5)

[Hoare, 1981] C. A. R. Hoare, "The Emperor's Old Clothes," *Communications of the ACM* **24** (February 1981), pp. 75–83. (Chapter 5)

[Hoare, 1985] C. A. R. Hoare, *Communicating Sequential Processes,* Prentice Hall International, Englewood Cliffs, NJ, 1985. (Chapter 10)

[Hoare, 1987] C. A. R. Hoare, "An Overview of Some Formal Methods for Program Design," *IEEE Computer* **20** (September 1987), pp. 85–91. (Chapter 12)

[Holzner, 1993] S. Holzner, *Microsoft Foundation Class Library Programming,* Brady, New York, 1993. (Chapter 7)

[Honiden, Kotaka, and Kishimoto, 1993] S. Honiden, N. Kotaka, and Y. Kishimoto, "Formalizing Specification Modeling in OOA," *IEEE Software* **10** (January 1993), pp. 54–66. (Chapter 3)

[Horgan, London, and Lyu, 1994] J. R. Horgan, S. London, and M. R. Lyu, "Achieving Software Quality with Testing Coverage Measures," *IEEE Computer* **27** (1994), pp. 60–69. (Chapter 13)

[House and Newman, 1989] D. E. House and W. F. Newman, "Testing Large Software Products," *ACM SIGSOFT Software Engineering Notes* **14** (April 1989), pp. 71–78. (Chapter 14)

[Howden, 1987] W. E. Howden, *Functional Program Testing and Analysis,* McGraw-Hill, New York, 1987. (Chapter 13)

[Humphrey, 1989] W. S. Humphrey, *Managing the Software Process,* Addison-Wesley, Reading, MA, 1989. (Chapter 2)

[Humphrey, 1995] W. S. Humphrey, *A Discipline for Software Engineering,* Addison-Wesley, Reading, MA, 1995. (Chapter 2)

[Humphrey, 1996] W. S. Humphrey, "Using a Defined and Measured Personal Software Process," *IEEE Software* **13** (May 1996), pp. 77–88. (Chapter 2)

[Humphrey, Snider and Willis, 1991] W. S. Humphrey, T. R. Snider, and R. R. Willis, "Software Process Improvement at Hughes Aircraft," *IEEE Software* **8** (July 1991), pp. 11–23. (Chapter 2)

[Hwang, 1981] S.-S. V. Hwang, "An Empirical Study in Functional Testing, Structural Testing, and

Code Reading Inspection," Scholarly Paper 362, Department of Computer Science, University of Maryland, College Park, MD, 1981. (Chapter 13)

[IEEE 610.12, 1990] "A Glossary of Software Engineering Terminology," IEEE 610.12-1990, Institute of Electrical and Electronic Engineers, Inc., 1990. (Chapter 5)

[IEEE 1028, 1988] "Standard for Software Reviews and Audits," IEEE 1028, Institute of Electrical and Electronic Engineers, Inc., 1988. (Chapter 5)

[IEEE 1058.1, 1987] "Standard for Software Project Management Plans," IEEE 1058.1, Institute of Electrical and Electronic Engineers, Inc., 1987. (Chapter 8)

[Isakowitz and Kauffman, 1996] T. ISAKOWITZ AND R. J. KAUFFMAN, *IEEE Transactions on Software Engineering* **22** (June 1996), pp. 407–23. (Chapter 7)

[ISO 9000-3, 1991] "ISO 9000-3, Guidelines for the Application of ISO 9001 to the Development, Supply, and Maintenance of Software," International Organization for Standardization, Geneva, 1991. (Chapter 2)

[ISO 9001, 1987] "ISO 9001, Quality Systems—Model for Quality Assurance in Design/Development, Production, Installation, and Servicing," International Organization for Standardization, Geneva, 1987. (Chapter 2)

[ISO-7185, 1980] "Specification for the Computer Programming Language Pascal," ISO-7185, International Standards Organization, Geneva, 1980. (Chapter 7)

[ISO/IEC 1539, 1991] "Programming Language Fortran," Second Edition, ISO/IEC 1539, International Standards Organization, International Electrotechnical Commission, Geneva, 1991. (Also published as ANSI Standard X3.9-198-1992.) (Chapter 7)

[ISO/IEC 1989, 1997] "Committee Draft 1.1, Proposed Revision of ISO 1989: 1985, Programming Language COBOL," JCT1/SC22/WG4, International Standards Organization, International Electrotechnical Commission, Geneva, 1997. (Chapter 7)

[ISO/IEC 8652, 1995] "Programming Language Ada: Language and Standard Libraries," ISO/IEC 8652, International Organization for Standardization, International Electrotechnical Commission, 1995. (Chapters 6, 7, and 12)

[ISO/IEC 12207, 1995] "Software Life Cycle Processes," ISO/IEC 12207, International Organization for Standardization, International Electrotechnical Commission, Geneva, 1995. (Chapter 3)

[ISO/IEC 14882, 1998] "Programming Language C++," ISO/IEC 14882, International Organization for Standardization, International Electrotechnical Commission, Geneva, 1998.

[IWSSD, 1986] Call for Papers, Fourth International Workshop on Software Specification and Design, *ACM SIGSOFT Software Engineering Notes* **11** (April 1986), pp. 94–96. (Chapter 10)

[Jackson, 1975] M. A. JACKSON, *Principles of Program Design,* Academic Press, New York, 1975. (Chapter 12)

[Jackson, 1983] M. A. JACKSON, *System Development,* Prentice Hall, Englewood Cliffs, NJ, 1983. (Chapters 10, 11, and 12)

[Jacob, 1985] R. J. K. JACOB, "A State Transition Diagram Language for Visual Programming," *IEEE Computer* **18** (August 1985), pp. 51–59. (Chapter 10)

[Jacobson, Christerson, Jonsson, and Overgaard, 1992] I. JACOBSON, M. CHRISTERSON, P. JONSSON, AND G. OVERGAARD, *Object-Oriented Software Engineering: A Use Case Driven Approach,* ACM Press, New York, 1992. (Chapters 3, 11, and 12)

[Jain, 1991] R. JAIN, *The Art of Computer Systems Performance Analysis: Techniques for Experimental Design, Measurement, Simulation, and Modeling,* John Wiley and Sons, New York, 1991. (Chapter 10)

[Jeffrey, Low, and Barnes, 1993] D. R. JEFFREY, G. C. LOW, AND M. BARNES, "A Comparison of Function Point Counting Techniques," *IEEE Transactions on Software Engineering* **19** (May 1993), pp. 529–32. (Chapter 8)

[Jensen and Wirth, 1975] K. JENSEN AND N. WIRTH, *Pascal User Manual and Report,* Second Edition, Springer-Verlag, New York, 1975. (Chapter 7)

[Jézéquel and Meyer, 1997] J.-M. JÉZÉQUEL AND B. MEYER, "Put It in the Contract: The Lessons of Ariane," *IEEE Computer* **30** (January 1997), pp. 129–30. (Chapter 7)

[Johnson, 1979] S. C. JOHNSON, "A Tour through the Portable C Compiler," Seventh Edition, UNIX Programmer's Manual, Bell Laboratories, Murray Hill, NJ, January 1979. (Chapter 7)

[Johnson, 1997] R. E. JOHNSON, "Frameworks = (Components + Patterns)," *Communications of the ACM* **40** (October 1997), pp. 39–42. (Chapter 7)

[Johnson and Ritchie, 1978] S. C. JOHNSON AND D. M. RITCHIE, "Portability of C Programs and the UNIX System," *Bell System Technical Journal* **57** (No. 6, Part 2, 1978), pp. 2021–48. (Chapter 7)

[Jones, 1978] T. C. JONES, "Measuring Programming Quality and Productivity," *IBM Systems Journal* **17** (No. 1, 1978), pp. 39–63. (Chapter 5)

[Jones, 1984] T. C. JONES, "Reusability in Programming: A Survey of the State of the Art," *IEEE Transactions on Software Engineering* **SE-10** (September 1984), pp. 488–94. (Chapter 7)

[Jones, 1986a] C. JONES, *Programming Productivity,* McGraw-Hill, New York, 1986. (Chapters 8 and 13)

[Jones, 1986b] C. B. JONES, *Systematic Software Development Using VDM,* Prentice Hall, Englewood Cliffs, NJ, 1986. (Chapter 10)

[Jones, 1987] C. JONES, Letter to the Editor, *IEEE Computer* **20** (December 1987), p. 4. (Chapter 8)

[Jones, 1991] C. JONES, *Applied Software Measurement,* McGraw-Hill, New York, 1991. (Chapter 8)

[Jones, 1994a] C. JONES, "Software Metrics: Good, Bad, and Missing," *IEEE Computer* **27** (September 1994), pp. 98–100. (Chapter 4)

[Jones, 1994b] C. JONES, "Cutting the High Cost of Software 'Paperwork'," *IEEE Computer* **27** (October 1994), pp. 79–80. (Chapter 8)

[Jones, 1994c] C. JONES, *Assessment and Control of Computer Risks,* Prentice Hall, Englewood Cliffs, NJ, 1994. (Chapter 3)

[Jones, 1995] C. JONES, "What Are Function Points?" http://www.spr.com/library/funcmet.htm, 1995. (Chapter 8)

[Jones, 1996] C. JONES, *Applied Software Measurement,* McGraw-Hill, New York, 1996. (Chapters 2 and 7)

[Joos, 1994] R. JOOS, "Software Reuse at Motorola," *IEEE Software* **11** (September 1994), pp. 42–47. (Chapter 7)

[Jorgensen and Erickson, 1994] P. C. JORGENSEN AND C. ERICKSON, "Object-Oriented Integration Testing," *Communications of the ACM* **37** (September 1994), pp. 30–38. (Chapter 14)

[Josephson, 1992] M. JOSEPHSON, *Edison, A Biography,* John Wiley and Sons, New York, 1992. (Chapter 1)

[Juran, 1988] J. M. JURAN, *Juran on Planning for Quality,* Macmillan, New York, 1988. (Chapter 2)

[Kampen, 1987] G. R. KAMPEN, "An Eclectic Approach to Specification," *Proceedings of the Fourth International Workshop on Software Specification and Design,* Monterey, CA, April 1987, pp. 178–82. (Chapter 10)

[Kan et al., 1994] S. H. KAN, S. D. DULL, D. N. AMUNDSON, R. J. LINDNER, AND R. J. HEDGER, "AS/400 Software Quality Management," *IBM Systems Journal* **33** (No. 1, 1994), pp. 62–88. (Chapter 1)

[Karlsson and Ryan, 1997] J. KARLSSON AND K. RYAN, "A Cost-Value Approach for Prioritizing Requirements," *IEEE Software* **14** (September/October 1997), pp. 67–74. (Chapter 9)

[Karolak, 1996] D. W. KAROLAK, *Software Engineering Risk Management,* IEEE Computer Society, Los Alamitos, CA, 1996. (Chapter 3)

[Kazman, Abowd, Bass, and Clements, 1996] R. KAZMAN, G. ABOWD, L. BASS, AND P. CLEMENTS, "Scenario-Based Analysis of Software Architecture," *IEEE Software* **13** (November/December 1996), pp. 47–55. (Chapter 11)

[Kelly and Sherif, 1992] J. C. KELLY AND J. S. SHERIF, "A Comparison of Four Design Methods for Real-Time Software Development," *Information and Software Technology* **34** (February 1992), pp. 74–82. (Chapter 12)

[Kelly, Sherif, and Hops, 1992] J. C. KELLY, J. S. SHERIF, AND J. HOPS, "An Analysis of Defect Densities Found during Software Inspections," *Journal of Systems and Software* **17** (January 1992), pp. 111–17. (Chapters 1 and 5)

[Kemerer, 1987] C. F. KEMERER, "An Empirical Validation of Software Cost Estimation Models," *Communications of the ACM* **30** (May 1987), pp. 416–29. (Chapter 8)

[Kemerer, 1993] C. F. KEMERER, "Reliability of Function Points Measurement: A Field Experiment," *Communications of the ACM* **36** (February 1993), pp. 85–97. (Chapter 8)

[Kemerer and Porter, 1992] C. F. KEMERER AND B. S. PORTER, "Improving the Reliability of Function Point Measurement: An Empirical Study," *IEEE Transactions on Software Engineering* **18** (November 1992), pp. 1011–24. (Chapter 8)

[Kernighan and Plauger, 1974] B. W. KERNIGHAN AND P. J. PLAUGER, *The Elements of Programming Style,* McGraw-Hill, New York, 1974. (Chapter 13)

[Kernighan and Ritchie, 1978] B. W. KERNIGHAN AND D. M. RITCHIE, *The C Programming Language,* Prentice Hall, Englewood Cliffs, NJ, 1978. (Chapter 7)

[Kerth and Cunningham, 1997] N. L. KERTH AND W. CUNNINGHAM, "Using Patterns to Improve Our Architectural Vision," *IEEE Software* **14** (January/February 1997), pp. 53–59. (Chapter 7)

[Khan, Al-A'ali, and Girgis, 1995] E. H. KHAN, M. AL-A'ALI, AND M. R. GIRGIS, "Object-Oriented Programming for Structured Procedural Programming," *IEEE Computer* **28** (October 1995), pp. 48–57. (Chapter 1)

[King, 1988] D. KING, *Creating Effective Software: Computer Program Design Using the Jackson Methodology,* Prentice Hall, Englewood Cliffs, NJ, 1988. (Chapter 12)

[King and Schrems, 1978] J. L. KING AND E. L. SCHREMS, "Cost–Benefit Analysis in Information Systems Development and Operation," *ACM Computer Surveys* **10** (March 1978), pp. 19–34. (Chapter 4)

[Kitchenham and Känsälä, 1993] B. KITCHENHAM AND K. KÄNSÄLÄ, "Inter-Item Correlations among Function Points," *Proceedings of the IEEE Fifteenth International Conference on Software Engineering,* Baltimore, MD, May 1993, pp. 477–80. (Chapter 8)

[Kitchenham, Pickard, and Linkman, 1990] B. A. KITCHENHAM, L. M. PICKARD, AND S. J. LINKMAN, "An Evaluation of Some Design Metrics," *Software Engineering Journal* **5** (January 1990), pp. 50–58. (Chapter 12)

[Kitchenham, Pickard, and Pfleeger, 1995] B. KITCHENHAM, L. PICKARD, AND S. L. PFLEEGER. "Case Studies for Method and Tool Evaluation," *IEEE Software* **12** (July 1995), pp. 52–62. (Chapter 4)

[Kitson, 1996] D. H. KITSON, "Relating the SPICE Framework and the SEI Approach to Software Process Assessment," *Proceedings of the Fifth European Conference on Software Quality,* Dublin, Ireland, September 1996. (Chapter 2)

[Kitson and Masters, 1993] D. H. KITSON AND S. M. MASTERS, "An Analysis of SEI Software Process Assessment Results: 1987–1991," *Proceedings of the Fifteenth International Conference on Software Engineering,* Baltimore, MD, May 1993, pp. 68–77. (Chapter 2)

[Klatte et al., 1993] R. KLATTE, U. KULISCH, A. WIETHOFF, C. LAWO, AND M. RAUCH, *C-XSC: A C++ Class Library for Extended Scientific Computing,* Springer-Verlag, Heidelberg, New York, 1993. (Chapter 7)

[Klepper and Bock, 1995] R. KLEPPER AND D. BOCK, "Third and Fourth Generation Productivity Differences," *Communications of the ACM* **38** (September, 1995), pp. 69–79. (Chapter 13)

[Klunder, 1988] D. KLUNDER, "Hungarian Naming Conventions," Technical Report, Microsoft Corporation, Redmond, WA, January 1988. (Chapter 13)

[Kmielcik et al., 1984] J. KMIELCIK ET AL., "SCR Methodology User's Manual," Grumman Aerospace Corporation, Report SRSR-A6-84-002, 1984. (Chapter 12)

[Knuth, 1968] D. E. KNUTH, *The Art of Computer Programming, Volume I, Fundamental Algorithms,* Addison-Wesley, Reading, MA, 1968. (Chapter 10)

[Knuth, 1974] D. E. KNUTH, "Structured Programming with **go to** Statements," *ACM Computing Surveys* **6** (December 1974), pp. 261–301. (Chapter 6)

[Konrad et al., 1996] M. KONRAD, M. B. CHRISSIS, J. FERGUSON, S. GARCIA, B. HELFLEY, D. KITSON, AND M. PAULK, "Capability Maturity Modeling^{SM} at the SEI," *Software Process—Improvement and Practice* **2** (March 1996), pp. 21–34. (Chapter 2)

[Korson and McGregor, 1990] T. KORSON AND J. D. MCGREGOR, "Understanding Object-Oriented: A Unifying Paradigm," *Communications of the ACM* **33** (September 1990), pp. 40–60. (Chapter 6)

[Kramer, 1994] J. KRAMER, "Distributed Software Engineering," *Proceedings of the 16th International Conference on Software Engineering,* Sorrento, Italy, May 1994, pp. 253–63. (Chapters 10 and 12)

[Kurki-Suonio, 1993] R. KURKI-SUONIO, "Stepwise Design of Real-Time Systems," *IEEE Transactions on Software Engineering* **19** (January 1993), pp. 56–69. (Chapter 4)

[Lamport, 1980] L. LAMPORT, "'Sometime' Is Sometimes 'Not Never': On the Temporal Logic of Programs," *Proceedings of the Seventh Annual ACM Symposium on Principles of Programming Languages,* Las Vegas, NV, 1980, pp. 174–85. (Chapter 5)

[Landis et al., 1992] L. LANDIS, S. WALIGARA, F. MCGARRY, ET AL., "Recommended Approach to Software Development: Revision 3," Technical Report SEL-81-305, Software Engineering Laboratory, Greenbelt, MD, June 1992. (Chapter 3)

[Landwehr, 1983] C. E. LANDWEHR, "The Best Available Technologies for Computer Security," *IEEE Computer* **16** (July 1983), pp. 86–100. (Chapter 5)

[Lanergan and Grasso, 1984] R. G. LANERGAN AND C. A. GRASSO, "Software Engineering with Reusable Designs and Code," *IEEE Transactions on Software Engineering* **SE-10** (September 1984), pp. 498–501. (Chapter 7)

[Langtangen, 1994] H. P. LANGTANGEN, "Getting Started with Finite Element Programming in DIFF-PACK," The DiffPack Report Series, SINTEF, Oslo, Norway, October 2, 1994. (Chapter 7)

[Lantz, 1985] K. E. LANTZ, *The Prototyping Methodology,* Prentice Hall, Englewood Cliffs, NJ, 1985. (Chapters 3 and 9)

[Larsen, Fitzgerald, and Brookes, 1996] P. G. LARSEN, J. FITZGERALD, AND T. BROOKES, "Applying Formal Specification in Industry," *IEEE Software* **13** (May 1996), pp. 48–56. (Chapter 10)

[Leavenworth, 1970] B. LEAVENWORTH, Review #19420, *Computing Reviews* **11** (July 1970), pp. 396–97. (Chapters 5 and 10)

[Lecarme and Gart, 1986] O. LECARME AND M. P. GART, *Software Portability,* McGraw-Hill, New York, 1986. (Chapter 7)

[Lederer and Prasad, 1992] A. L. LEDERER AND J. PRASAD, "Nine Management Guidelines for Better Cost Estimating," *Communications of the ACM* **35** (February 1992), pp. 51–59. (Chapter 8)

[Ledgard, 1975] H. LEDGARD, *Programming Proverbs,* Hayden Books, Rochelle Park, NJ, 1975. (Chapter 13)

[Lee and Tepfenhart, 1997] R. C. LEE AND W. M. TEPFENHART, *UML: A Practical Guide to Object-Oriented Development,* Prentice Hall, Upper Saddle River, NJ, 1997. (Chapter 11)

[Lejter, Meyers, and Reiss, 1992] M. LEJTER, S. MEYERS, AND S. P. REISS, "Support for Maintaining Object-Oriented Programs," *IEEE Transactions on Software Engineering* **18** (December 1992), pp. 1045–52. (Chapter 15)

[Leppinen, Pulkkinen, and Rautiainen, 1997] M. LEPPINEN, P. PULKKINEN, AND A. RAUTIAINEN, "Java- and Corba-Based Network Management," *IEEE Computer* **30** (June 1997), pp. 83–87. (Chapter 7)

[Leveson, 1997] N. G. LEVESON, "Software Engineering: Stretching the Limits of Complexity," *Communications of the ACM* **40** (February 1997), pp. 129–31. (Chapter 1)

[Leveson and Turner, 1993] N. G. LEVESON AND C. S. TURNER, "An Investigation of the Therac-25 Accidents," *IEEE Computer* **26** (July 1993), pp. 18–41. (Chapter 1)

[Levi and Agrawala, 1990] S.-T. LEVI AND A. K. AGRAWALA, *Real Time System Design,* McGraw-Hill, New York, 1990. (Chapter 12)

[Lewis et al., 1995a] T. LEWIS, H. EL-REWINI, J. GRIMES, M. HILL, P. LAPLANTE, J. LARUS, B. MEYER, G. POMBERGER, M. POTEL, D. POWER, W. PREE, R. VETTER, B. W. WEIDE, D. WOOD, "Where is Software Headed?" *IEEE Computer* **28** (August 1995), pp. 20–32. (Chapter 1)

[Lewis et al., 1995b] T. LEWIS, L. ROSENSTEIN, W. PREE, A. WEINAND, E. GAMMA, P. CALDER, G. ANDERT, J. VLISSIDES, AND K. SCHMUCKER, *Object-Oriented*

Application Frameworks, Manning Publications, Greenwich, CT, 1995. (Chapter 7)

[Lewis, 1996a] T. LEWIS, "The Next $10{,}000_2$ Years: Part I," *IEEE Computer* **29** (April 1996), pp. 64–70. (Chapter 1)

[Lewis, 1996b] T. LEWIS, "The Next $10{,}000_2$ Years: Part II," *IEEE Computer* **29** (May 1996), pp. 78–86. (Chapter 1)

[Lichter, Schneider-Hufschmidt, and Züllighoven, 1994] H. LICHTER, M. SCHNEIDER-HUFSCHMIDT, AND H. ZÜLLIGHOVEN, "Prototyping in Industrial Software Projects—Bridging the Gap between Theory and Practice," *IEEE Transactions on Software Engineering* **20** (November 1994), pp. 825–32. (Chapter 9)

[Licker, 1985] P. S. LICKER, *The Art of Managing Software Development People,* John Wiley and Sons, New York, 1985. (Chapter 4)

[Lientz and Swanson, 1980] B. P. LIENTZ AND E. B. SWANSON, *Software Maintenance Management: A Study of the Maintenance of Computer Applications Software in 487 Data Processing Organizations,* Addison-Wesley, Reading, MA, 1980. (Chapter 15)

[Lientz, Swanson, and Tompkins, 1978] B. P. LIENTZ, E. B. SWANSON, AND G. E. TOMPKINS, "Characteristics of Application Software Maintenance," *Communications of the ACM* **21** (June 1978), pp. 466–71. (Chapters 1 and 15)

[Lim, 1994] W. C. LIM, "Effects of Reuse on Quality, Productivity, and Economics," *IEEE Software* **11** (September 1994), pp. 23–30. (Chapters 7 and 8)

[Lim, 1998] W. C. LIM, *Managing Software Reuse,* Prentice Hall, Upper Saddle River, NJ, 1998. (Chapter 7)

[Linger, 1980] R. C. LINGER, "The Management of Software Engineering. Part III. Software Design Practices," *IBM Systems Journal* **19** (No. 4, 1980), pp. 432–50. (Chapter 10)

[Linger, 1994] R. C. LINGER, "Cleanroom Process Model," *IEEE Software* **11** (March 1994), pp. 50–58. (Chapter 13)

[Linger, Mills, and Witt, 1979] R. C. LINGER, H. D. MILLS, AND B. I. WITT, *Structured Programming: Theory and Practice,* Addison-Wesley, Reading, MA, 1979. (Chapter 5)

[Liskov and Guttag, 1986] B. LISKOV AND J. GUTTAG, *Abstraction and Specification in Program Development,* The MIT Press, Cambridge, MA, 1986. (Chapter 6)

[Liskov and Zilles, 1974] B. LISKOV AND S. ZILLES, "Programming with Abstract Data Types," *ACM SIGPLAN Notices* **9** (April 1974), pp. 50–59. (Chapter 6)

[Liskov, Snyder, Atkinson, and Schaffert, 1977] B. LISKOV, A. SNYDER, R. ATKINSON, AND C. SCHAFFERT, "Abstraction Mechanisms in CLU," *Communications of the ACM* **20** (August 1977), pp. 564–76. (Chapter 7)

[Littlewood and Strigini, 1992] B. LITTLEWOOD AND L. STRIGINI, "The Risks of Software," *Scientific American* **267** (November 1992), pp. 62–75. (Chapter 1)

[London, 1971] R. L. LONDON, "Software Reliability through Proving Programs Correct," *Proceedings of the IEEE International Symposium on Fault-Tolerant Computing,* March 1971. (Chapters 5 and 10)

[Long and Morris, 1993] F. LONG AND E. MORRIS, "An Overview of PCTE: A Basis for a Portable Common Tool Environment," Technical Report CMU/SEI–93–TR–1, Software Engineering Institute, Carnegie Mellon University, Pittsburgh, January 1993. (Chapter 14)

[Longstreet, 1990] D. H. LONGSTREET (Editor), *Software Maintenance and Computers,* IEEE Computer Society Press, Los Alamitos, CA, 1990. (Chapter 15)

[Loukides and Oram, 1997] M. K. LOUKIDES AND A. ORAM, *Programming with GNU Software,* O'Reilly and Associates, Sebastopol, CA, 1997. (Chapters 4, 14, and 15)

[Low and Jeffrey, 1990] G. C. LOW AND D. R. JEFFREY, "Function Points in the Estimation and Evaluation of the Software Process," *IEEE Transactions on Software Engineering* **16** (January 1990), pp. 64–71. (Chapter 8)

[Luckham and von Henke, 1985] D. C. LUCKHAM AND F. W. VON HENKE, "An Overview of Anna, a Specification Language for Ada," *IEEE Software* **2** (March 1985), pp. 9–22. (Chapter 10)

[Luqi, 1989] LUQI, "Software Evolution through Rapid Prototyping," *IEEE Computer* **22** (May 1989), pp. 13–25. (Chapter 9)

[Luqi and Royce, 1992] LUQI AND W. ROYCE, "Status Report: Computer-Aided Prototyping," *IEEE Software* **9** (November 1992), pp. 77–81. (Chapters 3 and 9)

[Mackenzie, 1980] C. E. MACKENZIE, *Coded Character Sets: History and Development,* Addison-Wesley, Reading, MA, 1980. (Chapter 7)

[Mancl and Havanas, 1990] D. MANCL AND W. HAVANAS, "A Study of the Impact of C++ on Software Maintenance," *Proceedings of the IEEE Conference on Software Maintenance,* San Diego, CA, November 1990, pp. 63–69. (Chapter 15)

[Manna, 1974] Z. MANNA, *Mathematical Theory of Computation,* McGraw-Hill, New York, 1974. (Chapter 5)

[Manna and Pnueli, 1992] Z. MANNA AND A. PNUELI, *The Temporal Logic of Reactive and Concurrent Systems,* Springer-Verlag, New York, 1992. (Chapter 5)

[Manna and Waldinger, 1978] Z. MANNA AND R. WALDINGER, "The Logic of Computer Programming," *IEEE Transactions on Software Engineering* **SE-4** (1978), pp. 199–229. (Chapter 5)

[Mantei, 1981] M. MANTEI, "The Effect of Programming Team Structures on Programming Tasks," *Communications of the ACM* **24** (March 1981), pp. 106–13. (Chapter 4)

[Mantei and Teorey, 1988] M. M. MANTEI AND T. J. TEOREY, "Cost/Benefit Analysis for Incorporating Human Factors in the Software Development Lifecycle," *Communications of the ACM* **31** (April 1988), pp. 428–39. (Chapter 3)

[Maring, 1996] B. MARING, "Object-Oriented Development of Large Applications," *IEEE Software* **13** (May 1996), pp. 33–40. (Chapter 1)

[Martin, 1985] J. MARTIN, *Fourth-Generation Languages, Volumes I, II, and III,* Prentice Hall, Englewood Cliffs, NJ, 1985. (Chapter 13)

[Martin and McClure, 1985] J. P. MARTIN AND C. MCCLURE, *Diagramming Techniques for Analysts and Programmers,* Prentice Hall, Englewood Cliffs, NJ, 1985. (Chapter 12)

[Martin and Odell, 1992] J. MARTIN AND J. J. ODELL, *Object-Oriented Analysis and Design,* Prentice Hall, Englewood Cliffs, NJ, 1992. (Chapters 11 and 12)

[Mathis, 1986] R. F. MATHIS, "The Last 10 Percent," *IEEE Transactions on Software Engineering* **SE-12** (June 1986), pp. 705–12. (Chapters 1 and 2)

[Matsumoto, 1984] Y. MATSUMOTO, "Management of Industrial Software Production," *IEEE Computer* **17** (February 1984), pp. 59–72. (Chapter 7)

[Matsumoto, 1987] Y. MATSUMOTO, "A Software Factory: An Overall Approach to Software Production," in: *Tutorial: Software Reusability,* P. Freeman (Editor), Computer Society Press, Washington, DC, 1987, pp. 155–78. (Chapter 7)

[Mays, 1994] R. G. MAYS, "Forging a Silver Bullet from the Essence of Software," *IBM Systems Journal* **33** (No. 1, 1994) pp. 20–45. (Chapter 2)

[McCabe, 1976] T. J. MCCABE, "A Complexity Measure," *IEEE Transactions on Software Engineering* **SE-2** (December 1976), pp. 308–20. (Chapters 12 and 13)

[McCabe, 1983] T. J. MCCABE, *Structural Testing,* IEEE Computer Society Press, Los Angeles, 1983. (Chapter 13)

[McCabe and Butler, 1989] T. J. MCCABE AND C. W. BUTLER, "Design Complexity Measurement and Testing," *Communications of the ACM* **32** (December 1989), pp. 1415–25. (Chapter 13)

[McConnell, 1993] S. MCCONNELL, *Code Complete: A Practical Handbook of Software Construction,* Microsoft Press, Redmond, WA, 1993. (Chapter 13)

[McConnell, 1996] S. MCCONNELL, "Daily Build and Smoke Test," *IEEE Computer* **13** (July 1996), pp. 144, 143. (Chapters 3 and 4)

[Mellor, 1994] P. MELLOR, "CAD: Computer-Aided Disaster," Technical Report, Centre for Software Reliability, City University, London, UK, July 1994. (Chapter 1)

[Mercurio, Meyers, Nisbet, and Radin, 1990] V. J. MERCURIO, B. F. MEYERS, A. M. NISBET, AND G. RADIN, "AD/Cycle Strategy and Architecture," *IBM Systems Journal* **29** (No. 2, 1990), pp. 170–88. (Chapter 14)

[Meyer, 1985] B. MEYER, "On Formalism in Specifications," *IEEE Software* **2** (January 1985), pp. 6–26. (Chapter 10)

[Meyer, 1986] B. MEYER, "Genericity versus Inheritance," *Proceedings of the Conference on Object-Oriented Programming Systems, Languages and Applications, ACM SIGPLAN Notices* **21** (November 1986), pp. 391–405. (Chapter 6)

[Meyer, 1987] B. MEYER, "Reusability: The Case for Object-Oriented Design," *IEEE Software* **4** (March 1987), pp. 50–64. (Chapters 6 and 7)

[Meyer, 1990] B. MEYER, "Lessons from the Design of the Eiffel Libraries," *Communications of the ACM* **33** (September 1990), pp. 68–88. (Chapters 6, 7, and 15)

[Meyer, 1992a] B. MEYER, "Applying 'Design by Contract'," *IEEE Computer* **25** (October 1992), pp. 40–51. (Chapters 1, 6, and 14)

[Meyer, 1992b] B. MEYER, *Eiffel: The Language,* Prentice Hall, New York, 1992. (Chapters 5, 6, and 12)

[Meyer, 1996a] B. MEYER, "The Reusability Challenge," *IEEE Computer* **29** (February 1996), pp. 76–78. (Chapter 7)

[Meyer, 1996b] B. MEYER, "The Many Faces of Inheritance: A Taxonomy of Taxonomy," *IEEE Computer* **29** (May 1996), pp. 105–108. (Chapter 6)

[Meyer, 1997] B. MEYER, *Object-Oriented Software Construction,* Second Edition, Prentice Hall, Upper Saddle River, NJ, 1997. (Chapters 1 and 6)

[Mili, Mili, and Mili, 1995] H. MILI, F. MILI, AND A. MILI, "Reusing Software: Issues and Research Directions," *IEEE Transactions on Software Engineering* **21** (June 1995), pp. 528–62. (Chapter 7)

[Miller, 1956] G. A. MILLER, "The Magical Number Seven, Plus or Minus Two: Some Limits on Our Capacity for Processing Information," *The Psychological Review* **63** (March 1956), pp. 81–97. (Chapter 4)

[Mills, 1988] H. D. MILLS, "Stepwise Refinement and Verification in Box-Structured Systems," *IEEE Computer* **21** (June 1988), pp. 23–36. (Chapter 4)

[Mills, Basili, Gannon, and Hamlet, 1987] H. D. MILLS, V. R. BASILI, J. D. GANNON, AND R. G. HAMLET, *Principles of Computer Programming: A Mathematical Approach,* Allyn and Bacon, Newton, MA, 1987. (Chapter 5)

[Mills, Dyer, and Linger, 1987] H. D. MILLS, M. DYER, AND R. C. LINGER, "Cleanroom Software Engineering," *IEEE Software* **4** (September 1987), pp. 19–25. (Chapter 13)

[Mills, Linger, and Hevner, 1987] H. D. MILLS, R. C. LINGER, AND A. R. HEVNER, "Box Structured Information Systems," *IBM Systems Journal* **26** (No. 4, 1987), pp. 395–413. (Chapter 4)

[Mione, 1998] A. MIONE, *CDE and Motif, A Practical Primer,* Prentice Hall, Upper Saddle River, NJ, 1998. (Chapter 7)

[Mishan, 1982] E. J. MISHAN, *Cost–Benefit Analysis: An Informal Introduction,* Third Edition, George Allen & Unwin, London, 1982. (Chapter 4)

[Misra and Jalics, 1988] S. K. MISRA AND P. J. JALICS, "Third-Generation versus Fourth-Generation Software Development," *IEEE Software* **5** (July 1988), pp. 8–14. (Chapter 13)

[Modell, 1996] M. E. MODELL, *A Professional's Guide to Systems Analysis,* Second Edition, McGraw-Hill, 1996. (Chapter 10)

[Moder, Phillips, and Davis, 1983] J. J. MODER, C. R. PHILLIPS, AND E. W. DAVIS, *Project Management with CPM, PERT, and Precedence Diagramming,* Third Edition, Van Nostrand Reinhold, New York, 1983. (Chapter 8)

[Monarchi and Puhr, 1992] D. E. MONARCHI AND G. I. PUHR, "A Research Typology for Object-Oriented Analysis and Design," *Communications of the ACM* **35** (September 1992), pp. 35–47. (Chapters 11 and 12)

[Monroe, Kompanek, Melton, and Garlan, 1997] R. T. MONROE, A. KOMPANEK, R. MELTON, AND D. GARLAN, "Architectural Styles, Design Patterns, and Objects," *IEEE Software* **14** (January/February 1997), pp. 43–52. (Chapter 7)

[Mooney, 1990] J. D. MOONEY, "Strategies for Supporting Application Portability," *IEEE Computer* **23** (November 1990), pp. 59–70. (Chapter 7)

[Moran, 1981] T. P. MORAN (Editor), Special Issue: The Psychology of Human-Computer Interaction, *ACM Computing Surveys* **13** (March 1981). (Chapter 4)

[Moser and Nierstrasz, 1996] S. MOSER AND O. NIERSTRASZ, "The Effect of Object-Oriented

Frameworks on Developer Productivity," *IEEE Computer* **29** (September 1996), pp. 45–51. (Chapters 7 and 8)

[Mowbray and Zahavi, 1995] T. J. MOWBRAY AND R. ZAHAVI, *The Essential CORBA,* John Wiley & Sons, New York, 1995. (Chapter 7)

[Munoz, 1988] C. U. MUNOZ, "An Approach to Software Product Testing," *IEEE Transactions on Software Engineering* **14** (November 1988), pp. 1589–96. (Chapter 14)

[Musa and Everett, 1990] J. D. MUSA AND W. W. EVERETT, "Software-Reliability Engineering: Technology for the 1990s," *IEEE Software* **7** (November 1990), pp. 36–43. (Chapter 13)

[Musa, Iannino, and Okumoto, 1987] J. D. MUSA, A. IANNINO, AND K. OKUMOTO, *Software Reliability: Measurement, Prediction, Application,* McGraw-Hill, New York, 1987. (Chapters 4 and 13)

[Musser and Saini, 1996] D. R. MUSSER AND A. SAINI, *STL Tutorial and Reference Guide: C++ Programming with the Standard Template Library,* Addison-Wesley, Reading, MA, 1996. (Chapter 7)

[Myers, 1975] G. J. MYERS, *Reliable Software through Composite Design,* Petrocelli/Charter, New York, 1975. (Chapter 6)

[Myers, 1976] G. J. MYERS, *Software Reliability: Principles and Practices,* Wiley-Interscience, New York, 1976. (Chapter 13)

[Myers, 1978a] G. J. MYERS, "A Controlled Experiment in Program Testing and Code Walkthroughs/Inspections," *Communications of the ACM* **21** (September 1978), pp. 760–68. (Chapter 13)

[Myers, 1978b] G. J. MYERS, *Composite/Structured Design,* Van Nostrand Reinhold, New York, NY, 1978. (Chapter 6)

[Myers, 1979] G. J. MYERS, *The Art of Software Testing,* John Wiley and Sons, New York, 1979. (Chapters 5, 13, and 14)

[Myers, 1989] W. MYERS, "Allow Plenty of Time for Large-Scale Software," *IEEE Software* **6** (July 1989), pp. 92–99. (Chapter 8)

[Myers, 1992] W. MYERS, "Good Software Practices Pay Off—or Do They?" *IEEE Software* **9** (March 1992), pp. 96–97. (Chapter 4)

[Myers and Rosson, 1992] B. A. MYERS AND M. B. ROSSON, "Survey on User Interface Programming," *Proceedings of ACM SIGCHI Conference on Human Factors in Computing Systems,* Monterey, CA, May 1992, pp. 195–202. (Chapter 9)

[Naur, 1964] P. NAUR, "The Design of the GIER ALGOL Compiler," in: *Annual Review in Automatic Programming, Volume 4,* Pergamon Press, Oxford, UK, 1964, pp. 49–85. (Chapter 10)

[Naur, 1969] P. NAUR, "Programming by Action Clusters," *BIT* **9** (No. 3, 1969), pp. 250–58. (Chapters 5 and 10)

[Naur, Randell, and Buxton, 1976] P. NAUR, B. RANDELL, AND J. N. BUXTON (Editors), *Software Engineering: Concepts and Techniques: Proceedings of the NATO Conferences,* Petrocelli-Charter, New York, 1976. (Chapter 1)

[Neumann, 1980] P. G. NEUMANN, Letter from the Editor, *ACM SIGSOFT Software Engineering Notes* **5** (July 1980), p. 2. (Chapter 1)

[Neumann, 1986] P. G. NEUMANN, "On Hierarchical Design of Computer Systems for Critical Applications," *IEEE Transactions on Software Engineering* **SE-12** (September 1986), pp. 905–20. (Chapter 6)

[Neumann, 1995] P. G. NEUMANN, *Computer-Related Risks,* Addison-Wesley, Reading, MA, 1995. (Chapter 1)

[New, 1992] R. NEW, Personal communication, 1992. (Chapter 5)

[Nielsen, 1993] J. NIELSEN, "Iterative User-Interface Design," *IEEE Computer* **26** (November 1993), pp. 32–41. (Chapter 9)

[Nissen and Wallis, 1984] J. NISSEN AND P. WALLIS (Editors), *Portability and Style in Ada,* Cambridge University Press, Cambridge, UK, 1984. (Chapter 7)

[NIST 151, 1988] "POSIX: Portable Operating System Interface for Computer Environments," Federal Information Processing Standard 151, National Institute of Standards and Technology, Washington, DC, 1988. (Chapter 7)

[Nix and Collins, 1988] C. J. NIX AND B. P. COLLINS, "The Use of Software Engineering, Including the Z Notation, in the Development of CICS,"

Quality Assurance **14** (September 1988), pp. 103–110. (Chapter 10)

[Norden, 1958] P. V. NORDEN, "Curve Fitting for a Model of Applied Research and Development Scheduling," *IBM Journal of Research and Development* **2** (July 1958), pp. 232–48. (Chapter 8)

[Norusis, 1982] M. J. NORUSIS, *SPSS Introductory Guide: Basic Statistics and Operations,* McGraw-Hill, New York, 1982. (Chapter 7)

[Oest, 1986] O. N. OEST, "VDM from Research to Practice," *Proceedings of the IFIP Congress, Information Processing '86,* 1986, pp. 527–33. (Chapter 10)

[OMG, 1993] "The Common Object Request Broker: Architecture and Specification (CORBA) Revision 1.2," OMG TC Document 93.12.43, Object Management Group, Framingham, MA, December 1993. (Chapter 7)

[Onoma and Yamaura, 1995] A. K. ONOMA AND T. YAMAURA, "Practical Steps toward Quality Development," *IEEE Software* **12** (September 1995), pp. 68–77. (Chapter 5)

[OpenWindows, 1993] *Solaris OpenWindows User's Guide/OpenWindows 3.1,* Prentice Hall, Englewood Cliffs, NJ, 1993. (Chapter 7)

[Orfali, Harkey, and Edwards, 1996] R. ORFALI, D. HARKEY, AND J. EDWARDS, *The Essential Distributed Objects Survival Guide,* John Wiley & Sons, New York, 1996. (Chapter 7)

[Orr, 1981] K. ORR, *Structured Requirements Definition,* Ken Orr and Associates, Inc., Topeka, KS, 1981. (Chapters 10 and 12)

[Ottenstein, 1979] L. M. OTTENSTEIN, "Quantitative Estimates of Debugging Requirements," *IEEE Transactions on Software Engineering* **SE-5** (September 1979), pp. 504–514. (Chapter 13)

[Parikh, 1988] G. PARIKH (Editor), *Techniques of Program and System Maintenance,* Second Edition, QED Information Services, Wellesley, MA, 1988. (Chapter 15)

[Parnas, 1971] D. L. PARNAS, "Information Distribution Aspects of Design Methodology," *Proceedings of the IFIP Congress,* Ljubljana, Yugoslavia, 1971, pp. 339–44. (Chapters 6 and 12)

[Parnas, 1972a] D. L. PARNAS, "A Technique for Software Module Specification with Examples," *Communications of the ACM* **15** (May 1972), pp. 330–36. (Chapters 6 and 12)

[Parnas, 1972b] D. L. PARNAS, "On the Criteria to Be Used in Decomposing Systems into Modules," *Communications of the ACM* **15** (December 1972), pp. 1053–58. (Chapters 6 and 12)

[Parnas, 1979] D. L. PARNAS, "Designing Software for Ease of Extension and Contraction," *IEEE Transactions on Software Engineering* **SE-5** (March 1979), pp. 128–38. (Chapter 2)

[Parnas, 1990] D. L. PARNAS, "Education for Computing Professionals" *IEEE Computer* **23** (January 1990), pp. 17-22. (Chapter 1)

[Parnas, 1994] D. L. PARNAS, "Software Aging," *Proceedings of the 16th International Conference on Software Engineering,* Sorrento, Italy, May 1994, pp. 279–87. (Chapter 1)

[Parnas and Weiss, 1987] D. L. PARNAS AND D. M. WEISS, "Active Design Reviews: Principles and Practices," *Journal of Systems and Software* **7** (December 1987), pp. 259–65. (Chapter 12)

[Parnas, Clements, and Weiss, 1985] D. L. PARNAS, P. C. CLEMENTS, AND D. M. WEISS, "The Modular Structure of Complex Systems," *IEEE Transactions on Software Engineering* **SE-11** (March 1985), pp. 259–66. (Chapter 6)

[Paulk, 1995] M. C. PAULK, "How ISO 9001 Compares with the CMM," *IEEE Software* **12** (January 1995), pp. 74–83. (Chapter 2)

[Paulk et al., 1993] M. C. PAULK, C. V. WEBER, S. GARCIA, M. B. CHRISSIS, AND M. BUSH, "Key Practices of the Capability Maturity Model, Version 1.1," Report CMU/SEI-93-TR-25, ADA263432, Software Engineering Institute, Carnegie Mellon University, Pittsburgh, February 1993. (Chapter 2)

[Paulk, Weber, Curtis, and Chrissis, 1995] M. C. PAULK, C. V. WEBER, B. CURTIS, AND M. B. CHRISSIS, *The Capability Maturity Model: Guidelines for Improving the Software Process,* Addison-Wesley, Reading, MA, 1995. (Chapter 2)

[Perry, 1983] W. E. PERRY, *A Structured Approach to Systems Testing,* Prentice Hall, Englewood Cliffs, NJ, 1983. (Chapter 12)

[Perry and Kaiser, 1990] D. E. PERRY AND G. E. KAISER, "Adequate Testing and Object-Oriented Programming," *Journal of Object-Oriented Programming* **2** (January/February 1990), pp. 13–19. (Chapter 13)

[Peterson, 1981] J. L. PETERSON, *Petri Net Theory and the Modeling of Systems,* Prentice Hall, Englewood Cliffs, NJ, 1981. (Chapter 10)

[Petri, 1962] C. A. PETRI, "Kommunikation mit Automaten," Ph.D. Dissertation, University of Bonn, Germany, 1962. (In German.) (Chapter 10)

[Petschenik, 1985] N. H. PETSCHENIK, "Practical Priorities in System Testing," *IEEE Software* **2** (September 1985), pp. 18–23. (Chapter 13)

[Pfleeger and Hatton, 1997] S. L. PFLEEGER AND L. HATTON, "Investigating the Influence of Formal Methods," *IEEE Computer* **30** (February 1997) pp. 33–43. (Chapter 10)

[Pfleeger, Jeffery, Curtis, and Kitchenham, 1997] S. L. PFLEEGER, R. JEFFERY, B. CURTIS, AND B. KITCHENHAM, "Status Report on Software Measurement," *IEEE Software* **14** (March/April 1997), pp. 33–43. (Chapter 8)

[Phillips, 1986] J. PHILLIPS, *The NAG Library: A Beginner's Guide,* Clarendon Press, Oxford, UK, 1986. (Chapters 6 and 7)

[Pittman, 1993] M. PITTMAN, "Lessons Learned in Managing Object-Oriented Development," *IEEE Software* **10** (January 1993), pp. 43–53. (Chapter 8)

[Pollack, Hicks, and Harrison, 1971] S. L. POLLACK, H. T. HICKS, JR., AND W. J. HARRISON, *Decision Tables: Theory and Practice,* Wiley-Interscience, New York, NY, 1971. (Chapter 10)

[Ponder and Bush, 1994] C. PONDER AND B. BUSH, "Polymorphism Considered Harmful," *ACM SIGSOFT Software Engineering Notes* **19** (April, 1994), pp. 35–38. (Chapter 6)

[Porter, Siy, Toman, and Votta, 1997] A. A. PORTER H. P. SIY, C. A. TOMAN, AND L. G. VOTTA, "Assessing Software Review Meetings: Results of a Comparative Analysis of Two Experimental Studies," *IEEE Transactions on Software Engineering* **23** (March 1997), pp. 129–45. (Chapter 5)

[Poston and Bruen, 1987] R. M. POSTON AND M. W. BRUEN, "Counting Down to Zero Software Failures," *IEEE Software* **4** (September 1987), pp. 54–61. (Chapter 5)

[Poulin, 1997] J. S. POULIN, *Measuring Software Reuse: Principles, Practice, and Economic Models,* Addison-Wesley, Reading, MA, 1997. (Chapter 7)

[Preece, 1994] J. PREECE, *Human-Computer Interaction,* Addison-Wesley, Reading, MA, 1994. (Chapter 9)

[Prieto-Díaz, 1991] R. PRIETO-DÍAZ, "Implementing Faceted Classification for Software Reuse," *Communications of the ACM* **34** (May 1991), pp. 88–97. (Chapter 7)

[Prieto-Díaz, 1993] R. PRIETO-DÍAZ, "Status Report: Software Reusability," *IEEE Software* **10** (May 1993), pp. 61–66. (Chapter 7)

[Putnam, 1978] L. H. PUTNAM, "A General Empirical Solution to the Macro Software Sizing and Estimating Problem," *IEEE Transactions on Software Engineering* **SE-4** (July 1978), pp. 345–61. (Chapter 8)

[Quirk, 1983] W. J. QUIRK, "Recent Developments in the SPECK Specification System," Report CSS.146, Harwell, UK, 1983. (Chapter 5)

[Quirk, 1985] W. J. QUIRK (Editor), *Verification and Validation of Real-Time Software,* Springer-Verlag, Berlin, 1985. (Chapter 5)

[Radin, 1996] G. RADIN, "Object Technology in Perspective," *IBM Systems Journal* **35** (No. 2, 1996), pp. 124–26. (Chapter 1)

[Rajlich, 1985] V. RAJLICH, "Stepwise Refinement Revisited," *Journal of Systems and Software* **5** (February 1985), pp. 81–88. (Chapter 4)

[Rajlich, 1994] V. RAJLICH, "Decomposition/Generalization Methodology for Object-Oriented Programming," *Journal of Systems and Software* **24** (February, 1994), pp. 181–86. (Chapter 3)

[Ramamoorthy and Tsai, 1996] C. V. RAMAMOORTHY AND W.-T. TSAI, "Advances in Software Engineering," *IEEE Computer* **29** (October 1996), pp. 47–58. (Chapter 1)

[Rapps and Weyuker, 1985] S. RAPPS AND E. J. WEYUKER, "Selecting Software Test Data Using Data Flow Information," *IEEE Transactions on Software Engineering* **SE-11** (April 1985), pp. 367–75. (Chapter 13)

[Reifer, 1986] D. J. REIFER (Editor), *Tutorial: Software Management,* Third Edition, IEEE Computer

Society Press, Washington, DC, 1986. (Chapter 8)

[Reiss, 1990] S. P. REISS, "Connecting Tools Using Message Passing in the Field Environment," *IEEE Software* **7** (July 1990), pp. 57–66. (Chapter 14)

[Rettig, 1994] M. RETTIG, "Prototyping for Tiny Fingers," *Communications of the ACM* **37** (April 1994), pp. 21–27. (Chapter 9)

[Riehle, 1991] R. RIEHLE, "A Space for CASE," *HP Professional* **5** (July 1991), pp. 40–47. (Chapter 14)

[Rochkind, 1975] M. J. ROCHKIND, "The Source Code Control System," *IEEE Transactions on Software Engineering* **SE-1** (October 1975), pp. 255–65. (Chapters 4, 14, and 15)

[Rosenblum and Weyuker, 1997] D. S. ROSENBLUM AND E. J. WEYUKER, "Using Coverage Information to Predict the Cost-Effectiveness of Regression Testing Strategies," *IEEE Transactions on Software Engineering* **23** (March 1997), pp. 146–56. (Chapter 15)

[Ross, 1985] D. T. ROSS, "Applications and Extensions of SADT," *IEEE Computer* **18** (April 1985), pp. 25–34. (Chapter 10

[Rothermel and Harrold, 1996] G. ROTHERMEL AND M. J. HARROLD, "Analyzing Regression Test Selection Techniques," *IEEE Transactions on Software Engineering* **22** (August 1996), pp. 529–51. (Chapter 15)

[Royce, 1970] W. W. ROYCE, "Managing the Development of Large Software Systems: Concepts and Techniques," *1970 WESCON Technical Papers, Western Electronic Show and Convention,* Los Angeles, August 1970, pp. A/1-1–A/1-9. Reprinted in: *Proceedings of the 11th International Conference on Software Engineering,* Pittsburgh, May 1989, pp. 328–38. (Chapter 3)

[Rumbaugh et al., 1991] J. RUMBAUGH, M. BLAHA, W. PREMERLANI, F. EDDY, AND W. LORENSEN, *Object-Oriented Modeling and Design,* Prentice Hall, Englewood Cliffs, NJ, 1991. (Chapters 11, 12, and 14)

[Russell, 1991] G. W. RUSSELL, "Experience with Inspection in Ultralarge-Scale Developments," *IEEE Software* **8** (January 1991), pp. 25–31. (Chapter 5)

[Sackman, 1970] H. SACKMAN, *Man–Computer Problem Solving: Experimental Evaluation of Time-Sharing and Batch Processing,* Auerbach, Princeton, NJ, 1970. (Chapter 8)

[Sackman, Erikson, and Grant, 1968] H. SACKMAN, W. J. ERIKSON, AND E. E. GRANT, "Exploratory Experimental Studies Comparing Online and Offline Programming Performance," *Communications of the ACM* **11** (January 1968), pp. 3–11. (Chapter 8)

[Saiedian and Kuzara, 1995] H. SAIEDIAN AND R. KUZARA, "SEI Capability Maturity Model's Impact on Contractors," *IEEE Computer* **28** (January 1995), pp. 16–26. (Chapter 2)

[Saiedian et. al., 1996] H. SAIEDIAN, J. P. BOWEN, R. W. BUTLER, D. L. DILL, R. L. GLASS, D. GRIES, A. HALL, M. G. HINCHEY, C. M. HOLLOWAY, D. JACKSON, C. B. JONES, M. J. LUTZ, D. L. PARNAS, J. RUSHBY, J. WING, AND P. ZAVE, "An Invitation to Formal Methods," *IEEE Computer* **29** (April 1996), pp. 16–30. (Chapter 10)

[Sammet, 1978] J. E. SAMMET, "The Early History of COBOL," *Proceedings of the History of Programming Languages Conference,* Los Angeles, 1978, pp. 199–276. (Chapter 13)

[Schach, 1992] S. R. SCHACH, *Software Reuse: Past, Present, and Future,* Videotape, 150 mins, US-VHS format. IEEE Computer Society Press, Los Alamitos, CA, November 1992. (Chapter 7)

[Schach, 1994] S. R. SCHACH, "The Economic Impact of Software Reuse on Maintenance," *Journal of Software Maintenance: Research and Practice* **6** (July/August 1994), pp. 185–96. (Chapters 7 and 8)

[Schach, 1996] S. R. SCHACH, "The Cohesion and Coupling of Object," *Journal of Object-Oriented Programming* **8** (January 1966), pp. 48–50. (Chapter 6)

[Schach, 1997] S. R. SCHACH, *Software Engineering with Java,* Richard D. Irwin, Chicago, 1997. (Chapter 7)

[Schach and Stevens-Guille, 1979] S. R. SCHACH AND P. D. STEVENS-GUILLE, "Two Aspects of Computer-Aided Design," *Transactions of the Royal Society of South Africa* **44** (Part 1, 1979), pp. 123–26. (Chapter 6)

[Schach and Wood, 1986] S. R. SCHACH AND P. T. WOOD, "An Almost Path-Free Very High-Level

Interactive Data Manipulation Language for a Microcomputer-Based Database System," *Software—Practice and Experience* **16** (March 1986), pp. 243–68. (Chapter 9)

[Scheffer, Stone, and Rzepka, 1985] P. A. SCHEFFER, A. H. STONE, III, AND W. E. RZEPKA, "A Case Study of SREM," *IEEE Computer* **18** (April 1985), pp. 47–54. (Chapter 10)

[Schmid, 1996] H. A. SCHMID, "Creating Applications from Components: A Manufacturing Framework Design," *IEEE Software* **13** (November/December 1996), pp. 67–75. (Chapter 7)

[Schmidt, 1995] D. C. SCHMIDT, "Using Design Patterns to Develop Reusable Object-Oriented Communications Software," *Communications of the ACM* **38** (October 1995), pp. 65–74. (Chapter 7)

[Schneidewind, 1987] N. F. SCHNEIDEWIND, "The State of Software Maintenance," *IEEE Transactions on Software Engineering* **SE-13** (March 1987), pp. 303–310. (Chapter 15)

[Schneidewind, 1994] N. F. SCHNEIDEWIND, "Validating Metrics for Ensuring Space Shuttle Flight Software Quality," *IEEE Computer* **27** (August 1994), pp. 50–57. (Chapter 5)

[Scholtz et al., 1993] J. SCHOLTZ, S. CHIDAMBER, R. GLASS, A. GOERNER, M. B. ROSSON, M. STARK, AND I. VESSEY, "Object-Oriented Programming: The Promise and the Reality," *Journal of Systems and Software* **23** (November 1993), pp. 199–204. (Chapter 1)

[Schulmeyer and McManus, 1987] G. G. SCHULMEYER AND J. I. MCMANUS (Editors), *Handbook of Software Quality Assurance,* Van Nostrand Reinhold, New York, 1987. (Chapter 5)

[Schwartz and Delisle, 1987] M. D. SCHWARTZ AND N. M. DELISLE, "Specifying a Lift Control System with CSP," *Proceedings of the Fourth International Workshop on Software Specification and Design,* Monterey, CA, April 1987, pp. 21–27. (Chapter 10)

[Seitz, 1985] C. L. SEITZ, "The Cosmic Cube," *Communications of the ACM* **28** (January 1985), pp. 22–33. (Chapter 5)

[Selby, 1989] R. W. SELBY, "Quantitative Studies of Software Reuse," in: *Software Reusability. Volume II: Applications and Experience,* T. J. Biggerstaff and A. J. Perlis (Editors), ACM Press, New York, 1989, pp. 213–33. (Chapter 7)

[Selby, Basili, and Baker, 1987] R. W. SELBY, V. R. BASILI, AND F. T. BAKER, "Cleanroom Software Development: An Empirical Evaluation," *IEEE Transactions on Software Engineering* **SE-13** (September 1987), pp. 1027–37. (Chapters 3 and 13)

[Selic, Gullekson, and Ward, 1995] B. SELIC, G. GULLEKSON, AND P. T. WARD, *Real-Time Object-Oriented Modeling,* John Wiley and Sons, New York, 1995. (Chapter 11)

[Shapiro, 1994] F. R. SHAPIRO, "The First Bug," *Byte* **19** (April 1994), p. 308. (Chapter 1)

[Shaw, 1984] M. SHAW, "Abstraction Techniques in Modern Programming Languages," *IEEE* Software 1 (October 1984), pp. 10–26. (Chapter 6)

[Shaw, 1990] M. SHAW, "Prospects for an Engineering Discipline of Software," *IEEE Software* **7** (November 1990), pp. 15–24. (Chapter 1)

[Shaw, 1995] M. SHAW, "Comparing Architectural Design Styles," *IEEE Software* **12** (November 1995), pp. 27–41. (Chapter 7)

[Shaw and Garlan, 1996] M. SHAW AND D. GARLAN, *Software Architecture: Perspectives on an Emerging Discipline,* Prentice Hall, Upper Saddle Valley River, NJ, 1996. (Chapter 7)

[Shen, Conte, and Dunsmore, 1983] V. Y. SHEN, S. D. CONTE, AND H. E. DUNSMORE, "Software Science Revisited: A Critical Analysis of the Theory and Its Empirical Support," *IEEE Transactions on Software Engineering* **SE-9** (March 1983), pp. 155–65. (Chapter 8)

[Shepperd, 1988a] M. J. SHEPPERD, "An Evaluation of Software Product Metrics," *Information and Software Technology* **30** (No. 3, 1988), pp. 177–88. (Chapters 8 and 13)

[Shepperd, 1988b] M. SHEPPERD, "A Critique of Cyclomatic Complexity as a Software Metric," *Software Engineering Journal* **3** (March 1988), pp. 30–36. (Chapter 13)

[Shepperd, 1990] M. SHEPPERD, "Design Metrics: An Empirical Analysis," *Software Engineering Journal* **5** (January 1990), pp. 3–10. (Chapter 12)

[Shepperd, 1996] M. SHEPPERD, *Foundations of Software Measurement,* Prentice Hall, Upper Saddle River, NJ, 1996. (Chapter 4)

[Shepperd and Ince, 1994] M. SHEPPERD AND D. C. INCE, "A Critique of Three Metrics," *Journal of Systems and Software* **26** (September 1994), pp. 197–210. (Chapters 8 and 13)

[Sherer, 1991] S. A. SHERER, "A Cost-Effective Approach to Testing," *IEEE Software* **8** (March 1991), pp. 34–40. (Chapter 14)

[Sherer, Kouchakdjian, and Arnold, 1996] S. W. SHERER, A. KOUCHAKDJIAN, AND P. G. ARNOLD, "Experience Using Cleanroom Software Engineering," *IEEE Software* **13** (May 1996), pp. 69–76. (Chapter 13)

[Shlaer and Mellor, 1988] S. SHLAER AND S. MELLOR, *Object-Oriented Systems Analysis: Modeling the World in Data,* Yourdon Press, Englewood Cliffs, NJ, 1988. (Chapter 11)

[Shlaer and Mellor, 1992] S. SHLAER AND S. MELLOR, *Object Lifecycles: Modeling the World in States,* Yourdon Press, Englewood Cliffs, NJ, 1992. (Chapters 11 and 12)

[Shneiderman, 1980] B. SHNEIDERMAN, *Software Psychology: Human Factors in Computer and Information Systems,* Winthrop Publishers, Cambridge, MA, 1980. (Chapter 1)

[Shneiderman and Mayer, 1975] B. SHNEIDERMAN AND R. MAYER, "Towards a Cognitive Model of Programmer Behavior," Technical Report TR-37, Indiana University, Bloomington, IN, 1975. (Chapter 6)

[Shooman, 1983] M. L. SHOOMAN, *Software Engineering: Design, Reliability, and Management,* McGraw-Hill, New York, 1983. (Chapter 13)

[Shriver and Wegner, 1987] B. SHRIVER AND P. WEGNER (Editors), *Research Directions in Object-Oriented Programming,* The MIT Press, Cambridge, MA, 1987. (Chapter 6)

[Silberschatz and Galvin, 1998] A. SILBERSCHATZ AND P. B. GALVIN, *Operating System Concepts,* Fifth Edition, Addison-Wesley, Reading, MA, 1998. (Chapters 5, 10, and 12)

[Skazinski, 1994] J. G. SKAZINSKI, "Porting Ada: A Report from the Field," *IEEE Computer* **27** (October 1994), pp. 58–64. (Chapter 7)

[Smith, Kotik, and Westfold, 1985] D. R. SMITH, G. B. KOTIK, AND S. J. WESTFOLD, "Research on Knowledge-Based Software Environments at the Kestrel Institute," *IEEE Transactions on Software Engineering* **SE-11** (November 1985), pp. 1278–95. (Chapter 10)

[Sneed, 1995] H. M. SNEED, "Planning the Reengineering of Legacy Systems," *IEEE Software* **12** (January 1995), pp. 24–34. (Chapter 15)

[Snyder, 1993] A. SNYDER, "The Essence of Objects: Concepts and Terms," *IEEE Software* **10** (January 1993), pp. 31–42. (Chapters 1 and 6)

[Sobell, 1995] M. G. SOBELL, *A Practical Guide to the UNIX System,* Third Edition, Benjamin/Cummings, Menlo Park, CA, 1995. (Chapter 4)

[Sparks, Benner, and Faris, 1996] S. SPARKS, K. BENNER, AND C. FARIS, "Managing Object-Oriented Framework Reuse," *IEEE Computer* **29** (September 1996), pp. 52–61. (Chapters 7 and 8)

[Spivey, 1988] J. M. SPIVEY, *Understanding Z: A Specification Language and Its Informal Semantics,* Cambridge University Press, Cambridge, UK, 1988. (Chapter 10)

[Spivey, 1990] J. M. SPIVEY, "Specifying a Real-Time Kernel," *IEEE Software* **7** (September 1990), pp. 21–28. (Chapter 10)

[Spivey, 1992] J. M. SPIVEY, *The Z Notation: A Reference Manual,* Prentice Hall, New York, 1992. (Chapters 3 and 10)

[Stankovic, 1997] J. A. STANKOVIC, "Real-Time and Embedded Systems," in: *The Computer Science and Engineering Handbook,* A. B. Tucker, Jr. (Editor-in-Chief), CRC Press, Boca Raton, FL, pp. 1709–24. (Chapter 12)

[Stefik and Bobrow, 1986] M. STEFIK AND D. G. BOBROW, "Object-Oriented Programming: Themes and Variations," *The AI Magazine* **6** (No. 4, 1986), pp. 40–62. (Chapter 6)

[Stephenson, 1976] W. E. STEPHENSON, "An Analysis of the Resources Used in Safeguard System Software Development," Bell Laboratories, Draft Paper, August 1976. (Chapter 1)

[Sternbach and Okuda, 1991] R. STERNBACH AND M. OKUDA, *Star Trek: The Next Generation, Technical Manual,* Pocket Books, New York, 1991. (Chapter 2)

[Stevens, Myers, and Constantine, 1974] W. P. STEVENS, G. J. MYERS, AND L. L. CONSTANTINE,

"Structured Design," *IBM Systems Journal* **13** (No. 2, 1974), pp. 115–39. (Chapter 6)

[Stocks and Carrington, 1996] P. STOCKS AND D. CARRINGTON, "A Framework for Specification-Based Testing," *IEEE Transactions on Software Engineering* **22** (November 1996), pp. 777–93. (Chapter 13)

[Stroustrup, 1991] B. STROUSTRUP, *The C++ Programming Language,* Second Edition, Addison-Wesley, Reading, MA, 1991. (Chapters 6 and 12)

[Symons, 1991] C. R. SYMONS, *Software Sizing and Estimating: Mk II FPA,* John Wiley and Sons, Chichester, UK, 1991. (Chapter 8)

[Takahashi and Kamayachi, 1985] M. TAKAHASHI AND Y. KAMAYACHI, "An Empirical Study of a Model for Program Error Prediction," *Proceedings of the Eighth International Conference on Software Engineering,* London, 1985, pp. 330–36. (Chapter 13)

[Tamir, 1980] M. TAMIR, "ADI: Automatic Derivation of Invariants," *IEEE Transactions on Software Engineering* **SE-6** (January 1980), pp. 40–48. (Chapter 5)

[Tanenbaum, 1990] A. S. TANENBAUM, *Structured Computer Organization,* Third Edition, Prentice Hall, Englewood Cliffs, NJ, 1990. (Chapter 6)

[Tanenbaum, 1996] A. S. TANENBAUM, *Computer Networks,* Third Edition, Prentice Hall, Upper Saddle River, NJ, 1996. (Chapter 7)

[Teichroew and Hershey, 1977] D. TEICHROEW AND E. A. HERSHEY, III, "PSL/PSA: A Computer-Aided Technique for Structured Documentation and Analysis of Information Processing Systems," *IEEE Transactions on Software Engineering* **SE-3** (January 1977), pp. 41–48. (Chapter 10)

[Tepfenhart and Cusick, 1997] W. M. TEPFENHART AND J. J. CUSICK, "A Unified Object Topology," *IEEE Software* **14** (January/February 1997), pp. 31-35. (Chapter 7)

[Tevonen, 1996] I. TEVONEN, "Support for Quality-Based Design and Inspection," *IEEE Software* **13** (January 1996), pp. 44–54. (Chapter 5)

[Thayer, 1988] R. H. THAYER (Editor), *Tutorial: Software Engineering Management,* IEEE Computer Society Press, Washington, DC, 1988. (Chapter 8)

[Thayer and Dorfman, 1990] R. THAYER AND M. DORFMAN, *Tutorial: System and Software Requirements Engineering,* IEEE Computer Society Press, Los Alamitos, CA, 1990. (Chapter 9)

[Thomas, 1989] I. THOMAS, "PCTE Interfaces: Supporting Tools in Software Engineering Environments," *IEEE Software* **6** (November 1989), pp. 15–23. (Chapter 14)

[Tichy, 1985] W. F. TICHY, "RCS—A System for Version Control," *Software—Practice and Experience* **15** (July 1985), pp. 637–54. (Chapters 4, 14, and 15)

[Tracz, 1979] W. J. TRACZ, "Computer Programming and the Human Thought Process," *Software—Practice and Experience* **9** (February 1979), pp. 127–37. (Chapter 4)

[Tracz, 1988] W. TRACZ, "Software Reuse Myths," *ACM SIGSOFT Software Engineering Notes* **13** (January 1988), pp. 17–21. (Chapter 7)

[Tracz, 1994] W. TRACZ, "Software Reuse Myths Revisited," *Proceedings of the 16th International Conference on Software Engineering,* Sorrento, Italy, May 1994, pp. 271–72. (Chapter 7)

[Tracz, 1995] W. TRACZ, *Confessions of a Used Program Salesman: Institutionalizing Software Reuse,* Addison-Wesley, Reading, MA, 1995. (Chapter 7)

[Trammel, Binder, and Snyder, 1992] C. J. TRAMMEL, L. H. BINDER, AND C. E. SNYDER, "The Automated Production Control Documentation System: A Case Study in Cleanroom Software Engineering," *ACM Transactions on Software Engineering and Methodology* **1** (January 1992), pp. 81–94. (Chapters 5 and 13)

[Turner, 1994] C. D. TURNER, "State-Based Testing: A New Method for the Testing of Object-Oriented Programs," Ph.D. Thesis, Computer Science Division, University of Durham, Durham, UK, November, 1994. (Chapter 13)

[UML, 1997] UML Notation Guide, Version 1.0, www.rational.com/uml/start/notation_guide.html, 13 January 1997. (Chapter 11)

[van der Poel and Schach, 1983] K. G. VAN DER POEL AND S. R. SCHACH, "A Software Metric for Cost Estimation and Efficiency Measurement in Data Processing System Development," *Journal of Systems and Software* **3** (September 1983), pp. 187–91. (Chapters 8 and 13) [van Wijngaarden et al., 1975] A. van Wijngaarden, B. J. Mailloux, J. E. L. Peck, C. H. A. Koster, M. Sintzoff, C. H. Lindsey, L. G. L. T. Meertens, and R. G. Fisker, "Revised Report on the Algorithmic Language ALGOL 68," *Acta Informatica* **5** (1975), pp. 1–236. (Chapter 2)

[Verner and Tate, 1988] J. Verner and G. Tate, "Estimating Size and Effort in Fourth-Generation Development," *IEEE Software* **5** (July 1988), pp. 15–22. (Chapter 13)

[Volta, 1993] L. G. Volta, Jr., "Does Every Inspection Need a Meeting?" *Proceedings of the First ACM SIGSOFT Symposium on the Foundations of Software Engineering, ACM SIGSOFT Software Engineering Notes* **18** (December 1993), pp. 107–114. (Chapter 5)

[von Mayrhauser and Vana, 1997] A. von Mayrhauser and A. M. Vana, "Identification of Dynamic Comprehension Processes during Large Scale Maintenance," *IEEE Transactions on Software Engineering* **22** (June 1996), pp. 424–37. (Chapter 15)

[Wahl and Schach, 1988] N. J. Wahl and S. R. Schach, "A Methodology and Distributed Tool for Debugging Dataflow Programs," *Proceedings of the Second Workshop on Software Testing, Verification, and Analysis,* Banff, Canada, July 1988, pp. 98–105. (Chapter 5)

[Walker, 1992] I. J. Walker, "Requirements of an Object-Oriented Design Method," *Software Engineering Journal* **7** (March 1992), pp. 102–113. (Chapter 12)

[Wallis, 1982] P. J. L. Wallis, *Portable Programming,* John Wiley and Sons, New York, 1982. (Chapter 7)

[Walsh, 1979] T. J. Walsh, "A Software Reliability Study Using a Complexity Measure," *Proceedings of the AFIPS National Computer Conference,* New York, 1979, pp. 761–68. (Chapter 13)

[Ward and Mellor, 1985] P. T. Ward and S. Mellor, *Structured Development for Real-Time Systems. Volumes 1, 2 and 3,* Yourdon Press, New York, 1985. (Chapter 12)

[Warnier, 1976] J. D. Warnier, *Logical Construction of Programs,* Van Nostrand Reinhold, New York, 1976 (Chapter 12)

[Warnier, 1981] J. D. Warnier, *Logical Construction of Systems,* Van Nostrand Reinhold, New York, 1981. (Chapters 10 and 12)

[Wasserman, 1985] A. I. Wasserman, "Extending State Transition Diagrams for the Specification of Human-Computer Interaction," *IEEE Transactions on Software Engineering* **SE-11** (August 1985), pp. 699–713. (Chapter 10)

[Wasserman, 1996] A. I. Wasserman, "Toward a Discipline of Software Engineering," *IEEE Software* **13** (November/December 1996), pp. 23–31. (Chapters 1 and 2)

[Wasserman and Pircher, 1987] A. I. Wasserman and P. A. Pircher, "A Graphical, Extensible Integrated Environment for Software Development," *Proceedings of the Second ACM SIGSOFT/SIGPLAN Software Engineering Symposium on Practical Software Development Environments, ACM SIGPLAN Notices* **22** (January 1987), pp. 131–42. (Chapter 14)

[Webster, 1995] B. F. Webster, *Pitfalls of Object-Oriented Development,* M&T Books, New York, 1995. (Chapter 1)

[Wegner, 1989] P. Wegner, "Dimensions of Object-Oriented Modeling," *IEEE Computer* (October 1992), pp. 12–20. (Chapter 7)

[Weinberg, 1971] G. M. Weinberg, *The Psychology of Computer Programming,* Van Nostrand Reinhold, New York, 1971. (Chapters 1, 4, and 13)

[Weinberg, 1992] G. M. Weinberg, *Quality Software Management: Systems Thinking,* Volume 1, Dorset House, New York, 1992. (Chapter 8)

[Weinberg, 1993] G. M. Weinberg, *Quality Software Management: First-Order Measurement,* Volume 2, Dorset House, New York, 1993. (Chapter 8)

[Weinberg, 1994] G. M. Weinberg, *Quality Software Management: Congruent Action,* Volume 3, Dorset House, New York, 1994. (Chapter 8)

[Weinberg, 1997] G. M. Weinberg, *Quality Software Management: Anticipating Change,* Volume 4, Dorset House, New York, 1997. (Chapter 8)

[Weller, 1993] E. F. Weller, "Lessons from Three Years of Inspection Data," *IEEE Software* **10** (September 1993), pp. 38–45. (Chapter 5)

[Weller, 1994] E. F. Weller, "Using Metrics to Manage Software Projects," *IEEE Computer* **27** (September 1994), pp. 27–34 (Chapter 8)

[Wells, 1996] T. D. WELLS, "A Technical Comparison of Borland ObjectWindows 2.0 and Microsoft MFC 2.5," www.it.rit.edu/~tdw/refs/om.htm, February 5, 1996. (Chapter 7)

[Weyuker, 1988a] E. J. WEYUKER, "An Empirical Study of the Complexity of Data Flow Testing," *Proceedings of the Second Workshop on Software Testing, Verification, and Analysis,* Banff, Canada, July 1988, pp. 188–95. (Chapter 13)

[Weyuker, 1988b] E. WEYUKER, "Evaluating Software Complexity Measures," *IEEE Trans. on Software Engineering* **14** (September 1988), pp. 1357–65. (Chapters 8 and 13)

[Wheeler, Brykczynski, and Meeson, 1996] D. A. WHEELER, B. BRYKCZYNSKI, AND R. N. MEESON, JR., *Software Inspection: An Industry Best Practice,* IEEE Computer Society, Los Alamitos, CA, 1996. (Chapter 5)

[Whitgift, 1991] D. WHITGIFT, *Methods and Tools for Software Configuration Management,* John Wiley and Sons, New York, 1991. (Chapter 4)

[Whitten, 1995] N. M. WHITTEN, *Managing Software Development Projects,* Second Edition, John Wiley and Sons, New York, 1995. (Chapter 8)

[Wiest and Levy, 1977] J. D. WIEST AND F. K. LEVY, *A Management Guide to PERT/CPM: With GERT/PDM/DCPM and Other Networks,* Second Edition, Prentice Hall, Englewood Cliffs, NJ, 1977. (Chapter 8)

[Wildblood, 1990] A. WILDBLOOD, "Ada Reuse: The Promises Ring True," *Defense Science* **9** (April 1990), pp. 38–39. (Chapter 7)

[Wilde, Matthews, and Huitt, 1993] N. WILDE, P. MATTHEWS, AND R. HUITT, "Maintaining Object-Oriented Software," *IEEE Software* **10** (January 1993), pp. 75–80. (Chapters 13 and 15)

[Williams, 1996] J. D. WILLIAMS, "Managing Iteration in OO Projects," *IEEE Computer* **29** (September 1996), pp. 39–43. (Chapters 8 and 11)

[Wilson, Rosenstein, and Shafer, 1990] D. A. WILSON, L. S. ROSENSTEIN, AND D. SHAFER, *Programming with MacApp,* Addison-Wesley, Reading, MA, 1990. (Chapter 7)

[Wing, 1990] J. WING, "A Specifier's Introduction to Formal Methods," *IEEE Computer* **23** (September 1990), pp. 8–24. (Chapter 10)

[Wirfs-Brock, Wilkerson, and Wiener, 1990] R. WIRFS-BROCK, B. WILKERSON, AND L. WIENER, *Designing Object-Oriented Software,* Prentice Hall, Englewood Cliffs, NJ, 1990. (Chapters 1, 11, and 12)

[Wirth, 1971] N. WIRTH, "Program Development by Stepwise Refinement," *Communications of the ACM* **14** (April 1971), pp. 221–27. (Chapters 4 and 5)

[Wirth, 1975] N. WIRTH, *Algorithms + Data Structures = Programs,* Prentice Hall, Englewood Cliffs, NJ, 1975. (Chapter 4)

[Wohlwend and Rosenbaum, 1993] H. WOHLWEND AND S. ROSENBAUM, "Software Improvements in an International Company," *Proceedings of the 15th International Conference on Software Engineering,* Baltimore, MD, May 1993, pp. 212–20. (Chapter 2)

[Wolberg, 1983] J. R. WOLBERG, *Conversion of Computer Software,* Prentice Hall, Englewood Cliffs, NJ, 1983. (Chapter 7)

[Wong, 1984] C. WONG, "A Successful Software Development," *IEEE Transactions on Software Engineering* **SE-10** (November 1984), pp. 714–27. (Chapter 3)

[Wood and Silver, 1994] J. WOOD AND D. SILVER, *Joint Application Design: How to Design Quality Software in 40% Less Time,* Second Edition, John Wiley and Sons, 1994. (Chapter 9)

[Woodcock, 1989] J. WOODCOCK, "Calculating Properties of Z Specifications," *ACM SIGSOFT Software Engineering Notes* **14** (July 1989), pp. 43–54. (Chapter 10)

[Woodward, Hedley, and Hennell, 1980] M. R. WOODWARD, D. HEDLEY, AND M. A. HENNELL, "Experience with Path Analysis and Testing of Programs," *IEEE Transactions on Software Engineering* **SE-6** (May 1980), pp. 278–86. (Chapter 13)

[World Book Encyclopedia, 1996] *World Book Encyclopedia,* World Book-Childcraft International, Inc., Chicago, 1996, Volume 14: N–O, p. 552–53. (Chapter 11)

[Yau and Tsai, 1986] S. S. YAU AND J. J.-P. TSAI, "A Survey of Software Design Techniques," *IEEE Transactions on Software Engineering* **SE-12** (June 1986), pp. 713–21. (Chapter 12)

[Young and Gregory, 1972] D. M. YOUNG AND R. T. GREGORY, *A Survey of Numerical Mathematics, Volume I,* Addison-Wesley, Reading, MA, 1972. (Chapter 6)

[Yourdon and Constantine, 1979] E. YOURDON AND L. L. CONSTANTINE, *Structured Design: Fundamentals of a Discipline of Computer Program and Systems Design,* Prentice Hall, Englewood Cliffs, NJ, 1979. (Chapters 6, 10, and 12)

[Yourdon, 1989] E. YOURDON, *Modern Structured Analysis,* Yourdon Press, Englewood Cliffs, NJ, 1989. (Chapters 4, 10, and 14)

[Yourdon, 1992] E. YOURDON, *Decline and Fall of the American Programmer,* Yourdon Press, Englewood Cliffs, NJ, 1992. (Chapter 2)

[Yourdon, 1996] E. YOURDON, *Rise and Resurrection of the American Programmer,* Yourdon Press, Upper Saddle River, NJ, 1996. (Chapter 1)

[Zage and Zage, 1993] W. M. ZAGE AND D. M. ZAGE, "Evaluating Design Metrics on Large-Scale Software," *IEEE Software* **10** (July 1993), pp. 75–81. (Chapter 12)

[Zelkowitz, Shaw, and Gannon, 1979] M. V. ZELKOWITZ, A. C. SHAW, AND J. D. GANNON, *Principles of Software Engineering and Design,* Prentice Hall, Englewood Cliffs, NJ, 1979. (Chapter 1)

INDEXES

AUTHOR INDEX

This index includes only authors and references cited in the actual text.

D

E

F

G

H

I

J

K

L

M

N

O

P

Q

R

S

T

V

W

Y

Z

SUBJECT INDEX

C

D

H

I

J

K

L

M

N

O

P

Q

R

S

T

U

V

W

X

Y

Z